Wireless Internet Applications and Architecture

Building Professional Wireless Applications Worldwide

Mark Beaulieu

Addison-Wesley

Boston • San Francisco • New York • Toronto
Montreal • London • Munich • Paris • Madrid
Capetown • Sydney • Tokyo • Singapore • Mexico City

The publisher offers discounts on this book when ordered in quantity for special sales. For more information, please contact:

Pearson Education Corporate Sales Division
201 W. 103rd Street
Indianapolis, IN 46290
(800) 428-5331
corpsales@pearsoned.com
Visit AW on the Web: *www.aw.com/cseng/*

Library of Congress Cataloging-in-Publication Data

Beaulieu, Mark
Wireless Internet applications and architecture : building professional wireless applications worldwide / Mark Beaulieu.
p. cm.
Includes bibliographical references and index.
ISBN 0-201-73354-4 (alk. paper)
1. Personal communications service systems. 2. Wireless communications systems. 3. Internet programming. 4. Application software. I. Title.
TK5103.485.B43 2001
384.5—dc21

2001046323

ISBN 0-201-73354-4
Text printed on recycled paper
1 2 3 4 5 6 7 8 9 10—CRS—0504030201
First printing, December 2001

Contents

Foreword

Everything is converging today.* Computers and telecommunications; semiconductors and systems; psychology and medicine. But I am interested in a specific convergence – one that will change the lives of many of us in the next decade or so: the convergence of wireless and the Internet.

What a contrast between two industries! On the one hand, we have the Internet, just a few years old, still bubbling and boiling, still trying to decide what works and what does not; on the other hand, we have the telecommunications industry, which started 125 years ago when Alexander Graham Bell called out to Watson, and the wireless industry, which started 105 years ago when Marconi made his first transatlantic "call."

I work and live at the nexus of both of these industries, and I'm amazed to discover that, in many ways, the industry exemplified by this exciting Internet industry is more mature, more sound, as well as more dynamic and effective than the wireless industry. The Internet industry is attuned to the market, and has the potential of serving a wide variety of applications with an even broader variety of solutions and marketing approaches. Consider the contrast further.

We wireless people are consumed with technology. We talk in acronyms – TDMA, CDMA, TDD, FDD, 2G, 3G, UMTS, and on and on. We spend more energy battling each other than we do trying to grow our markets. Instead, we should be talking about services that people want and need, about the devices that will make peoples' lives more productive. When the wireless industry finally matures, we will stop using technical terms like *cellular, broadband,* and *WAP* to describe consumer services and end the wasteful "air interface wars" of the past decade.

Is the Internet world better? Well, it does have its share of acronyms and technobabble, but because the Internet is an open platform, it has the freedom to focus on real problems, to create and search out markets and then to make those markets work. And, it has the freedom to go out of business when the businesses and markets do not work as you hoped and expected. That is how free enterprise works and is the real secret behind the success of the Internet.

So, do we need to converge wireless and the Internet? Of course! There will not be a real Internet for people until the Internet can be delivered untethered with its full potential.

The wireless Internet of the future will be an open platform that harnesses the creativity of thousands of application providers who have figured out how to serve large specialized market segments with new devices, services, and content that just cannot be delivered any other way. They are not universal systems that try to do all things for all people. They are focused on one market – wireless Internet – for people who need wide bandwidth and always-on capability, who can benefit from the freedom to be anywhere while they communicate.

The Internet has the capability of bringing new levels of productivity, enjoyment, and convenience to vast constituencies. I am talking about delivering a myriad of applications, services, and contents to a wide variety of consumers. I am talking about a heart patient whose life can be saved by a single high-speed burst of data that sends vital signs to a doctor. I am talking about services and content that help people to live longer and to enjoy that longer life. To serve consumers well, these emerging applications depend on key technical attributes of wireless networks.

- *Always on.* People have neither the time nor the patience to wait for a dial-up connection, or the money to pay for a high-speed connection while they are not using it.
- *Speedy connections.* Wireless broadband takes about 20 seconds to download a 5-minute song at 1 megabit per second, or a few seconds to send a picture. Consumers will not wait longer.
- *Freedom to move.* A wireless connection is essential; and that connection has to be everywhere. People want to talk, but not while chained to a wall. They want freedom to be anyplace.

Of course, the price of these services, devices, and contents must be low enough that large numbers of consumers can enjoy them. And that means no installation, no technician visits. You have to be able go to the store, buy, take home, and operate everything. What I'm describing to you is a future Internet, an untethered Internet, an Internet unhindered by the closed platform and the walled garden, an Internet that needs no connection to a wall. That world is coming, if we have some faith in the future.

What does this mean to those of you in the business world? Disruptive concepts like smart antennas, spatial processing, and the open platform are going to create new opportunities for new companies that will force existing companies to do some things differently. They will, over the next five to ten years, profoundly change both the manufacturing and service elements of the telecommunications industry. The beneficiary will be the consumer, who will have more choices and more opportunity for a better life.

This revolution, and it truly is that, will take many years, and the book you are now holding in your hands will help you to understand what's coming in the world of wireless and give you tools to create and build great applications for this revolution.

Martin Cooper
CEO and Chairman
ArrayComm, Inc.
Inventor of the portable cellular phone

Preface

Living the Wireless Life

Building wireless applications for businesses and consumers is as challenging for me today as it was in the early 1990s. Today's challenge: Given a miniature device, microscreen, and low data-transmission rate, figure out how to deliver interesting and useful mobile applications. This means being a detective to discover the identity of the mobile person. It also means living the wireless mobile life, with all its devices. These are the vital parts of the ongoing stories wireless developers get to tell.

There is a magic point in mobile wireless development when, as you are building, you find the medium of wireless. Often at that point, what you build no longer makes sense on the PC desktop. Using wireless handhelds, Web phones, pagers, voice portals, and radio-based appliances, you can provide personal services that no one on the Internet has ever seen. You create. You find purpose. Newfound purposes and new wireless content can challenge and change the way traditional "unmobile" businesses operate.

Your customers, and most people, already use the conventional Internet. But when they are mobile, with wireless Internet devices, they use a new breed of information and services. If you can tune in to how a mobile business works and see what a person on the go actually needs, then you will begin to understand why engineers are building innovative and powerful wireless applications.

When I speak with new engineers and wireless clients, I naturally start with devices and move on to wireless networks and applications. It seems that the less the audience knows, the more eager we become to teach. I am always tempted to fill them in on the advantages of CDMA, SMS, XML, i-mode, GPS, HDR, 802.11a . . . until at some point, I can see that my audience is lost. As Miles Davis once said, "If you understood what I said, you would be me." Everyone wants to know wireless technology, because people are ready to build the wireless Internet and would like to know all the rules. Yet, I have found that long speeches saturate any listener. A book is my way to slow down and give the reader the time to measure out what he or she wants to know. Upon reflection, that is how I learned the wireless Internet – over time, in successive overlays of wireless concepts gained from professionals and practice. I thought it best to produce this for you in the same way – as a progressive set of illustrations and explanations of the key ideas, experiences with mobile users, the thinking that goes into a wireless application, and source code learned from wireless projects worldwide. Each overlay helps form a better engineering practice, improves client communications, and helps you do your best work.

Our job is to make new things. To bring things into existence, there is no substitute for downloading wireless device emulators, writing code, hacking databases to mobilize them, and watching it all come together as a new wireless Internet service. This is a time when open source and wireless technology are restructuring the Internet. The world has become an exchange for wireless professionals who are fast at work and are willing to share knowledge.

Some of the best wireless applications may have been written years ago; others are yet to be. In anticipation of great future wireless technology, I summon many good years of lessons from the wireless industry and have tried to capture inspiration from the best, for I have worked with the best. My early years at General Magic, Sony, and Motorola were spent helping produce intriguing wireless consumer and business applications. As a result, this book offers knowledge from great engineers, masters in telecommunications, programmers of key applications, hackers of mobile content, designers of great interaction interfaces, and builders of smart wireless architectures. You will see why professional developers see that the wireless Internet, not the PC Internet, is already the primary access method in Japan and Europe, and is emerging in North America. Producers of wireless applications in the wireless hot spots of Tokyo, Taiwan, San Diego, and Finland talk about their mobile wireless applications, practices, essential principles, rules of thumb, and ideas.

My main goals are to help you understand key wireless ideas, speak the correct language, and make relevant wireless applications and architectures. The critical telecommunications and computer concepts will give you the edge to build current and next-generation wireless services. Some wireless technology may change, but basic concepts and principled thinking should remain the same and give you a solid footing.

As a project team learns a common language, it can rapidly build effective products to create the "houses" of the mobile wireless world. The mobile user is a visitor to the "wireless house." This book is written for those who will build that house.

— •— •—• —•— —••• • •— ••— •—•• •• • ••—

To decipher this, see the "International Morse Code" section in appendix A.

What This Book Covers

To make good, perhaps great, wireless Internet applications is our goal. To help you understand the technology of two industries equally well, this book tells the story of telecommunications and the Internet. If you are a software programmer, an experienced engineer, or an interested executive manager, this book explains and illustrates the key technologies in a uniform manner. It is for you, your team, or your interested clients who like being well informed. It shows how wireless applications on every major platform are developed, and it explains the central issues of wireless architecture. Perhaps you need to tell your boss about why you needed to buy this book.

Wireless Internet Applications and Architecture is comprehensive. It covers the core telecommunications and computer technologies and many wireless software techniques, applications, and architectural standards in one place. This book discusses wireless hardware, software, network, and new content from a neutral point of view; it is not wedded to one device or technology. If you are working on a wireless project, the information in this book can save time in the process because it lists the resources you will need and shows how experts solve the tough problems. It contains invaluable contributions from developers working on existing and emerging wireless technology, who shared some examples of their wireless applications. It explains the wireless XML, Java, and Web tools and content production techniques.

To get the big picture, we show wireless networks, the programming model for devices, and wireless Internet applications close up. Web cell phones, handhelds, pagers, voice portals, and Web PCs are examined in detail. This book dissects the new classes of mobile wireless applications for professionals and general consumers. Two special features of this book are the rare source code in Part II (industrial location-based algorithms fundamental to content and services) and the section "Rebuilding Your Web Site" in chapter 18, which explains how to transition your Web site to the wireless Internet.

This book appears at an interesting time, when the world's telephony and computer standards are converging to deliver a wireless digital carrier. It shows developers how to use the new portable communication devices to connect mobile users with purposeful wireless applications and personalized content that originates entirely from the Internet. The good news for developers is that wireless Internet development is largely an extension of familiar Web site engineering. Server engineers will learn the many new and changing standards and find out in detail the best ways to reach all the wireless targets. Mobile end users' requirements are new to many developers. This book teaches skills and techniques such as persona development to help you understand, discover, invent, and deliver a new personal technology that has already changed parts of the world.

Wireless Internet Applications and Architecture, an ideal companion for the single-platform development book, provides a full context for wireless development. This book covers essential aspects of popular wireless development environments and wireless servers. It is helpful in understanding embedded wireless systems, such as an in-car dashboard navigator, satellites, and other "closed" systems. The book takes a quick but important look at fixed wireless systems such as MMDS. The focus remains, however, on mobile systems that developers are programming today.

After you read this book, you should be able to explain wireless technology, be able to produce good wireless applications, and know what it takes to build servers and make long-term architectural decisions. This book also serves as a continuing wireless applications reference.

How This Book Is Organized

To help you understand, write, and build wireless applications, the book is divided into three parts. Essential wireless themes, however, are woven throughout.

Part I introduces the wireless Internet, language, and core concepts. In the first part, you are the general developer, learning the sometimes confusing language and technical issues of wireless computing and communication development. The part begins by describing the trends, forces, and organizations that are shaping the growth of the wireless Internet.

Part II shows how to create wireless applications and how to make them better. In the second part, you are the application developer, learning how to build great wireless applications. This part walks you through key applications for the Web phone, the handheld, the pager, and the voice portal. The chapters examine how to construct messaging, browsing, interactive, and voice portal applications by showing application code and examples of mobile content. Wireless projects are described fully with diagrams, examples, and source code. By building a few of these projects (this book looks at a series of them), your skills will mature and you will learn to make sound architectural decisions.

Part III examines the components of wireless architecture. In the third part, you are the architect, learning the principles of wireless architecture and how servers for multiple wireless devices are built. These chapters describe wireless standards and practices, as well as the effect wireless architectural elements have over time. This part of the book goes beyond wireless applications to provide a more comprehensive set of technical standards and useful reference materials that people throughout the computer and telecommunications business use. It has been organized sequentially from long-term to short-range issues for the architect who must make lasting decisions. Whereas Part II shows single wireless client applications, Part III looks at the back-end server and multiple-client solutions. It is for the software engineer who is looking to become an architect, to advance a relationship with senior design members, or to understand how to make significant development decisions for wireless applications and servers.

The appendices offer a broad range of resources. They contain references such as the FCC spectrum allocation and a "tip sheet" for looking up auctions or examining unallocated spectrum. There are some "retro" resources commonly used in wireless projects today. For example, ASCII is used in byte encoding for WAP; Morse code is used in messaging; and Soundex encoding is handy for wireless text messaging. The appendices also include information about wireless research, standards bodies, and companies, as well as lists of written resources in books, periodicals, papers, reports, and articles on the Web.

Although the content of this book is presented in three parts, each part contains important wireless concepts that developers tend to overlook, but that deserve discussion. Each theme is introduced as a subject, then applied, and finally deployed. For example, in Part I you discover wireless location-based applications. In Part II you see how to develop them with source code to key industrial algorithms. In Part III you can go on to understand GPS satellites, what the FCC docket says about E911 requirements and their Revision Order schedules to 2006 for handsets and networks, and the alternatives to consider. Another important theme is the uniqueness of the mobile audience, which is introduced in Part I. Part II shows how the audience can be characterized as personas. Part III continues with a wireless publishing model, personalization engines, and transcoding architectures to support real identities.

Acknowledgments

This book, a core dump for me, is the life work of many others. I would like to acknowledge those who have contributed to the substance of the book and especially those who have spent time reviewing the wily drafts that were transformed into these typeset pages.

My many thanks for the assistance and suggestions of the following reviewers: Dan Witmer, the honorable and tireless telecommunications sergeant of wireless application developers in the trenches, whose many stories color these pages; Kenneth Bowen, a technician who lives the quotable life, for the colorful use of language that is the code of culture; Keith Bigelow, for shoving *The Inmates Are Running the Asylum* in my face; Dennis Portello, for his many technical i-mode insights; James Murphy, the professional teacher with a never-ending Zen to learn, for increasing awareness of how the book reads; Christopher Reed, the dangerous hillbilly of wireless, a humanely great instructor, for his unstoppable passion to get things right; Andrew Harding and Robert Sese, diligent engineers, who provided challenging remarks while reading a difficult draft; the always critical

Roland Alden, who poured a gallon of useful battery acid on the manuscript; Bob Bourbonnais and Carolyn Yount, whose edits helped voice portal developers; Bill Day, for his views of Sun J2ME; Scott Lincke, for Palm product information; Bob Badavas, for experienced views on vertical markets; Debra Voisin, for her information design outlook that is all about dance; Robert Reimann from Cooper Interaction Design, for helping to communicate persona design clearly; Martin Cooper, for making me think twice and giving personal time to help me understand the substance and the future of wireless technology; Kevin Kelley and David Brandos, for many improvements on telecommunications; Robert Roche, for interpretations of U.S. spectrum; Henrik Sidebäck, for the view from Sweden; Lusman Winarto, for erudite responses; Fran Rabuck, for keeping me on my toes with technical details; Mika Könnölä and Eero Teerikorpi, for security details and a finer Finnish perspective; and Tom Wheeler, for many helpful political and well-considered business views.

Special thanks for the gifted developmental edits of Kitty Jarrett, who seemed to know what I was saying in the greenest of drafts; to Stephane Thomas, an editor with never-ending positive energy; to Laurel Kline, for imparting the ways of FrameMaker; and to Rand McKinney and K.S., for calling a spade a spade and taking the entire rough work seriously; to Joan Flaherty, whose copy-editing skill makes even a tired author enjoy reading a sentence one more time; to Rosemary Michelle Simpson for turning the book inside out with her marvelous view of indexing; and to the many other professionals at Addison-Wesley. Finally, I must thank Lutris Technologies for a culture that promotes its writers, and QUALCOMM, a company busy making the future of the wireless Internet happen.

A family is a gift. Most of all, I thank my family. In the midst of writing a book, the subject can take over your soul. While the family was sleeping, I am told, I bolted up saying, "Yes! Without wires, it is possible." Only a family understands. My youngsters, Joshua, Brian, and Sarah, kept me up on the coolest wireless technology. They showed me how fun a Nokia phone can be and were constant reminders of the vitality of music. My father, Richard Beaulieu, a Signal Officer and a gentleman, took me to work one day and gave me a peak at the SAGE Iconorama system when I was a boy, when impressions count most. My mother, Lorraine Beaulieu, gave me my first break as an artist and kept me honest, "a wireless . . . what?" And my wife, Joanna – my reason for reason.

Part I

An Introduction to Wireless Internet

> In a few years more than 60 percent of all Web transactions will be triggered by wireless devices, making mobile eCommerce a tremendous opportunity for businesses to provide new personalized, location-based services over the Internet.
>
> *– Mark Hanny, Vice President of IBM's Web Integrator Initiative*[1]

The Internet. When most people think of the Internet, they think of the wired Internet. The Internet is still largely a world of large screens, big disk drives, Ethernet wires, and browsers to look at Web sites, email, and high-speed connections. There is another emerging world of the Internet that is built and behaves differently: the wireless Internet.

For some years wireless software engineers, communication architects, interaction designers, and mobile content experts have been building a world of wireless Internet applications. This is a world without a mouse; no wires – just batteries; people walking about with handheld screens, sometimes using a miniature keyboard; a small screen browser to look at Web sites; and short messaging, where voice matters and where everything must weigh less than a pound or it has no use. Good mobile wireless applications often serve needs more directly than a lumbering laptop or desktop application.

The wireless Internet is the network of radio-connected devices and servers using voice, information, and other Internet services. Its origins and its services cover both the computer and telecommunications industries. With the birth of the wireless Internet, the telecommunications industry has definitely accelerated the access points to the Internet. Almost every Internet service is being made ready for the wireless Internet. Industry, government, standards bodies, and commercial enterprises are preparing the way for an enormous upgrade of cellular phone services for a wireless Internet. Ultimately it is all one Internet – wired or unwired. But the wireless part of it has very special properties, reaches a different class of end user, and provides revenue opportunities not at all like the wired Internet.

To get on the wireless Internet is an objective for many companies. Businesses with Web sites can open a "wireless channel" and provide customers with mobile commerce, or mCommerce. Customers use wireless devices to access the Internet services of a business. Using wireless protocols, customers run applications that range from messaging, to Web browsing, to all kinds of interactive applications and transactions. mCommerce is an evolution of eCommerce (electronic commerce). Both terms express the market and technology, but mCommerce has a startling property.

The remarkable thing that interests companies is that *mCommerce puts customers in stores; eCommerce keeps people out of them*. A customer in front of a personal computer, or PC, looking at your company's digital storefront is not the same type of customer as a mobile customer. Mobile customers use a wireless locator to find your store. Perhaps they have searched for nearby products, and your store has them. Some wireless devices can actually make purchases on the spot. So, mCommerce is a bit of a hero for many businesses with real storefronts in this Internet economy. To a developer, the server can handle electronic transactions and logic the same way that a customer can use either the traditional Internet-wired channel or the new Internet-wireless channel.

Conventional eCommerce sites use the wireless Internet too. Amazon.com lets you purchase books online with a Web browser. Using a wireless server, companies branch off the main site to let customers purchase books using a microbrowser on their Web cell phones. Like all good mCommerce sites, Amazon lets buyers customize their mobile pages so they do not have to type in so many things when they are on the go.

Whether you are developing applications, a wireless information service, or interactive wireless games, understanding the wireless Internet is important. If you thumb through the pages of this book, you will see the key diagrams and headline topics that can help you "get in the game." Part I encompasses telecommunication and computer technology, and the two form the roots of the wireless Internet. Diagrams of hardware, software, networks, and content are the props of the wireless Internet acted on a world stage by developers, organizations, countries, and impressive technology companies. In a proverbial battle between voice and data to set standards for universal service, the incumbent voice market has the numbers, but the data market has the advantage in efficiency, value, and multipurpose utility.

1 Chapter

The Wireless Internet World Stage

Today, many businesses are aware that if they do not have a wireless branch for their Internet business, they will not be able to reach half of their potential customers by the end of 2003. Most wireless connections to the Internet in 2005 will run faster than the wired cable and DSL service of today. Not waiting for the better technology, millions of people worldwide are using Web phones and wireless handhelds to access the Internet. Nations and corporations are making enormous efforts to establish a wireless infrastructure, including declaring new wireless spectrum; building new towers; and inventing new handsets, high-speed chips, and protocols. At stake is the future primary access to the Internet.

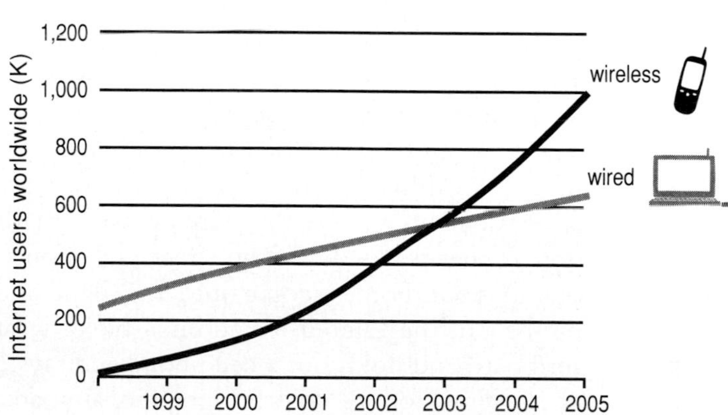

Figure 1 Wireless devices overtake the Internet
(*Source:* Copyright © 2001 Motorola, Inc. All rights reserved.)

By most estimates, one billion people will have access to all parts of the Internet by the end of this year. One billion wireless Internet-ready devices will be produced by the end of 2003 as wireless devices overtake the Internet (Figure 1).[1] Two billion wireless mobile users worldwide will exist by the year 2010 according to the UMTS Forum, which represents the global mobile wireless industry. We will examine more expert forecasts later.

The Internet: From Wired to Wireless

Although the Internet has been in common use for only a relatively short time, people are ready to take it a step further, to take it on the road with them and make the Internet accessible anytime and anywhere. It was not so long ago that handwritten letters were the only means of personal long-distance communication. Printed news was the only way to find out what was going on. It really was less than ten years ago that the wired Internet became available, affordable, and usable by the average citizen, and here we are wanting more.

The simplest definition I ever heard of the Internet is: "Everyone's computer connected." The Internet is an ever-expanding connection of worldwide networks that offers a wide range of information and services. Through a mix of public and private networks, personal computers (PCs), file servers, printers, and many other devices are interconnected. People use Internet services to send and receive email, chat online, take a tour of the world from a Web browser, log in to remote computers, download cool applications, shop online, listen to music and share pictures, watch digital videos, and talk with people and computers. Internet application developers see these Internet services as corresponding to technical protocols and standards that range from the Post Office Protocol (POP) to VoiceXML. Many of these Internet protocols are the same for the wireless and the wired Internet. Most protocols are based on the tested and proved Internet-woven world of physical wires that connect fixed terminals. The major exception to this is the low-level radio protocols. Together the wired and the wireless Internet are connecting more of the world every day. (A detailed list of Internet services appears in chapter 15, section "Internet Services and Protocols.")

As they plan with Internet standards, build new wireless technology, and operate over the airwaves, many organizations are envisioning changes to infrastructure to support new wireless services for their customers. But some visions are vexed. The truly mobile user for whom the wireless Internet is being built is often being misled. Worldwide, false expectations are being set up as some major television advertisements poison the wireless well. In the United States, a guy in a black trench coat walks down the street and shouts up to apartment dwellers, "Come out of your homes, come into the light and browse the Web with your cell phone." In the United Kingdom, a bloke wearing a psychedelic scarf rocks on a surfboard and holds out a cell phone and says, "Come surf the Internet." As pretty as it seems, today's colorful, graphic, animated PC Internet that people see on their desks at home or in the office is really nothing like the mobile wireless Internet. Although you could have a snappy, colorful, animated screen, when you are traveling, it gets in the way. The truth is that travelers want less, not more. They need quick access to direct information so they can move on. A wireless Internet service had better have something to say, a reason to use it, and something new for the mobile user. Television advertising doesn't show the revolutionary pioneers of wireless who have used their small devices daily. In certain places around the world, travelers get messages, share mobile information, and discover nearby places on small wireless devices. It is a world of personal mobility that many have heard about but few have experienced.

What Internet services can you get on wireless devices, and what devices are available? Depending on where you are, the networks offer widely varying features, capacity, and coverage. The class and quality of services are significantly different in Europe, Japan, and the United States. Early wireless users are experimenting with new services, the most popular being messaging, followed by access to World Wide Web content via microbrowser screens. A microbrowser is a small version of a Web browser that first appeared on Web phones. A small family of devices is currently being used to access the Internet wirelessly, as we shall see later in chapter 3, the section "Six Wireless Device Families Mobilize the Internet." Briefly the devices and their services are:

- *Web phones:* The most common device is the Internet-ready cellular phone, which we call a Web phone. There are three major Web phones: the U.S. HDML & WAP phone, the European WAP phone, and the Japanese i-mode phone. With them, you can exchange short messages, access the Web with a microbrowser, and run personal service applications such as locating nearby items of interest. Most Web phones work only when they have a network connection. Newer advanced Web phones can run applications.
- *Wireless handhelds:* Another common device, the wireless handheld, such as a Palm, can also message and use a microbrowser. The industrial handhelds, such as a Symbol or Psion, can perform very complex operations such as completing orders and taking customer signatures. They have the advantage of working offline.
- *Two-way pagers:* A device used often in business is the pager. The most popular is the two-way pager because it lets you receive and send a message as well as use a microbrowser.
- *Voice portals:* A recent innovation is the voice portal, which lets you have a conversation with an information service by using any kind of telephone or mobile phone.
- *Communicating appliances:* Such electronic devices are outfitted with wireless technology that can participate in the Internet. Examples include wireless cameras, watches, radios, pens, and many other devices.

- *Web PCs:* The standard Internet-connected personal computer is still used as an access method to mobile accounts, wirelessly or not.

Initially people use wireless devices to complement wired Internet services. The popular rush to the wireless Internet is being catapulted by sales of Web phones. In addition to voice, these phones run simple Internet services over cellular phone networks. Their use for voice and data is based on a steady evolution of communication and mobile computing technology.

A Short History of Wireless Networks and Devices

The wireless Internet comes to us from both the computer and telecommunications industries. Each industry has set important precedents that form the wireless landscape of today. In the late 1970s, entrepreneurs contemplated the creation of the personal computer. Meanwhile a national cellular phone system was being planned. Far before these new devices and networks would be built, however, communication technology had a history rooted in wireless technology.

Our wireless era is a second coming. The word wireless was in general use by 1915 to describe Marconi's "syntonic wireless telegraph," which he patented in 1896. The original diagram used in his 1902 lecture is shown to the side. This early radio freed the world from a landscape dominated by the poles and wires of Morse's telegraph, which had been in use since 1843. Using the same International Morse Code, the operator tapped out the messages of the electronic communication revolution and dit dit dit dah (V) would no longer need a wire. Marconi's wireless clicking system used radio waves. Like any new technology, the wireless telegraph was put into service to do the work of the old. However, it was not long before the medium of radio was recognized. On 15 June 1920, the first public song recital was broadcast from Britain using a Marconi 15-kilowatt telephone transmitter. From then on, the digital clicking business became the analog talking and music business. Radios were a consumer hit by 1930. If you had a wireless radio receiver, you had "a wireless."

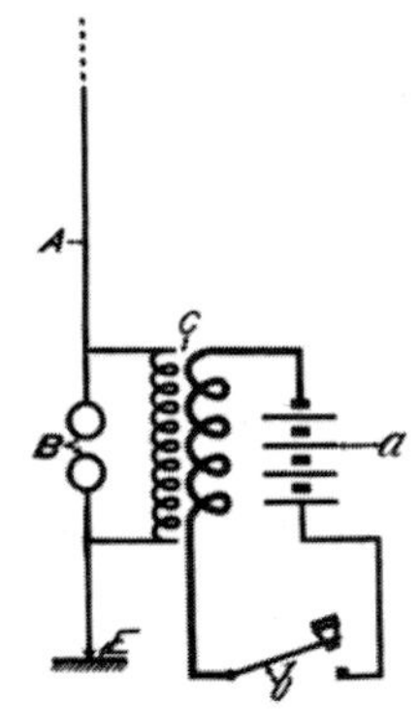

The Invention of the Cellular Phone

In 1934 the U.S. Congress created the Federal Communications Commission (FCC). This took over the role of the Federal Radio Commission, which had been formed in 1927. Previously, in 1918, President Wilson had put the feuding telephone and telegraph industries under control of the Post Office. The FCC, in addition to regulating landline interstate telephone business, began to manage the national radio spectrum. It also made international treaties because radio signals do not stop at the border. The FCC designated no radiotelephone channels until after World War II.

Portable communications systems have been under development since the 1940s when military radio required a man to backpack hefty gear. Replacing the backpack "walkie-talkie" was the Handie-Talkie with a long whip antenna, the SCR-536 (Signal Core Radio made by Galvin Manufacturing, now Motorola, Inc.). The mobile radio made it possible for signal division personnel to coordinate and command battle movement over a one-mile, line-of-sight AM radio band. Mobile terminals were too big and bulky for civilians to carry, however. In 1962 an automated telephone system for car phones appeared and was known as the Improved Mobile Telephone System (IMTS). This 23-channel system required a high-powered 200-watt transmitter to be located at the highest point in a city. Soon, small citywide networks of radiophones were operated for public safety. Mobile terminals were made available for automobiles and trucks, and the CB radio and the "car phone" radio became the wireless device of the early 1970s.

In 1973 Martin Cooper stood on a Manhattan street corner to make a phone call. In his hand was a 30-ounce device he had designed for Motorola. With this device, christened DynaTAC, Cooper had made the world's first portable cellular phone call. Ironically, one of the first people to receive one of his calls was the head of research at Bell Labs. Bell Telephone had a regulated monopoly on the telephone business, and it was "illegal" to introduce competing phone technology. Motorola showed that another company could produce viable public wireless telephone technology and tested a four-cell network in Washington, D.C., in 1974. It pioneered the chief distinctions of a cellular system, specifically, signals could be handed off and the channel could be reused in the same area for another call.

After years of study, the first national network that went live was the Japanese analog cellular system in 1979. To some people in the United States, it was like the Sputnik going up: another nation was leading in the technology of the future. In 1981 the FCC established rules that agreed with AT&T's plan for a national mobile phone network and calculated that the United States would need at most a system no larger than 300,000 subscribers, which was the total number of U.S. doctors, lawyers, and realtors. It was assumed only these professionals could afford such a network. The market was expected to grow as large as a million subscribers by 2000. This resulted in the Advanced Mobile Phone Service (AMPS). In 1982 the U.S. Department of Justice, headed by U.S. District Court Judge Harold Greene, broke up the Bell telephone monopoly into one long-distance company, AT&T, and seven "Baby Bells." After a historic 1984 consent decree, the company was forced to spin off its local phone companies, and the FCC issued an arbitrary set of rules to control ownership and operation of cellular networks.

Between 1983 and 1984, the FCC used comparative hearings to select the licensees in the top 30 markets for the new 800 MHz to 900 MHz spectrum for mobile phones. (MHz, or megahertz, are spectrum frequencies for radio transmission and are technically explained in chapter 3, the section "The Language and Science of the Wireless Internet.") For the lesser markets, where there was more than one applicant, the FCC used lotteries to determine the prospective owner. To "foster competition," in each market the FCC set aside two blocks: System A and System B. The A block was for new wireless companies and the B block was for conventional wireline companies. The landline companies received free B block licenses. Bidding companies were expected to compete by offering better prices and building more towers. To this day, when you buy a phone, an operator goes to the Network Access Management, or NAM, fields of your cellular phone to register preference for sysa or sysb. In the San Francisco Bay area there was Cellular One System A and GTE MobileNet System B.

The early 1980s continued the era of the car phone, which cost around $3,000. A car phone was glamorized in television shows such as *Hawaii Five-O* when Steve McGarrett would talk into something the size of a shoebox.

The United States and Europe have had completely opposite approaches to running cellular networks. The U.S. government on the one hand fostered free-market diversity and on the other artificially required that the technology live a long life for "the public good." When color TV came to market, the FCC required that television operators transmit a color signal that worked on black-and-white sets. Today, the FCC also mandates that a cellular operator must continue service for 10 years after the last subscription is sold.

In contrast to the U.S. approach, the Europeans mandated one unified network. In the 1980s, each European country had its own wireless analog standard. In 1990 the European Economic Union resolved there would be one standard – GSM, or Groupe Speciale Mobile. They allocated new spectrum frequencies while the old frequencies continued to operate. With GSM, many operators tore down and replaced tons of legacy cellular network gear throughout Europe. People had to throw their old phones away to get multinational coverage. Over the same spectrum, they rebuilt 900 MHz GSM towers (now expanded to 1800 MHz). Today GSM is used in many parts of the world.

Some U.S. companies invented a similar standard, Time Division Mobile Access (TDMA), in the early 1990s to replace the AMPS cellular phone system. (By the way, all these terms – AMPS, GSM, CDMA – are different national cellular air interfaces, and are explained as part of the section "Network Evolution:1G, 2G, 3G," in chapter 4.)

CDMA Networks: The Genius of QUALCOMM

In 1989 a small U.S. company called QUALCOMM demonstrated Code Division Multiple Access (CDMA), a totally new cellular technology based on military spread-spectrum technology. CDMA transcended GSM and TDMA technology by providing clear voice and a low-power, dynamic signal ideal for data. The conventional 900 MHz networks were already in use and QUALCOMM had nowhere to run in the United States. It looked around the world and found Korea to be a home to bring up an all-CDMA network in 1993.

In 1994 the FCC announced auctions for the new spectrum at 1900 MHz that could carry Personal Communications Services (PCS.) This time the rules of the auction effectively prohibited current owners of cellular phone companies from bidding because the FCC restricted anyone from owning more than 45 MHz of spectrum – a spectrum cap. The landline baby Bells had plenty of cash to burn and made deals with a number of spectrum winners. QUALCOMM was very smart. It had anticipated the 1900 MHz spectrum play on the PCS auctions. On the auction block were two parts of PCS spectrum – wideband for phones and narrowband for pagers. Of the 26 PCS phone markets, QUALCOMM was able to get 14 to go to CDMA. This included "PrimeCo" (Nynex, Bell Atlantic, US West, AirTouch, and Ameritech). Sprint was a major PCS auction winner. PacBell was too, although it later became a GSM company. The remaining PCS phone markets went TDMA, thanks to Craig McCaw who had started his empire with family money years before, and was now the owner of 84 old and new licenses. Later he sold his equipment and networks to AT&T, who spun out AT&T Wireless in 1999.

The FCC deregulated the carrier spectrum in 1987 (docket 87390) permitting TDMA, GSM, and CDMA air interfaces to run at any spectrum area. However, the auctions forced "competition" to take place with two carriers from a wireline and a wireless carrier in each area. Each one could only afford one air interface. This is how weird demi-regulation gets. In San Francisco a Cellular One is a System A operator running TDMA. But if you go to Los Angeles, then Cellular One is a System B operator but runs only CDMA. Because these two air interfaces are absolutely incompatible, subscriber phones advertising PCS service operated in only one geographical area. A cellular PCS phone would always fall back to the nationwide AMPS network since all PCS phones were dual mode. Even today in the United States, you can mistakenly buy the "wrong phone" and the "wrong network plan"; it all depends on where you travel. Of course, using cellular phones during international travel has its own charms.

The United States is going through a wild wireless saga of different standards and technologies. QUALCOMM successfully established a strong CDMA standard. World courts have upheld the QUALCOMM's original patents on CDMA, which it now licenses worldwide. The company recently spun off all its physical instrumentalities and is in the business of inventing and licensing complex signal technology to improve telecommunications and motion picture systems.

In retrospect, it is fortunate that the U.S. "free market" prevailed and that, unlike Europe, the FCC did not mandate a national standard. We would never have CDMA today. The irony is that CDMA, this dark-horse technology, rejected in the beginning, is now the basis for all 3G networks worldwide – most commonly as wideband CDMA, or W-CDMA. CDMA technology is so important we cover it throughout the book.

The Handheld Communicator and the PDA

The computer industry of the 1960s and 1970s was dominated by the big iron of mainframes and minicomputers. On April 1, 1977, the personal computer market was born with the Apple II. It turned out that making smaller iron was an even bigger business as PCs became more than computing machines. By the 1980s, the PC evolved to include sound cards; large, color screens; and CD-ROM multimedia technology under the thinking that a digital convergence of publishing, computers, and communications was taking place. Only partially realized then, this theme continues, with streaming multimedia as the "new" over-the-air wireless Internet multimedia technology. In the 1990s, new companies began to challenge the makers of personal computers and phone handsets. The even more miniature wireless communication devices were able to make wireless connections to the Internet. These new companies, such as RIM, Palm™, Kyocera, and Handspring™, work as small-iron chefs, feverishly perfecting their silicon and telecommunications hardware for customers on the go. Research In Motion (RIM) is a Canadian company that produces superb two-way pagers.

In the time line of mobile wireless Internet devices (see Figure 2), before miniature wireless Internet devices could be built, the computer industry and the telecommunications companies, or telcos, crossed paths many times with many networks and devices. The progressive miniaturization of the computer led to the first portable computer of the late 1980s. Practically speaking, in daily use, the early portables were too heavy to carry and too costly to build, the screen was poor, the computer was slow, and the battery life was extremely short. Voice was completely ignored. A small set of companies built industrial handhelds, identifying early business applications, and meeting early stages of success. They established vertical markets, which are commercial markets that specialize in applying technology to one kind of business. Vertical markets define the beginning of almost every new technology. Products from this market are seen today as industrial handhelds in use by workers at airport car rental agencies, and as electronic hand-carried clipboards used by packaging people on their delivery runs. Companies such as Grid, Go, Slate, and Eo, the early makers of tablet and notebook-style portable computers, are no longer in business. Symbol (who absorbed Telxon) and Intermec (who absorbed Norand) continue to make the "heavy-duty trucks" of the wireless Internet. The range of these markets is covered in chapter 5 in the section "Wireless Vertical Market Interactive Applications."

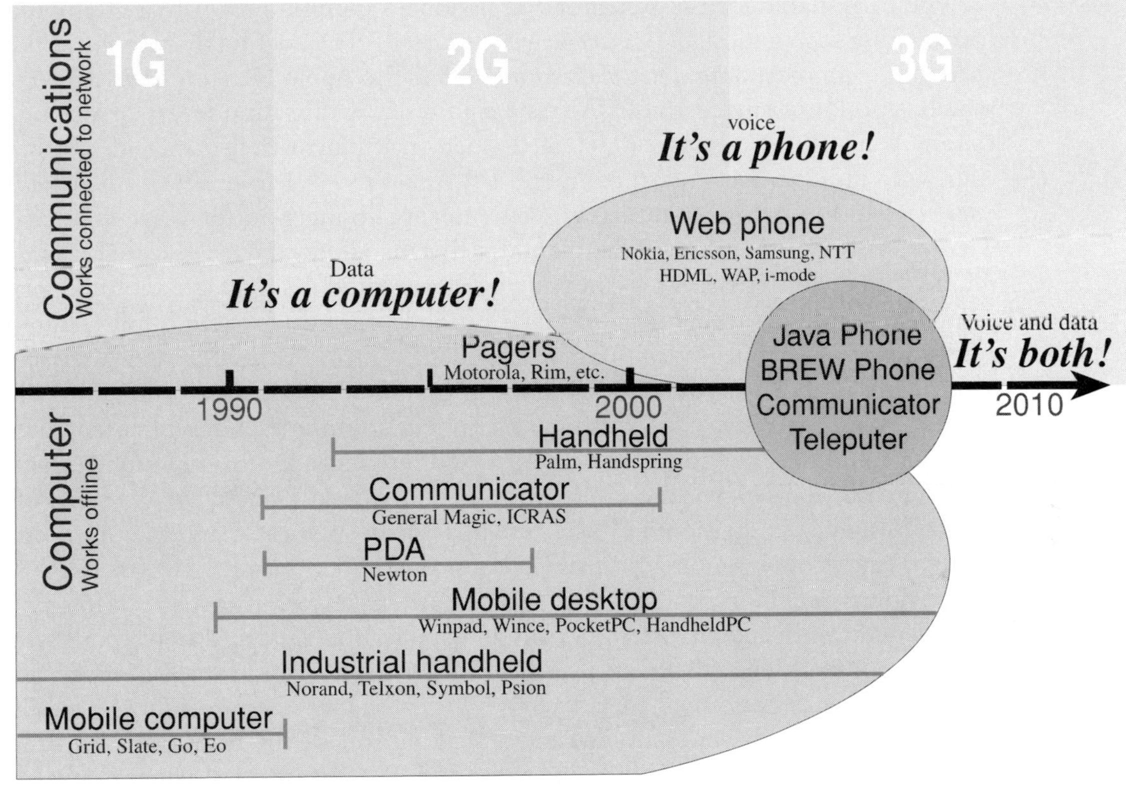

Figure 2 Time line of mobile wireless Internet devices

Throughout the 1990s, the computer companies emphasizing data and the telcos emphasizing voice led the early starts and limited successes of the wireless industry. With few efforts toward harmonization, each industry reinvented technology and opposed every other technically. Although the telcos tried to do it on their own, the network for data transmission definitely favored the Internet defined by the computer industry. As for the computer industry, even its best devices were no match for the robustness, simplicity, and maturity of radio technology of the telcos. To rule their voice and data kingdoms, the telco and computer industries produced ever-smaller digital media-delivery devices, some dedicated, some cross-bred; examples are workstations with telephones, telecalculators, handwriting tablets, Teletext, and nomadic computers. Most were technolocutions, or odd names for technologies that are not understood. Technolocutions are often based on names of familiar technology (for example, "horseless carriage" to describe the automobile, "iron horse" to describe the locomotive, and "radio pictures" to describe the television).

The early name for the miniaturized handheld communicator that attempted handwriting recognition, the *personal digital assistant* (PDA), definitely belongs in the gallery of technolocutions. First realized in 1993 as the Apple Newton MessagePad™, which is no longer made, the PDA was put into service for unique personal applications. While the Newton team created a personal information handheld, another team who built the Macintosh computer left Apple in 1991 to produce a *communicator* – a handheld that assumes a wireless Internet connection for voice and data. That team became General Magic and its first handheld device featured a telephone connection and slots for extensible hardware modules such as radio modems. The General Magicians heroically defined a mobile operating system, a full-featured communication architecture, power management, and a new mobile user interface. Their early mobile data devices, marketed as the Sony MagicLink™ and Motorola Envoy™, could not live long without a wireless communications infrastructure. Neither could the Newton. The market also suffered a lack of useful mobile content standards. The Newton division was shut down and General Magic spun off the communicator division as ICRAS, which made vertical market applications for its Data Rover handheld. Unable to update its hardware, in 2001 ICRAS closed down operations, and General Magic now makes voice portal technology.

Old desktop operating system designs and application models do not work well for the handheld. The Microsoft Corporation has tried many times to market its Windows operating system as a handheld device. Palm, Inc., was successful specifically because it realized that mobility is centered on personal content quickly available in handy hardware. The familiar mechanics of the Windows operating system actually got in the way of mobile use, requiring too many steps to get something done. With a one-button cradle, the Palm Pilot™ could copy all the familiar content of your PC into a handheld device. Until 1997 the only way to get wireless data was through a data modem or a pager. The Web phone changed all that.

The Convergence of Voice Networks with Web Phones, Handhelds, and Pagers

The world's wired phone system is out of whack with its primary user. The phone network was originally designed for human conversation; by 1994, however, if you looked at the actual traffic running through the phone network, you would see that half of it was not people talking but computers exchanging data. The system engineered to keep a steady circuit open between two parties was not good for the primary end user who prefers little bursts of intense information with long pauses in between. As the Internet grew to gigantic proportions, the act of browsing the Web through dial-up modems swamped phone networks.

Faced with the pressure to change, the telcos were forecasting a systemic decline in the use of voice and decided to add new capabilities to their networks. The telcos reengineered and upgraded the network to connect machines better.

The telcos also sponsored the opportunity for a new device. By 1997, a little company called Unwired Planet worked with telcos to install, free of charge, a microbrowser in cellular phones so voice subscribers could cruise the Internet. SprintPCS underwrote a lot of the initial development. A number of European telecommunications companies convinced Unwired Planet to recast the technology as the Wireless Application Protocol.

Appearing in 1998, the Wireless Application Protocol (WAP) is the basis for the small-screen Web phone found in European and some U.S. phones. The computer industry had its PDA, and the telco industry had its WAP. The popular *Doonsebury* cartoons that used to make fun of difficult PDA handwriting recognition could just as easily apply to the challenges of application complexity and text entry on the WAP phone's numeric keypad. Although Unwired Planet and WAP cellular phones failed to take off, the Web phone would find its day in the land of the rising sun in 1999.

Important economic and social barriers hold back the transition of cellular phones as computers. Unlike the wired network primarily filled with data, the cellular network is filled with voice. According to the FCC, only two percent of wireless mobile traffic is currently data. How tempting it is for telcos to continue profiting from voice subscribers. Throughout the 1990s, the telcos upgraded 1G analog cellular to 2G digital cellular, making the networks ready for data. But rather than pioneer the inevitable trends toward digital traffic, the telcos simply added subscribers. The cellular voice market is still the primary dollar attractor, and it is how most people continue to use the wireless networks. Most telcos still consider data an upsell to their phones.

The social factor is also a barrier. People like talking, perhaps too much so. They tolerate cell phones with poor quality of voice (QoV) – noisy line, sound delay, clicking, chirping. This brave desire to speak and listen despite all technical challenges is deeper than we think. It is epic mythology: 2700 years ago, an ancient poem of Homer tells of a homeward-bound odyssey where the hero asks to be rope-tied to the mast of his ship to endure the speaking and singing Sirens. "So they sent their ravishing voices out across the air and the heart inside me throbbed to listen longer."[2] The gallantry reminds us voice can be so powerful a force that it can prevent even heroes from ever reaching their destination. Voice continues to keep not only cellular telcos but also subscribers away from their digital destinies. Not to worry. Youth have found new magic in digital messaging on their Web phones. Consider the father in the United Kingdom who receives some typical advice from his teenager about cell phones. "Hey, Dad, why are you using your cell phone to talk to someone when you can send them a message?" Voice. How old-fashioned.

According to the forecasts of the leading handset manufacturers, beginning in 2002 every digital cell phone made will be Internet-enabled. Already, people buy more Web phones than computers. Affording a $100 device cannot compare to a $1,000 PC, but today people are buying voice and status first, data second. Any forecasts of wireless devices paving the way for the new Internet have to be taken with a grain of salt.

The voice networks are changing, and for good reason. One of the nearly forgotten features of the Nextel cellular phone is a "walkie-talkie" protocol called the Integrated Dispatch Enhanced Network (iDEN), which lets subscribers talk to others who use that network without having to dial them. Initially used for dispatch, this service became popular in business. In personal radio, subscribers with the same two-way radios can talk freely to each other up to two miles away without need of a relay tower. People are beginning to find out what engineers know regarding the value of data in voice networks: a system out of touch with its purpose is highly inefficient. The waste is enormous. When we compare voice to text using a wireless carrier, the words spoken take up far more space than if they were typed as text. Using the same circuit with conventional wireless modulation, you can speak for one second or transmit 250 words of email. Compared to wireless data, voice is a luxury. Although tempting to use, voice is wasteful in utility. Although it is easier to talk than type, it is faster to read than listen.

Because people like talking, using their PCs, and accessing the Internet, they are giving the telcos a run for their money. Over the Internet, people make voice calls using Voice over IP (VoIP) to eliminate charges for long-distance telephone calls. This can be done from PCs and now with new wireless IP phones that replace old office phones. PC-to-phone calling services such as Dialpad.com, PhoneFree.com, MediaRing.com, and Net2Phone offer free, unlimited phone calls within the United States. Millions of users place calls over the Internet. An effort called Enum combines phone numbers with Internet IP address numbers so you can call computers. (ENUM is covered in Part III, chapter 22.) Although the call is free, not everyone likes VoIP calling because the quality of the connection is not predictable: the QoV from echoes and voice delays is poor, the equipment is expensive, and they are not easy to make. For the consumer, VoIP calls require a personal computer, an Internet connection, a sound card, a microphone, speakers, and, for best quality, a headset. In most cases, the caller must install specific software. Cisco, AT&T, and WorldCom are all making mobile IP cellular phones that use wireless connections inside a business. Originally, VoIP delivered cheap minutes, but the new Internet voice systems are able to offer new services and applications that lead to profitability.

In 1999 Web phones achieved popularity in Japan with the explosive growth of i-mode – the sensational always-on packet digital service (discussed later in this chapter, under "The i-mode Story.") The wireless Internet is an international medium that fills the air not only with talk but also with all manner of digital content. Successful wireless businesses in Europe and Asia are now providing valuable lessons about appropriate wireless applications and the infrastructure required by wireless technologies. These new Internet-enabled cellular Web phones are gradually expanding market size by adding new services. However, the surprising new use of these Web phones, especially in Europe, is not for talking but for typing.

Messaging on Web Phones

The most popular use of the new European cellular phones is not cruising the Web, but exchanging simple messages with the Short Messaging Service (SMS). SMS is built into the entire European GSM cellular phone system. Messaging as a replacement for voice is very popular, in spite of the effort to create SMS messages.

Typing messages into a WAP phone is conceptually similar to hand cranking the engine of the first automobile. Better a sore thumb than a broken arm. Have you ever tried to do email on a cell phone? Hit the 4 key two times for "H" and the 5 key two times for "I." That was "HI." Now type in a Web address. For many, this thumb wrestler's dream is not a problem. For others, it is a keyboard version of annoying phone mail systems: "Press 1 for service, press 2 for returns..." The messaging software is crude, the screens are small, the numeric keyboard is difficult. It is a cranky beginning for an alternative to voice. As the wireless industry begins to design for a portable Internet experience, the solution may move out of the hands of the telco and handset manufacturers, back into the hands of the new handheld computer companies. The RIM pager with its small keypad is promising.

The SMS method is store and forward. Store-and-forward messages reach their destinations in the amount of time required to pass through the network. SMS service lags in many countries, especially messages going overseas. Only a paging network guarantees rapid message delivery. Web phones try to do the work of pagers, but the phone network is encumbered by voice priority calls. The pager market is in decline. However, we are seeing a comeback in two-way pagers, the preferred devices of many business professionals. Paging has an illuminating history of international use that is handy for wireless application developers to know.

A Brief History of Paging

Paging is built on its own valuable wireless networks. North America has enjoyed a long era of two-way paging networks; the European Public Paging Association (EPPA) only recently completed successful lobbying for approximately 800 KHz of spectrum for a back channel. The new wireless Internet pagers make use of networks with return channels for two-way messaging. But it was not always that way.

The pager was the first wearable personal communicator. It found its first use in vital services. For medical care, hospital staff and doctors could be notified immediately. For emergency services, fire and police personnel could be summoned quickly.

The first large, citywide public paging service was launched in New York in 1961. The original pagers were one-way and produced a tone alert. If you got a page, you had to find a telephone and respond. If you wore a pager in public, this meant you were a very important person, with life-saving ability. The Netherlands started the first national public paging service in 1963. Soon tones gave way to special paging codes. The first digital paging code developed in North America in the 1970s were entirely numeric. While U.S. national standards were emerging throughout the 1970s and 1980s, local individuals applied for citywide licenses and erected a single transmitter to serve their town. Large paging companies bought up all these civic paging operations over time. Two of these U.S. paging systems were added to the British Post Office (BPO) network when it was launched in 1973.

By 1976 the BPO realized that its customers and the number of pagers per radio channel needed to be increased for their national system. For economic reasons, a numeric paging system was required. In 1976 manufacturers and industry association representatives from Europe and the United States investigated the selection of a paging code standard and established the Post Office Code Advisory Group (POCSAG). In 1978 the final report was published and bound in a blue cover. For 20 years the paging Blue Book defined the POCSAG code that became a de facto world standard. The International Telecommunications Union (ITU) officially accepted it in 1981. The POCSAG code supported tone, numeric, and alpha paging. It significantly improved battery life and channel capacity over all previous codes.

The POCSAG code supports many millions of pagers with a relatively low number of transmitters to reach a nationwide population. European operators provide one frequency with complete personal roaming. The national 931 MHz paging frequency in the United States allowed a similar national service. By 1998 more than 100 million POCSAG pagers were in service in almost every nation. Meanwhile some countries began using a European paging service called Eurosignal. The pagers were specified to be four-channel units operating at 87 MHz using an analog sequential tone signaling protocol.

Although POCSAG was used worldwide, it was not an official European standard approved by the organization of European Post, Telephone and Telegraph administrations organized in France as CEPT, or the Conférence des Administrations Européenes des Postes et Télécommunications. However, Eurosignal was a European standard. As a result, some of the largest European countries, notably France and Germany, were very reluctant to introduce POCSAG paging. This reluctance to introduce this standard contributed to Europe's losing the worldwide race for paging penetration, allowing the United States and Asia Pacific countries to rapidly overtake the conflicting European standards in paging.

The Second-Generation Pager Standards Battle

The CEPT organization began work in 1985 to develop a unified European paging code standard. It was approved in 1993 by the European Telecommunications Standards Institute (ETSI) as the Enhanced Radio Message System (ERMES). The ERMES code was to be a digital code based on POCSAG. Like Eurosignal, it would harmonize a set of 16 operating frequencies, from 169 MHz to 169.8 MHz. The ERMES code specified a standard signaling structure to allow roaming. It defined multicasting for easier distribution of messages. ERMES battery life and alpha text-messaging characteristics were superior to those of POCSAG. These advantages were to be gained at the expense of many more transmitters (as a result of a much higher signaling bit rate), which were necessary to support long text messages. However, there was no improvement in the more popular short numeric message capacity, and the standard focused on a large code overhead necessary to support multifrequency roaming with codes for 32 countries. It proved too difficult to get ERMES widely accepted; large countries had nationwide single frequencies for paging allocated in the 280 MHz and 930 MHz bands; it was not marketed in cities and small towns, which were offered only the new service. Even with ITU endorsement, it could not compete with dominant numeric paging market requirements.

The alphanumeric paging code FLEX, originating from Motorola USA in 1993, has become the de facto world standard. Although FLEX is similar in format and structural characteristics to ERMES, it addresses many of the weaknesses. FLEX has a lower code overhead because it avoids multifrequency roaming in the basic code. This gives it an improved alphanumeric message capacity. A dynamic choice of signaling bit speeds from low POCSAG up to higher ERMES rates gives it a better match between local population needs and transmitter requirements.

Third-Generation Pager Standards and Two-Way Paging

The current trend in paging is to use a return path, also called an uplink channel. A paged person can reply, effectively creating an email system. In addition to direct delivery of full-body email messages, new paging services allow automatic roaming across large continents, an increase in capacity, and a far richer response capability. With more choices than an email reply, advanced paging can operate as an application by continuously sending and receiving information between parties.

Third-generation paging services were first introduced to the North American continent in 1995 by Mtel/SkyTel and are currently used by more than one million subscribers. The most popular paging network protocols are based on the FLEX forward channel protocol in combination with a return channel called ReFLEX. In North and South America, harmonized forward and return channels have been allocated in the 931 MHz and 901 MHz bands, respectively, while in

Europe harmonized forward and return channels have been allocated by the CEPT in the 169 MHz and 867 MHz bands, respectively. Few European countries have implemented the return channel, however, making two-way paging a rarity in Europe. The EPPA Web site is at <http://www.eppa.net>.

Wireless Networks

Pagers, wireless handhelds, and Web phones all interconnect through the Internet. They transmit wireless data over the air to a tower that connects to the wired Internet, eventually reaching a Web server somewhere in the world.

Three industries are competing to define the wireless Internet. Each industry wants to mold the Internet to its own image. To the *computer* industry, everything looks like software and databases to users. To the *telecommunications* industry, everything looks like a voice call to subscribers. To the *media/publishing* industry, everything looks like a content channel to a media audience. Each industry differs in the ways revenue is generated, customer loyalty is maintained, and systems are planned, built, and operated. Overall, it can be said that the wireless Internet is moving from controlled, proprietary industrial systems to universal, openly defined digital networked systems. The mobile audience is sometimes called users, subscribers, or audience depending on the industry model. The computer and telecommunications industries set the technical stage for the market. Media publishing – professional and amateur – is the emerging digital industry that contributes the greatest value to the Internet.

For many years, the telecommunications and computer industries have used their respective phone and computer network backbones in different ways to do the same thing: The computer industry uses Voice over IP (VoIP), the telco industry uses data overlays on voice channels. Each industry uses common digital networking standards that are more Internet centered. When everything is digital, there is no difference if the bits that pass between two people are spoken or emailed. How the bits must bounce and rebound shapes the medium of the wireless Internet. To uniquely identify any wireless device, the computer network uses an IP address and the telco uses a telephone number. Each number is treated differently technically and for billing purposes. Although voice and data are well defined by each industry, each uses its favorite technology.

Computer, radio technology, and battery technology are beginning to come together. Small devices are built with digital computer and radio signal-processing architectures that are able to handle both voice and ever more personal information. An important emerging branch of the wireless Internet is the so-called third-generation (3G) packet-switched cellular networks. For the most part, people use two-way pagers for messaging, cell phones for microbrowsing, and handheld devices for interactive applications. Even when each device has its own wireless network and different software, underneath all the content is the same. Common content, easily produced, is the cardinal value of the wireless Internet.

Software and Content That Make Hardware Useful

A wireless application is software that runs on wireless devices or servers to exchange content over a wireless network. Content is delivered through wireless applications. The progressive popular choices of content delivery are through voice call, messaging, browsing, interactive wireless, and conversational voice portal applications.

Although a voice call may solve immediate needs, messaging is often more effective. Developers often overlook messaging in wireless projects. Messaging is the basis for many collaborative business and personal uses. Many European developers instinctively build SMS dialog-style applications rather than browser applications for Web phones.

Mobile customers view miniature versions of Web sites via microbrowsers. But microbrowsing is not like PC Web browsing. A microbrowsable site is simple to access and read. A successful microbrowsable site redefines the standards of conventional surfable Web sites that have grown heavy with complex layouts, excessive graphics, and numerous pages and links. With some effort, Web content can become more informative when it is personalized. Developers write content for these microbrowsers in HDML, WML, cHTML, and XHTML Basic (markup languages are covered in the section "The Markup Languages of Wireless Publishing" in chapter 5).

The interactive applications and transactional systems are very useful to business. Wireless business applications can be as specific as vertical market dispatch applications, or comprehensive systems. mCommerce, or mobile commerce, could just as easily mean miniature commerce. Applications are small, billing is measured in fractions of a penny, and access is through devices that fit in your hand. To involve a mobile user, you have to reduce transactions to short, ordinary text. Although the Web phone has given new access to Web sites and increased the number of potential customers, the handheld is showing some of the more compelling mobile uses. Regardless of the application, to say something to, or do something with a person on the go, you have to get to the point quickly.

The chief devices for wireless applications are Internet-ready Web phone, especially good for voice, and the wireless handheld, especially good for data. There is a tendency to be either-or. Should we develop for the handheld or the Web phone? Wireless system architectures often side with either voice-based telecommunication or data-based computation. Although there is a temptation to be an engineering loyalist to one industry, and there is a general lack of harmonized standards among the industries, you can develop good wireless Internet software to serve both.

Some telcos deliver wireless applications and content in a proprietary manner. Sprint and British Telecom have packaged a Web phone with a service plan that reaches select Internet service destinations. Rather than study the dynamics of the Internet content model and user base, the telcos are remolding the Internet into their own image. Telco subscribers get well-chosen but selective access to the Internet, sometimes called a "walled garden" model. Alternatively, on nontelco devices, such as handheld and pager devices, people access the wide, open Internet where end-user experience differs enormously. Not everyone has the patience or the budget to explore the wireless Internet, so the telco's walled garden model has value. However, wireless subscribers want easy and open access to the Internet, which is one of the conclusions of i-mode.

The World Wide Web's success does not stem from the innovations of either the computer or the phone industry, but from a simple publishing model. In 1990 a simple Web browser was invented to plainly present documents. It used an ordinary publishing language with a magical link notation so that by clicking on linked text or a graphic target in the document, you leapt over the Internet to another server that showed related documents. This publishing language, Hypertext Markup Language (HTML), has been upgraded to an Extensible Markup Language (XML). XML and its variants comprise the base for generating everything from portable data to wireless mobile voice-based and even video-based documents. These open standards are used worldwide on the Internet.

Mobile users need traction, not distraction. Traction means going somewhere; the more effort you put into moving, the farther you get. Personal wireless applications help travelers in many ways. Valued wireless technology provides identity and individuality; it delivers mobile content that is personal and succinct. All good mobile information is personal, contextual, and relevant. When I am on my way to work, all I need to know is if the train is late. I do not need to see an interactive Web browser picture of moving train maps or long schedules. I need a simple piece of information: Is my train on time? Since new devices know the time and the place, developers can grant this wish almost magically. Location and time combine to give other information greater personal relevance. They are the hallmarks of mobile content. Mobile applications accomplish things that cannot be done on a PC desktop. Personalization is a way to set up a Web site to filter large amounts of content. The use of time of day and location can filter even more. Mobile Web sites benefit from being far more user-centric. Mobile utility is a "direct-drive" application for the traveling user. Traction is the attraction.

The new mCommerce systems will challenge the ways operating eCommerce systems are built and operated. We already know that mobile technology keeps people active, while PC technology keeps them in their seats. At the risk of inventing more technolocutions, the new wireless mobile era goes so far as to call for an mUser, and for industries to be called mMail, mBusiness, mBanking, mPublishing, mKiosk, and mGames. These odd names probably will not stick – but the mobile-oriented industries they represent are being built around the world today.

The World Wireless Scoreboard

Japan was the first country to establish significant wireless Web phone applications and content. The Europeans also have a healthy Web phone market. Although commercial wireless systems are used widely in the United States, the popular Web phone market is in relative infancy. It comes as a shock to many to learn how far a lead the general overseas wireless markets have over the United States. Global wireless maturity (Figure 3) is measured by the age of the wireless standards in use, number of subscribers using them, available spectrum, territorial coverage, wireless devices per capita, infrastructure, cross-industry participation, number of new devices in the market, and working national services. World wireless technology adoption appears to roll out from east to west. Looking at the world wireless scoreboard, analysts see Japan is number 1, Europe is number 2, and the United States is the third world wireless Internet trailer. Analysts say the Japanese and Koreans are about 6 months ahead of the Europeans and at least 24 months ahead of the United States.

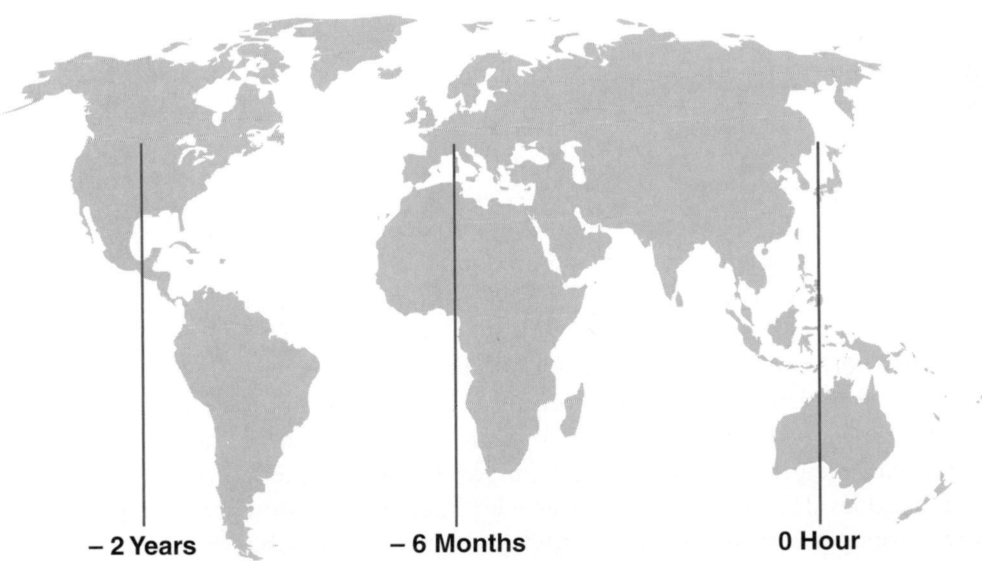

Figure 3 Global wireless maturity. With regard to 3G spectrum, the United States is at least two years behind Japan.

Michael Porter offers a more comprehensive analysis of the dynamics of global wireless technology's maturity in markets in his "Case Study of Finnish Wireless Cluster," which is included in the White House report on 3G.[3] In essence, he notes there are economic clusters like that in Finland that feed upon their own success. Participating in a cluster offers advantages in perceiving new technology and in operational or delivery possibilities. Clustered firms are often able to perceive new customer needs more clearly and more rapidly. Moreover, new business formation occurs more readily in economic clusters, because the barriers to entry are lower there than elsewhere. The required assets, skills, inputs, and staff are readily available at the cluster location and are easily assembled there. On the opposite end of the spectrum are countries that are able to exploit the advantage of wireless technology. Nations such as China that have few phone lines, no Internet infrastructure, and no complex bureaucracy for administering landline access are leapfrogging straight to wireless Internet technology.

The Japanese are clearly ahead according to Bill Gates. In his .NET introduction, Gates stated that DoCoMo had the most successful wireless technology on the planet.[4] Makers of great miniature consumer technology, the Japanese's chief advantage was to appreciate the simplicity of the Internet model and to create the simplest means by which developers could offer Web content to mobile users. The reality today is that Japanese businesses are offering next-generation wireless services that are not even on the drawing boards of most U.S. corporations. To understand the reasons for the many Japanese advantages, read "The i-mode Story" later in this chapter.

Europe provides examples of leading wireless usage and application maturity. The Nordic countries have an especially high penetration of mobile phones. The entire European Economic Union unified all air interfaces in 1990 through GSM. It is the most popular worldwide wireless cell phone standard. Built into it is the extremely popular SMS, or the Short Message Service.

The United States is experimenting with many powerful wireless technologies. There are many fragmented and incompatible wireless networks, but this will clear up. After all, when the telephone was invented in the late 1800s, there were three telephone networks in New York, and none of the telephones operated on the other networks. Today, as if the lack of national standards were not enough of a barrier, the U.S. pricing system prohibits rapid expansion. Meanwhile companies using their own equipment and wireless networks to provide unique commercial advantages are creating small wireless vertical markets.

How does this affect the developer who intends to create wireless applications? As a developer writing wireless software applications and building wireless content, you are insulated by high-level protocols from the underlying wireless hardware and wireless network protocols. However, some awareness is required to support new handsets, emerging networks, and the mix of coverage, new features, and network-specific protocols.

World Spectrum Auctions

Wireless devices require wireless networks that operate on assigned frequencies of spectrum. Spectrum, as we shall examine later in the section "The Language and Science of the Wireless Internet" in chapter 3, is the available electromagnetic area for airwaves. Currently, the wireless radios in devices are built to tune into only one part of the spectrum. Spectrum is a limited resource. As wireless spectrum is used up worldwide, licenses for new spectrum have to be assigned. Many governments put a frequency spectrum up for sale and auction it off to the highest bidder. Other governments award licenses outright – a practice referred to as a beauty contest. The companies with the best financials, technical capabilities, and public service record are chosen.

The total wireless spectrum can be summed up internationally as gross bandwidth allocated in each country. In the global wireless bandwidth allocation in 2001 (Figure 4), many countries have twice the wireless spectrum that the United States has. In the United States, a spectrum squeeze is in effect for a number of reasons. The United States has the largest television spectrum in the world, leaving little room for wireless communications. The FCC also sets a 45 MHz ownership cap on spectrum. There is no cap in other countries, where successful individual carriers operate as much as 100 MHz of spectrum.

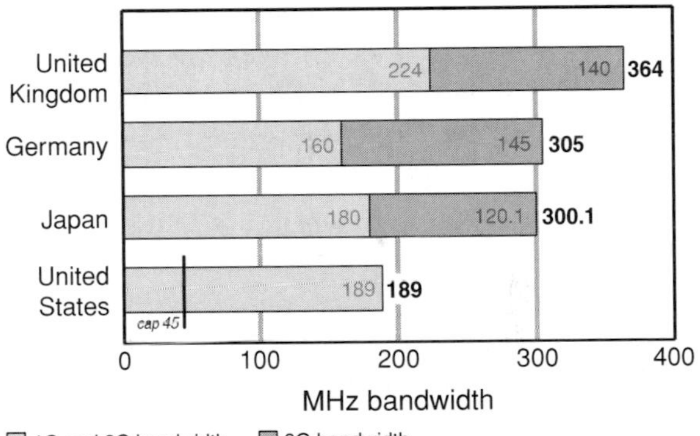

Figure 4 Global wireless bandwidth allocation in 2001 (*Source:* Cellular Telecommunications and Internet Association)

Owning megahertz is a big business. Wireless operators in the United States earned $238 million of revenue per MHz under the existing spectrum allocation of 1999. At the beginning of 2001, telcos had spent more than $110 billion worldwide to buy 3G licenses around the world. In Europe, Germany, the United Kingdom, and the Netherlands, license auctions raised US$82.5 billion. World wireless 3G licenses are being auctioned for advanced wireless services called International Mobile Telecommunications 2000 (IMT-2000) and Universal Mobile Telecommunications System (UMTS). While the United States continues the debate over possible next-generation spectrum, the Europeans have completed most of their 3G auctions and awarded licenses. The Japanese, well ahead of everyone, did a great job of planning consumer IMT-2000 3G services to launch May 31, 2001.

The United States continues to fall behind other parts of the world, in part because of legislated policy and the penalties of the regulated free market. As other countries build 3G technology and market services to the rest of the world, the current plan is for a U.S. 3G auction to take place no earlier than 2002. This may require a prior auction to recover unused television spectrum or the resale of occupied spectrum. The last major U.S. wireless auction sold the Personal Communications Services (PCS) licenses in 1995 and 1996, worth $11 billion.

The total worldwide cost to build 3G may reach as high as $751 billion, according to market researchers Herschel Shosteck Associates.[5] For a detailed account of auctions, international spectrum, and the U.S. position, see "3G Spectrum Auctions" in chapter 16.

Wireless Content and Applications around the World

The Internet is by nature global, and your content reaches all popular devices and networks, whether you intend it or not. In anticipation of the 3G economy, there is much to learn from succeeding applications. It is important for wireless developers to look all over the world at places wireless activity is taking root. The early wireless economies show wireless information and business applications are the strongest starting point. As the market matures, wireless information portals evolve into distinct services and specialized content. Some particularly stellar examples are Japanese wireless service, European banking, and the U.S. wireless industrial applications.

Types of Wireless Content

The progression of technology that made the wired Internet successful is the same for the wireless Internet. The Internet started with email. The wireless Internet began with messaging, added small Web page browsing and access to online databases, and finally became interactive with logical applications such as inventory checking and illogical ones such as games. Sophisticated applications synchronize and manage content. One way to evaluate wireless applications is by the unique content they deliver. The following popular wireless content sources have different purposes.

- Messaging – 50 words or fewer for person-to-person communication
- News – headlines and paragraph synopsis to stay informed
- Stock quotes, company headlines – making decisions
- Sports scores, player backgrounds – social participation
- Yellow Pages – finding a business

- Navigation – getting directions
- Transportation updates – traffic, public transport, airline information

Because mobile users have limited time, they will not ponder large bodies of content and will generally avoid complex wireless streams that require negotiation and input. Comparative shopping or data collection applications are suitable only for audiences who are locked into long commutes. Wireless advertising is unlikely to succeed because mobile use is very directed and subscribers are paying by the second. People do not like to pay for things they do not ask for. The mobile wireless user can receive content that takes advantage of a special characteristic of wireless networks – the wireless network can correlate time and location.

To make wireless mobile transactions useful requires the participation of other companies for the application to really take off. For example, to get a service such as checking into a hotel in Europe as you connect with a GSM Web phone from the back of a taxi requires travel agencies, hotels, and taxi services to commit to infrastructure. Infrastructure includes not only a secure technical and useful design solution but also standards of operation, training of staff, and system maintenance. It is necessary that everyone use a common or interoperable technology.

Early Public Wireless Systems: i-mode, WAP, Palm™

When we look at world use of the wireless Internet, we see many kinds of users and systems. North American business users in industrial markets primarily use wireless Ethernet. But the number of subscribers is small. Figure 5 shows global wireless Internet use as of November 2000; the largest subscriber base is the Japanese consumer market, which uses i-mode. According to Eurotechnology.com,[6] Wireless Internet subscribers are distributed as follows:

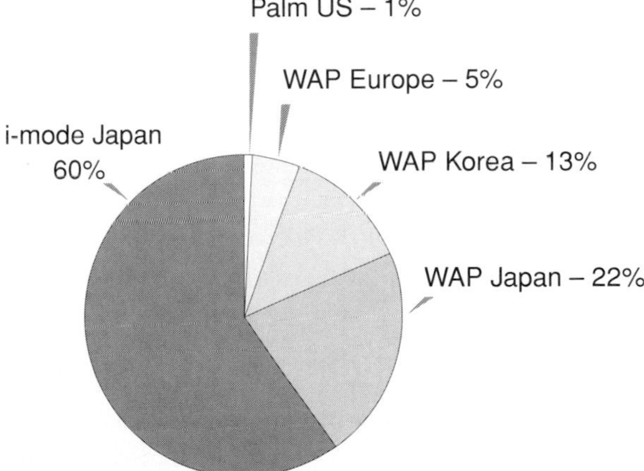

Figure 5 Global wireless Internet use as of November 2000 (*Source:* Based on information from Eurotechnology-Japan Corporation)

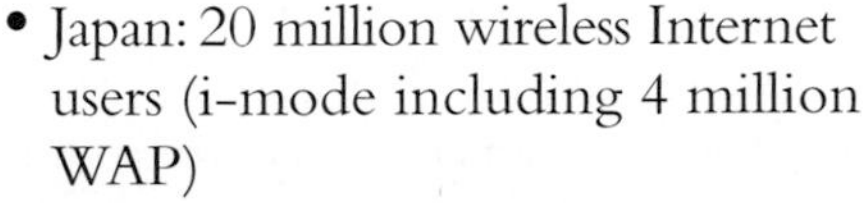

- Japan: 20 million wireless Internet users (i-mode including 4 million WAP)
- Korea: 2 to 3 million wireless Internet users (WAP)
- Europe: 1 to 2 million wireless Internet users (WAP)
- United States: 0.5 million wireless Internet users (Palm including 0.2 million WAP)

Let us look a little deeper at the Japanese, European, and U.S. markets and see what is making each one tick.

Japanese Wireless Applications

Start at the top. The most successful wireless Web phone technology on the globe is the i-mode service in Japan. Since mobile wireless callers from Japan can look at your wireless Internet site, you will want to know how to reach them. Examples of i-mode are shown in "Writing i-mode cHTML Applications for Wireless Browsing" in chapter 10.

It is helpful to understand the accomplishments of i-mode. Table 1 gives the result of a short survey of Japanese wireless applications as of 2000, showing entertainment in the lead. Before this, the Japanese market showcased Personal Handyphone™ modem service, which delivered information and news to early wireless business markets. It is helpful to take a closer look at the i-mode technology to understand how this wireless market works.

Table 1 Japanese wireless applications

Application	Dominant Example	Use
Entertainment transport updates	Games	64%
Information	News agents	21%
Transaction	eCommerce	9%
Database	Corporate Internet access	6%

Source: Copyright © 2001 NTT DoCoMo, Inc. All rights reserved.

The i-mode Story

The most popular wireless data service on the planet is i-mode, developed by DoCoMo (which means "anywhere" in Japanese), a subsidiary formed in 1992 from Japan's largest telecommunication service provider Nippon Telegraph and Telephone Corporation (NTT). NTT is a national telco and handset maker. i-mode (the *i* stands for information) is a wireless technology and service mark. The i-mode service, begun February 1999, enables users to access Internet services via their cellular i-mode phones. This is the largest wireless society of subscribers, and it is increasing at the rate of 50,000 new users per day. It is oversubscribed, often chokes the Sun servers, and is used everywhere in major Japanese cities. Many global Internet content companies, such as CNN in Atlanta, originate as i-mode services. This is how many Japanese got their Olympics news. This i-mode application is in chapter 10, the section "i-mode and the Olympics."

Japan envy is no substitute for learning from the world's most successful wireless technology. To begin with, NTT has a good understanding of wireless Internet service and has a good business model. It is sobering that national telcos and handset companies who started service a year ahead of DoCoMo and invested at least ten times more capital do not have even one-tenth of the subscribers. i-mode appealed to eight million subscribers in 18 months. With each subscriber, on average, signing up for three additional services at $1 per month per service, NTT DoCoMo earns $36 per year per subscriber in incremental business. Why is i-mode so popular, and what are the key lessons to learn?

Figure 6 An i-mode phone (*Source:* Copyright © 2001 NTT DoCoMo, Inc. All rights reserved.)

Walking down a Tokyo street, a first impression is that everyone is using *keitai* (cell phones), especially the i-mode phone (Figure 6). They are everywhere, in use all the time. Women wear them around their necks like jewelry. For good reason, they are perhaps the most beautiful handsets ever designed. The Japanese perfection of miniaturization is from another world. They are thin, very light, often pearly white with beautiful tiny color screens and battery life exceeding 260 hours. Keitai are works of art. At the center of the action is an i-mode button, which connects a handset to the Internet. i-mode is an always-on service, meaning you do not dial in to get it. It comes to you. This is because the network is entirely packet based, not circuit switched like the rest of the world's 2G networks. People are accessing more than a dozen i-mode search engines and sites that give miniature views of such things as sports scores, stock trading, banking, weather forecasts, maps, concert tickets, train timetables, recipes, restaurant coupon discounts, and horoscopes.

When you talk to the Japanese, they say these appealing services solve many of the problems encountered using the PC Internet. The wireless Internet is a real option for those who never cared for PCs, could not afford them, had difficulty using them, or simply did not have any space at home. Computers are found in 13 percent of Japanese households. Wireless Internet ketai are used by well over 25 percent of the population. Japan has some 20 million Internet users, with 3 million to 4 million accessing it from home and the rest from offices.[7]

How many i-mode subscribers are there? DoCoMo, like other successful networks, knows that people like to see themselves. One of the fun things about i-mode is it posts its subscriber numbers at <http://www.nttdocomo.com>. As of July 2001, there were 25 million subscribers and more than 37,000 i-mode sites, including 1,420 preferred sites. Some 1,600 Web sites offer application downloads for their i-appli Java service.

Access to Japanese Web sites is very simple, and there are fun things to do for the commuting workers who take hour-long train rides. People send all kinds of avatars, or animated cartoons, that represent services and users via email attachments. Tamagotchi, the digital pet craze, lives in i-mode. The maker, Bandai Company, ships a different animated character every day to every i-mode phone of registered pet lovers. This service, along with others that Bandai offers over i-mode, brings in more than 2 million subscribers, each paying about $1 a month.

Subscribers who enter a four-digit PIN typically can purchase items over an i-mode phone. Since the cellular provider already has the subscriber's personal and billing information, the system avoids data entry and the risk of passing on credit-card information. Payments appear on the phone bill, often posted by a third-party, as we shall see.

Technically, i-mode 2G service has a transmission speed of 9.6 kbps. The i-mode service uses compression technology to increase the volume of data that is transmitted, and the underlying packet-switching system makes efficient use of bandwidth. Email is limited to about 250 characters per message, but you can scroll through consecutive messages. i-mode also uses SSL, or Secure Socket Layer, provided by RSA, and uses Sun Solaris servers on the back end.

Lessons from Japan's i-mode Success

The big secret to the success of i-mode is that Internet developers can put their Web site content online with few changes. In addition, if you keep a customer on the air, DoCoMo or a third party will give you the major cut of the transaction. But it is worth thinking about other Japanese merits:

- Packet-switched service is always connected.
- Attraction comes from personal value, not Internet hype.
- The service is a viable national technology enclave.
- Content makers are given choices.
- The microbilling economy encourages consumer purchasing.
- Simple Internet standards make everyone's work easier.
- Subscribers use quality handsets.
- Complete products are offered from the carrier.

- Satisfied subscribers get what they want.
- A mature commercial infrastructure contributes to use.

Let us look at each of these qualities.

Constant Connection

Subscribers leave their i-mode phones on all the time, as long as the batteries are charged. They pay only when information is exchanged. The constantly connected subscriber lives in an information-rich world. Since data moves in packets, as it does on the Internet, many more people can access the network simultaneously than if they were only making called connections. A profound point about this packet system is the elimination of consumer labor to access the network. Subscribers do not have the typical 30-second to 60-second dial-up service to check to see if anything is there.

Personal Value, Not Internet Hype

According to Takeshi Natsuno, media director at NTT DoCoMo in an interview in March 2000, "We wanted to attract ordinary people, not techies. So we never used words like *Internet* or *Web*."[8] In the United States and Europe misleading advertising continues for the "Internet in your hand." The smart people know they do not want the Internet in their hand, and the uninformed do not know what you are talking about anyway. In Japan operators keep the sites simple and focused, and the technology hidden. There is no separate dial-up into the Internet, and there are no long Internet addresses to remember; keywords and short menus work well enough.

A Viable National Technology Enclave

DoCoMo's cellular voice and i-mode service is nationwide, covering 98 percent of Japan. This is an area roughly the size of California. Subscribers get perfectly matched hardware, software, and content. The network and device standards are harmonized. DoCoMo keeps strict design control over supplier handsets so there is little confusion for the consumer. The service was planned to use a specific device and a specific digital wireless network, and to deliver the general content of the Internet. Unlike in the United States, the air interfaces work equally well everywhere.

Choices for Content Producers

Subscribers are offered a premium area that provides special customer care, featuring specially produced content, and a higher billing plan. Callers are also offered any wild content that exists on the Internet. A subscriber can get a trusted service or something creative and original – something the Internet is known for.

Microbilling Economy

Ten Yen-Mail is a popular low-cost Internet mail service. For 10 yen, or US$0.08, customers send and receive email of up to 2,000 alphanumeric characters that is delivered within 12 seconds from any Internet provider's server. Web content is transferred at higher speeds for subscribers of the preferred services. For messaging and Web content, subscribers are charged only for the amount of information they retrieve, not the amount of time they are online. The low basic subscription fee of $3 per month gives you an i-mode email address. Most extra services are $1 per month per service. Middle-tier content providers that produce traffic for the carrier get, through third-party billing, a small cut of the carrier's revenue from subscribers' fees. Anyone who produces interesting content can make a microcent that can be multiplied by millions of subscribers.

Simple Internet Standards

Many existing Web site operators are launching i-mode–enabled sites because it is quite simple to convert existing Web pages to an i-mode–formatted page. The market grows because everyone can bring content to bear rapidly. More than 50,000 i-mode sites were made available in 2001. Developers use the Compact HTML, or cHTML, markup language that works with the NetFront Browser. Both language and browser were designed by ACCESS Company, Ltd., for DoCoMo. The strategy of using familiar standards and a clear Internet publishing model is different from inventing a brand-new complicated technology that would require new gateways and consortiums for global adoption that must prove their value in the market.

Quality Handsets

The i-mode handsets are works of art and standardized. i-mode–capable phones are preloaded with a menu and simple directions. Handset excellence leads the market by capturing the imagination of potential buyers. The simplicity of Japanese keyboard entry is an often overlooked phenomenon. For the calligraphic Japanese language, keyboarding has always been complex. On regular computers, their input method is to have a key entry sequence. Beginners look at pop-ups of the predictive code completions. But experts know the keys. The Japanese are already familiar with this style of code entry. All phones have a predictive lookup input system, unlike Western designs that have crude tri and quad tapping per key.

Complete Products from the Carrier

Subscribers have comprehensive billing. They do not worry about configuring for different providers or configuring software, as is the case in other parts of the world. A user follows the prompts that appear on the device without having to worry. The handset maker goes the distance to ensure utility.

Satisfied Subscribers

The Japanese application market has an enormous number of choices. It has evolved to match consumer interest. As Table 1 shows, at the beginning of 2001, the i-mode application breakdown is 64 percent entertainment, 21 percent information, 9 percent transaction, and 6 percent database. This translates largely to games, newsagents, eCommerce, and corporate Intranets.

A Mature Commercial Infrastructure

The Japanese commercial infrastructure includes hotels, restaurants, taxi companies, banks, all of which involve transaction and personal communication responsibilities demanded by an i-mode society. These companies have call centers that are ready for mobile use. A particular i-mode feature that content providers make use of is the `phoneto` tag, which allows a user to place a voice call to the company hosting the Web page. This may not seem like much, but the subtle point is that someone at the server company takes the call. The "mobile service" branch of a company is already on board with a corporate mobile service response infrastructure.

Understanding the i-mode Economy

The i-mode economy is lucrative and very sophisticated. It will generate more than $4 billion this year. But it was a transition for DoCoMo, who first tested the market with DoPa, a vertical market service for businesses in the mid 1990s. "We went from volume to value, from the voice to the nonvoice connections market," said Mr. Kouji Ohboshi, chairman of NTT DoCoMo, April 5, 2001, in an interview with the Japanese press.

DoCoMo's i-mode planning group knew that it needed a portal to attract users and a menu bar to make it easy to look for information. DoCoMo helps its official content providers customize their i-mode Web sites. Official provider sites can be accessed directly from DoCoMo's i-mode menu, and official providers can charge a monthly fee for a service. DoCoMo handles the collection as part of its monthly billing. In addition to making money from subscription airtime charges, DoCoMo takes a 9 percent commission for content and transactions. NTT makes most of its money through airtime charges and the volume of data sent and received. In January 2001, NTT introduced i-appli in a new service to provide applications for its new i-mode phones that run Java applications.

It is not just DoCoMo, but also the third-party billing agencies that make it work. When an i-mode subscriber accesses an interesting service from a phone that is not in the i-mode "preferred group," the subscriber may see a screen that asks, "Do you want this cartoon service for $1 a month?" If the viewer accepts, the charge is appended to the DoCoMo bill. DoCoMo takes its 9 percent, and the rest of the revenue is split between the content provider and the billing aggregator.

A more thorough analysis of wireless business models is covered in the section "The Site: Wireless Business Models" in chapter 16.

The Future of i-mode: Competition and 3G

The future of i-mode is very ambitious. According to Yoshinori Uda, Senior Executive Vice President, NTT DoCoMo announced the 3G version of i-mode to begin trials in May 31, 2001 under the name of FOMA, or Freedom of Mobile multimedia Access. FOMA is the Japanese W-CDMA service from DoCoMo. It will add advanced Web access, image and music distribution, and video conferencing. By the end of 2001, FOMA should be generally available. DoCoMo plans to invest US$1.4 billion in the spring of 2001 to build FOMA service. Through 2004, it plans to roll out a national network estimated at US$8.8 billion.[9]

DoCoMo believes there will be a progression of wireless products to grow from human to human, human to machine, to machine to machine. The human-to-human variety is conventional phone calling. Human-to-machine interaction involves a person speaking to a voice portal or using a Web phone browser to interact with a server. Machine-to-machine interaction is using a cell phone to make transactions with another device, or having software-programmed agents perform tasks with other software agents. Although the Japanese market by 2010 will reach 120 million people, the total market is expected to include 360 million wireless devices, three times the population. DoCoMo plans to offer the world its mobile multimedia networks and a range of devices.

DoCoMo's 3G FOMA prototype handsets are for manufacture and license – a small basic handset, visual phone, and a data terminal. All IMT-2000 terminals are intricate devices with a large color display and small cameras. Some use separate radio-connected components. The basic FOMA phone features voice, high-speed data at 384 kbps data downlink, 64 kbps data uplink, and still color pictures. The visual FOMA phone (Figure 7) features voice, a small camera, high-speed data, still picture, and video transmission. One model is a three-part device. A phone radio communicates with a picture on watch, a PC function body, and a handset antenna. The data-dedicated FOMA terminal has a large screen and offers data access only. NTT plans its new i-mode service to run with Java-capable phones that have unique applications.

Figure 7 Visual FOMA phone (*Source:* Copyright © 2001 NTT DoCoMo, Inc. All rights reserved.)

NTT DoCoMo continues to develop strategic partnerships and operating agreements with key companies. At the end of 2000, NTT made a $9 billion investment in AT&T Wireless to introduce i-mode into the United States. The service will not meet with much success operating over AT&T's older TDMA circuit-switched technology; however, AT&T Wireless may begin deploying 3G W-CDMA networks beginning in 2002 with rapid expansion thereafter.

Although DoCoMo was the first company to offer a wireless Internet access service, another Japanese company, KDDI (the merger of KDD, DDI, and IDO), runs its own packet network that offers WAP and operates at a speed of 14.4 kbps. Japan Telecom, like many other companies, is testing new 3G services for use in 2001. DoCoMo accesses cHTML over its own packet-switched air carrier Personal Digital Cellular (PDC). Rival KDDI accesses WML over its cdmaOne air carrier. As of fall 2000, DDI and IDO have more than 400,000 subscribers, mostly using dial-up email service. With the introduction of the new 3G packet network, cdmaOne users who purchase new phones will be able to stay connected just like i-mode subscribers. Officially, DoCoMo says it will migrate from cHTML to XHTML Basic with a contingent agreement from the WAP Forum.

As Japan is running out of wireless bandwidth for its current cellular network, it has been aggressive in pushing for early adoption of the new third-generation standard. DoCoMo plans to introduce 3G with a starting speed of 64 kbps. Its i-mode service brand will be upgraded to fit W-CDMA, or wideband CDMA – the high-speed spread-spectrum protocol designed by QUALCOMM. DoCoMo modifies and includes W-CDMA in the chips it manufactures. The final transmission speed is planned to reach 2 Mbps in 2003.

Yokosuka Telecom Research Park is the site where Nokia, Ericsson, Motorola, Lucent, and QUALCOMM conduct experiments with DoCoMo on W-CDMA. Japanese companies have key advantages: NTT DoCoMo has the rights to the chipset, mounting, and miniaturization technologies. Other Japanese companies such as Matsushita Communication Industrial (Panasonic), Fujitsu, Mitsubishi Electric, and NEC have been fine-tuning miniaturization techniques in cell phones since 1995. They are world leaders in providing sleek, lightweight handsets.

European Wireless Applications

Europe is also establishing wireless technology. In Europe, many developers implement a message-based version of their application and then a microbrowser version. But a study of the evolution of the market is illuminating. Durlacher (1999), a marketing research firm, in its 1999 Mobile Commerce Report did some careful analysis of mCommerce in Europe. It defined mCommerce as any transaction with a monetary value that is conducted via a mobile telecommunications network. The infant European wireless market had generic information applications in 1998 when mCommerce totaled $323 million. More than 90 percent of the applications were wireless information services. The balance was financial, auto navigation, business applications, and customer relationship management. But, as Table 2 shows, the European wireless applications projected for 2003 forecast specific services expected to yield $23,600 million. Although European applications are

Table 2 European wireless applications 2003

Wireless Application	Use
Advertising	23%
Finance	21%
Shopping	16%
Information	11%
Business	8%
Car navigation	8%
Customer relationship	7%
Entertainment	6%

Source: "Durlacher Mobile Commerce Report 1999." [Online]. Available: <http://www.durlacher.com/fr-research-reps.htm>.

perhaps six months to a year behind the Japanese in wireless deployment, the Europeans are leaders in wireless banking and financial applications.[10]

European Wireless Mobile Portals

Europe has an unusual concentration of wireless mobile portals. The services and content provided by the mobile portals are tracked in detail by gsacom. The company studied seventy portals and organized them into six main categories:

- Communication and community – email, calendar, and chat
- Information – News, weather, directories
- Lifestyle – Listings of events, restaurants, movies and games, betting
- Transaction – Banking, stock trading, purchasing, and auctions
- Travel – Listings of hotel, flights, timetables, and tourist guides
- Other – Personalized service, location-based services, device-dependent functions, auctions, and advertising

To find excellent information for the study of wireless portals, go to the Web site <http://www.gsacom.com>.

WAP Applications

A Wireless Application Protocol (WAP) site is remarkably small on a Web phone. In Europe, it is the most popular way to microbrowse Web sites. WAP specifies a wireless application framework and network protocol for low bandwidth wireless Internet devices such as Web phones, pagers, and handhelds. WAP predominantly targets Web phones, and the standard does a passable job of unifying a large set of international cell phones. The WAP Forum, a large consortium of telcos and computer hardware and software manufacturers, defines the WAP protocol. The standard was derived from the work of a U.S. company called Unwired Planet, now called Openwave. (Knowing the successive names of the company – Unwired Planet, Phone.com, and Openwave – helps you to recognize their products.) In North America, the original wireless gateways of Phone.com connect with the popular UP.Browser (Unwired Planet) microbrowser, which is burned into the ROM of 90 percent of U.S. Web phones. In Europe and Japan, the WAP gateway connects with a WAP microbrowser, for example, the AU-Systems browser from Ericsson. Openwave.com continues to influence the direction of WAP through its participation in the WAP Forum, although these two entities appear to be going in different product directions.

Viewing WAP Sites from a PC

What are your favorite WAP sites? Everyone can name favorite Web sites, but you may not have started your list of best WAP sites. You do not have to own a WAP phone to see them. All you need is a PC. Figure 8 shows a small WAP site on a Web phone; it comes from <http://www.gelon.net>, one of many WAP portals. You pick from many popular Web phone emulators to explore the hundreds of WAP sites. The emulators are handy for developers who want to quickly check their finished sites on newly appearing devices. Of course, a real Web phone is the only true test of a WAP site. When you name your site, note that Web addresses with fewer characters, such as ayg, igo, or nextel, are easier for people to type and reach. If you study these sites in detail, you will want to study the European or Asian WAP portals, which are far more developed than in North America.

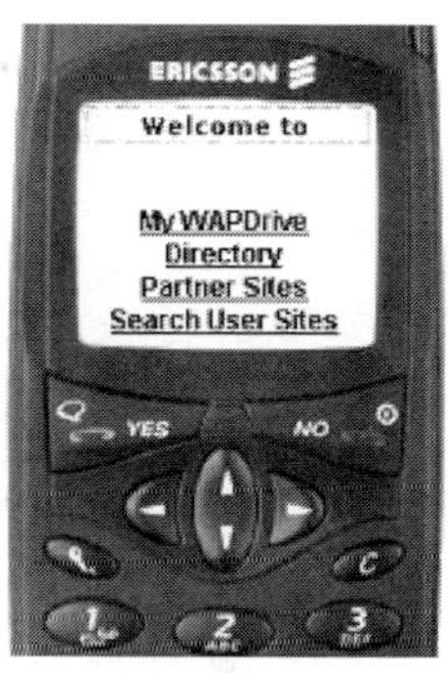

Figure 8 A WAP site on a Web phone (*Source:* Copyright © Telefonaktiebolaget LM Ericsson. Photo used with permission.)

Pros and Cons of WAP

The Wireless Application Protocol provides a reasonable standard to deliver small amounts of meaningful text to the mobile user who wants to carry only one wireless device – a Web phone. Developers using WAP Forum WML and Openwave.com HDML can make useful Web phone applications.

Designing for WAP is a very disciplining experience. Some developers say WAP is too complex. Others say WAP may have set the bar too low by accepting too small a screen and too many variations on keyboard input and display from handset manufacturers. They compare WAP phone capabilities to the capabilities of a Palm handheld and Pocket PC and conclude handhelds are better data devices. But WAP devices do voice.

According to some developers, "WAP is a necessary pothole to fill." The relatively small number of WAP sites continues to be a challenge for the WAP Forum. The huge adoption of the simpler i-mode system has developers debating the merits of WAP worldwide. Developers do have to labor to convert their Web sites to generate the unique content in Wireless Markup Language (WML). Doing so requires new authoring tools, server software, client software, textbooks, and education. WAP needs far more technical training than i-mode needs. As the WAP handset makers "innovate," developers have to keep track of all the flavors of microbrowser and gateway. You can write applications so that it serves most handsets and gateways. However, customizing for each cellular device can be a significant improvement for the user. Another issue is that, unlike for i-mode, to secure large WAP applications, you must license the intellectual property from various parties in the WAP Forum – gateways, security code, and so on. The Openwave WAP gateway is different enough from the Nokia gateway that large servers have to handle responses differently.

Table 3 shows early WAP customer comments drawn from articles in publications ranging from the *Wall Street Journal* to metropolitan newspapers. People accessing WAP shopping sites say applications are difficult to use. This could be from a poor application design that shows too many choices. Users say their phones freeze up. In this case, the "cache must be cleared," and customers have to reset the phone. These problems have happened to enough people, often enough to warrant many articles in major newspapers, magazines, and newsgroups. Developers often bear the brunt of complaints better directed at hardware and the realities of today's 2G networks. The lesson for wireless developers is to proceed with caution and apply good design skills appropriate to the mobile world.

Table 3 Early WAP customer comments

Pro	Con
The sites with mobile content are useful.	The screen is too small; I cannot read text.
WAP offers Internet access while not at my desk.	I get lost using the microbrowser.
WAP uses an industry-standard phone browser.	It's not easy to use.
It provides a useful design for a narrowband wireless network.	Access to information takes too long.
WAP works with many Web phones.	I cannot access my favorite sites.
	Private WAP gateways are long-distance calls.
	The application has too many screens.

Another issue for WAP is security. The deployed WAP design relies on a WAP gateway translation that takes a Wireless Transport Layer Security, or WTLS, to decrypt the signal where data stands in the clear and then to re-encrypt it in SSL to continue on the Internet. This is corrected in WAP 2.0 with Dynamic Proxy Navigation, which allows the device and the server to agree on an end-to-end security path. This solution may be adopted some time in 2001 or 2002.

European Wireless Banking

Nordic countries have a long history of electronic and wireless banking leadership, showing large numbers of customers using sophisticated wireless financial and banking applications. By 2000, more than 30 banking groups in Finland offered wireless banking services. Successful financial services have been early adopters of technology. The harsh lesson of the ATM (Automatic Teller Machine) market was that institutions that did not offer direct banking lost significant market share. The efficiency of ATM banking was not only a bottom-line advantage, but also a customer convenience. Today WAP banking and brokerage services are offered to customers for the same reasons. To banks, wireless applications are multichannel strategies to reach customers and increase business. They have found investors given a handset do more day trading. To develop a wireless economy, the participation of banks encourages commercial institutions such as hotels and stores to provide wireless services.

Nordic wireless phones are everywhere in Scandinavia. The Finnish company Nokia and the Swedish company Ericsson are leaders in the European Web phone market. The Scandinavian countries have the most cellular phone users per capita in the world. Because Finland is a leading creator of wireless technology and operates a mature wireless market economy, Hewlett-Packard moved its wireless division to Finland in October 2000.

Merita is a leading Finnish bank with a history of introducing automated banking throughout the 1990s. In 1999 it introduced the Solo WAP banking service across the Scandinavian banking system. Solo uses Nokia, Ericsson, and Siemens handsets and offers banking service in three languages. The traffic for Solo is substantial. The electronic customers include Merita in Finland (845,000), Nordbanken in Sweden (460,000), and Unibank in Denmark (200,000) for a combined 1.5 million customers in 2000.[11] Combined they perform 4.3 million banking sessions per month. Like banking via the ATM, mobile banking requires a customer to enter a username and a Personal Identification Number, or PIN. This is the same user authentication used by Etrade and many other wireless functions. Although SMS is popular, banking customers prefer WAP browsers. Customers are annoyed at the typical connection time of 30 to 40 seconds, but they anticipate a 2.5G network that will provide immediate access.

As Scandinavian banking fully anticipates a mobile business economy, its progress can also be explained by the hard work in defining industry standards. A Nokia-secure WAP banking gateway uses Mobile Electronic Transactions (MET) to provide a common framework for mCommerce. Key elements include a common syntax for secure transaction including payments, the storage of keys, and certificates. Ericsson, Motorola, Nokia, and others have been instrumental in defining commerce standards for making transactions on the move. They founded the Mobey Forum for banking mobility on May 10, 2000. (Visit <http://www.mobeyforum.com/> for more information.)

All GSM phones use a Subscriber Identity Module (SIM). Handset makers are experimenting with WAP Identity Module (WIM) chips. These chips provide special security and storage for the end user. Some phones have external readers, and others have integrated dual slots for RSA SecureID chips.

Banking Customer Study

The Solo WAP banking applications include accounts, payments, foreign payments, credit card information, investments, shopping, email, news checking, savings, money transfer, customer service, interaccount money transfer, and ticketing.

Shortly after introduction in 1999 Solo performed a banking study of more than 100,000 customers. The largest groups of users were professionals in information technology, service, and retail business. The majority of these customers like to get information in the morning and complete transactions in the evening.

Customers were asked where they used mobile wireless service. Their answers from most to least popular places were at home, at a summer cottage, at work, in a hotel on a business trip, in the car, at an airport, and on public transport. The typical WAP phone user in this study does not take public transportation. These WAP customers like the independence and control of being able to pay bills while on business trips or on holiday. Feeling they could manage time and finances better, they view their WAP phone as a "remote control of life." It helps them avoid waiting in lines to buy things. Customers identified with a sense of participating in the "new economy." On the other hand, customer fears included losing their Web phone and thinking someone could get into their accounts. However, bank analysts believe that credit cards are easier to lose and at greater risk for abuse. Most of the surveyed customers feel that the bank should cover any phone abuses. Despite many reported usability problems, customers do find value in the service.

The Wild, Wild Wireless United States

By most accounts, the United States lags far behind the working wireless economies of Japan and Europe. To its advantage, the U.S. invention of CDMA is the basis for the world's 3G networks. The United States flies a constellation of global positioning satellites to give the world a wireless location infrastructure, and it has some of the highest-speed wireless networks. Yet the United States does not provide predictable national data and voice coverage.

Even after the United States resolves basic issues such as offering 3G spectrum, a thriving wireless marketplace requires the cooperation of many companies. Hotels, banks, and transportation systems already participate in the wireless market in Japan and Europe. In the United States, there are many provincial opportunities where enclaves of wireless technology provide exceptional local value.

While the Europeans have reached agreement on one wireless network standard, the United States operates many. Companies are pitted against one other. If it were a movie, this would be a Western full of big old bosses in control, gunslingers proving their bravado, upstart outlaws passing through town, sheriffs aiming to do right, and pioneers and settlers just trying to raise a family and make a living. Amid the potshots and cavalry charges, local stories fill the town newspapers of the new frontiers while the fate of a nation is at stake.

The shootout over the standards, towers, and spectrum is becoming intense. The Metricom low-cost, high-speed Ricochet modems offered high data rate connections. QUALCOMM offers a new technology like CDMA and HDR, displacing TDMA and older data networks. Arraycomm has shown powerfully smart I-BURST antennas, and Mitsubishi SWIFTcomm is building a new high-speed network called IPMA that might outdo them all. (These networks are compared in chapter 17, Table 36 "Wireless Data Protocols.")

If wireless is so great for the world, why is not wireless everywhere in the United States yet? Because the land is so big, it costs a telco plenty. It is estimated that for one network operator in the United States to upgrade to the first phase of 3G service the cost is between $500 million and $600 million. This involves raising towers and adding new technology to each one. The cost of building a network from scratch is between $5 billion and $10 billion. Regulation, competition, pricing, and territoriality are further barriers. The saga of U.S. communications history explains why things are the way they are. You can buy a cell phone with data service in San Francisco that by FCC regulation will not work in Los Angeles. Two perfectly respectable wireless phone air interfaces – well-established TDMA and technically superior CDMA, both originated in the United States – are totally incompatible and overlap on two parts of the FCC spectrum. The European GSM air interface brought into the United States recently requires a special phone to use both GSMs.

Paying for a wireless data call when traveling can be like the old Western story where a gold miner is charged $5 for an egg. In most countries, you pay to originate a call. In the United States, the called party also pays for the call, and then pays for data. The U.S. cell phone data rates are among the highest in the civilized world. I am always amazed at my wireless bills and wonder what it will take to convince telcos to lower rates to start this market. Wireless Internet service plans add data charges to the base plan. Data calls are typically priced by connect time and data transmitted. Over time, the telcos may curb their need for immediate profits so that a volume-pricing plan can start the U.S. wireless market and produce a longer chain of revenues. However, the United States is a huge territory to cover with limited cellular towers badly in need of upgrading. At best, the United States can be thought of as a wireless network of select cities. Service is spotty even in a city with coverage. You can ride 10 miles beyond a city line and find you are no longer a wireless citizen.

The telecommunications infrastructure is huge and moves slowly even when it is no longer "protected to recover costs" as a monopolistic regulated business. In the free market, there is a two- to three-year lag from the first release of a standard such as CDMA to when it becomes available to the general public. It takes time to get a spectrum license, deploy enough towers, produce the chips, upgrade software, change out circuit board line cards in towers, and build handsets capable of using the new technology. Upgrading current customers to the new standard also factors into the timetable because there is a tendency to retain and grow the preexisting market. If it ain't broke, don't fix it.

Another barrier to growth has been intense competition in the computer industry. It is well documented that companies with older technology have been able to restrict and eliminate new entrances. For example, Microsoft heavily influences the development community. It had the effect of terminating the entrance of new mobile systems such as the GO PenPoint tablet by countering with a quickly invented pen-based system. Ironically, ten years after that market could have started, Microsoft is showing a TabletPC to be available in the near future. Hindsight is deceiving, however. GO, Slate, Grid, and EO would probably have failed had there been no Microsoft because their products did not work smoothly. Also, to stay in business they needed a viable startup model such as Palm provided by founders like Jeff Hawkins, who later founded Handspring. Interestingly, GO attempted to hire Mr. Hawkins when he worked at Grid. He developed his idea much later and undoubtedly reacted to the problems with the TabletPC. In the end, Palm, Inc., may have needed GO's failure to help point the way.

Slowing the advance of the wireless Internet is the telcos' instinctive reaction to preserve the voice market. Incumbents (TDMA and GSM carriers) want nothing more than to keep things the way they are. In the telco boardroom, executives wish for more spectrum, but they know giving customers data access is the larger growth market. The clamor for a wireless Internet is drawing attention. This data-intense market will thrive on efficient air interfaces.

Wireless Development in the United States

The U.S. Internet is currently very wired and PC-oriented. It is common for wireless devices to synchronize data from an Internet-wired PC. Another reason people resort to wired connections is that wireless connections are often unavailable. In the United States, Web phone access is through custom-built and licensed gateways. In North America, cellular network plans are expensive. The U.S. billing plans are out of line with international practice, where the called party does not pay. Wireless developers in North America consider the following options:

Use data networks. The U.S. mass market offers wide-area data networks that can be accessed by some Web phones. Most handhelds using wireless modems support these networks, including those with the Palm OS® and PocketPC OS®. Rather than use a wide area network (WAN), many businesses use a local area network (LAN). This is popular with industrial handhelds like Symbol.

Build your own towers for handhelds. To eliminate wireless service charges, companies buy their own wireless access points and position them around their building or mount them on vehicles. These access points talk to wireless LAN cards on the handhelds. This eliminates monthly bills, and provides enormously superior data throughput. The payback time of buying towers and wireless cards relative to wireless subscriber networks is often within two years. Application development is the greatest expense.

Use two-way pagers. Unlike the rest of the world, the United States offers a well-developed paging back channel for two-way paging. Neither Web phones nor handhelds are paging devices. Mobile applications with urgent data such as financial applications are well served by paging networks. The RIM 957 is a solid design with good North American national coverage.

Use alternative networks. In the developing American free market it is sometimes useful to take advantage of emerging high-speed networks such as Ricochet, IxEV, or I-BURST. These provide alternatives to common slower air interfaces and their data overlays. Beware that early wireless network technology depends on the providing company's ability to move from the technology stage to a broad commercial stage. In order for their technology to gain enough market share to survive, towers have to be deployed over many locations.

Explore location-based services (LBS). All networks depend on some degree of location positioning information. Obviously, cell-phone billing and the mechanics of call handoff use location, although details are usually kept private. In the United States, developers are well advised to develop lines of location-based services and to geocode their content to make it available for public location-based systems. (Location-based applications are covered throughout the book.) General location services are a special opportunity being driven by the wide availability of Global Positioning Systems (GPS) and, more important, the FCC E911 mandate, both covered in chapter 17, "Anticipating Location-Based Network Features."

Use middleware. Middleware companies, such as Broadbeam, Aether, AvantGo, and GoAmerica, provide many services and intermediate system software that can cut transmission costs for data over voice networks by compressing the data call when subscribers use email and browsing software. Middleware features are covered in chapter 18 under "Wireless Middleware for Large Systems."

Global Wireless Internet Development

Developing wireless Internet applications or serving wireless content worldwide is easy to do over the Internet. A developer should take advantage of the different networks, protocols, and Web languages. North American networks support handhelds and pagers best. Asian and European markets are geared to Web phones. Developers should also take advantage of European SMS messaging protocols built in to the entire GSM network. The European devices by Symbian such as the Ericsson R380 Web phone and PSION handhelds are popular and have special features (described throughout Part II). WAP phones look at Web sites formatted in WML. There are more Japanese than European WAP sites. In Japan, i-mode is king of service and requires a site be shown as cHTML Web pages. To offer combined services for all networks, protocols, and applications requires structuring your server (covered in chapter 18, the section "Building Servers and Matching Client Applications").

Wireless Internet Projections

It is important to consider the stakes in the wireless Internet. In the United States in 2000, 37 percent of the population used a cell phone with only 0.3 percent getting Internet access.[12] A survey of forecasts of the top marketing research firms (e.g., International Data Corporation, Durlacher, Strategis Group, and Gartner) reveals that by 2005 more people will use the wireless Internet than the traditional wired Internet. Averaging recent forecasts, I arrived at the following estimates:

- 2004 – 29 million U.S. wireless Internet subscribers
- 2004 – 47 million European wireless Internet subscribers
- 2005 – 500 million worldwide wireless Internet subscribers

According to multiple industry reports, the general annual mCommerce revenue for the United States is $10 million. For Europe, it is $15 million. For Japan, it is $400 million. mCommerce is eventually expected to dominate PC-oriented eCommerce. By 2004, combined revenues of mCommerce and eCommerce are expected to weigh in at $1.2 trillion, according to International Data Corporation (IDC).[13] Location-based services, the surprise wireless technology that makes applications location aware, is estimated to generate $4 billion in the United States and $30 billion worldwide by 2004 according to SignalSoft.[14]

In Japan, Internet connections are made predominantly with cell phones rather than PCs. The Japanese government forecasts that in 2010, 120 million Japanese, or almost the entire population, will own a handset.[15] Since many people will own more than one, Japan's market potential is estimated at 360 million units. A Japanese industry association has a bold forecast for wireless market revenue:

- 2000 – $20 billion mobile Internet business of the $50 billion telecom revenues
- 2003 – $60 billion mobile Internet business of the $100 billion telecom revenues[16]

The operating systems market for cellular phones is expected to be worth more than $1 billion in 2004. It is also important to look at the growth of content. At the beginning of 2001, there were

- 21,000,000 Internet Web sites
- 22,000 i-mode sites
- 4,000 WAP sites

The fact that the telephone industry will make only Internet-capable wireless cellular phones after 2001 will probably affect the design of future landline telephones.

Wireless LANs are low cost and high powered. They are revolutionizing office and home systems and are very popular in U.S. business. Computerized offices and enterprise campuses use the wireless Ethernet to connect to the Internet. Bob Badavas, Chief Executive Officer of Cerulean Technology (now part of Aether Systems, Mobile Government Division), says that the market for wireless LAN is largely hidden from most wireless developers.[17] Many companies such as Cahners In-Stat Group, Price Waterhouse, IDC, and Frost & Sullivan forecast wireless Ethernet manufacturer revenues. A current Frost & Sullivan report on wireless Ethernet reveals the following revenue forecasts:

- 2000 – $600 million
- 2002 – $884 million
- 2005 – $1.6 billion

It is also forcast that worldwide shipment of wireless LAN equipment in 2001 will increase to more than 73 percent, according to a report from IDC.[18] It forecasts higher revenues:

- 2000 – $1 billion
- 2005 – $3.2 billion

The Chief Information Office (CIO) has a job to extend the enterprise to the workforce. Desktop workforces are about as productive as they will ever be. The mobile workforce is another issue. In large companies, about 30 percent of a workforce changes every six months. The conventional enterprise changes project teams, transfers personnel, and retrofits offices. Mobile wireless systems can decrease operating costs, and they can improve productivity. A wireless company is in a unique position. "He who gets closest to the customer wins," says Badavas. The wireless LAN marketplace will explode over the next three years with a combined annual growth rate greater than 75 percent, according to the HiperLAN2 Global Forum.[19] (Business vertical markets are covered in chapter 5, "Wireless Internet Applications and Content.")

Standards Bodies and Consortiums

When a technology first begins to develop, companies create their proprietary ways of doing things, and their products are not necessarily compatible. When the three competing telephone networks were invented and rolled out in New York in 1890, the telephone from one network could not call anyone on the other network. That is where standards come in – to allow different technologies to work together.

Wireless systems require specific radio frequencies, hardware devices, radio towers, software, and specially formatted content. To try to bring together divergent air carriers, wireless device manufacturers, or wireless content formats, many important standards align networks, hardware, software, and content and build the wireless market. Once models are defined, then interoperable equipment and services can be targeted. When technology standards are clear, well grounded, and simple, everyone has a part to play and markets grow wildly. Well-considered standards can provide generations of use. To drive the industry and establish standards to harmonize usage, there are many powerful worldwide organizations, industry consortiums, companies, and standards bodies to register standards and work together as international organizations.

Internet Standards

The most influential Internet body is the World Wide Web Consortium (W3C). The W3C was founded in 1994 by Web technology pioneer Tim Berners-Lee. The W3C registers the working standards called Recommendations, which apply to, for example, HTML and XML. The Internet Engineering Task Force (IETF) issues Requests for Comments, or RFCs, that are the written definitions of the protocols and policies of the Internet. In response to RFCs, notes and proposals are posted at the W3C. The IETF is funded by the Internet Society (ISOC). The Internet Assigned Numbers Authority (IANA) administers IP addresses and the InterNIC does domain naming.

Technical Standards

One of the most authoritative world bodies is the International Telecommunications Union (ITU), located in Switzerland. The European Telecommunications Standards Institute (ETSI) has transferred most of its work to the ITU. Since spectrum licenses are legally required for equipment to operate correctly without interference, national government agencies often confer with the ITU to agree on the frequencies. Wireless air carrier standards are registered with the ITU, where they are called Interim Standards (IS); for example, CDMA is registered as IS-95. The Institute of Electrical and Electronics Engineers (IEEE, pronounced "I triple E") defines key digital transmission standards, for example, IEEE 802.11b for the wireless Ethernet.

3G Standards

The third-generation network requirements are specified by international organizations. The ITU defines the two most common standards, IMT-2000 and UMTS. These are largely the same. IMT-2000 stands for the International Mobile Telecommunications 2000 and is focused on services. The number refers to the year, the frequency bands, and the data rate for 3G. It is used more often in Asia. UMTS is the Universal Mobile Telecommunications System and focuses on frequencies and technical features. UMTS is used in Europe, refers more to spectrum, and is defined by the European UMTS organization. Ad hoc groups like the UMTS Forum support 3G-related organizations. (See chapter 16, the section "The 3G Wireless Internet" for a more thorough description of these standards.)

Consortia

Companies band together, usually behind a lead company, to establish important standards. The Bluetooth Special Interest Group is a consortium spearheaded by Ericsson to promote the Bluetooth low-power radio standard. The IEEE carried this over as its 802.15 standard. The WAP Forum is a consortium primarily formed by telcos that defines the Wireless Application Protocol for Web phones. Its primary language, Wireless Markup Language, is proprietary, unlike the i-mode markup language cHTML, which is registered with the W3C.

The entire cast of worldwide influential standards makers, wireless companies, and their Web sites are listed in Resources at the back of the book.

Getting Ready for a Wireless Future

> The future has already arrived. It simply comes to different places at different points in time.[20]

There is nothing truer for developers than the fact that the wireless Internet is happening all over the world and that new technology and business opportunities are arriving in different places, at different times, and in different degrees. As you plan and build, what are the best ways to know of the advancing technology and business opportunities? Conventional wisdom says to read marketing research reports, expert books, and industry magazines; visit wireless portals; attend trade shows; study the competition; listen to experts; and talk to friends already in business. There are deeper sources of inspiration.

We may be on the verge of an information renaissance. Its ignition depends on a number of factors. Finding the roots of rebirth dormant in communication and Internet origins uncovers a range of stimulating forces. A past model of dramatic cultural change is the activity in Western culture that led to the Renaissance in the late 1400s. Simultaneous discoveries, a capital economic model, and artistic growth in all levels of society brought on the great changes. To prepare for a wireless future, consider forming a strategy based on the forces that precipitated the earlier Renaissance.

Travel to discover. People in some cultures live in the future already. The time machine door is open; all you have to do is step in. As described earlier, the wireless Internet in Japan is said to be 24 months ahead and Europe is 18 months ahead of the United States. Talk to scouts, make direct contact by email, read studies, and find out about foreign successes like Japanese i-mode and European SMS. How is it used? What lessons can be learned? Above all, travel and see it. To view another future arrival point, interview early adopters using new applications or talk to youth who send messages on stylish phones.

> By 1400, journeyers braved sea and land traveling long distances to find new lands and peoples. The explorers observed new practices and established foreign trade routes exchanging foods, spices, fashion, art, music, science, ideas, and cultural values. The continued adventure stimulated societies on both ends of the path.

Study research labs. What is the science, the new technology, and where is it headed? Study research and, if possible, visit the leading research labs. Great labs today include MIT Media Lab, SRI International, Yokosuka Research Park, Xerox PARC, major chip producer's labs, and startups. They explore new forms of transcodable communication and optical radio nets, and make strange things like "radio paper." The scenes of invention and experimentation are educational, military, and commercial. They give inspiring insights and early lessons.

> The Renaissance study of Arabic universities unveiled basic knowledge that stimulated many scientific advances. The Persians had also expanded upon many of the Greek teachings that had been cast aside. Expertise from any source was realistically studied and applied to all forms of living. Understanding technical manuscripts and foreign teachings retrieved lost expert knowledge and led to new scientific concepts.

Observe real models. It is important to observe research and technology to bear practical fruit. Military and industrial institutions found practical benefits from wireless technology many years ago. Having seen what works, large corporate campuses now use wireless laptops to connect to the institution's network. Industry applies wireless technology to deliver packages and process returns of rental cars.

Just as personal computers were an attempt to give everyone his or her own mainframe, the miniature handheld delivers powerful industrial and military mobile capabilities. Observing the present chips and base technology in production offers new possibilities. As with any attempt to bring fire down from the mountain, you have to see the flame first. Before us is a new human model based on activity and information in motion.

> Artists, including Da Vinci, actually looked at a human body before drawing it. This socially unacceptable practice of objective observation was articulated in perspective, a method of drawing, born in a new way of seeing making Art a science. The restoration of perceptivity, of objective and rational approaches to the arts and sciences unseated prevailing behaviors, practices, and laws.

Excavate the past. The best may have come before us. Sometimes at the origin of a technology, elements are overlooked in favor of others that have led to early successes. Often many forgotten elements are critical later as the dominant technology matures. There is much to learn from the General Magic user interface, the user conceptual model, and communications architecture. GO, an early mobile device company, produced powerful models of social computing and a mobile workforce. The Apple Newton™ component objects were among the best interface designs ever. Buried with these elder technologies are many fine concepts. When the long lost memories and methods of earlier civilization are recovered and reborn, they can challenge "modern" thinking enough to restore valuable practices and stimulate new ones.

> To stand on European city ruins was a starting point for Italian Renaissance architects such as Alberti and Brunelleschi. Architects considered the possibility that earlier life and buildings held hidden values. The quest of some Renaissance

> architects included excavation, careful reconstruction, and understanding earlier classical life. The Italian Renaissance rediscovery of Roman and Greek architecture revealed "new" living patterns successful for earlier generations. Greek writing, restored from foreign sources, fortified science, and philosophy. The rediscovered ancient philosophical school and science of Aristotle influenced many. The restored Greek view supplanted many of the Latin practices of the times.

If you travel and explore, observe and see, research and study, excavate and restore, you are on the road to building a better wireless solution and creating a new wireless culture. These strategic activities leading to growth formed the basic pattern behind the Western Renaissance. In the production of wireless technology, the classic practice of apprenticeship, of learning from somebody who allegedly already knows, could be helpful in today's research lab. In the past, apprentices sometimes worked with quacks; but some discovered masters, and learning from them was invaluable.

The wireless Internet era is in many ways a rebirth of the imagination of earlier computer and telecommunications periods of invention. As technologists and business professionals anticipate the future, they travel, observe, examine, and excavate in order to uncover the richest of worldwide resources.

Living Wirelessly

To live the wireless life firsthand is important, for it is not enough to study wireless technology. To get any feeling for it, use a Web phone, a handheld, a two-way pager, a voice portal, a wireless camera. Try various services. Personal travail is the way to become informed and passionate about improving the wireless world. The journey can be interesting, but it is not the reward. Fully mobile pioneers are not content to create a new world. The end of their journey is the created land worth the beginning of a thousand journeys. The wireless Internet is the backdrop for a potential global renaissance that affects you, your family, your neighborhood, your education, your job, your government, and your world.

2

Chapter

The Needs of the Wireless Internet User

As we look at people using wireless technology, it is useful to examine their relationship with technology over time. Good developers are able to move beyond the fresh discovery of technology to its valuable application for popular and personal needs. Wireless technology has a special audience. To develop lasting wireless Internet technology, it is important to experience a mobile user's viewpoint and to know what is valued about the mobile wireless Internet.

We Are at the Beginning

It is a common mistake to assume that because people can use cell phones to browse the Internet, the wireless Internet is a consumer market and therefore you should build consumer Web sites for phones. Not so. While it is true that the consumer market for voice cell phones is maturing, the Internet use of phones is in its infancy. When telecommunications advertising tells people to "come out of your homes and into the light and use your cell phone to surf the Internet," it is a recipe for disaster. For the consumer, the mobile experience is nothing like the desktop Internet experience. Nor is its purpose.

The Technology Adoption Curve

Wireless technology is no different from any other new technology that works its way onto the world stage. It starts crudely, finds some initial uses, and eventually becomes widespread. It is critical to know where you are with respect to the maturity of the technology. Understanding which stage technology is in tells you not only the components to use, but for whom you are building your technology and what services they want. At each level of technology, a different kind of person uses it. Most developers are being told to build products for an advanced consumer market. They do not realize we are at the beginning of a curve, where there is the most room for great invention: Wireless Internet in the early 2000s is a hobbyist, youth, and special-case business market. This is when reputations and industries are born.

Do not confuse the consumer market for cell phone voice with the technology stage for wireless data. Our current position on the wireless Internet technology adoption curve is apparent in Figure 9. It is based on a line of thinkers from Everett Rogers, Geoffrey Moore, Paul Saffo, to David Liddle who showed how technology develops in society. The difference in psychology of the buyers and the purpose of the technology changes significantly over time. Technology has a trajectory of innovators, early adopters, early majority, late majority, and finally laggards. Liddle simplified this to explain that a technology is first proven experimentally, then justified economically in business use, and then established as a commodity with standards and cost reductions to become a consumer reality.

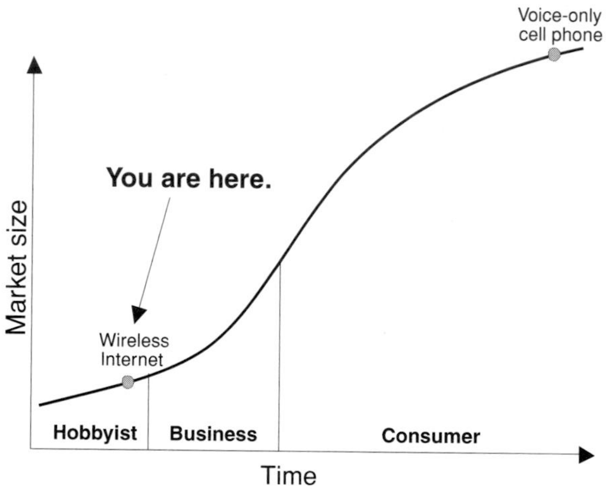

Figure 9 Wireless Internet technology adoption curve

As technology matures, so does the audience for whom you build it. When the technology is new, then the first audience you should build for is the hobbyist. Only these earliest experimenters will stand the pain of "cranking up a horseless carriage." When the technology finds its first application, then you need early adopters inside a business or government agency. Businesspeople will put up with noisy, but high-capacity heavy-duty trucks that move cargo. It is up to technologists to demonstrate value. If they do, then a business can justify buying expensive engines and long-lasting tires, establishing fuel supply, building roads, writing its own maps, and crafting its own signs. Finally, for a mature market, the developer can build for a consumer who will enjoy multiple benefits of a fully defined, standardized, and pervasive technology such as the automobile industry. In this mature phase, many different businesses play a part to sustain a vibrant market. The shift of building for the hobbyist, then a business, and then a consumer is called "crossing the chasm," which has been studied carefully by Geoffrey Moore.[1]

Entering the Market at the Right Point on the Curve

In the beginning, a technology appears to come and go before it explodes as a market. There have been countless starts of disruptive technologies. Disruptive technologies, well studied by Harvard Business School Professor Clayton Christensen, can transform the ratios of labor, capital, materials, and information that make the products and services of a company.[2] Many disruptive wireless technologies that vied to alter the marketplace value of industries are now vestiges of computer companies and telcos. For computers, handwriting recognition was thought to be the disruptive technology to give the advantage to users of mobile computing. The pioneer handhelds – the Go PenPoint™ and the Apple Newton™ – failed. General Magic forced their wireless communicator straight to the consumer market before solving the business requirements of wireless infrastructure and data billing – a legacy to their ICRAS spin-off, which repositioned its handheld wireless technology to early business vertical markets.

To a developer, it makes sense to build first for the youthful, the hobbyist, and early business, not for the pragmatist or general consumer. If you try to rush ahead to the general consumer, then acceptance is often denied. Consumers will complain strongly, as we hear about Web phones with small screens, long waits to connect, and unsatisfactory content. The popular and profitable wireless market i-mode in Japan started out on the right foot with a model for a youthful, hobbyist market. As we read, i-mode is already moving across the technology adoption curve into the mainstream to become a valuable business asset of the wireless Internet.

An important strategy in the development of wireless technology is appreciating the shift in adoption from hobbyist, to vertical market, and finally to horizontal market applications. A vertical market is a dedicated business market. *Vertical market applications* first address very specific business needs for a particular company or industry. The applications provide a clear benefit through higher productivity or other competitive advantage. Over time, the technology is improved and the advantages are more generalized. Vertical markets often become horizontal markets. A *horizontal market application* crosses many vertical markets and is a general commodity. It is an inevitable trend for most technology as the business changes from high margin to high volume.

An example of this progression is the growth of the word processor markets. In the 1970s, companies built dedicated word processing systems for business. These were vertical markets. Later in the 1980s, the word processor became a horizontal market application that could run on any computer. Another example of vertical to horizontal progression comes from telecommunications. iDEN originally was a dispatch radio network. Technically, it still is an Enhanced Specialized Mobile Radio (ESMR), but it is now a popular WAN cellular standard charted by the FCC like all the other subscriber cellular services.

Today in the United States, most industrial wireless applications serve vertical markets. An example is the customer processing when you return a rental car at an airport. Agents use wireless devices to verify and track package delivery after your signature is taken. Another vertical wireless market is dispatch management, which uses wireless devices to send field workers to assignments. Still another is law enforcement where officials use wireless devices to record infractions and print tickets. Established wireless vendors aspire to address larger horizontal markets. A broad spectrum of business users can use wireless communications across many lines of business. (See Figure 28 for a diagram of wireless vertical markets.)

The transition to horizontal markets can occur when wireless communication is fairly inexpensive, broadly deployed, and easy to use, and once a large number of off-the-shelf applications are available. Japan is rapidly undergoing the transition to an early horizontal consumer wireless market.

With early technology, you have to accept that infrastructure is not developed. Without support, you should have no grand illusion that the world wants it. You are "ahead of your time" with respect to society's ability to accept early technology. You might have invented the automobile, but without gas stations and roads (you mean I have to invent that too?) then it cannot take off in any major way. In wireless, we do not even have good automobiles for the consumer. Hobbyists travel a wireless highway in need of development, and although they run out of gas (batteries) far too often, the hobbyists and not the consumers will tolerate it.

Recognizing early technology, you can construct local applications that appeal to the youth market, hobbyists, and vertical market business segments. As global standards and technology mature, time your readiness to leap to the next phase, which is the early consumer horizontal market. Consumers are ready in Japan, some are in Europe, but they will not be for a few years in the United States.

Mobile Users Are the Secret

As secret as the mystery of an Egyptian hieroglyphic is the nature of the people who use the wireless Internet. Unlocking their mobile behavior is a challenge, and there are some interesting revelations that experienced wireless developers share. Starting with the obvious: Users are mobile and what they keep on their person is important. What is that person's identity?

It cannot be stressed enough how different and how misunderstood the mobile user is. This person drives personal content, wireless applications, and even mobile hardware. Any great wireless project allows discovery time to explore and define the mobile personality. In all my wireless years, the one lesson that recurs continuously is that the well-understood mobile user makes mobile applications. Yet almost every engineer new to a wireless project makes the same mistake – move a desktop application to the hand space; it fails. How come?

It is a mistake to fight a new war with the weapons and strategy of the last. Mobility is an advantage, in the same way that the new tanks of World War II proved to have decisive advantage over long, expensive lines of fortifications that some countries built. French planners thought the Maginot Line would delay the enemy long enough to build trenches – a World War I strategy. The secret of the tank was not so much its being "armored mobile artillery"; it was the *radios inside* that coordinated their striking power. It is questionable that Microsoft yet understands mobile users, even after five bombardments of "Windows everywhere" – Winpad™, WinCE™, PocketPC™, HandheldPC™, and Talisker™. The message remains, "Don't change how you work." Put simply, a desktop does not make sense in your hand. The lesson from Palm, Inc., that Microsoft Corporation did not learn is that a desktop slows down mobile users. Paramount to mobile use, personal data comes first. As the world learned quickly, mobile warfare is different. History shows that those who understood the field of mobile warfare prevailed.

"How not to write Windows software?" That is the question. Indeed, when there were only PCs, developers for the first Palm Pilot™ carried small blocks of wood all day long, pretending to be mobile users in anticipation of the device that would one day make them rich. They did very PC kinds of things and took meticulous notes about what they were doing and expecting to get done. Mobile existence, they found, was different from PC existence. Mobile users work with notes, not documents. They think on their feet. They do not do spreadsheet analysis. They make a point rather than dazzle with presentation technology. They tap on a screen; they do not click with a mouse. They scribble, they do not type. They revel in the utility of personal information, always with them. Information takes on a different character, as mobile use shows.

Mobile use is at first entirely strange to conventional software engineers and interface designers. Even software engineers on the wireless warpath are shocked when they put down their emulators and actually walk about and use wireless devices. Even then, engineers do not really understand the application they have made unless they are in sync with the real users and what they are trying to get done. Mobile users are unique. They do not program, they do not think software is an art, and a good number do not even use PCs. Because they are walking about, they are busy and will not give full attention to any gadget. They expect to complete tasks in seconds and minutes. When a mobile user catches a quick ride in a taxi, with a sandwich in one hand, talking to a friend, and casually using your wireless application – that is the real world.

Desktop programmers create, and most PC users expect, "an altar" to ritualistically work in low light in a quiet place before a large screen, paying full attention to the monitor, invoking long incantations of peculiar commands. To get these command sequences right, users are assisted by lengthy documentation and online help. But mobile reality is choppy and sudden. Your application is way down on the priority list of things that will get users' attention. These users have no time, so whatever you do had better be direct, simple, and useful. The point is that your application is not supposed to command stunning attention. It is to simply fit in with a mobile lifestyle, as transparently as possible. This kind of thinking is so different from approaches to the desktop that it is hard to convey to designers and engineers. Mobile users are often in social situations. In front of another person, the software needs to operate faster than on a desktop. In usability studies, the longest a user will wait when mobile is roughly one-third of the time he or she will tolerate on a desktop. As a person takes notes when someone is speaking, keeping up is barely possible on paper; with electronic ink, it is next to impossible and it looks awkward. A key realization is that when information is on you and around you, you begin to think differently. A person will cut corners and do what is necessary. The key challenge is this: What can a person do with a wireless device that cannot be done on a desktop?

Line-busting applications are one of a new class of mobile wireless business applications. Almost as if on a stage, new mobile business users act out their service using portable devices as props. In the line-busting prototypes at General Magic, we built a new service for Peet's Coffee, various airlines, and retail businesses. Retail personnel normally work behind a counter where transactions are limited by the few cash registers available. With line-busting applications, when lines of customers build up, the staff can come out from behind the counter, take orders, process customers, and break up lines. The receptionist can be with the customer. Developers complete handheld applications with wireless Internet connections. The roving register is no longer a desktop application. For the new mobile business, the era of roving is arriving.

World Mobile Use

Using wireless handhelds on the go, businesspeople directly access succinct parts of company data. Japanese commuters are entertained on long train rides with i-mode cell phones. European friends and family are unified by SMS messaging. Banking customers use Web phones to perform complete banking services – everything from getting a payroll check electronically, to looking at balances, to transferring funds. North American handhelds and pagers routinely perform vertical market tasks.

With wireless applications, innovative developers are placing useful mobile content in the pockets of end users. They cleverly take advantage of the specific time of day, location, and personal interests of the mobile user. In motion, people write on, talk to, and type on small wireless devices. People use them to take pictures, sense scan codes, swipe card stripes, interrogate badges, and perform rapid transactions with other wireless devices. Networks of people in the mobile infosphere use devices that sense the world and one another, and perform direct transactions.

Subscriber or User?

The face of the mobile audience deserves depiction. The telecommunications companies portray them as subscribers. The computer companies think of them as users. While both are correct, mobile wireless applications are best built for people with real identities. If possible, use the active name of the profession when addressing mobile users. An application for wireless stock traders should be built for investors, not users. In this book, the term *traveler* is often used rather than *user* or *subscriber,* although specific identities are used when possible. The correct name should permeate your documentation and the way your team members and clients talk about the project.

You Are the Next Wireless Application

Where you are and when you are there can be magically pulled out of the air and combined with content to make relevant mobile applications. Knowing the personality of the audience is very useful in making decisions about the utility of the technology. A good wireless project ideally matches content to a personality. Because this traveling person is different, his or her interface should be different. Simplicity and directness work best. Developers can benefit from working directly with travelers who live a mobile reality. Development teams can also use the skills of an interaction designer who can articulate mobile personas.

A special practice in producing wireless applications for a mobile audience is developing personas. A *persona* is the characterization of the most important mobile user for your wireless application. Making personas helps developers recognize the goals and interface values of a traveler who uses mobile services. This requires study to produce the best possible direct interaction with content. Substance rather than fancy graphic form is what matters. The personal values of software and content are important for the interaction designer to characterize. In fact, personalization engines made popular with custom shopping application servers are increasingly important for wireless servers. (The methods that interaction designers use to produce useful characterizations of the mobile audience are covered in chapter 6, the section "Personas.")

The Secret Initiation

Mobility creates an opportunity for developers to provide relevance and identity in their applications for the mobile end user. The way I think of the task of building applications is, I am on a mission to work directly for stock investors, building inspectors, home care nurses, restaurant diners, and business travelers to give them something they have never seen, sometimes something the world has never seen. I work for them; they inspire me; they tell me their secrets; they are the boss, not anyone else. They are the only ones who will teach me what mobile wireless makes possible. They become my friends, and they initiate me into the world of mobile use. Here are two important lessons they have taught me so far:

1. *Speak in my language.* Be familiar with my words, my images. Use a model about how I work with my friends, my business. As an investor, I work with trading portfolios, not file systems. As a nurse, I work with patient clipboards, not user input and output systems. That logo is my company – I own a piece of it and I am proud of it. Stick with the metaphors of my profession. A note of caution to developers: Although it is tempting to transcend metaphors to create an original digital application, it is much safer to use something familiar. It is easier for Intuit to get people to use a checkbook metaphor than it is to invent and then train them on some new imaginary personal banking system.
2. *Information, when it is on me, is different.* Information when it is with me is mine. Information on a desktop is someone else's. You had better give me something useful if I am going to keep it in my hands all the time. I like a handheld because my data is with me. The Palm handhelds have four physical buttons that give direct access to what I use most often. I will only carry about what is critical. Layers of windows and menus get in the way. I want simple delivery of content important to me.

Making Applications Personal and Easy

Location matters. It is a continual theme in wireless applications. A person can depend on a wireless device to explore a new city, locate a business, and arrange to meet someone. A popular wireless service shows nearby cafes in response to a typed zip code. The service is useful, but the user need not enter a zip code – the device knows where it is. Cell phones already know where they are to compute roaming charges. They are also required to provide location for emergencies. (In chapters 5, 7, and 8 we show how to write useful location-aware applications.)

Time matters. Web phones ensure the accuracy of time. People on the go appreciate exact time. Perhaps the ticking clock counting air minutes makes everyone more aware of time. If your content is marked with exact time codes and event date codes, you are off to a good start. Time really matters to mobile users, and they have increased requirements of wireless services. Your service will need improved accuracy and validation of content, and it will need a higher level of maintenance. To deliver mobile precision, most databases need serious upleveling since they were designed to deliver content based on older publishing and distribution models. For example, travel guides and databases rarely record the hours of a place. A fair percentage of their content is out of date. Mobile databases require updates that are more frequent and a model for self-regulating content (covered in the section "Gauging the Frequency of Wireless Publishing" in chapter 20).

Time can take advantage of XML in your service. XML is used to encode data such as calendars and events from multiple sources so they can be shared and coordinated. Meanwhile back at the PC, when people are planning, times may need conversion to the local time depending on the user's mobile location.

Personality and individuality matter. Personal information management is a key application on mobile wireless devices. It turns out that the PC is a good place to let users make their grand mobile plans. Given a large number of restaurants in a city, the traveler might want to download and be updated about nearby places that fit within a certain price range, cuisine, or level of quality. Personality of the owner counts both in application design and underlying content. Mobility should simplify choices. Transactions must be simple. There is no time to fill out forms. Many wireless transactions are tied to a trusted Internet member service. Amazon establishes their membership system from the PC. The entire set of forms for one-click shopping information is filled in ahead of time on a PC. Customers simply identify themselves via a username and password. i-mode is simpler yet – one field for a four-digit PIN. After signing in, the system brings forward preferences and can streamline transactions with automatic billing information already stored.

What Mobile Users Say

The use of wireless technology is in its infancy, and users new to the technology often heap on complaints. In the wireless industry, the hobbyist knows that battery charges last a short time and wireless coverage is limited. But consumers expect more. The rollout to consumers has largely kept wireless technology local. Figure 10 shows a "wall of wireless complaints" that were first heard in the early

♦ This device is too heavy, too expensive. ♦ I am waiting until Windows works on my phone. ♦ Network charges are too high. ♦ This handheld desktop is not like my PC. ♦ There is no infrastructure. ♦ The wireless network is too slow. ♦ The software is not useful. ♦ I cannot get to the Web site I want. ♦ Coverage is too limited. ♦ It drops my calls when I am moving. ♦ This device is mobile, but it does not communicate. ♦ I lose all my data when the battery dies. ♦ Battery only lasts for half a day. ♦ I have to carry too many devices. ♦ There are too many screens to navigate. ♦ It is too hard to use. ♦ The PC is better. ♦ I cannot remember the Web phone function keys. ♦ The screen is too dim. ♦ The fonts are too small, I cannot read the text. ♦ I get lost navigating the application. ♦ I cannot access the Internet sites I want. ♦ I cannot see the screen as I talk. ♦ The device is too slow. ♦ Personal wireless service plans are not available when I roam. ♦ Fear, uncertainty, and doubt about what Microsoft might do. ♦ This application runs differently on each device and I get confused. ♦ Technology is too immature. ♦ There is too little content available. ♦ It does not work in other countries. ♦ I have to recharge too often. ♦ It takes too long to get a connection. ♦ There is no service in my area. ♦ Billing plan outside my area is too expensive. ♦ New services are not available on my device. ♦ I have to rekey address and phone numbers from the wireless device into another. ♦ I do not want to carry another device. ♦

Figure 10 Wall of wireless complaints

days of the wireless industry. Some are barriers to the broader adoption of wireless technology, but many can be overcome.

A litany of techno-grief is to be expected with any new technology. In the days of the first horseless carriages, there were no "self-starters." That wall of complaints might have included "The crank, it's hard to wind the dad-blermed thing." ♦ "There are no fuel stations outside the city." ♦ "This automobile drives poorly over a horse trail, and tire punctures are a chore." ♦ "I could sure use a good road map." Early automobiles were definitely contraptions only for locals whose only solace on bad days was to hear the neighborly wisdom, "Your auto is scaring the horses. Get a horse." How the world changes when industries evolve.

There are good reasons for complaints about wireless technology. But there are things you can do about it. Complaints that the screen is too small, that text is too small, or that keyboards are ineffective can be levied against the handset manufacturers. But you can use large fonts and provide simple numeric choices. That Web phone bills are too high is a flaw in telco market planning. But you can use handhelds or pagers instead. Over time, the industry "listens" to customers. As technology and infrastructure improve, the market grows. Until then, being forewarned when you build wireless applications is a good survival tactic. Listen to the complaints, steer around as many of these traps as you can, and be resourceful to avoid creating grief. (Some positive guidance awaits you in chapter 6, especially the section "Wireless Developer Best Practices.")

Mobile User Identity

Whatever users say, good or bad, the key effect of the digital network is the opportunity for rapid feedback when the content's producer and its consumer are brought closer together. In electronic networks, the cause and the effect happen so close to each other that it redefines commercial and personal relationships. The wireless Internet is different from the 1960's world of Marshall McLuhan, where identities were overrun by broadcast and mass media networks. During a televised interview on CBS in the 1960s, McLuhan observed:

> We are on the air. And on the air, we do not have any physical body. When you are on the telephone or on radio or on TV, you do not have a physical body; you are just an image on the air. When you do not have a physical body, you are a discarnate being and you have a very different relation to the world around you. And this I think has been one of the big effects of the Electric Age. It has deprived people really of their private identity.

Reversing this trend is the wireless mobile Internet that grounds an individual in personal and physical experiences. It is not like the "immersive" electronic media – the telephone, television, or PC network where the user is engulfed.

Unlike prior electric networks, the wireless Internet enhances physical presence. It underscores active personal identity. Manifesting presence is a direct and personal process as mobile users operate a bewildering array of devices. Fortunately, engineers can cut through this bewilderment with a few central concepts that unify all of the wireless equipment and technology, which we address in chapter 3.

3

Chapter

The Equipment and Technology of the Wireless Internet

The wireless Internet depends on many different devices. Each device depends on a wireless network that connects to a server. Everything is based on the underlying physics of radio technology and the science of network transmission technology. Becoming familiar with the "terminals" of the network is a good place to begin.

Six Wireless Device Families Mobilize the Internet

Hurricanes of wireless devices connect to the wireless Internet. Basically, these devices let people send messages, access a mobile Web site, use interactive services, or converse. Perhaps increasing the confusion, each company – Sun, Symbian, Microsoft, Palm, Motorola, RIM, Kyocera, and the list goes on – provides its own view of the "universe of devices." Practically, developers must reach beyond vendor categories to provide popular service. It is necessary to take a device-agnostic or a "Swiss-neutral" viewpoint to match the reality that engineers find in the server room where many devices hit their servers. Six wireless device families (Figure 11) provide a useful model for engineers to sensibly develop solutions for the wireless Internet. Each family of devices has general characteristics and a primary programming technique. From this overall model, content providers can deliver and engineers can write appropriate device and server applications.

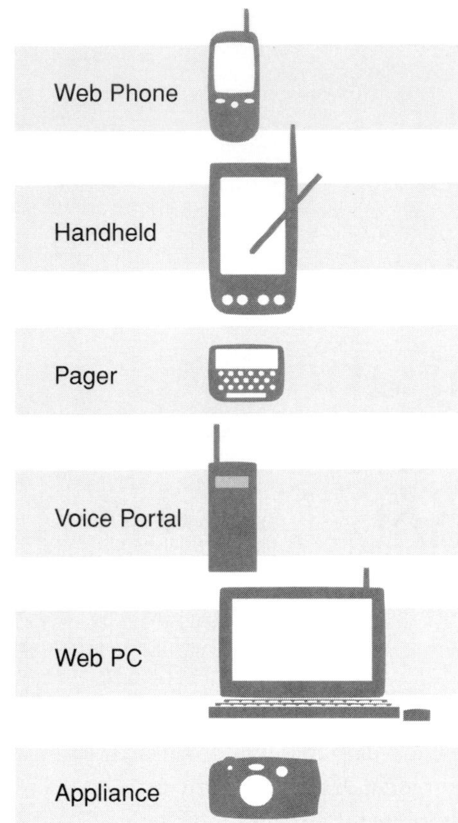

Figure 11 Six wireless device families

Sometimes wireless development projects access only one of these devices. A business might be able to afford only one class of device or may have been sold a "voice only" or "paging only" solution. Perhaps a back-end server was designed specifically to reach only handhelds. This is now a temporary condition. Internet businesses originally directed to PCs are looking to add wireless capacity. The capability to accommodate every possible wireless device family extends the maximum reach of your service. Wireless architecture has come a long way to let your server connect with both wired and wireless devices simultaneously. It is helpful to understand each device and the wireless development method, one at a time. As a software or content engineer new to wireless development, you probably know the PC, but you might not know the character and advantages of the mobile device families.

Web Phones

Remember calling on a telephone wired to a wall? Now that phones are cellular and mobile, making a voice call is not enough. Cellular phones are rapidly being transformed into portable wireless networked computers. A *Web phone* is a modified cellular phone with display hardware and Internet access software. Web phones are in use all over the world. Handset makers plan to make only Internet-ready cell phones beginning in 2002. A Web phone can make a traditional cell phone call, but it also contains a microbrowser, special keys, and some memory to connect to the Internet. Web phone characteristics (Table 4) are common to most manufactured devices, but they all have different names. Key cellular phone makers call the Web phone a *handset* or *mobile terminal*. Symbian calls it a *WID*, or Wireless Internet Device. The Japanese call it an *i-mode* phone. Europeans call it a *WAP* phone after the Wireless Application Protocol. Sun Microsystems calls Web phones a *CLDC,* or Connected Limited Device Configuration, family of devices with a *MIDP,* or Mobile Internet Device Profile. Most devices talk to public cellular networks, but the new mobile *IP Mobile Phone* from Cisco "talks" to private computer networks. Analysts also use the term *smart phone*, and others have their own favorite names. Engineers

Table 4 Web phone characteristics and manufacturers

Names	Features	Makers
Web phone WAP phone i-mode phone MIDP on CLDC WID Smartphone Java phone BREW phone IP Mobile phone MSU Terminal	Voice Limited messaging Limited Internet access Small display Phone keypad for input Limited data access Must be connected Voice command	Nokia, Ericsson, Motorola, Sony, Samsung, Kyocera, NTT DoCoMo, Nextel, SprintPCS, Alcatel, Cisco, Broadcom, AT&T

(you gotta love us) have names like *MSU* for Mobile Subscriber Unit, or the ever-popular *terminal*. Although I cannot remember anyone saying, "I'll call you on my terminal."

The Web cell phone is the primary international wireless Internet device. The Japanese use beautiful color i-mode phones. The Europeans use WAP phones for messaging. In North America, people use all kinds of Web phones. At the beginning of 2001 there were 600 million cell phones, and of these, 10 percent were Internet-enabled. In 2005 there are expected to be a billion Internet-capable Web phones.[1] People buy these primarily for voice calls, but they are starting to use the Internet access features. Web phones can browse parts of the Internet. They also send and receive short emails. Messaging is a key feature of mobile devices. Whereas handhelds and pagers often have full text keyboards, most cell phones have only a small numeric keyboard. Although it is challenging to enter text on most cell phones, the Europeans, who transmit an enormous amount of Web phone messages, have made a game of it – gisting. The art of transmitting the gist of a message is to send the fewest letters and still make sense.

While adults value the voice part of the phone, the younger audience finds value in messaging and accessing the Web. The Web phone microbrowser is a very small version of a PC Web browser. A microbrowser typically shows only the text parts of a Web site. There are many ways to make Web sites ready for these Web phones, as we shall see.

Web phones form a category that includes every device from the basic Internet-enabled phone, to the advanced smart phone, and to the smarter phones to come. Cellular phones are evolving in each part of the world every year. Smart phones download and run programs. The screens grow larger, and more memory and storage is built in. The upper bounds of phone intelligence are still being stretched. Cellular phones have some simple advantages over the PC: You never have to boot them and when they are in range of a tower, they reset their exact time including time zone. The smartest Web phones combine the features of handhelds, such as a large touch-sensitive screen, functional keyboard, and complete operating systems that execute applications. Only recently have some kinds of Web phones been designed to be programmable, such as the Palm Powered™ Kyocera smartphone, the Motorola and Mitsubishi Java-enabled phones, the Ericsson Symbian class phones, the Microsoft "Stinger," and QUALCOMM BREW™-enabled phones. These programmable Web phones run a Radio Operating System (ROS). The ROS allows limited access to the device and can provide communication functions not available on computers. Whether an operating system (OS) or an ROS, the best mobile systems conserve power during every operation and never lose data.

Handhelds

The wireless device that gets most of the work done in the United States is the handheld. The *handheld* is a small computer with a programmable operating system, storage, a full keyboard, and a large screen. Many have touch-sensitive displays. Some handhelds have slots to add various peripheral cards. Handheld family characteristics and manufacturers (Table 5) offer a wide range of qualities.

The handheld is also called a *PDA*, or Personal Digital Assistant; a *Communicator* by General Magic and Symbian; a *CDC* platform by Sun; an *HPC*, or Handheld PC, by Microsoft; and a *palm-top* by some analysts. When the handheld has voice and computerlike processing power, it is a *teleputer*, the term used by telecommunication visionary George Gilder. It is an all-around service device for the wireless Internet. In 2000, there were 10 million handhelds, 3 percent of which were Internet-enabled. By 2006, the forecast is for nearly 40 million Internet-enabled PDAs.[2]

Table 5 Handheld characteristics and manufacturers

Names	Features	Makers
Handheld	Medium computation	Palm, Handspring,
PDA	Good messaging	Hewlett-Packard,
Communicator	Internet access	Symbol, Psion,
CDC	Medium display	Intermec,
HPC	Touch screen	Compaq,
Palm-top	Full keyboard	Casio, etc.
Teleputer	Significant data storage	
	Handwriting recognition	
	Peripheral cards	
	Works offline without connection	

There are two kinds of handheld – the industrial and the consumer handheld. The main difference is the environmental packaging. Both are programmed in a similar way. The handhelds used by the consumer and small businesses are largely based on the Palm OS and Microsoft WinCE OS. The industrial handheld shown to the side is rugged and is used in business. Makers of industrial handhelds like Symbol, Psion, Intermec, Itronix, and Husky and others are listed in chapter 19, in Table 44 "Industrial handheld manufacturers and devices."

Although both types of handheld are designed to work offline, in a connectionless mode, the industrial version rapidly connects to wireless networks as needed usually over a local area network (LAN) rather than the commercial wide area network (WAN). Without a connection, a handheld has enough storage for a mobile worker to complete tasks. This is not like a Web phone, which always requires a connection to be useful. The handheld is often designed with enough memory to store and enough power to operate on an entire week of work.

Handhelds can be thought of as miniature PCs. However, one great improvement over the PC is that they are instant-on devices. They do not take 5 minutes to boot up. Many have special storage technology so that they never lose any user data.

Wireless handhelds are information-centric devices. Large screens, full keyboards, and computer architectures let handhelds run complete applications. The PDA handheld first featured a touch-sensitive screen that permits users to write in "electronic ink." This lets businesses capture customer signatures. With handwriting recognition, or HWR, software, well-formed scribbles can be converted to text. Although keyboards are faster for input, HWR suits the style of many on-the-go mobile users. In time and motion studies, typing on a projected keyboard is significantly more efficient than handwriting recognition. A handwriting expert can often keep up with typing speed, but as soon as a mistake is made, input slows down significantly. Correcting text is quicker using a keyboard because tapping backspaces is faster than having to reposition a cursor and then handwrite the connection. This kind of problem is easily identified with usability technique, which is covered in chapter 21 in the section "Measuring Interfaces." For Asian languages, HWR is a divine feature because their character sets are larger than any keyboard. Asians use a complex character substitution method when tapping keys to compose native Kanji. Japanese type in Katakana and Hiragana, the phonetic forms of their language, which is more suited to keyboards. Stroking letters in Kanji is much faster than piecing together the characters from a Western keyboard. The Chinese use BoPoMoFo (these four syllables are like saying ABCD), a phonetic form of Mandarin dialect.

Some handhelds can establish quick wireless links to other handhelds, PCs, printers, or other devices, often using IrDA (infrared) or Bluetooth (short-range radio) technology. New features are constantly being added to the handheld, although most of the interesting ones have been pioneered already with military and industrial handhelds. These advanced systems perform precision GPS location and barcode scanning, and integrate transparent voice service over WANs or LANs.

Handhelds are versatile. Most can be reconfigured to connect with a wireless Web phone network or a corporate wireless Ethernet LAN. They send and receive files as well as email over the Internet. If they are configured to use a wireless cell phone network, they typically use a dial-up connection. The current handhelds are designed to pull, not to be pushed, devices. This information means the owner has to initiate all requests for content. Handhelds require users to make a connection to the wireless network and see what is out there. Handhelds are not signaling devices like pagers and newer Web phones that have content pushed to them. Paging systems have packets pushed to the device and the network is said to be "always on." Some handhelds can connect to a paging network, but they require special modems to receive pages or alerts.

The handheld has a proprietary but programmable OS to run applications and store data. Nearly infallible use is a benchmark for the industrial-class device that must operate for many days in hot and cold environments without recharging. Mobile serviceability depends not only on battery life, but also on the operating system's use of power. An operating system that does not conserve electrical power rigorously rarely lasts more than a full day of continuous field use before it must be recharged. Another power conservation solution for low-cost handhelds is the use of masked Read Only Memory (ROM). This kind of memory is fixed and can only be read. The limitation of masked ROM is that the software on the chip cannot be upgraded.

Expandable handheld computers are the most valuable. Many Symbol devices, the Compaq iPAQ™, and all Handspring Springboard™ devices have either slots or infrared ports to use peripherals. Devices with slots for removable cards can use the latest card technology, thus providing expandable modules for handhelds (Figure 12). These include laser scanners to read barcodes; card readers to let you swipe plastic cards; Global Positioning System (GPS) radio cards to read satellite signals to give you location; camera cards to take pictures; and antennas to communicate with all kinds of networks. Many handhelds use a standard PCMCIA, or Personal Computer Memory Card International Association, which comes in type 1, 2, and 3 thicknesses. By using a standard, devices can use a world of standard off-the-shelf PC-card devices. Newer connectors include Compact Flash and Secure Digital.

Successfully used in the industrial handhelds for many years, multiform modules became a key distinction for Handspring, Inc. The device improved on the family of handhelds offered by Palm, Inc., by giving it a modular slot so it could be reconfigurable. The slot in the handheld by Handspring does not use a PC-card specification, so it cannot use the many off-the-shelf mobile peripheral

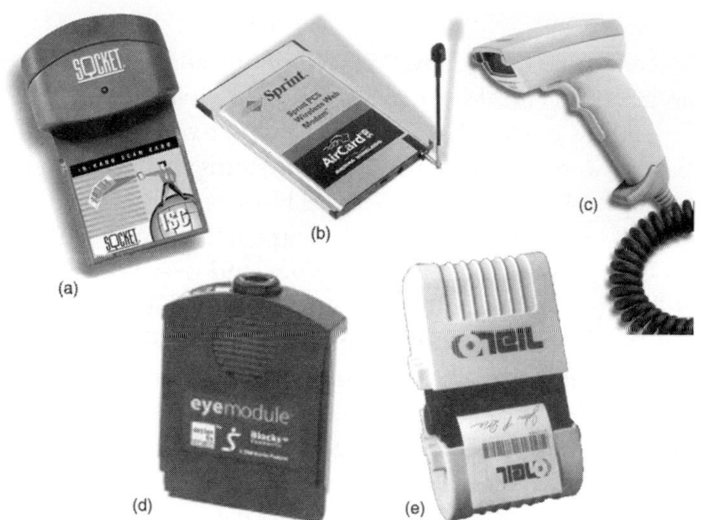

Figure 12 Expandable modules for handhelds used in key wireless applications include (a) a barcode scanner, (b) a data modem, (c) a handgun barcode scanner, (d) a color camera, and (e) a wireless printer (*Sources:* (a) and (c) Copyright © 2001 Socket Communications Inc.; (b) Copyright © 2001 Sierra Wireless, Inc.; (d) Copyright © 2001 Handspring, Inc.; (e) Copyright © 2001 OneilPrinters. All rights reserved.)

devices. The proprietary slot requires peripheral makers to retool to build add-ons exclusively for Handspring products. Handspring does see to it that first-class plug-and-play drivers come with the modules. Multifunctional design is expected to cross over to cell phones. In 2000, handheld makers Symbol and Motorola announced a half-billion-dollar joint venture to produce multifunctional wireless scanning components to be available on special Motorola phones and other devices.

Most popular handhelds like the ultrathin Palm V, the versatile iPAQ PocketPC, and the affordable Handspring Visor™ include Personal Information Management (PIM) functions. The PIM suite includes schedules, contacts, address books, and to-do lists. These can synchronize with the information on a PC. Palm, Inc., pioneered full-copy synchronization of PC data. Synchronization, shortened in conversation as *sync*, lets a person take a snapshot of PC data, work mobile, and then upload changes. With a wireless modem, a person can sync over the air. Industrial applications go a step farther. They transparently connect with a group server to dynamically share information pools with the field team. The best industrial handhelds have communication software built in that lets them freely switch access to public cellular or private LANs. These PIM and sync features are starting to appear on some cell phones.

Pagers

Many wireless applications seem to be directed to Web cell phone and handheld use, but one device is a hidden gem. It is ideal for rapidly and inexpensively exchanging data. A *pager* is a small wireless device that uses a paging network to send and receive data. Originally, pagers were one-way messaging systems that sent paging codes to a subscriber (see chapter 1, the section "A Brief History of Paging").

Pager characteristics (Table 6) include some interesting varieties. Most people think of a "pager" as a *one-way pager* that beeps the owner and displays a paging code. But the *two-way pager,* introduced by Motorola and Skytel and made popular by RIM, has changed everything. An *uplink pager,* also known as a *pinger* or *beacon,* is a low-powered, one-way sending pager that transmits telemetry and sometimes location. Uplink pagers are commonly used for asset management such as tracking vehicles, major equipment, and even pets and children. *Active badges* are one-way pagers used in offices to track employees.

Today's pager operates over WANs on their own wireless data networks. Pagers are sometimes overlooked because much of their functionality is being incorporated into cell phones. However, pagers have some unique features. A chief advantage is their low-cost, time-sensitive data signaling. Signaling is the means of sending messages when they are ready. Most users think of this as alerts, which they receive if they instruct an information system to alert them if anything changes or is new. For example, a personal stock portfolio might have a trigger set to fire a message alert when something changes. The pager is signaled immediately. Handheld networks generally have no such feature and Web phones are occupied with voice traffic and do not have as strong a reception to ensure that vital messages transmit. Pager indoor coverage is significantly better than cellular phone reception. Another feature of pagers is that they are always on, unlike other wireless data devices that require dialing up to learn if there is new information. Besides signaling, some of the impressive features of the pager are two-month battery

Table 6 Pager characteristics and manufacturers

Names	Features	Makers
Pager Two-way pager Uplink pager Pinger Beacon Active badge	Excellent messaging Limited Internet access Small display Full keyboard Excellent reception Requires a connection Long use without recharge	RIM, Motorola, Glenayre

life, extremely small for portability, global coverage, good indoor access, and inexpensive billing. Pager bills are roughly one-fifth the average cellular phone bill.

Email is the most used application on the Internet, and it should come as no surprise that this would be true for wireless Internet. But email is store and forward; that is, you get mail only when you dial up and poll your service. Pagers wake up when a message is available and receive packets when they are pushed to the device. Pagers are largely found in the U.S. market. After many years of growth, in 1997 the U.S. pager market finally flattened, the uptake being replaced by cell phones that incorporate messaging and pagelike services. In 1995 the United States pioneered return path/channel paging, also called two-way paging, and the European paging industry has spent many years trying to lobby for a return channel. Almost every European digital phone implements Short Message Service (SMS). A U.S. version of SMS is available on most cellular networks. Unlike a pager, SMS does not guarantee the message will sent on time. While the United States has been content to have a separate paging channel, the Europeans have looked more carefully at the limits of paging service. Not only are they integrating paging into their networks, but they are specifying a new packet pushing protocol (PUSH) that not only signals devices but provides a response protocol. In the long run, the future wireless 3G air interface defines an always-on network where received messages can be signaled to the device, essentially working as a paging network. On the other hand, it will take a long time before 3G coverage will reach as many places as the paging networks.

The top two-way pager manufacturers are RIM and Motorola. There are also companies that produce paging modules for handhelds such as Glenayre Technologies. We will look at programming the RIM 957 Java kVM later in the applications section. Modern two-way pagers can almost be classified as handhelds for functionality. They are fully software programmable. Two-way pagers use a data-paging network. Pagers are meant to be portable and purposeful messaging devices. Pager modems can turn configurable handhelds into full-fledged pagers. A good example is the @ctiveLink™ pager from Glenayre, an add-in for the Visor™. Motorola's new Accompli™ 009 Personal Interactive Communicator has a small paging keyboard and color screen, and sends messages over GSM and GPRS. Like RIM's pager modem, it features the standard PIM applications.

For the wireless Internet, we group paging, messaging, and signaling as messaging applications. This is an evolutionary step beyond pure paging networks that only alert users. Pagers are ideal as inexpensive and low-power wireless devices. For receive-only, one-way paging, you can get global service from satellites. When wireless networks begin to accommodate packet switching, we'll be able to page almost any wireless device.

Voice Portals

A *voice portal* is a natural voice interface that runs on a server to give you a dialog. It listens to your speech, calculates a reply, and then speaks a response. Any telephone system, wired or cellular, can use a voice portal. The appeal of voice portals is their accessibility by more than 2 billion wired phones. There are far more phones, including old analog cellular phones and newer Web phones, than any other wireless technology. In 1999 U.S. consumers conducted $430 billion in commerce over the phone, more than ten times worldwide Web purchase.[3] The leader of this market, Nuance, sees the Internet as the voice Web to enable vCommerce, or voice-driven electronic commerce. The number two company is Speechworks, which specializes in voice recognition. Other voice portal service providers include Tellme, Portico, Wildfire, and BeVocal.

Table 7 lists voice portal characteristics and manufacturers. A subscriber dials into a voice portal and speaks in full sentences. The response to the natural dialog is from a natural-sounding or synthesized personality. The voice portal listens with voice recognition software and responds with speech synthesis software. The interaction is not perfectly natural, but it is effective. Using a voice portal, you might ask it, "Give me directions to the nearest ATM"; the voice portal would speak back locations. Or you might ask it, "Please call my mom," and it would look up the phone number and place the call. The standard way for wireless developers to offer their Web site voice portal service is through VoiceXML, the voice extensible markup language. The art of speech application design requires listening and speaking customization and is covered in chapter 14 in the section "Developing Voice Portal Applications."

Voice activation, voice portals, and intelligent voice response are related technologies. *Voice activation* is a feature of some handsets to recognize key words with a limited vocabulary. *Voice portals* listen to complete sentences and use complex logic to determine intent and produce a humanlike conversation. It is a full generation beyond intelligent voice response (IVR). IVR uses simple, voice tree systems. The voice portal listens to full sentences, thinks deeper, speaks in well-formed sentences, and permits a somewhat simplistic verbal dialog. While IVRs operate

Table 7 Voice portal characteristics and manufacturers

Names	Features	Makers
Voice Portal vCommerce	Limited messaging Limited Internet access Voice interface Requires a connection Connection from any voice phone	Nuance, Speechworks, Tellme, BeVocal, Wildfire, General Magic

by the user's response to prompts – "Dial 1 for information, Dial 2 for service" – in a sometimes annoying and cryptic hierarchy of possible responses, voice portals operate in response to you, to your voice. For example, using a voice portal, you can say, "Open my address book" or "Give me today's hockey scores" at any time. If you have programmed the voice portal correctly, it responds with the correct information.

Voice portals are interesting for three good reasons:

1. They can reach a larger number of wireless voice devices.
2. They are the best technology for people who prefer to listen and talk rather than read and write.
3. They can use any handset or telephone in any country.

Handset makers do not have to build different keyboards for each nationality. In fact, a next-generation voice portal phone might have neither buttons nor displays. You ask it to reach a service. If you need a display, you can use a Bluetooth or WiFi network, and direct visual material to any displaying device within 10 meters.

Why should developers consider implementing a voice portal? It is a potential mass market. It is a great solution for those who cannot use wireless data devices with small screens and tiny keys. Some people are verbal. Some situations do not allow keying in responses. Verbal exchange, when intelligently designed, is perfectly fine. Drivers in vehicles often cannot (and, indeed, should not) use their hands, so voice is ideal in this environment. According to the Cellular Telecommunications and Internet Association (CTIA), 80 percent of cellular phone use takes place in a car. The need for mobile communication is essential, but drivers who do not pull over to handle important conversations can cause accidents. Overzealous lawmakers are beginning to conclude that it is not possible to talk safely to anyone while driving.

Why should developers avoid implementing a voice portal? Not everyone likes to talk all the time. And for those who do, conversations take time. Although a voice portal is ready to listen to every word at any time, a vocal dialog takes a while to complete. It is often quicker to display a menu. If there are many choices, then callers have to wait to hear them all and perhaps ask them to be repeated in order to compare choices. It is like being in a restaurant and a waiter speaks a twenty-item menu. It is faster to "go back" on a visual system than on a "speaking" system. The programming for voice portals is a challenging art. Licensing quality component services for voice portals such as listener and speaker elements can be expensive.

With a voice portal, the entire dialog engine runs on a server. Will it ever run on the phone? There are two barriers. Verbal dialog engines require an enormous amount of processing power to deliver a natural conversation. Even if you had that power, native languages and professional vocabularies are unique and changing. Each Web site or industry group defines its own language. Open working groups are helping to establish common vocabularies based on XML. Downloading a new language or speech tree before using a new service could be prohibitive because its data might be too large for the device's memory and further cause long download times and costs.

Good voice portal solutions provide a powerful, well thought-through command language that lets users cut through the normal flow of dialog and layered decision trees. This quickly delivers the end result to the advanced subscriber and is often part of a customer care call center.

In making conversational applications that use voice portals, it is possible to include a real person rather than a synthetic personality. This model was colorfully established in the 1987 *Max Headroom* TV series where field reporter Edison Carter kept vocal contact with the dispatcher, Theora, in a back office. She worked as a dispatch agent, keeping track of things and using her computer to figure things out for her mobile colleague. She would occasionally consult the artificially subintelligent personality Max Headroom – the synthetic persona of Edison. (The series is remembered at <http://www.maxheadroom.com>.) The OnStar™ system in General Motors vehicles uses this model. Car owners connect with a real customer agent who will help explain things. The customer agent uses an Internet computer to solve problems for drivers in need of directions, car repair, roadside emergencies, and other automotive services. Having a real person online to support a wireless data application is a practical solution to many vexing problems with field force wireless deployments.

Web PCs

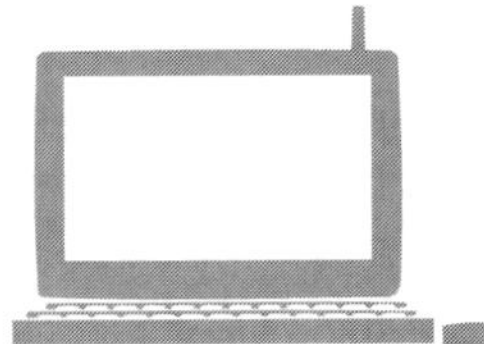

Personal computers are not particularly mobile, but they are an important part of a personal mobile application. The PC is often used as a springboard for a handheld device. They are useful for wholesale Web site access that can be accessed later by mobile devices. Web PC characteristics (Table 8) include not only desktop but also laptop machines. I suppose anything is wireless if you slap an antenna on it. But PCs and even laptops have proved to be poor mobile devices. At best, they can be put on wheels and treated as mobile stations as long as they are near a power supply. For the home healthcare market, Fujitsu mounted a flat screen PC on wheels in the mid 1990s. Microsoft is now working on a tablet PC. As full featured as any laptop, this one is lightweight, has a rich handwriting interface, and is easy to hand over to other people to use.

Running a colorful Web browser from a desk is another part of many mobile users' lifestyles. Using the larger screen lets people gather mobile content or set up

Table 8 Web PC characteristics and manufacturers

Names	Features	Makers
PC Laptop TabletPC	Maximum computation Full Internet access Used to set up mobile accounts Mobile servers Poor mobility	IBM, Dell, Gateway, Sony, Toshiba, Sun, VALinux, Apple, Compaq

options within a mobile portal. By taking the time on the PC, they can simplify choices when they are on the go. From their PC, users can hit a mobile Web site or a wireless channel portal like AvantGo. There, they check off the mobile functions or content they need. When they sync their devices with the channel portal, it fetches all the content, formats it, and transfers new content to the device.

Conventional Web sites are beginning to provide a mobile start page. From the PC, mobile users expect to set up a working mobile relationship to the rest of the site. They often personalize and streamline their interests to access the parts they need when mobile. For example, on Yahoo, people access their personal mobile portal pages to determine the devices they will use and the services they will see when they are mobile.

Most mobile users know what they want. They already are familiar with Web sites and are not asking to browse them from their wireless devices. It takes too long and costs too much. It is best that you extend the high-level mobile utility of your site. Provide simple transactions on the field and detailed ones on the PC. In marketing-speak, a Web site offering mobile customization lets you "extend your reach and maintain the online relationship."

Of course, the PC is the primary programming platform for developers. It is remarkable for its ability to be reprogrammed to perform an enormous range of functions. It can run popular operating systems like Windows, Linux, Solaris, or Macintosh. The PC will run a wide variety of software applications and production tools. It can generate code and data for wireless devices. The PC is used to write software directly for wireless devices, as well as produce content for the servers. Many PCs also operate as servers providing Internet content for both wireless and wired devices.

The operation of the wireless and the wired PCs is almost identical. The wireless laptop is a little more interesting, but from the viewpoint of the wireless Internet, it is nothing more than an oversized handheld.

For some people, the PC is their first Internet device. On the other hand, for people living in Asia or Europe, a Web phone or other wireless device may be their only Internet connection. For those with PCs, elaborate mobile content can be prepared. In addition to customizing mobile pages for later use, people can mark up content and build small mobile databases of information that can be used when the people are mobile. For example, travelers planning to visit a destination can designate an area where they will be and compare restaurants, hotels, and events to form an active list. This can be pulled together and put on the device or consulted later as a virtual guide.

In industry, dispatchers use the PC to coordinate wireless devices in the field. From a central control facility, administrators use PCs to connect enterprise services with wireless clients. By the end of the decade, most PCs will have a "wireless broadband" connection that will be faster than today's wired office PC. The recent Bluetooth wireless standard lets PCs share the antenna of a cellular phone to exchange both voice and data. This makes them effective as reference devices within the wireless Internet.

Communicating Appliances and Other PC Devices

With declining sales in the personal computer industry, many consider this a post-PC era. Consumer electronics devices are being produced as low-cost, dedicated Internet devices, some of which are wireless. Playing on the "Intel Inside™" marketing campaign, Intel is planning an "Intel Outside" campaign that targets these new devices. The generic name *iAppliances*, Internet appliances (perhaps better called information appliances), refers to specialized gadgets designed as a single application. Communicating appliances characteristics and manufacturers are geared toward delivering Internet access for specific purposes, as Table 9 shows. iAppliances are not like personal computers that are adaptable, configurable, and reprogrammable. iAppliances often have an experimental Web-top user interface that borrows heavily from existing Web PC desktops. iAppliances connect with the Internet and are dedicated to a channel with specific content. If you want to play Internet radio on your home stereo, why buy a PC to watch a color screen to listen to a radio station?

Table 9 Communicating appliances characteristics and manufacturers

Names	Features	Makers
Embedded computer iAppliance Webpad WebTV Wireless cameras Cellular watches eBook	Purposeful computation Limited Internet access Special function devices	Kodak, Microsoft, Ricoh, startup companies

The catalog of Internet devices is quite rich. There are electronic book readers, tablets, electronic picture frames, email stations, and Internet radios. WebTV provides television and limited Internet access. As a family of wireless devices, communicating appliances largely fit our application model as handhelds that have proprietary OS devices. Few of these are programmable; however, you can reach most with your content.

Content access devices are a strong direction for future Internet developers who are engineering technology to originate content rather than software applications. Most software is embedded in these devices, although some are programmable. The webpad, a large slatelike device being made by many manufacturers, is programmable under contract with the manufacturer. Webpads are a bit heavy and have short battery life, but are useful for limited mobility and are often considered a consumer home appliance. Another domestic iAppliance is the consumer eBook that is forecast to command a $500 million market in 2004, compared to the $8 billion market for paper books today. Telcos and computer industries continue to miniaturize features to the point of becoming fashionable and wearable. Today smart watches, watch cameras, paging jewelry, and headset earrings can combine the urgency of messaging, condensed views of email and pictures, and short pagerlike services. Some devices use the Bluetooth wireless standard that replaces cables and connectors and permits them to exchange and synchronize data with other nearby devices. Developers who want to deliver or receive Internet content from these domestic devices will need to contact the vendor to understand the specific data stream, device software, and wireless network protocol.

Wireless Networks That Support Wireless Devices

Developers often have to compare devices to decide which are appropriate for a wireless project. But the comparison is complete only when you evaluate the underlying wireless network. Beware of using Web phones and handhelds in time-sensitive applications without complete knowledge of the signaling network. Paging networks treat data in a timely manner. Web phones do not signal for data unless the network is designed for it. Even then, data takes lower priority than voice. Depending on your network, you may have to build or buy push services.

As much as we want to compare devices and their qualities, the reality is that you have to look carefully at the underlying wireless network that each device operates with. Usually a wireless device operates on only one wireless network. Because public and local area networks are so different, especially in the United States, the best advice is to understand network differences in protocols, coverage, voice qualities, and data qualities before settling on a device.

Limited coverage and availability are realities of wireless networks. If you are sitting in an underground parking garage in San Francisco, you will not receive wireless coverage. If you are in the elevator of a high-rise building, you will not get service. For most people at their desk at work, in basements, or inside many buildings, there is too much interference from concrete and steel. In big cities there are "wireless shadows" that limit access to all wireless devices. Even if you set up your own wireless LAN, the signal will not reach everywhere inside your building. Great advances are being made with digital signal processing to dramatically increase signal sensitivity, but this will take some time to develop.

Another network variable is capacity. Try placing a phone call at a large trade show like COMDEX or CTIA after a big announcement, or calling from a stalled freeway or any well-populated area. When everyone goes to the air at the same time, the cellular towers reach their capacity quickly. These are annoying and, we hope, temporary conditions of the wireless world. The most useful networks support both voice and data, are always on, and are IP based. A pager is always connected to its network and operates in low-power mode ready to receive data.

Because most people have to live with one device, devices must be compared. Text entry is a differentiator. If users are expected to perform a fair amount of text entry, a handheld device works better than a Web phone. Some two-way pagers have useful keyboards. For more exotic functions like recording a customer's signature or reading inventory barcodes, then only a configurable handheld will do. Devices have different abilities to handle voice and data. Most can access the public wireless carriers; however, most handhelds can access the LANs with higher data rates. Most handhelds require making a connection to establish service. This is unlike pagers and cell phones, which operate in low-power mode to be signaled by wireless networks to alert or ring the owner with important information.

A simplistic but useful summary of wireless devices would be: For a high-volume corporate data device, use a handheld. For simple nationwide Internet access and voice calls, use a Web phone. For low-cost access to important data, use a pager. To reach everyone who has a phone, use a voice portal. And always let the PC manage the wireless account. Of course, the entire line of devices can be supported with the right server architecture, as we shall see in chapter 17.

The One Essential Device

Out of my pockets, I pull a Web phone to take calls, a pager to receive and reply to urgent messages, and a wireless handheld with my favorite wireless Web browser, schedule, and phone numbers. I look up phone numbers on my handheld and then key them into my phone. Email addresses I have to punch into my pager. And in each city I visit, some devices get wireless network connections and others are mute. You never know. When I travel to Europe or Asia, then I need to pull my SIM chip out of my phone. The geeks are gawking at the spread of technology. Coming soon are ideal wireless devices. They harmonize data and voice technology and use the many wireless networks of the world. One approach is to make a super smartphone or a communicating handheld. On the other hand, given technology like Bluetooth, multiple devices might simply share a common handset, handheld display, and antenna, each subdevice doing what it does best.

The business market is certainly looking to conserve expenses by providing one ideal device. In early 2001, two new form factors were introduced to the market. A series of handheld-compatible phones were produced by Kyocera culminating in the Kyocera QCP™6035 smartphone (Figure 13), and a phone-compatible handheld was introduced by Handspring as the VisorPhone™ (Figure 14). Other companies followed suit. Motorola introduced a pager with a phone, and SprintPCS introduced a cell phone with a handheld. A general emerging design direction for small devices is to have interchangeable and separable subdevices. This is the architecture of industrial handhelds as well as the Handspring product platform and is suggested by Bluetooth device configurations.

Figure 13 Cell phone with a handheld
(*Source:* Kyocera QCP™6035 smartphone courtesy of Kyocera Wireless Corporation.)

Mobile workers often need to use voice and data. Enterprises do not want to pay for multiple devices or to train employees to use each device. We now see portable phones with efficient low-power Java kernels. They can run high-level applications and still work as cellular phones. New operating systems can process data and take a voice call simultaneously. Some executives are pushing for a network computer, others for a smarter phone, and others have pushed on to the inevitable future where hundreds of millions of small wireless bitstreaming subdevices deliver much needed integrated voice and data services.

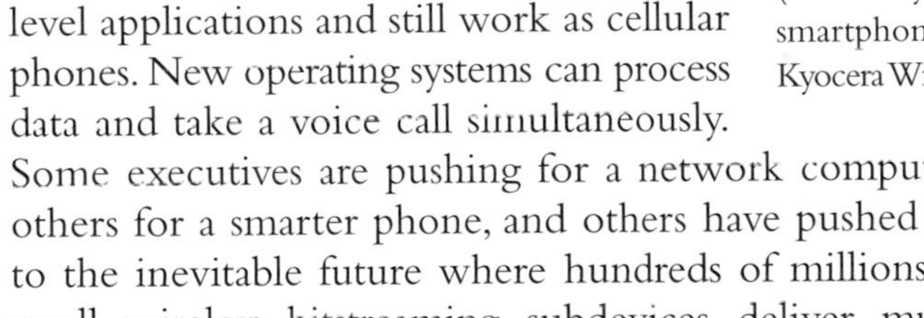

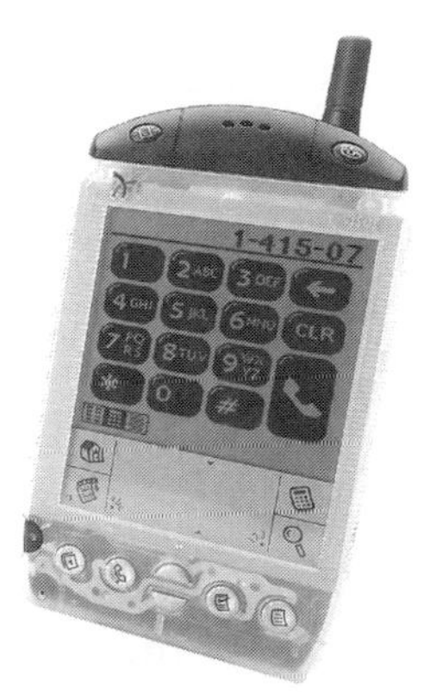

Figure 14 Handheld with a cell phone
(*Source:* Handspring VisorPhone™ copyright © 2001 Handspring, Inc.)

Java phones are early teleputers that deliver combined voice and data services over a wireless Internet-work. A Swiss army knife capable of voice, data, and paging requires a lot of power. Without proper energy management and battery design, a combination device may not be portable. As the wireless Internet evolves, essential devices will emerge. Until then, consider working with the best qualities of each wireless device over its associated network.

We have looked at the broad range of wireless devices people have in their hands today. The next step is to look inside these devices to understand the necessary physics and science. This will let us appreciate the distinctions among various wireless networks and devices, and perform basic estimations of their use.

The Language and Science of the Wireless Internet

Wireless devices deliver different qualities of voice and data over the air. These qualities are based on the physics of radio waves and the science of the spectrum. Based on these principles, telecommunications and computer technologies rule the wireless Internet industry. Many software developers are familiar with computers, bytes, and programming languages. But these new wireless devices are based largely on the ideas and language of radio physics. This is the basis for building wireless technology and understanding spectrum, bandwidth, and quality. A closer look at the physics will help you understand the boundaries of the technology.

Wireless Spectrum

The electromagnetic spectrum, or simply spectrum, is the entire range of energy waves over which communicating devices transmit. The electromagnetic spectrum (Figure 15) is assigned common groupings of energy waves, commonly called airwaves, that make up bands of the spectrum. Over the airwaves, TV, radio, cell phone, or any wireless Internet devices communicate with a transceiver. Each kind of transceiver uses dedicated frequency ranges that are measured in Hertz (Hz); 1 Hz is one cycle per second. The spectrum of airwaves is ordered by frequencies. To the left end are the long, low-power, low-frequency waves. The spectrum increases to the right with high-energy, extremely short waves. When

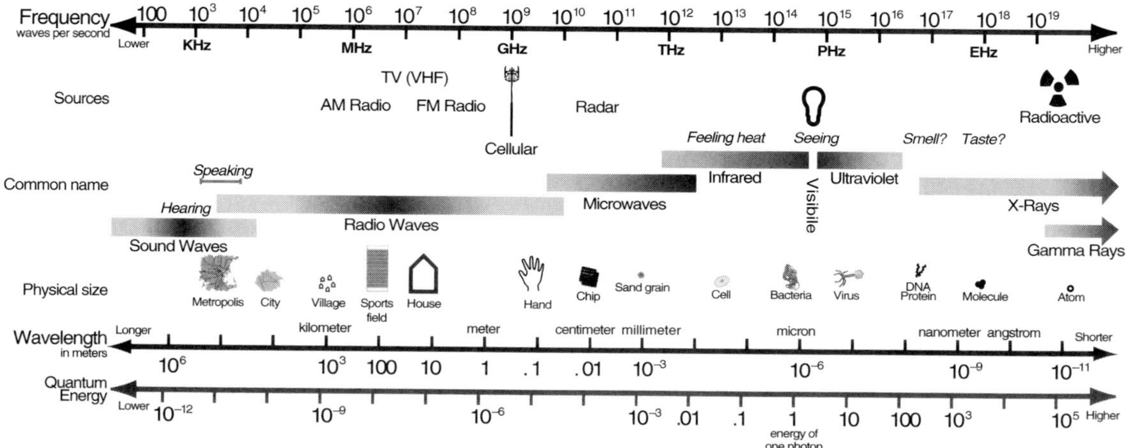

Figure 15 Electromagnetic spectrum

you listen to FM radio at 88.5 on your dial, the station is transmitting to your radio at 88.5 MHz, or megahertz, that is, 88.5 million cycles per second. The higher a radio technology is on the spectrum, the more power it requires.

Some interesting properties of the spectrum are that higher frequencies travel shorter distances. They take more power to transmit; with enough power, they can be life threatening. Higher frequencies can be modulated to carry more bits per second than longer waves, but they are subject to atmospheric interference. Broadcasters generally prefer owning a lower frequency because it costs less to transmit a signal, it carries farther, and it is generally "safer."

The U. S. Federal Communications Commission (FCC) and similar agencies around the world break up the spectrum and assign bands for specific purposes. Bands are ranges of frequency with common names. Worldwide bodies such as the International Telecommunications Union (ITU) also make frequency agreements so devices will operate clearly worldwide. Regulating radio interference is necessary so that wireless devices do not interfere with one another. To prohibit interference from a neighboring transmitter, the FCC restricts bands of coverage. Hundreds of these bands that have general names are shown at the back of the book in appendix A, under "FCC Spectrum Allocation."

The owner of popular mobile cellular bands must obtain an FCC license, which guarantees the owner exclusive use in a territory. Other parts of the spectrum go unlicensed such as the Instrument Medical Scientific (ISM) at 2.4 GHz and Unlicensed National Information Infrastructure (U-NII) at 5 GHz. Unlicensed sections of the spectrum are open to use by any transmitting device. It may interfere with, or more colorfully expressed, step on the signal of another wireless device. With intelligent signal processing, interference conflicts can be minimized.

Over time, the FCC licenses higher and higher spectrum with wireless technology. In the 1980s the FCC licensed 800 MHz for cell phones; this part of the spectrum sits above the established AM and FM spectrum. When cellular spectrum was used up in 1996, the FCC auctioned off the higher-spectrum 1900 MHz licenses to operate at a lower power range called Personal Communications Services (PCS). Your cell phone today typically uses either the 800 MHz or the newer 1900 MHz band of the spectrum to transmit. A "dual-band" cell phone can use either of these parts of the spectrum. Typical frequency and spectrum expressions (Table 10) are the common language of engineers. In the tradition of counting by thousands, 1000 Hertz is 1 kilohertz (KHz); 1000 KHz equals 1 megahertz (MHz); 1000 MHz equals 1 gigahertz (GHz). A PCS cellular phone can be said to run at 1900 MHz, or 1.9 GHz; they are the same. If you are using a wireless handheld device, most local wireless transmissions take place at 2.4 GHz; however, you might see it expressed as 2400 MHz. The complete list of prefixes for words that measure magnitude appears in appendix A under "Bits, Hertz, and Prefixes of Magnitude."

Table 10 Expressions of frequency and spectrum

Spectrum in Hertz	How It Is Said and What It Means
1.9 GHz = 1900 MHz	"One point nine gigahertz equals nineteen hundred megahertz." This is where CDMA PCS operates on the spectrum.
2.4 GHz	"Two point four gigahertz" is an unlicensed ISM band. It is used by wireless Ethernet, Bluetooth, HomeRF, and other protocols.

When we say that a PCS phone operates at 1900 MHz, that is a rough number sometimes written as circa 1900 MHz (*circa* is Latin for "around," meaning "approximately"). The actual PCS range is 1850 MHz to 1910 MHz for the transmitter and 1930 MHz to 1990 MHz for the receiver. Named intervals of spectrum are often called a band. The PCS band runs from 1850 MHz to 1990 MHz; the difference of 140 MHz is called bandwidth.

Bandwidth and Data Rate

Bandwidth measures the difference between the upper and lower ranges of a spectrum frequency. It is the area in which licensed signals are transmitted. The wider the bandwidth, the larger the number of callers or amount of data you can pass. Although bandwidth traditionally describes the width of a spectrum channel for wireless Internet engineers, bandwidth also measures data capacity. For a wireless device, the bandwidth indicates how many bits can be transferred per second. Eight bits equals 1 byte. One byte of storage measures 1 character. To compute storage and file sizes (in bytes) on computers from telecommunications, you have to divide the number of bits by 8 (Table 11).

If your data rate is 9600 bits per second, that means you can send or receive 1200 characters per second. However, the number of user bits – the actual useable data – is always lower because of header, error checking, and billing information in the stream. Most telecommunications traffic uses traditional 8-bit frame characters. However, the double-byte Shift JIS characters in Asian markets use 16-bit character frames, as do international Unicode characters.

Table 11 Calculating communication and storage sizes

8 bits = 1 byte	All telecommunications network rates are measured in bits per second; computers measure storage in bytes.

Talking Bits

The "b" used in communication measurements is sometimes innocently confused. You are reading 9.6 kbps, but engineers express data rates (Table 12) like kbps as *bits per second* – never bytes per second. Telecommunication language is always spoken in bits not bytes.

Typical Web phone data rates range from 9.6 kbps to 14.4 kbps. Even at 9.6 kbps, you do not get to use those 9600 bits. You can use only about half of those bits because many bits are used for routing, addressing, security, and error correction. Pager and handheld modem data rates run as high as 19.2 kbps. New U.S. and European cellular data protocols increase the data rate to 144 kbps and beyond. While the standard for third-generation data rate is 2 Mbps, high data rate (HDR) sustains 2.4 Mbps, and wireless Ethernet is 11 Mbps.

Data in Information Theory

Information theory is a fascinating and complex subject that explains cryptography, the ability of signals to carry content, and many important fundamentals in communication science. Information theory was invented by Claude Shannon, who passed away in 2001. After doing work related to classified code breaking in World War II, Shannon performed signal systems and information theory research for Bell Telephone Laboratories in Murray Hill, New Jersey. Shannon's law states that channel capacity is related directly to the product of bandwidth and the logarithm of the signal-to-noise ratio. It defines the maximum rate at which data can be communicated over a given communications channel. In the simplest of reductions of a perfect and simple channel,

1 Hz = 1 bit.

This is a useful working equation to estimate the maximum amount of data you can get from a basic telecommunications band. For example, the typical 20 Hz AMPS band can carry only about 20 kbps of data. But a 1 Hz wave is not

Table 12 Common data rate expressions

Data Rate	How It Is Said and What It Means
bps	"Bits per second."Never say bytes. Bps is the data rate of a network.
9.6 kbps	"Nine point six kilobits per second." An average cellular data rate is 9600 bits per second.
2000 kbps = 2 Mbps	"Two thousand kilobits per second equals two megabits per second," which is the target data rate for third-generation networks.

what it used to be. In newer modulation and compression techniques, it is possible to encode four or more times the capacity in the wave oscillation.

Converting Voice to Data: Hertz to Megabits

Cellular networks carry both voice and data. The human voice can convey understandable speech in 300 Hz to 3300 Hz. Telephone companies use 4 KHz as the allocated bandwidth for speech. Using a digital telephone network with conventional modulation, a key equation shows the conversion of average talk bandwidth with the conventional amount of data that can be transferred:

4 KHz talk = 64 kbps data.

Another way to express this is that through the 4 KHz of spectrum through which we speak in 1 second, a telephone converter passes 64 kilobits of data. One conclusion from this "talk to text" equation shows how efficient data is relative to voice. Using digital-to-analog pulse code modulation (PCM), one channel can convert one 4 KHz voice channel by chopping 1 second into 8,000 samples. Any sample is 8 bits, or 256 values, which results in an encoding of 64,000 bits of data per second. Divide 64,000 by 8 to convert bits to bytes, and that is the number of computer text characters – 8000 bytes or about two pages of book text per second. The cellular data rate and amount of text transferred (Table 13) vary depending on the carrier technology. In the United States, T1 lines are commonly used for both voice and data. T1 can carry 24 voice calls, each at 64 kbps equaling 1.544 Mbps data.

You can see voice is not very efficient relative to data, although there is something to be said for the music in voice. There are many techniques to compress data or enlarge a 4 KHz channel.

Table 13 Cellular data rate and text transfer

Data Rates	Text Transferred
4 KHz = 64 kbps	The average wired talk bandwidth is 4 kilohertz. In 1 second of speech on a phone network, 64,000 bits of data or two pages of book text can be transferred, using conventional wired modulation technology.
14.4 kbps	The maximum wireless data rate over current-generation public air carriers is 14.4 kilobits per second, equivalent to 2000 characters per second.
9.2 kbps	The average wireless data rate over current-generation public air carriers is 9.2 kilobits per second, equivalent to 1000 characters per second.
T1 = 1.5 Mbps	"T one" lines carry data 1.5 megabits per second or about 188,000 characters per second.

Bandwidth of Telco Data Pipes

Bandwidth for Internet data is like plumbing – the wider the pipe, the more data you can send. The telecommunications industry has standardized on these "pipe sizes." The common U.S. standard of wired transmission is T1 – the T stands for *trunk line*. A trunk bundles many smaller lines. T1 typically bundles 24 voice calls or 1.54 million bits per second. Most offices use a fractional T1 line rate for Internet data. Common trunk rates (Table 14) use different international standards to carry data over a wire. North America uses the T hierarchy, Japan uses the DS hierarchy, and Europe uses the E hierarchy. Their scales of service are different from that of T trunks. A T1 line is the same as DS1, digital service level 1. You sometimes see F rather than T. F stands for fiber, but the scale of services is the same as the trunk lines. OC is optical carrier used in all the newest fiber technology. The complete international hierarchy list is in chapter 17, the section on "Evaluating Wired Bandwidth."

Wired bands The telcos and cable television market use common terms to describe the bandwidth of their signals. Although useful in planning wired bandwidth capacity, these terms have little or nothing to do with the wireless bands. A wired *narrowband* is less than or equal to T1, or 1.5 Mbps. *Wideband* is greater than T1, or 1.5 Mbps, up to T3, or 45 Mbps. *Broadband* is greater than T3 and includes Digital Subscriber Line (DSL), Integrated Services Digital Network (ISDN), or cable modems. Broadband is a wide area communications channel of significant bandwidth that carries multiple signals two ways and is used in video cable systems. Broadband carries multiple channels, while *baseband* is a wire with a single service. A LAN is a wired baseband that handles a single, digital channel able to access multiple devices. A typical baseband Ethernet or token ring network runs between 10 Mbps and 100 Mbps.

Table 14 Common trunk rates

Wired Network			Data Rate
DS0[a]			64 kbps
DS1	T1[b]		1.54 Mbps
DS3	T3		45 Mbps
		E1[c]	2 Mbps
		E3	34 Mbps

a. DS = Japanese digital service.
b. T = U.S. trunk.
c. E = European trunk.

As far as wires go, there are powerline systems that run data over conventional electrical wires. Electrical utility powerline data operates at 2 Mbps. Asymmetric Digital Subscriber (ADS) line runs at 384 kbps to 24 Mbps, and TV cable modem coaxial cable has a data rate of 384 kbps to 48 Mbps. Optical fibers have a data rate of 622 Mbps and better.

Wireless bands A set of names that engineers use for emerging wireless bandwidth are not yet defined. These terms are in flux. As defined by the FCC in 1996, *wireless broadband* is 200 kbps or better in both directions. The term *broadband* is often used for data bandwidth wider than a voice call. Although it has a number of meanings, when wireless engineers speak of broadband, they mean wireless broadband rather than the 45 Mbps or greater wired broadband multichannel service. In conversations about wireless bands, engineers rarely use *wideband*. Today's cell phone wireless bandwidth is implemented as a sub-narrowband network and is sometimes called *wireless narrowband,* referring to data overlays of circuit-switched cellular phone data at 14.4 kbps or slower.

Common wireless data rates and devices (Table 15) are highly variable. As of 2001, the Web phones, handhelds, and pagers use different networks with different bandwidths. A more comprehensive table of comparative data rates appears in chapter 17 in the section "Worldwide Wireless Data Migration."

As we will see later, data networks are bound not only to spectrum but also to territories. Japan and Europe are well covered, but the North American wireless coverage patterns are confined mainly to large cities and airports. Even when a U.S. or Canadian license for spectrum is granted, few companies have the resources to cover North America. It usually takes many years to bring up towers, which usually cover large cities first. It is sometimes important to advise your clients on actual network territorial coverage and deployment plans, especially if they have to commit resources to specific devices. If your client operates in the San Francisco Bay Area, the speedy Metricom was useful. But if the client works in cities where Metricom had no coverage, then you had to use another system.

Table 15 Common wireless data rates and devices

Wireless Data Rate	Wireless Device
9.6 kbps	Web phones
14.4 kbps	Pagers, Web phones
19.2 kbps	Pagers
128 kbps	Handhelds using Ricochet
11 Mbps	Handhelds using a wireless LAN

To make wireless broadband terminology more "interesting," former fixed wireless services are experimenting with mobile terminals. These services currently require dishes or line-of-sight (LoS) antennas. They are useful as fixed wireless Internet "on ramps" and provide service. For the technically minded, all these fixed wireless access services are grouped under the IEEE 802.16 standard. The three most prominent broadband wireless access (BWA) technologies are:

- *Local Multipoint Distribution Service (LMDS)* is a low-power broadband, point-to-multipoint technology. This fixed wireless service can deliver up to 155 Mbps data at a radius of 2 km to 8 km and operates at from 29 GHz to 31 GHz.
- *Multichannel Multipoint Distribution Service (MMDS),* popular with Sprint and WorldCom (MCI), delivers data at 750 kbps to 11 Mbps with a range of 35 miles supporting 100,000 subscribers. Other vendors get a 100 Mbps data rate over shorter ranges. MMDS operates between 2 GHz and 4 GHz making available 186 MHz of spectrum.
- *"Wireless fiber" microwave transmission* steps up to 155 Mbps with a range of 3 to 5 miles. It operates between 24 GHz and 39 GHz making available over 1 GHz of spectrum. At these high bands, powerful wireless systems are being tested at data rates in Gbps. At this frequency, the signal experiences severe loss in bad weather.

Channels are subdivisions of spectrum used by an operator to connect subscribers. An operator with a wireless license divides that spectrum to obtain as many subscribers as possible. Channels subdivide bands. There are many schemes to share channels and they go by names like FDMA, TDMA, CDMA, and GSM. We will study each of them soon, but the important point to know is that callers share a limited number of channels on an assigned spectrum bandwidth.

When you communicate wireless data, the more bits, the better, right? Yes, but the more bits you take, the less bandwidth there is for other wireless callers in your area. In high-traffic areas, you will sometimes get good performance, but often experience long unpredictable waits. This is network latency.

Latency and Quality of Service

The terms *delay* and *latency* are often used interchangeably. *Delay* is a fixed waiting time to get network response. Delay is apparent in high-altitude satellite links where two speakers have to wait a second to hear a response. Delay is a raw limitation of a medium. There is nothing you can do about it. You can adjust for latency. *Latency* measures the elastic time it takes to get a network response. Latency and delay timing (Table 16) are often expressed in milliseconds (ms).

Table 16 Latency and delay timing

Latency	How It Is Said and What It Means
1000 ms = 1 second	"One thousand milliseconds equals one second." A half second delay is equal to 500 milliseconds, or 500 ms.
150 ms	"150 milliseconds" is the expected roundtrip latency of a standard voice network. It should never exceed 400 ms.

Latency can be thought of as delay, but unlike raw wait time, latency has an unpredictable range of waiting times due to changing variables.

Latency is a common occurrence in many technologies. A disk drive's latency is the time it takes to rotate to seek data. Latency of a network implies the reserved power of connections, which are inhibited by many factors. Network router latency is caused by route table lookups and header conversions. A network connection that is busy serves its subscribers slowly and is said to have high latency. It generally improves when fewer subscribers are on the air. Accumulated delays compound latency. In the multitasking operating system in networks, a context switch causes users to experience lags as the system moves from one piece of software to another. As a network switches and caches, it can give rise to higher levels of latency. Latency is a critical measure of a voice network. The latency of a voice network is expected to be 150 ms but not to exceed 400 ms. This is a measure of the quality of service (QoS). *QoS* is a telco industry term that refers to the operational quality of a network. Telco engineers take pride in their networks that meet the *five nines* of QoS; that is, a service operates at 99.999 percent of expected performance. Of course, six nines are better.

Using higher capacity networks and adding basestations can increase the traffic. Developers can take some steps to combat latency. Simplifying Web pages shortens over-the-air load time. Sensitivity to page latency is more pronounced in wireless applications as increased traffic slows down overall service. On a Web phone, it can take 10 to 30 seconds to request consecutive pages of a story. This latency issue, if you do not address it, will cause subscribers to move to a better service. Middleware can minimize latency and is covered in chapter 18 in the section "Wireless Middleware for Large Systems."

4

Chapter

Wireless Networks

Spectrum is the magic medium that now connects wireless technology more and more through the Internet. The construction of wireless applications depends on utilizing various ranges of spectrum and changing generations of wireless transmission technology. The wireless digital network uses mobile cellular concepts such as handoff and spectrum reuse. The wireless network also uses layered protocols to manage the development of services. Networks are evolving from analog circuit-built connections to digital IP packet-switched connections that increase spectrum efficiency and maximize subscriber voice and data capacity. Keeping voice clear and increasing data loads put a special quality demand on the many wireless networks.

The Three Wireless Internet Networks: WAN, LAN, and PAN

The wireless Internet is broadly defined by three kinds of wireless networks. The power ranges of wireless networks (Figure 16), which are in descending order WAN, LAN, and PAN, form a bubble of usable energy patterns around a traveler. A differing range of wireless towers – cellular towers, basestations, and access points – serves each wireless network. These antennaed transceivers communicate with all manner of wireless devices, exchange data or voice with them, and then transmit that information through relays and cables eventually back to the wires of the Internet.

The most powerful network is a wide area network (WAN), which is a licensed public wireless network used by Web cell phones and private radio frequency

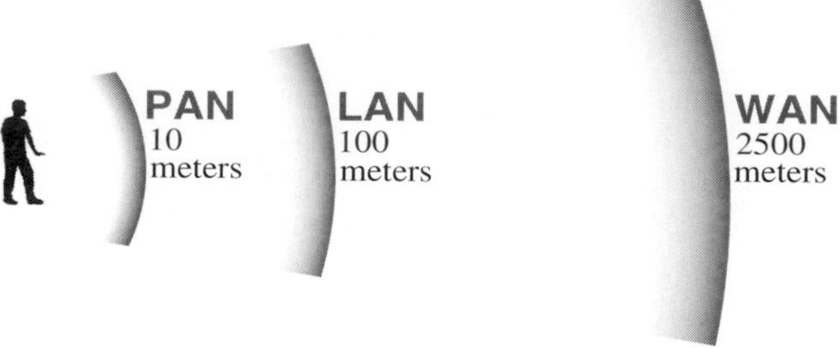

Figure 16 Power ranges of wireless networks

(RF) digital modems in handhelds. The cellular tower has the most powerful signal; it can range up to 10 miles. WAN carriers provide public service for cell phones. They are heavily regulated and licensed to specific territories. Over the public wireless network, cell phones and handhelds with radio modems all have antennas that talk with *towers*, or as they say in the U.K., masts. WAN cellular towers come in three power configurations: macrocell, microcell, and picocell. *Macrocells* are the standard cellular tower. They are sometimes called supercells. For high-density areas, one macrocell is replaced by many microcell towers, which use lower power to connect more callers in an area. Moving down the power curve, the basestation, sometimes called a *picocell,* can be installed in buildings.

The next most powerful network is the wireless local area network (LAN), which operates on unlicensed spectrum. It is used most often by computers and handhelds and by some experimental cell phones, but not by pagers. LANs are used in private business and at home. They have a range of up to 100 meters. The transmitter for a LAN is called a basestation and is typically mounted in buildings. Some companies use only laptops with wireless LAN cards to connect to the company network.

Finally, we have the very low-powered short-range personal area network (PAN), which operates on unlicensed spectrum and has a range of up to 10 meters. The low-power transmitter was called a wireless access point, but the later acronym WAP almost always means Wireless Application Protocol. Although sometimes called basestations, wireless access points are now often called simply access points (AP). A PAN does not need an access point. Devices can connect directly to send voice and data if they have PAN transmitters. When used in personal computers, a PAN replaces short cables or connectors that, for example, attach computers to printers or keyboards to computers. In mobile devices, the PAN is used to perform transaction, data exchange, or voice relay functions. Because LANs and PANs use the same band of unlicensed spectrum, they compete, overlap, and occasionally interfere with one another.

All wireless devices have one thing in common: They are radios. This is an important observation to keep in mind. Each family of wireless device usually connects through its own wireless radio network. Wireless devices can use large, public, cellular phone networks, private in-building wireless networks, or room-wide networks typically with one radio and one antenna. We are just beginning to see devices that have multiple antennas. A WAN, LAN, and PAN device could tri-cord a wireless connection to anywhere on the wireless Internet.

The facts of life are that the network operators, not the handset makers, set the market rules. The carriers determine which handsets will operate on their networks. This is unlike the PC market where hardware is independent of the network. Fundamentally, the wireless network is the cause and the wireless devices are the effect.

From Analog to Digital Networks

Cellular phones have evolved from first-generation analog to second-generation digital networks. Just like computers. There were analog computers before digital computers. At Southwest Research Institute in San Antonio in the 1960s, as a guest from high school, I met scientists who showed me the analog computers they used in primate research to simulate various behavior models. An analog computer was made of electronic circuits that were patched with cords and for which you had to build specific electronic circuits to perform different calculations. Complex oscillation and voltage differences could model physical situations, readings could be taken, and what-if analysis could be done by changing resistance or increasing voltage. There was no software other than documentation of the circuit diagrams.

Using specialized digital circuitry that is software programmable, you can process digital signals beyond the capacity of analog circuitry. Compared to analog technology, digital provides higher quality, greater flexibility, fewer errors, and simpler means of replication. Cellular networks also share the same dramatic difference between their analog and digital construction.

Digital sampling (Figure 17) is a technique to encode sound as digital signals. When you listen to an AM radio station, the analog signals modulate a smooth carrier wave generated from a tower. Cellular phones modulate electromagnetic radio waves over their frequency of carrier. Sampling the signal is a key digital technique.

Let us say a fraction of a second's worth of speech is transmitted. Vocal tones are digitized by sampling and converting them to bits. Bits are then encoded as pulse code modulation

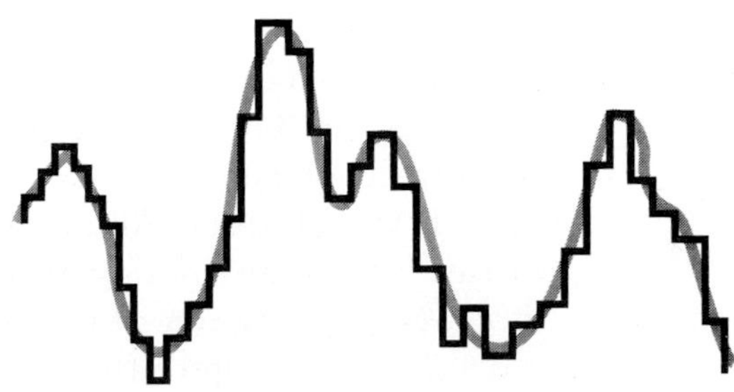

Figure 17 Digital sampling

(PCM). Here is how it works. If you are sampling a wave, you measure the strength (amplitude) as an 8-bit code. The sampled bits 11000000 become a number, 192, which is the PCM number that encodes the previous bit stream. That is what the *C*, code, in PCM stands for. Telco PCM quantizes 64,000 bits every second to represent speech. PCM can be sampled at other rates. Digital encoding is the basis for the cellular networks of the second and third generation. Telecommunication companies are exploring entirely new techniques to modulate the carrier in order to transfer more data.

For digital networks such as CDMA, the voice signal is sampled, compressed, and transmitted, and software is used to rebuild the signal. Digital networks have advantages over analog networks when signals fade. As signals fade and lose strength, digital signals can often be reconstructed using digital technology. Analog circuitry simply cuts off. In the reconstruction of the faded digital signal, there is more information available to fix errors. Also, digital signals can be scrambled, making them more secure. Another plus for digital signal sound processing is the wider dynamic range for volume and greater range of frequency for tone, which gives a clearer, more natural voice. Digital cellular signals sound stronger.

Modulation is a key part of the efficiency of radio transmission. The number of modulation techniques is extraordinary. The simplest techniques used in common radio are AM and FM. Amplitude modulation (AM) simply varies the strength of a signal to convey tone. Frequency modulation (FM) fixes its amplitude and adjusts the difference between each frequency wave to convey information. Phase modulation (PM) plays with the exact shape of the frequency wave and is used in current wireless transmission technology. Until recently, Shannon's law of information implied you could not exceed 1 bit per Hertz, meaning that if you had a 20 kHz channel to talk with, you could not exceed a data rate of 20 kbps. However, recent modulation techniques to phase and polarize waves allow more bits per second in the oscillating wave. Sideband energy is generated outside the frequency when the wave is heavily reshaped. There are many competing variants of these new forms of modulation, a promising one being Orthogonal Frequency Division Multiplexing (OFDM). Other techniques include Gaussian Minimum Shift Keying (GMSK), M-ary Bicoded Keying (MBCK), Quadbit Amplitude Modulation (QAM), Quadrature Phase Shift Keying (QPSK), Differential Quadrature Phase Shift Keying (DQPSK), Vector Orthogonal Frequency Division Multiplexing (VOFDM – Cisco), and Coded Orthogonal Frequency Division Multiplexing (COFDM – Radiata). All of these techniques break the frequency into multiple carrier signals, transmitting overlapping components of the wave in parallel. This increases the bit rate. A review of some of these new air carriers and their bit rates is developed in chapter 16, the section "4G, New Spectrum, and Emerging Wireless Air Interfaces."

Two-Way Communication Signals

What makes cellular radio different from broadcast radio is the ability to receive as well as transmit a signal. The two general techniques to coordinate sending and receiving signals are *Frequency Division Duplex (FDD)* and *Time Division Duplex (TDD).*

Frequency Division Duplex is a communication protocol that uses two frequency bands. All licensed cellular WANs use FDD. In these cellular calls, the *paired band* is a set of coordinated transmission signals with one band to transmit (uplink to a tower) and the other to receive (downlink from a tower). For example, a PCS network uses a set of paired bands; the uplink is near 1850 MHz and the downlink is near 1990 MHz. The lower band is always for the handset transmitter because the phone uplink can use the lower part of the spectrum where the waves travel farther. This is because lower frequencies take less power to transmit.

Time Division Duplex is a communication protocol that shares the full band for sending and receiving. Almost every wireless LAN uses unlicensed TDD. TDD has a great advantage over FDD when it comes to data. TDD can dynamically allocate the amount of spectrum needed to send or receive data. FDD bands are symmetric, and it assumes that the sender and the receiver will use the same amount of spectrum. This is true with voice, but not with data. At least ten times more data is downloaded than is uploaded in average use. TDD can take advantage of the fact that more data can be sent from the tower, which conserves spectrum. FDD will waste the uplink spectrum capacity for data. As WAN systems evolve to carry more data, they may rely on the more spectrally efficient TDD.

Advances in Antenna Signal Design

Since all wireless devices are radios, they use antennas. Towers have a much stronger signal than battery-powered devices. Any antenna transceiver drops off over distance exponentially (to the fourth power!) until it becomes too weak to use.

Omnidirectional transceivers connect to antennas to radiate power and receive any signal in a sphere around the tower. All cellular WAN systems have a *control channel* part of the spectrum that probes the comings and goings of devices. The control channel signals devices about to make or take a call. When a handset is ready to talk, the tower transfers the control channel to the *transmission channel.* As mentioned previously, the two transmission channels for WAN phones are the send (uplink) and the receive (downlink) channel. The control channel must be omnidirectional. But once a device is located and transmission takes place, then the continuous use of an omnidirectional antenna wastes power. Newer antenna designs and signal-processing systems are radically improving energy efficiency and subscriber capacity. Directional transceivers can focus antenna power in a sector. They can also be designed to process the incoming and outgoing transmissions better. Perhaps the most promising are the spatial processing systems, which are covered later in the section "Spatial Processing and Smart Antennas" in chapter 5.

Telco and Internet Networks

Before settling on a device, it is useful to know wireless networks by their engineering and practical differences in coverage, transmission efficiency, voice qualities, and data qualities. Most wireless Internet devices operate within only one wireless network. The wireless networks differ widely. At the most basic level, there are analog and digital networks. These networks can be circuit based or packet based. Circuits guarantee a two-way connection and are used in most cellular voice calls. Packets are efficient at sending data immediately and are used in i-mode and paging networks. Almost every industrial wireless application uses a packet-based LAN. In time, this will matter less because future wireless networks are destined to become packet switched. Your professional network evaluation will be necessary to build systems for users who page, browse, interact, or converse with wireless systems.

Telcos and the computer industry officially define networks in two ways. The formal definition of the *Internet network* is a collection of host computers that can communicate directly. Telcos define the *telco network* as a series of interconnections. In all cases, these global networks connect to terminals. Each of these industry networks has its own wireless air interface and protocols for voice and data.

If you use a Web phone or make a phone call in the United States, you access the Public Switched Telephone Network (PSTN). In Europe you access the Post Telephone and Telegraph (PTT). Each is a combination of local, long-distance, and international phone networks. Across the world, these telco networks formally register their standards with the ITU to keep specifications clear for interoperability.

Internet networks also have important distinctions for their subsidiary networks. They often use a telco backbone, but they also have standards for data interchange registered with the ISO, IEEE, and the W3C. The Internet is known as global public network, but companies provide intranets and extranets, which also involve wireless devices. An *intranet* is a portion of the Internet that runs behind a firewall and is visible only by company employees. An *extranet* is a secure part of the Internet viewable only by people with accounts, typically vendors or customers. A so-called business-to-business, or B2B, application is typically built on top of an extranet.

Circuit-switched and packet-switched networks (Figure 18) use a telco switch to send voice calls through the telephone network and data transactions to the Internet. If you use a pure digital system, such as a Cellular Digital Packet Data (CDPD) modem, then you are accessing the wireless Internet without switching. However, the next-generation wireless network is moving from a telco-defined, circuit-switched system to an entirely Internet-defined, packet-switched protocol system. Generally, circuits provide low latency and packets provide higher bandwidth.

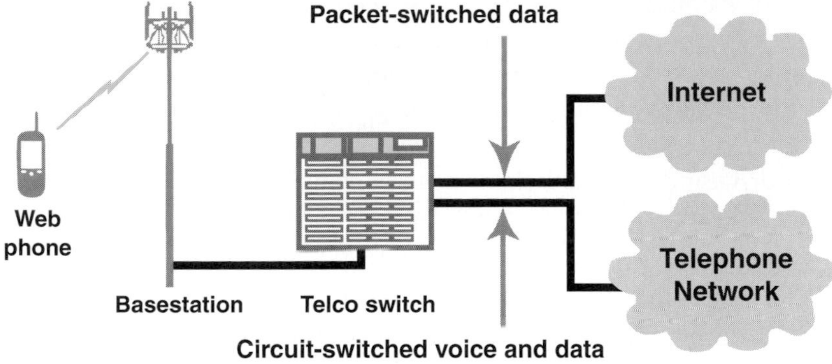

Figure 18 Circuit-switched and packet-switched networks

Voice circuit switches can transmit data, but for data subscribers the results are often the worst of both worlds – long latency and low bandwidth.

Comparing Circuit-Switched and Packet-Switched Networks

There are two network architectures for communicating devices: the telco-favored circuit-switched network, which connects voice phones, and the computer industry–favored packet-switched network, which best connects digital computers. Although the existing wireless network infrastructure is largely voice-centric and circuit switched, the wireless industry is squarely moving to a fully digital, packet-switched network using the same protocols that power the Internet. What are circuit-switched and packet-switched networks?

- A *circuit-switched network* builds up a circuit for a call, establishes a dedicated connection of circuits between points, and then tears it down. A circuit connection forms a single path between the caller and listener that lasts the entire time that both parties are on the call. You are guaranteed this circuit regardless of whether you are talking, sending data, or are silent. Examples of circuit-switched devices are telephones, cellular phones, Web phones, and dial-up modems. In order for Web phones to access data, their voice-grade circuit switches use data overlays that run on top of the established circuit.

- A *packet-switched network* routes IP-addressed data packets between points on demand. Packets are routed through multiple paths. It is how the Internet works. Packet-switched networks exchange variable amounts of data or voice packets. These packets can come in large bursts, typical of data, or in steady little streams, typical of voice. Data can be transmitted almost immediately because no call setup is involved. This quality is referred to as "always on" and provides continuous use. Such connections are best suited for personal messages, stock information, file transfers, and other Web microbrowsing where the connection is infrequent, but the amount of information transferred can be large.

An analogy to driving a car will help you understand the efficiency of packet switching. Imagine you were to drive from New York City to San Francisco. On a circuit-switched system you would first clear and keep one lane open for the entire drive. On a packet-switched network you just drive from city to city taking the best lane at each point until you reach your destination. During a traditional circuit-switched phone call, the network must build the connection, guarantee it, and tear it down after a call. All circuits must be recovered after use. The number of active circuits limits traffic on the network. As calls keep circuits open during long silences, this technique is especially wasteful and congests wireless networks. The packet network is filled only when packets are sent or received. Most packet networks can dynamically allocate bandwidth to transmit short bursts of data. The circuit-switched technique has a fixed size for bandwidth and works like a fixed-size water pipe that can only trickle so much data at a time. Finally, the billing on packet-based systems is based on characters transmitted – a simple calculation. For circuit calls, the minimum billing unit is often 1 minute, yet devices trying to establish a connection consume half the first minute, and billing plans with variable times on them are not received well. Companies cannot build reliable budgets with variable expenses, so circuit-based wireless networks with different roaming policies are difficult to do business with. Packet-switched connections tend to be more robust because a communications problem may require that a packet be resent, whereas with a circuit-switched connection the entire connection may have to be reestablished if a call is dropped. On the other hand, a reliable circuit is often the best way to guarantee that time-based content such as a music or video stream will arrive without interruption during a connection. Improved Internet protocols now keep packets in order and get around resending packets that can break up voice or streaming multimedia. These are some of the good reasons that the wireless Internet is becoming packet switched.

Phone Numbers and IP Addresses

To guarantee a unique connection, there are phone numbers and Internet Protocol (IP) addresses. In an ordinary cell phone call, a person enters a phone number and the network builds a circuit to the calling party. Phone numbers uniquely identify devices on a worldwide circuit-switched network. A global telephone number is called a Mobile Station International Subscriber Directory Number (MSISDN); it concatenates codes for country, exchange, local exchange, and subscriber. It looks like +44-408-731-3300, the phone number for Yahoo.

To make an Internet connection, a person enters an IP address. The network finds the device that matches it and responds by routing packets to it. An IP address is 32 bits long (4 bytes) and is global. It is expressed in dotted-quad format, for example, aaa.bbb.ccc.ddd. The first half of the number is the Net-ID, which identifies a network to which the host computer is attached. The second half is the subnet mask that includes the host ID, a unique number given on the network. For example, the IP address for Yahoo's Web site is 204.71.200.75. You could enter the dotted-quad address, but most people usually enter www.yahoo.com, the Web domain name. A Web domain name is used in the Uniform Resource Locator (URL), an explicit address to access the resource on the Internet. A Domain Name Service (DNS) router resolves the first part of a URL name to an IP address. The URL concatenates an Internet service, a computer, a domain name, and a file location on the computer. For example, <http://www.amazon.com/news> uses the http protocol to access the Web server at the amazon.com domain and then requests the default Web page in the news subdirectory. Technically a URL is a type of Uniform Resource Identifier (URI). A URI is a more general Web address that allows optional directives. For example, adding the short string `?city=paris&restaurant="chez%20jenny"` after the URL can direct a Web server to further resources. Another type of URI is the Uniform Resource Name (URN), which refers to a persistent and always available Internet resource. The URN is used by libraries or publishers and is becoming more important in wireless networks to establish reliable locations for moving sources of content.

Globally, a phone number is guaranteed unique on existing circuit-switched networks and an IP address is guaranteed unique over the packet-switched Internet. All wireless Internet devices require a packet-switched protocol; although overlays to circuit-switched networks can behave like IP devices.

Who creates the numbers? Phone numbers are assigned through the North American Numbering Plan Administration (NANPA). IP addresses are assigned by the Internet Corporation for Assigned Names and Numbers (ICANN). Many other companies will register domain names, but only ICANN can give out IP addresses.

Comparing Networks by Software Stacks

When you look at how applications use computer networks, there are two general methods of operation – client/server and peer-to-peer. In the client/server model, the source system makes a request, and the destination system returns a response. Most wireless networks use the client/server method. An alternative to this master/slave relationship is letting applications establish a peer-to-peer connection. Peer-to-peer networks guarantee a connection so that applications between the two systems operate at a peer level and can call each other and exchange data directly. Wireless devices obtain service from either a wireless telco or a data carrier network. Each network has its own data protocols, spectrum, billing plan, data rates, devices they can talk to, and coverage territories. (Wireless network architectures are compared in Part III.) For now, lets examine the technical elements of networks.

Software development often relies on components; networks operate as a *software stack* of layered protocols. The software stack explains important distinctions regarding various wireless Internet protocols like WAP and i-mode service. Software engineers who write wireless code sometimes have to program to one of these layers. To understand the idea of layered abstraction, consider the way software operates in computers. Programmers write software programs in languages like Java or C++. Compilers convert the language to lower-level libraries of command instructions and data. A computer executes only the instructions and data at the lowest layer. At this level, the program is nothing but an assembled collection of instructions and data locations. Computer instructions are part of the Central Processing Unit's (CPU) machine instruction set, shifting memory registers and creating temporary logical circuits upon which the microprocessor and other chips operate. At the bottom level, above the silicon circuits, is machine code. No one today writes at the machine-code level – pure sets of 1s and 0s that shift and change in memory – although the first programmers used to throw the binary switches to run programs when computers were invented.

This entire process of layered abstraction is a good way to view how a wireless network delivers content to devices. The wireless device can make high-level Application Programming Interface (API) requests that actually generate transportable bit streams that are sent over the air to be reassembled on the responding server miles away. Wireless servers operate on lower network protocols to examine user agent headers to establish device protocols and formats. They establish a session, manage application resources, and at a lower level handle the connection stream and process data and security packets. And the progression continues.

The Seven Layers of the OSI Model

Sometimes we look at modular parts of a system to understand how to build them. For example, wireless devices connect with servers and wireless server applications use databases. The interoperation of different systems can also be understood by investigating how the network connection operates. In 1974 the International Standards Organization (ISO) specified the seven-layer model called the Open Systems Interconnect (OSI) seven-layer model to define network communication. It defines communication software services and their protocols by layer. Each layer provides services that are needed by the next layer. An OSI layer has interfaces that support an upper layer, but the mechanics and operations in the responsible layer must be completely independent from any other. The responsibilities of each layer are defined by the OSI standard.

This model is also a useful way to compare wireless networks. Together the layers of the OSI model are commonly called a software stack in network architecture. For example, the server stack is often compared with a WAP stack or an i-mode stack. (The WAP and i-mode security stack are described in Part III, "Wireless Internet Architecture.")

The OSI seven-layer model (Figure 19) not only distinguishes layers but also shows how data moves from a source server to a destination wireless device. The OSI model layers are numbered from 1, the bottom (most primitive) layer, which is the physical transmission media (e.g., wire, fiber, or air), to 7, the highest layer of the model where application processes execute and transform information. Layer 6, the presentation level, manages the information that the application layer either operates on or references during communication. Layer 5, the session level, provides services needed by protocols in the presentation layer to organize, synchronize, keep resources ready, and manage initiation and closure of data exchange. These three layers, 5 through 7, are the application layers that lie on top of the transport layers.

The session layer lies on top of the transport level, layer 4, which provides and ensures reliable and effective data transfer. The Transmission Control Protocol (TCP) and User Datagram Protocol (UDP) are defined at the transport level. Gateways operate at this level to convert the transport protocols from one system to another. One key protocol of the Internet is Transmission Control Protocol/Internet Protocol (TCP/IP). The TCP divides information into pieces and puts destination addresses on each piece. The IP can take a piece, look at the address, and route it to an Internet destination.

Level 3, the network level, provides a means of connectionless-mode transmission among transport entities. It makes transport entities independent of routing and relay considerations associated with connectionless-mode transmission. Internet

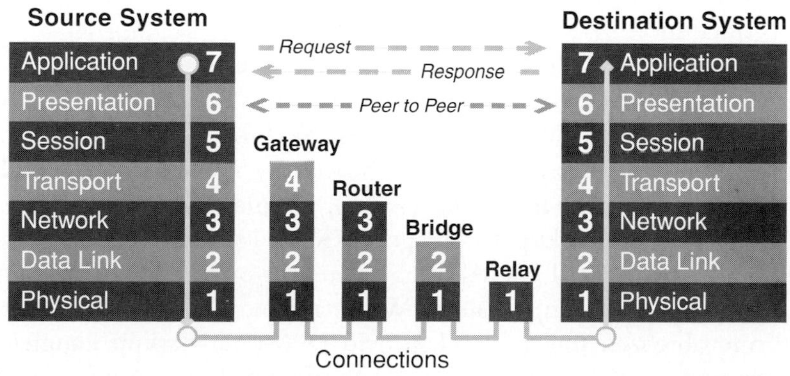

Figure 19 The OSI seven-layer model

Protocol for Ethernet allows network and internetwork addressing. Routers operate at the network level to direct traffic toward devices. Layer 2, the data link level, provides functions and procedures for connectionless-mode transmission among networks such as CSMA/CD for Ethernet. Hardware bridges, also called switches, connect networks at the data link level. Finally, the physical level, layer 1, provides mechanical, electrical, radio frequency means to activate and deactivate physical transmission connections between data links. Repeaters, signal amplifiers, or hubs "stretch the wire," or make the final physical connection to a terminal device.

For wireless Web development, we are interested in the top three layers of the OSI reference model, often called the application space. This leaves the lower four, the transport layers, to do most of the work between machines. Ethernet and Bluetooth protocols are focused on the lower transport layers.

As mentioned, Internet hardware is built to support the OSI model. Gateways translate one system to another at the transport level. The router is concerned with addressing translations of message streams. The bridge, also called a switch, segments traffic for its nearby systems. The relay, or hub, can add power to a signal. As a hub, it fans it out to terminals. There are now wireless versions for all these boxes. A key distinction between wired and wireless Internet is the introduction of handoff. Mobile wireless devices are allocated specific spectrum channels. The switch can reallocate the traffic channel segments that would be fixed addresses in wired networks.

Wireless OSI Layers

Commercial wireless networks also use the OSI model. The WAP Forum defines its very own WAP stack. NTT DoCoMo defines i-mode layers with little invention. A comparison of wireless OSI layers (Table 17) shows equivalencies of Internet, WAP, and i-mode systems. While i-mode follows the Internet OSI layering very closely, the WAP layers take liberties to reinvent protocols. Let us crawl through the layers once more.

As an OSI-defined network stack, the top of every wireless model is layer 7 where the popular microbrowsers operate. In WAP, this is the UP.Browser (Unwired Planet); for i-mode, it is the popular Access NetFront i-mode browser.

Next is the presentation level, layer 6 of the OSI model. The WAP Forum calls this the Wireless Application Environment (WAE). In practice, all developers know this to be the Wireless Markup Language (WML). Having a site generate WML content as well as traditional HTML Web content is one of the first assignments of many wireless engineering projects. WML is not all there is, however. The current UP microbrowser interprets Handheld Dynamic Markup Language (HDML), the forerunner to WML. At this level, i-mode developers use Compact HTML (cHTML) interpreted by the Access NetFront Browser.

Table 17 Comparing wireless OSI layers

OSI Layer	Internet	i-mode	WAP
[7] Application	IE browser	NetFront browser	UP browser
[6] Presentation	HTML	cHTML	WML
[5] Session	HTTP/HTTPS	HTTP/HTTPS	WSP
[4] Transport	TCP/UDP	TCP/UDP	WTP/WTLS/WDP
[3] Network	IP	IP	IP
[2] Data link	ATM	PDC-P	PPP
[1] Physical	SONET	RF (i.e.,WCDMA)	RF (i.e., CDMA)

Programmers work at layer 7 of the network stack to write wireless applications for a WAP microbrowser or SMS messaging. Programmers and Web coders work at layer 6 to write a markup page in WML in the WAP stack. Engineers work at layer 5 to manage the application. Architects have knowledge of all levels.

As we move down the WAP stack to level 5, the Wireless Session Protocol (WSP) and Wireless Transport Layer Security (WTLS) define the session layer. WAP has three specifications that define the transport layer: WTP/D, WTP/T, and WTP/C. The task of WTP/C is to provide a reliable connection-oriented service to the upper layer. WTP/T provides a reliable transaction-oriented service suitable for Web browsing. WTP/D provides a datagram service. WTP/D is replaced by UDP when a gateway converts between WAP and an IP network. i-mode uses SSL for security.

The Network, Data Link, and Physical layers perform the radio connection between a device and a transmission tower. Special pieces of hardware translate signals and protocols, but translation is not always necessary. If there are no intermediary gateways, routers, bridges, or repeaters to connect systems, then you can have a direct peer-to-peer connection, as is the case in Personal Radio and PAN. OSI peer-to-peer communication means two systems use layers 6 and 7 to communicate directly. The rich technical details are covered in the section "OSI Bottom-Layer Secure Architecture," in chapter 15.

The Network's Effect on Society

A physical network enables a social network. It is important to observe the effects of networks on people. The more you understand the compelling qualities that draw people to networks, the more subscribers you have. The more subscribers you have, the greater the compounded value of your network. Marshall McLuhan, the famous Canadian communications media expert, first observed the effect of networks. He said that the instantaneous feedback loop created between your business and your audience creates a new kind of commercial relationship and a new set of responsibilities for the operation of a business. He also pointed out that participation is global with electronic networks, that the new interconnectedness is similar to life in a small village, and that the quest for electronic identity is a necessary outcome of networks that increase in value when more people are connected.[1] (A deeper analysis of network effects is covered later in chapter 21, "Anticipating the Personal Value of Networks.")

The social distinction offered by using different network technologies is enormously significant. People who use packets connect easily and rapidly, and increase the tempo of relationships. The distinction continues in the way institutions let their constituencies use network technology. The ways that companies engage media broadcasters to relate to their consumers is completely changing society and the media business. The difference between traditional broadcast and cellular Internet is that broadcast towers speak; cellular towers listen.

WANs: Citywide Towers Serve Nationwide Networks

WAN

- 500–1900 MHz
- 9600 Kbps
- 2500 meters

Cellular WANs have evolved considerably since their commercial introduction in the 1980s. WAN towers form territorial grids that define their network coverage pattern. It is helpful to understand the various generations of WAN technology that use radio spectrum. When you hear the term *3G,* it refers to a third-generation WAN that optimally handles voice and high data rates through a digital packet-switched network. The wireless applications you can write for a WAN, such as microbrowser, Java phone, and messaging applications, are governed by the mobile qualities of this cellular network.

Towers Power the Mobile Spectrum

Take a moment as you walk about a city or travel along a highway to look up at the light poles, telephone poles, and building tops. You will see the new wireless technology – strange new antennas and the little boxes we call basestations and wireless access points, which are the transmitters of the wireless era often attached to their own tower. The cellular WAN tower (Figure 20), often called a Base Transceiver Station (BTS) by telecommunication engineers, seems to be everywhere. These towers are different from TV and broadcast systems that have come before. Like big TV towers, cellular towers communicate on a specific frequency of the electromagnetic spectrum. While the power of AM radio or TV VHF broadcast transmissions radiate hundreds of miles, the wireless cellular WAN towers use very low power to extend not much farther than a mile. There may be a hundred cell towers in the same footprint of a standard broadcast tower. One key difference between broadcast and cellular is the signaling. Cellular towers use two-way signaling. In

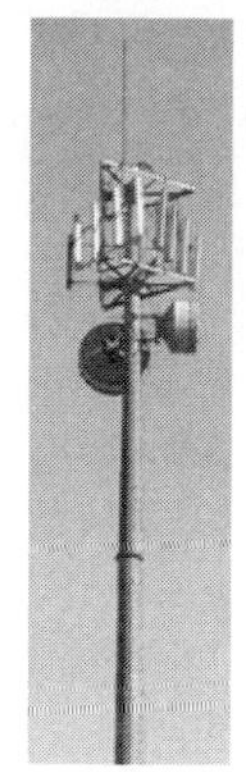

Figure 20 Cellular WAN tower

other words, cellular towers speak and listen. Broadcast towers can only speak.

Towers, especially broadcast and microwave transmitters, radiate a lot of electromagnetic power, so do not get close to them. In the wintry wars of the last century, radio transmitters could melt snow, and soldiers would get near the transmitters, microwaving themselves to get warm, only to find problems later with cancer and light radiation poisoning. Cellular towers use far less power, but you still want to keep a distance.

Compared to broadcast towers, cellular WAN towers are lower power. The energy is good enough for short-range transmission. They use interactive signaling that allows multiple callers to receive as well as send. Precellular citywide send-and-receive radios could at best handle up to one hundred radio devices. To reach the thousands of wireless devices, cellular tower grids (Figure 21) are efficiently planned to maximize coverage. To minimize cost, the cellular towers are clustered and wired back to Basestation Controllers (BSC), which convert the wireless call to a telephone call. The entire grid of towers and controllers links back to a telephone exchange called a Mobile Switching Center (MSC), more formally called a Mobile Telephone Switching Office (MTSO). The MSC switches calls, and tracks and bills users. The physical locations and the capacity of towers depend on the kind of radio carrier and the techniques for passing a caller from cell to cell. In older cellular systems, one-third of the capacity was intended for people talking, one-third for people entering the cell, and one-third for people leaving the cell, without trying to reuse frequencies. Second-generation networks have improved call handoff and frequency reuse, as we shall see soon.

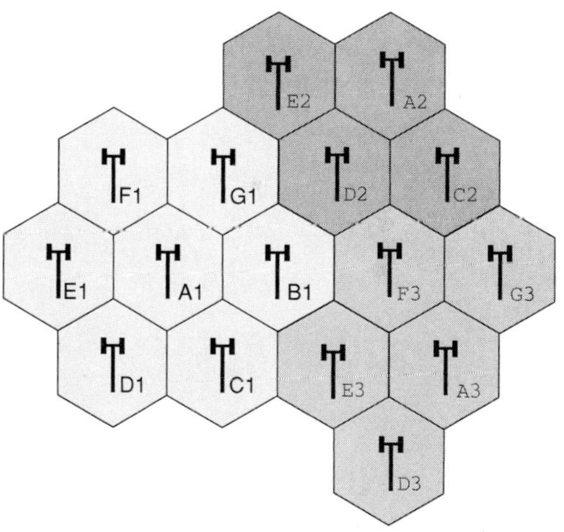

Figure 21 Cellular tower grids

Cell Phones and Handhelds as Radios

Cellular phones are essentially radios. The cellular Web phone operates over a moderately powerful licensed and regulated frequency to exchange voice and data with a cell tower. The typical range is from 500 to 1000 meters in a metropolitan area. Large, rural cells reach 2500 meters. Cell phones work as two-way radios. Like radios, all wireless devices work only where signals can penetrate. In a building, for example, they usually work best near windows. They often do not work deep inside a building, on lower floors, or in elevators or underground garages. The common wireless handheld uses a low-power modem either built in or attached. Handhelds with modular connections can slip in either a WAN or wireless LAN modem, usually for data exchange. Recently they can also support voice connections.

Mobile Cellular

When your cellular phone is in motion, your call has to be managed from one cellular tower to another. Generally, the faster a radio device moves, the lower its data rate. Whether you are sitting at a desk, walking about, or commuting on a train, the quality of service (QoS) and effective bandwidth vary. People in motion often experience dropped calls. QoS variation is graded by the speed of the traveler. 3G radio interfaces are standardized to achieve transmission rates of at least 144 kbps as a baseline for continuously mobile environments (e.g., highway traffic speed), 384 kbps for limited mobility (e.g., speed of a bicycle), and 2 Mbps for low mobility (e.g., walking or fixed service). In next-generation networks, enhanced roaming is the ability to move transparently among all these modes and various commercial and private networks while keeping an ongoing call, but its success depends on how cellular call management and billing is implemented.

How a Cellular Call Works

Cellular phones are radio telephones that send and receive signals even when you are not talking. When a cell phone is turned on, it operates in low-power mode as it listens for a control signal. The control signal is actually a different band from your voice-transmission channel. The microcomputer in the device directs the radio to tune to the strongest signal on one of many data-only channels known as paging channels. These channels are never heard; they just broadcast signaling codes to any listening cellular phone. To make a call in North America, the subscriber enters a phone number and presses the Send button. In less than a second, the cell phone automatically transmits the number being called along with both the Mobile Identification Number (MIN), a 24-bit representation of the telephone number of the caller, and the Electronic Serial Number (ESN), a 32-bit number that identifies each cell phone. This information is processed at the Mobile Switching Center (MSC). The MSC is connected to every cell tower in the system and manages all voice and data movement. It checks the caller for a valid MIN/ESN pair and logs the billing of the call, as well as lets the call continue by building a circuit between the caller and the receiver. It orders the caller's cell phone to change to a voice channel, connects that voice channel to the landline telephone network, and dials the number into the network. The rest of the call is conducted as though it were an ordinary landline phone call. When the cell phone subscriber hangs up, an electronic disconnect is transmitted and the MSC disconnects from the landline network. It marks the transmission channel as free for another call.

A call to a cellular subscriber is conducted in much the same way. Once again, a mobile cellular device is tuned to its signaling channel. The MSC transmits the cellular telephone number on all signaling channels. When the called unit responds with a signal, then the MSC sends a signal to the cellular unit to cause the phone to activate a bell, such as the ever-popular turkey warbler, or a modern ring tone. When the phone is answered, it is directed to a free talking channel and the conversation can begin.

As a subscriber moves about the city during a phone call, the MSC measures the quality of the signal. If there is deterioration because the caller moves from one cell to another, a handoff to a new channel occurs with no interruption to the call. *Handoff* is the process of automatically passing the call from one transmitter to the next. Figure 22 shows a car moving away from the weaker tower A1 into the range of the stronger tower B1, which requires cellular handoff. An analog handoff is directed by a data signal burst at a frequency that cannot be heard on the voice channel in a protocol called a "blank and burst." This effectively mutes the voice signal in the handset as it decodes the data. This happens in less than 1/8 second so neither party hears a gap in conversation, although an astute listener might notice a tiny gap in the conversation. It is not unusual for several handoffs to occur in a minute, as the subscriber vacillates between cell boundaries.

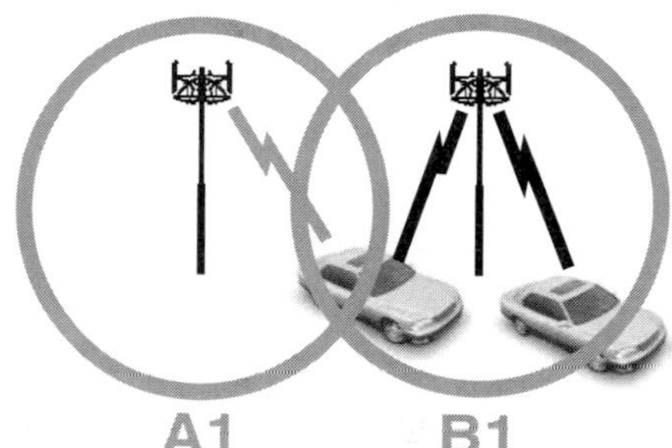

Figure 22 Cellular handoff

For all practical purposes, the cellular system keeps track of the location of every subscriber who is talking on any channel. When the system determines that a subscriber has moved out of one cell into another and executes a handoff, the MSC control center notifies the mobile telephone on a signal channel to change the frequency to the next channel that corresponds to the new cell. At the same time, the MSC transfers the conversation to that channel. The mobile device uses the new radio channel frequency of the next tower. Call uncovering is critical in handoff; it is the restoring of your previously used channel to the cell tower left behind.

So far, we have talked about circuit-switched cellular phones, but handoff quality is also critical to wireless data networks that are packet switched. Mobile applications that use LANs must hand off transmission of packets of data with the aid of wireless hubs and routers that control moving devices in the same manner as WAN towers.

Connecting to the Internet

After contact is made with a cellular tower or basestation, where does it go? The connection continues through either the backbone of the Internet or digital phone system network (see Figure 18). This runs through underground wires, between microwave dishes, and inside optical fiber. Here communication is managed by systems like ATM (Asynchronous Transfer Mode), SMDS (Switched Multimegabit Data Services), Synchronized Optical Network (SONET) Rings, or Frame Relay. ATM packet-switched networks transfer data at 622 Mbps to 13.22 Gbps. SONET manages optical fiber data between 51.8 Mbps to 13.22 Gbps. Newer SONET rates use OC768 at the high end at 40 Gps. OC stands for Optical Carrier. In the United States, we connect through SS7, IS-41. In Europe, GSM connects to Mobile Application Part (MAP). Wireless application developers rarely see this kind of "plumbing." The call eventually reaches the wires of the Internet and continues through gateways, proxy, Web, and application servers.

The Three Generations of WAN Air Interfaces

Cell phones and wireless devices transmit on frequency spectrum just like radio stations do. A WAN frequency band is licensed to a company. The company selects an *air interface*, a low-level protocol that connects its cellular tower to the devices over the licensed frequency. The evolution of air interfaces (Figure 23) began with

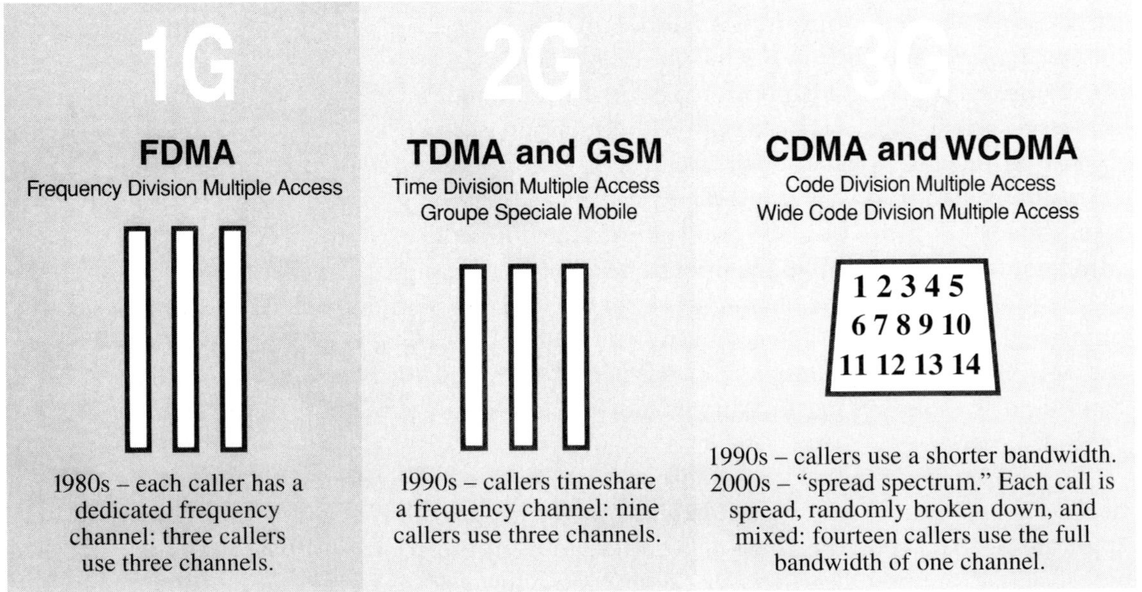

1G
2G
3G
FDMA
Frequency Division Multiple Access
1980s – each caller has a dedicated frequency channel: three callers use three channels.
TDMA and GSM
Time Division Multiple Access
Groupe Speciale Mobile
1990s – callers timeshare a frequency channel: nine callers use three channels.
CDMA and WCDMA
Code Division Multiple Access
Wide Code Division Multiple Access
1 2 3 4 5
6 7 8 9 10
11 12 13 14
1990s – callers use a shorter bandwidth.
2000s – "spread spectrum." Each call is spread, randomly broken down, and mixed: fourteen callers use the full bandwidth of one channel.

Figure 23 Evolution of air interfaces

popular air interfaces that originated in the 1980s. They would timeshare the spectrum to cell phones, the way mainframes used to timeshare terminals. There were many variations on this timeshare frequency managed air interface until a totally alien interface came along called CDMA. It spread a call randomly throughout the available spectrum. Overall, air interfaces have evolved to consume less power, increase signal quality, and accommodate more subscribers per band. High-level application software is largely independent of the bottom level of the OSI stack where air interfaces live. But to use a real Web cell phone, not a software emulator, you will run into these air interfaces. You may need to know which WAN air interface works with which devices when you buy a cellular plan and make decisions for clients. Air interfaces have different data rate capacities, security, performance, and geographic areas of operation.

Network Evolution: 1G, 2G, 3G

Global air carrier interfaces have evolved from a first-generation (1G) voice-only analog network to our current second-generation (2G) digital network. The emerging third-generation (3G), high-speed data and voice network has many grand features. Each generation can handle more subscribers, who generate more revenue. One generation does not wipe out the previous; rather a 2G tower operates next to a 1G tower, usually at different parts of the spectrum. Since it takes a while to install new hardware, cellular devices are made to *fall back* to use the more pervasive previous-generation network.

1G Networks

- Circuit-switched network
- Analog signals
- Voice only
- AMPS in United States

First-generation analog cellular networks were built strictly for voice calls in the early 1980s. All 1G networks are based on Frequency Division Multiple Access (FDMA), an air interface that guarantees a dedicated frequency and circuit to each caller. The Japanese began national service in 1979. The U.S. service, Advanced Mobile Phone Service (AMPS), operates at 800 MHz. Each country had its own 1G air interface protocol. Some examples are Total Access Communications System (TACS), Extended Total Access Communications System (ETACS), Nordic Mobile Telephone (NMT-450 and NMT-900), CNetz, MATS-E, and Radiocomm. Nearly half the world's cellular phone owners still use the basic 1G analog cellular technology in fallback mode.

Some cellular operators, anticipating the next-generation digital network, upgraded to protect their cellular network investment to provide some of "tomorrow's" services that their customers demanded such as callerID. Another reason for upgrading from AMPS was that handsets were easy to clone; a legitimate caller's identity codes could be fraudulently copied to make free calls. The upgrade from analog cellular is D-AMPS 136, or Digital AMPS – but that is all second generation.

2G Networks

- Circuit-switched network
- Digital signals
- Voice or data overlay
- 9 kbps or 19 kbps
- Dial-up service

The 2G air interfaces are digital cellular. They were all brought to market in the early 1990s. This second generation includes data services, fax, and email. Almost every wireless device sold in 2001 uses one of the second-generation air interfaces (i.e., TDMA, iDEN, CDMA, PDC, or GSM).

The first North American 2G digital air interface was Time Division Multiple Access (TDMA). It originally operated at 800 MHz. Where 1G FDMA provides an exclusive frequency, TDMA lets multiple callers time-share a frequency band. A TDMA call is sliced into a series of time slots. Each caller gets one time slot at regular intervals. It makes more efficient use of available bandwidth than FDMA. The current ITU standard is TDMA IS-136, which evolved from IS-56. (*IS* stands for Interim Standard.) AT&T Wireless is the largest TDMA operator. TDMA networks can support circuit-switched data at 9.6 kbps, though most carriers have opted for CDPD, a separate data overlay. The 1996 spectrum auctions for Personal Communications Services (PCS) let TDMA operate at 1900 MHz, but CDMA, a powerful new air interface almost synonymous with PCS, won many of the auctions.

Groupe Speciale Mobile (GSM, sometimes translated as Global System for Mobile Communications) is the European implementation of services that uses a TDMA air interface. GSM operates at 900 MHz and 1800 MHz throughout Europe. GSM unified the many incompatible national first-generation systems. The Economic Union decided on GSM in 1990; it is the European air interface that has been exported successfully to the rest of the world as the most popular 2G air interface. It actually precedes the U.S. TDMA introduction. GSM introduced frequency hopping. This lets phones switch the call frequency many times a second for security. GSM also introduced the simple two-way messaging standard, Short Message Service (SMS), that has proved very popular. AMPS had 3 slots per channel, TDMA has 6, and GSM has 8. GSM supports circuit-switched data services up to 14.4 kbps. The U.S. GSM 1900 MHz network is incompatible with the European 1800 MHz network. Only a multimode phone will operate between the two networks.

Code Division Multiple Access (CDMA) is patented by QUALCOMM Incorporated and was commercially introduced after TDMA. CDMA runs in the Americas on PCS 1900 MHz and some older 800 MHz frequencies. It is a radically different air interface, using military spread-spectrum technology. A CDMA tower and phone break a transmission into random pieces and space it out over the entire allocated 1.25 MHz bandwidth. The randomly spread frequencies are transmitted all at once. Over the air, it is secure. Unlike old AMPS phones where anyone can use a frequency scanner to listen in, CDMA is next to impossible to detect. If you turn on a frequency analyzer, you will see only a noise floor buildup

Table 18 CDMA qualities

Low power use	Higher data rate
Secure spread-spectrum signal	Improved handoff, subscriber capacity
Dynamic "bursty" signal ideal for data	Sound quality

as multiple callers appear. The separation pattern, or "code," is used to break up and reassemble the signal. Because CDMA spreads fragments over a larger frequency band, it is significantly more power efficient than TDMA technologies. This conserves battery life and is safer. CDMA escapes from rigid time slots, is dynamic, and can allow for variable sized bursts of data. Although GSM and TDMA are well evolved, CDMA has many advantages that they do not (see Table 18).

If you were to take CDMA quality claims into a court of law, arguments would break out over definitions of standards, statistics of use, and various performance criteria. In the end, all air interfaces evolve, each looking more like its competitor. But two qualities where CDMA appears to have the leading edge are data handling and power efficiency. CDMA does not use a timing advance that breaks calls into fixed sizes. It can dynamically scale the signal over the available bandwidth. This makes it ideal for data bursts, and efficient data carriers are key to the wireless Internet. Finally, it should be noted that GSM can actually run on CDMA, although the original tests were considered threatening to the GSM/TDMA stakeholders. The CDMA Development Group site is <http://www.cdg.org>.

Personal Digital Cellular (PDC) is the national air interface in Japan introduced in the early 1990s. PDC is a TDMA technology over which the popular i-mode service operates at 700 MHz to 800 MHz. It does not hand off between cell towers. PDC is not used anywhere else in the world, and the Japanese are moving directly to a third-generation W-CDMA. Personal HandyPhone Service (PHS) is their wireless data network. Arraycomm antennas connect PHS data modems in handhelds and notebook PCs. In December 1998 the PHS network was upgraded to 64 kbps.

Alternative WAN Air Interfaces: iDEN and TETRA, PMR and TETRA

In addition to AMPS, TDMA, CDMA, and GSM for cellular use, spectrum is licensed for mobile radio on ships, planes, citizens band radio, and so on. These are not as popular as cellular air interfaces, largely because they require dedicated equipment and offer lower-quality voice and service. The good news is that these have very low billing charges. The "FCC Spectrum Allocation" in appendix A charts all the alternative uses of spectrum.

A very important network is the Specialized Mobile Radio (SMR) spectrum, which is regulated as a mobile radio dispatch service for closed user groups such as taxis, civic personnel, and professional field forces. The SMR network goes by the name of Personalized Mobile Radio (PMR) in Europe. The European ETSI implemented its PMR as the Trans European Trunked Radio (TETRA) network.

The most popular version of an SMR in North America is the Enhanced Specialized Mobile Radio (ESMR) network, iDEN, the Integrated Dispatch Enhanced Network designed by Motorola. This TDMA digital air interface has excellent channel reuse and offers many cellular services previously reserved for PCS cellular systems.

Unique to TETRA and iDEN networks are the following services not found on conventional cellular phones:

- Direct phone-to-phone connection. Like walkie-talkies, these phones are always on to exchange phone messages immediately without dialing.
- Group calling. Using a common dispatch code, callers press a dedicated button to speak. Anyone who shares that code on the circuit can listen and respond.

Marketed as Direct Connect® for business users, iDEN subscribers simply tap the Connect button to transmit similarly to transmitting with a walkie-talkie. iDEN circuits form an immediate shared channel for phones using the circuit. Sharing voice or data circuits with callers has proved very successful in business applications and is a primary feature of the new QUALCOMM QCHAT™ service. The iDEN communications system combines into a single network the capabilities of SMR dispatch, WAN cellular calling, short messaging service, and both circuit-switched and packet-switched data. Nextel Online℠ was launched April 2000 to provide wireless Internet service for iDEN business customers. Packet data uses a single 25 KHz channel that offers data speeds of 19.2 kbps. iDEN originally operated from 450 MHZ to 900 MHz with current network operators delivering service over PCS 1900 MHz spectrum.

Nextel is the dominant carrier of the Motorola iDEN protocol. Other iDEN carriers include Southern LINC, which uses the iDEN network for traditional dispatch service in the Southeast United States; Pacific Wireless Technologies, which deploys an iDEN network in central California; and Tellus, the Canadian telecommunications carrier.

Nextel combines billing features, a near-nationwide footprint, handsets, and iDEN service. Nextel continues to compete successfully in the mobile telephone market. Nextel is the seventh largest mobile telephony provider in the United States and the second fastest growing operator. Nextel lists 8 million U.S. iDEN subscribers in September 2001. The iDEN network is capable of providing access to approximately 73.3 percent of the U.S. population. Nextel has the highest

Average Revenue Per Unit (ARPU) in the industry, reaching $74 per subscriber per month during 1999.[1]

TETRA is a highly secure network that requires the receiving phone to prove its identity. TETRA operates at 400 kHz, which gives towers a 100 km radius. It is mainly for police and emergency use. TETRA can transmit data at 36 kbps. TETRA cell phones can operate in ambient listening mode, meaning operators can listen even when the phone is switched off – useful in emergencies. One of the largest European TETRA suppliers is Dolphin, and one of the largest U.S. TETRA suppliers is Motorola. The North American TETRA subsidiary is NATF. A key site is <http://www.tetraforum.org>.

3G Networks
- Packet switched
- TDynamic allocation of voice or data
- Transparent roaming
- Quality sound and video
- Data transmission at 2 Mbps
- Indentification of caller location
- W-CDMA, CDMA 2000, TDD, UWC, FDD air interfaces

Third-generation networks are designed to support digital packet cellular. 3G is the world's first all wireless bit stream network intended for global coverage. 3G is the wireless Internet transmitting voice, data, photos, audio, and video – all bits running on a wireless packet-based cellular network. 3G has some remarkable features: it is always on; it has data rates beginning at 2 megabits per second; it and allows easy transparent roaming from network to network. It is largely based on CDMA technology and benefits from the many CDMA features. The higher data rate is better than the speed at which most consumers experience wired access to the Internet, making possible video and multimedia services.

Transparent roaming (also called transient roaming) is the ability to continue a data or voice call over multiple networks without dropping the call. A person could smoothly communicate while traveling between home and office, traveling the streets, visiting the countryside, and working at a business through interoperable handoffs among networks. 3G IMT-2000 allows transparent handoffs between terrestrial and satellite connections. This also includes passing a call from a WAN tower to a domestic wireless LAN basestation, a PAN home consumer cordless phone receiver, or any wireless company PABX. The specifications for 3G Digital Enhanced Cordless Telephone (DECT) allow for this. Even in a 3G world, if you cannot pay for each call, your connection is not made. Mobile billing using the wireless Internet can be complicated because payment agreements must match a wide variety of tower and handset technology. Theoretically, 3G connections are handed over to corporate wireless LANs, for which no billing meter ever runs.

With the evolution of the wireless Internet, the differences from the wired Internet narrow. Both give an always-on data and voice service. The era of circuit-switched calls is coming to an end.

3G Air Interfaces

There are five official air interfaces specified for 3G. The first and second generations of wireless were designed primarily to support voice using circuit-switched technology. The third generation of WAN is engineered to carry all digital media including voice using an Internet packet-switched network. In spite of the many exotic 3G features, the primary motivation for deploying it, as it is for every generation of WAN, is to add voice subscribers. To keep subscribers, all 2G air interfaces have an upgrade plan to get to 3G. The five 3G air interface standards proposed by the ITU in May 2000 were:

- W-CDMA
- CDMA MC
- TDMA Single Carrier
- TD-CDMA/TD-SCDMA (TDD)
- FDMA/TDMA (DECT)

It is up to the owners of the new 3G spectrum to determine which air interface they will support, but a CDMA-type carrier is the recommended standard. The new commercial 3G WAN transmitters being built in Japan and Europe use W-CDMA. The predominant worldwide air interface for 3G appears to be CDMA-based because of its spectral and power efficiencies. Many companies are licensing QUALCOMM CDMA patents to implement their own versions of CDMA. Global implementations for CDMA-based technologies may turn out to be sadly incompatible. Rather than wait to see who wins the air interface standards battle, advanced radio technology like Software Defined Radio (SDR) and adaptive antennas may provide worldwide compatibility. The five interfaces and the migration path from 2G is detailed in chapter 16 in the section "The Five 3G Air Interfaces."

WAN Channel Capacity for Data

It is important to know the theoretical data capacity of WAN networks. Each air interface fits within a regulated amount of bandwidth. Bandwidth channel capacity for data (Table 19) shows that the data rate in bits per second is a somewhat smaller number than the original Hz allocated. The width of any spectrum band can be expected to deliver that many bits. This simple data rate rule of thumb is based on some gory details.

Table 19 Bandwidth channel capacity for data

Air Interface	Regulated Bandwidth	Simple Data Rate
1G AMPS	30 kHz	20 kbps
2G PDC	25 kHz	20 kbps
2G TDMA/GSM	30 kHz	20 kbps
3G CDMA/EV	1.25 MHz	2 Mbps
3G W-CDMA	5 MHz	4 Mbps

Recall from our quick romp through telecommunications physics that the information equation 1 Hz = 1 bps sets the maximum we can get from spectrum. This is the maximum limit for simple modulation used in WAN systems. After taking a bandwidth and subtracting the guard band and the error-correction overhead, you get the effective capacity. Two factors generally cancel each other out – general channel sharing (divide by 8) and hardware compression (multiply by 8). Using a full channel for data means that no one else can use the channel, so the truly effective rates are often about one-third of the simple data rate. Other compression techniques can increase the data rate.

WAN Messaging, Paging, and SMS

Messaging is a primary activity of networks. It is the dominant feature of pagers, and a popular feature of Web phones and, to a lesser extent, handhelds. Pagers operate over their own networks and are popular in North America. Recent pagers use the two-way ReFLEX paging network and the Motient and Mobitex data networks. Paging guarantees an alert within 30 seconds anywhere on the paging network, some of which are global.

In Europe, the Short Message Service (SMS) is a standard part of GSM and provides pager-like messages. It is low cost and widely available. In Europe, GSM handsets that receive only SMS messages are called Terminate Only handsets. Handsets that handle two-way SMS messaging are called Terminate and Originate handsets. SMS is store and forward and runs as lower priority to voice traffic. SMS activity can be retarded in a highly congested area. Most European countries have speedy implementations that deliver messages in seconds. In other countries, delivery may take a full hour; going overseas, it may take a day. A GSM SMS message operates over the control channel rather than the main transmission channel. It sends 300 bits per second over a low-priority control channel interlay. Although an SMS protocol was specified in the U.S. PCS network, no carrier implemented it initially. After its popularity in Europe, it is now implemented in most U.S. WAN networks. In the United States, Nextel, AT&T Wireless, and GSM providers like VoiceStream Wireless offer two-way SMS. SMS networks have different limits on message size, and GSM's is 160 characters. The full list of character lengths appears in the section "Messaging Networks and Protocols" in chapter 17.

SMS is good for fun and games, but if you need guaranteed messages, you should consider paging networks. Paging networks such as ReFLEX have evolved to deliver the widest coverage and best emergency notification service. To make reliable professional network messaging applications over a WAN, the telcos are promoting a new standard called PUSH to ensure SMS performance with pager-quality alerts, message receipts, and richer responses. SMS is not only for messaging. Used in continuous transmission, SMS can serve as an application for developers. Examples are described in the section "Developing Pager Messaging, SMS Games, and Interactive Applications" in chapter 11.

WAN Data Networks

The generations of cellular technology have made spectrum more efficient for data. The technology that leads to digital spectrum efficiency has also increased the number of subscribers per channel. Until 3G is ready with its efficient voice and data qualities, 2G data overlays, alternative data-only networks, and 2.5-generation networks provide the best ways to handle data.

1G Data Network Overlays

First-generation networks were for voice only, but data can be sent over 1G networks with an old-fashioned data modem. A PC laptop or handheld becomes a wireless terminal with a data modem. These are inserted as PC cards or attached to the device with a serial cable. The cellular modem dangles off the PC, and is colorfully referred to as *soap on a rope*. This is cumbersome and not very mobile, but it does allow digital IP connections. Many wireless networks rely on an old AMPS data modem or a CDPD overlay that runs over AMPS. These use data modems such as a PCMCIA card and use interfaces such as ETC, ETC-2, MNPDEC, and TX-CEL. In olden times you had to dial into a modem pool – ⋆3282 (which spells out ⋆DATA). This causes the carrier to switch from analog to digital modem service. Generally, today's wireless data call is made automatically when the built-in data modem finds a channel in the air to connect with. Although it is convenient to have a wireless built-in modem, the availability of a modular PC card slot and soap-on-a-rope approaches lets you upgrade to faster modems and new networks as they become available.

U.S. 2G Data Networks

In upgraded first- and second-generation networks, data is typically sent as an analog overlay. In the United States, Cellular Digital Packet Data (CDPD) is overlaid on an AMPS voice circuit. Overlay use is like a gopher popping up its head to find an unused channel. When no one is talking, it grabs the channel and nibbles on the data overlay. When a voice call appears in the air, it ducks its head and waits for the next free space. The data overlay can never interrupt a voice call.

Today's common 2G narrowband, circuit-switched data pipes run at 9.2 kbps and have an upper limit of 14.4 kbps. A data-only protocol like CDPD runs a 19.2 kbps. There are three major data networks in the United States: CDPD, Mobitex, and Motient. None of these air interfaces are compatible with any of the others. From a software programmer's point of view, wireless data services are largely similar and usually need some low-level support to handle the data stream. Vertical market applications are commonly implemented on these data networks. The applications include fleet management and dispatch for field service organizations, remote telemetry, alarm monitoring and electronic funds transfer, and email and limited Web access for mobile professionals. Most carriers such as Mobitex offer flat-rate, "all-you-can-eat" pricing, but some still charge in message units for 1K of data. There are still some older plans that have prohibitive hourly unit prices, making them useless for consumer applications. A comparison of the data network and the devices they support is detailed in the section "North American 2G Data Networks: CDPD, Mobitex, and Motient" in chapter 17.

2.5G Data

An interim step to fully packetized 3G networks is the 2.5G wireless WAN additions. They are designed to operate in 2G network spectrum by using separate air interfaces to deliver higher data rates largely on European GSM networks. Although they exist alongside voice circuit systems, 2.5G networks still require a dedicated chip set for both network towers and handsets. They compete with the long-standing, low-band, data-only networks such as RAM Mobile Data (Mobitex), Motient, and even CDPD. 2.5G enables mobile services such as mobile banking, mobile shopping, and direct entertainment, and gives overall better Internet access.

Emerging wireless data rates (Figure 24) include a number of European GSM data upgrades. Each standard shows an average data rate on the bottom and a peak data rate at the top of its range mark. Peak rates are achieved only when there are no other callers using the tower. We see the future of wireless data standards as entirely packet switched.

High Speed Circuit-Switched Data (HSCSD) is the final circuit-switched data path for the GSM network. It works by adding together neighboring 14.4 kbps GSM time slots. The maximum combination is four slots, yielding a data rate of 56 kbps. Subscribers have to pay for each extra slot, so use is not widespread, especially considering that GSM networks are jammed with voice calls. An HSCSD circuit is theoretically well suited to videoconferencing and multimedia. For "bursty" data applications, the packet-switched air interfaces make far better use of the spectrum.

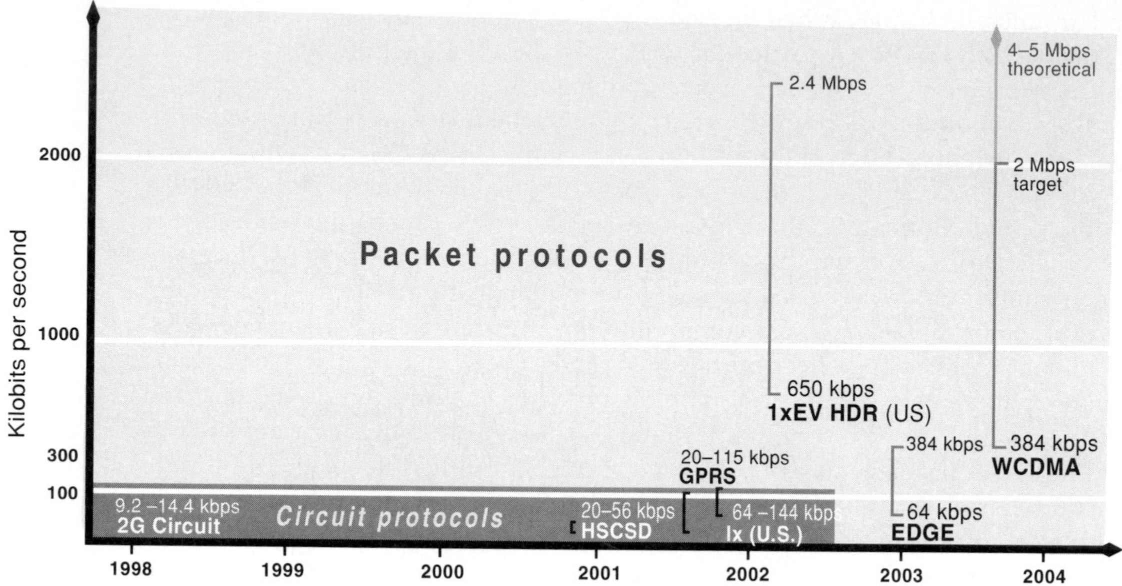

Figure 24 Emerging wireless average and peak data rates

General Packet Radio Service (GPRS) is the first implementation of Internet protocol packet switching to be used with GSM. It is also an upgrade for the IS-136 TDMA standard, popular in North and South America. GPRS was standardized by the European Telecommunications Standards Institute. The protocol starts at 19.2 kbps and has stepping rates that can potentially reach 115 kbps. GPRS combines neighboring 19.2 kbps time slots, typically one uplink and two or more downlink slots per GPRS tower. To use all the GPRS slots takes a lot of power, not to mention that it denies access by other subscribers. The effective GPRS systems of 2001, which deliver an average 20 kbps to 40 kbps of data, are T-Mobil in Germany and BT Cellnet in the United Kingdom. Subscribers observe that it makes WAP a significantly better experience. (More information about these devices is in the "GPRS Handsets" section in chapter 19.)

Enhanced Data for Global Enhancement (EDGE, originally Enhanced Data for GSM Enhancement) is a packet-switched technology that can operate by itself or work as a GPRS upgrade. This TDMA technology peaks at 384 kbps, although loaded tests show a subscriber will get about 64 to 100 kbps. EDGE can combine three voice channels to achieve its data rate. EDGE is a favorite standard of AT&T Wireless and is expected to be the data carrier for i-mode in the United States. The chief proponent of EDGE is the TDMA group the Universal Wireless Communications Consortium (UWCC). The UWCC Web site is <http://www.uwcc.org>.

With 2.5G data standards, carriers have to combine voice channels thereby reducing subscriber capacity. Operators are concerned about the expense and the potential loss of subscriber service in congested areas. On the other hand, these technologies are useful for 2G operators who do not hold 3G licenses.

3G Data

EDGE and GPRS were designed to operate with 2G networks. 3G UMTS (Europe) and 3G IMT-2000 (Asia) can use packet-switching technology over a W-CDMA carrier. But the data specifications for 3G are not clear. Although the marketing talk for 3G targets 2 Mbps, the technical specifications for the Japanese and European end game for data appear to stop at 384 kbps. As some European and U.S. operators are planning to install 2.5G technologies, some Korean and Japanese telcos are planning to go straight to 3G. Meanwhile some U.S. networks are planning a far more ambitious data standard called HDR that can reach peak data rates of 2.4 Mbps. Other air interfaces that use wireless spectrum efficiently for data and have reasonable data rates, which peak at 40 Mbps, come from companies such as ArrayComm and SWIFTcomm. Each builds its own high-capability, wireless data networks and data modems. It appears they will arrive much earlier than 3G, and in some cases may transcend the conservative 2 Mbps target data rate of 3G. Many of these newest networks only carry voice through packet and IP protocols. The emerging potentials of these networks are contrasted in the section "New Spectrum and Capacity Create New Wireless Applications" near the end of chapter 5.

The WAN air interfaces have evolved to use voice and data more efficiently. In lower power networks, data, rather than voice, has been the dominant interest. Although HDR appears well positioned to take the world stage, there is one significant alternative data network with no monthly billing charges, and an order of magnitude faster data rate – wireless LAN.

LANs: Blockwide Basestations Reach Business and Home

LAN

- 2.4 GHz
- 11 Mbps
- 100 meters

As we move down the power range from a public WAN, the next wireless footprint is the LAN, which has a range of 100 meters. When developers draw an application diagram, they might use the term *WLAN,* or wireless local area network. Because wired and wireless LAN protocols are interchangeable from an application viewpoint, it is simpler to say LAN. Companies connect computers and peripherals over a LAN private network. It almost exclusively uses the Ethernet protocol. Where WAN devices talk to a cellular tower, LAN devices talk to a basestation. For LAN applications, see chapter 12, "Developing LAN Interactive Applications."

Wireless Applications for Business

The wireless LAN for business provides the network for leading wireless business applications in the United States. Wireless business applications are important to the history of wireless applications. Recall from the diagram of the wireless Internet technology adoption curve (Figure 9) that technology moves from inventive uses to business purposes. Technology that has been proved to have business value moves more readily into mass consumer markets. Wireless LAN applications improve the accuracy of field interviews, accelerate report preparation, simplify review and approval process, and ensure more thorough incident and accident reports. Wireless LANs are used worldwide in markets that include retailing, transportation, distribution, manufacturing, parcel and postal delivery, government, health care, and education. Vertical wireless applications feature real-time data collection and access to mission-critical information.

Symbol is a leading maker of vertical market application hardware, namely, industrial handhelds with wireless functions. Symbol has made more than 10 million barcode scanners and mobile computers. Most industrial handhelds have built-in wireless LAN modems. On the lightweight side of LAN hardware is the consumer class of handhelds based on the Palm and WinCE operating systems. They are useful and are beginning to be designed well enough to perform the tasks of the industrial-grade devices. The LAN network is packet based and fully supports handhelds that can work standalone and offline. Handhelds routinely make intermittent wireless LAN connections to exchange data. The wireless LAN is sometimes isolated on company networks for security reasons. Security is generally implemented with a transmitter key for each wireless device and can also use over-the-air encryption software.

The handheld and LAN combination continues to prove valuable to enterprises. Many companies now uses antenna laptops with wireless Ethernet to connect the corporate network to basestations. If you need a data truck, use a LAN with a handheld. If you can get by with a data cart and can afford subscription charges, then a WAN application will do. A useful comparative study of WAN and LAN airline applications appears in the section "Comparing Wireless Devices" in chapter 9.

Wireless Ethernet

Greater wireless data bandwidth is the primary advantage of LAN. While WAN cell phone data trickles in at kilobits per second, LAN data is measured in megabits per second. The LAN is packet switched with coverage about a block wide. Wireless Ethernet operates on the spectrum at 2.4 GHz, which is an unlicensed Instrument, Scientific, Medical (ISM) band. Bluetooth devices and cordless phones operate at this frequency and can cause interference.

The most popular industrial worldwide LAN standard is wireless Ethernet, IEEE 802.11b. The well-understood Ethernet protocol makes software easier for Internet programmers. Most implementations use the Direct Sequence Spread Spectrum (DSSS), although the Frequency-Hopping Spread Spectrum (FHSS) is possible. IEEE 802.11 comes in a few data rates. The original 802.11 ran at 1 Mbps, stepped up to 2 Mbps, and was rife with vendor incompatibility.

Figure 25 Airport 802.11b basestation (*Source:* Photo courtesy of Apple Computer, Inc. Photographer, Mark Laita.)

The standard today for wireless Ethernet is 802.11b, said as "eight oh two dot eleven b," and is extremely compatible among vendors. A typical basestation operates at 11 Mbps and shares 255 devices. However, the individual handheld generally does not get more than 3 Mbps. The Airport 802.11b basestation (Figure 25) is commonly used to talk to PC and proprietary devices and has been one of the lowest priced 802.11b basestations in the market.

Wireless Fidelity (Wi-Fi, pronounced WHIFF-ee) is the commercially certified name for 802.11b. Wi-Fi products are tested and certified by the Wireless Ethernet Capability Alliance (WECA), which has done an excellent job of certifying interoperable 802.11b products. WECA's standard is rock solid and competing devices like modem cards are reliably interchangeable.

WECA is helping sponsor IEEE 802.11g, a Higher Data Rate wireless Ethernet that is expected to boost speed to 22 Mbps. This higher-speed version continues to operate at 2.4 GHz. The WECA Web site is <http://www.wirelessethernet.org/>.

Home Networks: HAN and SOHO

Two marketing terms, Home Area Network (HAN) and Small Office Home Office (SOHO), designate any wireless LAN that has been priced and designed to work with standard office equipment. These wireless networks connect home computers, printers, telephones, and other consumer devices. Home Radio Frequency, or HomeRF, is the popular wireless network forum led by computer and consumer electronic companies. Their key standard, which specifies both voice and data, is the Shared Wireless Access Protocol (SWAP). HomeRF also operates at 2.4 GHz and transmits data at 1 to 2 Mbps.

In September 2000, much against the wishes of the IEEE, the FCC cleared channels for the operation of HomeRF at 10 Mbps. HomeRF has a 50-meter range and can connect up to 10 devices including computers, telephone, home theater, and DVD. The SWAP standard combines LAN data technology and a TDMA extension that lets existing cordless telephones carry voice traffic using Digital Enhanced Cordless Telephone (DECT) protocols. Intel's AnyPoint™ wireless hub uses SWAP and requires each device participating in the network to have a wireless access point and a wireless card. The HomeRF Web site is <http://www.homerf.org>.

Building Your Own LAN Towers

You can offer wireless LAN to a business to eliminate per-minute charges, transmit far more data, make a secure network, and add many network services beyond the scope of WAN carrier abilities. Of course, you have to buy your own basestations. When "building your towers," that is, planning basestation locations, make sure equipment is positioned well, can handle capacity, and is tested for handoff. Basestations are typically placed at 100-meter intervals and located in room corners. Business is not alone in appreciating the advantages of a wireless local area network. Believe it or not, communities across the planet are putting their own 802.11b towers on rooftops to avoid steep telco charges and get superior Internet data service throughout their neighborhoods. They are not waiting for the telcos to drop their rates and build up to the data capacity perhaps five years from now.

The low-cost wireless basestations have sparked a wireless "air rush" as startup companies and telecommunication vendors lay claim to airports, hotels, and other public localities. Wireless mobile users with laptops and handhelds using wireless 802.11b cards connect to the global Internet. Although many companies have done this for their campuses, it is somewhat surprising to see groups in Phoenix, Arizona, San Francisco (SFLAN), London (the consume.net group), and even in Helsinki, marshal local businesses and citizens to mount arrays of basestations to provide free mobile Internet service. Building a grass-roots broadband network is reminiscent of the origins of the Internet.

Local Area Network Interference

Radio signals always run into naturally interfering obstacles; for example, street lamps emit radiation, and a damp tree can totally block a line-of-sight signal. The other radio interference is the greatest problem. Interestingly enough, IEEE 802.11b, HomeRF, and the new Bluetooth PAN networks all use the same unlicensed wavelength, as Table 20 shows.

This unlicensed band is where many other consumer electronics devices operate, thus creating many "mid-air collisions." The most notorious is the cordless phone, although microwave ovens have been known to generate radio frequencies that interrupt networks. To avoid interference, some network protocols hop from frequency to frequency. They *hop*, or switch, to one of the unoccupied 78 channels in the 2.4 GHz spectrum. They hop to avoid collisions or, more precisely, to recover from collisions. The air space of a busy office can get crowded and service can be denied.

Table 20 Wireless 2.4 GHz protocols

	IEEE 802.11b	HomeRF	Bluetooth
Speed	11 Mbps	1, 2, 10 Mbps	30 to 700 kbps
Use	Office or campus LAN	Home office, house, and yard	Personal Area Network
Range	100 meters	50 meters	10 meters
Frequency sharing	Direct sequence spread spectrum	Wideband frequency hopping	Narrowband frequency hopping
Backers	Cisco, Lucent, 3Com, Apple, Intel, WECA Consortium	Apple, Compaq, Dell, Motorola, Proxim, HomeRF Working Group	Ericsson, Motorola, Intel, Nokia, Bluetooth Special Interest Group
URL	www.wirelessethernet.com	www.homerf.org	www.bluetooth.com

IP Cellular Phones

The wireless LAN can also carry voice. One of the strengths of HomeRF is that voice, consumer digital video, and audio are specified in the HomeRF LAN. One proprietary implementation of voice stream overlays using wireless 802.11 is the Spectrum24 Network from Symbol Technologies Incorporated.

Cisco began providing mobile, wireless, Ethernet, cellular-style VoIP phones in 2001 to go with its IP Phone network. Cisco, Com, Alcatel, and Broadcom are offering wireless cellular phone service via VoIP to wireless Ethernet access points. Companies like Allied Riser expect to carry the service into vertical markets. AT&T and WorldCom are also producing an IP phone for mobile use. Most mobile IP phones use Session Initiation Protocol (SIP).

Next-Generation Wireless LAN

In addition to the ability to carry voice, another desired feature for a LAN is the implementation of location-aware protocols. Every new 3G WAN network is planning to use location-positioning equipment and assorted network protocols and algorithms to provide exact location to mobile users. The wireless LAN version may be easier since the LAN "cell" has a more limited radius. The task is to determine easily the GPS location of all wireless basestations.

Although 2.4 GHz standards conflicts are causing national headaches today, you can expect global migraines tomorrow. The FCC provided additional spectrum for unlicensed wideband operations in 1997. Both Europe and the United States have set aside a 200 MHz portion of the 5-GHz band, from 5.15 GHz to 5.35 GHz. The FCC calls this Unlicensed National Information Infrastructure (U-NII).

The fastest LAN yet is coming. In the LAN boxing rink, in one corner, weighing in at 54 Mbps, from the USA is 802.11a. In the other corner, weighing in at 155 Mbps, from Europe is HiperLAN2. HiperLAN2 appears to be designed to support more of the time-critical services of packetized voice and video than 802.11a supports. HiperLAN2 has stepping rates from 6 Mbps to 155 Mbps. On the other hand, it appears that 802.11a will probably reach a broader market first. The solution may take time to ensure that the QoS (Quality of Service) and required security features can deliver data, voice, and video well. Four U.S. companies – Flarion, Atheros, Radiata, and Texas Instruments – and SuperGold in Dublin, Ireland, are implementing 802.11a technology. Both networks will eventually exceed 100 Mbps, depending on the carrier modulation techniques such as OFDM, GMSK, MBCK, QAM, and QPSK (covered in chapter 4 in the section "From Analog to Digital Networks.")

HiperLAN2 technology tests began in Tokyo by DoCoMo in April 2001 under the product name *Biportable,* which stands for Broadband IP Platform with Optical and Radio Technical Ability. Biportable PDAs connect at 36 Mbps high-speed Advanced Wireless Access transceivers. Operating at the 5 GHz band, each access point can serve 122 users concurrently while connecting to a 1 Gbps optical network. This system conforms to the Broadband Radio Access Networks (BRAN) reference standard. BRAN is an ETSI standard for configuring towers and terminals for broadband wireless access. BRAN specifies three kinds of connection: a connection called HiperAccess from 5-kilometer tower to building roof basestation, a connection called HiperLink from basestation to access point, and a connection called HiperLAN from the last meter from access point to devices. HiperLink is a point-to-point connection that may use new 17 GHz spectrum. The HiperLAN2 Global Forum (H2GF) Web site is <http://www.hiperlan2.com/>. Realize that at these speeds with sufficient access points, there is no good reason to remain wired to the Internet, even with a desktop or workstation.

PANs: Roomwide Transmitters Coordinate Nearby Devices

PAN
- 2.4 GHz
- 700 Kbps
- 10 meters

At the bottom of the wireless power range is the Personal Area Network (PAN), where transmitters reach about 10 meters, the width of an average room. A PAN network operates with nearby devices to exchange data and voice, sometimes automatically. Unlike the WANs or LANs, PANs require no tower to operate. However, to connect back to the Internet, they can use differing network architectures. They most often use an access point like the TDK Bluetooth basestation (Figure 26). A synchronizing interface that connects a handheld with a PC creates a PAN, although these connections are mostly made via cable today. Wireless synchronization of voice and data is a requirement of modern PAN systems. A PAN

Figure 26 Bluetooth Basestation

allows nearby machines to communicate data and coordinate services over their wireless network. This set of complying machines is often called a *federation of devices*. Sets of devices uniquely define their own applications. PAN applications are covered in chapter 13, "Developing PAN Device Applications."

PAN Roomware Applications

Considering powerful mobile WANs and LANs, it might seem absurd to design a network with a short range. But consider the distance between a keyboard and a computer, or the distance between the computer and the printer. PAN systems are designed to link local devices without using a wire or having to plug in anything. PAN devices are driven largely by miniaturized form factors. Using many kinds of sensors, PAN systems will do something new – they will feed the wireless Internet, and add a new element to application architecture. The Swedish company Anoto is working with 3M on a radio pen that transmits, as it is being written, text or graphics to a nearby transmitter. The company Digital Ink is producing an electronic pen that transmits its writing with infrared. Other interesting PAN devices include sensors, scanners, monitors, magnetic card readers, wireless cameras, and wireless GPS antennas, which all conspire to increase the operating purposes of wireless devices.

Early PAN systems replace cables, allowing transparent synchronization of data and exchange of files. A PAN Web phone transparently passes voice or email between handhelds and laptops. As PAN devices go through a discovery protocol, they can form a federation of devices capable of performing their application. Discovery involves exchanging device identities and service capabilities between devices. It also means waking up any relevant information that may be available. Some simple examples of device federations are a handheld with a wireless scanner and a wireless printer to manage inventory.

The personal domain that a PAN creates, builds on peer-to-peer transfer of information. Early examples of PAN direct applications include scanning inventory, financial authorization, credit card terminal transactions, in-store bills payment, direct location and time tagging, personal medical monitoring such as a cardiac device sending medical data, automatic meter reading, toll taking, and asset location. On the horizon are location-based and remote control applications that will allow consumers to pass PAN transceivers and collect business information, electronic coupons, menus, or other "wireless data souvenirs." PAN users either transact immediately on the information or pass the data along to their personal servers for later use. Remote control PAN applications let a person use a wireless device to read room and device configurations, and present them as a map of options that can be universally controlled.

To achieve this level of wireless device control, a number of technologies have come into play including Bluetooth wireless technology for short-range radio voice and data connections, infrared technology for short-range infrared connections, Jini for software protocols of nearby devices, and RFID for automatic identification. Some devices have PAN technology built in; others require that you plug in a PAN device.

Bluetooth Network

The Bluetooth™[2] network is a low-power, personal, wireless voice and data network that has a range of 10 meters. A Bluetooth network, called a *piconet,* can connect eight Bluetooth devices. It features automatic synchronization and pass-through of a data or voice stream for all devices. Any Bluetooth connection can support both data (asynchronous) and voice (synchronous) communications with a total bandwidth of 723 kbps, which includes a 57.6 kbps back channel. Table 21 shows how Bluetooth channels can be configured to operate a 432 kbps symmetric data channel, three simultaneous two-way voice channels, or a streaming 723 kbps data stream.

Using a radio data protocol operating at the 2.4 GHz ISM frequency band, the Bluetooth network features a fast-hopping, spread-spectrum radio that operates with 1 milliwatt of power. It broadcasts a 10-meter, 0 dBm-range (dBm is decibels in milliwatts). The first version of the Bluetooth network is only point-to-point, although it specifies a point-to-multipoint broadcasting protocol. A Bluetooth piconet requires one master device and can serve up to seven slave devices. Up to ten piconets can coexist in one coverage range to form a Bluetooth *scatternet* that involves 80 devices. Bluetooth signals, like other LAN signals, can communicate through solid objects (unlike infrared signals that require an unobstructed line of sight to make a connection). Bluetooth version 2 describes a 100-meter, 20-dBm radius that puts it into the category of a LAN.

Table 21 Bluetooth data and voice configuration

Configuration	Data Rate
3 voice channels	64 kbps
Symmetric data	434 kbps
Asymmetric data	723.2 kbps & 57.6 kbps return stream

The Bluetooth name and trademarks are owned by Bluetooth SIG, Inc., U.S.A., although they were originally coined by Ericsson, the Swedish telephone equipment maker. The name comes from King Harald Bluetooth (Blåtand), who lived from A.D. 911 to A.D. 985 and united Denmark and Norway. He died in a battle against his son, Svend Forkbeard. The Bluetooth Special Interest Group (SIG) is a consortium that includes the founding members IBM, Ericsson, Nokia, Intel, and Toshiba; it has grown to include 2000 other companies including almost every phone and computer manufacturer and computer notables like Palm, Inc., and Microsoft Corporation. In December 2000, Ericsson transferred legal and manufacturing rights to Intel to increase capacity of production. Ericsson announced a WAP Bluetooth server at the end of 2000. This is an essential piece of technology for producing end-to-end solutions for Bluetooth application architecture. The Bluetooth Consortium SIG Web site is <http://www.bluetooth.com/>.

Bluetooth wireless technology is positioned to displace infrared data and is a good mechanism to synchronize devices, transfer files, and generally replace data cables. Its primary focus is to be the wireless connections among mobile devices, fixed computers, and cellular phones. The low-power radio module can be built into some mobile computers, cellular phones, printers, fax machines, and network connection points. Ericsson demonstrated an early T36 WAP Bluetooth phone in 2000, and other Bluetooth hardware manufacturers are producing basestations, plug-in PC cards, Universal Serial Bus cards, and slip-on wireless modules.

Bluetooth Profiles

Bluetooth devices fit in profiles established by the Bluetooth SIG. *Bluetooth profiles* are general characteristics for families of Bluetooth devices. Some, but not all, profiles can communicate data and voice. The Generic Access Profile contains all the Bluetooth protocols and possible devices. It includes some standard profiles:

- *Serial Port Profile* defines how devices can establish a serial connection over the radio link. This is mostly to support traditional serial data transfer.
- *Service Discovery Application Profile* establishes the "master" and "slave" relations and the pairing and bonding protocols of Bluetooth devices.
- *Generic Object Exchange Profile* is for the exchange of data based on the OBEX standard defined by IrDA.

Many specific Bluetooth devices also have profiles including those for telephony (cellular voice), intercom ("walkie-talkie"), and LAN access (data). Some of these are "ultimate," idealized profiles. As engineers say, No hardware is as powerful as that which has not yet been made, no software is as powerful as that which has not been written.

Bluetooth Interference and Security

Like 802.11 wireless Ethernet, the HomeRF and Bluetooth networks operate over the unlicensed 2.4 GHz radio band. Because the Bluetooth network uses very low transmission power, about 1 milliwatt, the more powerful signals from other devices may overwhelm its signal. Bluetooth protocols are supposed to hop around local interference sources, using a fast frequency-hopping scheme (about 1,600 hops per second spread over 79 channels). But that frequency-sharing scheme may still bump into nearby radios that are using the 802.11b direct-sequence scheme. The potential for interference remains an open problem.

The largest interference and security challenge to Bluetooth transmission comes from other Bluetooth devices. At the Monaco and the PCIA Bluetooth conferences in 2000, a popular device at the exhibition was always a Bluetooth "sniffer." These can look inside any nearby Bluetooth device. One of the most ironic things to see were exhibitors putting up shielding in efforts to make sure their devices did not talk to one another. At the 2001 CeBIT trade show in Hannover, Germany, 100 Bluetooth transmitters utterly failed to connect due to different versions of the Bluetooth standard and a massive amount of 2.4 GHz band interference. This unlicensed promiscuous network is certainly facing serious challenges. In a further strike against Bluetooth SIG, in the spring of 2001 Microsoft removed its planned Bluetooth drivers from its Windows platforms, saying that the maturity of Bluetooth wireless technology did not seem good enough. On the other hand, the new Microsoft operating system for small devices, Talisker, supports Bluetooth protocol.

A Bluetooth network certainly has the potential for interesting federations of coordinated devices. It has a discovery protocol and shares data and voice freely. However, completely secure data and voice traffic requires controls that are not well defined in the Bluetooth specification. Over time, encryption software and personal identity procedures should provide stability. Since each link is encoded and protected against both eavesdropping and interference, the Bluetooth network can be considered a secure short-range wireless network. Ensuring authentication and preventing impersonation are necessary for general use in consumer transactions.

When the Bluetooth network faces outward to a WAN, its data stream matches the conventional data rates planned for European 2.5G systems. EDGE data rates reach up to 384 kbps, which is a fair match for Bluetooth symmetric data channel. However, Bluetooth transmission can be overpowered easily by the standard indoor 3G data rates. The Bluetooth data rate cannot compare to conventional wireless Ethernet at 11 Mbps. But wireless Ethernet does not carry voice easily, so Bluetooth has its place. On the other hand, its low speed is one reason for the new specification for Bluetooth, IEEE 802.15.

IEEE 802.15 and the Bluetooth Network

IEEE 802.15 is the IEEE version of the Bluetooth specification. It serves two purposes. The first is to specify a version of the Bluetooth network that will be complementary to 802.11 wireless Ethernet. For example, the standard will allow 802.11 and 802.15 networks to alternate. The specification's second purpose is to amplify the Bluetooth ability to transmit 20 Mbps. This was driven in part by Eastman Kodak Company, which required a wireless format to support downloading photos from a digital camera – a task that requires more speed than the Bluetooth network delivers.

A Bluetooth PAN is convenient for passing conventional voice and small data streams. However, if it wants to play with emerging 3G data applications such as videoconference streaming media or take advantage of new wireless camera standards, it will need to be upgraded. The Bluetooth device forecast in 2001 is a $950 million market. By 2004, one billion Bluetooth devices are expected to create a $4.5 billion market, according to Gartner Research in 2000.[3]

Infrared Technology

Infrared is a popular way for handhelds to exchange data or to wirelessly print. The infrared mouse, keyboard, and consumer remote control have existed since the early 1980s. However, it was not until 1994 that an infrared standard was published by the Infrared Data Association (IrDA). Today the terms *IrDA* and *infrared* are almost interchangeable. Infrared devices use line of sight, exchanging data by lining up their infrared lenses, and have a typical range of 2 meters. They are often used to manually exchange information using strictly a point-to-point connection. Each device requires the same version of IrDA to operate. IrDA version 1.0 transmits data at 115 kbps and IrDA version 1.1 transmits 4 Mbps. More than 12 million laptops, printers, digital cameras, cell phones, pagers, adapters, remote keyboards, remote controlled TVs, and LAN access devices have implemented IrDA in 1999.[4] Most handhelds use IrDA to exchange data. The IrDA Web site is <http://www.irda.org>.

Jini

Sun Microsystems developed Jini, a set of protocols that allows devices to discover and join one another to share data and services. It is pronounced the same as "genie" and does not stand for anything – other than it starts with a Java J. This is neither a network nor a hardware standard, but it is an interesting experimental protocol. Jini runs on top of Java platform devices that can communicate over a network, thereby creating a federation of devices. Jini objects and code take 3 MB of space and are tested on lab equipment. Jini is a high-level service protocol that works compatibly with either the Bluetooth or IrDA low-level protocols. The Sun Jini Web site is <http://www.jini.org>.

Barcodes and New Radio Technologies

The barcode, printing, and portable collection terminal market is a $4 billion business in 2000, according to Symbol Technologies, Incorporated.[5] Printed barcodes are a print-and-scan technology useful in PAN architectures. They are useful in many inventory control and asset management applications. The PDF417 barcode (Figure 27) is already in use by the military and is now appearing in commercial use. It redundantly encodes characters, so a torn tag will retain integrity. It also encodes 2000 symbols; the industry staple CODE39 carries only 43 characters. The original Universal Product Code (UPC) stored only 11 symbols. Dense barcodes have the advantage in rapid customer processing because the checkout scanner no longer has to go back to a database to retrieve detailed package content or standard warning information.

Figure 27
PDF417 barcode

Although barcodes cost nothing to print, one of the limits of barcode use is that a line-of-sight scanner is required to read the code. Not so with radio-based scanners called interrogators. Some recently developed wireless technology provides low-cost printing of radio transmittable tags that can be read by interrogators.

Smart cards are stamp-sized chips that sometimes contain microprocessors. They are usually portable cards, although sometimes the card is embedded in a device. Smart cards can store subscriber security data or actual cash values like credit amounts, and are most often used as electronic tickets in mass transit or in telephone credit cards popular in Europe. There are many models of smart card: the Subscriber Identity Module (SIM), WAP Identity Module (WIM), and the new postage stamp–sized Secure Digital (SD), which is an industry answer to the SONY Memory Stick. All of these cards have toolkits and utilities that developers use to write software to access the megabyte-sized internal file system.

Radio Frequency Identification (RFID) tags are made as either active or passive technology. They are used largely in inventory control, package tracking, and proximity detection. RFID-tagged objects can be read with a PC card plugged into a handheld or from a basestation. There are many industrial makers with no apparent standardization. Any RFID interrogator within 30 meters can read an RFID tag in active mode.

Electronic Article Surveillance (EAS) systems use wireless technology to prevent theft. A low-cost tag strip or button is located on merchandise such as clothing, CDs, and books. When a large detection antenna located at a store's entrance reads a tagged device, an alarm is triggered. EAS antennas typically operate between 1.7 MHz and 8.2 MHz. Tags are deactivated at the cash registers.

Smart labels use very low-cost silicon chips that work as "antennas" that can be read over the air by an RFID interrogator. BiStatix™ by Motorola is a special format that lets you print your own BiStatix tags. The technology is being produced in conjunction with International Paper Company. While an RFID tag costs $.50 to $1.00, this new smart label costs a few pennies. You actually print the transponding antenna signature on a sheet of film called an interposer. The current tagging scheme permits a 96-bit signature.

Personal radio is another interesting kind of personal network technology that is used exclusively for voice. Subscribers use two-way radios for conversation. Personal radio is popular with traveling families and sports enthusiasts. People with these devices can be as far as two miles away from one another and not need a relay tower. These devices can theoretically perform LAN and PAN functions, although voice is the primary use now. As we move to 3G transparent roaming networks, one mode of communications devices already made possible with the Bluetooth protocol is in point-to-point contact, which completely avoids a relay tower, something that personal radio already does.

PAN Synchronizing Protocols

A series of protocols and standards are in use to synchronize data between Bluetooth and infrared devices. A key industry standard synchronization language, SyncML specifies at a high level how data can be exchanged and is covered in the section "SyncML" in chapter 5.

One underlying protocol for data transmission over PAN networks is OBEX (object exchange) specified by the Infrared Data Association; it can run over most transports like TCP/IP and the Bluetooth protocol. OBEX is a binary HTTP protocol. It is built into devices like PDAs such as the Palm Pilot, and select mobile phones from Ericsson, Siemens, and Nokia. Microsoft Windows 2000 also has built-in OBEX support. An Open Source version of OBEX is called Open OBEX. The document that describes OBEX is at the Web site <http://www.irda.org/standards/pubs/IrOBEX12.pdf>.

New wireless devices that actively connect through a PAN and relay to a WAN provide new sources of content to feed the Internet. The new content is likely to be images from cameras, real-time Bluetooth telemetry data from sensors and readers, data formats from scanners, and audio streams from microphones and video. The additional overlay of time- and location-stamped information is likely to be part of the content stream that ultimately provides a new basis for content usage.

5

Chapter

Wireless Internet Applications and Content

What do mobile users want to do, and what information is important to them? Wireless developers provide such an enormous amount of technology for so many uses that it is hard to say where to begin to provide the application and content solutions. Specific devices and networks to serve professional purposes support business applications. For consumers, the many programs, sub-applications if you will, range from the newest ring tone that identifies a person to a personal information application suite, all using a general device and network to organize life and communicate with others. The range of wireless applications is best understood in general groupings of programming models.

The bulk of what people do over the wireless Internet is to talk and exchange messages. Simple person-to-person messages. Other applications are increasing in popularity including Web browsing where content is held on a server, interactive applications that run programs on your device, and voice portals where applications are designed as dialogs. It appears now that the eXtensible Markup Language (XML) will play a strong role in all levels of application development and content definition. The new wireless network technologies are making possible a mobile user whose purpose and personality are realized through wireless applications and content.

The Four Wireless Internet Applications

In the broad view of wireless applications, a progression of applications follows the popular evolution of the primary wired Internet applications. To plan a wireless mobile application, there are four functionally different wireless application families: messaging, browsing, interacting, and conversing.

- *Messaging.* Using devices like the Nokia Web phone, RIM 957, or a Motorola pager, people send messages. They use Short Message Service (SMS) and other email protocols. The message channel is not just for messages. Developers write SMS applications, often with a SIM toolkit.
- *Browsing.* With microbrowsers people use their Web phones, handhelds, and pagers to read Web sites that developers write in simplified HTML, WML, cHTML, HDML, and XHTML Basic.
- *Interacting.* The large category of mobile interactive software is written by developers to run on the mobile device. This category is unlike the other application families. It does not require a connection. To work offline, professionals process records and gather information for business applications, and then connect as needed. Consumer Java Web phones run standalone games and personal applications. Software is made for the device.
- *Conversing.* In addition to calling someone directly, people can call into voice portals like Tellme and Wildfire to get information from Web servers. Software developers program voice gateways in VoiceXML and VML to listen and to speak in the format of a dialog.

The wireless Internet applications are ordered by popularity as well as their historical introduction. If you are developing a wireless network or launching a wireless channel from your server, you should consider the same progression. Mobile Web phone users expect these services. Like the successful origins of the Web Internet, early mobile applications are simple. Information is largely text based. The early audiences are those who know what they want to do. As reported in the *Daily Yomiuri,* "The Internet is a sort of window into a very bewildering array of options, and people are kind of at a loss as to what to do, whereas the cellular telephone offers a very finite, fixed set of clear choices, which is very appealing to Japanese consumers."[1] Successful mobile applications deliver simple choices and useful information.

Some marketing lyricist proclaimed that the great thing about wireless technology is that it moves applications off the desktop into the rest of your life. I am not sure that is a good idea. But having a usefully connected, well-informed mobile life is the right idea. Creating good wireless applications and useful content is the key.

Types of General Wireless Applications

The early consumer wireless applications have developed with unique mobile characteristics. As Figure 28 shows, in the U.S. mobile market, early wireless applications predictably favor email and personal applications. Wireless location is at the bottom presumably because the service was rarely offered in 2000.

Strategis Group estimates that there are 32.3 million potential mobile data subscribers, or 25 percent of the U.S. workforce. But small-device wireless applications, unlike desktop applications, are specially positioned to take advantage of elements such as location and simple transactions.

Another look at wireless business applications can be derived from the early wireless companies that are largely following the Internet market:

- *Full portals:* Yahoo! Amazon, AOL
- *Information:* News, sports, weather, entertainment
- *Activities:* Tickets, games, music, betting
- *Services:* Stock trading, air travel
- *Commercial:* Inventory, inspection, ticketing, service

A typical aggregation of mobile wireless business service might include traffic, stock quotes, flight information, business directory, and directions by car or by foot.

Table 22 gives yet another look at international wireless Internet usage. According to this study, messaging will remain the dominant application and

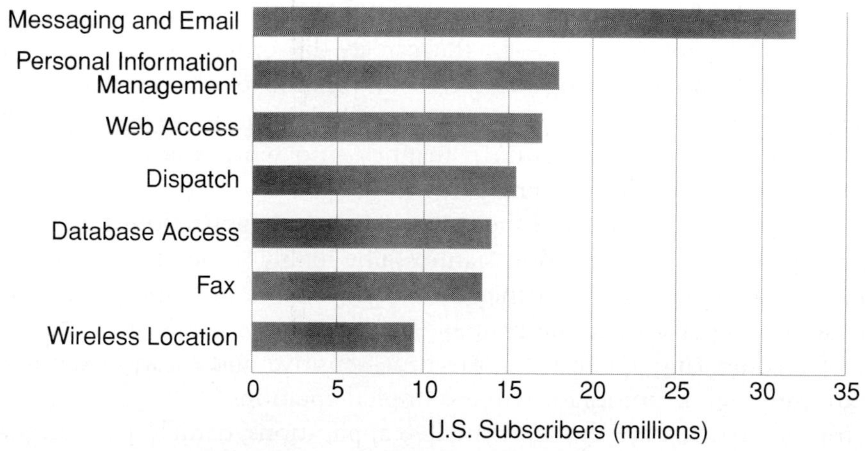

Figure 28 The U.S. mobile data market by application (*Source:* Strategis Strategic Information Services, Inc,. 2000.)

Table 22 Forecast of worldwide users (in millions) of wireless Internet applications

Service	2001	2002	2003	2004	2005	2006
Messaging	275	467	700	922	1154	1445
MCommerce/retail	44	126	225	360	454	551
Financial services	149	265	410	598	771	935
Enterprise intranet	22	53	88	142	154	192
Internet browsing	94	154	250	428	654	924
Navigation/LBS	72	217	432	748	1181	1502
Entertainment	174	292	434	631	836	999

Source: ARC Group 2001.

include email, SMS, and FAX. Over time the use of devices for mCommerce becomes as prominent as messaging.

Information becomes a service. This is the conclusion of the study of first wireless markets discussed in chapter 1 in the section, "European Wireless Applications." The early market offers general aggregated access to information often via a wireless portal. The market soon matures and wireless services differentiate. They become application specific, unique publishing channels, specialized interactive services, and transactional systems.

Location, Time, Personalization, Simple Transaction

One of the keys to dynamic mobile content is presenting to subscribers highly relevant personal service information – in the car, in the office, on the street, at home. Information is useful during the travail of vacation or the excitement of work. Wireless content can take into account the caller's location, personal preferences, and the time of day. Information is mapped into what is around, what is open, what is interesting to the traveling person.

Figure 29 give us a closer look at the value of wireless applications ranked by location, time, personal, and transaction features. The highly valued features of the mobile audience include location of the subscriber, timeliness of information or service, the ability to personalize the content, and the ability to perform a simple transaction. By comparing applications, the time-sensitive and location-sensitive industries are early opportunities for wireless implementations.

At the top of the chart are the most suitable applications, namely, navigational direction and location followed by transportation updates, arrival, and departure times for planes, trains, and other mass transit. At the bottom are the general or national services that are not as interesting as something that has local appeal. Of

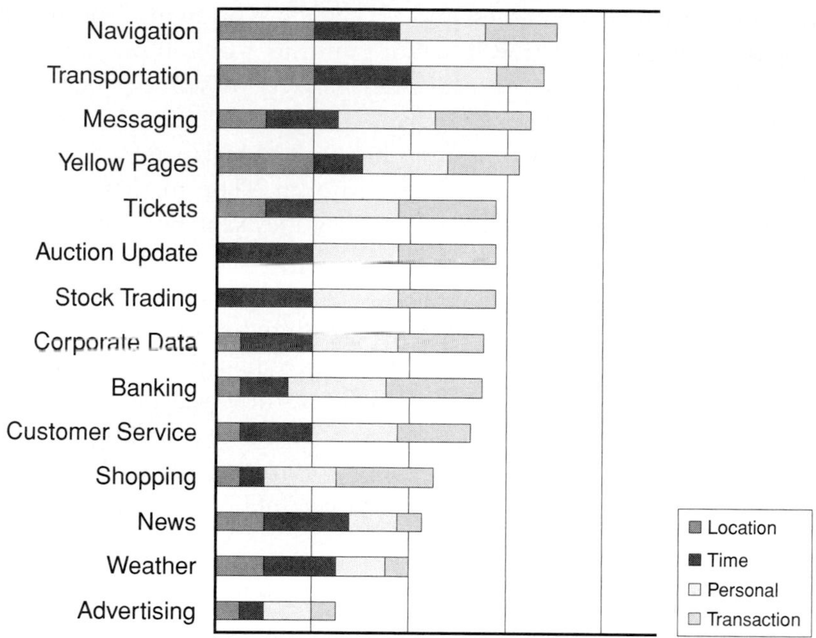

Figure 29 Wireless applications ranked by location, time, personal, and transaction features

course, any one of these categories can be recast to become more personalized, location valuable, time sensitive, and transaction simplistic.

Messaging

In all wireless data applications, text is the most common medium – unstyled, short, ordinary text with the message up front. The medium offers efficiency and ease of transmission. Its brevity suits the short amount of time an on-the-go user has. Effective messages get to the point and can be acted on.

The most used computer application is email. Corporations as well as families use email to stay connected. Two-thirds of the U.S. workforce uses email. Every world survey shows it to be the most frequently used and the most essential application. Email, newsgroups, and postings add a valuable human quality to any Web site as the network of viewers become aware of each other and their participatory effect. It may come as no surprise that email is the number one starting point for wireless. But emails and their attachments are a bit much to read on a small device. They eventually overrun memory and, because the cost is figured by the letter, they become very expensive. Messaging rather than email is what mobile users do.

The value of ordinary wireless text messaging is evident worldwide. Ten billion emails and messages are sent every day. AOL says it transmits 1 billion messages per day worldwide.[2] Reportedly, 200 billion SMS messages will be sent in 2001. The average European subscriber sends more than one a day.[3] The GSM Association says 15 billion SMS messages are sent each month.[4] DoCoMo Japan says i-mode subscribers send more than 3 billion messages per month.[5] The market research firm In-Stat predicts that the number of wireless messages sent per month will balloon to 244 billion in December 2004.[6]

Wireless messaging is one of the most important systems for developers to understand. It is heavily used to circumvent the voice system because calls are very expensive. Just as important, messages get through even when the person is not available. Text gets to the point. Pure and simple ASCII, the good old American Standard Code for Information Interchange, is the base 8-bit text coding used in mobile messaging. Globally the messaging system recommended is UNICODE, the 16-bit version that represents all the world's languages. However, i-mode currently uses Shift-JIS double-byte codes.

Signaling and Messaging

Wireless email and messaging systems depend on underlying tools like decision support, message confirmation, and "push" messaging. For example, replying to an email from a Web phone can be difficult. Most North American carriers offer messaging on today's Web phones for a fee, but every service is different. In Europe, SMS is a standard part of the GSM phone service. SMS is low-priority store-and-forward text that arrives when it can. It requires special software to correctly write out SMS and manage the transmission and responses. For handhelds and pagers, email response is more traditional. Web phone and handheld mail often requires a dial-up connection to a circuit-switched network. Unless you have a paging channel or a packet-based wireless air interface, you will not get urgent text on time. For some wireless applications, the most important part of messaging is its speedy delivery and signaling the end user that a message is important or merely present. This is especially true in financial applications. An incoming alert tone might signal the need for a business approval, arrival of an important delivery, the latest subscribed information, a timely summarization, or a reminder of an appointment. Signaling is part of the pager network and its functionality is generally available on WANs. However, signaling is a rare feature for handhelds that are designed to work offline. With a handheld, a mobile user opens a connection and checks on email or exchanges Internet content as needed. Handhelds are offline most of the time. In time-sensitive networks, this one factor rules the handheld out of many solutions. Instead, paging devices such as the RIM are often used because they are always listening to paging channels in low-power mode.

Push Protocol

Today on most Web phones or handhelds people have to dial up to see if anything is ready. This is called a *pull* model. For important messaging applications, such as sending urgent messages or financial alerts, a push technology is required. This can be successful with signaling protocols and paging codes over a paging network. From an application server's viewpoint, messaging pages are sent like email, and receipt confirmation of the message is often critical. From an end user's viewpoint, the user is alerted when the device is signaled to receive a page. However, not all devices or wireless networks support paging. Pagers and cell phones constantly listen for a paging control signal. A handheld with a data modem is optimized to use a higher throughput data channel, and its architecture does not provide the power to be on all the time to listen for a control signal. It relies on the owner to "dial up" for service.

WAP phones count on a data signaling protocol to provide pagelike services. While GSM already has a built-in SMS store-and-forward message service, a push protocol is required to move packets of data to devices and alert the receiver to ensure transmission of important information. The most common form of push technology uses SMS. Push was first defined in WAP 1.2 by the Push Access Protocol (PAP). Push can be better than paging because it defines a rich menu of interactive responses. Few operators have implemented the push model largely because of the expense and administration of this dedicated server, and the complexity for developers to support it. For many subscribers, SMS service is good enough.

Advanced messaging systems are becoming very useful. Alert messages can be triggered from servers and messaging applications can be written so that information can be acted on from within the message. Decision support text messaging systems are important to corporations. These commercial information systems can send a message that includes embedded options and multiple replies. For example, a message could ask for a decision and have approval or disapproval buttons directed to multiple parties. Special sign-and-return components are also part of commercial messaging systems. List servers send brief news items to newsgroup subscribers. The challenge is to keep the payload for a mobile device small.

Unified Messaging

People have multiple numbers and email addresses for home and business. Each voice, text, and fax system has its own store-and-forward management system and user interface for retrieval. Most ring or alert you that new content is ready. And what do mobile users do when traveling? They most often have to connect to each service to get various messages and documents. The need for unified service is clear.

It is probably best for now that a person on the go has a separate mobile email address for messaging. Others can choose an email address for sending them documents and long explanations or choose a mobile address for the short, urgent, or time-sensitive messages. Let the sender decide. In the long run, one of the goals of UMTS is to bring together all messaging, paging, email, voice, and fax systems into one unified, digital mailbox service. This *unified messaging* is not simple, as we will discover when we explore architecture further.

Microbrowsing Web Sites

After messaging, browsing content is the most popular wireless application. The great advantage of the wireless browser is that your content will run on many different devices. Developers do not need to directly program the device. Wireless Web content is generated from markup languages on the server. Most development for these pages is not done on the device at all, but on the server. It is similar to making standard HTML Web pages; however, you typically use a device emulator to make sure the pages appear and can be navigated correctly.

It is important to rescale your thinking about presenting content from a Web site. Web site servers deliver large-screen content to PC browsers and small-screen content to microbrowsers. Designers once used every possible screen color and dynamic animation in a Web browser. Now they work with gray-scale microbrowsers to convey simple content. These Web pages allow 4 lines of text, 20 characters wide, without color. The basic U.S. or European Web phone can hold only 1000 bytes. Japanese Web phones can handle 2000 bytes. Developers in the United States most commonly write WML and HDML, and XHTML Basic markup. These languages present text with little styling and provide a minimum of navigation. The Web page can embed links to other sites and call buttons to other phones.

Read-Only Publishing

The most effective cell phone applications are effectively read-only, meaning there is no upstream content you expect users to spend time supplying. Do not expect text input from the field, especially if the mobile device is a cell phone. Mobile users like messaging, news, and very basic content access.

Experienced engineers and new wireless teams often make the mistake of thinking they can simply convert original Web pages with text entry fields to Web phone–usable pages. This is technically easy to do and awful to see. Using conversion tools, developers zip through a Web site and show their manager that the project is done in record time. Unless you pay wireless end users to use this product, they will probably not use it. You have to rethink their needs for mobility and consider how to save them time with a mobile design.

If possible, redesign forms so that text is presented in lists to choose from rather than have open fields to type into. Mobile users find entering text very frustrating even when text entry technology is good. If they must enter text, then allow the input to be saved so it can be reused. Consider presenting text pop-up lists. These can be customized on the server. Even two-way pagers can use this strategy. Mobile wireless text is first a publishing medium. The first need is to simply make your Web content mobile and available.

Dynamic Content

Dynamic content is the programmed presentation of Web data, generated at the server with variables that can be controlled by the user, often in real time. Whereas static content is the retrieval of Web pages from a file system, dynamic content is the presentation of generated pages in memory, based on the changing logical use of the data. On simple static content Web sites, a browser request is routed to a file on disk and sent back with many elements stored on the file system. On a dynamic content site, it is said to be database-driven and requested pages are formed in memory filled in part by making database calls for content, with rarely a hit to the file system. A simple example of dynamic content is the banner of a Web page that comes from a system (ad management) that is entirely different from the content on the rest of the page. No page remains the same.

One of the chief advantages of dynamic content is that developers do not have to write so many Web pages. You do not use the file system for each page; rather, you generate through programming, the entire Web page in memory before sending it to a requesting browser. Consider a Web site that listed every shop in a metropolitan area. You could build a Web site with one page for each shop – the method of static HTML content. You could write 4000 pages or, with dynamic content, you need write only 1 page. The site server fills in the page on the fly with a call to the commerce database. Because pages are dynamic, mobile users can influence Web pages as they move about. Your server can construct interesting pages based on the personality, the location, and the time zone of the mobile user. Dynamic content is particularly effective not so much in Web browsing, but in interactive applications.

Interacting with Applications

Beyond messaging and browsing are interactive applications. This is the most complex level of wireless development and is appropriate for handhelds and large-memory devices. Unlike for the other application families, developers must write code for the client device, which requires their familiarity with the underlying OS of the mobile device. Many interactive applications require a server to exchange data. Emerging applications must be designed to operate distributed, work peer to peer with other wireless devices, or perform transactions using added security software.

The tools for this kind of development provide access to the operating system of the client device. The development environment involves a programming language like Java for J2ME libraries and C++ for the Palm OS®, and, of course, the emulators for the device. The way the wireless network operates is largely abstracted in the programming library you must learn for each device.

The standard bundled Personal Information Management (PIM) handheld applications include address book, date book, to-do list, memo pad, calculator, mail, and expense report. These synchronize with a desktop version of a different application that uses the same content. Newer software designs perform over-the-air synchronization against, for example, shared group calendars and contacts lists. PIM applications are a good beginning for wireless interactive applications.

Wireless interactive applications let you perform special operations such as signature capture, scanning verification, and barcoding. They typically make use of an onboard database that works with a remote server. Although you can do many interesting things on a programmable device, not every wireless device can execute your interactive code. The chief disadvantage of a wireless interactive application, compared to a browser solution, is that whatever you write will run on only that one device, although there are some tools that help you reach a family of devices. You also have to distribute the software to the client. Interactive applications make sense when the client for whom you are building the application has a fixed set of wireless devices. Written to operate on the client device, interactive applications are the standard in industrial vertical markets.

Wireless Vertical Market Interactive Applications

Vertical markets are highly specialized markets that have a domain of expertise and a unique solution. Unlike horizontal market applications such as electronic mail, wireless vertical markets (Table 23) have their own applications. A common example of wireless vertical market solutions is the processing done when a customer returns a rental car at an airport. An agent uses wireless devices to check the car and print a receipt on the spot. Other examples are package delivery where a signature is taken, dispatch management where wireless devices send field workers to assignments, and law enforcement where officials scan in information, make records on wireless devices, compute results, and print tickets on the spot. Vertical markets have the advantages of providing a complete solution and avoiding the marketing costs of rolling out a general market technology that must address a wider range of possible uses.

There are three mobile vertical market segments. The first wireless vertical application area is for *mechanized* applications, which are found in the transportation and logistical supply industries. These applications typically monitor and process large inventories. There are many opportunities here using new low-cost GPS tracking chips, high-density barcodes, and radio ID locators. The second vertical

Table 23 Wireless vertical markets

Scope	Mechanized	Field Force	Institutional
Group	Transportation and logistics	Mobile workforce	Health care, public safety, finance
Industry	Motor carriers, air couriers, retail distribution, travel, manufacturing, distribution, third-party logistics	Route distribution, field service, insurance, public and municipal service, utilities, inspection	Home health care, clinical patient care, pharmaceuticals, ticketing, fire control, pretrial court records, banking, and securities
Applications	Pickup and delivery, fleet management, vehicle maintenance, car rental return, package delivery, signature capture	Sales force automation, field service reporting, merchandising, building inspection, insurance reporting, punch list, customer relationship management, enterprise asset management	Patients' records, pretrial processing, ticketing, brokerage

application area is *field force* applications, which are suitable for the mobile workforce divisions of large companies. It uses wireless technology to manage and coordinate people, their tasks, and personal inventories. Established applications in this segment are Sales Force Automation (SFA), Customer Relationship Management (CRM), and even lowly punch list applications, such as those for building inspectors so they simply inspect and punch certification checklists. There are new wireless opportunities in merchandizing, such as efficiency improvement using PAN and peer-to-peer synchronization technology. The third wireless vertical application area is *institutional* and involves health care, public safety, and large bureaucracies. Key opportunities in this sector are supplying lower cost, lighter systems with higher speed wireless services to shovel more of the required amount of administrative material.

Real-time data collection, tracking of materials, and access to mission-critical information are the mainstays of wireless business solutions. One specialty is Enterprise Asset Management (EAM), which involves the tracking, movement, and updating of information about equipment and materials. Workers can view work orders and the list of materials for all work orders, as well as access individual corrective procedures to maintain any piece of equipment.

Developers program the majority of interactive applications for handhelds. Unlike handhelds, most Web phones are not programmable and have little storage to work offline. Wireless handhelds operate offline and connect intermittently, often over a wireless LAN. Through years of purposeful use, many handheld mobile user interface components have evolved.

You can specialize in niche vertical markets that often require specialized development. Home health care is an example of a niche vertical market. To build a wireless system for home health care, you consult with an expert practicing nurse, you research all the details of the standards required for gathering data and printing legal forms. You analyze the workflow of nurses who work in this area and style the application in a way that makes sense to them and saves their time.

As we explained, the technology adoption curve tells us that for early technology to succeed beyond the hobbyist stage, it must find at least one business market to demonstrate value. Once cost is justified, the applications can move from a singular vertical market in a horizontal manner to other business markets and possibly to a consumer commodity market. Examples of making this technological transition from a single to a broad market are those who observe the utility of a military or large industrial system and then implement it in a broad manner. It is sometimes easiest to bring fire down from the mountain. If you are willing to search, there is much to find and learn from established wireless vertical market systems.

Wireless vertical markets are developed by companies that combine technology for a business purpose. They are often justified in a return-on-investment (ROI) plan that prices the solution at a margin where the application often pays for itself within two years. Here is an example. Traditionally, field-based personnel such as law enforcement officers return to headquarters to complete reports and use agency systems. Handheld access can provide accurate, up-to-date information, capturing a lot of the detail in the field as it happens. Since more than three-fourths of a department's operating budget is typically consumed by personnel costs, any demonstrable solution that saves time and increases quota yield per shift hits the bottom line.

Many of these ROI systems are "paid off," the application has proved value, and the customer is ready to grow. Established vertical markets are open to competitive, lower cost wireless technology solutions.

What was once vertical can become horizontal. For example, large wireless dispatch control systems are specific and use expensive gear. But many small businesses could achieve the financial benefits of these large systems. A smaller dispatch-oriented system could be based on modern, widely available, lower cost wireless gear.

Emerging Collaborative and Synchronized Applications

We are entering the era of social applications. Unless blocked by security and privacy systems, any device can potentially connect with any other over the wireless Internet. An original peer-to-peer application – walkie-talkie voice calls – serves as a simple example of a collaborative application. Some families today use personal radios that give family members the ability to coordinate activity. Businesses with field personnel are beginning to share wireless data as well to accomplish collaborative goals. Conventionally, clients communicate with a server. However, wireless devices can operate directly with one another without using a server or even a relay tower. These often result in peer-to-peer connections and are part of the promise of Bluetooth networks.

With data, sharing and exchanging content are primary values. Napster-like access to music, collaborative shared workspaces, and synchronized group tasks require interactive software and local storage. To take a poll of people or to vote on issues with wireless devices in forums is also highly desirable. The wireless network technology to handle massive voting in dense areas is often a barrier, unless a packet-switched wireless network is in use.

The military and high-end commercial field force applications make much use of real-time synchronized applications. In these applications, wireless devices synchronize and share large common data pools and task codes. All subscribing members communicate and interact with instantaneous updates from distributed servers. With their "moving radars," a team's members have a means to track and converge on whatever interests them and their network. Advanced systems use a specialized radio net that secures encrypted bandwidth. But one key technology is differential data exchange to provide nearly instantaneous distributed changes. The other key technology for coordination is dynamically distributed servers that replicate a common frame of reference at any time.

Software Distribution and Provisioning with Middleware

If you think about it, any organization that uses hundreds of low-cost wireless devices has some special challenges. Keeping costs for airtime down is always an issue. The model of every device and the version of every piece of software have to be kept in line and synchronized in mass. The administration of hardware and software is a business in and of itself. Administrators have to update and distribute software. For large installations, wireless devices must be *provisioned*, meaning the exact model of wireless device has to have a precisely matched version of software, and it has to be shipped and be useable almost immediately, which means account and security settings have to be configured.

Middleware companies provide software and services that tie together applications, the underlying operating system, and the wireless network. Some middleware companies, such as AvantGo, expedite data transmission by providing subscribers a "channel" that uses software on the client device and the server to cache and compress subscribed streams of wireless content. Middleware minimizes page latency and saves billing cost by compressing wireless transmissions. Some compression schemes can triple the data capacity over the air. They do this by simplifying routing, grouping data blocks, and eliminating redundant housekeeping parts of the packet protocols. Many middleware companies can also distribute and provision software on large numbers of wireless devices with administrative software. For example, ScoutWare from Aether Systems lets administrators inspect the file directories of handhelds and distribute software across the entire base of machines. Software provisioning and distribution tools are two of the many helpful functions supplied by third-party wireless middleware companies such as Broadbeam, Aether, AvantGo, and GoAmerica.

To upgrade a device's underlying software, the device must be programmable. The operating system on a wireless device runs from either a programmable Flash ROM, which can be upgraded, or a masked ROM, which cannot be changed. Most Web phones are made with masked ROM and their operating systems cannot be changed. The good points about masked ROM devices are that they are not subject to viruses and are very cheap to build. Unfortunately, you have to throw your phone away to get new features. Handhelds often come in Flash ROM and masked ROM forms, so you must check. Upgrading wireless applications is a simpler matter. Unlike low-level system software, applications use highly variable amounts of available memory. Wireless software distribution can be downloaded via cable, sent over the air perhaps as an email attachment, or pushed onto the device with secure middleware software. It is important to assure users that they are securely receiving the right software and the right version of it.

Wireless Games

Wireless games are not only fertile examples of interactive applications, but they also attract one of the most sought after early market audiences – the youthful and hobbyist. The youth of the world enjoy portable gaming. They have bought 65 million Nintendo Game Boys and download games on their Web phones by Nokia and handhelds by Palm, Inc. According to game analysts, gamers in pursuit of electronic entertainment constitute 80 percent of North American youth. The wireless game market by 2005 is expected to be $6 billion, twice the size of the portable game market in 2001.[7]

There are new gaming models made possible by wireless devices. Wireless game play can move desktop play to an outdoor recreation. Gen-Y players use WAP phones to play games such as nGame's Alien Fish Exchange, which is a mix of Pokemon and the virtual pet Tamagotchi. In this wireless game, players breed fish on a moon orbiting Jupiter for restaurants across the galaxy that are looking for rare species to feed their customers. Even more popular is the i-mode trout fishing game where patience is a virtue. But the wireless games have just begun and offer incredibly rich opportunities for wireless Internet developers. The early market for the young gamer and the hobby experimentalist is awash with new ideas that take advantage of mobile wireless devices in their own right. Pokemon, with its trading of characters, had fun inside and outside the game. Location-based Easter egg hunts and survivor hide-and-seek games are examples of mobile fun. Meanwhile, conventional wireless game portals are being made for such epic Internet role-playing games as Everquest, for which a monthly subscription fee is charged. Network games that run on the Internet can last forever and now directly involve any real point on Earth.

There are gamers and there is gaming. The adult gaming industry is experimenting with wireless casino games and connections to the popular games of chance. They are simple to implement, although security, game play authentication, and banking issues are a larger part of the game. While expanding the gaming industry with wireless is inevitable, the early volume market will clearly favor the youth market, which is primed for early technology.

Wireless Interface Components

Gamelike interactive components for wireless handhelds were pioneered with the Apple Newton® MessagePad®. It turns out that mobile users need well-designed, highly intuitive, simple, fun-to-use components for mobile applications. Animated calendars to set appointments and keyword list selectors that dynamically change based on use are examples of objects that simplify multiple types of mobile data input. Components provide a standard way to do things and can be reused on multiple platforms. Some components are unique to field applications. Signature capture is not found on the desktop and it lets people sign documents on handhelds with "electronic ink." The interesting components provide gamelike data entry. The highly visual way in which end users choose a date on the Newton or Palm handhelds is simply not available with conventional Internet desktop applications, where people are expected to use a keyboard. As Java phones appear, they too will require such components. Of course, all wireless devices need security components.

Wireless Multimedia

The multimedia industry depends on underlying formats. Downloadable MP3 music files are a worldwide phenomenon of interest. In the United States, the iPAQ and PocketPC handhelds have MP3 players. Over-the-air retrieval of audio is only practical on a 2.5G or 3G network. On the other hand, it is realistic to download files to a PC and cable them over to a handheld. Today the Japanese market features audio, pictures, and slow stream video for wireless networks. Japanese Telecom and NTT DoCoMo are building faster networks to download personal music for their millions of cell phone customers. The new lineup of i-mode phones feature cell phones with built-on cameras. Other companies working on interactive radio and personal audio are RealAudio, Savos, Vitaminic, and qSent.

On the Palm network, ActiveScript Flash can transmit animation streams. Emerging multimedia formats are covered later in this chapter in the section "SMIL and Flash for Streaming Media."

Conversing via Voice Portals

Voice applications are generally being offered as complete office portal services rather than select server applications. With a voice portal, business subscribers can access address books and their phone lists, have the service place calls, read their mail, and get stock quotes. The implementations can be pricey, but they are justified in large-scale projects such as call centers. Smaller developers can look forward to using voice portals as service extensions to their site from select vendors.

Voice portal applications can be written fairly easily. By using a VoiceXML markup language, your application makes use of special intermediate software that runs on a voice gateway. The voice gateway handles both speech recognition and voice synthesis. You can throw as much money as you want at each component. Speech-recognition systems can be used that understand basic commands or complete sentences. Voice synthesis, sometimes called text to speech (TTS), can be augmented by having voice talent make recordings.

The VoiceXML conversational application is structured as a voice interface to a dialog. There are three main items to consider: prompts, grammars, and dialogs. A prompt is an audio message played by the system that appears as a line in the file. A grammar comprises the words or phrases spoken by users in response to the prompt that the voice portal listens for. The dialog controls which prompts are played, which grammars are active at any given point, and the overall conversational flow. Some very useful and free tools such as Nuance V-Builder™ let developers convert HTML pages in a drag-and-drop manner into sequential dialogs.

Matching Applications to Wireless Devices

Today's wireless 2G Internet finds messaging, information browsing, interactive, and conversational applications suitable for specific devices, each with a unique programming model. The two-way pager is well suited for a wide range of wireless data applications on existing networks. Wireless interactive applications are powerful and require custom production and are a smaller market than pagers. Web content is relatively uniform for any device and does not require customization to accommodate the operating system, nor does it require the consumer to download an application. Browsable Web content is also virus free, a favorite observation of security analysts who do not like the idea of having to download software to run a security application. Conversational interfaces with voice portals have the same safety property.

On a mobile device, the end user has very little time to input information. It is important to consider restructuring content so that users can view it easily with choices presented rather than requests that need input and roundtrips to determine the options. The simplest approach is to consider making wireless content a read-only experience. It is physically easier for mobile users to check off multiple choices than to fill a blank field with text. It also makes back-end processing easier. It is a common mistake for programmers to port their existing Web forms applications. It is simpler to consider that the mobile audience for content expects a wireless publishing medium. The interactive parts that require input should be reduced to the simplest level, only one or two transactions.

As a developer managing and delivering content, you want to reach every wireless device without worrying about details. The good news is that you do not have to worry about wireless air interfaces. CDMA, TDMA, or GSM or their data cousins CDPD, Motient, DataTAC, and GPRS should make little difference to your programming efforts. They are lower-level network protocols well abstracted by APIs. On the other hand, when people buy a Web cell phone or handheld, all of a sudden they have to shop through this list. In the real world, air carriers have different connection speeds, billing plans, and coverage. To reach a wide range of devices in the best manner possible, you will need to program, which is the subject of chapter 18, "Building Servers and Matching Client Applications."

The Markup Languages of Wireless Publishing

XML

You have probably written HTML Web pages. If not, you certainly have gone to a Web browser and selected the "view source" option to see how they are made. For wireless Web browsing, there are many markup languages to consider.

A *markup language* is a document format that defines content and style. It is designed to be read by a browser that interprets the codes for style and content in order to display or print the content. It is not at all like a computer language, such as Java or C++, that runs as a program. Markup languages are a mix of text and style commands that tell a browser how to present output for either a screen or a printer. Markup languages simply define content with style.

The most interesting language of all is the eXtensible Markup Language (XML). It describes data without style. XML syntax can also define other markup languages. It is the root language for modern Internet browsers, big and small. Internet servers worldwide use XML as the base to exchange protocols and data. This language is also the emerging language of wireless publishing, and its derivative languages are used in all wireless browsing technology.

All wired and wireless content originates from Internet servers. Most people with PCs use a Web browser to contact a site. If they have Web phones or handhelds, they use a microbrowser to view a site. Phone makers burn microbrowsers into silicon that reads markup languages. All kinds of browsers depend on the server content to be formatted in a standard markup language.

XML defines portable structured information. It is ideal for wireless publishing and for messaging. The entire Microsoft .NET initiative uses XML as a cornerstone for storing document files, the electronic exchange data, and Smart Tags. Smart Tags are intelligent cut-and-paste XML-tagged data.

From the point of view of a content producer, XML has many familiar properties of HTML. But HTML has a fixed number of styles. With XML, you can define your own style tags. This enhances distinctions in style and efficiency of content transmission. XML is also a means to publish data directly, without the overhead of style. New wireless devices without microbrowsers, such as Java phones and pagers, can receive data with standardized XML data streams.

Understanding Microbrowser Markup Languages for Devices

Developers have been producing Internet Web sites in one standard markup language, HTML, since the early 1990s. A typical Web browser, such as Internet Explorer or Netscape Communicator, interprets HTML Web pages pretty much the same way, so if you write HTML once, it works on most every kind of PC. The mechanics for creating wireless markup are very similar, but the interpretation on wireless devices is not as consistent.

Wireless devices challenge the conventions of Web pages. As simple as it might be to use only HTML, it makes poor sense for mobile users with Web phones to view such pages. The power of the Palm over the Microsoft mobile products explains the difference. When people are mobile, they need something short and personal. They just do not have time to marvel at dazzling artwork or complex documents on the go. They find great value in information synchronized with sources of data they care about. The interface for mobile use is also quite different, requiring simple presentation and active navigation.

Wireless developers have been using four page markup languages: WML, HDML, cHTML, and simplified HTML. These deliver wireless Web pages to microbrowsers built into Web phones. Some microbrowsers can also be downloaded to handhelds and pagers. Most embedded microbrowsers read only one of those formats, although the new ones are multimode.

- U.S. Web phone developers write in HDML and PQA. PQA, the Palm Query Application, uses a subset of HTML and is the chief browsing language in the Palm handheld market.
- To reach European WAP devices, developers write the Web sites in WML. The WML microbrowser is licensed by the WAP Forum.

- To reach i-mode Web phones, developers write Web content in cHTML. The original cHTML microbrowser, NetFront, was written by Access Japan for NTT DoCoMo.

Some telco server gateways attempt to perform conversions with mixed results. Do not forget classic HTML. It is common for Web phone sites to have PC Web pages made so that mobile users can personalize their Web accounts for mobile use. Also, some large-screen handhelds can view HTML sites.

HTML: The Original Web Page

The Hypertext Markup Language (HTML) is the lifeblood of the Internet. Almost every Web page is written in HTML. Almost any document written in HTML is viewable equally on a Macintosh, PC, Sun, or Linux computer. An important contribution to the success of HTML is that the "source code" is always available to any Web browser; the user simply selects the "view source" menu command.

When HTML was invented, the Internet Web was born. But the language also required the inventor Tim Berners-Lee to create a Web server and a browser to view it. While working at CERN in 1990, he defined HTML, URL, and HTTP standards. Later he established the World Wide Web Consortium (W3C), of which he is now a director.

HTML is a remarkably simple language – simple enough for the entire world community of developers to understand. So that the world could use it easily, the standard was openly published by the W3C. The very last version of HTML is 4.1. The successor to this language, endorsed by the W3C, is the new language XHTML. It is the same as HTML, except that it uses a well-formed XML language. Professional developers value XHTML for its precision and the fact that any text can be validated as "correct" by a parser. XHTML gets around the complex whomper-jawed style of conditional writing to let it appear the same on different browser implementations. The HTML and XHTML specification Web site is <http://www.w3.org/MarkUp/>.

XML: A Universal Web Page

HTML provided a simple, serviceable start to the Internet, but it had limits and the features could be extended only by committee. Beginning in 1996 the W3C began studying HTML and its cantankerous predecessor, the Structured Generalized Markup Language (SGML) publishing standard. The result was new extensible language, XML, which was released by the W3C in February 1998 with the following features:

- *Data separation.* Data can be represented without concern for presentation.

- *Extensibility.* New commands can be added. It can also be produced in modules.
- *Acceptability.* A growing number of XML schema repositories have backing from major companies such as Microsoft, IBM, and Sun.
- *Simplicity.* The language is text based and easy to read.

The origin of XML was a grand reflection on HTML and all other markup languages. One of XML's powers is that it is a metalanguage; that is, it is able to construct others languages and extend them. It can define all the parts of a language, such as tags and attributes. From XML, all markup languages can be generated. One of the first XML-derivative languages is the Wireless Markup Language (WML), used in WAP.

Being able to simply describe data is helpful for different databases, programs, and file systems that store data in different ways. Just as Java was a portable computer language, XML is a portable data language. Being a raw data language, XML is very useful in mobile wireless systems. It provides a simple means for various devices, applications, and servers to exchange information. Industries can now define their own portable XML languages and data definitions.

XML is also a vocabulary for data. If you look at an XML document, then the layout of the XML data must be defined. The first line at the top of any XML file designates a Document Type Definition (DTD). A DTD refers to a file somewhere on the Internet that is the structural XML specification for the components of the file. DTDs are now being enhanced to become XML schema. Both have standards committees of specialized organizations familiar with the vocabulary and storage issues of their profession. Each committee arbitrates the finalized DTD and XML schema for industries such as geography, chemistry, architecture, and real estate. Only DTD is universally accepted.

We already said that a major difference from HTML is that XML does not specify style. This raises a question about how style is used. XML explains what something is, not how it looks. XML data is tagged by name, so outside of the XML file, there are other files or methods that can define what to do to style the tagged data. One common technique is the use of XML Style Language (XSL). XSL and other style techniques such as Document Object Model (DOM) handling are discussed in chapter 18, in the section "Implementing Wireless Application Servers." The XML Web site is <http://www.w3.org/XML/>.

HDML Grows into WML

Developers in the United States often provide Web sites for Web phones in two similar formats, Handheld Dynamic Markup Language (HDML) and Wireless Markup Language (WML). Whereas the publishing model for HTML is a single Web page, these two languages use a deck of cards metaphor.

In 1997 Unwired Planet (UP) made the UP browser to read its new HDML language for small-screen Web phones. By giving this microbrowser away freely to handset makers, the UP HDML microbrowser was burned into the ROMs of at least 90 percent of the U.S. Internet-ready phones. When Web phones are used in Internet mode, the UP browser logo appears on the opening screen. The HDML format is in use by AT&T PocketNet and Sprint Wireless Web, and there are sites like Amazon that are HDML only. The open W3C submission of HDML is at <http://www.w3.org/Submission/1997/5/>.

After HDML was on the market for a year, handset makers decided to standardize their microbrowser. Telcos started a consortium called the WAP Forum, which commissioned Phone.com (formerly Unwired Planet, now Openwave Systems) to generalize HDML. Designed by committee, WML version 1.2 was defined in June 1999 and it heavily resembles HDML. The WAP Forum also provides WAP gateways and secure servers, one of the more popular being the Nokia ActivServer. WAP phones connect through WAP gateways to reach either a final WAP server or a developer's Internet site that has WML-formatted pages. A telco WAP gateway generally converts between HDML and WML markup languages to match the phone's microbrowser. But the conversion does not always come out right because there are so many versions of HDML and WML microbrowsers and gateways. If you had to pick one language, it would be WML, because you have a better chance of conversion with WML than with HDML.

WML is a private standard and it requires permission from the WAP Forum to see it. You can fill in electronic permission forms at <http://www.wapforum.org>. Many beginning developers avoid the registration process by going to WAP Forum member sites that have an easier starting point. A useful member site is <http://developer.phone.com/dev/ts/htmldoc/40/wmlref/>.

WML defines an entirely new publishing model of presenting a deck of cards that subscribers can shuffle through. The stated purpose of this design was to prevent roundtrips to the server. However, it turns out pages can be built more easily in a far simpler cHTML markup language.

The i-mode Standard Compact HTML

The markup language that delivers most of the wireless world's Web content today is Compact HTML (cHTML). This simple language was developed by Access Japan, which developed the matching NetFront browser that is found in every i-mode phone. The cHTML standard was introduced via the W3C in 1998 and is posted on the Web for all to see. The language is used worldwide, although for the longest time only a Japanese i-mode phone browser could see it. If you use an i-mode phone, you are looking at a site emitting cHTML, a simplification of HTML designed for Web phones. What is useful about cHTML is that it is very easy for a

Web developer to make. cHTML avoids advanced HTML features like tables, cascading style sheets, and dynamic scripting. This has the effect of simplifying the load of detail that appears on a phone. The Compact HTML language Web site is <http://www.w3.org/Submission/1998/04/>.

XHTML: The Next Web Page

The W3C now recommends that XHTML replace HTML as the world's Web browser language. XHTML 1.0 was a reformulation of HTML 4.01 in XML. XHTML is well-formed HTML that uses XML rules. Using XHTML you cannot write confusing Web pages, miss closing style marks, or put the content out of order so that it might accidentally be interpreted in different ways. In other words, text must be strictly composed XHTML and can be validated by software tools.

Developers have built empires from simple HTML Web pages, and the tradition will continue with XHTML. These PC-directed pages are large and fancy, using complex features that need a high-powered CPU to present complicated dynamic formats. Obviously, these are not practical on devices with small displays. At a minimum, Web designers are encouraged to scale down XHTML content for mobile use, as they do for a Palm handhelds and Pocket PCs. The XHTML feature-rich language is not particularly well matched for the lean requirements of mobile use. The functionality of XHTML to construct rich and complex pages is overkill for mobile devices, so XHTML has been divided into modules. Mobility demands basic simplicity and directness of information, and the module of XHTML that does this is XHTML Basic. The specification of XHTML is found at <http://www.w3.org/TR/xhtml1/>.

XHTML Basic 1.0 for Mobile Devices

As mentioned, XHTML is a replacement for HTML. XHTML is a huge specification, about 400 pages long. But small wireless devices are no place for overlapping windows, cascading menus, or frames. To answer this, XHTML Basic was defined as a proper subset of XHTML for mobile application presentation, including Web phones.

Figure 30 shows the migration of markup languages, with XHTML Basic as the stated future direction for WML developed by the WAP Forum and cHTML developed by DoCoMo. XHTML Basic does not allow frames, but it does allow simple tables, an improvement on cHTML. The W3C released XHTML Basic in December 2000; it is defined at <http://www.w3.org/TR/xhtml-basic/>.

The new trimode browsers that support XHTML, WML, and cHTML were introduced in 2001 as the Openwave Mobile Browser and the Access Compact NetFront Plus Browser.

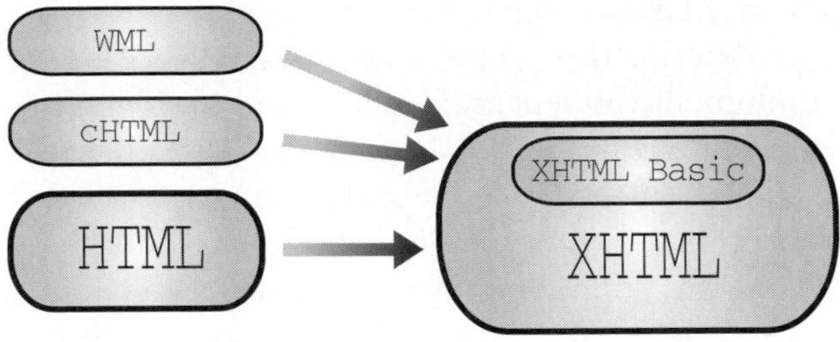

Figure 30 Migration of markup languages

Which Mobile Language Is Best?

It is important to reach the mobile user who sees you only with a small screen. A thoughtful reduction of your content can save the mobile customer's time. Avoiding excess style and useless data also helps users avoid paying for extra over-the-air time.

If you want to meet the market, however, you want to provide your content through the popular mobile markup languages. The majority of U.S. handhelds and pagers are prepared to see simple forms of HTML via Palm PQA. To reach Web phones, 90 percent of U.S. mobile phones read HDML, although WML is coming on strong. Because HDML and WML are very similar and telco gateways generally convert between the two, if you have to choose one, go with WML. Realize that although phone sales are significant, HDML and WML browsers on phones go largely unused.

The world's most used wireless markup language is cHTML. In the fall of 2000, when 15 million people were using i-mode gateways in Japan, only 200,000 people worldwide were counted using WAP gateways.[8] The greatest revenue-producing markup language is cHTML; with Asian exposure, this can be a highly beneficial venture. In Europe, WML is the common language for cell phones. In the United States, it is HDML and some WML. Do not forget that if your application requires signaling, then a large-screen pager such as the RIM BlackBerry 957 might work best. Handhelds and large pagers can download almost any browser.

Finally, there are emerging XML browsers that format displays on devices like Java phones. These appear to have the most promising potential of all because the content is more simply generated, over-the-air data is minimized, and the effort of computing the presentation moves from the server to the mobile device. We will look at programming each markup language and device later in Part II.

SMIL and Flash for Streaming Media

Synchronized Multimedia Integration Language (SMIL, pronounced "smile") is a language for authors to write interactive multimedia presentations. It is also defined by an XML grammar. Using SMIL, an author can describe the temporal behavior of the objects and media streams in a multimedia presentation, associate hyperlinks with media objects, and describe the composition on a screen. SMIL is a language for choreographing multimedia presentations where audio, video, text, animation, and graphics are combined in real time. SMIL enables authors to specify what should be presented when, enabling them to control the precise time that a sentence is spoken and to make it coincide with the display of a given image on the screen. The definition allows SMIL timing and synchronization syntax and semantics to be reused in other XML-based languages. SMIL components should be used for integrating timing into XHTML. It may be that a SMIL "Basic" will be required to perform efficiently over the stringent network requirements of mobile devices. The SMIL Web site is part of <http://www.w3.org/AudioVideo/>.

A commercial language called FLASH from Macromedia does a very efficient job of streaming animations well and is now being made ready for mobile devices. We will look at multimedia applications later in Part II.

VoiceXML for Voice Portals

VoiceXML™ is a global standard for programming voice portal components to create audio dialogs; it is defined by the W3C. VoiceXML is a trademark of the VoiceXML Forum. This language is not to be confused with VoIP, or voice over IP, which is a low-level protocol defining how voice traffic can be moved over Internet packet data networks. VoiceXML evolved from voxML, a voice standard that was implemented by every company in a different way. VoiceXML provides a common standard for developers to define a dialog for phones and specifies the framework for a voice browser and speech synthesis as markup languages. The VoiceXML Forum is an industry organization founded by AT&T, IBM, Lucent, and Motorola. The organization specifies voice portal development standards at <http://voiceXML.org>. The formal W3C specification of VoiceXML is found at <http://www.w3.org/Submission/2000/04/>.

Software Independence with XML Servers

When you manage and deliver content, you want to reach every wireless device without worrying about details. First-time developers as well as major companies have made the mistake of automatically translating their HTML into WML, HDML, and cHTML. It just does not work. Even if scaling down pages could work, the pages would not meet the needs of the mobile traveler. Information pages for the active user are different from Web pages for general browsing. Architects have stepped back to think about this. One chief conclusion is that content should be encoded in XML. From the one portable XML source, an application server can transmit XML or dynamically present the page for each markup language required.

The Future of Wireless XML and Data

XML is a promising medium for the exchange of data. It is an ideal way to structure interactive applications and works as a mobile content language. Used intelligently, it can couple efficiently with presentation formatting on wireless devices.

A person can read XML, unlike proprietary binary database formats; but XML does not use storage efficiently. Since it can represent different data sets, XML schema groups define industry DTD and XML schema that will represent their data. An XML schema gives companies a common vocabulary. Because XML can define raw data without interference from style, wireless technology companies are looking to send and receive portable data in the XML format. XML schema are a useful way to define a data format and exchange data between devices and servers.

Another beneficial aspect of XML is the ability to exchange data with different pieces of software used by different companies using standards such as SOAP and UDDI, which are covered later. The "cut-and-paste" method used in software will get much smarter. Software with embedded XML tags will reassemble itself when it appears in different software.

Wireless XML browsers are an emerging solution. They use wireless XML to exchange dynamic information efficiently. This stream is freed from having to transmit Web browser markup, the standard technique used by Web servers today. XML sync is being pioneered in new Java phone applications that use XML browsers. Official synchronization of XML between the wireless device and server can be accomplished with a new synchronization standard, SyncML.

SyncML

Data synchronization is a key element of mobile applications. In the wireless Internet, synchronization is the process of making data sets on various devices and servers become identical. Technically this is replication, since synchronization is the generation of events at precisely the same instant. But many devices may not be online, and there are many machines involved in generating events that intermittently have to be synchronized. Synchronization has the added effect of replicating data, so if you lose a machine, you have not lost your data; it still resides someplace else. The general process is popular on the handheld by Palm, Inc., with the HotSync® process. Palm also defines a conduit protocol over which programmatic low-level synchronization of the device and the server take place.

Synchronized Markup Language (SyncML) is an open standard defined by the SyncML Forum, which comprises more than 600 companies. The forum's founders demonstrated SyncML working on competing platforms at the SyncML Supporter Summit in Los Angeles, California, on June 26, 2000. A good synchronization protocol permits changes on any machine to be made automatically on all other participating machines. It also does a very good job of resolving conflicts when the same records have been updated differently in different places. Since it is a high-level standard, it can exchange data over any network. SyncML enables synchronization over fixed networks, infrared, cable, or Bluetooth. Any XML language can be written for efficient exchange of data between two points. SyncML can efficiently deal with special challenges of wireless synchronization. It can minimize the use of bandwidth, operate well on connections with low reliability, and alleviate high network latency by submitting only differences rather than full record sets.

SyncML is ideal for exchanging many wireless application data formats. Any personal information (e.g., email, calendars, to-do lists, contact information, and other relevant data) can be made consistent, accessible, and up to date, no matter where the information is stored. Mobile information synchronized with any network can enhance the group value of personal applications with remote synchronization. For example, a calendar entry that a person on a business trip makes on a mobile device is equally available to a secretary in the network.

If you were to diagram devices and servers in a mobile wireless information architecture, then the SyncML data synchronization protocol fits right in. It defines workflow for communication during a synchronization session when the mobile device is connected to the network. The protocol names and identifies records, lists common protocol commands that will synchronize local and network data, and resolves data synchronization conflicts. The Web site is <http://www.syncml.org/>.

The Importance of Being Simple

One accidental lesson taught by Mr. Berners-Lee is that a pent-up world full of content can be released with very simple technology. By contrast, advanced multimedia authoring systems and complex imaging languages like Display PostScript were the rage of the computer industry.

Over the years, the Internet has connected millions of people to leverage collective global talent. People produce and connect with their favorite content. If the Internet is "everyone's computer connected," then Napster, Gnutella, or Free.net have opened some important channels. Willing end users allow their computers to share content and software directly with other foreign disk drives over the Internet. In a mass wireless society, interconnecting new content source gives the network increasing points of opportunity for an "information age." Mobile devices are the moving eyes, ears, and hands of the wireless world, feeding content through XML media streams and connecting to the sources of recently fed content. Over a wireless Internet, we begin to live in a world with *every radio simply connected and every antenna available.*

If we have learned anything about the power of our electronic broadcasting and digital networks over the years, it is that content is the driving force. Content of the network is what keeps people interested, and wireless developers can mediate it. The telcos have a destined part to play – the business of keeping people on the air. Developers' and carriers' viewpoints benefit from the simple invitation to be part of people's lives. The charm of the i-mode view is that it lets the world use all of its resources to produce many lines of content in a simple manner.

Personal Content Drives the Wireless Internet

Wireless devices and applications enable content to flow. The secret of the future wireless industry lies more in content than in any other factor. Content, a fancier word than *data,* and more far-reaching than information, is the digital media that originates from stored or live sources. Most Internet content comes from stored locations on a database or a file system. But content can be originated live from the field, for example, a video stream, voice conversation, or live telemetry from devices.

The key to success in the digital industry is observing the obvious mechanics of the market; content runs on software that runs on hardware. The emphasis on data and not software or hardware is a significant dynamic. Why is the Palm handheld fundamentally unique? Some say it is the specialized hardware. Others observe the unique mobile software. These are both important, un-PC advantages. The fundamental reason that the Palm handheld is unique is that *your data is with you.* In a split second, you take action because information is at your fingertips wherever you happen to be. Data in an easily available, mobile form is the prize. In the wireless world, having your content everywhere is highly valued.

Figure 31 shows the growth of hardware, software, and content in industries that now broadly form the wireless technology market. Content gets to end users wherever they happen to be using commodity software and commodity hardware exclusively designed for mobile use. Hardware is a software multiplier and software is a content multiplier. Each multiplies the number of successive sales of the supported technology by a factor of 100 or better. A simple example of the multiplier market dynamic is the relationship between CD players and recorded discs. Intuitively you know that for every player owned there are many dozens of CDs. Likewise, for a computer hardware platform, there are many pieces of software, and from one email software program, you generate hundreds of messages. For every finished published book, the world produces ten thousand more personal documents.

It is the business of wireless networks to keep people on the air with content. Telcos get to charge them time, whether the transmission is in voice or bits. It is the personal digital traffic over the wireless network that is the prize. In the era of

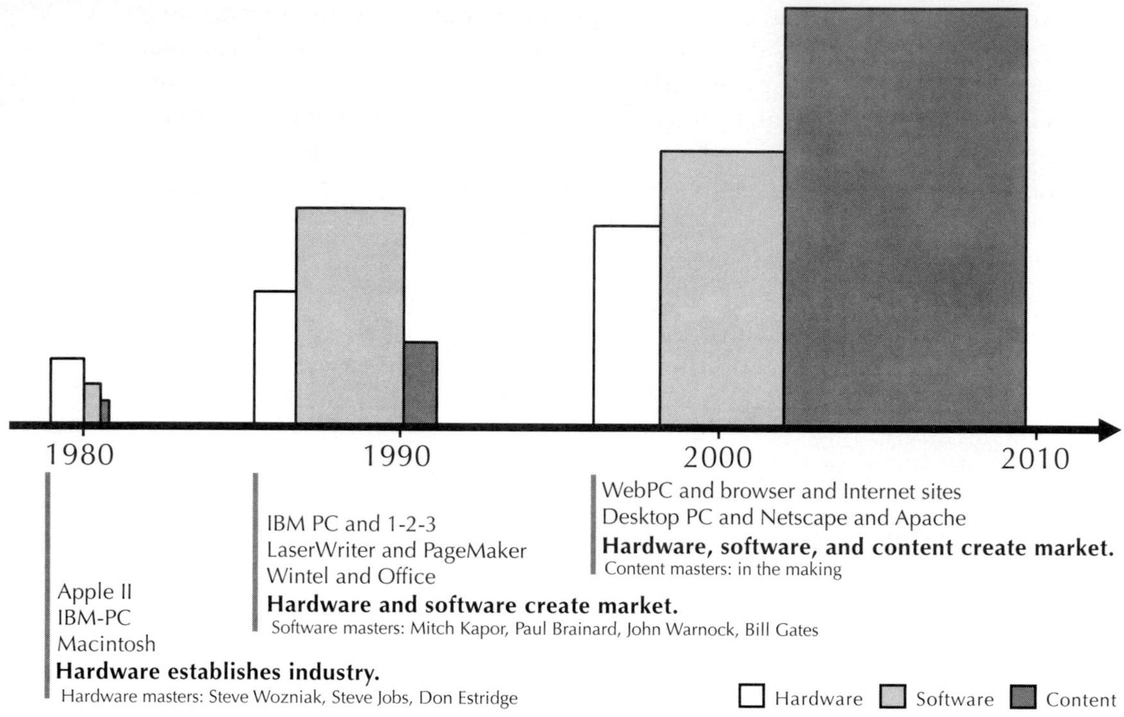

Figure 31 The growth of hardware, software, and content with market leaders and innovators

the wireless Internet, content, software, and hardware sell one another, but the larger capital market is renewable content. The intertwining of all three is now the basis for what might be called the 3G economy; but it was not always that way.

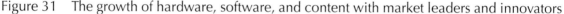

The dynamic market and technology for hardware, software, and content have evolved significantly. In the late 1970s and early 1980s, personal computer companies created a market that stemmed from the zeal of radical engineers in an era of the "home computer revolution." Their "power to the people" mission was to give everyone a mainframe. Hardware can go only so far. Soon businesses discovered that software and hardware really sell each other. So much so that by 1985 it was well understood that the spreadsheet Lotus 1-2-3™ sold the IBM PC and that PageMaker™ sold the Macintosh and the LaserWriter. Those were the days of the "killer app," an application so new and powerful that it drove hardware purchases. The combinations of software and hardware produced a computing solution not available on any previous generation of technology at any price. Dan Bricklin's VisiCalc, an electronic spreadsheet, was a true invention. No such tool even existed on a mainframe. It was such a valuable tool that it was the reason for many businesses to get personal computers. But it took more than software alone.

Lotus realized this, refined the software, and made a brilliant marketing bundle with the IBM PC. The term *killer app* has stuck. The spotlight moved from hardware to software, but the two formed the market. IBM and its continued focus on hardware resulted in loss of significant market share because IBM didn't catch on to the industrial shift to software and PC development tools that Microsoft understood so well. The bottom line is that hardware was simply a multiplier for the larger capital market of software.

In the 1990s, Microsoft developed a market based on standardized software that leveraged myriad hardware combinations. Microsoft Corporation became the software king, supplying the primary operating system licenses and key software applications that evolved into the Microsoft Office application software suite. But the market expanded further and the spotlight shifted from software to content as the ultimate multiplier.

The shift to content happened in 1995 when a simple-as-can-be Web browser kicked open the door with an ordinary method to put anyone's content online. Worldwide, no less. This new digital publishing model used a Web browser to view Web-served content. Web businesses, dot coms, were born overnight, delivering content and services to PCs. Content is now a main wireless focus in business and can give companies better market positions and help them focus priorities on data and information. Content hackers are nothing compared to data hackers. The hackers of content, the new digital media experts, are now at the center of the wireless world's spotlight, as software becomes a commodity and content becomes a sought-after value. The trio of hardware, software, and content define today's enormous dynamic market.

Searching for the Killer Application of Wireless

As the Cellular Telecommunications and Internet Association (CTIA) has said, it is important to think in terms of providing useful services, not killer apps. Some analysts think that companies are trying to relive the early days of computers, to find the killer app and find that powerful combination of hardware and software. But the dynamic today clearly spotlights content. It might be said that the browser was the last killer app. It jump-started the World Wide Web and, according to George Gilder, ended the computer industry.[9]

When people say that the killer application for wireless is email or the killer app is text, or that it is voice, they are right to point out the import of these primary media. But these are media, not applications, and as applications they would not be particularly interesting. As the Internet and even the Palm handheld have made clear, content is the primary value in modern markets. For the wireless mobile Internet, the power combination that defines the capital market is content, software, and hardware. All three are essential. However interesting wireless devices or mobile software may be, they are merely vehicles for personally useful content. Personal content is the prize. Wireless Internet content provides the transcending value that is replacing the significance of prior generations' technology.

Companies that are aware that the success of hardware depends on the success of software that depends on the success of content, and that all three form the wireless mobile market, are preparing new products and alliances. It explains why successful hardware makers invest and provide developers with proper software and content tools. A Software Development Kit (SDK) is necessary to build special-purpose applications inside an Integrated Development Environment (IDE). Developers use these tools to build applications that transform content with the help of databases. Emulators simulate an entire wireless device environment and interaction flows. The far-sighted vendors provide Rapid Application Development (RAD) tools to build wireless applications in hours instead of weeks. The great RAD tools let you form software and connect to live content sources while exploiting the underlying hardware features. All of these tools accelerate the vendor's position and a developer's ability to produce great wireless applications. Successful wireless solutions exploit the hardware and software feature set. Location-based displays, locators, and Bluetooth control devices provide functions that transform the nature of content.

Collaboration and synchronization are key dimensions of mobile data utility. The Palm handhelds have shown the value of this many times over. Synchronization honors the value of content. Synchronization, or sync, has a useful side effect: If you lose a device or a server goes down, the user has a replica of data on another machine. Data is rarely lost – a comforting relief from an era of crash-prone desktops. Some key wireless applications – messaging, microbrowsing, personal management of data, synchronized record handling, and interactive locators – are all vehicles for content. And content now defines the wireless market dynamic.

It appears that content is the driving cause for the success of the Internet. In the wireless Internet, this same content is more refined. One of the key distinctions of mobile content is that it can be location based, time based, and matched to the personality of the mobile end user.

All three – hardware, software, and content – must be technically conceived in a mobile operational environment. Multiplying content is the outcome, the purpose, and the market.

Valuing Personal Wireless Content

Content is the largest digital business there is. For a simple reason – the resource never ends. It is always being updated. Compared to commercial publication, personal publication generates far more volume over digital networks. Wireless content (i.e., conversation, messages, notes, information, and digital media), not software or hardware, is the driving force behind the wireless Internet marketplace. What will determine the value of the wireless Internet economy is not data, but personal data; not information, but relevant personal and targeted business content. Personalization, customization, and individuation are key. Mass-market industries are beginning to be supplanted by highly personalized service-oriented industries. Today on the Internet, people can build their own travel plans, design their own shoes, be their own DJs, publish their own art, and write their own guides. An interesting effect of personal applications is that they often create a fiercely loyal network of users.

As wireless networks are able to carry more bits in the air, Internet appliances such as wireless cameras, Internet radios, and onsite videos will make an ever-stronger case for content as the prime factor in the 3G economy.

Moral of the story: If you want to make it big in the wireless Internet, move into the content spotlight, become a data hacker, and master databases, XML tools, and content personalization techniques. Let content multiply the value of your software, which will multiply the value of your hardware and increase the total value of the mobile user network you are creating.

Location, Time, Personalization, and Simple Transactional Content

Today's wireless Internet content includes maps, voice, images, and animation, yet text is the most efficient and widely delivered medium. All of these media have added mobile-specific qualities. A good way to think about this change in content is to ask, What can mobile users do that cannot be done at the desktop? Creating relevant personal information for the wireless traveler is a useful way to explore the distinguishing elements of location, time, personalization, and simple transaction. Developers need to think like the mobile user about the convenience of relevant content while driving a car, working through the day in the office, walking the streets, being at home, and traveling. Wireless content can take into account the caller's location, time of day, and preferences to show what is around, what is open, and what is interesting.

Location is a unique feature of mobile wireless devices and is becoming a widely available technology feature. Beginning in 2001 and running through 2006, the FCC implements Phase 2 of the E911 mandate. (E911 stands for emergency calls made by dialing 911.) Over this span of time, an increasing precision of caller location must be automatically provided for emergency use. Emergency police, fire, and medical teams can then find and assist people in danger. The E911 timetable, ranging from 300 to 10 meters, appears in Table 38, "FCC E911 Phase 2 calling precision schedule," in chapter 17.

The location technology used for emergency calls was derived from military purposes. The precision technology of the Global Positioning System (GPS) is based on a system of 24 U.S. satellites orbiting Earth. Traveling armies (and even consumers) can receive latitude, longitude, altitude, and the precise time for their current location. Content encoded with these points is said to be geocoded. Precision geocoding is encoded as terrain maps onboard cruise missiles that, in conjunction with GPS satellites, can reach very exact targets. Commercial geocoding companies have refined the database technology for civilian use.

The race to provide precision location technology is on. The smart wireless handset makers and network companies are scurrying to provide customers the best precision location technology. The cellular phone network provides location information. A person's wireless device can certainly be a lifesaver in emergencies. If a person can be found for tragic reasons, then how about reversing the purpose? Let the person find things for festive and happy ends. The traveler may want to quickly find a family member or pass on his location to friends. Wireless applications include locating nearby businesses, directions to destinations, and noting interesting locations on the way. It can be as simple as communicating "come get me here." There are clearly privacy issues because these devices can be used to locate and monitor unwilling or unknowing owners. As with callerID, people will probably be given the choice to opt out of location features.

Showing Location

Many grateful lives will be saved using E911 location services. Although fear, danger, and tragedy may start this location-oriented market, it is clear that pleasure, possibility, and delight are the consumer values that will sustain it. With pleasurable travel goals, the life of the person on foot can change significantly. Using location-based services (LBS), the viewer becomes location-aware of content, as she is interactively informed about nearby targets of interest and their locations.

In Japan, the train system provides a location-based service on Web phones. It reports times, destinations, and arrival status to busy commuters. In the United States, taxis in Boston drive around with digital roof signs that change based on where they are and the time of day. Cabs are equipped with wireless Internet GPS. When they are in Chinatown, the billboards read in Chinese. When it is day, the displays show ads for shopping; late at night, they change to bars and entertainments. Many handheld location applications, such as Where2Go, show where the public restrooms are in major cities. It rates them as well. For whatever purpose, the greater the precision, the better the service. As wireless devices and network services compete for location precision over the coming years, so must editors of content. As you develop wireless content, expect calling devices to increase to pinpoint accuracy in the coming years. If your mobile users can be tracked, give them the power to track. You can inform callers of their locations, show them where the nearest objects of interest are, and compare nearby elements. In order to do this, the content used in location-based applications must be geocoded in a database. Geocoding shows latitude and longitude rather than a street address. This is necessary for giving directions and showing maps. As a handheld

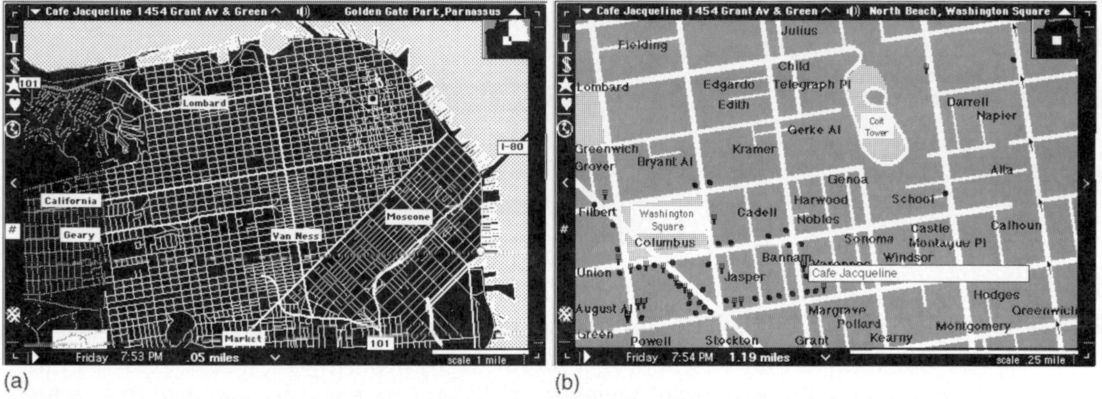

(a) (b)

Figure 32 Handheld restaurant guide shows *(a)* a map with the location of the Café Jacqueline in an area of San Francisco, and then within a minute, *(b)* it zooms into the street on which the cafe is located. (*Source:* Courtesy of Digital Lantern)[10]

restaurant guide zooms to a destination (Figure 32), geocoded restaurants appear on street maps. The underlying restaurant data is geocoded so their locations can automatically appear. The traveler gets their locations from the network or the device.

Showing the Time

Location information often implies time. For example, upon locating a service, it is often important to know when the service is open. Why mention a restaurant if it will close in 10 minutes? Mobile travelers are also limited by time. For example, they need a nearby gas station that is open now. Time schedules are also important. In the old world, it was good enough to post a long table of public transportation. A rider most commonly wants to know, "Is my train arriving on time?" Providing relevant times for events is a subtle differentiator between a good and a poor wireless content service. Although mobile travelers need immediate information, they still need to plan. The large-screen PC is better suited for the many variables in scheduling and planning, but these plans can be made ready for mobile use.

Showing Personality

Figure 33 shows an example of a personalized restaurant guide implemented for bitmap handheld displays. Traveling diners might have their own best lists. In Figure 33*a*, the traveler has requested information on the most romantic restaurants in San Francisco; in Figure 33*b*, the traveler has requested more information about one of those romantic restaurants. There is a wealth of information – general area of the city, street address, the fact that is will be open for 3 more hours, telephone

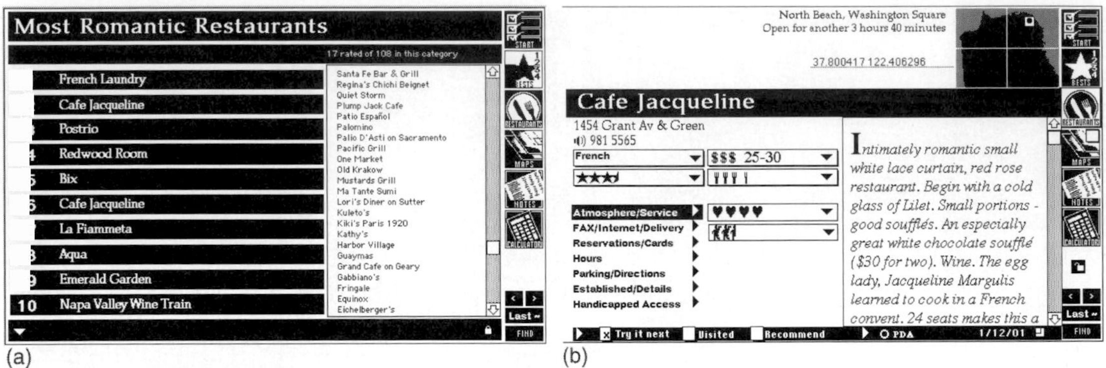

(a) (b)

Figure 33 Personal lists and restaurant reviews: *(a)* The list received in response to a request for most romantic restaurants in San Francisco, and *(b)* specific information about one of the restaurants on the list. (*Source:* Courtesy of Digital Lantern)[11]

number, price range, amenities, as well as a review. A traveler can tap markers that appear at the bottom of the review screen to make personal notes about this restaurant. Such "best" lists can be exchanged and collected. The diner ratings and personal reviews can also be entered. They serve as a private reference and tip sheet. The favorites are social items exchanged at home and abroad, by voice or by beaming.

As the mobile nature of data changes, wireless developers paint information displays with the new pigments of content. For example, you can tell the traveler that a restaurant is "open for another 3 hours 40 minutes," rather than make the traveler work to figure out the information with a conventional table of opening and closing times. As you see in the thumbnail map, the guide shows location. The actual geocode (37.800417 122.406296) for the restaurant is a token piece of geographical information just for show. Key location algorithms of this application and the outline for a dozen more location-based applications appear in "Primary Location Applications" in chapter 8.

Developing Content

The key content engine for a developer to master is the SQL database. Since XML defines portable data, it is also important to understand that language and its many components such as XML schema declarations. It is useful to plan enterprise architectures that use XML vocabularies and spoken command vocabularies used in voice portals. The language for content is captured in W3C XML schema repositories.

After C and C++, the most practiced programming language in the world today is Java, the portable, high-level language used widely over the Internet. The Java kernel operating system (kVM) on wireless handhelds and Web phones and the recent BREW™ application execution environment allow a far richer set of interactive experiences than has been found on Web phones or pagers so far.

Sophisticated content delivery also requires knowledge of application server components that manage users and their preferences. The emerging encoding of the Internet bit stream now consists of digital media stream formats and protocols. In addition to traditional markup languages are the new time-based voice and multimedia protocols such as FLASH, SMIL, VoiceXML, and VoIP. We will see later in Part II that developing personal content requires the construction of a persona, the cultivation of information design principles, and skillful mobile content database designs.

The New Content

Ninety-nine percent of wireless Internet content does not even exist yet. It will be created by the patterns of people on the go. Content developers will create powerful new systems for the wireless Internet industry. Until then, there is a lot of resampling from previous formats. There are many emerging economic opportunities and legal issues.

Today's content was not created for wireless devices. It is often resampled to fit on the small screen, and there are useful database techniques to facilitate this. A good example of this is the widely transmitted *TV Guide*'s national data feed distributed to newspapers, magazines, and broadcast stations. The synopsis for each show is partitioned into four sets, ranging from a full paragraph, to a sentence, to a phrase, to no more than three words. The content is scaled into place depending on the receiving publication.

In mobile environments, the data might need to be processed and converted for use. For example, you may need to recode times for quick and efficient comparative computation; you may need to add specially indexed columns for preference filters; you may need to tag free-form textual keywords to match personal indexes so that the server will rapidly respond to mobile users' requests. To provide proximity services, databases need to record geocoded locations, timestamps, and appropriate personality preference data. Combined with the proper software, correctly constructed mobile content can deliver superior value.

As roving crowds inspect the world with their trusted wireless devices, a change in content service and information flow takes place. The increased frequency of publication and the importance of greater data precision are required to match the values of the mobile audience. People become source points, feeding the Internet with their digital content. They can be included within a wireless publication by an extended editorial relationship with the reporting readers. The network of users forms the base of the application. Group broadcast subscriptions are a popular location-based application for "celebrity sightings" in Los Angeles and New York City. Subscribers who see celebrities submit a text message to the group server. All members get a broadcast message as sightings come in.

The mobile audience is largely undiscovered territory. The experienced ones know what they want, and you must understand and support them. The conceptual model of roving subnetworks of people coordinating and using their wireless devices to discover the infosphere and new aspects of one another is an important piece of architecture to grasp. Mobile users may work from big-screen PCs grazing Web sites, earmarking the content for mobile use where they convert choices to active steps. When they are out and about, they expect a reduced mobile interface to use their content as they planned.

Ultimately, a primary source of content will be the artists, personalities, and other creators of digital content. We look through movies at our stars, listen beyond radio programming to hear personalities, and read past pages to understand writers. Whoever or whatever is at the other end of the wireless Internet should have as rich a human quality as our engineering will allow.

New Spectrum and Capacity Create New Wireless Applications

A massive changeover in wireless technology is taking place. Developers who make wireless Internet applications are preparing for it. Industry and governments are all making way for 3G networks and infrastructure. Using new spectrum and new wireless air interfaces, companies are creating a global wireless Internet of immense power. By 2005, most people will experience wireless connections that are faster than today's desktop connections. The always-on, packet-switched broadband spectrum will connect a new breed of wireless devices to optical networks delivering waterfalls of content. The feeding of the Internet with PAN devices full of personal digital content will form user-driven architectures and new applications.

Internet developers are in a good position to play on the emerging wireless Internet because, wired or not, all content is entirely Internet served. The essential mobile wireless Internet applications are more personal than a pocket watch.

CDMA and HDR versus GSM and EDGE

The advertised end game for the 3G wireless Internet, as shown in wireless data rates in Europe and the United States, is a third-generation, always-on, 2 Mbps, transparent roaming wireless network. It is built out of a backbone that runs Internet packet-switched protocols. While the maturity of European and Asian wireless markets are perhaps two years ahead of the United States, in 2002, U.S. wireless technology is letting all wireless devices make an order-of-magnitude jump over them all (Figure 34). Everyone talks about a 2 Mbps data rate target for 3G, but you have to look at the evidence of chips in production and hardware devices being built. Wireless data rates in Europe and Asia show that the peak rate for

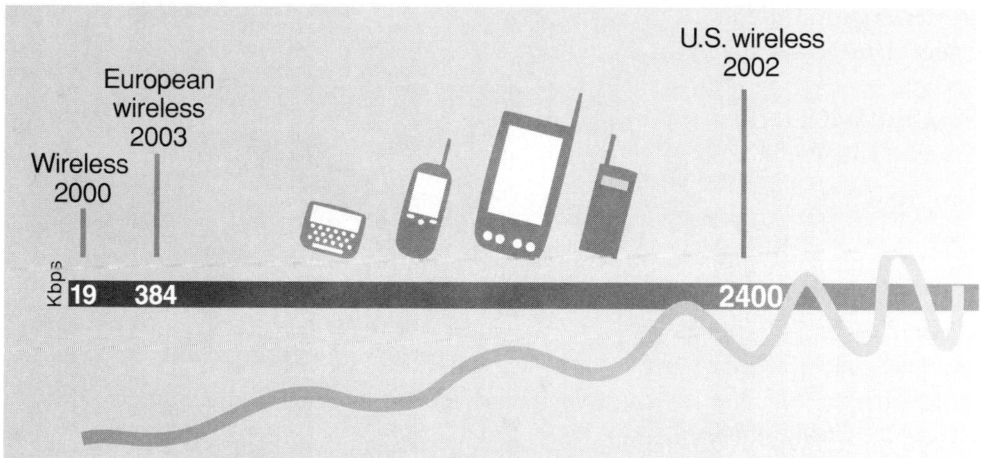

Figure 34 Wireless data peak rates in Europe and the United States

wireless WAN technology is EDGE, which tops off at 384 kbps by 2003. Meanwhile, companies in the United States have completed making chips and antennas that meet and exceed the 2 Mbps target for 2002.

The CDMA company QUALCOMM produces high data rate (HDR) chips that can reach a 2.4 Mbps peak wireless connection. To appreciate how fast this is, consider the fastest personal connection in an office; a T1 connection is 1.5 Mbps. To be fair, these are peak rates. Peak rates are based on one device using the maximum channel capacity. In a realistic test, an average cellular connection "on a good day" is likely to run 40 kbps using GPRS, 100 kbps using EDGE, and 800 kbps using HDR. Also to be fair, your DSL or T1 fractional line generally does not exceed 400 kbps.

HDR, also known as 1xEV (enhanced value), is a packetized data air interface invented by QUALCOMM. Its peak data rate is 2.4 Mbps; an average service load is around 650 kbps. HDR achieves data rates and performance levels that 3G targets, and it can be implemented on top of 2G networks. It is useful for fixed, portable, or mobile applications. HDR will effectively be introduced in 2002 and should be apparent by 2003 after enough EV line cards are in place in the towers. Analysts are saying that EDGE technology will probably take a year longer than 1xEV to roll out.

Emerging Wireless Network Technology

As U.S. 3G spectrum takes its time to come into view, some early companies are using multiple parts of the commercial spectrum, raising their own towers, and offering their own low-cost networks. Clearly, there are too many incompatible air carriers using different generations of technology and spectrum to get general service. But data carriers offer useful local service.

Ricochet MCDN

Metricom Incorporated invented Ricochet Microcellular Data Network (MCDN), more commonly called the Ricochet Network. The network operated with its network modem in select U.S. cities providing a data rate of 128 kbps. Metricom's original data modem was introduced in 1996 and became popular with laptops. The Ricochet network was designed to operate over three bands – the regulated 900 MHz band and unlicensed 2.4 GHz bands, as well as the licensed 2.3 GHz Wireless Communications Systems (WCS) band. As a low-power technology, the microcells operated within a radius of 500 meters. They were typically mounted on lampposts, where the MCDN cells would uplink to their master or wireless access point (WAP), which connected to the fixed wire network.

Spatial Processing and Smart Antennas

To wring every bit out of the wireless spectrum and dramatically enhance signal quality, companies such as Arraycomm and Rangestar make improved hardware, namely, smart array antennas that include a digital signal processor (DSP), which can adapt to the frequency and sensitivity of radio signals and dynamically process the radio spectrum. Rangestar makes custom smart antennas and transceivers that dynamically adjust the focus of a transmission. This is very different from the sector antenna approach used by WAN cellular operators. Smart antennas can also increase the number of callers in an area, permit a higher data rate, conserve energy, and reduce interference. They use techniques like adaptive beam formation and diversity antennas that use a DSP to selectively combine signals.

Older engineers remember the phased array antennas that were used as far back as World War II, which were simple smart antennas. Typical cellular radio stations broadcast radio-frequency energy over wide areas. The only useful part of that energy is the tiny part that reaches the antenna of the cellular phone that is connected. The rest of the broadcast energy is wasted; it interferes with others, limits the number of conversations in a given area, and pollutes the radio frequency environment. The result is less reliable service for fewer subscribers. Much modern smart antenna technology literally delivers energy where it does the most good.

The "smart antennas" are based on a technology adaptive array processing to allow the station to listen to a specific user and to reject other users who might interfere. It becomes possible to communicate with more than one person at the same time in the same cell and in the same channel, just as long as all the people occupy a different space. ArrayComm trademarks this combination of spatial processing and smart antenna as IntelliCell®.

In adaptive array processing systems, a traditional single antenna is replaced by an array of antenna elements. The output of these elements is digitally processed in real time to determine how to combine signals of each antenna element to support a desired conversation while rejecting all others. Instead of broadcasting an individual user's information all over the map, the array effectively delivers RF energy to that user alone; it avoids sending energy to other receivers using the same radio channel. Reception is reciprocal; the adaptive processing system listens only to desired signals and rejects others. The result is the ability to conduct significantly more conversations in any given area in a given amount of radio spectrum.

ArrayComm i-BURST is an implementation of IntelliCell and can sustain a 1.2 Mbps connection, although it can reach 40 Mbps. It is scheduled for deployment in 2002 in Europe. ArrayComm also has more than 50,000 basestations deployed in Asia using the IntelliCell process. Their antennas also support the Japanese Personal HandyPhone Service (PHS). IntelliCell processing is effective inside buildings. Sensitive receivers coupled with intelligent processing can increase the reception range of GPS satellites and terrestrial radio towers.

Lower-powered antennas are the basis of Bluetooth transmitters, and companies like Rangestar are offering a combination WAN and Bluetooth package. Developers can build new wireless applications for wireless devices that can simultaneously use WAN and PAN connections for voice and data applications far and near.

SWIFTcomm IPMA is an experimental network and can reach 20 Mbps. Like any wireless network, it requires a unique built-in or add-on data modem and network of towers. As a new technology, it has limited geographic availability. Unless network operators put up towers to support these standards, the technology will be of little value.

The many emerging wireless air interfaces such as MMDS and UWB that operate on different parts of the spectrum are thoroughly discussed in chapter 16 in the section, "4G, New Spectrum, and Emerging Wireless Air Interfaces."

Software-Defined Radio

It is a wonder that world travelers have any success using cellular technology because there are so many conflicting WAN air interfaces and billing systems. All cellular phones in production today are at least *dual-mode,* meaning they can operate on a 2G network like TDMA at 1900 MHz and when the towers are not available fall back to 1G AMPS protocols at 800 MHz. To help international travelers, Motorola has designed a world phone that operates as a GSM *tri-band* phone. It can offer GSM 900/1800 MHz in Europe and GSM1900 MHz in the United States. It does not use AMPS or CDMA. International billing and calling comes at a heavy price. For example, when my friends from France were visiting with their GSM world phone, even though they were two blocks away, I had to dial France, and we both paid long-distance phone bills to talk. A recent technology called SDR may finally harmonize diverse standards and simplify billing.

Software-defined radio (SDR) chip sets combined with adaptive antennas can theoretically provide access to any air interface and spectrum in the world. SDR is able to download a complete operating system and programmatically change frequency and air carrier protocols. Over a WAN, an SDR can potentially interoperate on any continent. Although today's SDR is meant for a predefined mode operation, it eventually can download new or upgraded operating systems. SDR is both a handset and basestation technology that is estimated to be in more than half of all WAN systems by 2004. A true SDR can upgrade the entire phone operating system and air interface from a carrier network. For example, a traveler dropping into Europe or Asia could have her phone convert from CDMA to GSM or PDC. Where travelers would normally be out of service, they could get a message from the local carrier offering to download their GSM service for their stay. Elaborate applications such as foreign language translation could also be part of an SDR download. This could translate billing rates and information when mobile. Although an SDR open architecture for a reconfigurable wireless technology is noble, the FCC will not yet certify an SDR that can sweep spectrum. The SDR Forum is <http://www.sdrforum.org>.

The Shock of Digital Capacity

With the Internet, people spend more time hitting foreign disks and databases than accessing their own. Optical net data rates and huge Internet data stores are creating an Internet backbone and storage network of extraordinary capacity. *Within five years, the ordinary consumer PC will have a terabyte disk drive.* That is 1000 gigabytes. This is based on the long-standing trend that disk area density doubles every year. Wireless devices will draw on digital capacity using wireless networks with ever more powerful data rates. *Within five years, the ordinary consumer PC laptop will have at least one antenna.* The wireless PC will get better service and a higher data rate than today's wired system. The future proliferation of wireless devices will provide many more sources of wireless content. Wireless streaming media and digital broadband will probably augment, if not replace, broadcast radio and television transmission as we know it today.

Broadband optical backbones handle enormous amounts of traffic. Optical fiber is being deployed at an enormous rate. Optical fiber the length of the United States is laid down every day – over 4000 miles a day. Optical fiber offers the fastest high-bandwidth transmission technology we know of currently. A Lucent 864 strand optical cable is able to carry 28.6 petabits per second. A petabit is one million gigabits. This was the entire monthly traffic of the Internet in 1995. In current tests, an optical 10 Gbps signal travels 3000 km without a repeater using waveguide fabrication of the optical fiber. We cover data architectures to support this kind of capacity later in the section "Heavy-Duty Application Servers" in chapter 18.

The latest optical networks are beginning to use the new Internet protocol IPv6. IPv6 is the base protocol for Internet2 that also goes by the name of NGI, or next-generation Internet. IPv6 dramatically increases the quality of service with error correction and precise two-way timing services. IPv6 is examined later in the section "The Internet of the Future" in chapter 22.

Digital services that are no longer circuit-based or proprietary will be integrated more easily on the new IP-based wireless Internet. On a packet-switched network, everything is bits bringing together voice, email, faxing, and other common Internet services. Transparent roaming between networks is in the cards. 3G wireless networks and applications should integrate a personal lifestyle. Over a long conversation, a person in his office talks on a office PBX, takes a taxi, and arrives at a countryside house. Today this would mean making separate calls involving DECT, LAN, WAN, satellite feed, and HomeRF transmitters. Keeping the billing perfectly straight and handoffs across all cell towers are still formidable issues. Today's devices usually listen to only one wireless network. RIM BlackBerry pager is only a WAN machine. Although it reads messages, it cannot easily read your office email, which needs to be forwarded and have attachments stripped off. When the pager is in your office, the antenna cannot grab the office 802.11 LAN signal.

The 3G aims to integrate all calls in a packet-switched network with interoperable handoffs. Companies like Symbol, Cisco, and Sierra Wireless give wireless devices multiple wireless carrier architectures for WAN, LAN, and PAN networks. Globalstar cellular phones operate over a WAN and a Satellite Area Network. Reading a changing location-based personal newspaper might someday be more than a novel experience. A goal of ITU IMT-2000 and an extraordinary business opportunity is to bring together diverse telecommunication and Internet services into one useful package, which we discuss later in the section "Universal Messages" in chapter 22.

3G Wireless Applications

Abundant storage and enormous digital bandwidth will lead to an unparalleled exchange of digital content. Faster networks increase wireless bandwidth and access. Developers have many opportunities to embody content and create new applications to amuse and inform people. As Martin Cooper has said, "Bandwidth is awareness."[12]

There are many devices to feed the Internet. Wireless microphones, cameras, and scanners are the instruments of new applications. Communicating devices of the future will switch among voice, information, pictures, video, and radio. They set up private digital circuits for mobile users to speak and share information. New devices are used as locators, radars, remotes, and active assistants. World corporations are about to experience disruptive change as developers work to deliver the following essential 3G emergency, professional, and consumer wireless applications that challenge the premises of businesses.

Locators. Grateful lives are saved as cellular phones transmit precise accident locations. Using the same technology, people can use mobile maps as they travel to find locations, locate nearby friends, and keep tabs on the kids. The synchrony of nearness will come from GPS and PAN applications.

Telemedicine. There is a shirt available today that measures 39 vital body functions of its wearer that can be transmitted remotely to a hospital. People can make an office call where all that information is available to their doctor in seconds and that allows the caller to see the doctor's face as the diagnosis comes back. Experts in the field of telemedicine say such applications represent a potential hundred billion dollar market.

Games. Two teenagers on two distant parts of the planet play a game. They have no geographic boundaries, no political boundaries, and no language boundaries. They are playing and they are communicating. The social impact is far more profound than that of simply playing games.

Music and video. When Sony sells a CD or DVD, it is not selling discs, it is delivering music. When that music can be delivered wirelessly directly into a Sony Walkman, it has a different business premise. If you can download a five-minute song in a matter of seconds, people may never buy a CD again. XM Internet radio and Sirius Satellite radio are new digital distributors. Wireless digital video will likely replace televised broadcast signals.

Cameras. Does Kodak sell film and chemicals or do they deliver images? You can now buy cameras that, after you take a picture, allow you to push a button and have that picture, in a matter of seconds, downloaded to your Web site so that other people can look at it. A journalist can download a picture or a streaming video clip directly to an editor so that it appears on a news broadcast in seconds. New capacity digital cameras like the Foveon, wireless Internet cameras from Ricoh and LightSurf, suggest new servers and applications. Analysts expect at least 80 million people worldwide will transmit mobile wireless photos by 2003.

The Near Future of Wireless Technology

The powers of the wireless Internet are about to be revealed. In anticipation of the 3G economy, wireless Internet developers are busy filling the engineering potholes of our times for markets barely defined. Other developers are innovating with lasting wireless technology concepts. The future is arriving in various parts of the world against an enormous backdrop of world 3G spectrum auctions, hundreds of thousands of ever more miniature new wireless Internet devices, and a free-for-all of new transmission standards. An incredible switchover is about to take place. By the end of 2001 in the United States, the E911 mandate accompanied by the recently freed GPS signaling had made location-based services an essential part of any wireless content server. As Web phones become locators, wireless content can play on a new radar screen. A free-for-all in wireless options will be available in major cities at first. All of a sudden 3G wireless cellular networks will come online worldwide, increasing subscriber capacity and new levels of performance by using new digital devices that will be viewed as providing remarkable services.

Nothing will be more significant to the wireless industry than the changeover to 3G, made possible by the new broadband wireless air interfaces and optical backbone technologies. It is now clear that ordinary wireless carrier technology of the near future will exceed the fastest connection speeds of the wired desktop PCs. Transmission speeds are astounding. High-bandwidth optical connectors make possible the movement of large storage to remote corners of the Internet and wide area servers. Technology continues on an incredible growth path, transforming the computer and telecommunications landscape, forever making the Internet a wireless entity. It is the new terrain for wireless developers.

Building the Wireless Internet

It takes computer and telecommunications engineers to build the key technology that make wireless Internet applications possible. There are many profitable and useful wireless application examples already. The United States has achieved technical supremacy in many wireless technologies: CDMA air interface, high-speed wireless data chips, smart antennas, spatial signal processors, and GPS location services. Europe has proved the value of a unified GSM standard and SMS messaging. Japan has constructed beautiful Web phones, proved the essential value of keeping wireless content simple with cHTML, and showed the value of an always-on, packet-switched i-mode service.

This new wireless Internet industry is finding the right interplay of hardware, software, content, and network technology. 3G has to be more than a 2G model made large. 3G is a pervasive consumer opportunity that has evaded the computer industry. The first interesting wireless technologies will appeal to the amateur, the hobbyist, and youth, followed by money-saving solutions that will give innovative businesses an advantage. In all cases, mobile users are the key to successful applications. All over the wireless Internet, they use variations of the key families of wireless Internet devices – Web cell phones, handhelds, pagers, voice portals, communicating appliances, and the Web PC.

Computers were designed with a hard-wired bus architecture. Everything is physically connected. The telco network is rigidly designed to guarantee circuit connections. The Internet was a hard wire attached to a computer to browse the Web and get email. Now millions of people are using wireless services. They want to get on the "wireless bus." The hard and fast telco PSTN wiring system is challenged by a packet-switched backbone always full of bits. The wires are disappearing and computer components, once attached and wired to the CPU bus, are going away. Desktops of icons are being pulled apart and recast as new forms of application and sources of content. Useful components of code and data are finding new purpose in an architecture that is shared and coordinated. File systems store data hundreds of miles away and can be accessed at speeds faster than an attached disk drive over a computer bus. As storage flies out the window, so do other parts of conventional computers and cell phones.

The *exploded icon* is the governing image of the wireless Internet. Devices are being forged to interconnect over a new wireless bus. The technology icon of their former singular selves is being decimated. A PC may no longer have a disk, and, let loose of wires, it may no longer have a proper screen, keyboard, or mouse. Peripherals may be shared across multiple devices the same way printers are shared today. The icon of the cellular phone, a handset with an antenna and keypad, is about to explode. Bluetooth casts the antenna as a shared peripheral, sends the screen here, and projects the microphone there. A nearby keyboard or hand screen may work just fine to control the handset, if there is one. A wireless Internet industry may emerge in which each vendor makes its best piece of hardware. Every scattered thing appears to have one thing in common – an embedded radio that makes it part of a communicating network. The adoption of a mobile wireless bus breaks forever the conventional desktop, enterprise network, and server architectures. This collapsing reconstruction of architecture – the mobile application network of devices – is where we are headed in Part III, "Wireless Internet Architecture."

At the center of the wireless Internet is a content revolution. It is the XML Internet realized with a billion devices times a billion calls as a billion people communicate. Although the future suggests interesting devices and networks, we can learn from the small, widely used wireless work engines of today.

Even if you are not a revolutionary, there is important work to be done. In Part II we take apart some wireless applications and some mobile content, and show how developers build something new, real, and useful for the ever more mobile Internet world.

Part II

Wireless Internet Applications

A *wireless application* is software that runs on a wireless device that exchanges content over a wireless network. The actual wireless applications are distinguished from one another based on the wireless devices, networks, and application families, which we covered in Part I and summarize in the following list.

Devices
- Web phone
- Handheld
- Pager
- Voice portal
- Web PC
- Communicating appliances

Networks
- WAN
- LAN
- PAN

Applications
- Messaging
- Web browsing
- Interacting
- Conversing

It is time to look more closely at wireless applications that perform messaging, Web browsing, and other interactive and conversational functions. To understand which devices work best, which networks can deliver good service for what mobile audiences want to do, and the extra technology that can be applied, it is helpful to see real applications, to consider the thought behind their development, and to learn how they are made.

There is a nearly universal process to develop wireless applications that run on the wireless Internet. The wireless development method we show in Part II works for a 3G Web phone microbrowser over a W-CDMA network, a handheld interactive business application over a wireless Ethernet LAN, an interactive Java phone MIDlet over a WAN, a pager over a Motient network, or even a voice portal using AMPS.

Many developers first think that their wireless cell phone applications have to connect to some entirely foreign back-end modem bank they have to learn about, or that they have to program for some special communications server. That is not the case at all. Wireless applications are generally fielded from the same Web server that PC Web browsers read from. All content originates from the Internet. A Web phone microbrowser fetches Internet Web content that is generated from a Web server. It is the server that supplies the content stream to the wireless application. Most of the development for the Web phone page design is actually done on the Web server.

Wireless applications are different from PC applications in that the guts of the content are expected to reside elsewhere. Standalone PC applications like spreadsheets continuously operate on local storage, whereas wireless applications operate temporarily and connect to exchange their underlying data at a moment's notice. Personal mobile devices often include personal information management (PIM) applications such as address books, contact lists, and calendars. PIM applications synchronize with a PC using a cable. The PC acts as a personal hub to send to and receive from other parts of the Internet. Synchronization can occur over the air with a PAN or LAN, although WAN synchronization can be expensive. Distributing and coordinating data, such as a group calendar, is an emerging form of wireless application. The content may be coordinated with a master calendar server or simply be distributed, perhaps using SyncML.

To learn the process of wireless development, it is helpful to understand the business case. Look for this in chapter 16, in the section "The Site: Wireless Business Models," where we cover the business reasons for building the application. Assuming there is a business justification or motivation, then the wireless device, network, and application must be selected and developed. In chapter 6, "Concepts for Working with Wireless Applications," we show the universal project development process used for an Olympic Event WAN browsing application, a WAN handheld travel guide, a LAN interactive building inspector application, a PAN device application, an SMS messaging application, and a voice portal horoscope application. Each project involves four steps:

1. *Introduce the person.* Start wireless projects by identifying the mobile user. Successful developers take time to characterize a persona, introduce themselves to mobile users, and become familiar with their patterns of work.
2. *Build the content.* Build a database with real content first. Real content that appears early in a project will drive many later decisions. Content is the stuff that users gather, send, and receive. The detailed form of content, such as text or geocodes, should relate to the user persona study.

3. *Develop the application.* The logic of the way the content is or will be used comes next. This involves techniques for creation, access, navigation, and ordering of the application and its content. This stage typically uses simulators.

4. *Use a real wireless network and device.* Exactly how the content is styled and how the interface is physically controlled are refined at the end of the development process. At this point, exceptions are made for unique devices. The majority of text in this part covers implementation techniques for the unique devices of each network.

Often users think of applications by their real-time and offline qualities. WAN-based systems like Web phones require a constant real-time connection. LAN-based systems like handhelds are designed to work offline. Devices and networks give an application either a real-time or a delayed quality. Messaging applications may need real-time connections to be able to "chat." But most people use the mailboxes and answer when they can. Browsing the Web for real-time information obviously needs a connection that a passive offline browser does not require. Interactive applications on handhelds are designed to work exactly the same offline or when they are connected and can exchange data. In conversational applications, a direct call is common but voice mail can effectively accomplish the same thing. To the user, the many timely kinds of wireless connections are all various forms of personal connection.

6
Chapter

Concepts for Working with Wireless Applications

Our working knowledge of wireless Internet so far is a mix of concepts and trends. Trends such as "people will use more wireless devices than wired ones" help motivate and anticipate, but they do not really help us understand the principles to write software or deliver wireless content.

"To work for my wireless company, you should be familiar with these ideas," said the director. From this point forward we add the details of an application to the idea. There are six central ideas we have covered that you should know about and that we will illustrate.

1. *The person is mobile.* Seems obvious. This idea changes everything once you understand it. The wireless Internet keeps people in motion. Once a person is mobile, the wireless content becomes personal. The unique qualities of personal behavior are established in the section "Mobile Users Are the Secret" in chapter 2. The practice is discussed in "Defining Your Mobile Audience" in this chapter.
2. *Six devices mobilize the Internet.* Wireless devices need to be unified from a programmer's point of view. The characteristics of the Web phone, handheld, pager, voice portal, communicating appliances, and Web PC are introduced in "Close-up Characteristics of Wireless Devices" in chapter 9. A server solution

unifies them all, as we will see in chapter 18, "Building Servers and Matching Client Applications."

3. *Four wireless applications drive the wireless Internet.* Wireless application programming models include messaging, browsing, interacting, and conversing; they are compared in chapter 5. Programming examples of these applications appear throughout Part II.

4. *Three networks form the wireless Internet.* The three Internet networks are WAN, LAN, and PAN; they differ in power, regulation, and data rates. The key network advantage is the packet-switched network over the circuit-switched WAN network. Applications are grouped by networks in chapter 4.

5. *Mobile content defines the wireless business.* The value of content over software and hardware is detailed in chapter 5 in the section "Personal Content Drives the Wireless Internet." XML content defines portable data independent of style. Mobile content values of location, time, personalization, and transaction are covered in detail in chapters 7 and 8.

6. *Make location-based wireless applications and maximize mobility.* The mobile person wants relevant information. Developing location-centered applications gives them place and time, and can often be personalized. Examples appear in chapter 5 in the section "Showing Location" and in chapter 8, the section "Primary Location Applications."

Underlying terminology like *Mbps, MHz, 3G, 2G, 1G, CDMA, GSM, TDMA, AMPS* are introduced in chapter 4. The physics of the wireless Internet are covered in chapter 3 in the section "Wireless Spectrum."

Remembering That Small Is Beautiful

Software engineers coming from the world of a large, blazing, color screen, a rip-roaring 80 GB drive, 40 MB applications, and a two-foot long keyboard, look aghast at dim screens of little cell phones, pagers, and handhelds. Yet, how long would you last if you had to tote all that gear wherever you went? In motion all the time, you would appreciate lightness, smallness. Top mobile engineers design small systems, giving users what they want, at the moment, wherever they are. These new engineers live by a different code. Think small.

The U.S. auto industry provides an example of a move from large to small. In the 1950s the U.S. car industry had reached the zenith of large, stylized muscle cars that consumed maximum fuel and had wildly changing styles year after year. Under the hood, their engines needed frequent maintenance. Tires had to be replaced every year. The Europeans brought to market a totally counterculture

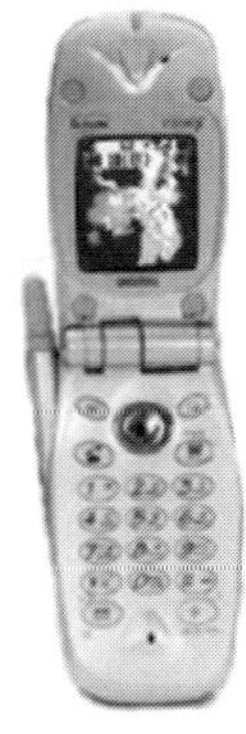

Think small.

It may not be much to look at. But beneath that humble exterior beats an air-cooled engine. It won't boil over and ruin your piston rings. It won't freeze over and ruin your life. It's in the back of the car, where the weight on the rear wheels makes the traction very good in snow and sand. And it will give you about 29 miles to a gallon of gas.

After a while you get to like so much about the VW, you even get to like what it looks like.

You find that there's enough legroom for almost anybody's legs. Enough headroom for almost anybody's head. With a hat on it. Snug-fitting bucket seats. Doors that close so well you can hardly close them. (They're so airtight, it's better to open the window a crack first.)

Those plain, unglamorous wheels are each suspended independently. So when a bump makes one wheel bounce, the bounce doesn't make the other wheel bump. It's things like that you pay the $1663* for, when you buy a VW. The ugliness doesn't add a thing to the cost of the car.

That's the beauty of it.

Figure 35 Examples of compelling mobile devices. The Europeans establish a useful consumer technology as the North Americans produce business systems. The Japanese are thinking smaller still. Pictured beside the VW ad are a Nokia phone, a Nextel HDML phone, and an NTT DoCoMo i-mode phone. (*Sources:* Advertisement copyright © Volkswagen of America, Inc.; Nokia phone copyright © 2001 Nokia Corporation. Nextel HDML phone copyright © 2001 Motorola, Inc. NTT DoCoMo, Inc. Printed with permission. All rights reserved.)

alternative vehicle, the VW Beetle, now revived in modern styling. The original VW was a shocking innovation. The technology changed automotive history and the honest understated advertising campaign changed marketing history. Rather than flashy and powerful, the German automobile was simple and adequate. The engine was the showpiece; it was gas efficient, air cooled, and mounted in the rear. What engineer could conceive of this? The homely VW was the original work of Ferdinand Porsche. His design used significantly fewer parts and simple systems that required lower maintenance than other automobiles. By eliminating the water pump, out went radiator failure. The suspension and tire system lasted an unheard-of 40,000 miles before a change.

Small hardware that runs all by itself is beautiful. Examples of compelling mobile devices (Figure 35) like the VW Bug have very small and efficient qualities. Unlike laptop PCs, the Web phone features a power-efficient operating system that runs for a much longer time before having to "fill-up" with a charge. It knows the time of day and knows where you are. It does not take three minutes to reboot. It is instant-on. Compared to the personal computer world, the wireless Internet is counterculture. It has its own content, its own culture. The vibrant mobile cultures do not care so much about "the Internet" as about utility and information. (Remember the i-mode story in chapter 1.) The counterculture inspires new ways of thinking about the possibility of communication and computation through the guise of mobile use.

When you think small, you make needless choices go away. When you work mobile, you do very specific bottom-line tasks. Good applications operate mostly as a wireless publishing channel. When you work offline and disconnected from the server, your system transparently queues messages and data. When the connection appears, it synchronizes updates, regardless of whether it is WAN, LAN, or PAN. At least that is how the professional systems work. Even system software is automatically updated over the air. Small wireless applications make use of one-click transactions. Ironically, to personalize wireless preferences for their small devices, users often work with their mega-gigabyte PC to set values and get content from large Web sites.

The relationship between the beautiful PC screen and the Spartan wireless small screen is like that between the muscle car and the VW Bug. A reminder of mobile utility (Figure 36) is that technology can be small and ugly, yet very reliable, taking you to useful places. Both the VW and its business model changed the standards of the world automotive industry. With the end of thinking in terms of "this year's model," it became necessary to produce only one repair manual and only one line of parts. This simplified manufacturing, inventorying, selling, and delivery to any place in the world. It was radical. It was simple. It was small.

Companies that took the trouble made a great leap forward with the Internet. The wireless Internet is another opportunity to eventually double the size of their

It does all the work but on Saturday night which one goes to the party?

Once upon a time there was an ugly little bug. It could go about 27 miles on just one gallon of gas. It could go about 40,000 miles on just one set of tires. And it could park in tiny little crevices no bigger than a bug.

It was just right for taking father to the train or the children to school. Or for taking mother to the grocery store, drugstore, dime store and all the enchanting places mothers go when everyone else is working.

The ugly little bug was just like one of the family. But alas, it wasn't beautiful.

So for any important occasion the poor ugly little bug would be replaced. By a big beautiful chariot, drawn by 300 horses!

Then after a time, a curious thing happened. The ugly little bug (which was made very sturdily) never got uglier.

But the big beautiful chariot didn't exactly get more beautiful. In fact, in a few years its beauty began to fade. Until, lo and behold, the ugly little bug didn't look as ugly as the big beautiful chariot! The moral being: if you want to show you've gotten somewhere, get a big beautiful chariot. But if you simply want to get somewhere, get a bug.

Figure 36 A reminder of mobile utility (*Source:* Copyright © Volkswagen of America, Inc. Printed with permission. All rights reserved.)

public. There is special work involved in building the small application, although a wireless application and a Web-based application "can share the same garage." Mobile and wired development have many common engineering properties. To think small, however, companies have to think hard about what functions their users most want and use; companies must take a fresh look at the mobile customer. When mobile people use a computer socially, their purposes are different from when they are desk-bound. Sometimes they enjoy new utility provided by GPS, Bluetooth, scanners, or expandable modules. But the vital beep of unglamorous paged text often brings smiles.

Today's Internet video commercials often excite us to ill-conceived impossible futures; meanwhile the mobile wireless applications in actual use are being produced for a revolution that is not televised. Utility often battles glamour. How could a simple technology like the 1959 Volkswagen succeed against the muscle of Detroit? Volkswagen, with an annual advertising budget of $800,000, faced enormous U.S. automotive marketing campaigns such as the one that spent $8 million in four months for a car called the Edsel. Even with all that "convincing advertising," the Edsel went nowhere. Buyers understood the differences and small thinking prevailed.

Perhaps success depends on how you think about your mobile business. Steve Case, founder of AOL, built the largest media company in the world on slow dial-up connections (less than 56 kbps), which 88 percent of people in the United States experience as their Internet connection in 2001. People find great value in basic technology. Journalists and analysts often chronicle the disadvantages of wireless technology. In their jolly jaded confidence, they assert that people need powerful devices and faster connections. But a shrunken graphical supercomputer with a powerful connection is not useful on the road; nor is it likely to solve mobile problems. It is likely to slow you down. Mobile users need on-the-spot personal information from handy wireless devices. They need less, not more. This is new territory and a development team that is knowledgeable and focused on wireless possibilities can help discover the best purpose of a mobile application.

Much of the world either has a PC or does not need one. Many parts of the world find success in the wireless Internet as smaller, more efficient wireless devices connect simply with institutions that supply content and services. The makers of the technology and the culture that uses it understand that small is beautiful. This direct thinking has led to generous adoption rates in Japan. Must we wait for the gas-guzzling, power-hungry vehicle when it is clear that a small Bug will do?

"Thinking small" is the basis for a new wireless culture that experiences good mobile applications. It finds that Web sites waste time; simple text makes the point; direct personal applications work best; information about location and personalized data is an advantage. Thinking small is about messages and notes, not

Table 24 Features of wireless devices compared to features of PCs

Wireless Small Talk	PC Big Talk
Battery life in days	Power supply in minutes for blackouts
Small and portable	Big and powerful
Weight in ounces	Weight in pounds
CPU functions in silicon	CPU functions in memory
Fits hand, fits pocket	Fits under a desk
Storage in megabytes	Storage in gigabytes
Memory in megabytes	Memory in hundreds of megabytes
Screen visibility, lines	Screen size 19" or bigger, millions of colors
Personal content	Enterprise application software
Touch screen	Three-button mouse with thumbwheel
Small keyboard	100 keys + 12 functions on 18"-wide keyboard
Network always on	Network always on
19.2 kbps or faster	128 kbps or faster
Coverage	
Voice clarity	

email and documents. The wireless features listed in Table 24 are for those who think small and talk small. A typical mobile traveler's feeling about mobile devices is, "The cool thing about my Web phone is that when I get off a plane, it sets the time automatically. It knows where it is. I do not have to boot it up. It does not crash. I can use it in more places than my PC. My important information is with me, as I need it. It is always on, I am always connected, and it fits in my pocket like car keys."

Miniaturization is certainly the key trend in digital device manufacturing. Some say that cellular phone screens are too small. While these developers wait for the screen to come, leading engineers see a minimalist opportunity to build mobile wireless applications that are small and powerful. It is a design opportunity that does not come often. In a small text space, one can communicate simply and to the point of necessity. The challenge for developers is to determine essentially what people want when they are on the go and arriving at specific places.

Experiencing Wireless Development

Wireless developers are quick – quicker than most Internet Web developers. When my business partner Roland Alden and I worked at Metatext Corporation, which made prepress software, we had a standing rule in software development: When you write software – even after an hour of work on something new – always leave your work ready to be shown. This is a great survival skill. Picture the outcome always; never leave a process undone. "Getting things going" is articulated well in the book *Extreme Programming* (XP). XP deconstructs classic front-loaded programming software lifecycles. The goal is to make new technology products come to market quicker. XP authors Kent Beck and Erich Gamma explain the development process as a successive set of user stories immediately addressed with spikes. A spike, a rapidly developed software solution that technically solves at least one of the stories' key challenges, advances a project rapidly. This successive evolution of stories and spikes defines a product by first exploring what can be done, committing to what will be done, and then steering the body of work to a destination.[1]

Guiding the larger project requires great management of resources and timing. Initially the inventor's approach to see what can be made with available technology is to explore alternatives. To reach a large audience, however, many professionals are required to produce, distribute, and maintain a working product. The large-scale projects are similar to a film production model; a script and storyboard plan all the shots so that when the special gear and paid professionals show up they can rapidly produce the piece with little time wasted. Speaking of paid professionals, key wireless talent is required to produce the project and here is the cast of characters and their roles.

Wireless Core Team

Most of the work in wireless Web companies is done by professionals with wireless job titles and task responsibilities. One of the rarest talents that a wireless team manager can hire is the interaction designer (Figure 37).

Wireless team composition now includes a wireless architect, an interaction designer, a wireless client and server programmer, and a mobile content developer, in addition to people who perform other traditional software development roles. Because this industry is so content-centric, an editor and creative talent are also needed to keep people on the air.

A small team has the flexibility and speed to develop wireless projects. Certainly companies have complex wireless projects that require organizing an army of people to build and provision specific hardware, engineer special-purpose software, uniquely secure content, and provide special support and training. But the wireless market has no room for very complex systems that take a year to build. The technology changes are so dramatic that any long-term deployment is likely to mire an organization in an outmoded system. By and large, the wireless market is evolving to allow more of a mix and match of hardware makers, component software producers, and new content providers to work in shorter production cycles using tools for instantaneous distributed change.

Many companies that add a wireless channel to their Web sites get by with a small wireless team, although they can get help from the outside from those skilled in wireless ways. To do a first-class wireless job, your project will require both new and traditional talents. The new wireless talents – the wireless architect, mobile interaction designer, wireless programmer, and mobile content developer – engage for brief periods during a project. The interaction designer should be consulted during the entire process.

The *wireless architect,* also called a wireless systems analyst, is able to assess an existing system and make recommendations about how to open wireless channels. Architects make high-level technology decisions largely based on current realities and pending developments. They keep an ear to the ground for the wireless industry changes coming in the near future. They are valuable because they track the wireless Internet industry and responsibly select a wireless architecture that permits anticipated growth.

The *interaction designer* is the most unique talent for a wireless project. These people are rare and are more often contracted from consulting or design firms. They understand both small screen design and mobile audience purpose. Understanding goal-oriented audience motivations, as well as processes for information design, persona, scenario, and storyboard development, is their specialty. Interaction designers own the "user experience" throughout the project. For wireless Internet projects, they observe and interview real mobile end users in the mobile environment. They are often active personalities, perhaps interested in drama and dance, and are physically available to work out in the field with mobile users. Successful projects allow these professionals to work with the whole team to keep them in touch with end users' needs during the development process. What makes interaction designers unique in mobile design is their understanding of action. They often go outside to work with the mobile audience using devices for their mobile information.

WANTED
Interaction Designer
for Wireless Applications

Looking for a creative interaction designer to work as usability specialist, committed to a career in wireless applications and new consumer technology interfaces. Opportunity to invent new applications involving location-aware services, personalization, time-sensitive and synchronized applications with emerging wireless devices. Has familiarity with Web applications and has designed interfaces for at least one client wireless device – WAP phone, handheld, pager technology in either industrial or consumer applications. Has designed mobile applications for at least a few of the following language platforms WML, cHTML, XML, HTML, PQA, Java. Can contribute to mobile information architecture and take full charge of illustrating storyboards and writing scenario-based narratives. Will construct mobile personas, and have mobile audience-profiling skills. Game design experience also worthwhile. Bonus if you have experience designing Bluetooth, GPS, SyncML, applications or have experience in messaging, microbrowsing, or interactive wireless applications for wireless portals. You will communicate as part of a team with both customers and engineers to explore new solutions.

Figure 37 A want ad for a designer with rare but essential talents

The skilled *wireless programmer* knows client and server development. Server-side work is often done in Java, although a Microsoft.NET language also works for Intel servers. Wireless device programming is often necessary and requires familiarity with the software development kit and language for the device. This can be C++ or Java. Since wireless applications can run the gamut from messaging, to browsing, to interaction, these software engineers usually have a specialty. Messaging requires knowledge of paging, mail server protocols and push technology, and involves development on the server. If the messaging response is complex, then client software development is also required. To program for the wireless browsing model, the wireless programmer works entirely on the server where knowledge of the markup language and the dynamic binding to the database have to be developed. For an interactive solution, programming is generally synchronized between the client and the server. Specific wireless applications require skills such as game engineers possess.

The *mobile content developer* is aware that having your information on you is one of the key advantages of wireless. These developers participate in the information design along with the interaction designer. They can rapidly build prototype databases with realistic content to feed a prototype. Content developers realistically size the data and traffic requirements, generate database schema, use SQL databases, represent data as XML, can generate a DTD or XML schema, and advise how content can be presented dynamically through the server. They are concerned with data synchronization and representation on the wireless device and the server. Sometimes XML schema has to be created, but this requires research to work well with participating companies. Mobile content developers help partition data for partial mobile use. They often have to repurpose databases by adding location, time, personalization fields, or tables for mobile use. Security and privacy issues are also important, often involving collaboration with a wireless security engineer who works on the server. Content experts may also be consulted to make decisions on the sources and character of the data for mobile use.

Finally, for voice portal projects it is important to engage the services of *linguists*. They understand many of the finer issues of listening and speaking. Simple things like pauses, pacing, and diction help make a conversational application work well. If you are hiring, an ideal candidate is a linguist who has programming skills. A linguist with VoiceXML skills fills a similar role to a Web designer with HTML skills. The "out-of-the-box" voice portal uses a synthetic speaking engine. Although it works, it is not as warm and friendly as you might want. If you want to make your site sound professional, you need to hire vocal talent to replace and augment the computer-generated text to speech (TTS), with recorded speech and prompts. You will probably also need to hire a recording engineer and book time in a recording studio.

People with traditional software development talents also take on wireless responsibilities. The project manager understands and communicates the new wireless development method mentioned earlier. Managing the wireless process involves the internal development team and possibly external clients. The process sets the schedule for dependencies, deliverables, and roles engaged in building the product. The manager coordinates deliverables from the development team. Day to day this involves the management of the progression of the mobile design, the implementation of client and server software, monitoring mobile content development, and championship of and sensitivity to the popular use of the new wireless channel. Certainly, traditional engineers are involved in server development and security issues. The quality assurance staff involved with an early view of the storyboard development can be very helpful. They will certainly give important feedback during the many tests and deployments of wireless devices. Developers can use third-party wireless testing organizations to offload the complexity of the testing process. Training is important because much of the world needs education on the limits and capabilities of the wireless Internet. Support is also useful to keep deployed systems operational.

The Process for a Universal Industry

Earlier we talked about getting things going. This is the right attitude of experienced professional developers: Let me at it. But to appreciate the universe, you have to step back a bit to look at how things come to be and how they go.

The fashioning of a wireless industry borrows from telecommunication, computing, and even publishing traditions where creative observations of cliché needs are manufactured into an archetype of utility. Telcos always talk about *plan, build,* and *operate.* Of course, the project has many steps. The "operate part" is new to many computer software engineers. The computer industry is used to construction cycles. Software development takes a project through *concept, prototype, planning, production, final testing,* and *maintenance.* Software engineers are often unaware of the people that actually use what they make. Yet an audience has ongoing technical needs that require continued engineering and development. Typically, when it comes time to build version 2 of software, an entirely new team is formed, cut off from the audience that is using the product.

The product itself has a lifecycle. I think the wireless Internet industry realizes that digital content benefits most from a strong participatory relationship between the technology providers and the mobile users. Telcos know that operation is the critical element of sustaining a business and healthy media publishers build circulations based on an audience that expects more.

Creative and Realistic Beginnings

A great idea or even a simple observation of needs can be the origin of a new wireless application. A playful SMS game, an interactive model of a city, or some utilitarian idea about the use of Bluetooth, voice, GPS, or other technology can spark a prototype that goes quickly to development and production.

Realistically, a project needs a technology and business concept to justify expenses before development can begin. Commercial wireless development often takes the concept or prototype and matches it with a wireless business model. The business-interested developer can study "The Site: Wireless Business Models" in chapter 16 to determine appropriate models. On the other hand, the wireless work may be handed to you via a request for proposal (RFP). This is a commercial statement that frames a concept to be developed, to which a development team responds. Whatever the cause, the project manager draws up a set of product requirements; however, this is often exploratory and requires some investigation of the scope of the project and the users.

During the investigation of project scope, some inspired ideas are generated; however, the purpose in the beginning is to understand mobile user tasks and gather customer requirements. Feasibility is quickly explored and hopefully useful discoveries are made.

A wireless architect makes early decisions including confirming the target audience and target devices and networks, and determining any third-party or internal tools that engineers need to build. They sometimes make recommendations about the process to ensure the ongoing life of the product through operation.

We are still forging a universal process for wireless development. Fortunately, the wireless development method is fairly solid. In the making of wireless projects, the wireless team moves through development phases in a special order.

The Wireless Development Method

The development method is special for wireless projects (see Figure 38) and resulted in very successful, quick production of wireless applications for Sony New Technology communicators and General Magic wireless vertical market applications throughout the 1990s. It involves the following key steps.

1. *Study the mobile user.* The interaction designer identifies and studies the audience. The mobile user drives the actual application with the interaction designer's creation of a persona, the primary typical user, and the scenarios in which the persona acts. A wireless architect then reviews the persona, the potential devices, networks, and messaging, browsing, interacting, or voice applications. The interaction designer determines suitability from a user's standpoint. The architect determines feasibility from a technical standpoint and produces a *wireless application plan* that serves the mobile user, while the interaction designer produces an information design for the content and storyboards that outline the flow of mobile activity.

2. *Create a mobile database with content.* The mobile content developer takes the persona study and application plan to develop an information design. XML

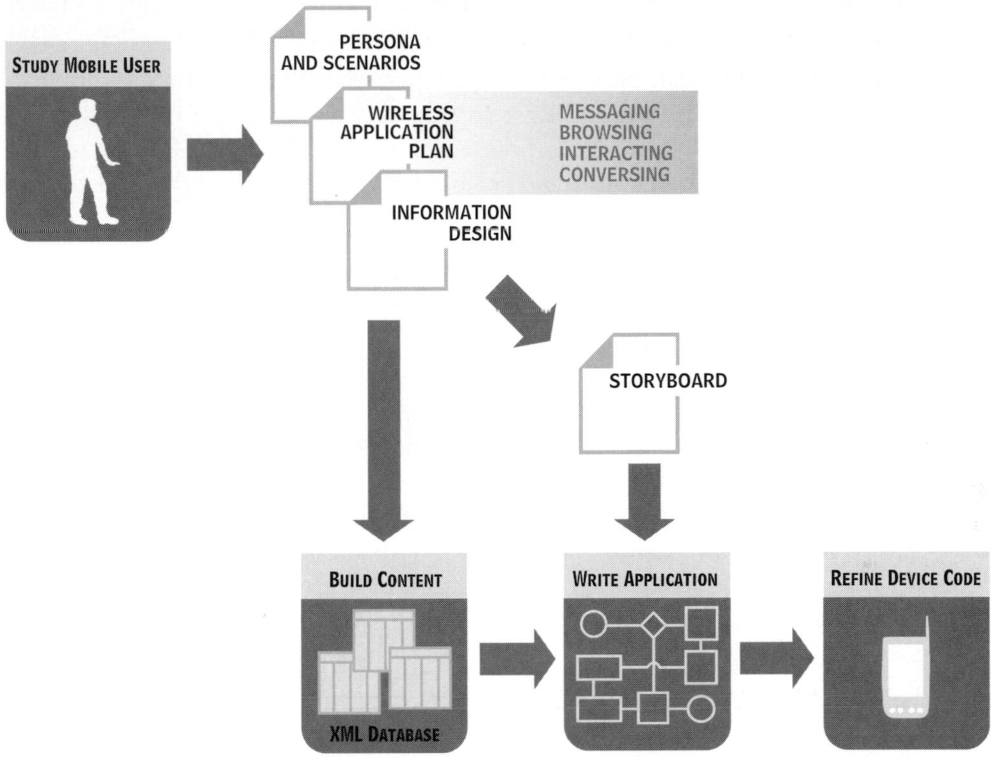

Figure 38 Wireless development method

suitability is examined for both the wireless application and server utilization. Content is loaded for use during early development.

3. *Design a logical application.* The wireless programmer quickly lays out a working model suggested by layouts drawn by the interaction designer. Universal to wireless is the next step. A developer fires up a simulator, builds wireless screens, and codes business logic while attached to real content.

   The major components in the application are:

   a. *Wireless field application.* The primary application for the mobile user on the go is the focus of a project. Many early wireless projects stop here and do not include the next steps, which are necessary for mature wireless applications.
   b. *Back office administrative application.* You may have built an incredible wireless application, but remember that someone must manage the mobile user content on the server. Some engineering thought must be given to building

useful tools with a good interface and to the necessity of administrative involvement to maintain a wireless system.

   c. *Design a Web PC start page.* If it is appropriate to the persona and application, a personalized Web PC start page is added where the user sets up an account and personalizes the mobile application. This can let the mobile user administer the account and set up a mobile site to make it ready for mobile use.

4. *Use a device.* A consumer device using a real wireless network exercises the application. A good test uses the scenarios established when the persona was created. Ideally, the device is put into the hands of a real mobile user who matches the persona. Real content can then be generated.

The wireless project quickly gives you one mobile user, one working database, one application, and one wireless device to show off. But you take time continuing to enhance the content and the application. Unlike most software projects, wireless development often requires quality assurance testers up front in the design process. Experienced quality assurance professionals are aware of the potential mobile audience and help the interaction designer with insights into the persona profile.

You have noticed in the process that the emulators and devices appear later. Ideally, you have an open-ended wireless contract to select the correct network and device after you have studied the mobile user. Quite as often for commercial reasons, the wireless hardware and networks are fixed before the project begins. In either case, a wireless application plan is produced and signed off. You need to know what tools to get for your development platform. Tools are listed by device later. Ideally, each wireless device requires its own storyboard. The storyboard will show how content is displayed and how input and navigation work based on the characteristics of the device.

Wireless Demo

To show the world that small is beautiful, a demonstration or prototype is often required that is the basis for the final application. A prototype of the application, a demo, or a pilot test of a working sample is helpful to establish the working nature of the solution and show this example to investors or participants. This often takes the form of a demo that can inspire the beginning of project. A great wireless demo (Figure 39) largely involves stage production skills. Unlike PC demos where you can use a large projection monitor, wireless demos should move around with real devices and close-ups. It is important to avoid using a device emulator. It is more effective to show the application running with an occasional camera close-up of the real data appearing on the wireless device and changing on a PC "big board." By big board, I mean a large control room–style information display that is being updated in real time as wireless devices make changes from the floor.

The complete business operational plan, completed designs, and a production schedule are required. This happens some time before making a prototype and definitely before production. Just as in making movies, wireless development requires a well thought-out storyboard and a detailed set of working plans. A solid requirements plan and architectural description can save a fortune.

In production, professional application and content teams write large amounts of code and collect or repurpose content. With a plan, teams go about their work on devices and servers, and content is often generated during production. Without a plan, production can come to a standstill as people go in different directions. The software cycle approaches completion with rounds of testing that include ever-larger audiences. Finally, the product can be planned for distribution where any steps for provisioning are made.

- Easy-to-explain overview
- Real devices, not emulators
- Real wireless network
- Active use cases
- Live stage presence
- Big board view of changing wireless transactions
- Serious content
- New datatypes
- Multiple wireless users
- PC Web interface tool
- Elmo or wireless camera for close-ups.
- 5 minutes or less

Figure 39 Recipe for a great wireless demo

Some large organizations actually provision the devices and the wireless service for their customers. *Provisioning* makes available to a customer a tested package including the right wireless device, compatible peripherals such as memory cards and earplugs, the right version of the software, and any account setup. When the customer receives the shipment, it works right out of the box. Wireless provisioning is a large task that can include hundreds or thousands of users each month.

Wireless Developer Best Practices

There is a saying that best practices are used because no one paid an engineer to figure out how to do it right. *Best practices* are professional guides that help professionals avoid doing things that waste time and money and help them produce high-quality products. Recall the wall of wireless complaints in chapter 2 (Figure 10); you want to resourcefully overcome objections of early wireless technology. To avoid those traps during the course of development, experienced developers keep in mind a number of general lessons to improve the quality of their wireless applications.

- Design mobile database and load sample content early.
- Use interaction design to minimize navigation and eliminate unnecessary tasks.
- Use information design to simplify content.

- Use big fonts as often as possible.
- Simplify the content with unformatted text in short sentences.
- Design black-and-white composition first. Gray, not color, screens are the first market.
- Explore mobility. Play with portable information. Forget the PC Web model.
- Identify core business utility and key transactions.
- Characterize only the mobile audience and get early participation.
- Convert all input text fields to choices and buttons, if possible.
- Save the user's time.
- Review for consistent navigation and layout.
- Do not mix interfaces (i.e., voice, gesture, keying text); stay in one medium.
- Allow for misspelled input.
- Make error messages clear, helpful, and actionable.

If you resourcefully steer around limitations and provide a meaningful implementation, then users say good things about the wireless Internet.

Defining Your Mobile Audience

It is important to clearly identify a primary user and the primary device. As we work in product teams, and concentrate on deadlines and flowcharts and build wireless applications with new technology, it is easy to lose sight of the end customer. Although many wireless engineering teams forget for whom they are making products, they have the ability to liberate the user. A usability specialist or an interaction designer is usually in charge of developing a profile of the end user to help a wireless team recognize the mobile user and individual needs.

It is important to feel that you are building for someone real. Andy Hertzfeld, co-inventor of the original Macintosh Computer, suggests that you build something new for yourself first. Care about your invention and think about improving its purpose to give your life advantage. If you take your work to heart, you might actually start dreaming about it, rather than have a nightmare about avoiding it. Pride comes with making something useful. But you really have to take this observation further; otherwise, you will build something that only an engineer will love. When you move to the goal of building for other people, creating something for a business person or an average citizen, it is important to realize that you are not one of them. You need to set someone else up as the model to use your invention in order to make sure you are not just kidding yourself. This model goes by the name of persona. Let your persona dictate the necessities that will be the mother of invention.

The technology and the mobile audience for wireless applications are very new. They are significantly different from what has come before – for you and everyone on the team. A successful practice that informs developers and qualifies the audience is the identification of the mobile persona. There are three basic steps to studying the mobile user.

1. Develop a persona.
2. Describe scenarios.
3. Create storyboards.

From this work, engineers can build products. Jeff Raskin expresses a working sense for mobile usability when he says, "An interface is humane if it is responsive to human needs and considerate of human frailties."[2] Wireless interfaces need to be both useful and able to recover quickly from human errors. It takes a special sense to know how to design so that the right wording and the right functions can be used, and so that recovery from their misuse can be graceful.

Personas

As we have said, the mobile user needs to be defined. There is some confusion about the identity of the mobile end user. One of the causes for bewilderment is that the kinds of users differ with respect to the maturity of the technology. The point of the technology adoption curve is that you begin defining your audience generally as hobbyist, business, or consumer by knowing the point in time of your technology. You apply that technology to the appropriate audience. One surefire technique that clarifies the audience and gives you important development tools is the building of a persona.

A *persona* is a single, concrete characterization of someone who uses an application. There can be three or four of them, but a project always needs at least one primary persona. The creation of persona involves the identification of the typical personality, the writing of a background, a description of characteristics and actions that define the "presence" of the personality, a photograph or illustration of the person, and a "day in the life" of the persona that shows typical activities. This is not a real person, and the picture should be anonymous. It is important that this persona be introduced without explicit reference to your proposed technology. Later in scenario writing, we envision the persona using the wireless technology.

The invention of a "wireless mythology" of a mobile user performing actions is the art of building personas and scenarios. The persona's spirit lives throughout the project. Once a persona is defined, traditional development questions are often resolved by simple reflection and discussion, and answers to the question, "Would Maria (the persona) like this feature?"

An interaction designer is usually in charge of constructing personas. A brief persona description and sample scenarios together guide the wireless project during design and development and are often delivered to a client along with the design deliverables.

A persona is not a real person but a specific characterization of a class of people and their usage patterns for a particular application. A persona must be embodied in a realistic depiction, however. For your wireless application, personas become invocations of the use. They can inspire team members who are often energized by the mascot mythical figure while the project is being developed. This hypothetical mobile user is the result of a merged set of demographic identities for which you build the wireless application. Once constructed by the interaction designer, the persona provides a realistic quality for the wireless team and the client. A persona, although fictional, has a realistic personality. At a minimum, the profile for the persona should have:

Figure 40 "Maria King" persona. (Photograph by Mark Beaulieu.)

- *Name:* Maria King
- *Title:* Senior Account Executive, Navco Manufacturing
- *Picture:* See attached (Figure 40).
- *Biography:* 32 years old, MBA, mother of 2. See attached.
- *Personality:* Likes profession. Reads *WSJ*. See attached.
- *Goals:* Gain corporate visibility. Improve abilities. Show bottom-line value of all technology.

A short one- or two-paragraph biography for the persona is important. The first paragraph of a persona introduces the person and his or her life, without reference to your technology. It is fair to say that in the early phase of the wireless industry, no one really knows the fundamental qualities of the brand-new technology or what the mobile user wants.

Goals and Tasks

Goals are key elements of personas. Goals spring from the persona's identity. Goals are personal and often embrace professional objectives. Once goals are stated, a design team can help the end user achieve them. It is part of the fun of the mobile design challenge. One look at military wireless mobile goals can be an eye-opener.

Soldiers who use mobile wireless technology have very definite goals. Recently, the U.S. Defense Advanced Research Projects Agency (DARPA) sponsored the development of the Situational Awareness and Information Management System (SAIM). The system feeds wireless battlefield data to soldiers. The program is intended to create an "information bubble" to serve soldiers in action. "On the battlefield, you don't have time to browse," stated Prasanna Mulgaonkar, SRI International lab center director on the project. He stated there are four fundamental issues that a soldier wants to know at all times:

1. Where are my buddies?
2. Where am I?
3. What's going on?
4. What do I do next?

The litany of mobile battlefield goals of a soldier transcribes to civilian activity. The coordinated needs of a mobile field force often have the same goals. Everyone needs location and direction.

The needs of a person on the go are certainly different from the person sitting at a desk. The early success of the Palm handhelds largely comes from the company's respect for the fundamentally different needs of the mobile user. Therefore, when developing wireless projects, think of the persona as the spirit that builds your application. You write the code, modify content, and deliver the service to this persona. Working for the mobile persona and being in touch with his or her content is how great applications are written.

It is likely that each of your projects will be for a different kind of end user. The personalities change from the experimental technical crowd, to the ordinary business professional, to the liberal early consumer, to the easy-going mass population, to the late-adopting conservative where nothing can go wrong. Development teams that go to the trouble of defining mobile personas often find projects exceed the project's stated goals. The design firm Cooper Interaction Design makes a very strong practice of goal-oriented design. Its site is <http://www.cooper.com>.

Studying Persona

Look forward to starting new wireless projects with one mission. Find the elusive mobile personality in the act of achieving goals. Like a detective, you observe and write down notes about real end users as they complete central tasks. You want to distill the successful qualities of this persona. Tasks can be derived from goals, and are prioritized by them as well. Mobile users are the true clients. A good way to begin is to become familiar with customer demographics. Read users' letters and understand surveys to get an idea of the baseline of the audience. Notice their jargon, their interests, their short-cut notations, their language, their imagery, their concerns, their intent, and their goals. Pay attention to their words and the order in which they do things. Observe their locations, time-sensitive needs, and personal activities. You will see a real difference between building for an installed PC base and building for a new pool of mobile users.

The investigation of the persona often requires interviews. Here are some key questions that are answered in this book: What content interests your audience? How dynamic is this content? Does it require heavy user interaction? You also want to find out when and where they will use the data. Are they at home, at work, traveling for business, or on vacation? You also need to determine the networks that are available geographically. Will the audience remain in a specific area or travel among regions? If they are traveling, what networks are available at home, at the destination, and en route? All these questions were answered for the Nokia mobile user study in chapter 1 in the section "European Wireless Banking."

You want to get a broad feel of the user base to characterize audience by their personas. Understanding identities and personas is key to giving your product personality and purpose. If you do so, your product may not work for everyone, but it certainly will work for these people. You should collect the few key personas you need, but you and your team then need to reduce the collection to one primary and no more than two, possibly three secondary personas. Over time, the persona study will become your jargon, your notation, your language, your imagery, your concerns, and your goals.

Your job is to create a purposeful network application for personas. Once you have identified them, you put into place the simplest mechanisms for the persona to achieve his or her goals. Beyond the generic persona, you can add customization to help end users designate their identities. People signify their personalities with the details of content and you can often take advantage of local time and physical location.

Although it may be fine to think of your end user as a consumer, that is not enough definition to guide your application. You need to come out of the fog of marketing demographics and into the light of a crisp characterization. You may need a skilled writer to help you write a simple narrative. A persona needs enough detail so everyone has a feeling for this person. Turn the average mobile corporate user into Maria King, Field Account Executive for Navco Manufacturing. Her goal is to be visible in her large company and her tasks are to keep its customer banking networks operational and give the best service she can. She covers the San Francisco Bay Area field accounts for the ATM line of her banking products and services. She spends most of her time upgrading network products. She is also mother of two and has a Web phone to keep in touch with the family as well as get updates from the field as schedules change. She cares that her phone is dependable and keeps her in touch reliably. She turns off her phone so as not to be disturbed. Between meetings she checks voice mail, completes decisions with the company messaging system, and sets up her meetings for later in the week.

For vertical market handhelds, your average field professional becomes Bob Hurley, Field Service Technician for Aimless Networks. His goal is to be a productive installer and not work overtime so he can enjoy his family life. He drives a company Ford van six hours a day managing work, taking a regular lunch, and getting back to the family for dinner. He installs six network converters a day and uses his phone sometimes to borrow inventory from nearby drivers. He uses a truck-mounted detachable handheld that has voice. He checks off his installations and when he docks his device, it automatically recharges and updates the dispatch list after every call, alerting him only if a change to schedule takes place.

You will make discoveries as your personas teach you what works and what does not. Users think in terms of the problem that they are trying to solve, and not in terms of how to use the tool to solve the problem. The best tools are transparent to the users. Whenever users have to stop to figure out how to use the tool, they get sidetracked and frustrated, forgetting the problem they are trying to solve. Having an eye out for the customers as they go wireless with your application, you can often observe common patterns of use. With willing users, you can explore with them how best to save time. As much as possible, reduce instrumentality, and cut out what you can. Observe user repetition, what they consider as favorites, and come up with ways to "remember repeated patterns." There are obvious points in software where users should not have to type in information that is well known. Make capsulated "one click" buttons of operations. Streamline steps. If choices get too complex, consider laying them out on a Web site for customer preselection before going mobile. This is a successful strategy of the mobile portals from Oracle or Yahoo!

The Finer Points of Persona Development

Focus groups that look at a project after release often reveal that technology was not being sensitive to real users in the first place. Sometimes focus groups are needed, but try to avoid them. Instead, do your real user focus work up front. Again, before any development, be sure to model users as personas. Two major qualities come to mind in defining your audience – strength of nerve and strength of imagination. It is easy to be overwhelmed when you observe so many mobile users, work with differing client personalities, and are busy developing your team's various technical and creative talents. It takes a lot of energy and inspiration to conduct the development process. Even with great ideas, you have to make hard decisions to be productive. Be bold; have no fear. Conventional wisdom often fails to exploit new technology. It is important to either inculcate creativity yourself or have trusted people on your staff who are tuned into the shape of things to come. Insensitivity to the imagination of your audience is a cause of many lost opportunities.

You should get to know your audience. You may know that you will support active interfaces and construct direct designs. But personal detail is helpful. Begin by reading client demographics, users' letters, and surveys. Understand identities and personas so you can get a feel for the breadth of your solution. Read their jargon, write their notation, use their imagery, and live in their world enough to sense their needs. Meet real users and profile their goals to help characterize the audience as personas. You want to have a real "Maria King" tell you how doing some wireless task truly saves her time. The motivation is not so much to help you figure out an engineering solution, but to put you in a position of continually feeling good about helping people live better lives. In any case, field testing an application and noting actual behavior are great tools for identifying possible usability improvements and alternatives that improve an application. For more information on this subject, see the section "Demographics, Profiles, Personas, Identities" in chapter 21.

Voice Portal Personas When it comes to developing voice applications, the persona study does not change. However, it is worth noting the points in the persona's life where he or she has time for conversation. Voice portal applications can start as dialogs outlining subject and flow. Later, refinements for natural speech and alternative forms of dialog can be developed. As mentioned, linguists are very useful in the refinement of the project.

Using Professionals as Personas and in Your Project The ability to rapidly construct meaningful personas and useful scenarios is as important a resource to a wireless project as a good engineer. If you can hire an interaction designer or a design firm, they will save you a fortune in downstream project expenses. Although most of their work is done up front, having an interaction designer and project manager advocate the personas and their needs during the course of development can short-circuit many "misinformed" engineering decisions. Beyond personas is reality. If you do not have an interaction designer for persona creation, because having a full-time person may not be cost effective, it may be useful to contract for this service. Useful examples of persona development appear in chapter 9 of Alan Cooper's book *The Inmates Are Running the Asylum.*[3] To help you learn from actual users, quality assurance experts provide excellent end user feedback. Employing seasoned quality assurance professionals early in new technology projects can also be very helpful. Usability experts sometimes apply sophisticated techniques to verify their interfaces, as we discuss in the section "Measuring Interfaces" in chapter 21.

Relevant Content Personas may want personalization, locality, and time relevance, but they always need a navigation model that makes sense to their world. A multimedia interface designer once designed a kiosk interface that would present a library of fish to fishermen. She came across an idea for a conceptual model by observing her audience. Every fisher knows that fish are drawn to favorite stream locations – fishing holes. She used the fishing hole as a navigational and retrieval model. The kiosk was very popular. Unfortunately, thoughtless models are easier for careless engineers. I am thinking of a wireless traffic-reporting system. A group was given the goal of providing mobile traffic reports to wireless WAP commuters. The engineers simply took the traffic streams and presented the entire list of bulletins for the audience to browse. The engineers did their job and in record time. But this delivered only raw content from a traffic-monitoring agency. The content did not match the world of the driver. Without thought given to organization and relevance, the content will not find its target. Drivers had to repeatedly find what was in their area by accessing bulletins to see if the areas they were traveling through were mentioned. This wireless service was too much work for a driver and had no mobile following. The solution needed a more personal model based on the driver's world. If content is to be valued for being location-based, time-sensitive, and personalized, then how better to find out what this means than by spending time with the people who use it and care about it?

Creating Scenarios

A *scenario* is a concise description of a persona using technology components to achieve a goal. The scenario considers how the mobile user handles the hardware, how the application is operated, and how the content is used. There are at least two primary types of scenarios to consider: the daily use case and the necessary use case.

Daily Use Case Scenarios

It is important for a team to list all the possible requirements for a product, but the chief focus should always be on the central actions the person is doing with this product most of the time. Functions that are used every day should be handy. Products often make the mistake of providing all the possible functions up front. If many daily operations are used, then design a progressive disclosure of functions. Hide away the sometimes used functions, but put the most used information and functions in a space that is easy to get to. Signify location, time-relevant, and personal needs. Define where and when the application is used. Observe people acting out their data. Europeans have done a stellar job of this. By doing more with less you can see successful WAP and i-mode applications where the user moves from an airport to a taxi to a hotel – checking in, planning an evening, and so on. This solution can involve related wireless companies, for example, those that complete wireless transactions.

What a person does most often in a wireless application should be presented foremost in the interface. Making phone calls or reading email is a common wireless activity. Supporting the most needed functions is a primary design task in building the wireless application. Reading a daily use case scenario, one should easily see the most used functions actually solving the persona's goals.

Necessary Use Case Scenarios

As mobile users need less-common features, you provide them in a place that is not on the main path of choices in the interface. Complexity is best progressively disclosed to the user. For example, reading email is on the main path because it is used every day. Replying to email is on the main path. Composing email is not on the main path. This capability should be a short step away from the main path so it can be found and used when needed. The users should be able to figure out how to do it without external help from other users or manuals.

When composing a scenario, meet real users and profile their goals. Use their language. Learning from this approach means moving around while using actual wireless phones, not simulators.

Creating Storyboards

With the scenarios in hand, and sometimes with a conceptual sketch from the wireless application plan, and an information design outline, an interaction designer can draw a storyboard. A storyboard diagrams the entire story of use, one screen at a time, and shows the display, navigation, and interaction for the wireless device. There are three things to keep in mind: the mobile user conceptual model (process), the display the user sees (output), and the command system through which the user operates the system (input). The screens are laid out in order, with navigational options indicated.

Getting to know your eventual user is the essential beginning of storyboards. It is also worth consulting a wireless architect who can illustrate the general sequence of use for a wireless device and network model that will fit your case. Complex wireless projects have multiple storyboards, but it is best to focus on the storyboard for one primary wireless device. When you get more experience, you can consider the major and minor devices – the primary work going into the PC that has a high screen density and a pointing device and the mobile screens that have low screen density and some standard command buttons. As you will find out, presentation, input, and navigation vary greatly among mobile devices.

Figure 41 shows the storyboard for WAP email application login, including the key navigational Web phone screens. At Lutris Technologies, where this application was made, the storyboard was taken from a high-level site map that outlined the pages that would appear within the WAP email system. Note how attention in this storyboard is spent not on graphics and colors, but on fields and links.

Tools for creating this storyboard could be PowerPoint™ or Visio™, which let you rapidly lay out the text and graphics of the application. PowerPoint is useful because you can embed fields and links to simulate the application.

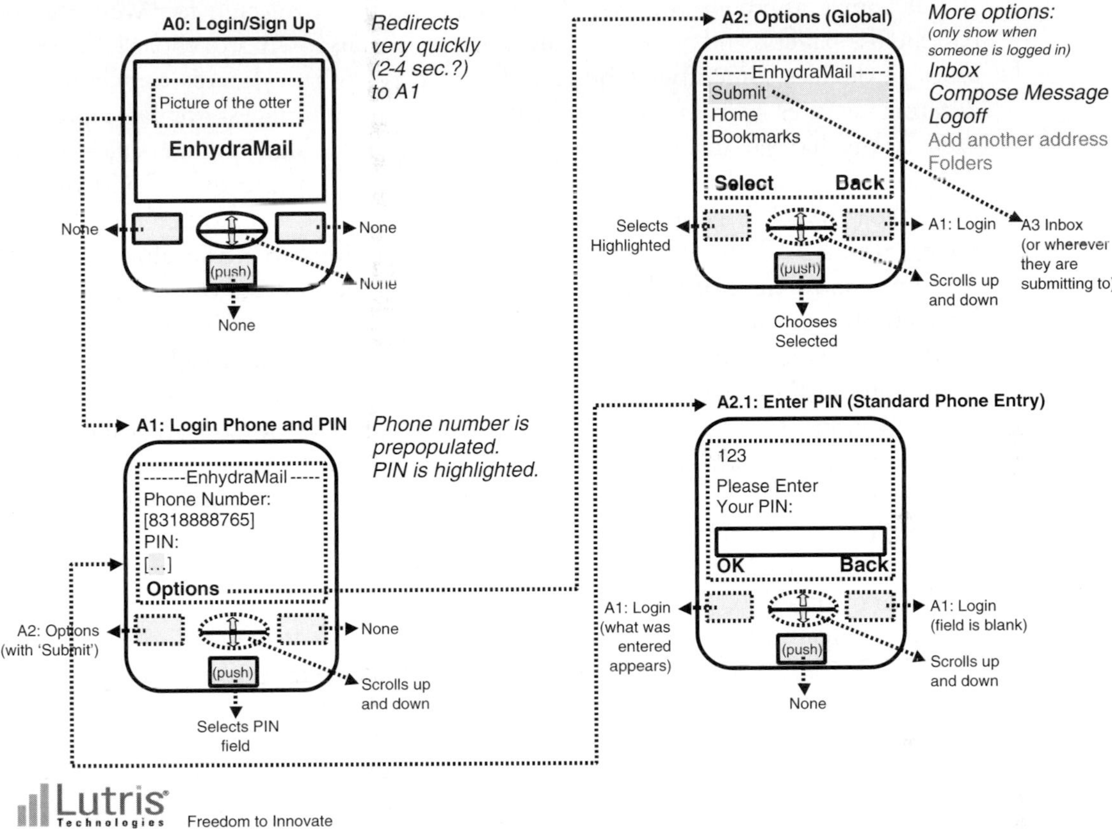

Figure 41 Storyboard for WAP E-mail application login (*Source:* Lutris Technologies, Inc. Reprinted with permission.)

Activity Diagrams with Storyboards

A PC-style storyboard approach is often a problem. Mobile users do not like to navigate hierarchies. They are used to a flow of control. To help advance storyboard design, developers often provide activity diagrams for the mobile user application, as shown in chapter 21, Figure 109 "Activity diagram for a wireless location application."

A wireless system can require two storyboards – one for the mobile field persona and one for a business console persona. The console provides means to administer the account, set up personalization, or prepare content for mobile use. The administrator usually needs only an HTML PC screen. The mobile user clearly needs a storyboard for mobile use. He or she may also need an HTML PC screen to set up mobile preferences.

Of course, there are four wireless mobile families to design for: Web phones, handhelds, pagers, and voice portals. Each needs its own storyboard. Different types of devices sometimes require different types of storyboards to accomodate different features such as screen size, functions, and interfaces. For large projects, each family has variants; for example, a Web phone design is necessary for both WML and i-mode. But the best strategy is to focus on one device and make it work well first. The general navigation can be transposed to other mobile platforms, although there are many fine-grained decisions to make along the way. You must show the primary distinctions of the wireless device on its storyboard.

Web phones can do HTML and handhelds by Palm can do WML, so decisions need to be made up front about appropriate markups and approaches. Ultimately, it is less about the language you use for your device and more about the presentation and input. The plan and the storyboards must be definitive. To reach a truly global audience, you will have to design custom presentations for the families of devices. For an American audience, a PQA is often the best answer, especially if the application is complex and requires a lot of user interaction. For the Europeans, the solutions are more often SMS and WAP.

A handy usability statistic is, the maximum tolerable wait time for a mobile device is one-third of what people will tolerate for a PC. When the user is in motion, responses must come quicker. And a skilled wireless designer will make some decisions to decrease the number of steps. Of course, more steps will be eliminated in testing. Storyboards can go through a round of "paper testing," a practice of quality assurance personnel who take each scene and run it before potential users to evaluate flow and consistency. Storyboards finally go to the engineering team to implement.

Location-Based Scenario

The Wayfinder Scenario (Figure 42) is another example of persona development. Passing through airports, people often have difficulty finding the services they need. The availability of these services, as well as how to get to them, is not obvious. Enter our new persona, Angela, a 31-year-old public relations consultant who is based in Los Angeles, but who has to travel during the week to visit customers. Her *goals* are to be on time always for client meetings, to travel without hassle, and to not feel stupid. Her *scenario* is: Angela is on her way to Seattle and has a 30-minute layover in an unfamiliar airport. She wants to grab a cup of coffee before she heads to her connecting flight. The storyboard shows that on her handheld, Angela uses the list screen to look up the service she wants (Figure 42, board 1). After choosing a service, Angela sees the map screen (Figure 42, board 2), and

After Angela arrives, the airport map and service details are downloaded to her PDA via a wireless local area network. Angela quickly finds her favorite coffee shop in the list.

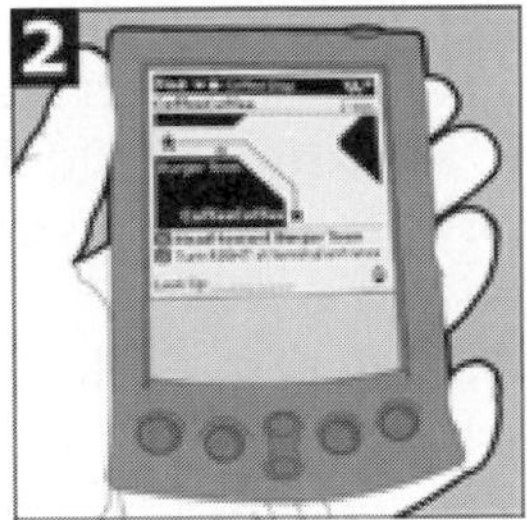

The Wayfinder shows Angela the nearby coffee shop and exactly how to find it with handy landmarks indicated on her map.

Angela follows the directions the Wayfinder gives her, and successfully finds the coffee shop. Soon she enjoys a double-tall, fat-free mocha latte grande.

Figure 42 The Wayfinder Scenario (*Source:* Courtesy of Cooper Interaction Design, Inc.)

then a close-up of the map (Figure 43). It shows her position, her destination, and major landmarks on the way. She can navigate by looking at the map or by following the simple directions to her destination (Figure 42, board 3).

The Wayfinder's design can be validated against Angela's goals. To meet Angela's goal of getting to her meetings on time, we made the Wayfinder interface simple and quick to use, with only two screens. To help her travel with as little hassle as possible, the Wayfinder includes a complete service database of the airport she is currently visiting, with reliable directions and information. Note the critical role of content to this application. To ensure that Angela never feels lost or confused, the idioms of the Wayfinder interface are familiar, consistent, and easy to use, even in an unfamiliar airport. The Web site for the continuation of this scenario is available at <http://www.cooper.com/concept_projects.htm>.

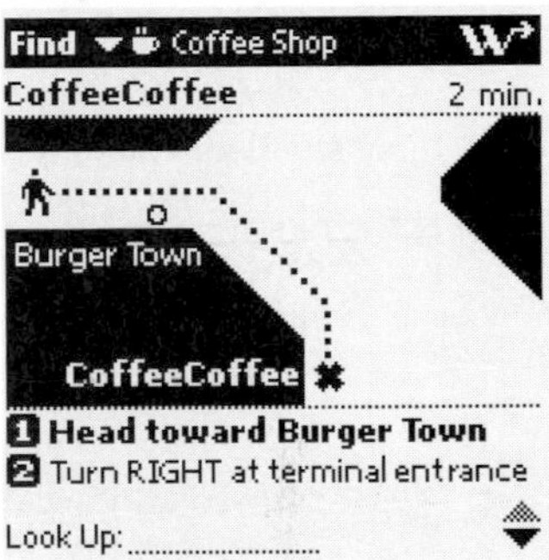

Figure 43 Wayfinder close-up of Figure 42, board 2 (*Source:* Courtesy of Cooper Interaction Design, Inc.)

Using the Wireless Application Plan

If your team is new to wireless development, then a short conceptual sketch showing all the wireless components can help everyone out. This *wireless feasibility study* is usually made by a wireless architect or an experienced engineer. They know the correct notation and familiar text. The conceptual diagram illustrates the mobile user, wireless devices, wireless networks, a server, and content sources. It shows everyone a first idea of overall use – the flow of the application and the content movement, as well as a sense for the number of devices to acquire for development. General drawings of both the end field use and the administrative operations should be made. The conceptual diagram is brief. The conceptual diagram is not the "day-in-the-life" scenario, but a quick technological explanation of the system. It illustrates general operations and serves as an overview within the wireless architect's *wireless application plan*.

The wireless architect formalizes all parts of the feasibility study. While the storyboard writer will refer to the study, the wireless architect refers to this diagram and adds the correct layers such as the details of security or synchronization. The architect further illustrates how actions originate and responses are generated. As an alternative to the narrative text in the feasibility study, a timing diagram can show how data moves through the system over time.

When you are starting a wireless project, it is important to understand what you will use. A wireless application plan includes the special qualities of the primary device hardware, the presentation and interactive parts of the software, the specific wireless network, the nature of the data, a solution for how the content is to be used and managed, and the software tools you will use.

The network for the wireless application and its mobile database require construction notes because they must work together. As we will see in the coming chapters, the approach you need to take when developing for a WAN network is considerably different from the approach you take when developing for a LAN network. The wireless network protocols require different efforts to handle data and ensure security. The Web phone handset requires constant connections and has a much more compact interface, providing for greater mobility and lighter content. It deserves a direct and simple interface access. LAN devices are much more like computers, have greater capacity, large screens, and high data exchange rates, and can work offline.

Sometimes with your wireless application plan you can invent wireless applications, at other times you are responding to the market. Regardless, the application must match the maturity of your audience. Recall the technology adoption curve in chapter 2 (Figure 9). Applications historically mature with the declining technical sophistication and increasing service expectation of the audience. An early market application such as a youth portal makes sense. Early vertical market businesses match individuals with directed purposes. The quality of a wireless travel guide suitable for the early-adopting business person is different from that of a consumer variety.

In planning for specialty functions of wireless applications, you must anticipate further tasks. Proximity, location-based service, time-based tracking, notification, and alerting are valuable in a mobile on-your-person device. To get these functions, you may have to produce or buy wireless technology tools. You need to consider not only the wireless application, but also the day-to-day operation for most wireless systems that involve content. Other tools and components required for wireless development that support text messaging, personalization, location, calendars, and other content include servers, gateways, and special engines. They are covered in chapters 18, 19, and 20.

Feedback: The Beginning and the End of Testing

Wireless connections may operate in one city and fail in another. It is best to test in a variety of physical locations. Conditions vary widely in wireless. For instance, you may be able to simulate the loss of a connection between modem and basestation by removing the modem's antenna while it is communicating. Or you could move your application out of your coverage area as you use it.

If you are using middleware that employs a server at a central site, test it under the load of multiple mobile stations as they simultaneously access it. Developers find differences in the ways operators process the signal.

Final validation of a wireless solution means that you must test the solution in the primary use locations. Wherever you expect your primary population to use the application, testing and refinement for deployment are essential. For example, if your wireless application is expected to be used along interstate roads, then make sure the towers are there to support it with the devices you are recommending. Another example is a congested airspace like in New York City or Los Angeles. You may find when you are testing the air that TDMA or CDPD circuits are in fact saturated during the expected peak hours of use. You may need to recommend switching to another data network and set of wireless devices to satisfy local customers. The actual traffic of devices affects the way you optimize your server.

The best Internet developers have made the medium work for them by involving the audience in the solution. Often real users make observations and recommendations about the service. Many changes can be made in short order without costly redistribution. The speed by which a site generating content can reach users who can then respond to it creates a feedback loop, which is unique to the medium of the Internet. This is not merely an editorial loop; it is a service loop, and that can lead to an evolved system. A resourceful development team can quickly post a wireless Internet system and, with skilled design, make changes to improve it while the system is on the air. This means that many a wireless system can be brought up in short order, thereby delivering value to the audience without having to wait the traditional cycle for a full battery of tests to be signed off, delaying market availability and early to market advantages.

As the wireless service becomes maintainable, it is important to provide a feedback mechanism where customers make useful suggestions for the general benefit of the network. You have effectively created a wireless network channel that connects mobile users in such a short feedback loop that response and change are immediate.

Exploiting Mobile Operation

It is very important to have someone assigned to observe the mobile customer periodically during the actual use of the wireless service. This person observes usage, detects unexpected values, and voices evolving goals of the mobile end user. The focus is no longer on planning and building, but on operation. Looking at how editorial, administrative, customer service, or customer support units operate in an organization provides some examples of mechanisms that are necessary for any business to survive and cary on a relationship with its "audience."

This follow-up not only shows you care about the customer, but that your organization is ready to provide industry leadership in what may be a new and legitimate business opportunity. Internet Web sites are able to do this all the time because their business is electronic and easy to change. As you seek to qualify your wireless network, keeping a flexible resource in reserve is key, thus permitting the wireless architecture to grow. The total value cannot always be foreseen.

Although Internet Web sites are able to change in short order, changing navigation and placement on a small wireless device can be very disorienting. This is because mobile applications use a command system that is learned by the mobile user. It is recommended that a pilot audience test system changes before issuing releases.

Innovative companies hold in reserve the resources to grow after deployment. It takes observation and intelligence to recognize how your applications are actually being used. More than once, consumers have been attracted to qualities of an application that had nothing to do with the original engineering plan. The trick is to care about the life of the product and exploit the serviceable value. Your company may let you observe and make changes beyond the initial release. Staying in the loop with the mobile user is the best way.

Wireless Development Tools

You can lay out and test an interface design in the presentation mode of PowerPoint, and on Apple computers with HyperCard and SuperCard. However, there are special third-party wireless development and design tools available and coming to market. Wireless handheld and handset companies like computer companies offer an SDK. They sometimes include it in an integrated development environment (IDE). These tools let you write applications, call operating system functions, and round out the software development production process. Every successful handset and handheld maker offers an SDK and support program, usually with the cooperation of a software tools company like Microsoft or Metrowerks. Many devices, like those of the Symbian family, can be programmed in multiple programming languages. But not all runtime programs you make will work within the popular operating system. For example, although you can program a Linux application for a popular handheld, your end user may not want to install Linux because it takes some programming skill. It will also kill any of the other PocketPC applications.

Today's popular wireless programming languages are C, C++, and Java. Writing code on an SDK must be tested on the target device. To speed this up, the SDK provides emulators that simulate the device on a PC. Many emulators let you debug the device memory model from the PC as well. Within the operating system of the wireless device are libraries of code with special application programming interfaces (APIs), the most obviously unique being the phone call interfaces for the telephone. Well thought-out handheld devices offer libraries that include communications, data handling, and synchronization. They provide a mobile interface and mobile components, and some define a high-level application control. The most advanced tools are Rapid Application Development (RAD) tools, which can save weeks of time. If the manufacturer does not have a RAD tool, check the third-party tools. We will look at many of the best tools in the next chapters.

Foundation tools are sometimes required. And you need good engineers to build them. Foundation tools are core pieces of software that let you produce other parts of the system and end up helping to make the entire wireless system work. This may mean having to write modules of code for your device, which could include memory managers, XML parsers, display components, Bluetooth drivers, mapping modelers, and record synchronization subsystems. It could also mean having to build special system tools. For example, for your application to deliver wireless content, you may need tools for the content experts. These back-office tools help collect source information, "clean up" odd pieces of data, and maintain the integrity of the content. It is worth pausing to consider if they are necessary. They do take time to build, however, they often improve the quality of content or save time when the system is deployed. Of course, you can spare engineers the task of inventing tools by checking on commercial as well as Open Source suppliers. You can often download trial versions of tools. Then you can determine if they are good enough or if engineering needs to go the extra mile to create special quality tools.

7

Chapter

Developing Wireless Content

After you understand the personas of mobile users, it is best to understand their content. There is nothing cooler than inventing content that people really enjoy using. There is nothing more impressive than working with massive databases that represent entire worlds of information. Developers often get to define new data types and invent software to transform the data to make it personally relevant. Content creates the underlying value of the wireless Internet, as described in chapter 5, the section "Personal Content Drives the Wireless Internet." Before we write the mobile wireless application, it is important to develop a realistic working body of content. Generating wireless content involves some understanding of how to create and use text, geocodes, event time codes, and personalization data types.

The key engine for content is the database. Mastering database skills is essential to developing wireless content. Databases are set processors. They handle sets of information with a uniform command language that is far more efficient that any programming effort.

In this chapter, we look primarily at basic content as it relates to browsing, active wireless applications, and text messaging systems. We discuss content partitioning, which is a common wireless database distribution technique. In the near future of the wireless Internet, content will be drawn largely from wireless Internet devices, and will require special encoding for later retrieval.

Getting Started with Content

Content is a broad term. Technologists often prefer the word *data*. Technically, *data* is the representation of something. Content and information are uses of data. *Information* is structured data that has relevant value for an audience. *Content* includes information, programmable code, traditional data, and raw media including real-time streams such as conversations.

Content is the most important part of a wireless application. Content is the payload for which a mobile user will wear a device virtually at all times. Wireless Internet content includes maps, voice, images, animations, and text, which is the most efficient, widely used data type.

For the wireless era developer, content hacking skills are as important as code hacking skills. Projects sometimes make use of *content experts,* who are authorities specializing in the sources of various content. These professionals can add credibility to your sources. On the other hand, people who use the content reveal many useful commonsense insights. Make use of professional field forces also. They can tell you which qualities of the content are important and which are not.

Mobile applications make frequent use of location, time, and personal values to create a new form of content. Mobile yellow-page directory entities have geocodes, hours of operation, and often a rating scheme. These data values match the relevant personal interests to produce tailored individual content streams. This individualized content is the basis for personal applications. New wireless devices become the data sources that feed the wide area, local, and personal networks. Underlying databases, that are constantly being accessed and changed with personal data increase in value. Through the seasons, well-maintained content becomes a significant asset.

Good content is what people are willing to pay over-the-air time for. To a large degree, content is generated pretty much the same way for the wired and wireless Internet. From a Web server, a static Web page is delivered from the server's file system. With a little more work, the developer can program a server that is data-driven. Data-driven Web servers fill Web pages with content by making calls to a database. The advantages are clear. Rather than build 10,000 Web pages to display national hotel information, only a few model pages are built which make calls to an underlying database. Developers typically implement this with .ASP, .JSP pages, or even in Perl. HTML is the final form that a conventional Internet Web site delivers. Many wireless sites transmit WML, HDML, or cHTML. However, XML is becoming the general language to transmit and exchange data. A receiving XML browser can format XML content. For the content producer, XML provides new choices in portable publishing. Unlike HTML and WML, which have a limited number of tags, XML is customizable and extensible. You can define your own tags, your own vocabulary. The advanced sites are application servers that deliver dynamically generated wireless content to all forms of devices, which we address in Part III.

Content Professionals

Before designing a database, collecting the content, or writing the application, an information design is composed that will set priorities on the qualities of the content. Content generation and management require wireless professionals with specific production and operational roles. In traditional media businesses, reporters, editors, disc jockeys, and news anchors are in charge of collecting, correcting, and dispatching content. As a wireless information service, your wireless content operation may be a small. Like the situation at a radio station, there may be only one "DJ of content" who needs to have a dynamic personality and rapport with the audience to keep sources and edits for the wireless mobile audience up to date. Like any other publisher, a wireless information service has an audience that values good content. The editor/DJ manages sources of content that have degrees of authority, reliability, credibility, utility, and style qualities, which we hope are encoded in your database. Editors may also have to resolve issues of copyright or permissions that accompany content and source business.

Information Architecture and Information Design

Information workflow of a content system must be planned for an information service to operate. An information architect will specify how data is collected, its sources, and the ways it will be modified and presented. This person evaluates all parts of the data gathering and information flow through customer delivery. The information architect works with an interaction designer who has studied mobile end users, has constructed primary personas and scenarios, and then produces a storyboard proposing the exact layout of information per device. The information designer makes decisions about the best way to organize the content. One person, as the grand information designer, often does all three tasks.

Information design is perhaps one of the most critical of the wireless arts. *Information design* is the practice of organizing bodies of information in ways that users understand. It is the art of making simple conceptual models for deep content. In short, it is information communication. It is also the study of how to organize and present information so that it can be accessed and understood easily. An example of good information design is the organization of telephone directories. A directory can be ordered alphabetically (e.g., white pages) or by class of service (e.g., yellow pages). Everyone is finding out now that for a mobile guide, the information is better organized by location. Using a mobile application, people most often simply want to know what is nearby.

The practice of information design distinguishes the types of media (i.e., verbal, visual, metaphoric, narrative, and animated) and now includes multimedia that must often synchronize sound and image. The practice includes information classification as well as information organization. It is used to organize content in a database and provide a conceptual model for the user, and can affect menu design, word choices, and most everything a mobile user and a database designer see. Information designers use some common groupings.

- Alphabet — A to Z or Soundex
- Association — Personalized categories, specifically important to the owner
- Category — Formal or common topics
- Continuum — Magnitudes such as biggest to smallest, warmest to coolest
- Frequency — Most used first
- Location — Office plan or nearby geographically
- Number — Population and quantity
- Random — Sampling for effect
- Time — Seasonal, weekly, daily, hourly, momentary

Information design visualizes the quantity and the qualities of information. Thematic graphic techniques for presenting information are often popular with information designers. The design of instructions is also a part of the practice. Information design can be entertaining as long as it does not destroy the informative value of the underlying communication.

An important step in information design is the examination of all content to group it into the most useful categories. In the creation of an interactive restaurant guide, Digital Lantern assembled a huge amount of information: dining reviews, ratings, private reviews, sound bytes, restaurant addresses, phone numbers, maps, and what hours restaurants are open. A skilled information architect, Nathan Shedroff, reduced this incredible collection of information to three ideas – people, restaurants, and maps. The information design provided both a database schema and the primary interface for the mobile application. One of the key advocates of information design is Shedroff's mentor, Richard Saul Wurman, who has written at length about the subject. As designer of the SMART Yellow Pages®, Wurman's team used many techniques to reduce the immense content to useful new forms. Another illuminating source is Edward Tufte, the great teacher of information design theory. He reminds us of the techniques for representing information directly, truthfully, and simply – great virtues for the mobile representations of information.[1]

Interesting information designs deal with the best way to present massive amounts of information. Consider the indexing at <http://www.newspapers.com/>. In January 2001, it listed all the world's newspapers with a useful information design, using the following categories:

- *Natural groupings* – Top 10, in your area, U.S.A. only, international only
- *Maps* – By country, by state
- *Topic and source* – Entertainment, business, and TV news
- *Age group* – College, kids, seniors
- *Alphabetical* – Text search, of course

The utility of content can be measured by market acceptance and the number of subscribers who participate. Participation may involve having subscribers also be "authors." Some may take on roles as sources of content in the wireless operation; however, creating mobile content is an art and the interaction designers are the primary artists. Interaction designers and the people who use the content all need a mobile content engineer to make it work. Engineers have learned that when they dump content to small wireless screens automatically, they need the information designer to provide an orderly succession and give purpose to content that has meaning for the mobile user.

General Values of Wireless Content

When you get content ready for wireless systems, there is a range of common to exotic media types you can use. Text is the fundamental basic medium for mobile wireless. It is quickly understood and easily made. On the other hand, other sources of content are very rich. The new wireless technology is able to capture time and location. The new wireless devices can capture and transmit interesting media like audio, pictures, and video.

Precision can distinguish wireless content companies. Some wireless devices report location better than others, but it also requires precise content to make it all work. Some companies care about giving better organized, quality content to consumers. Giving a store location to your mobile traveler as a ZIP code is different from showing the location within 10 meters. The application interface is programmed differently. And the data collected is more refined. A lot of the content that has regular or frequent changes, such as changes of location and time, will have to be corrected. The idea is to design an application that will embody an underlying content system and will respond to change and increased precision.

Another observation about content publishing is that consumers of digital networks favor more frequent publishing. The frequency of publishing, how often content is published, actually changes the nature of the content. (We explore this issue with the wireless publishing models in chapter 20, the section "Gauging the Frequency of Wireless Publishing.")

Not all organizations can measure up to the extra work. But a well-crafted system can go a long way toward handling the extra load. Whatever publishing frequency your system and staff can support – hourly, daily, weekly, monthly, seasonally – your audience will consistently expect wireless service at those intervals.

It is important to recognize that your audience is a source of content. This may not be obvious in content publishing. But it is a reality of personal mobile wireless systems. People have opinions and a desire to upload what they have to say. It is important to provide a mirror, because your audience members like looking at themselves. If you allow participation in the content, you can increase your following. Amazon's main goal is to sell books and other products, yet its database is much larger than a sales machine. Among other things, Amazon's database lets people review products. It provides readers links to other reviews in the Amazon network.

3G Content

Sending pictures, animations, videos, audio, and voice requires that developers encode these larger media types in their databases. If the Internet is any indicator, personal media and individual reporting of personal events will become more popular with wireless devices, requiring these richer media forms.

Synchronized Multimedia Integration Language (SMIL) is a means to encode time-domain media in your database for later presentation. It is especially useful for multimedia. It is good for sending a "voice-over" that is synchronized with pictures. This could be broadcast in a streaming format via a nearby Bluetooth digital projector. SMIL authoring tools are listed at the W3C, although RealAudio, Microsoft, and Apple Computer make encoding tools that send streams in SMIL. The SMIL output is often sent to a Java Applet SMIL player.

Another content format you can keep on your server is Macromedia® Flash™, a popular streaming animation standard that is finding its way onto wireless devices. As an XML language, Flash can be generated from a server as a stream that can be consumed by the ActiveScript presentation language from Macromedia on devices.

Wireless applications actively use industrial data; for example, customer signatures are taken, calculations are made from fields, item identification codes are scanned, and real-time telemetry is gathered. To complete the wireless application, devices send the data to standard server databases. A small database is often needed on the device. There are many issues of synchronization and data type equivalency that need to be resolved. Synchronization tools can ensure that the latest copy of the data on the handheld and the latest copy of the data on the server agree.

Text: The Medium of Wireless

Mobile users often produce most of the text in a wireless system, and it is important to understand their encoding and techniques for mobile text presentation. Text messaging is the lifeblood of the Internet. After voice, text is the most commonly transmitted medium over wireless networks. Text messages are very useful and economical. Unlike Web pages, they do not "mesmerize" a traveler; they are the simplest way for people to convey intent. In Europe, the first applications are not WAP, but SMS. A key change for most wireless developers is to think in terms of telegraphic messages rather than long and complete explanations. At first, it seems like a slaughter of language. But short bits are all that people on the go have time for.

Using Journalistic Style

Many professions and techniques produce text that wireless systems can take advantage of. These techniques include the journalistic style of writing (i.e., creating stories the same way that newspapers do), creating text notation systems, and gisting messages.

Newspapers organize the text of a story in a very efficient way to accommodate their busy and diverse group of readers. A headline tells the reader what the story is about, and the first paragraph, the *lead*, compresses the entire story (i.e., gives you the gist of it). A good lead paragraph contains the who, what, where, when, how, and why of the story. The rest of the article develops the details and tells a full story as space permits If it is a late-breaking story in a paper going to press, then room is made for the essential lead material. Another good example of this style of communication is the executive summary of a report or business plan. In developing wireless news, it is a good idea to follow the newspaper style of presenting text. Say the most important things first, and then explain why.

In mobile messaging systems, you need to convey the substantial summary first and then continue the story in detail. If you do this, readers have the option of grasping the basics from the lead. You let them decide whether to spend more time reading to learn the whole story. This is a civil conservation of their time. They do not feel forced to read volumes to get the needed information.

Writing a Message

Crafting billions of SMS and pager messages is largely a personal art. Message writing is probably only taught in military schools. Good messages cut to the quick. Your name is the first thing a reader wants to know. The subject field expresses your substantial meaning. Messages should lead with a stamp with time and location, which are important in later references to the message. So far you are transmitting who, what, where, and when. Although some messages are signals and commands, a personal message has three parts. The first part establishes a context, often referring to the last contact, and makes a request. The body expands the subject, giving the reason for details subordinate to the request. The closing resonates a call to action, stating the action you expect the reader to take. It may end with an invitation to respond that the message is understood and a confirmation that said actions will be executed. A personal signature is important. Handwritten messages can be expressive, but not very transportable or legible. It is useful to add a dimension of emotion through various symbols.

Using Text Symbols

Wireless users are surrounded with text notation and symbols. They are used to common symbols. Some systems have a text notation to streamline the service. For example, stock trading, airports, rating systems often use a compressed notation to indicate values. Many industrial trades have their own symbols, terms, and language that you may need to uncover. Many "power" end users find these languages endearing and efficient.

- MSFT, CSCO, and RHAT are stock exchange symbols.
- SFO and LAX are airport codes.
- GT TH MSG is a gisted SMS message.
- 345.56, 978.34 are library call letters for books.
- :-) is an emoticon.
- •••• •• is "hi" in Morse code.

Sometimes it is wise to use well-known symbols to save time. People learn the Palm Grafitti® handwriting recognition system. The stenographic style saves the time it would take to write formally correct calligraphic marks.

In the long run, text input and voice input can be developed as a command language that drives an application. If you are defining an XML vocabulary, you might interview the domain experts of your application to uncover the jargon and notation. A judicious selection of commands can provide shortcuts that give users powerful advantages.

Messaging the Gist

In email and messaging among friends, there are creative practices that make messages personal. Sending gisted text, Morse code, and emoticons are common techniques. A recent trend in cell phone messaging is the practice of sending the gist of a message. *Gisting* is the art of sending the message as soundable fragments. "GT TH MSG" is short for "Get the message." People like this because gisting takes less time than thumbing in the full message on a phone keypad. The original Soundex compression rules are helpful here. To compress a text message, always use the first letter of any word, but eliminate following vowels or repeated consonants. Gisting text messages also includes folding words, for example, "CU@LNCH" for "I will see you at lunch." They read like early Western Union telegrams, which removed unnecessary words. After a while, a gisted message works like paging codes with a meaning special to the community of readers.

Gisting saves time, and is part of the play people have with SMS messaging; but there are other text messaging techniques such as sending emoticons and Morse code. Emoticons have been used in email since the beginning and can indicate how people feel about things. Hobbyists use Morse code to sign messages or hide small notes. For more information on these techniques, appendix A contains sections on "Soundex for Gisting," "International Morse Code," "Emoticons," and "Tempo."

Encoding Text

There are many text-encoding standards for wireless text. In low-level WAP development, text and commands are converted with the WAP ASCII byte-encoding scheme. You can read a WAP book for the gory details. It is critical so we have included the ASCII table in appendix A. For the Java phones, the text-encoding standard is ISO-Latin1.

Wireless text messages are usually transmitted using older, simpler 8-bit ASCII formats, a subset of UTF-8. Unicode is preferred to ASCII because, as a 16-bit data type, it can represent all the written languages in the world. WML supports ISO10646, which is identical to Unicode 2.0. To reduce the extra byte overhead on a low-bandwidth wireless network, UTF-8 is the default. Example 1 shows the ISO Unicode encoding override for WAP; it cancels the WML default and requests 16-bit encoding for WML.

Example 1 ISO Unicode encoding override for WAP

```
<?xml version="1.0" encoding="ISO-10646-UCS-2"?>
```

The encoding for Asian markets is seldom Unicode. i-mode uses Shift_JIS, an older double-byte text format for Asian languages. Still other documents are stored in Big 5, the Chinese-centered encoding. On Asian Linux and Java servers, the most common encoding is EUC-JP. The Japanese language is actually composed of Latin (called Romanji), Hiragana, Katakana, and Kanji characters.

It is important to encode the right character in your Web page, database, or message file. Here are the various codes for the letter *a:*

Encoding	**Representation**
Latin Display	a
ASCII Hex	0x61
Decimal	97
Binary	01100000
Octal	140

But when we go to double-byte Asian, the encoding gets a little more complex; all values are hexadecimal, with the exception of the cHTML example.

Kanji Display	今
Unicode (UCS-2)	\u4ECA
Shift_JIS	8DA1
EUC-JP	BAA3
Big 5	A4B5
cHTML Escape	今 (decimal)
UTF-8	E4BB8A

Using CDATA

In wireless markup languages, the simplest way to pass text through the browser interpreter without worry about the special markup characters is to use CDATA for blocks of text. Everything between the start tag <![CDATA[and the final tag]]> will be passed on without translation by the markup parser.

Geocodes, Time Codes, and Personalized Data

Wireless devices and networks that provide time and location are very useful. Servers combine this with personalization. The rapid delivery and speedy access to small bits of mobile time, location, and personal information can exhaust servers and databases, so content encoding must be efficient. It is useful to understand the sources of this new content, the data types, and special things you can do with a database.

All about Geocodes

Precision location-based wireless applications use geocodes to locate people, buildings, streets, and places of interest. Locating any point on Earth is based on locating the latitude, the longitude, and, in some cases, the altitude. As a reminder,

Figure 44 Geocodes are given as points of latitude and longitude

latitude forms ladders north and south and the longitude measures the longer degrees east and west. Geocodes are given as points of latitude and longitude (Figure 44). The angles of measurement north and south of the equator are the latitude with the North Pole at 90 degrees, the Equator at 0 degrees, and the South Pole at –90 degrees latitude. The angles of measurement east and west are the longitude. Looking down on the counterclockwise spinning Earth, the starting point of longitude is the line drawn down from the North Pole, through the Royal Greenwich Observatory in London, England, continuing to the South Pole. This is 0 degrees longitude, also called the Prime Meridian. It is also where the clock is kept for Greenwich Mean Time, GMT. Longitude goes east up to 180 degrees and it goes west to –180 degrees. The overlap of 180 degrees west and –180 degrees east is the International Date Line in the middle of the Pacific Ocean.

A *geocode* is the latitude, the longitude, and sometimes the altitude that fixes an exact location on the surface of Earth. Another word for geocode is *latlon*, short for "latitude and longitude." Geocodes are typically a pair of 14-byte strings that contain one signed decimal per coordinate. Latitude is always presented first. An example of the decimal geocode is 36.973200 - 122.02458. Geocodes show the decimal geocode as well as the traditional nautical geocode, which is given as the latitude in degrees, followed by 0 to 59 minutes, followed by 0 to 59 seconds. An example of a nautical geocode is 36°58'24" N by 122°01'28" W. Since base 60 is not easily computed, everything is in decimal geocodes. The precision of geocodes in databases and telemetry devices is always important to keep in mind. You do not want to send someone into the ocean who needs to be on the beach.

Location in Geocodes

To offer location-relevant data, you need to use the form that works with wireless handsets. These latlons often require that the database be geocoded. *Geocoding* is the insertion of latitude and longitude values for objects in your database. Geocoders can convert values for such things as street addresses, phone numbers, latitude-longitude pairs, zip codes, and named locations. You can use a geocoding service or a geocoded database, or buy or build a geocoder. I have made my own geocoder; here is how.

Geocodes are often obtained by converting a street address using a large mapping database that has already noted the latitude and longitude of each street segment. Developers for U.S. location-based applications can start with all of the streets in the country that have been geocoded. This information is in the public domain. Although the United States Geological Survey (USGS) has interesting mapping, including topological mapping, what you need is the U.S. Department of Commerce's Topologically Integrated Geographic Encoding and Referencing (TIGER) files. These files contain descriptions of points, lines, and areas on Census Bureau maps. Each segment of a street, river, or railroad has a precise latitude and longitude. These were made to help take the census, for the post office to determine zip codes, and for Congress to determine boundaries for electoral districts. The TIGER/Line files, produced by the U.S. Department of Commerce, are the data source for most Geographic Information Systems (GIS). GIS companies reprocess these TIGER files to produce their own brand of national geocoded data and corresponding geocoders.

Geocoded streets as TIGER records (Example 2) contain latitude and longitude coordinates, Federal Information Processing Standard (FIPS) codes identifying geographic census areas, blocks of address ranges, ZIP codes, and other political district data. Note that geocodes are measured in decimal rather than nautical form. TIGER files are available on CD-ROM from the Bureau of Census. The Web site is <http://tiger.census.gov/>.

Example 2 Geocoded streets as TIGER records

```
10005 106530810 D Injun Joe Road A41 16324 16328 22 95959
06060570579209092090 0008 0008 667 667 - 121019465+39282619-
121018050+39279698
10005 106530811 D Injun Joe Road A41 16330 16330 22 95959
06060570579209092090 0008 0008 667 667 - 121018050+39279698-
121017664+39278582
10005 106530812 D Rock Creek Road A41 16814 17032 16703
16995222295959959 06060570579209092090 0008 0008 668 667 -
121019343+39282810 to 121019563+39286624
```

TIGER data is all ASCII encoded. Some companies have cleaned up these files, straightened roads, and added GIS data. Companies have also begun to provide international geocoded databases because public domain street databases do not exist anywhere but in the United States. Some commercial sources for enhanced international geocoding include ESRI, Navigation Technologies, and

ETAK. Other companies that add services such as map generation, directions, and area searches include Kivera, Televigation, MapQuest, and Vicinity.

You can start geocoding from scratch by reformatting TIGER files. Typically, you remove political data, reformat street names, align street segments, and optimize the storage format. By interpolation, you can perform the key geocoding functions. Depending on what you want to do, many third-party Geographic Information Systems can import data files directly. ESRI provides GIS software for map and other processing applications. Oracle provides a geospatial-processing component to use when you need to perform rapid comparisons on large geocoded data sets. Vicinity provides a patented rapid computation model to deliver nearby elements already geocoded in your database. GIS systems are discussed further in the section "Using Location" in chapter 8.

Time in Content

Showing awareness of time in your application is meaningful and often requires special data encoding. Time, especially real time, can be tricky for wireless applications. Mobile devices and storage servers use their own clocks. When the servers and devices are thousands of miles apart, it is important to keep the time relevant to the traveler. This often requires conversion because time depends on location. There are two general forms to record time. A *timestamp* records a full calendar date and time to the second. A *time code* measures time intervals to the millisecond. You need to be very clear in specifying the precision required for the date, the time, and the duration.

Computations with timestamps can be difficult when the precision of the sources differs. Some data encodings are good to the nearest month; others are good to the nearest second. Use common sense to code software; but in gathering content, always get the most precise time code possible. For example, a store may be open Fridays, Friday afternoon but not Friday morning, or may open Friday at 11:30 A.M.. Your database will have more value, and can be used for more kinds of applications when you can deliver precise data. Later on, you can write functions that degrade precision if needed, but you cannot add precision later. The traditional timestamp supplies a time and date value as defined by your database. If you are getting time-coded information from many sources on the Internet, you need to normalize time by Greenwich Mean Time, and sometimes you have to record the location so use of the data will make sense.

For time-based content, time codes are used. Time codes accompany events or real-time media in motion. Time codes can be used to control durations of overlapping media. This is different from traditional date and time data types in databases. The Synchronized Multimedia Integration Language (SMIL) is a means to present encoded time-domain media. SMIL Time codes (Example 3) were developed by the Society of Motion Picture & Television Engineers (SMPTE, pronounced SIMP-tee). The SMPTE defines time codes in SMIL as frames per second – 24 frames per second for film and 30 frames per second for video. In SMIL, `clip-begin` is an attribute that specifies the beginning of a continuous media clip as an offset from the start of the media object.

Example 3 SMIL Time codes

```
clip-begin="smpte=10:12:33:20"
Hours ::= 2DIGIT        (0.23)
Minutes ::= 2DIGIT      (0.59)
Seconds ::= 2DIGIT      (0.59)
Frames ::= 2DIGIT       (0.23)|(0.24)|(0.29)
Subframes ::= 2DIGIT    (0.99) hundredths of frame
```

Time-based data and multiple media combinations of data require special consideration within the database. Conventional databases simply store quantitative information. Precisely timed data has different uses and requirements because the retrieval and networks mechanisms can interfere with the timing. Media stream data is often served and indexed as large objects. The IBM/Informix database coined the term *BLOB,* or binary large object, which many developers use to refer to media objects.

Simultaneous Media

If you design an application that simultaneously uses voice and data, then the timing requirements for data must be studied. For example, on a Cisco IP Phone, as a user takes calls she sees associated information on the faceplate in real time. Taking a live call, processing a recorded message, and using other IP services have different screens and options associated with them. These are transmitted to the user as coordinated transactions of visual data and accompanying voice streams. These can be very effective in reducing confusion and saving time, but careful analysis of the state of the user transaction is required. It is advised to steer clear of combined media interfaces without exhaustive study. These systems are hard for most people to learn because there is no convention for knowing when the verbal or the visual interface is dominant.

Personalizing Content

There are no well-established methods of personalizing content. Subjective personal values can be encoded, however. A personalized application requires a representation of the user's identity and a representation of the subjective values of the content. Some wireless sites allow users to define their own profiles, while others automatically deduce values through use. One problem with automatic systems is they can easily make false assumptions of value and interest. They sometimes shut users out of the range of useful choices. Programmers try to combat this by offering user-definable profiles. This customization step is a necessary part of personalization. Although laudable, it has been proved time and again that most people will not set profiles.

Database designs can base user profiles on original persona studies. A personal profile can be used to build a table of extended user attributes, a table that defines group preferences, tables of content attributes suitable for matching to user attributes, and filters to assist the matching process. In the flow of a wireless application, after user authorization is matched on a security table, then the prior session information is restored.

At the core of a content personalization system are a user profiling system, a ranking system, and a content profiling system. Personal attributes can streamline content choices or generate additional options. Generating further choices is a fine art. Often it is based on history of the individual and others who are like the individual in a technique called collaborative filtering.

The use of location, time, and personalized values as facets of content give it relevant personal dimensions. Mobile yellow pages have database columns with name, category of product, geocodes, value, price, service features, and hours of operation; a consumer rating scheme can provide matches that suit personal interests. When you have a commerce Web site or a very large body of content, then personalization engines and content management engines are essential. For more information, see the section "Personalization Engines" in chapter 18.

Structuring Content

Information professionals develop wireless content with databases, publishing tools, and a healthy respect for the architecture of information. Wireless information portals or wireless information services depend on specialists that can structure information.

Wireless information relies on databases to deliver mobile content. Structuring content uses classic database techniques. Either a mobile content engineer or database administrator will define data types, build and relate tables, and partition containers of content for small mobile devices. These definitions and structures are derived from the information design and a database design. The data may ultimately appear as XML when the server sends the content along the way. If you implement XML on your server, then you must make sure the client's wireless device knows what to do with it.

Partitioning Wireless Data

Who knows how much data your mobile audience may see at any given time? The 1200 byte capacity of a HDML Web phone, a 4 MB store on a handheld, or a 256 MB memory of a laptop can receive increasing amounts of content. You must engineer your database to deliver variable-sized content.

Small devices and slow networks require you to partition data. *Partitioning data* means grouping it into bundles that are tailored for the target. Content providers often partition data into useful sizes before transmission. The goal is to provide a scalable content stream that is generated automatically from the database. There are a few good techniques for partitioning data.

To partition data for small wireless devices and networks, *not merely the presentation, but the database content itself has to be structured differently.* Consider lists. You might be able to list twelve popular products easily within a 12-line handheld display. On a 4-line display, you might need to make four groups that link to pages of three per group.

Consider news. For a handheld, you can send a headline and the first 30 characters of each article. You can let the user pick how many articles to see, maybe sort by date or subject, and still have space for popular quick news links. On a Web phone, you can probably send only the headlines. What to do?

Some developers try restructuring content automatically with third-party translation tools. For example, they convert HTML to WML. Although these languages can convert markup codes, they simply cannot sensibly break down content. These translators cannot partition the data. Partitioning generally requires either an editor or someone familiar with the content and its importance. These professionals can create distinctions necessary for the navigation of the content and its organization, or perhaps they can reclassify the content.

One way is to structure content. Text written in journalistic (newspaper) style with the important matter up front is always guaranteed to have a useful first paragraph. A partitioning algorithm can cut the rest. The charm of this approach is that mobile readers can pretty much get what they want quickly. If they have a larger device, they can read on.

Another way is to structure scalable content. Staff editors can partition content by producing multiple-sized stories. This can be semi-automated. On television broadcasts, television-listing information is presented to viewers. This comes from a content feed that is a partitioned stream. On any given day, the content feed provides listings for all networks not only for television viewers, but also to newspapers and magazines. If you looked at the actual content feed, you would see that it is a series of synopses partitioned progressively into four or more ever-smaller formats. You might see a show described in one long paragraph, in one long sentence, in 32 characters, or in three words. You take what you need.

Another way is to structure content with embedded key words. To do so, give the user a set of key words, and have editors make sure all content is tagged with these attributes. That way mobile readers or their software agent can filter content that matches their interests. The chances of matching content are better if a real editor can examine and tag text. This approach depends on an information designer's having properly identified useful categories for classification and retrieval.

Delivering Wireless Content from Databases and Servers

The primary data engine underneath a wireless server is a SQL database. A database is a collection of data efficiently designed for quick retrieval. Almost every commercial Web database uses SQL, which is a relational database language that uses short commands to transform sets of data.

When a mobile content expert works with SQL, he often works with a traditional database administrator (DBA) who helps define a data schema, builds tables and indexes, and specifies relationships among tables. Working largely from an architectural requirements document and perhaps a storyboard, the content and database specialists look at both the end users' requests on the data and the internal operational system for creating and managing data. Using a storyboard, the team can decompose tables of information into fields of data. The DBA will list fields in a table as columns of a specific data type and size.

Consider the mobile delivery of national news to a mobile user who wants stories about a particular city. The solution might require that the database extract headlines and the first paragraph of any story keyed to the area. The story database might include tables that define the full articles, authors, filing dates, and editorial approval. The database design can detail tables for customer-facing use and then for internal operational use. Externally, a story could be pegged with subject fields. Internally, the story might have editorial staging, as well as source and production values. This can often be defined quickly and tested independently of having to use the actual news database.

It is easy to make a prototype of application data with simple SQL databases like MS Access. To power large Web sites, the working prototype can be quickly scaled up to an established SQL database, such as Oracle, DB2, MS SQL Server, Informix, or Sybase. Each vendor SQL database differs in dialect, and they are not interchangeable. To allow uniformity, most sites establish a connection to the database with a sequence of calls using ODBC or JDBC.

Database-driven dynamic content is very important for any Web server, wireless or not. But wireless content is often more dynamic. In the content server example showing access of SQL data (Example 4), a story is retrieved from the database and presented in HTML; it ends with `<br>` tags. This example builds a headline and a lead paragraph, and then identifies an author by calls to the news records of a database.

Example 4 Content server example showing access of SQL data

```
/* This IIS .ASP wireless Web content server code generates the most
recent stories about a city. This only presents the first paragraph of
an article. The CITY is passed in as a query string of the form
URL?CITY="Santa Cruz" (usually by a Web phone microbrowser) */
```

```
CITY = Request.QueryString("CITY")

SQL="SELECT ID, CATEGORY, TITLE, CITY, STATE, AUTHOR, AUTHORDATE,
HEADLINE, ARTICLE, FROM STORY WHERE (CITY = '" & CITY & "') AND
(CATEGORY = CITY) ORDER BY AUTHORDATE DESC"

RS.Open SQL
if RS.EOF = False then
  RS.MoveFirst
  Response.Write RS.Fields("HEADLINE ") & "<br>"
  Response.Write LeadParagraph(RS.Fields("ARTICLE")) & "<br>"
  RS.Fields("AUTHOR")
End if
RS.Close
```

After the database is designed, then real data is needed. Each table needs a realistic number of records loaded with practical content. This is called load testing. Record loading is often an art in itself. After the tables and data types are built, then some thought goes into converting existing or making original content. Existing data sources often come by converting CD-ROMs, downloading from the Internet, or connecting to other legacy databases. Search engines routinely dredge the Internet for data; extracting content requires special parsing tools.

Describing Data with XML

Using journalistic style to present a stream of text is easily handled by XML. On wireless handhelds, XML news stories will probably have tagged the <who>, <what>, <when>, and <where> elements. Readers can order information by these categories, too. In other mobile applications, where planning and coordination are important, XML DTD and encoding of data can be especially effective across multiple databases.

Finally, content needs to be simple for wireless use. Wireless data sizes are ultimately measured by the time it takes to load the page. Traditional Web sites allow a maximum time, often 3 seconds, for a page design. Obviously, this depends on the connection. Simplifying the page design and eliminating complex elements shortens the transmission time. This can be appreciated only by using real devices.

Repurposing Databases with Geocodes

In the examination of source materials for repurposing as a database, data types often have to be converted. The useful fields in the sources must be formatted to the right data type and length. As the system is deployed, original data is added and changed. Content is sometimes simulated to do load testing, but with new data types like geocodes, fields must be created and new content generated for these new fields.

If you were building a mobile business directory, you would want to load test a large geocoded database against a typical number of users. To build the data in the first place, you would convert a list of business street addresses to geocodes. Whether you use a geocoder, use a service, or perform your own conversion with TIGER files, the outcome is a set of X (latitude) and Y (longitude) points for each business. When the database has useful geocoded points, you can give wireless directions to the businesses listed, generate maps of these businesses, or tell mobile travelers which businesses are nearby by using proximity algorithms, which we address in the next chapter.

8

Chapter

Putting Location, Time, Personalization, and Transactions to Use

To create a distinguished mobile application that uses location, time, and personalization, and perhaps performs a simple transaction requires some understanding of how people use these elements. The experienced wireless developers will tell you that the goal of the application determines the content. The content determines the functions. Geocodes, timestamps, and customizable filters are among the many functional elements in wireless applications. To help people live a more relevant mobile life, these elements are put to use in many interesting ways in wireless Internet applications.

Using Location

Location not only allows people to find you, but also allows you to find people. Part of the intent of many teenagers' evening cell phone calls is to simply find out where their friends are. Determining location is the basic point of many calls and messages.

Security and privacy are added issues for location-based wireless applications. A Palm handheld user can ask where the nearest grocery store is, but first the user has to press an onscreen button labeled "Find me." For privacy reasons, the dialog includes notification that your location information will be transmitted. Upon acceptance, the service figures out what cellular tower the person is using and returns with information for the area.

Information, when it is with you, is different. This is a defining advantage for the wireless developer. While the E911 mandate creates a condition for early location-based opportunities, the innovative companies are busy making the market happen by refining the precision for location technology. Using GIS databases for industrial applications, we get an early insight into the important assets of location-based services and content.

GIS and Location Servers

Many professionals use a Geographic Information System (GIS) to process large amounts of geodata and build a large-scale location-based server with hundreds of thousands of points. A GIS stores information about the world as data sets. These data sets are often presented as thematic layers overlaid one upon another. Common GIS thematic layers (Figure 45) are related by geography. This simple but versatile concept has proved invaluable for solving many real-world problems from tracking delivery vehicles, to planning the locations of new buildings, to modeling city simulations. A similar overlay idea is common to any travel guide that must show shops and street maps, and be aware of the traveler and other similarly minded explorers. The previously mentioned TIGER files are good sources for GIS overlays for streets.

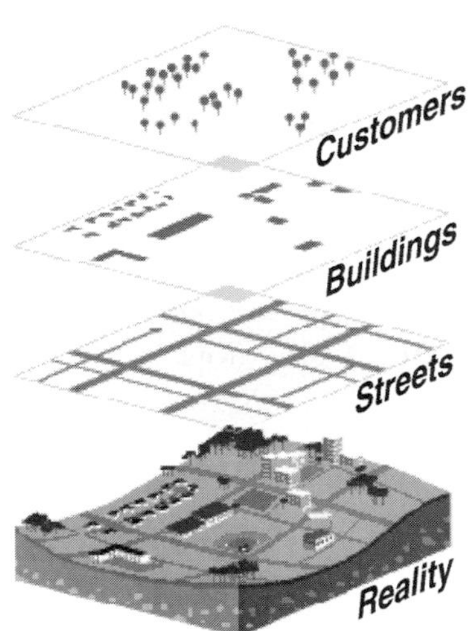

Figure 45 Common GIS thematic layers (*Source:* Graphic image supplied courtesy of ESRI.)

A number of location service companies provide telcos and developers with positioning information and interfaces for location-based services. These companies work actively with telco operators to provide positioning equipment that will provide caller location services. These location services deliver the geographic locations of mobile callers. Some companies also provide location-based services and content-to-end user applications. As a developer, you should contact the companies, obtain their interfaces and documentation, and participate in their pilots. As you might guess, most of these systems are XML based. Location positioning companies such as SignalSoft and Cell-Loc, have their own protocols and offer various telco stages and content supplier partnerships. See Table 40 for the full list of "Location Service Providers," at the end of chapter 17.

GIS systems use geocoded data in multiple databases to perform strategic analysis. For example, to determine the best location for a new store routinely involves spatial analysis of competitive stores relative to available population.

Industrial Location-Based Applications

The Trimble navigator surveyor and Symbol fleet tracking applications were pioneer location-based wireless applications in use by field forces in the early 1990s. Today there are many industrial applications. Vehicles with onboard GPS transceivers transmit their geocoded telemetry to a monitoring dispatch application. Dispatch software lets operators track busses, taxis, and fleets. Motion picture studios record GPS on location to help post-production editors reconstruct scenes. Field workers and government agencies use handhelds with GPS receivers to map underground pipes, plan street maintenance, and check light poles.

Primary Location Applications

To a traveler, location can mean a point, a region, a distance to travel, or a whole set of possible targets. Location-based applications can therefore have many uses and means of navigation. People get around by using multiple location hierarchies such as street address, geographical location, and neighborhood. All three are used to refer to destinations. To navigate a location-based application, many interfaces drill down to more detailed maps. Abstractly, location-based applications match users' needs to physical services available.

Location is precisely defined as a geographic place measured by latitude and longitude. But not everyone thinks in terms of latitude and longitude. People in a plane, in a package delivery truck, in the back of a taxi, or walking on foot have different ideas about how to get around. A street address, or better, street and cross street names work for a taxi driver. Citizens refer to neighborhoods and local landmarks. Mail delivery people think by zip code and street. Good geocoding engines can translate among latlon, common names, zip codes, and even telephone numbers. Which one you use depends on what mobile users already have available and where they need to go. The trick is to convert the now present latitude, longitude, and possibly altitude available on new wireless devices into the other types of geocoded information.

ALI Networks and GPS Devices

To develop location applications, position determination hardware, algorithms, and geocoded content need to be brought together. The E911 mandate refers to Automatic Location Identification (ALI) technology being in place to work. This can be implemented either by the network, which can triangulate location, or with the handset, which can have a GPS device. Implementing ALI with the GPS device is more expensive, but it gives much higher precision. To get the best service, a GPS device needs to work with ALI towers.

Sometime GPS is built into a device and sometimes a GPS receiver card has to be added, usually to a handheld. GPS receivers take at least two minutes to acquire the satellite signals when the device is turned on. Part of acquisition is downloading the ephemera almanac of where the satellites should be located to assist the GPS signal computation. The GPS receivers compute precise orbital data (ephemeris) and clock corrections for each satellite. To speed things up, many complying ALI WANs keep track of the latest ephemera used by their location-positioning equipment. ALI networks in combination with the new GPS handsets can give locations to within 10 meters in seconds. Each ALI system combines handset and network technology in different ways, yielding differing levels of precision. The catalog of techniques and precision is found in the section "Anticipating Location-Based Network Features" in chapter 17.

Emergency!

The early market for location-based services (LBS) is born from fear, not from pleasure. As with many creative inventions, the LBS systems were developed in response to need, rather than desire. The first location-based market for Web phones in the United States is based on emergency services. These are mandated by the U.S. Congress and implemented by the FCC as the E911 mandate. The purpose is to provide the caller's location in life-threatening situations. When a caller dials 911, the call is sent to a Public Safety Answering Point (PSAP). In a matter of seconds, the call has been appended with the current latitude and longitude of the caller's location, and the time of call. While listening, the PSAP agent can forward the precise location to fire, medical, or police agencies. The initial location applications are lifesavers for the stranded or endangered subscriber. Building these applications involves working with the location service providers and telcos, although secondary emergency products and services are clearly needed. The level of precision necessary gives the location within 300 meters.

Immediate Request Services

Not every wireless location-based application needs to be an emergency. An entire class of applications to help callers requesting service can provide immediate responses from supporting services. The traveler may need roadside service, dispatched transportation, or rapid delivery of a product. The only difference from emergency service is that instead of calling a PSAP, the call goes to a company for service and the caller's location is voluntarily disclosed.

If you think about it, a "Taxi come get me here" service could be the simplest location application. Nothing more need be said. A location-aware taxi dispatch application ideally returns to the caller a message saying, "Stay put, taxi 2 is on the way and should be there in 7 minutes." The software at the dispatch center needs to be able to take the request, and perhaps an associated validation. The caller's software only need bind the current location from onboard GPS or through network location technology. The necessary level of precision gives the location within 30 meters.

Directional Services

Using the Internet to get directions is common. When a person is traveling, the need can be urgent. A mobile user can speak to a voice portal, "I am lost; how do I get back to the freeway?" Or the person can request directions from a handheld. Another great time-saver is giving the phone number of the destination. A good geocoder can convert a landline phone number to either a street address or a lat-lon and return directions. If the caller is using a GPS device rather than an ALI network, the speed of travel can be calculated exactly, and the time of arrival can be estimated. If the application is smart and the content accurate, it can determine how many minutes before a business opens or closes as well.

Getting there is important, but what is on the way is interesting. In route planning, especially for longer trips, landmarks and waypoints are noted. Interesting sights can be shown in the plan or en route. New land-based applications use only landmarks. A traveler may want shortest or most scenic alternative routes. The traveler may also need alternative routes as road conditions change. Factoring in traffic conditions during the route computation can generate optimal routes. Real-time traffic information is important during commuting to forewarn of route conditions and avoid congestion.

The level of precision for directional services in vehicles indicates the location within 50 meters. With "dead reckoning," deducing direction by the history of travel and the vagaries of the actual streets, this precision can be interpolated from a larger network signal that affords location to within 300 meters. This degree of precision does require high-quality street-mapping data on board the traveling vehicle to be effective.

Identity Applications

Employees with Radio Frequency Identity (RFID) tags, Bluetooth badges, or smart labels can be identified for security and administrative purposes. Bar codes and radio transponders attached to items such as packages and vehicles provide identity and incidental location for security, survey, administrative, and general information applications. Identity applications are primarily an accounting and security tool. A good example is the automatic toll card reader installed on bridges to scan passing cars that have an electronic beacon card. Railroads have been using these for years to track rolling stock. Store inventory is regularly tagged. In all cases, a nearby interrogator reads the object tag to determine the location and time. The precision of the tracking and locating varies among tagging systems.

The radio technology is entirely proprietary for identity applications. There are no standards and you have to write custom software for every solution. Often, the identity code of a handheld, Web phone, or pager can be used as a tracking token.

Tracking Services

Tracking services provide location and ongoing telemetry about the target. Automatic Vehicle Location (AVL) is an entire industry based on mobile applications for fleet management and truck routing. Tracking can also serve personal purposes. Knowing when a child strays beyond the neighborhood is an obvious consumer location-based application. Tracking pets, family members, or anything that can move requires a real-time tracking and logging database that is tied into business logic and a messaging system. Clearly, theft detection and recovery of vehicles or other assets can make use of tracking applications.

Some devices that developers can consider for tracking are an uplink telemetry pager that has GPS. If the area is small and well bounded, Bluetooth, Wireless LAN, or RFID might be used in a location-sensing network. Otherwise, pingers or GPS-enabled handsets will work. Tracking can obviously raise privacy issues that need to be resolved with appropriate sensitivity.

An obvious location task is bound to be the answer to, "Where did I leave my handheld?" Many people have called their cell phones to find out where they left them. The precision of 100 meters for industrial tracking applications is not fine enough for many consumer applications, which may require location within 10 meters, depending on the goal of the tracking application.

Messaging Locations with List Servers

The locations of constantly moving valued assets can be transmitted to interested parties through messaging systems. Group broadcast subscriptions are a popular location-based application for "celebrity sightings" in Los Angeles and New York City. Subscribers who see celebrities submit a text message to the group server. This application makes use of a list server so that all members get a broadcast message as sightings come and go. This makes use of a highly active network of interested users providing useful and accurate input. The information precision is usually limited by the callers' common knowledge of locations of business names, street addresses, and neighborhoods. When geocoding techniques are applied, the given location may be from 100 to 500 meters of the place; the precision is improved if the caller is using an ALI network or a GPS device.

Friend Finder

Using active badges today, applications query the locations of the owners. Taking this a step farther with WAN GPS, in a variant of chat rooms, people of similar cast can make their presence known. At a mall or generally public place, travelers can discover and chart the presence of people with possibly similar interests. Friends and family already use devices like personal radio or even cellular phones where the most often spoken question is, "Where are you now?" which obviously can be answered before it is asked with location-based networks and devices. In social situations as strangers start up conversations, people may well be able to use their wireless devices to begin the relationship. People beam business cards with standard handheld technology. A friend-finding application requires precision of location to be in the 100 to 300 meter range.

If a person can be related to anyone else on the planet through a chain of six people who know one another in between, the so-called six degrees of separation, then friends are likely to be closer than you think. If only the social genealogy were mapped on the wireless Internet. Two nearby Bluetooth owners might find out their common friends quite quickly to establish rapport.

Area Information

Civic information or commercial guide services can respond with a general tree of information about almost any locale. With the wireless Internet, this can be far more directed than a "Welcome to Paris" information directory. Much finer and more personalized local guides are possible. Amateurs and professional groups might share their tours of neighborhoods, museums, or shopping. Perhaps travelers walk through a historic park and can seek a special interpretation on their ordinary phones or display screens. Maybe the traveler wants an alternative interpretation for a zoo or art museum that only a fan on the wild Internet might provide. There are already wireless Internet guides that show where restrooms are in buildings. Businesses may offer improved reception information, thereby relieving secretaries from having to relay commonly known information like building locations, directions to offices, restrooms, elevators, and so on. A corporate tour of a building could be mapped and keyed to where the person happens to be. Area information access may become common – "Speak or dial ★INFO."

Area systems provide a blanket of information and can rely on geocoding to provide well-known points as landmarks. If the content is easy to update, then the currency of the data in frequent use and verification make the service more valuable. The location precision for area applications can run from 10 to 300 meters, although the generic set of information for the area is often good enough.

Proximity Applications

Providing a "Nearby" button is unique in mobile applications. Proximity services list many items around the caller. A good service lists what is open at that point in time. For example, an emergency-oriented proximity application should show not only the nearby gas stations, but also which ones are open. In order for your service to deliver nearby ATMs, hotels, and restaurants, all the points need to be geocoded in a database. Useful proximity information often needs to be combined skillfully with other information. For example, copier service technicians daily replace belts, filaments, and gears. Sometimes they need a rare part and they go to their delivery vehicle to find they have run out of that part. A simple proximity application shows nearby service technicians and vehicles that carry the part. To be useful, the location precision for proximity applications can run from 5 to 100 meters.

The Palm VII uses a network that can provide general location information. A programming example of how to obtain and use nearby location from a Palm OS is covered later in the section "Writing Palm Query Applications for Wireless Browsing Applications" in chapter 10.

Geospatial Information Models

A step up from area and proximity applications are geospatial information models. These contain precisely coded area information and can relate it via proximity searches to the traveler. Digital travel applications list sets of nearby hotels, restaurants, shops, and sights. The list of places in a large city can grow quite long. People use many meaningful ways to sort or compare this kind of information. One popular technique used by information designers is to compare information visually, typically on a geographic map. One interesting approach, if the device has the memory, is to download a city model that can operate as a dynamic starfield map. A *starfield map* depicts elements in various iconic forms like stars in the sky that take on meaningful shapes. The user can tap on buttons or sliders to see dynamic comparisons of various themes. One example of a digital guide that lets diners use their "food radar" as a starfield display is the Digital Restaurant Guide that appeared in *Wired Magazine*.[1] Continuing from the example, the location-based guide (Figure 46) shows restaurants lit up that are actually open. This can be done only with carefully encoded content and onboard algorithms that readily interpret the data. The traveler taps iconic buttons on the left to control the starfield. Each tap brings up different thematic icons, regrading the underlying information and presenting a different overlaid map.

Tapping any spot on the starfield map shows more information. The architecture runs a dynamic city model on the laptop or a laptop synchronized with a server, holding all the combined content of the mobile users. Ratings were synchronized via email. It was originally implemented on HyperCard on the Apple PowerBook, and later redesigned for Java applets. In further advances, Self-Organized Maps (SOMs) integrate natural geographic spaces and spatial views of information about subjects of interest, as well as spaces for thematic interpretation for personal use. The precision for a geospatial model generally ranges between 5 and 50 meters from the location and coverage areas are typically a square mile.

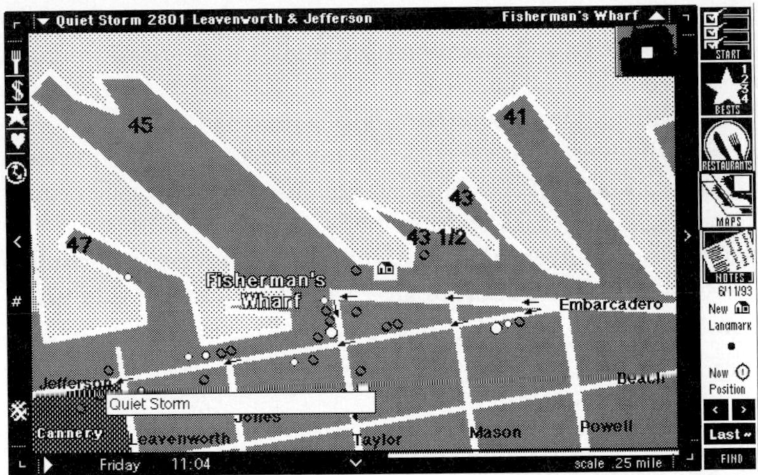

Figure 46 Location-based guide. In a starfield display like this one, locations of restaurants that are actually open are lit up.

Surveying the Neighborhood with Precision

To record, mark, and make precision maps was the mission of early GPS applications used in surveying. Much of the same survey technology – the surveyor's diary, precise times, and multiple location data points – are useful in creating "personal maps." Automatically noting time and location, mobile users can annotate elements in and around their area. Often presented in a map, the data points are encoded as latlon pairs, thus forming geocoded records. At any given latlon point, a timestamp, some telemetry, or a personal note can be transmitted. High-end GPS and ALI technology are necessary to get professional 1- to 3-meter mapping precision.

Surveyed areas let you go on to track assets, build accurate models, and provide the base over which other layers of a GIS content stream can give important information. One of the technical issues here is keeping different survey models in register; they often have different boundaries to describe information. Information on the "seams" can stay visible with the proper location-based rendering algorithms.

LAN and PAN Location Technology

The location-based market driven by the E911 mandate is directed entirely to WAN technology, yet most of the location applications discussed so far could be applied to LAN and PAN technology. A LAN usually has fixed basestations, and the geocodes for any node can be deduced with the proper software. The moving PAN can usually be located with reference networks.

LAN and PAN location systems are likely to become a significant new opportunity, especially if the WAN service charges for LBS applications are too high. It may be that charting the general area you live in and all the places of interest at home and work may be ultimately of more continuous use than the WAN location systems. Using fixed Bluetooth or LAN devices, you could create personal maps of your building or work area. For example, if you are creating a gallery tour guide, you can mark and organize works of art spatially.

It is interesting that, especially in the 3G transient roaming scenario, including these microcellular networks with the appropriate technology can provide precision location to within 1 meter.

Shared Locations

If you have a party at the Jazz Cafe tonight, you can give an address. Some people can get automatic directions to a destination. Others need directions from you; some only have telephones. To share destinations with a select set of people, each with a different wireless device, requires a special protocol and service. You can share a rich XML map as a graphic, text, or voice if you have developed the right server. As we find interesting things, we share maps and location information with network members, and it should make no difference what communication technology they want to use to see the shared view. Sometimes you may prefer graphics, at other times text, at other times voice. It all depends on the underlying XML location format you use. Sharing sets of locations is important for group applications and is as precise as the boundaries of the geocodes given. It is up to the receiver to apply the most precise interpreter of the geocoded destination. Shared location maps can be constructed and transmitted using WAN, LAN, and PAN equipment.

Geonetworks and Location-Aware Guides

Consider how your applications and content service can become location aware. Besides knowing nearby location services, people need to be able to compare what they find. Package delivery can now become package tracking, and this translates to customer confidence. Rather than support a customer call, you can design a system where customers can access information automatically, for example, to find the exact location of ordered merchandise.

A travel guide server provides mobile geoinformation. But it also must let travelers plan trips. The Vindigo mobile city guide has shown that at least one-third of people who request geocoded information are not in the area at the time. In other words, people need to be able to plan as well as receive direct service. To provide the many data elements and alternative routes in an exploratory format may be stretching the abilities of many portable devices. So much data would take a good amount of memory and a fairly large display space, making it suitable for PCs and handhelds.

Without automatic mapping tools, it takes a long time to develop maps and collect the underlying content for geospatial systems. The "spot business" – positioning elements for maps and geospatial systems – obviously requires intense maintenance. Streets, buildings, and points of interest come and go. Keeping track takes staff; however, in time, any device may constantly transmit geocoded marks with their telemetry, keeping the geoconceptual worldview correct. It is likely that having an electronic sign that transmits location and hours of operation may be a standard way the wireless Internet becomes a geonetwork. The architectural challenge is discussed in the section "Creating Self-Maintaining Content Systems" in chapter 20.

Latlon Proximity Algorithms

All location-based applications use proximity algorithms to compute distances between geocoded objects and to produce maps of nearby objects. The computation can be done in software code or on a database. The source code for both techniques follows.

Any engineer can determine the distance between two points by calculating a hypotenuse. But how do you determine distance with latitude and longitude? Location-based developers do it with geocodes. The algorithm for geocoded distance calculation (Example 5) shows you how to determine distance in miles, given the latitude and longitude of two points, using polar coordinate computation. This is a very efficient algorithm.[2]

Example 5 Algorithm for geocoded distance calculation

```
Function Distance (ByVal Lat1 As Double, ByVal Lon1 As Double, ByVal
Lat2 As Double, ByVal Lon2 As Double) As Double
' Calculates distance between two locations, given their latitude &
    longitude
Dim PI As Double
PI = 3.14159265359
Distance = 1.15 * (180 * (Arccos((Sin(PI * Lat1 / 180) * Sin(PI *
        Lat2 / 180)) + (Cos(PI * Lat1 / 180) * Cos(PI * Lat2 / 180) *
        Cos(PI * (Lon2 - Lon1) / 180))) / PI) * 60)
End Function
```

Often you have a set of objects stored in a SQL database and need to compute sets of nearby objects, for example, to find all the nearest businesses for a traveler. Rather than iteratively calculate, the best way to do this is to let a SQL database do the work. SQL geocode calculation for cities within 5 miles (Example 6) is the technique to compute objects local to a specified point. The SQL for this can be complicated, but it is nothing more than the base distance of the original polar calculation of the previous algorithm.

Example 6 SQL geocode calculation for cities within 5 miles

```
MileRadius = 5
LAT_CITY = RS.Fields("LAT")
LON_CITY = RS.Fields("LON")
CON_GEO = 1.15

SQL="SELECT ID, CITY, STATE, LAT, LON, ROUND(("&CON_GEO&" * 180 *
ACOS(SIN(PI() * LAT / 180) * SIN(PI() * "&LAT_CITY&" / 180) + COS(PI()
* LAT / 180) * COS(PI() * "&LAT_CITY&" / 180) * COS(PI() * ("&LON_CITY&"
- LON) / 180)) / PI() * 60), 1) AS DISTANCE FROM CITYNEARBY WHERE
("&CON_GEO&" * 180 * ACOS(SIN(PI() * LAT / 180) * SIN(PI() * "&LAT_CITY&"
/ 180) + COS(PI() * LAT / 180) * COS(PI() * "&LAT_CITY&" / 180) *
COS(PI() * ("&LON_CITY&" - LON) / 180)) / PI() * 60 <= "& MileRadius &")
ORDER BY "&CON_GEO&" * 180 * ACOS(SIN(PI() * LAT / 180) * SIN(PI() *
"&LAT_CITY&" / 180) + COS(PI() * LAT / 180) * COS(PI() * "&LAT_CITY&" /
180) * COS(PI() * ("&LON_CITY&" - LON) / 180)) / PI() * 60"
```

These location-based algorithms are used all the time on servers and sometimes by models that run on client wireless devices. Your working knowledge is incomplete if you know where things are but not when they are available for use.

Using Time

More wireless networks and devices now readily send and receive current time and location. Unlike your PC, a Web phone resets time automatically when it travels, and it keeps very accurate time.

With regard to content, mobile users need to know when services are available – what is open now, how soon will it open, or when it closes. A subtle point of programming, the application can distinguish when to use server time, device time, or destination time. For example, if your mobile user is in an airport planning to visit a city, it is universal to say that a show opens in 2 hours, 23 minutes, but if the city is in another time zone, the time would have to be normalized against GMT rather than use local time codes.

Recall that in Part I, we discussed an XML schema for events and calendars. This is becoming a standard way to overlay foreign event calendars with your own. For example, with XML a favorite sports team's schedule can be overlaid on the calendar on your handheld. The listings for the upcoming theater play dates or your department's business calendar could all be overlays. However, to synchronize business calendars and appointments depends on understanding the programmable interface to a corporate group calendar server as well as the use of portable protocols like SyncML. The API and XML schema are both needed.

Put a human slant on time. Present a relevant sense of time that people are familiar with. Tell the traveler that a service opens in 35 minutes rather than show a long table of hours that a place is open. A mobile user's morning life is different from the evening life, and the developer can offer time-sensitive customization.

Time-based storage is not as obvious as you may think, once you start doing interesting time-relevant content that works the way people think. How real time is used is different from the safe data typing of time in databases. Reality is telling. Developers encode and optimize time for retrieval. Consider the actual time a hotel restaurant is open. One may have hours from 7 A.M. to 10 A.M, 11:30 A.M. to 2 P.M., and then open for dinner from 5 P.M. to 2 A.M. The way you encode these intervals is critical, especially if you need to compare and graphically present many places simultaneously at any given instant. Time strings are easy to show, but are of little use if you need to perform comparative time calculations. If you need to calculate what is open now, or show for 200 nearby restaurants what is open, about to open, or closed, you need to have thought through a proper storage technique. And it gets interesting storing and then computing past midnight. The best way to store data is based on how it will be used.

International use of time can also require special attention. Both the United Kingdom and the United States use daylight saving time. All clocks are set back one hour on the last Sunday in October (at least until 2038). However, in spring when clocks are set forward one hour, people in the United Kingdom reset them on the last Sunday in March, whereas in the United States they reset the clocks on the first Sunday in April. So, clocks are out of kilter the last week of March and the first week in April. Crossing time zones can also be tricky for the mobile traveler.

Using Personalization

Personalization is an art, not a science. Being personal starts with simple things. Remembering names and saving a traveler's responses for reuse saves him or her the trouble of reentry. But true personalization assists the user in many ways, especially with regard to large bodies of content.

Getting software to match users and choices is quite challenging. As it comes time to write a personal application, a content engineer will have to set up a database with attributes that describe the users' interests and attributes that match the content. Added levels of user personalization include relevant descriptors for location and time.

Personalization systems have different functions for different types of customer roles. These customer roles can be anonymous browser, paying customer, business supplier, author of content, contributing editor, or administrator. Not everyone wants to be "personalized." Commercial sites often try to "convert" a browser to a shopper by offering better services. Your site can have different levels of interaction, depending on the needs of the user. The following progression of user participation is fairly standard for Web sites.

1. *Anonymous users* can be tracked as they move about the site. Their navigation and time spent can provide baseline traffic statistics.

2. If they elect to become *profiled users,* then you use a cookie where you can store history and select information that helps the users when they return. A *cookie* is a small piece of data that is collected from Web pages and can be stored by a browser on the client device.

3. If they are willing to become *identified users,* then demographic information can help them make better choices. All the cookie information and a longer history of identified users are stored by the service. This uses a full registration database.

4. Finally, *loyal users* can be part of special programs to reward valued participation.

Good applications start with customer identity. Applications work best with a secure user authorization system, but casual entrance using stored cookies is a good way to bring the user closer. Once a familiar user has entered, prior session information is factored into the session logic. Most personalization is implied. A key technique is *collaborative filtering,* which generates relevant possibilities. This can become a form of reference selling. It suggests alternative and related choices to the person interested in a product. This works by looking at patterns of people with similar interests. Collaborative filtering is often used on Web sites to suggest other music, books, or movies.

Another personalization technique is to let customers set filters to reduce large amounts of data. This is more commonly called customization (explicit personalization). Realize that most people will never fiddle with setting preferences. Never rely on the user's having to customize preferences to initiate service. The persona and scenarios should suggest user default values.

At the core of many personalization systems is a rating or qualification scheme. For example, Amazon records how people respond to the products they purchase and what they think about reviews.

In building personal applications, it is important to streamline user interactivity and manage security, identity, preferences, and interests. Because there are so many elements to coordinate, it is useful to consider using a personalization engine, which is covered further in "Personalization Engines" in chapter 18.

Using Transactions

The secret to mobile commercial applications is the direct transaction. A *transaction* is a sequence of operations that require completion. A business transaction must be completed or not performed at all. For databases, a transaction is either committed or rolled back. Classic examples of transactions are withdrawing money from a checking account and adding items to inventory.

Wireless transactions need to be simple. The number of steps to validate a user and perform a transaction are best reduced on the wireless application. Wireless transactions initially are for customers who know what they want. Most people know how to operate their automatic teller machines (ATMs) to see account balances or connect to the Internet to look up a stock quote, so that type of transaction interface is familiar. Security is often implemented with a personal identification number (PIN). This is preferred to entering both the user name and password because a PIN is quicker to enter. On the i-mode service, a simple PIN is entered for financial transactions. It is certainly a good enough security mechanism for common banking ATM machines. However, in wireless transactions, the server must also be able to identify the device before it can accept a transaction.

Security continues to be a challenge for commercial wireless applications. Almost every device and network has a unique set of security mechanisms. The Internet protocols HTTPS and SSL provide common security layers for some wireless devices. The WAP industry offers Wireless Transport Layer Security (WTLS), which requires an assured proxy server or secure WAP server behind a firewall to get an end-to-end connection. On the other hand, WAP is not necessary for security. The Swedish company TicketAnywhere has developed a technology for delivering secure transactions over IrDA and SMS from ordinary GSM phones. We will look at server security in Part III.

Since a wireless device is part of a network billing plan, transaction payments can be assured using the network operator. Wireless transactions require business and financial liability agreements. Credit card authorization, or any transaction fulfillment, works pretty much the same way on a server for PC and on wireless devices.

Some devices such as European WAP phones use a Security Identification Module (SIM), which adds authentication. For physical purchases, either a Bluetooth or WAN transmission from your handheld combined with a smart card can replace the credit card. Smart cards are generally bound to a service and have their own tokenizing protocol for commercial transactions. Industrial wireless LAN applications routinely take customer signatures written in "electronic ink" on a handheld to complete legally binding transactions.

To implement secure transactions, precision location, sufficient personal content, and time-sensitive services, it is necessary to understand wireless networks and the devices that connect to them. The next few chapters address the ways each wireless network connects devices with servers and the differences of each device within the WAN, LAN, or PAN. Most examples show transactions, location, customization, and time-sensitive content put to use.

9 Chapter

Getting to Know Wireless Networks and Devices

Knowing your users, their content, and some sense of the application you are building for them largely determines the range of suitable devices. The wireless application and associated quality of content largely determines which network and wireless devices work best. Now it is time to look more closely at how wireless networks operate and which devices are appropriate for those networks. For a developer to compare and recommend them, it is important to look at each one close up.

Most developers are tempted to shop for a device first, but they should fully consider the wireless networks before that. A wireless LAN is far more useful for a business application, as long as you do not have to go far from the basestations. Pager and data networks can provide assured time-sensitive data with handhelds, and advanced pagers require custom applications development but can work offline and run interactive applications. When the content or transaction is small and a WAN connection can be maintained, the Web phone works fine.

Earlier we looked at wireless devices in terms of mobile wireless families: Web phone, handheld, pager, voice portal, and communicating appliance (Figure 47). For the rest of Part II, we will omit the Web PC, and focus on the mobile families. As a communicator of digital content, you eventually want to be able to reach all the devices, but in the beginning, select one device and one network to thoroughly understand it. Get it working and get it working right. Before branching

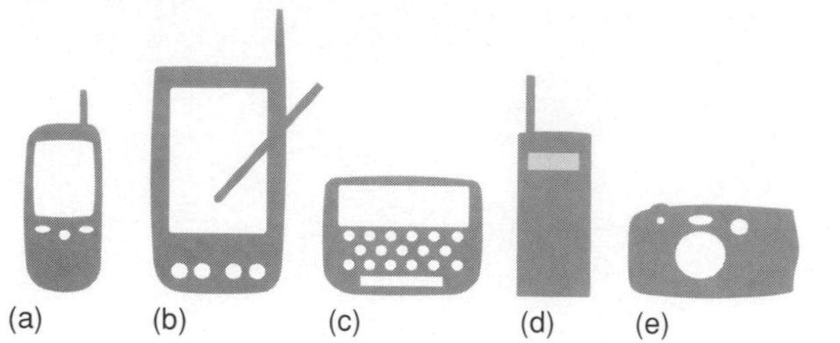

Figure 47 Mobile wireless families: *(a)* Web phone, *(b)* handheld, *(c)* pager, *(d)* voice portal, and *(e)* communicating appliance

out, test that device and make sure everything works well.

One aspect of many mobile devices is that they are often regarded as throwaways. Unlike a PC that you may keep for a long time, a wireless device has almost no value when the wireless network changes or is retired. The telco handset market conceives of Web phones as disposable. Web phones are replaced in two years by most owners. They are relatively cheap to make because most of the software is burnt into device-masked read-only memory (ROM). Unlike computers, Web phones do not have reconfigurable software. When the network changes, you must buy a new device. There is no upgrade path.

If you are new to this, make sure an application works with a target device and audience, then add others. To support multiple devices, use server strategies, which are thoroughly covered in chapter 18, "Building Servers and Matching Client Applications."

Comparing Wireless Networks: WAN, LAN, and PAN

The WAN, LAN, and PAN wireless networks connect devices with applications that also ran on servers. The publicly accessible WAN provides a low-bandwidth connection and charges for over-the-air connection time. While the three networks are largely independent, wireless devices are being made with multiple antennas to be able to connect to the appropriate network. The new 3G phones are being made with WAN and Bluetooth processors. Both WAN and LAN wireless networks connect wireless applications to servers. PAN wireless networks can also connect to servers, however, they are most effective talking device to device.

A WAN that connects WAP phones to a server (Figure 48) starts with a call from a WAP phone (or a handheld with a cellular modem). The connection to a public WAN tower uses a proprietary WAP protocol. Over the air, WAP exchanges binary tokens for WML strings. The phone request is then routed through a telco switch to a WAP gateway. The gateway recodes the data and continues passing the request through the Internet to a client server. The server interprets the request, finds the data, and passes back content as WML to the WAP gateway. The gateway recodes WML in binary form and passes it on to the WAP phone.

Handhelds have a much shorter path than WAP exchanges. A LAN connecting wireless Ethernet handhelds to a server (Figure 49) uses a basestation to make the

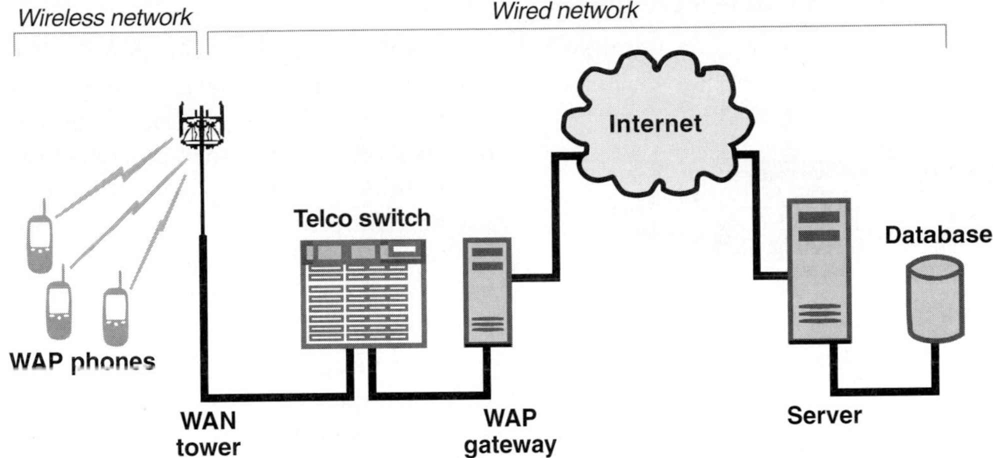

Figure 48 WAN connecting WAP phones to a server

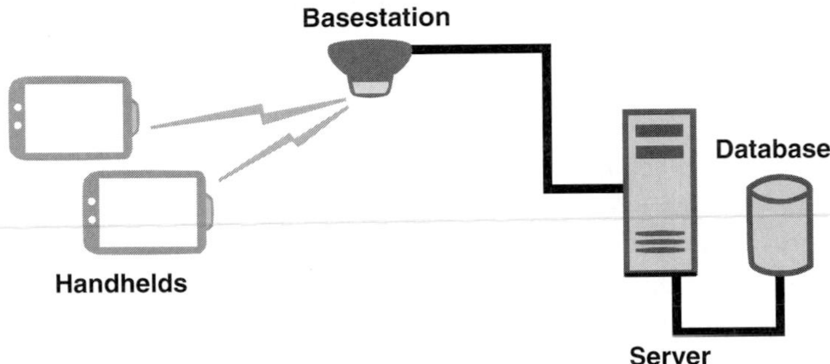

Figure 49 LAN connecting wireless Ethernet handhelds to server

wireless connection. The server typically runs a Java servlet and exchanges records with the handheld over the network using HTTP and TCP/IP. The handheld applications do not need a connection to be able to work; they simply use the connection to exchange data. The wireless LAN provides high-bandwidth connections, often at 3 Mbps or better in actual use.

Like the LAN, the PAN can also communicate with a basestation. However, a PAN connecting Bluetooth devices (Figure 50) lets local applications run peer to peer performing direct exchanges of data and services. Bluetooth transmits voice and data and is covered in detail in chapter 13 "Developing PAN Device Applications."

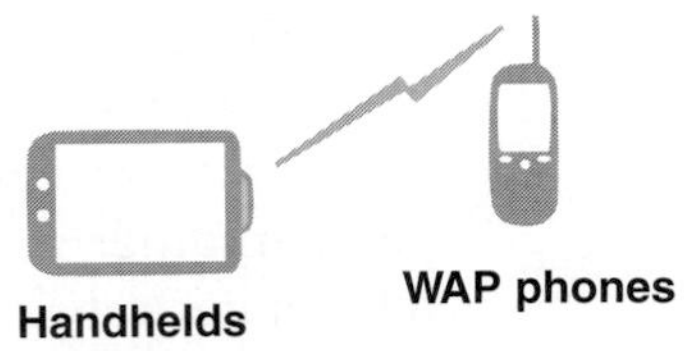

Figure 50 PAN connecting Bluetooth devices

Comparing Wireless Devices

A simple comparison of wireless airline information application shows some important differences between handhelds and Web phones. The most important one that bears repeating is that a handheld can work offline and make connections transparently. The Web phone requires a constant connection. The LAN, typically used by a handheld, is much faster. The DataRover handheld connecting to a LAN (Figure 51) lets airline processing agents work with lines of people. They check in passengers, take their luggage, check security, and generate boarding passes without a counter terminal. The devices use a wireless LAN that connects to an air reservations server and a commercial passenger processor. The LAN is necessary because the information must be high performance and real time. The basestation can transmit data at 11 Mbps. Handhelds reach any basestation within 100 meters. The basestation is wired to the LAN that reaches the server.

Form - AirCodes

Flight   Monday, April 3, 2000   Agent

Flight	Gate	Time	Arrive	Time
736	6	212P	SFO	633P
738	4	255P	SFO	707P
740	4	342P	SFO	800P
742	4	350P	SFO	810P
158	7	525P	SJC	946P
762	7	540P	SJC	1003P

DFW

Tap on flight for details & passengers

Figure 51 DataRover handheld connecting to a LAN (*Source:* Screen courtesy of General Magic, Inc.)

Let us look at a flight information system that runs on a Web phone using a WAN. A Motorola WAP phone connecting to a WAN (Figure 52) gets basic information across, however access times are much slower and the amount of information presented is relatively small. WAP access data is about 9 kbps over a public network. The WAP phone talks to a cellular tower that is attached to a telco switch. It passes through telco gateways before finally reaching the airline Internet server that keeps all flight information. Like a flight monitor, it provides up-to-the-minute information, but currently you have to make a request for each flight; it does not give updates of sudden changes. This device and network are useful for consumer gateway travel information but would never be able to check passengers in.

Figure 52 Motorola WAP phone connecting to a WAN (*Source:* Copyright © 2000 Motorola, Inc. All rights reserved.)

General Features of Mobile Devices

The early wireless devices are like the original VW bug. Wireless devices are ugly compared to the slick PC, but they take you places. The hardware, software, network, and content all form a wireless solution. When used for messaging, browsing, or interacting over a WAN network, these devices currently use a 2G circuit-switched data network. Circuit-switched nets are slow with data. With Cellular Digital Packet Data (CDPD) the average user experiences an effective data rate of 4000 bits per second. The recent introduction of CDMA 1x, which uses packet data, shows 64 kbps or better. The user experiences a wireless LAN transmission of about 3 Mbps so these applications can do almost anything in the 100-meter range of these basestations.

A few hardware elements affect the end solution, and each has a tradeoff. The heavier the battery, the longer the storage, but weight can be a barrier for prolonged mobile use. Obviously, the general memory and storage capacities of wireless mobile devices set limits on the size of applications.

Buying Devices

Developers know how to buy a computer, perhaps a Palm handheld, but few know what to do about a smart cell phone or a pager. Consumers are beginning to think of these as their next PC purchase. Of course, you need one to test with. The following conversation is a rather typical exchange between a salesperson and Mark, who wants to buy a Web phone.

MARK: My friends are using a cell phone to get on the Internet. Do you have any WAP or Palm phones?

SALESPERSON: WAP? I think we will have some of those next month. Perhaps you would like to see an X phone. It can do Y.

MARK: Cool. Your X does Y. Can I try it to hear a call, or can you show me the Internet?

SALESPERSON: No. You have to buy it and return it.

MARK: I see. Is X a triband phone that works in Europe or is this the CDMA phone with an XML microbrowser? Does it do T9 so I can do email? What is the calling plan and coverage?

SALESPERSON: Uh, well, uh, you have to buy a one-year plan. That is $$ for the 200 minutes, except on Friday and then ... $$$ $$$. I think there is an extra charge for Internet. Here is a map that shows coverage.

MARK: I see. What is your coolest phone? *Salesperson hands a Z to Mark, who takes it, frowns, and returns it.*

MARK: Wow, the Z. That phone only works 45 minutes before the battery dies. Thank you very much.

I recommend researching and buying devices online, noting the following characteristics:

- *Long-life battery.* Ironically, wireless depends on one wire – the one that delivers electricity to a battery recharger. Battery lifetime is still the limiting checkbox of every wireless device. Although pagers can go up to two months, many Web phones last no more than one day of constant use. Ideally, a device should last one week with average use.
- *Small, light, and portable.* Devices should fit nicely into your hand or in a pocket. They should weigh 10 ounces or less to satisfy a wide range of mobile users. Although professionals like heavy-duty tools, no matter how useful mobile technology may be, workers often leave behind the heaviest gear.
- *Extensibility.* The best devices have slip-in cards and add-on sleds that simply work without installation by the user. Visor allows add-in cards, and industrial handhelds use industry-standard, off-the-shelf PCMCIA cards. These turn your device into, for example, a bar-code scanner, camera, or card reader.
- *Memory.* Web phones have a typical working memory footprint between 128 and 512 KB. Handhelds have a special OS and a variable storage range typically between 2 MB and 8 MB. Handheld memory can be extended with flash cards that can range from 4 MB to 128 MB. There are now recent PCMCIA flash cards for handhelds that work as persistent memory up to 6 GB. Of course, these units draw more power. Power dramatically limits mobile utility. The CPUs of wireless devices have various speeds. The Web phone processor typically runs between 1 and 10 million instructions per second (MIPS). Meanwhile, handheld CPUs can process 30 to 100 MIPS. By comparison, an ordinary Web PC typically runs at 800 MIPS.
- *Software.* Onboard software is worth noting. The Openwave UP browser and messenger, Microsoft Mobile Explorer, and handheld PIM applications all define standard applications that users expect. Advanced systems let developers distribute applications over the air.

A full comparison of wireless devices and networks is helpful before acquiring or recommending gear. With the breathtaking pace of invention, it is wise to do an across-the-board review of the landscape changes every four to six months. The Internet has useful sources such as the wireless branch of CNET and the wireless developer portals that offer lists of devices and compare features, user ratings, and prices. It is a start at least.

Wireless service coverage must also be anticipated in development. Determine what local carriers support your device and what billing plans you must initiate to get service. Internet service is usually an extra, and sometimes there are options within those plans. This absolutely affects testing. Your end customer may be overseas using a native wireless protocol and device that as you develop, you cannot access. You can make great progress by running an emulator; however, someone local must test the actual product.

Understanding Mobile Operating Systems for Interactive Applications

As a developer, you will probably not look at an operating system unless you are writing an interactive application that runs on the client device. Many small wireless devices have operating systems burned into a masked ROM that cannot be upgraded. The Motorola Radio Operating System (ROS) is embedded on Web phones. The bottom-dollar versions of the Palm OS also use masked ROM. Masked ROM devices are cheaper, but the only option for a change in the operating system is to throw the device away and get a new one. A flash ROM device costs more, but a new OS can be "flashed" onto the ROM.

Mobile operating systems (Table 25) abound. Wireless applications make different requirements from the underlying operating system. Usually, messaging and browsing are standard and you will not really care what operating system runs on a device. Web phones and most pagers use a proprietary ROS that you cannot program. To program an interactive application, some devices can also run a secondary operating system such as the Java kVM and the Stinger OS. Phones usually let these operating systems run in a nearby processor space.

Handhelds have very complete operating systems with programmable libraries. You program interactive applications to produce features found on the hardware or within the network such as location access or scanner input.

Some handhelds can be initialized with different operating systems. Linux, the open source operating system, is popular with handhelds. Normally, the Compaq

Table 25 Mobile operating systems

Operating System	Manufacturer	Development Environment
Windows CE, Stinger OS	Microsoft	C++, VB
Palm OS	Palm	PQA, C++
EPOC, Pearl OS	Symbian	Java or C++
ROS	Motorola	Proprietary C
REX	QUALCOMM	Proprietary C
Java kVM	Sun	Java with J2ME
BREW	QUALCOMM	C, C++, or Java

iPAQ runs a PocketPC OS, but you can overwrite it with the Linux OS, which is available from handhelds.org. The new devices from Transmeta using the Crusoe processor can run PocketPC, Palm, or its own Midori Linux operating system. Linux on handhelds generally requires a lot of extra low-level support, but this means you get a lot of flexibility in implementation.

Most mobile operating systems are programmable in C++, for example, the Palm OS, the PocketPC, and the EPOC operating system found in the Symbian consortium machines. BREW™, the Binary Runtime Environment for Wireless, is a runtime environment, which lets you program applications for the device in object-oriented C.

Some devices are programmable in Java. The Java wireless phones, pagers, and handhelds all run a Java kVM. The Palm handheld can run the PalmOS and execute programs in a Java kVM. BREW can host a kVM and has third-party Java wrappers where the application can be programmed in the Java language

Usually a device is selected for network purposes and you have to write to the installed operating system. Sometimes you have the luxury of choosing. Here are some important differences for you to consider when comparing mobile operating systems:

Low power conservation. Instant on/instant off. No booting time and superb power management for the customer often means extra programming for the developer. Applications generally need to know how to "go to sleep," "wake up," and change behavior in "low power mode." Mature wireless operating systems take care of this for you with a persistent storage system. Extra concern must be given to secure data at various power levels.

Rich communications architecture. Some devices support a completely communication-independent interface to all forms of WAN, LAN, and PAN carriers. For each carrier, an engineer has to write drivers. Wireless interactive applications can get tricky when data can be in device memory, on device storage, at the WAN gateway, or on the content server.

Integrated multitasking communications is also a great benefit. Being able to browse a site, send email, and talk to someone simultaneously is valuable. Not that you will actively do all those things at once. Many Web phones will "throw away" your work when a phone call comes in. Allowing voice calls and data calls to coexist is one of the unique challenges of the new integrated networks. Generally a carrier network will only give a customer a single voice or a single data connection at a time.

Complete interface library. A good handheld can do everything from show large fonts to capture a handwritten gesture. As these wireless devices assume the role of a PC, a complete graphics library can make interactive applications easier to use than most others. Advanced devices have APIs for color, animation, MIDI sound, and voice. They expose the rich communication features of the underlying chipset.

The Java language and small device kVM have not taken care to support the minimal power management, real-time behavior, persistent storage requirements, universal communications architecture, wireless network connections, and the essential graphics mastered by the pioneering handheld operating systems.

The final word on operating systems is that you need good tools to program applications. Look for an SDK (Software Development Kit) and check the API libraries. Use a good programming language. Use an Integrated Development Environment (IDE) to manage the project, and if you are lucky, you might find a good Rapid Application Development (RAD) tool that will let you visually lay out the data and the application interface at the same time. They also generate the code and data! Ask your developer friends, go to conferences, or read up about wireless development tools at various wireless developer portals listed in the section "Developer Resources" in appendix D.

Close-up Characteristics of Wireless Devices

The wireless application you are planning to build is based on persona, scenarios, and information design. The application often determines the requirements for the wireless device. For example, a national financial application almost requires a paging network and pager to guarantee message arrival. Here are key application families to consider and recommended devices.

- For messaging applications, pagers are king. Most Web phones have some form of SMS and they are popular because, compared to voice, they save money. Phones are now appearing with large screens and full keyboards, putting them into the class of handheld designs. Paging networks guarantee messages, although some data networks approach their reliability.
- For Web microbrowser applications, the WAP phone, i-mode phone, and some remaining HDML phones view the corresponding WML, cHTML, and HDML pages. Handhelds and pagers often use the same phone-style microbrowsers.
- For interactive applications that can work without a connection, handhelds are the best because they have enough display, memory, and storage. Java and BREW phones are ideal for simple interactive applications.
- For voice portal applications, a Web phone, a handheld with a cellular WAN modem, or an ordinary telephone will work.

In Part I we looked at the general utility of wireless devices. In the forthcoming examination of Web phones, handhelds, and pagers we look closely at their characteristics. The display and input methods for each device are unique.

- *Display.* Web phones have a very small display space and some applications need a workable size to be effective. Most screens are monochrome. Handhelds can be half VGA size. Although they can have color, it shortens their battery life. Nonetheless, color screens have proved popular on Japanese Web phones. For animation and wireless digital video, the refresh rate of the screens must exceed the traditional 8 frames a second.
- *Keyboard.* Unlike the PC, most wireless devices do not have a pointing device – no mouse. However, there are many other wireless input devices – touch screen, thumb wheel, keyboard, and even handwriting recognition. Web phones have some control buttons and number buttons (0 to 9). Advanced phones use predictive text input. Handhelds typically have a projected keyboard that is touch sensitive. Pagers have a full microkeyboard, ideal for messaging. Some have Page Up and Page Down buttons, others use a thumbwheel scroller. Both input techniques let you cycle through various items.

The ability to perform both voice and data communications is desirable, but devices specialize in one or the other.

Web Phone Messaging and Predictive Input

Messaging is important on all Web phones. To enter text on a cell phone numeric keypad, how do you type the 26 letters using the 9 available keys? There are two common techniques: multitap and predictive input.

If you look at a cell phone, you will see that three or four letters are mapped for each number. The alphabet starts not with 1, but with the 2 key, which stands for ABC, and continues to the 0 key on most phones. Multitap entry is simple. To enter the letter C, tap the 2 key three times. Using a special technology called predictive input, tapping the 2 key means A, B, or C depending on the next key you type. Key sequences are mapped to words. *Predictive input* looks ahead and figures out what you are typing. A person can type in the full word on the numeric keypad; for example, "CAT" would be 228. Predictive text looks up all valid three-letter words that match 228, and then lets the person scroll through corresponding matches. Entering text on a cell phone is good in a pinch, but if your users are expected to perform a fair amount of text entry, a handheld device has better utility. The most popular version is Tegic T9, but the slightly more efficient Eatoni Wordwise is also promising. Motorola supplies iTap™.

Note that predictive keying is assumed in Asia. On PCs, Asian cultures are long used to complex character entry. Asian users constantly have to form key combinations and scroll choices to get Kanji. Regardless of your native language, when you have a small keypad, predictive input can save a lot of time when you are typing common words.

Web Phone Characteristics Based on WAP

Although there are hundreds of Web phone models, fortunately for developers, there are only a few Web phone markup page standards. If you are going to consider building a Web phone application, there are some general characteristics to consider. The WAP phone, i-mode phone, and HDML phone (Figure 53) all pretty much have the same displays and navigation buttons. Remember that Web phones, unlike handhelds, require connections to work. Web phones have little memory and limited bandwidth, and are largely text based. They support limited graphics. They are useful for simple messaging and limited browsing. It is generally wise to develop for the most popular phones rather than design for the lowest-common-denominator phones (4-line displays), which are phasing out rapidly. The new Java phone can also run interactive applications.

Display. The small page size of Web phone screens typically display between 4 and 12 lines. Each line is between 10 and 24 characters across. Pressing the scrolling button will show lines beyond the line limit of the screen. Long text is treated differently. Some phone browsers cut off text at the right edge of the screen, while others hold the remaining line, and let you scroll off the edge of the screen. Others animate long text, blinking the first part of the line and then the remainder. On some phones, you need to break your own lines on word spaces. This is true of i-mode where word-wrap is not implemented because the Japanese language

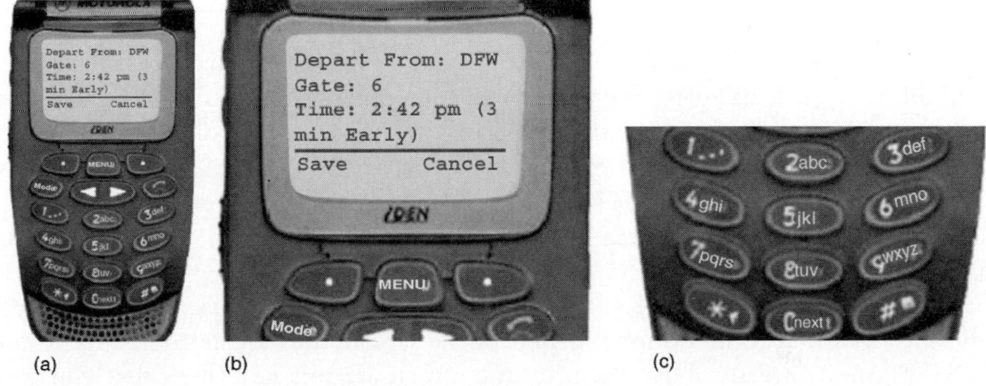

Figure 53 i-DEN phone (*Source:* Copyright © 2001 Motorola, Inc. All rights reserved.)

has no concept of a word space. Displays are generally growing larger. Fonts, both sizes and styles, are very limited. Developers usually have two sizes, one fixed and one proportionally spaced font. As a developer, you should keep in mind that short text expressions work best.

Navigation keys. All Web phones have a scroller, which may appear as an Up and Down tab, or Right and Left buttons. This scroller lets the caller navigate through a list and bring on to the screen the next line. Note that the UP.Browser always reserves the bottom line of the display for the status of a right and left choice. These two choices map to two hard buttons that appear directly under the screen. The default meaning that WAP specifies for these two are the Accept key (left soft key) and a Back key (right soft key). The other standard WAP keys are the Start Over key (often the Menu key), and the Scroll keys (usually Up and Down or Right and Left).

Keypad. Aside from the special WAP function keys, the phone pad is a 3 × 4 arrangement of numeric keys for dialing phone numbers. You can key the alphabet using the numeric keys 2 through 9. Alphabetic messages are keyed in by multitapping or, if you have predictive typing such as the T9 has, by direct typing. Multitapping may work differently on different phones. The 2 key will cycle through A, B, C, and 2. One new trend in Web phones is to have a much larger screen and to project the phone keys as a soft keyboard, just like handhelds do. Phones use a scroll key; they do not usually have a Next Page key. To get the user to move from one screen to the next, embed a navigation link in the markup language. All Web phones have a Menu button that can be used to bookmark the current site. This is most often implemented by using the press-and-hold method on the Menu key. When you press-hold the button, a dialog pops up and you name the site.

Programming WAP Phones

When developing general Web phone applications, try to use contextual navigation. It is better to keep a chain of associations going rather than design a large tree the user must navigate. Having people remember where they are in the tree of choices has not been successful. When laying out a screen display, make sure your most important elements appear at the top of the screen. Whatever appears later in the list must be scrolled up, and is often not seen or acted upon. WML screens that specify a TITLE tag do not always appear at the top of some phones, and you have to add that text to the display of some phones.

The typical WAP phone layout (Figure 54) has two hard keys, the Accept key and the Back key, at the bottom corners of the screen; they are always available on WAP phones. Directly above them on the screen are soft-key labels that you can set from WML tags. Because the two soft keys can be relabeled and have different meanings, the interface can change dramatically. This can be a source of confusion. It is best to keep the left key to mean Accept, Options, or Select. The left soft key always does something. The right key should mean go back, or cancel a choice. Keep in mind that soft keys perform actions, so if you label them, the labels should be verbs: Delete, Skip, Fax, and so on.

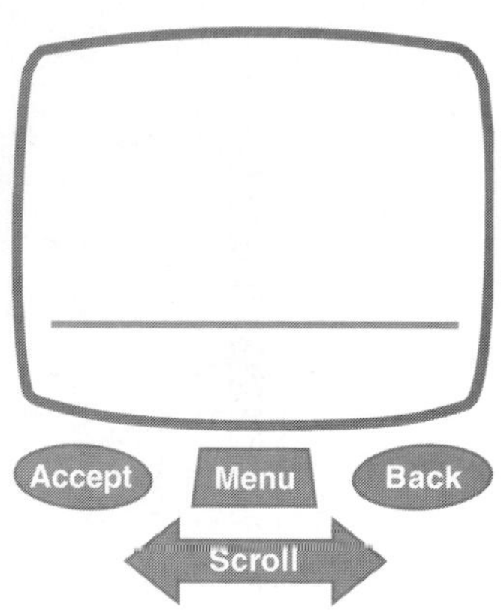

Figure 54 WAP phone layout

Most WAP phones support mapping within WML to the various hard buttons such as the Talk button, which makes a voice call. Browser-initiated phone calls do not return to the browser after the phone call. Incoming calls generally exit the browser. Other functions required by the WAP specification have hidden options and key combinations that are not easy to discover and require documentation. All phones support access to links. These are supposed to be accelerators for expert users, but most Web phone developers avoid these hard-to-learn, machine-specific features.

The minimum WAP phone has a display that is 4 lines deep and 10 characters wide, a vertical scrolling screen, ASCII text including uppercase and lowercase, an alphanumeric keypad with two soft keys under the display, and a menu key that must access the browser.

Accessing the Internet

We are all familiar with making a cellular voice call. You turn on the phone, key in the telephone number, hear a ring, and then speak. Making a "data call" to connect to the Internet is a little different on every phone. Generally, you press the Menu key to bring up a microbrowser display. You see few menus of Internet services. The display typically shows the telco default home page. You can scroll through their links and select one, the URL is transmitted to the server, and the Web site is returned 15 to 30 seconds later in the format for the Web phone. You can also enter a URL to view a site. It's a good idea to bookmark your test Web site to avoid repetitive keying of the URL. Bookmarking is usually done by holding down the Menu key.

Characteristics of Handhelds

The handheld is the "data truck" of the wireless industry. The leading maker of industrial handhelds is Symbol. Other companies that make industrial handhelds with many powerful features include Intermec, Husky, and the list continues in the section "Industrial Handhelds" in chapter 19. On the lightweight side of the business are the Palm OS® (Figure 55), PocketPC, and iPAQ handhelds.

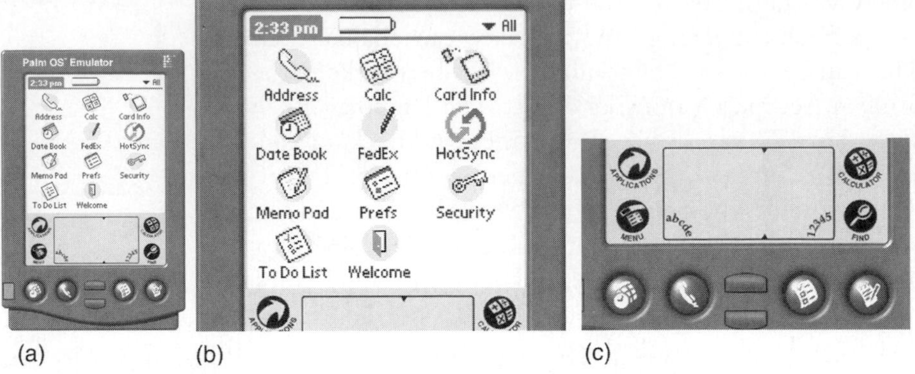

(a) (b) (c)

Figure 55 Palm™ Emulator (*Source:* Copyright © 2000, Palm, Inc. All rights reserved.)

The handheld is a useful portable data device that offers many PC-like features. It has been cultivated to work over a wireless LAN and to work as a first-class PAN device. It is not as good as a pager for messaging because it does not typically use a paging network. Voice is also an add-on for handhelds. Today's professional handhelds all have instant-on operating systems. A Compaq iPAQ can run a PocketPC OS or use a Linux OS, which is available from <http://www.handhelds.org>.

Display. Handheld displays range from 160 × 160 bits to 480 × 320, or half VGA screens. Most have gray-scale and color screens. Professional mobile users prefer to avoid color because the display uses too much battery and limits their mobile time. Also, color is not as sharp as the gray scale screen. Handhelds have a wide range of fonts and fairly comprehensive graphic libraries. The displays often function as the input device.

Input. Most handhelds have a touch-sensitive screen that lets mobile users tap on objects and use a projected keyboard for typing. Mobile users can take a stylus and draw or pen in a signature. The stylus is not special; anything will write on the touch-sensitive display. Sound is very important for feedback when you do not have physical keys to press. The PalmOS defines four standard buttons to start PIM applications: calendar, phone list, scheduling, and notes. Some handhelds include sophisticated MIDI and sound libraries for this purpose. Some handhelds have handwriting recognition software (HWR). After years of use, the Graffiti® software in the Palm OS has evolved to provide decent recognition.

Mixed-Function Handhelds

Some professional handhelds have configurable expansion modules. They can be configured for WAN, LAN, or PAN access with an add-on card. Other devices can be added such as scanners, barcode readers, GPS antennas, and even pagers.

Some of these modules are independently powered, and others can drain a battery in three hours of continuous use. Some new handhelds provide voice. The Visor handheld has a slot to add a cellular phone. Some Web phones add a handheld. The Kyocera smartphone and the Sprint PCS Touchpoint TP3000™ combine the Palm desktop with the cellular phone, giving these phones complete handheld functionality.

Characteristics of Pagers

The widely available data paging network gives great value to the pager by ensuring messages arrive on time. True pagers are on all the time. Messages get to you when they are sent. This is not like some attachable pager modems, handhelds, or Web phones that require dial up to get paging service. As we previously discussed (see the section "Pagers" in chapter 3), pagers are well suited for financial or time-critical applications. Pagers conceal a built-in antenna. They use power very efficiently and have a long battery life. Some one-way Motorola pagers can go two months between battery changes.

Motorola has traditionally been the leading maker of North American pagers. Most of the ones they have made are traditional one-way pagers that send alphanumeric paging codes. Today, the Canadian company RIM is leading the North American market with a family of two-way pagers like the RIM 957 Pager (Figure 56). The RIM two-way pager can send messages, browse the Internet, and execute Java applications. The popular RIM 957 full keyboard pager runs over the Mobitex network and charges about $40 a month to send email and access the Internet with the GoAmerica browser. Functionally comparable to the Motorola pagers, the RIM 957 pager has a larger keyboard and the software is easier to use.

Display. Pagers usually have small text displays. The RIM 957 displays 160 pixels by 160 pixels and shows a set of icons that represent underlying applications. At the top of the display is a small set of standard communication icons, which are seen on many Web phones. These indicate strength of connection and remaining

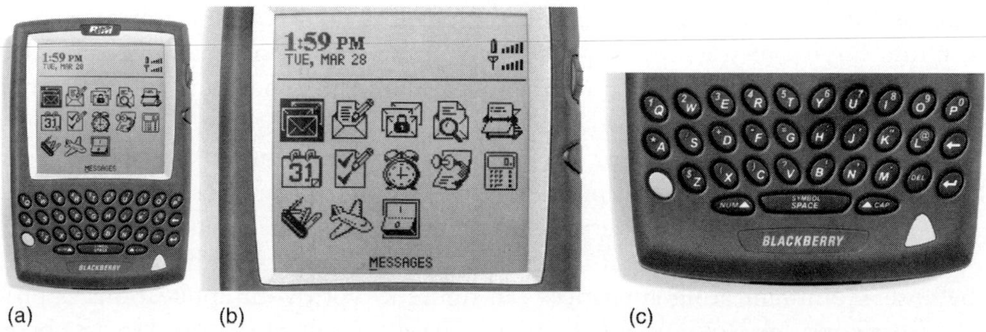

Figure 56 Rim 957 Pager (*Source:* Research In Motion. Used with permission.)

battery. When users hit your site with the RIM 957 and the GoAmerica browser, it is looking only for HTML sites. The RIM proxy server scales down any site before it hits the GoAmerica browser.

Navigation key. The thumbwheel dial on the right side of the RIM 957 functions as the pointing device. The thumbwheel can select icons on the desktop, traverse lists, and select fields on forms. When the thumbwheel is pressed, it selects and runs the current item. The GoAmerica browser uses the thumbwheel to scroll down beyond the screen.

Keyboard. The RIM pager has a full miniature QWERTY keyboard to enter text. It is ideal for mobile messaging. This is a special advantage over Web phones that have only numeric keys. The RIM has an orange key to the lower left that can access symbols and special functions. The power switch is the triangular switch on the lower right part of the device.

Characteristics of Voice Portals

Unlike the other devices, a voice phone system has no display or keyboard. The voice interface is entirely verbal. Some systems allow keypad response as an alternative to spoken responses at certain junctures of dialog. To write the code for a customer conversation, keep in mind that the voice interface relies on your conceiving a structured dialog of prompted requests and spoken responses. Developers write service prompts and tell the voice portal how to speak responses.

The significant distinctions in voice portals are in the quality of the speech recognizer and the speech synthesizer. Most of the voice processing happens through VoiceXML, which runs on the gateway of the voice portal provider. Much of the information about voice portals appears in chapter 14, "Developing Voice Portal Applications."

Characteristics of Communicating Appliances

Many single-purpose devices are being built with embedded radios to access the wireless Internet. These communicating appliances range from wireless cameras, to photo frames, to watches, to pens. Many are one-way terminals, meaning that they only send or only receive information. To build an application for a communicating appliance requires working with the vendor and its software developer program to get specifications for the protocols and media formats the device uses. Some use Bluetooth chips and profiles, others are proprietary Wi-Fi, and yet others use WAN access. Almost every recent digital device expects an IP connection.

Even if you cannot program these devices, you can work with the data stream they use. Communicating appliances can figure in with your applications as producers or consumers of content. Again, you have to contact the vendors to obtain the unique protocols, content capacities, and customer interfaces for these devices.

Getting Ready to Program Wireless Applications

As you get ready to write wireless software code, make sure you look over persona and scenario documents to understand the goals, utility, and expected operation. Look at the wireless application plan to check the type of device, network, and application. Look at the information design to understand the organization of content. Explore the content itself to see how much of what kind of material you will be making available. Look at all the sample screens of the storyboard or activity diagram to see what fields and navigation you will need to provide. If you are lucky enough to have an interaction designer, then talk with the person about user observations and any conceptual models that the end users may have about how they work. Content should also be ready before you program. This content usually lives on a database that is accessible from an Internet server. The server generates the wireless content for the wireless device. A WAN Web phone calls through the Internet to reach the server. A LAN handheld exchanges data through a wireless Ethernet network to a basestation that reaches the server. A PAN device connects through a Bluetooth network to a master access point that can reach the server. Regardless of the network, most wireless devices are now using IP addresses to connect and exchange data with back-end content servers.

Development Server and Tools

Wireless development tools are built for each device. Some tools are suited to different application families. Web browsing development tools are largely the same for all devices with emulator variations in the "skins," or the outer appearance, of the browsing phone. Voice portal tools are all unique, tuned heavily toward each vendor's voice service. Messaging tools for SMS make use of SIM toolkits. Interactive applications for client devices are the most specialized of all the application models. There is an SDK and an IDE for each device, whether it is a Psion, Symbol, Java phone, or RIM Pager. An SDK for the chosen device contains a full API library, emulators, and either code generators or object code libraries.

Develop sample content and load it into a database very early. Play with the data before you write the software to get a feeling for the quality of content you are expected to present and collect content.

Emulators are often used to help write your application. The emulator operates like the target device. *Like* is the key word. Emulators are developed through a code base different from the target devices. Emulators are notoriously inaccurate at predicting real behavior. On the other hand, emulators save time when you consider the steps involved in having to build, deploy, and then make a connection from a target wireless device. Few emulators match the quality of the real device. The display's appearance and the behaviors of scrolling, animation, and network performance are difficult to match correctly. There is no substitute for the real thing ultimately. If you skip early testing with a real device, you often miss some important lessons. A common mistake developers make with emulators is to use their keyboards so much that they are blinded by the challenge of mobile keying text and the constant need to keep keyed input as short as possible. Many emulators can also simulate the connection to the server and connection to the live database, an invaluable development tool. All device makers worth their salt can sign you up online to download their SDK and emulators.

Almost every application involves an Internet server. If you are making pages for a Web microbrowser or messaging application, all the work you do is for the server. To develop an interactive application, you must write software for the device. You often have to write corresponding parts on the server. The server development environment may be as simple as a file system serving Web pages or as complex as an application server accessing content in a database through programmatic calls to the data.

The wireless tools you need influence the way you work. An interaction designer may have produced wireless screens with a markup page editor like Front Page, Waptor, or GoLive. On the other hand, you might be lucky to have a Rapid Application Development (RAD) tool that reads your server database and builds device pages automatically. Most wireless programming systems have visual tools or command-line tools so you can edit projects manually. For example, a page editor can be drag and drop. But you can also edit WML code with a text editor. A semiautomatic approach often works best. Visual tools can be handy, but they often overlook specific details or programming abstractions that the underlying language allows. It is often necessary to edit low-level markup directly.

After you are satisfied the application is working well enough, then you need to get to a real device and test the real application over a real network under actual user conditions. The finished application must be posted to the right place on your server. Most programmers prefer developing wireless applications directly on the Web server. Otherwise, they work on their development computer and move files to the remote Web server. The server usually must be remotely restarted to allow the newly developed code to replace the running version. Advanced application servers have simple administrative interfaces to perform a "hot-swap" reset. Developers go in circles building and testing the server application with the emulator. You will learn quickly to keep roundtrips to the server down and transmit only the most essential data.

Keep in mind that travelers want to spend a short amount of time in the application. When they want a lot more depth, they will go to their PCs to access the server. The PC part of this application should be part of your total wireless application architecture.

After you understand how to program solutions for one delivery platform and network, then you can look at supporting multiple devices, multiple networks, and scale applications for high-volume traffic. High-traffic, multidevice systems require a different approach to writing the application and managing gateway caches, which is covered in chapter 18, "Building Servers and Matching Client Applications."

Real Applications

Now that you have some idea of the range of devices and networks, the remaining chapters of Part II show how to program wireless applications with specific examples. Each project is organized first according to the network and style of application that suit the common wireless devices used for that network. Networks come first because these define the data capacity that can be exchanged. Within each wireless chapter, all projects are structured in the same way.

- The title defines the network and application type. We show applications first by WAN, LAN, and PAN networks. The core wireless applications shown are browsing, interactive, messaging, and conversing.
- Devices and potential applications in the network group are explained. We usually look at the most popular or most powerful manufacturers' devices. The examples apply to pagers, handhelds, Web phones, or voice portal servers.
- Developer tools are listed, along with places to get them. These include client devices, emulators, code editors, operating systems, application tools, components, RAD tools, or special developer documents.
- Source code examples and excerpts are shown and discussed with relevant wireless content. These are oriented toward time, location, and personalized applications.

Let us look at the key examples of wireless Internet applications.

10

Chapter

Developing WAN Browsing Applications

When developers start writing small Web pages to extend Internet services to Web phones, pagers, and handhelds, they quickly discover how different such devices are from ordinary computers. Applications use little bits of data sent at low transmission rates to small screens. As with an ordinary watch, only a small but important piece of information is needed by a mobile user.

As you prepare an Internet Web site for wireless browsing access, consider that travelers will eventually see your site through small displays like the display on the Nokia 7110 WAP screen (Figure 57). The good news about writing a browsable application is you do not need to know about the low-level, dirty details of your wireless WAN – CDPD, CDMA circuit switch, GPRS, Mobitex, and so on. You simply write pages of markup language the same way you prepare HTML for PCs. Your project may designate multiple WAN devices such as Web phones and pagers that use a standard micropage markup language.

Figure 57 Nokia 7110 WAP screen
(*Source:* Copyright © 2001 Nokia Corporation. All rights reserved.)

As of 2001 the primary WAN markup languages are used everywhere in the world; however, the following languages are dominant in the following geographical areas:

- WML for WAP in Europe
- cHTML for i-mode in Japan
- PQA HTML and HDML in the United States

Examples of each language are covered in this chapter, although we use WML to include HDML because the languages are very similar. Because HDML is being phased out, we have included the URL for migrating from HDML to WML written by the inventors of HDML, Openwave Systems Inc. For each Web markup language, we will look at devices, tool kits, server setups, markup specifications, and sample application code. Java and BREW phones use a WAN network, and there is emerging interest in XML browsers for these devices. (For further information, see the section "Wireless XML Browsers" in chapter 11.)

WAP and i-mode Development

The Web phone in Europe is used for WAP applications written in WML. The i-mode applications are written in cHTML and are very popular in Japan. WML and cHTML are emerging as new cellular phone models begin to browse both kinds of site. For many years, most U.S. cellular handsets have microbrowsers that view only HDML, the predecessor to WML.

Recall that all Web phones can make a "data call" to a WAN tower (see Figure 48). The call continues through the Internet to make requests of your Web server for content. The request and the response are brokered by a WAP gateway that compresses the signal into binary byte codes. With i-mode, the connection is similar, except the gateway is simpler; the call passes through using SSL encryption end to end. Both types of Web phone have built in microbrowsers that read their own kind of Web pages. The phones also have a standard editor to read and send SMS messages. Lucky Web phone owners have predictive text input, which can speed text entry by anticipating your words. Some newer phones have both the microbrowsers and read new site content written in XHTML Basic.

General Wireless Tools and Where to Get Them

The Internet is a vibrant source of the latest tools. In addition to the sites sponsored by the network operators and manufacturers of devices, two useful general sites are <http://www.download.com>, which has many general-purpose tools, and <http://www.ayg.com>, which targets the wireless developer. To develop your application, you will also need Web phone emulators which are produced by the device vendors and software companies.

Wireless Application Development

When developing wireless applications for Web phones, consider the work of your team. Your Web phone screens are specified on a storyboard, but you may need an activity diagram to help you model the actual situation. Look at the persona goals, scenarios, and storyboards to get a sense of the purpose of this application. The details of the storyboard should clearly lay out screens, fields, and navigation. There may be remarks about setting any data validation for the fields.

Development of the application may require some trial and error because of the Web phones' limits on input, display, and content. Also it takes time to post your application to the network server for over-the-air development testing. To save time, it is good to do your thinking up front and have those designs to work with.

Content deserves special attention. Web phone browsers have a smaller screen size than Web PCs; therefore, if you have HTML, the content needs reduction. Although the storyboards should have things laid out, you may need to write partitioning algorithms on your server to measure data; the rule of thumb is 1K for WML and HDML and 2K for cHTML.

Directing Web Phone Application Flow

Mobile applications are workflow driven. This makes them different from PC Web designs. With PC Web browsing, developers are used to thinking in terms of data hierarchies that users will browse though. For wireless applications, you need to consider a mobile user's state of being – what will the person do next, given the immediate context?

Wireless developers who use PC Web concepts will lose users. Do not count on their paging back; it has been shown that requiring them to do so loses them easily. Use contextual navigation to stimulate a forward-directed flow of action to the user. Do not count on building your application to use a Back key, which is so readily available in WAP. It is typical in PC Web design to assume that people are used to hitting the Back key to revisit a page and explore it. But, having to go back over the air to retrieve previously seen content is costly. Create mobile value and structure for a mobile application by moving the user along with a natural flow. For example, if you look up a stock quote, give the investor an opportunity to look up a next stock quote from the results page that is being displayed. You would not want them to navigate back to the "quotes screen" to enter another stock's symbol to look up. The rule is, always show what most people will want to do next.

You may not be able to determine the true flow of action until you have interviewed mobile users or watched them to see what they are really doing and want to do with the application.

One thing for sure with WAP – you can easily design interfaces that make the user go in circles. The Back key should take the user to a logical and consistent place in the application at all times. WAP users, lost in navigation, often resort to resetting their phone, even though WAP specifies a Home key. The Home key is somewhere on the phone pad. It may be a combination function key + "1 key," making it next to impossible to remember. It all depends on the device. This is a continual challenge for WML developers. Each handset maker implements the navigational interface differently. This is unlike i-mode, which has a strong unified standard for all devices. Developers encode navigational links in the cHTML page.

Tips for Making Microbrowser Applications

The following tips are useful guides during wireless development:

- *Create an HTML start page.* If you have the time, allow entry to the wireless account from a PC to let the user input more extensive lists or to set up preferences. Internet users see the PC and the mobile device as two ways of connecting to the same place on the Internet.
- *Give 9 or fewer choices.* Give the user a preset list of options rather than have the user type in text. Since the keypad has numbers 0 to 9, the easiest thing is to let people type in one number. If the user must type, then try to keep the search to the first 1 or 2 letters of the key word. Present option lists with the most common choices at the top of the list, because on some displays the bottoms are cut off and have to be scrolled.
- *Use display.* Screen real estate has a premium value. Present the most important information first, just like in a newspaper article.
- *Use text.* Text is superior to graphics for mobility. Replace any graphics with text if possible. Consider the many ideas mentioned about using text in the section "Text: The Medium of Wireless" in chapter 7.
- *Help the user remember.* You are already trying to help the user minimize text entry, so look for opportunities to remember what users did the last time and provide choices where it makes sense.
- *Add links at the bottom of the page.* WML gives you only two soft keys and on some phones a Select button. cHTML uses ordinary page links. It requires no soft keys, but can remap all keys. Clearly, you need to add links and other actions. For example, in an email application, you might have the following at the bottom of your page: [Reply], [Forward], [Delete]. These will operate as buttons that when selected will perform the task you have indicated in your `href` statement.
- *Limit soft-key labels to five characters.* Most Web phones cannot display more than five characters in their soft-key label space. Shorten it to something meaningful, before the Web phone chops it off, perhaps making the term a mystery.
- *Replace text entry by choices.* Most phones have only a numeric phone keypad so use the keypad numbers 0 through 9 for key options. Applications should avoid requiring data entry. Every keystroke costs usability.

- *Get to the point.* Users can easily get lost in Web phone navigation. Try to organize your application to be as flat as possible, and ensure that the high-value areas of your applications are exposed immediately.
- *Partition content.* Some planning needs to go into how to provide useful bundles of data. On most WAP phones, in 1000 bytes you can present about eight useful Web phone screens. WAP WML compilers limit deck output to the capacity of the phone. A common maximum limit is 1492 bytes. It is recommended that your largest stack be 1200 bytes to allow for expansion of strings in transmission. Most developers are keeping WAP to 500 bytes. i-mode phones are rated up to 5000 bytes, but most developers keep the load down to 2000 bytes.

Writing WAP WML Applications for Wireless Browsing

There are a large number of popular WAP browser applications. These range from stock trading to information services. You write a WAP application in WML for mobile users to browse Web sites. WAP phones can process WML and the older HDML markup text. The two are very similar. Newer WAP phones also accept XHTML Basic.

The interpretation of WML files varies somewhat from one WAP microbrowser to another, from one phone to another. Developers are instructed by the WAP Forum to limit all cards to 1258 bytes per deck. Openwave's interface guideline is to partition information into 500-byte decks of cards because of network latency. WAP is complex, so remember that for every screen of text a user sees, there might be three times as much markup code to support it.

For graphics, WML images allow only a proprietary wireless bitmap (WBMP) image format. This is a simple monochrome, uncompressed bitmap. For color devices, the WAP Forum specifies the .PNG format. At a minimum, WAP phones have:

- 4 lines
- 12 characters per line
- WBMP graphics
- 1K memory for a WML deck

WAP Tools and Where to Get Them

The WAP Forum specifies the WAP protocol and the key WML specification. Openwave makes a useful server and toolkit. The Nokia Activ Server tools provide advanced security. The Nokia client emulator is shown in Nokia WAP 1.2 SDK (Figure 58). The following are the sources for these and related tools:

- <http://developer.openwave.com/> – The source for the updated Phone.com emulator for WML and HDML formats
- <http://developer.openwave.com/technotes/hdml2wml/index.html> – Migration guide to move from HDML to WML
- <http://www.wapforum.org> – WAP Forum specifications for WML
- <http://www.nokia.com> – WAP tools and server security that go beyond the WAP Forum
- <http://www.waptop.net/waptor/download.htm> – WAPtor page editor from WAPtop

Openwave™ has a number of tools including the Phone.com emulator. One of the great things about Openwave's WML emulator is that it is very forgiving. It provides good error messages, which are useful to beginning WML programmers. WAPtor is another freeware tool. This page editor for Web phones is very helpful in laying out the WML cards. It also validates WML pages. WAP Forum handset makers have their own special WAP emulators and servers. The Nokia emulator is one of the best.

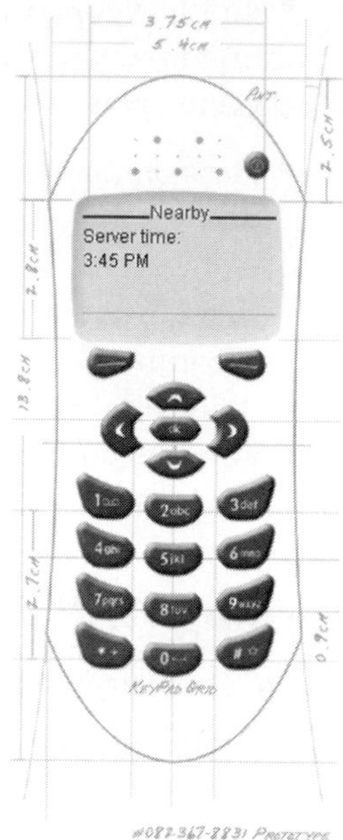

Figure 58 WAP 1.2 SDK Emulator (*Source:* Copyright © 2001 Nokia Corporation. All rights reserved.)

Write WML First, HDML Second

Your customers will be supported more broadly if, when writing for cell phones, you write to WML rather than HDML. Although HDML is the common standard in the United States and WML is the popular standard in Europe, WML is recommended. Although the HDML microbrowser is embedded in most U.S. phones, it is being phased out. Not to worry, many phones now carry a WML browser and an HDML browser. Also, many telco-deployed Up.Link™ and Openwave WAP gateways will attempt to convert between WML and HDML. The Sprint PCS HDML gateway will perform limited conversion of WML. But not all gateways do a good job. Although these two languages are similar, professional Web sites ultimately support an HDML branch. One reason is that HDML can be "ill-formed," but WML, as an XML language, must be formatted exactly right. This means that not all HDML content can be translated correctly for a WML browser. The WAP gateways support a different range of phone microbrowsers than the Openwave gateways support. After you have completed WML, if you have the resources, you should cover HDML. WAP servers also have dialects that treat WML differently. Working developers know they have to support HDML, WML, and Nokia WML. If you are looking for WAP security, you need an all Openwave.com solution, a Nokia server, or a third-party middleware security system behind your firewall.

WAP Directory Example: The Deck of Cards

Both WML and HDML structure their information like a deck of cards. This is in contrast to cHTML where all wireless information fits on one page. WML introduces new programming ideas to a markup language. It allows the creation of variables and the passing of values between cards. It has a special construct for handling soft keys, and has a convention for making telephone calls, to name a few of the stronger features.

Let us say you need to generate a small directory for your company. In the WAP directory example (Example 7), a WAP mobile customer is presented the full name of a business and then is given the choice of seeing the services for the business. Note that the most important services appear first. CARD 2 lists selection options. You scroll down to the option you want and press the soft key. Notice that the soft key says OK. This is the default phrase when you do not define the LABEL as we did in CARD 1. The DO statement is also able to pass the variable selected (ph, em, or ad) to the GO URL command. CARD 2 will transfer you to another URL within the site directory.

Example 7 WAP directory example: a deck with two cards

```
<WML>
 <CARD>
 <DO TYPE="ACCEPT" LABEL="Next">
 <GO URL="#card2"/>
 </DO>
 Wireless<BR/>Internet Inc.<BR/>Directory<BR/>
 </CARD>

 <CARD NAME="card2">
 <DO TYPE="ACCEPT">
 <GO URL="?send=$type"/>
 </DO>
 WI Services
 <SELECT KEY="type">
 <OPTION VALUE="ph">Phone</OPTION>
 <OPTION VALUE="em">Email</OPTION>
 <OPTION VALUE="ad">Address</OPTION>
 </SELECT>
 </CARD>
</WML>
```

Note that the third OPTION on card 2 does not appear on short screen devices. The user must scroll to see it. You can use a TITLE that will appear on the top of the current card. Some WAP developers often skip the TITLE because not all phones will show it. They present all the text for each card without a title. But a title is important. This is because titles can be bookmarked and this text appears on the bookmark list. So for a TITLE, choose 10 or fewer characters with some meaning. For a project, you should review the entire series of your titles. They need to be distinct enough to provide navigational sense to an end user.

WAP Soft Keys

A unique element of WML is the DO element. This tag lets you present users a labeled soft key. When they tap on it, the TASK is executed. Its general form is:

```
<DO TYPE="Action type" {LABEL="Label type"}>
<Task>
</DO>
```

where the elements are as follows:

```
Action type ::= (ACCEPT | OPTIONS | HELP | PREV | DELETE | RESET)
Label type ::= Text string or image
Task ::= (GO | PREV | REFRESH | NOOP)
```

The GO task is commonly used to send the user to a new URL. Note that it is a one-line statement that terminates with a close tag delimiter.

```
<GO URL = "Destination URL" />
```

Because it is a one-liner, you do not need the "/GO>" terminator. The next example of labeling and assigning a task to a soft key (Example 8) shows that the left ACCEPT soft key has been relabeled as Next. It is assigned the function of taking the user to the Coolsite URL and loading the greatapp.wml file.

Example 8 Labeling and assigning a URL to a soft key

```
<DO TYPE="ACCEPT" LABEL="Next">
 <GO URL="http://www.coolsite.com/greatapp.wml"/>
</DO>
```

Making a Phone Call from WAP Code

Of course, you should make use of the fact that the Web phone can make a cellular call, without having the user type in a number. Without any programming, on the new Web phones, if you receive an email with a phone number in it and you press call, the browser will parse for a phone number and dial it. In Japan, i-mode customers enjoy an automatic "dial the service" tag built into the Web phone page.

To program a phone number in WML or HDML, you can embed a phone link that calls the Wireless Telephony Application Interface (WTAI). A WTAI tag can dial numbers for your end user. Not all WAP phones support the WTAI interface, however. Beware that if you are using a translator, you must have all numbers. The WAP dialer will truncate alphabetic phone listings. When you place a call from your browser, the WAP browser typically goes to sleep and the Web phone goes into voice call mode. Assigning a phone number to a soft key in WML, HDML, cHTML, and HTML (Example 9) lets the user call from a micro browser. The WML Go command dials a call when the user presses the accept soft key labeled "Dial."

Example 9 Assigning a phone number to a soft key in WML, HDML, cHTML, and HTML

```
<!-- WML makes a phone call from accept softkey -- >
<do type="accept" label="Dial">
 <go href="wtai://wp/mc;8776110000"/>
 </do>

<!-- HDML makes a phone call from accept softkey -- >
 <ACTION TYPE="ACCEPT" TASK="Dial" NUMBER="8776110000">

<!-- cHTML (i-mode) makes a phone call from the number 3 key -->
<A href ="tel:8776110000" accesskey ="3">&#63881;Osaka</A><BR>

<!-- HTML for Kyocera smartphone URL based on RFC 2806, "URLs
     for Telephone Calls" -->
<tel:1(877)611-0000>
```

WML Variables

WML lets you define variables and use them again at runtime. Once a variable is defined, its scope is global to all decks and cards in that microbrowser for a whole session. Use the `setvar` tag to declare the name of the variable and then a value to assign to it.

```
<setvar name="varName"value="varValue"/>
```

where *varName* is the name of the variable, and *varValue* is the value you are assigning to it. Access the variable by using a $ prior to the variable name:

```
$varName
```

Variable names are strings that must begin with a letter or an underscore. The remaining characters may also include numbers. The example of using a variable in WML (Example 10) shows how in writing a travel guide a developer keeps the current location in a variable to head the guide and for use later to give the user location context.

Example 10 Using a variable in WML

```
<setvar name="city" value="Dallas"/>
<P>
$city Guide
<P/>
```

Setting up Your WAP Server

As you develop a WML application, at some point you will need to set up your server. In order for your Web server to return WML file streams, you not only have to create the markup <WML></WML> files, but you must also register the family of WML MIME (Multipurpose Internet Mail Extensions) types on the server. Once the server is configured, it is set up to serve WML files permanently. MIME forces requested file streams to behave as text, image, application, and so on. When WAP Web phones request a WML image or text or application from your Web server, the item will be sent back in the right way depending on the MIME instruction. Within Microsoft IIS, you access the properties of HTTP headers and set the File Types of the MIME Map. For a WAP server, there are six standard WML MIME types to register: wml, wbmp, wmlc, wmls, wmlsc, and dtd, as shown in Example 11 implemented for the Microsoft IIS server.

Example 11 Microsoft IIS setup for WAP document MIME types

```
Extension Mime
wmltext/vnd.wap.wml
wbmpimage/vnd.wap.wbmp
wmlcapplication/vnd.wap.wmlscript
wmlstext/vnd.wap.wmlscript
wmlscapplication/vnd.wap.wmlscriptc
dtdtext/plain
```

Apache can be entirely configured through the file httpd.conf, which is typically located in the apache/conf/directory or wherever Apache is installed on the server. The example of an Apache setup for WML document MIME types (Example 12) sets six MIME types. If you open httpd.conf in a text editor, you can scroll through and view the many Apache configuration directives. When you find a section where MIME types are declared, you can type in the five AddType MIME commands.

Example 12 Apache setup for WAP document MIME types

```
# AddType registers mime.types or
# coerces certain files to respond as certain types.
#
# WML/WAP types
AddType text/vnd.wap.wml.wml
AddType application/vnd.wap.wmlc.wmlc
AddType text/vnd.wap.wmlscript.wmls
AddType application/vnd.wap.wmlscriptc.wmlsc
AddType image/vnd.wap.wbmp.wbmp
AddType text/plain.dtd
```

The basic WML file is delivered to the microbrowser with MIME type text/vnd.wap.wml. Similarly, appropriate MIME types are passed for other WML variants. The .wmlc files would be compressed WML files; .wmls and .wmlsc represent WMLScript, the wireless scripting language and compressed WMLScript, respectively. Furthermore, WBMP files represent wireless bitmap files, the graphic format that the WAP Web phone supports.

Wireless Bitmaps

If you are using a Web phone, graphics should be used sparsely. Small logos can help reinforce service identity. Web developers are used to GIF or JPEG image files for desktop browsers. The WAP Forum defined a wireless bitmap, WBMP, as the only graphic format that a microbrowser will image. This uncompressed black-and-white image can be edited with new tools that now appear on the Web. For example, the declaration for a WBMP taxi image in Example 13 specifies the file in an IMG tag. As with all images, you should specify its alternative text meaning with an ALT tag. For microbrowsers that do not render the image, the alt value should not describe the image or name the file; it should provide a string that can substitute for the image.

Example 13 WBMP taxi image declaration with an alternate text tag

```
<img src = "taxilogo.wbmp" alt = "Taxi logo"/><br/>
```

Make DTD Local for Development

When you write WML or XHTML files, recall that the first line must refer to a valid DTD file. This file has to be loaded over the Internet. During development with an emulator, however, if you access this file it will slow you down. In fact, you may not have a Web connection during development. To speed things up, copy the DTD to a local project directory. This is best for testing. The wireless file will load the DTD from the Internet (Example 14) based on the first line of the file. The developer file will load DTD from a local computer (Example 15). Note the first line of the WML file uses a file:/// with three slashes instead of the http:// protocol. This makes the DTD file load much faster and without a connection in place. Of course, on a deployed system you must restore the Internet DTD reference.

Example 14 Wireless file will load DTD from the Internet

```
WML <!DOCTYPE wml PUBLIC "-//WAPFORUM//DTD WML 1.1//EN"
"http://www.wapforum.org/DTD/wml_1.1.XML">
```

Example 15 Developer file will load DTD from a local computer

```
<!DOCTYPE wml PUBLIC "-//WAPFORUM//DTD WML 1.1//EN"
"file:///wapdev/DTD/wml_1.1.XML">
```

Limit Your Screens

Web phones can be the source of useful or useless wireless applications. When applications fail, it is important to understand why. The WAN network is costly and if the application gets too elaborate, with too many screens to get what you want, then subscribers will not pay for it. There are some good lessons from consumer and business applications.

A recent restaurant review system was implemented with automatic tools on a WAP wireless portal (Figure 59). Without much thought given to a diner on the go, the system presented extensive screens of indexes and directories. This system could always return results, helping a person find a good restaurant, but as these screens show, it can take a lot of time the traveler might not have or want to spend.

Some people say using a WAP phone four-line display is like reading the newspaper through a straw. In this case, you want to give the mobile viewer sips not gulps. Use journalistic lead style and a directed, not a hierarchical, interface. It all comes back to good mobile design. The entire process has to be considered from scratch. Here is another case in point.

One business example with a happy outcome began with an early HDML phone implementation for a national field force of cable installers. The conversion of their dispatch software from familiar PC HTML to phone-based HDML ran over 100 phone screens. The field force reported frustration from trying to deal with simply too many screens. Installers going back up many navigation trees easily got lost. The HDML application required special training. They had to keep a manual at all times. They often reset their phones. The solution was to put the application on an industrial handheld that used wireless Ethernet. This communicated with the drivers' wireless truck basestation. The new application ran in fewer than ten screens. This was not only easier for an average cable installer to learn, but it cut out many of the costly WAN roundtrips sending and receiving screen data, which made the whole application run faster. If the users for whom you are designing need a data truck, consider a handheld and a LAN. If they can get by with a data cart and afford subscription charges, use a Web phone and a WAN.

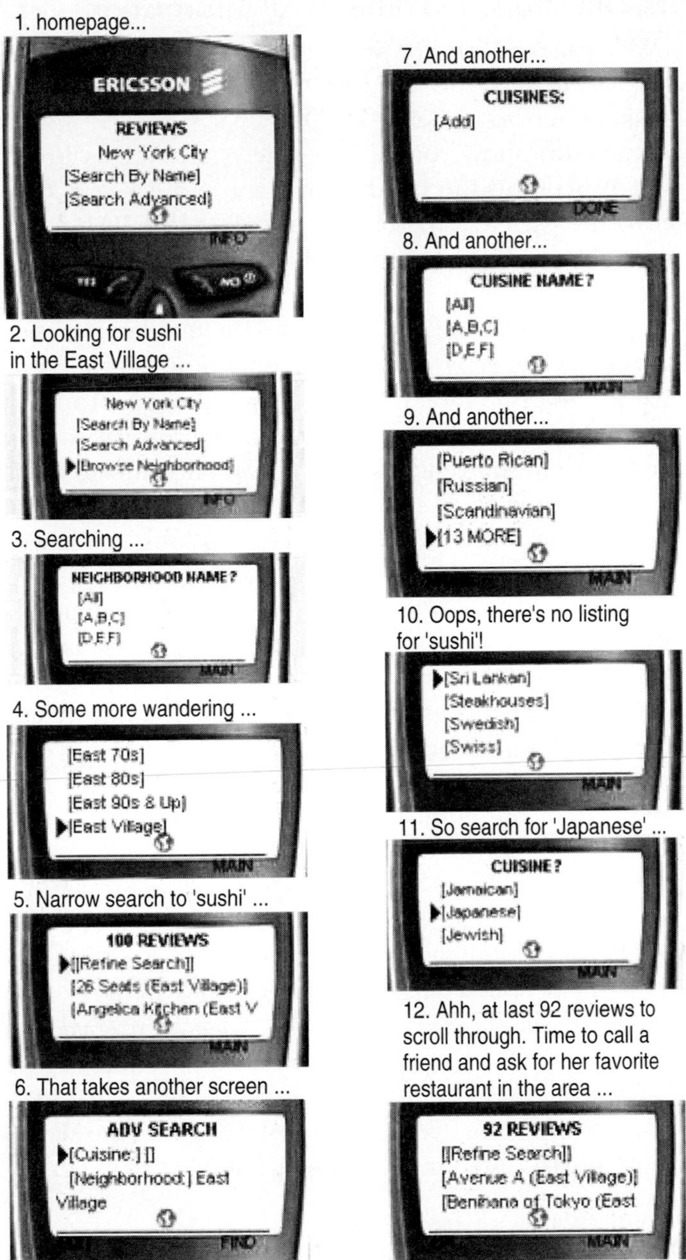

Figure 59 WAP screens (*Source:* Tiernan Ray/SmartMoney.com.)

More on Editors, Emulators, and other WAP Information

There are many Web page editors for WML. One useful shareware WML Web page editor is WAPtor. These editors validate WML since the pages are written in an XML language that refers to an XML DTD.

Development emulators show source code views, as well as provide various levels of debugging. When you fire up the emulator and direct it to your WML site, the phone shows the page and then lets you look at the WML source code.

As far as using WAP emulators, you might start with Openwave.com. The Openwave.com emulator is one of the best for beginners because it is the most forgiving. The site support is also excellent. While the emulator gives good error messages, it works in a very generic way and does not faithfully simulate the behavior of the many vendor phones. However, when it is time to approach a real device, you will want to use the emulator from the handset maker. To get faithful emulation you need to go to the vendor's Web site and download its emulator.

The Nokia WAP toolkit is good and can be modified to run on Linux. It has many features including detailed messages and lets you look at variables. It is the most truthful emulator for not only Nokia, but also Motorola phones. You can also download the Nokia gateway to test the whole loop from client to server.

WAP emulators can be used simply for checking. A very useful set of emulators hangs out at the informative WAP portal and search engine <http://www.gelon.net>. Using your Web PC, you can run its emulator to view your WAP site. The Web site also lists the latest WAP phone emulators.

Finally, you might want to look for a debugger to help you see what is going on inside the phone, when the emulators have done all they can. These can be licensed only by the handset makers.

Wireless developer support portals are used by many wireless developers to stay tuned to the Internet to find out about the latest technology, to exchange applications, and to get hold of development kits.

Many sources can help you when you are focusing on WAP development. Some useful books for developers are *The Wireless Application Protocol*[1] and *Professional WAP*.[2] The wireless developer portals are also very helpful for people with beginning and intermediate knowledge.

For other third-party emulators you can download, go to the Web; also check the wireless developer portals listed in "Developer Resources" in appendix D.

Writing i-mode cHTML Applications for Wireless Browsing

Japanese i-mode service delivers compact HTML (cHTML) content to phone microbrowsers. Even though they are not located in Asia, wireless Internet providers serve cHTML. The Internet is a global medium and for servers transmitting information worldwide, i-mode is just another page format. For example, CNN in Atlanta, Georgia, transmitted Olympic pages to CNN-owned servers in Japan in both Japanese and English. And it continues to do so. When a user requests a page, the request goes through DoCoMo and on to the CNN server at <http://mobile.cnn.co.jp>. Some i-mode sites are visible by Web PC browsers, although you will not be able to see some of the special characters. i-mode devices must use the Shift-JIS double-byte character encoding, which allows half-width kana characters as well as single-byte Latin characters. A minimal i-mode Web phone (Figure 60) has:

- 6 lines
- GIF images
- 2000 bytes per page
- 8 double-byte Asian or 16 single-byte Western characters per line

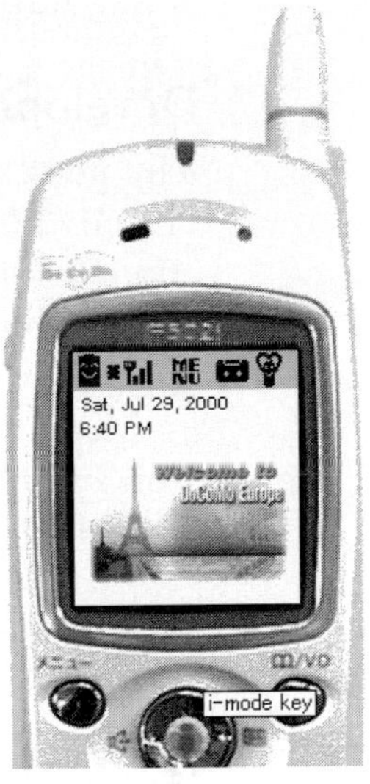

Figure 60 i-mode phone (*Source:* Copyright © 2001 NTT DoCoMo, Inc. All rights reserved.)

Note that text will not break on word spaces and wrap to the next line. You have to create your own word spaces. The maximum suggested size of a cHTML page is 5000 bytes, although developers recommend 2000 bytes.

i-mode Tools and Where to Get Them

To do technical server or browser development in i-mode requires a licensing agreement with DoCoMo, which provides all the documentation and necessary support. You can also contact third-party support companies that already have i-mode technical and commercial agreements. However, most developers can generate cHTML content fairly simply. If your content is interesting, you can charge people a small amount by agreement with DoCoMo or by using a third-party billing service. The following resources are helpful in making cHTML Web pages.

- i-mode cHTML markup is defined by the W3C, available at <http://www.w3.org/Submission/1998/04/>.
- DoCoMo cHTML tips are available at <http://www.nttdocomo.com/i/tagindex.html>.
- For an emulator, go to <http://www.docomo.fr/eng/europe/english_f502i.htm>.
- A Japanese tool is available at <http://www.asahi-net.or.jp/%7Etz2s-nsmr/soft/itool/download.htm>.
- An i-mode editor is at <http://www.wapprofit.com/products/i-modedownload.html>.

- Another good source viewable from Western browsers is <http://iseek.infoseek.co.jp>.

Developing i-mode Applications

The good news for application developers is that cHTML is good old (ancient) HTML 2.0 with a few added display features. There are many technical considerations in building i-mode applications. According to i-mode developers, they see connection times faster than WAP, so roundtrip conservation is not an issue. The markup is simpler in cHTML so more data can be sent than via a WML page.

Many i-mode phones show color. The lead advice is to make sure any image works in black and white first. i-mode has screens that are 2-bit black and white or 4-bit, 16-level gray scale, as well as 8-bit with 256 colors.

As for messaging, using an i-mode phone, you can send and receive i-mode email messages with up to 250 double-byte Japanese or 500 ASCII characters including spaces in the body of your message. Longer messages are cut off.

Security in i-mode is based on SSL and HTTPS, which is shown in Figure 87 in chapter 15. Most secure sessions begin with a subscriber's entering an assigned personal identification number (PIN). While some U.S. and European wireless efforts have concerns about security, the Japanese system seems to be running securely and smoothly.

Making i-mode Pages in cHTML

i-mode pages are written in cHTML. NTT DoCoMo defines two levels of cHTML: level one is supported by all i-mode phones, and level two is supported by the newer phones beginning with the 502i series phones. Although the size of i-mode documents can reach 5,000 bytes, it is recommended to keep them to 2,000 bytes. Unlike WAP, which has cards and decks, i-mode uses simple HTML pages one at a time. You build many cHTML pages with many links in each page for easy navigation, which would be faster than scrolling.

The differences between cHTML and HTML are worth noting. cHTML is largely a subset of HTML that omits many intricate features and adds a few new fun ones. cHTML eliminates the complex HTML features that would muck up a small, mobile display. In cHTML there are no JPEG images, no tables, no image maps, no support for multiple-character fonts and styles, no backgrounds, no frames, and no style sheets. It is remarkable how much can be accomplished with simpler protocols.

Several new features introduced by cHTML that are not part of HTML include an `accesskey` attribute, a strict implementation of header style tags, and the use of the emoji icon symbol set. Emoji icons (Figure 61), which display as unique character-sized graphics, can be summoned as special characters.

These new features are not part of the W3C Note on cHTML; and it is worth checking the DoCoMo Web site for the full list. Unlike WAP, i-mode applications can make use of true GIF images. The new `accesskey` tag is an XHTML attribute that is found in an `href` element. The entire i-mode keyboard can be remapped in this manner.

#	Image	Hex	Decimal	Title
1		F89F	63647	Fine
2		F8A0	63648	Cloudy
3		F8A1	63649	Rain
4		F8A2	63650	Snow
5		F8A3	63651	Thunder
6		F8A4	63652	Typhoon

Figure 61 Six of 166 emoji icons (*Source:* <http://www.nttdocomo.com/i/tag/emoji/index.html>. Copyright © 2001 NTT DoCoMo, Inc. All rights reserved.)

A cHTML Example: Subway Service

The i-mode cHTML for subway service (Example 16) shows a list of cities with subways and links to further Web sites for each city. This application could also link to another location in the page to save time, but the Web site does not manage that content, so a link exists instead. i-mode developers make use of linking within the page to minimize roundtrip access. Whatever does not display on the Web phone runs off the screen, and the mobile caller can scroll about the page.

Example 16 i-mode cHTML for subway service (*Source:* Copyright © 2001 NTT DoCoMo, Inc. All rights reserved.)

```
<!DOCTYPE HTML PUBLIC "-//W3C//DTD Compact HTML 1.0 Draft//EN">
<HTML><HEAD><TITLE>Subways</TITLE></HEAD>
<META <http-equiv="Content-Type" content="text/html;
                charset=SHIFT_JIS">
<BODY>
<DIV align="center">Subways</DIV>
<HR>
<DIV align="center">By Area</DIV>
<A href="http://www.xxx.co.jp/tko.htm" accesskey="1">
            &#63879;Tokyo</A><BR>
<A href ="http://www.xxx.co.jp/kngw.htm" accesskey ="2">
             &#63880; Chiba </A><BR>
<A href ="http://www.xxx.co.jp/chb.htm" accesskey ="3">
             &#63881; Osaka </A><BR>
<A href ="#toiawase" accesskey ="4">&#63882;Other Areas</A>
<HR>
<A name="Enquiry"></A>
If you are not in the areas listed above, Please select<BR>
<A href ="tel:0312345678">here</A> for inquiry by
        phone number or<BR>
<A href="mailto:Webmst@www.xxx.co.jp">here</A> for e-mail<BR>
</BODY>
</HTML>
```

Subways
By Area
1 Tokyo
2 Chiba
3 Osaka
4 Other Areas
If you are not in the areas lis ted above, Plea se select here for inquiry by phone number or here for e-m ail

Detecting i-mode calls is something you do on your server. It is important to identify the model of i-mode terminal with the user agent HTTP header (<HTTP_USER_AGENT>). By obtaining the HTTP header using CGI or an API call on your Web server, you can offer content that is maximized for viewing by individual i-mode terminal models. A full set of server detection techniques is covered in the section "Device Detection and Content Service" in chapter 18.

i-mode terminals are designed for use only with Shift-JIS encoding. Using the META tag, you can set the text encoding to Shift-JIS on your server. Note that i-mode terminals do not support the `http-equiv="refresh"` attribute.

The `accesskey` attribute designates a phone pad key that the user can press to select the item. This is used instead of moving the cursor to a link or form element. When written in cHTML, the `accesskey` can appear in the tags: <A>, <INPUT>, and <TEXTAREA>. You can designate any of the numbers 0 through 9 and the keys star, *, and pound, #, as an accesskey. Some i-mode terminals such as the 502i model do not allow star and pound keys to be used as access keys. Example 17, "Accesskey in i-mode," shows how to put up the picture of the numeral 1 with a location information flag to form a navigational link to the location directory.

Example 17 Accesskey in i-mode (*Source:* NTT DoCoMo, Inc.)

```
<!-- cHTML Navigate a link using the number 1 key. 63789 shows an icon
     of the number 1 and 63875 shows a location information flag.
 -- >
<A href ="/location" accesskey ="1">&#63879;&#63875;Location</A><BR>
```

Emoji i-mode Icons

Unique to i-mode is the definition of 166 emoji, or icons, that appear on handsets. Figure 62 shows 8 emoji icons. Icons can conserve display real estate because they represent multiple characters that would take up more space. It is best to insert the actual code into the document with an editor that can handle double-byte characters. These picture symbols are defined by double-byte SHIFT-JIS codes in the cHTML document. An editing tool that allows code input is helpful. With this method, six-byte decimal code is used (&#decimal code;) For example: `黎` designates the picture symbol in emoji slot 127, a box with the numeral 3.

#	Image	Hex	Decimal	Title
121		F983	63875	Location information
122		F984	63876	Free dial
123		F985	63877	Sharp dial
124		F986	63878	MopaQ
125		F987	63879	1
126		F988	63880	2
127		F989	63881	3
128		F98A	63882	4

Figure 62 Eight emoji icons (*Source:* <http://www.nttdocomo.com/i/tag/emoji/index.html>.)

i-mode and the Olympics

To give you some idea of i-mode markup, it is helpful to look at some production pages run during the 2000 Olympics. Note that the cHTML source code skips the DTD declaration. This elimination serves to squeeze those last few bytes out of the phones. The i-mode phones do not require it. When you are creating links, you must use the access key attribute of the tag to map phone keys to the document. DoCoMo suggests that you use its special emoji characters to show button numbers. It is a good idea to wrap only the special character and not the whole line when you are using an anchor; otherwise, scrolling will be slow. You will often see a `?uid=NULLGWDOCOMO` string on the menu URLs. This is for the DoCoMo/CNN registration system. Server-side includes can be used with cHTML because the content type for cHTML is the same as HTML. To also generate WML and HDML from the server requires some definite server tweaking.

The i-mode code and view of the Olympics home page screen in Example 18 shows the source file and the resulting display in Japanese. In the source code, you see the href links are tied to access keys that have been mapped to emoji icons. Also the Japanese katakana, hiragana, and Kanji characters are entered directly with the editor. Note that there are no word spaces in Japanese. In the display, the menu of events uses emoji-generated numbers and Japanese language. Emoji blocks work as underlined links because underlined links mess up the Japanese character set. This home page display links to all the news, business, sports, entertainment, travel, and weather events.

Example 18 i-mode code and view of the Olympics home page screen
(*Source:* Dennis Portello. Copyright © 2001 CNN, Inc. All rights reserved.)

```
<HTML>
<HEAD>
<TITLE>CNN - ﾒ榴{</TITLE>
</HEAD>
<BODY text="black" link="#000099" vlink="#333333">
<DIV align="center"><IMG SRC="/imode/images/cnn.gif" ALT="CNN"
 WIDTH="64" HEIGHT="30" BORDER="0"></DIV>
<!--#include virtual="/imode/jp/news_alert.html"-->
<HR>
<A href="/imode/jp/news_main.html" accesskey="1">□ </A> トップストーリー<BR>
<A href="/imode/jp/news.html" accesskey="2">□ </A> ニュース<BR>
<A href="/imode/jp/business.html" accesskey="3">□ </A> 経済<BR>
<A href="/imode/jp/sports.html" accesskey="4">□ </A> スポーツ<BR>
<A href="/imode/jp/ent.html" accesskey="5">□ </A> ショウビズ<BR>
<A href="/imode/jp/tech.html" accesskey="6">□ </A> テクノロジー<BR>
<A href="/imode/jp/health.html" accesskey="7">□ </A> 健康<BR>
<A href="/imode/jp/style.html" accesskey="8">□ </A> ファッション<BR>
<A href="/imode/jp/travel.html" accesskey="9">□ </A> トラベル<BR>
<A href="/imode/jp/weather.html" accesskey="0">□ </A> 天気  <BR>
<HR>
<!--#include virtual="/imode/jp/register.txt"-->
</BODY>
</HTML>
```

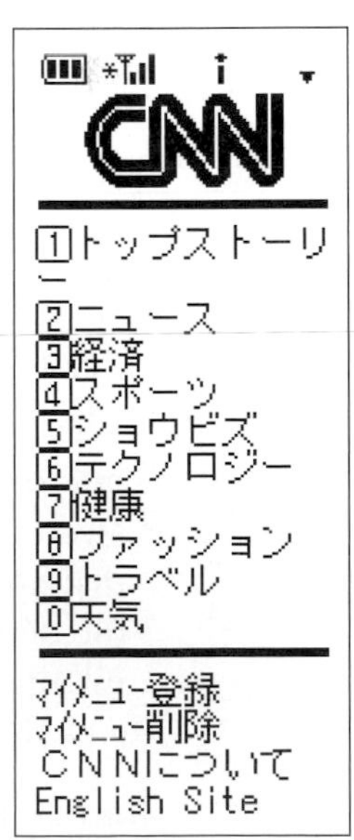

The i-mode cHTML code in Example 18 was edited with a Macintosh system using the BBedit 6 editor, as mentioned in the programmer's comments:

> I do all my development on Macs with the Japanese language kit installed and do all the testing on a PC running Win2k with Japanese as the default region but the language set to English. By the way, BBedit 6 from Bare Bones Software is a full double-byte text editor that comes with a WAP glossary. I did all the development of the i-mode site. Currently I've changed it to Chinese to work on a Chinese site.
>
> — Dennis Portello, Senior Developer, CNN

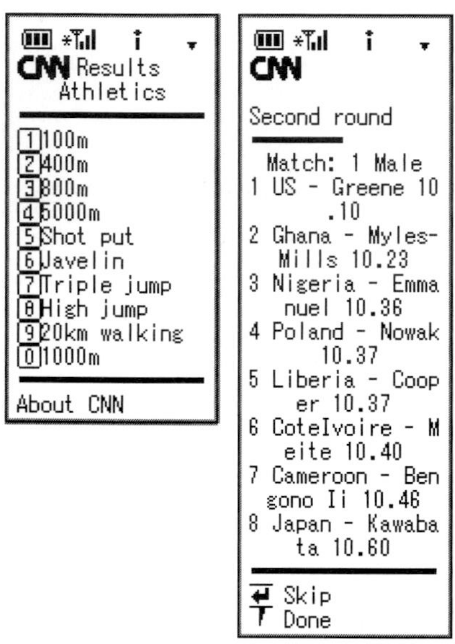

Figure 63 i-mode views of screens for Olympics results (*Source:* Dennis Portello. Copyright © 2001 CNN, Inc. All rights reserved.)

i-mode is for English mobile users as well. For example, in Figure 63 you can see the i-mode views of screens for Olympics results in English in continuing screens of sports pages. The 2000 Olympics results inform the visitors of the events, the country, the individual, and the timing results. Here we see current athletic events and results screens. Even though these screens "played" on phones in Japan, all i-mode content originated from the Internet headquarters of CNN in Atlanta, Georgia, USA. Files were transferred to servers in Japan for optimized traffic response.

Writing Pixo cHTML

Using open Internet standards such as HTML, cHTML, and ECMAScript, the Pixo Internet Microbrowsers provide access to the entire Web. It is very useful to look at the NTT DoCoMo i-mode sites written in cHTML. Pixo lets manufacturers and operators offer dual-browser wireless phones (i.e., cHTML/HTML and WML) to access WAP and i-mode content and services.

Pixo Tools and Where to Get Them

The Pixo developer site is <http://developer.pixo.com/>. The Pixo Internet microbrowser delivers a User-Agent header to identify itself to the server: `User-Agent: Pixo-Browser/2.0`. The microbrowser performs special tasks for Web pages that are specified as "PixoFriendly," including converting graphics to appropriate bit depths, displaying tables, and applying Pixo-designed functionality and formatting. To get these features, add the following markup between the opening and closing <head> element of each Web page:

```
<meta name="PixoFriendly" content="true">
```

When a phone with a Pixo Internet microbrowser sees pages that have this meta tag, it can make use of tables and other specially formatted data. As the Pixo Emulator in Figure 64 shows, you can test your site pages. The best advice for Pixo browser programming is to study cHTML and stay in touch with its Web developer program.

Figure 64 Pixo emulator (*Source:* Copyright © 2000 Pixo, Inc. All rights reserved.)

Writing Palm Query Applications for Wireless Browsing Applications

In the United States, travelers use Palm™ handhelds more than any other device to look at a Web site when mobile. There are a few ways to provide wireless content to owners of Palm handheld devices. The first and easiest wireless application to write to get coverage for your Web site is the popular Palm Query Application (PQA). This is also called Web clipping, which is for Web site browsing only. A fully implemented application is called a Web Clipping Application (WCA). A Palm VIIx™ handheld (Figure 65), or any device with Palm OS® version 3.5 or greater that has a Web browser, can reach your site with a PQA. The older masked ROM Handsprings do not work.

Figure 65 Palm VIIx™ handheld (*Source:* Copyright Palm, Inc. All rights reserved.)

AvantGo also makes a method that is simple to access if you download AvantGo's microbrowser. Without doing much of anything, your Web site is viewable by this HTML-oriented browser, which uses the AvantGo proxy server to pull together Web site material for your Palm handheld. By following the directions at <http://avantgo.com/developer/>, you can increase the effectiveness of your site.

The Palm OS devices are also good for interactive applications. We will look at writing those applications and the SDK tools for programming them in chapter 12, "Developing LAN Interactive Applications."

PQA Tools and Where to Get Them

Most developers simply use the Web Clipping Application (WCA), formerly called QA Builder, tool for PQA development, although you can also use a Palm emulator. WCA Builder is documented at <http://oasis.palm.com/dev/kb/faq/WebClipping/WCABuilder.cfm/>.

The Palm OS handheld devices are everywhere, using many wireless networks. The Palm VII™ handheld operates on Palm.Net®, which uses the Mobitex data network. The Palm V™ with OmniSky uses the CDPD network. The CDPD network delivers at twice the data rate of Mobitex, but the CDPD and Mobitex coverage patterns are different. Then there is Handspring Visor™, which uses Glenayre pagers and the ReFLEX network. A VisorPhone uses the GSM network. The Kyocera smartphone and the SprintPCS TP3000™ use CDMA networks. Regardless of the network, any Palm handheld with a microbrowser can reach your PQA site.

Developing PQAs

Most Web sites can offer a small snapshot of their content using a variant of HTML. The PQA gives a much larger view than a Web phone microbrowser. Palm devices also support location-based access for the PQA, which is detailed next.

While most Palm handhelds are equipped with a browser that lets mobile users navigate the Web and hit Web sites, the PQA is a way to download the top-level pages of a Web site to keep on a personal device. This lets users navigate the site offline and not waste the airtime getting familiar material. The PQA shows Web pages of a Web site especially built for a Palm handheld. When the person taps on a link, it launches an efficient Web request over the wireless Internet. Whereas a microbrowser typically caches pages of a site and then tosses them at the end of a session, the PQA is a hard-coded set of pages that represents the initial pages of a Web site and can be viewed offline at anytime.

With a PQA you can decide which parts of HTML will represent the site. One of the downsides of PQA is that it is difficult to use the Web data. Developers have to use the Copy Page command, which grabs an entire Web page, then whittle the page down with an editor. Mobile users can install a PQA with a HotSync® function or download them over the air from the Web.

How to Convert a Web Site to a PQA

End users can actually create their own PQA versions of a Web site, although it will be limited to the top-level pages. Developers can offer their own versions of their Web sites by designing their own PQAs.

It is fairly easy to understand how a PQA works. When the mobile user taps on a PQA icon, any Palm OS handheld loads and runs the Palm clipper software, which translates the encoded PQA HTML into a working Web page. The application runs like any Web application, making requests and responding.

To make a PQA, many developers use WCABuilder. It is both a Windows and Macintosh program that converts HTML codes and pictures to a PQA. WCABuilder is located on the Palm developer site. Basically, you work with an HTML 3.2 Web page and whittle it down with a Web page editor. Be careful to keep intact all the links or underlying anchors as you edit. Developers can simplify an existing set of Web pages to fit on a Palm OS device screen. This means using HTML 3.2 tags, and small graphics. When you are finished editing your Web pages, then run

WCABuilder. Point to the HTML source file and then press Build, which will grab all Web pages and images and form a file with a .pqa extension. Download this to the handheld, or post it to your Web site for others to download to their handheld devices with Palm OS software. The official source for writing a PQA is at <http://www.palmos.com/dev/tech/Webclipping/>.

PQA graphics can be as large as 153 × 144 pixels with four basic grays. Although there are color Palm OS handhelds, it is advisable to make graphics read in black and white so the images can be read by all devices. From the server, you can special-case color or black-and-white requesting devices. The values inside HTML are white #ffffff, light gray #c0c0c0c0, dark gray #808080, and black #00000000.

If you want to make your HTML file work as a PC Web file and a PQA file, then use the specific tag <SMALLSCREENIGNORE>, which tells a Palm device to skip parts of the Web page. This tag will be ignored by a PC browser. To program the handheld to ignore parts of a Web page (Example 19), use HTML code to print the headline text enclosed in the H1-style tag in all browsers. The microbrowser in the handheld will skip the long text sandwiched between the SMALLSCREENIGNORE tags.

Example 19 Palm HTML tag to ignore parts of Web page

```
<H1>Future Profiles</H1>
The committee signed the final agreement Monday.
<SMALLSCREENIGNORE>
The agreement went on to describe further the third and fourth
    conditions of the project.
</SMALLSCREENIGNORE>
```

Palm Mobile Components

Although the PQA relies on HTML 3.2, Palm has added some interesting new HTML tags to start applications and special components. Developers can get their Palm code to launch any of the internal applications. For example, a link can fire up the Palm address book if you use:

```
<a href="palm:addr.appl">Click here to launch Address Book</a>.
```

All the Palm applications have a four-letter extension: `palm:date.appl` launches the datebook, `palm:calc.appl` launches the calculator, and so on.

To take advantage of the Palm software components designed for quick handheld use, you can modify your Web form to use the DATEPICKER and TIMEPICKER components for INPUT. These nicely designed time and date interfaces vastly simplify input for mobile users.

Palm Location-Based Components

The Palm VII works as a location-based handheld. It can be programmed to send the traveler's current location. The Palm VII network, Palm.Net, is run by Mobitex. That network knows where the data modem is at all times. Mobitex can transmit the location of the nearest cellular tower that is transmitting your data. So, for example, when a person requests the nearest Starbucks, it is actually the Starbucks nearest to the cellular tower being called, which may be a few miles away.

You can access location-based information for the Palm if you have written your HTML forms with a "%ZIPCODE" input tag. Example 20 shows the source code and resulting view of the encoding for a Web page directed to a Palm VII. If you press the Nearby Food button, the zip code will be filled in by the Mobitex gateway by the time the request hits your server. The result is that if you query the request for ZIPMOBILE, it will return the zip code of the nearest cellular tower from which the handheld is making the request. Within your server, this can be matched to a zip code column in your database and return information about restaurants located in that zip code.

Example 20 HTML form code to obtain location

Nearby Food

```
<form method="post" action="http://www.xxxxx.com/scripts/foodform.cgi">
 <input type="hidden" name="zipmobile" value="%zipcode">
 <input type="submit" value="Find Nearby Restaurants">
</form>
```

Another useful Palm OS encoding is "%DEVICEID", which fills in the unique identity of the handheld. This helps to track a user's transaction.

For these Palm applications, your content need be geocoded only at a zip code level, so matching and sorting are easy. When the location precision provided by these handhelds improves, you will need to geocode content for latitude and longitude. (See the section on "Latlon Proximity Algorithms" in chapter 8.)

Web clipping with all its bells and whistles is a very popular way to make a Web site visible to Palm OS devices without a formidable commitment of developers' resources to build a fully interactive client application. There is even a Java development SDK for Palm handhelds. For more on the Palm OS Web browsing application development, visit the following sites:

<http://www.palmos.com/dev/tech/webclipping/gettingstarted.html>
Good tutorial for beginners

<http://www.kyocera-wireless.com/partner/sol_prov_form.htm>
For Palm telephony developers

11 Chapter

Developing WAN Interactive Applications in Java

Unlike the wireless Web browsing model where a developer's effort is simply to produce content on a server, interactive wireless applications require software to be built for the client device. Most cellular phones cannot be programmed, although the SIM toolkit is available for WAP phones. Recently, phones and pagers are offering Java™ programmability. A *Java phone* is a cellular phone that runs a Java virtual machine and executes Java programs. The RIM 957™ is a Java programmable pager introduced in 2000. New Java phones and pagers were introduced to the market in 2001.

Sun Microsystems, Inc., created Java as a network language. A smaller subset that can be developed in the Java2 Micro Edition (J2ME) is designed to work with wireless devices. The Sun Java classification of wireless devices (Figure 66) is a somewhat complex order of devices, development environments, and operating system standards. It may take years before Sun irons out all the acronyms (i.e., J2ME, MIDP, kVM, CLDC, CDC), configurations, and profiles to guide wireless developers with meaningful descriptions of the wireless landscape. The Java phone technology in some ways competes with WAP and i-mode. But to some degree the Java phone also competes with differing definitions of Java products from Sun. Java as a language now presents an incredible variety of dialects, platforms, and APIs: J2ME, J2SE, J2EE, PersonalJava, EmbeddedJava, JavaTV, JavaPhone, and the kVM, to name the most popular.

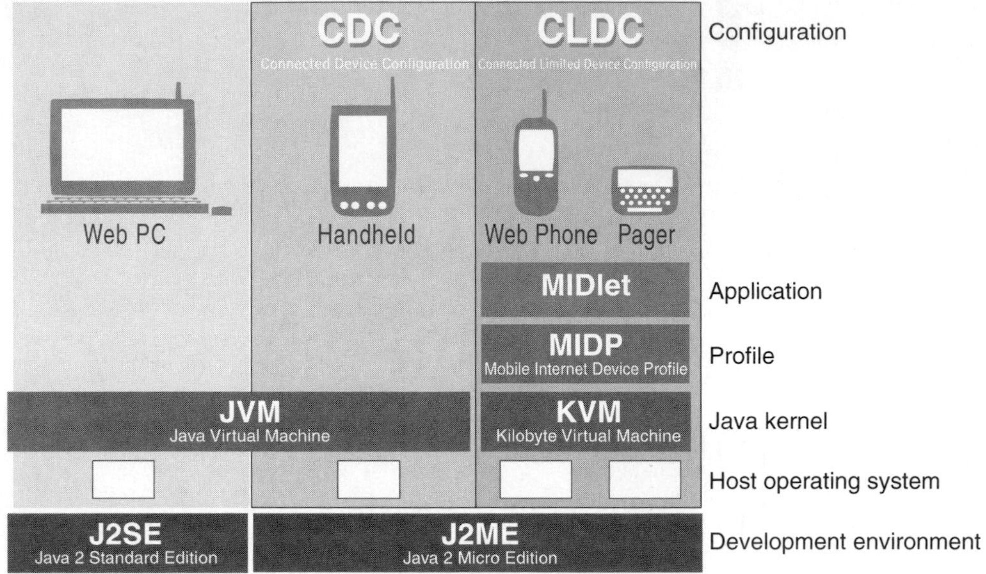

Figure 66 Sun Java classification of wireless devices

The key to understanding the Sun wireless Java space is held in the two families of devices on the low end – the Connected Limited Device Configuration and the Connected Device Configuration. Sun certifies both of them.

- *Connected Limited Device Configuration (CLDC)* devices run a kilobyte virtual machine (kVM). The kVM is a general name for the lightweight Java Virtual Machine. They have profiles like the Mobile Internet Device Profile (MIDP). CLDC devices usually have from 128 to 512 kilobytes of memory. Web phones and pagers are CLDC devices supported by a number of vendors. The LG Java Web phones appeared in 2000. In 2001, Motorola, Nokia, and DoCoMo marketed CLDC Java Web phones.
- *Connected Device Configuration (CDC)* devices run a Java Virtual Machine (JVM). CDC devices have 1 megabyte of memory or more. The Palm handhelds are supposed to have CDC profiles, however, most developers use the CLDC profile that uses the phone-style MIDP profile.

Both CDC and CLDC require the J2ME development environment, which attempts to bridge the differences among handhelds, Web phones, and pagers by producing Java programs. Java has always claimed to be a portable code model.

However, applications written for these small-scale Java devices will generally not run on any other Java device. This is largely because the low-end Java operating system kernel, the kVM, is being implemented as efficiently as possible and optimized for each device. A smart phone application will be extremely unlikely to work on a Palm handheld. There are programming techniques that are more portable than others, which we will discuss shortly.

Java J2ME Tools and Where to Get Them

Wireless Java developers can find a wide range of tools on the Web. The J2ME SDK includes a J2ME emulator, but you need a kVM from a vendor to run it. Here are sources for the major tools.

- <http://java.sun.com/j2me> – The generic toolkit from Sun. Vendors such as Motorola, Nokia, and RIM have their own J2ME tools. The Motorola and RIM tools are covered in the next sections.
- <http://www.kvmworld.com> – General source of information on the many kVM implementations.
- <http://kXML.enhydra.org> – Open Source client for a Java Phone XML parser.

Developing Java Wireless Applications

Why do people want wireless Java instead of SMS messaging or cHTML browsing? It is because they have to do applications that do not require a connection, are specialized applications beyond the scope of messaging and browsing, need extra security or other components, or want to run games or specialized software. By making the phone programmable and offering a widely used language to developers such as Java these applications can be written. Java devices are designed for sophisticated interactive applications.

Until J2ME and BREW™, the only programmability seen on Web phones had been through WAP WMLScript, which has very limited functions. Furthermore, WMLScript was designed so that most scripts have to execute on the WAP gateway – not very swift, as you might guess. Java is also free of the phone microbrowser. Microbrowsers, initially useful, are notoriously unpredictable at memory caching. Intelligent object caching is a key to efficient mobile use.

There are two important classes of interactive applications. A stand-alone application, such as a game, resides in memory. The other type of application connects to a server to provide updated information, such as a stock quote application that connects to a quote server.

J2ME Application Development

Writing Java in a J2ME SDK is not like programming desktop or server Java in a J2SE™ or J2EE™ SDK. J2ME was originally designed for iAppliances like television set-top boxes. J2ME now applies to standard wireless devices such as pagers and Web phones. J2ME produces Java applications that run on top of the kVM. The kVM implements only a subset of the Java Virtual Machine specification. J2ME features:

- Java language subset
- A virtual machine – kVM for a CLDC device and JVM for a CDC device
- Core classes and APIs
- Additional libraries for each configuration and profile
- Tools for deployment and device configuration including a verifier and a converter
- Configuration libraries (CLDC or CDC) and APIs for a family of devices
- Profile libraries and APIs for a vertical set of devices (e.g., the MIDP profile for Java phones)

In the case of wireless devices, the J2ME CLDC addresses characteristics such as battery operation, constrained memory, limited processing power, and low bandwidth, high-latency network connections.

The Sun J2ME application stack (Figure 67) shows that an application runs on a profile on a configuration on a kVM on a host operating system. The J2ME wireless toolkit defines MIDP for CLDC phones. The MIDP is a family and not device specific. MIDP must use HTTP, even if it is implemented over TLS/PDC-P or WAP. Nokia has to implement the MIDP APIs. Pagers and handhelds have another set of names that Sun has not made official.

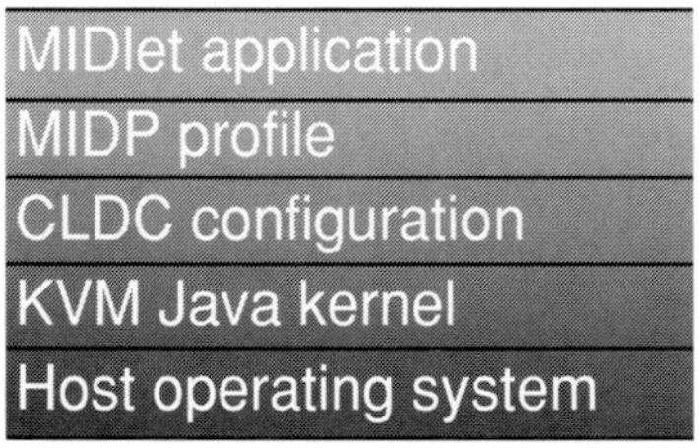

MIDlet application
MIDP profile
CLDC configuration
KVM Java kernel
Host operating system

Figure 67 J2ME application stack

Configurations provide common functions to a family of devices. J2ME can be deployed in multiple configurations. A configuration specifies minimum requirements for the virtual machine for devices with a similar footprint and functions. The CLDC reference was certified in 2000 for Java phones and pagers. Sun provides the reference model in its J2ME. The CDC reference from Palm, Inc., should eventually be certified.

Profiles are a set of class libraries and APIs that are built for devices in specific vertical markets. Profiles exist within a J2ME configuration. A profile can provide flexibility without loss of portability. A profile provides a user interface, input methods, persistence mechanisms, and so on. Profiles specify APIs and libraries for specific devices. They are defined through the Java Community Process (JCP). Motorola is the lead for the MIDP profile, although Nokia is a participant. The MIDP was certified after going through Sun compatibility tests.

Together the MIDP set of Java APIs and the CLDC provide a complete J2ME application run-time environment for Java phones. The MIDP specification defines the user interface, persistence storage, networking, and the application model. The MIDP storage model is a database, not a filing system.

The PDA Profile for the Palm OS® exists for CDC devices, in other words, handhelds. Other profiles under development are the Foundation Profile, which has no Graphical User Interface, the Personal Profile, which replaces Personal Java, and the Remote Method Invocation, or RMI, Profile to access very large machines.

MIDlet

A MIDlet is an application that runs on a Java phone. It is similar to an applet that runs in a browser or a servlet that runs on a server. All MIDlets are containers for code. Unlike applets, MIDlets do not need reloading. You download a MIDlet and store it. A MIDlet runs on top of the MIDP profile.

There are two ways to write MIDP applications for your CLDC. You can write applications that are either portable or device specific. MIDP application interfaces (Table 26) have a high-level API that ensures portability, and a low-level API that takes advantage of the characteristics of the device. Theoretically, if the MIDlet is written with only high-level MIDP APIs, it will run on any device in the MIDP family and possibly on any Java computer.

The application finally gets on a device by either cradle synchronizing or transmission over the air. The software distribution technique is up to the CLDC manufacturer.

Java provides improved memory management and cross-platform compatibility through the abstraction of a single small-footprint version of the JVM as the

Table 26 MIDP application interfaces

High-level MIDP API	Low-level MIDP API
• High level of abstraction with very little control over look and feel • High degree of portability across devices • Underlying implementation will do the necessary adaptation to device's hardware and native UI style. • Example: buttons, keys • Good for business applications	• Little abstraction • Provides precise placement and control of graphic elements and access to low-level input events • Not portable • Example: drawing functions • Good for games

kVM. To write Palm MIDlets you need Palm OS® v3.01 or higher. The distribution includes documentation, the kVM class library, and tools to package and install Java applications on devices with Palm operating systems.

The kVM is a lightweight JVM capable of executing Java programs. The CLDC kVM is designed specifically for small mobile devices with 16/32-bit RISC/CISC microprocessors, and with as little as 160 KB of total memory, of which 128 KB are for the virtual machine and libraries themselves. Aimed at the CLDC, the kVM is only 40 KB of object code. The kVM can be customized. Several Java language and virtual machine features have been made optional. A particular J2ME configuration defines which of these optional features must be included in the kVM implementation.

The kVM memory budget is to fit within a 128 KB footprint, of which 80 KB are needed for the virtual machine and the remaining space is reserved for application heap space. The garbage collection is small and simple. It does not move, uses single-spaced format, and marks and sweeps. It operates with heap sizes in tens of kilobytes and is handle-free.

If you install the developer's release of the kVM, you will see that some optional features are included in this implementation. Future configurations are likely to support a broader set of options. One of the goals of the kVM was to support incremental deployment of J2ME features, so a future kVM implementation should allow selection of added features. The following features are optional language elements: long, float, double, multidimensional arrays, recoverable handling of error classes, threads, event handling, JNI, class loaders, and finalization.

Most developers like the overall simplification of the Generic Connection Framework, which replaces 200 KB of network and storage libraries. One call, `Connector.open`, does it all.

- HTTP – `Connector.open ("http://www.site.com")`
- Sockets – `Connector.open ("socket://129.144.111.222:9000")`
- Communication ports – `Connector.open ("comm:0;baudrate=9600")`
- Datagrams – `Connector.open ("datagram://129.144.111.333")`
- Files – `Connector.open ("file:/personal.dat")`

Differences between DoCoMo i-appli and Sun MIDP

On January 26, 2001, DoCoMo started the mobile Java application market by introducing two Java phones, the i503f (Fujitsu) and i503p (Panasonic). These phones run Java applications in a branded service called i-appli. The market introduction began with 38 Java applets. These early Java applets include animated Mickey Mouse or Hello Kitty clocks, stock charting, karaoke, mapping, and arcade versions of Tetris, Space Invaders, and Pac-Man. All of the applets are 10 KB or smaller. The Japanese Java phones are able to download and store five applets in memory. Unfortunately, all the Mitsubishi phones that run Java were called back after a reset bug was discovered, but they were soon fixed and reintroduced.

To create an i-appli MIDlet, create a class that subclasses `com.nttdocomo.ui.IApplication` and override the public void `start()` method. The extra step you take when creating the MIDlet is to extend MIDlet from Sun's MIDP profile. Application descriptor files are specified by NTT DoCoMo's jam file. Sun MIDlets use a jad file.

J2ME Competitors

Sun is not the only producer of small Java environments. The first wireless Java phone, the Korean LG phone, did not use Sun "standards." It used its own Java subset. Here are other sources of environments that are similar to J2ME for wireless devices:

- J9 – IBM. The most evolved J2ME IDE is the Visual Age Micro Edition development environment. You develop under the VAME IDE. J9 is IBM's kVM that comes in five sizes.
- Waba – Wabasoft <http://wabasoft.com>.
- Jbed – Esmertec makes a Java compiler and JVM. With a compiled Java bytestream, an application runs on a Jbed JVM up to twenty times faster than a conventional JVM. Developers of code for the J2ME and MIDP can seamlessly switch over to Jbed Micro Edition CLDC and Jbed Profile for MIDP.
- Kada VM – Emworks produces a small proprietary Java VM.
- Redwave Onyx – Redwave Technology, Inc., produces the Java kVM called Onyx intended to match their Java Application Integration Development Environment (JAIDE) server; see <http://www.redwavetech.com/>.
- Hewlett-Packard's MicrochaiVM is a 20 KB kernel that uses a highly compressed form of Java.

Other commercial competitors to the Java kVM are QUALCOMM BREW and Microsoft Stinger with environments that can run applications on handsets.

Writing for the Java Phone

Java phones appeared from several manufacturers in 2001 including Motorola, Nokia, Ericsson, DoCoMo, and Siemens. The largest introduction of Java handsets was the Nextel i85s™ (Figure 68) and Nextel i50xs™ made by Motorola.

Motorola introduced the Accompli™ 008, a J2ME GPRS touch screen phone. Each manufacturer has a different J2ME development kit, although from a developer's point of view they are very similar.

The effective working memory is 640 KB, although preloaded applications usually take 120 KB. The target size for your application is expected to be 50 KB or smaller.

Figure 68 Nextel i85s™ (*Source:* Copyright © 2001 Motorola, Inc. All rights reserved.)

Java Phone Tools and Where to Get Them

The Sun Java site has a good introduction to programming with MIDP. The implementation for each wireless device is slightly different. You can get the early Kitty Hawk J2ME from LG that runs on the LG3000 phone in Korea. There are also the Palm, IBM, and now the Motorola J2ME implementations. For more information, visit these sites:

- <http://java.sun.com/j2me> – The generic toolkit from Sun
- <http://www.idendev.com> – For Motorola J2ME, kVM
- <http://kXML.enhydra.org> – Open source client XML parser
- <http://www.kvmworld.com> – General source of information

Palm and RIM BlackBerry also have a J2ME and kVM available from their sites. The RIM is covered in the section "Writing Java Code for Interactive Wireless Applications on a Pager" later in this chapter.

Inside Java Phones

The low-level phone software of the Motorola Java phone is partitioned into three parts. Java phone architecture (Figure 69) is a tripolar combination of a radio operating system (ROS) partition, a Java partition, and a WAP partition. The partitions are separated by iron walls. To ensure security, no APIs are exposed. The ROS partition handles all the low-level parts of the phone call, radio traffic, security, and billing. The WAP compartment operates the standard WML microbrowser and implements the WAP protocol stack. The software in the WAP partition is typically licensed by a company in the WAP Forum. The Java kVM runs in its own partition. Engineers from the handset company usually design the kVM as well as the ROS. This is how the three pieces of system software work together. On your phone, if you are in WAP mode and click on a link that refers to a Java MIDP application on the Internet, then your server responds with a .jad MIME request for the stored application on the server. This is an important

Figure 69 Java phone architecture

step, learned from i-mode use. The 200-byte descriptor file contains information such as size, capability, pricing, and so on. Customers might see a charge for the service presented on the display that is held in the descriptor. If they accept it, it downloads the file. When the file has arrived, the phone microbrowser passes it to the ROS, which invokes the Java run-time kVM that loads and executes the MIDlet code.

CLDC 1.0 has no floating point, no JNI, no reflection. It also lacks Remote Method Invocation (RMI), a mainstay of Java programming. However, a trick used by developers is to message a remote JNI in the cloud. Byte code verification is now improved with a preverifier. Reverification can be executed out on the network before the application arrives on the device. The code is full of the standard lines java.lang, java.util, java.io, and the extensions are all javax.microedition. ISO-Latin1 is the text standard required for CLDC. The early versions of CLDC J2ME also have no Java Telephone Application Programming Interfaces (JTAPI), which is required to generate phone calls from Java.

Standard MIDP methods include Start, Pause, Active, and Destroy. There is no Finalization. Because handsets are localized to their populations, you need to access native languages, which are made available through `System.getProperty`.

For more information on Java phone programming and J2ME visit:

- <http://www.billday.com> – Sun spokesperson for J2ME
- <http://developer.java.sun.com/developer/technicalArticles/wireless/midpgetstart> – Useful introduction to programming

Java Dependability and Security

To the telcos, a phone cannot crash. Yet this does happen to Java phones and WAP phones. (Pixo had a contest to see who could write the shortest line of Java code to crash a Java phone; there were many responses, some in one line of code). Telco operators are worried about the consumer expectation that the cellular phone has been and should always be a stable product. It is one of the reasons there is the three-way partition in Java phone architecture. Within the partition, only the device manufacturer can use the native file formats created. Software developers are prevented from accessing them.

End-to-end security is a top issue for Java phone projects. So far, there is no definite standard. One of the secure aspects of the system is that the Java phone will do byte code verification. Also, a MIDlet can access only its data and runs in its own memory. There is an allowance to bundle applications to form a MIDlet suite. These suites can be put into one JAR file and be allowed to collaborate. Sun worked on Kilobyte Secure Socket Layer (KSSL), which can be programmed to secure a connection over a TLS protocol.

Java MIDlet Server

To send a Java MIDlet from a server you need to provide not only the application, but also a JAD file. The JAD is the Java Application Descriptor for a MIDP application developed in J2ME. It precedes the transmission of a MIDlet and is typically a 200-byte descriptor file containing size and capabilities. If accepted, your server is to send the associated Java MIDlet. To configure your server to send Java phone MIDlets, use the following two lines of code.

```
MIDlet Descriptor    .jad   text/vnd.sun.j2me.app-descriptor
DTD                  .dtd   text/plain
```

Writing Java Code for Interactive Wireless Applications on a Pager

Pager messaging applications reach a wide network. One of the most popular devices you are likely to see is the Research in Motion (RIM) 957™ pager (Figure 70), which uses the BlackBerry™ email service over the Mobitex network. Aside from having an email client, the RIM messaging pager is programmable in Java. These applications run under the RIM kVM, as do all the PIM applications that come on the device. The general parameters for the RIM 957 device are:

Figure 70 RIM 957™ pager (*Source:* Copyright © 2001 Research In Motion.)

- 160 × 160 pixels
- 16 lines of text
- Full QWERTY keyboard

Pager Tools and Where to Get Them

The Web sites of the makers of the Research in Motion device and the standard tools are:

- <http://developers.RIM.net/handhelds> – RIM BlackBerry™ IDE for all lines of their pagers.
- <http://www.blackberry.net> – Developer support organization for RIM. This includes the C++ and RIM J2ME and kVM for its pagers
- <http://www.motorola.com/developers/wireless/> – Motorola Applications Global Network (MAGNET) manages the developer support programs for the Accompli™ 009 Personal Interactive Communicator and other pagers.

Developing Pager Messaging, SMS Games, and Interactive Applications

Messaging is used far more than Web microbrowsing, but the application is not much more sophisticated than a phone call transmitting information between a caller and a receiver. Wireless Internet developers are changing this.

Messaging control on the server to send an enterprise-to-person message or an important alert usually depends on integrating with a decision support system or a legacy messaging system. Although some pagers work as signaling devices, others have sophisticated two-way email and are part of a Lotus Domino or Microsoft Exchange solution. In Europe there are a number of innovative approaches to messaging using SMS messaging, and it is an open door to reapplication within North American paging systems.

Many Web phone developers begin with SMS messaging applications. In Finland wireless developers say that most companies are introducing SMS applications before WML or a WAP application. There are some practical reasons for this. In Europe all devices do SMS, and a small percentage do WAP. Messaging is a more flexible and useful format. There are more SMS devices than there are WAP devices, and the charges are far lower than for WAP access to a WML site. Messaging applications could be anything from a game to a business messaging system. SMS games are common and they are now being written with the messaging model.

Messaging can be thought of as an alternative form of looking at a browser application. It is a matter of breaking down what were formerly pages into messaging prompts and responses. Games as messaging applications rely on a game server to coordinate play and players. This is how popular games like Gladiator by JAMDAT Mobile and Trivia by Indiqu Mobile Entertainment Channels work. They are written as dialogs in message-and-response form. The Indiqu games work compatibly with an email, instant messaging, or SMS system. And they could just as easily operate over HTTP and use Web pages. Wireless game companies find wireless messaging devices and pagers ideal for moving messages fast and keeping the game going.

To develop interactive games and business applications that run standalone on a Java pager, you need good developer tools. The emulator for the RIM BlackBerry operating system is very sophisticated. It can simulate the target Java deployment environment and many real-world mobile conditions. You can test your application with this emulator that simulates variable tower strength. This tests if your software recovers from signal loss at any given time.

All RIM platforms are based on the Intel 386 and are multithreaded, multitasking operating environments that allow up to 31 simultaneous applications. A large number of APIs are available for developers within the RIM BlackBerry system API (Figure 71). These APIs include display, AutoText, on board applications

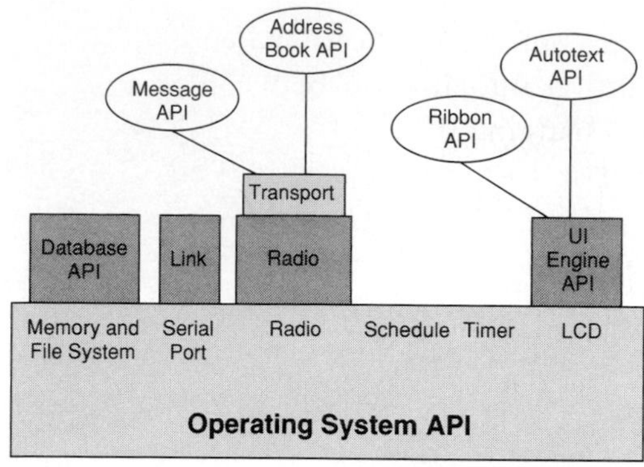

Figure 71 BlackBerry™ system API (*Source:* Copyright © 2001 Research In Motion.)

such as the address book, and email message handling. There is support for lower-level services like timers, scheduling, serial port, the thumbwheel, file system, memory, and so on. The RIM two-way pager works almost like a handheld; the SDK is designed for C++ and also has a Java 2 Micro Edition code library that supports the Sun MIDP.

In working with RIM, as with many paging systems, you do have to decode the 512-byte radio packets per application by assigning application. RIM low-level radio access (Example 21) uses standard C language buffering techniques to send radio packets. In J2ME, low-level access is available though a Radio class. However, the preferred method is to use the CLDC connector class to ensure portability.

Example 21 RIM low-level radio access (*Source:* Courtesy of Research In Motion.)

```
int SendPingToSelf (void)
{
  MPAK_HEADER header;
  char buffer[30];
  RADIO_INFO info;
  int SentTag;
  RadioGetDetailedInfo (&info);
  memset memset((unsigned char *)&header, 0, sizeof sizeof(header));
  header.Destination = info.LocalMAN; ;
  header.MpakType = MPAK_TEXT;
  SentTag = RadioSendMpak(&header, (unsigned char *)"This is a test", 14);
  if (SentTag SentTag >= 0){
     RimSprintf(buffer, sizeof sizeof(buffer), "Submitted tag = %d",
        SentTag);
     putline(buffer);
  } else {
     putline("Not sent");
  }
  return SentTag;
}
```

Wireless XML Browsers

XML has a special place in wireless technology. It is used heavily on servers and is a promising solution on wireless devices as well. Wireless Java developers have shown XML browsers on Java phones receiving XML streams over HTTP. The

XML stream is used to transmit and synchronize data. We will see how this works in a minute.

In order for browsers to work, the Web server computes the content and the display for every model of wireless device. Observe that for every piece of WML text the user sees, there is three times as much markup code to support it. The way XML works, you can transmit the XML data with no markup then combine later it with a corresponding style sheet full of markup code. An XML content stream can be sent to any device, which can then continue to format it to create a presentation. Developers are now exchanging pure wireless XML between the server and the wireless device. This is one of the special capabilities of the Java phone client and the Microsoft .NET servers.

XML exchange is not yet a standard of Java phones and other wireless devices. XML browsing is via XML streams sent over HTTP. The receiving device, such as a Java phone, has a lightweight XML parser to process the incoming XML stream from the server. The parser runs under the Java phone kVM to combine XML content with an onboard style sheet to generate conventional microbrowser pages or unique applications. This technique of constructing pages on the fly has powerful advantages when Web browsing; however, it presents a great challenge. XML browsers, just like MIDlets, have no standard user interface, which diminishes general use. Mobile user interface components are largely different from the PC variety. Consider how calendars and times are set, or signatures are captured. The mobile version is very different. The industry has not settled yet on a mobile browser. Engineers and designers creating their own Graphic User Interfaces (GUIs) will find this a blessing and a curse. This is new territory. Some lightweight XML parsers worth using are kxml, tinyXML, and wbXML.

Developing WAN Interactive BREW™ Applications in C++ and Java

QUALCOMM, Incorporated, supplies BREW™, or Binary Runtime Environment for Wireless, software for developers to create powerful next-generation applications. Applications developed using BREW allow end users to download them over the air through a telco carrier network. BREW applications run on all new QUALCOMM® CDMA chipset phones and use their many new features. Through a special application certification process, QUALCOMM asserts that programs are stable and guaranteed to not crash telephones. Compliance testing ensures a minimum level of application stability including basic functionality tests and verification by digital signature. The certification program provides telco operators with the comfort level they need before they introduce applications onto their networks.

brew™

BREW leverages the underlying QUALCOMM chip capabilities including Bluetooth, gpsOne, data access, MIDI, and MP3 processing. These are the Internet LaunchPad™ features that give end users many new 3G services. Developers write code with APIs that access the chip and the underlying REX operating system. These chip functions are shown in the MSM5500™ functional block diagram, (Figure 104), in the section "The Revolution in 3G Chips" in chapter 19.

BREW Tools and Where to Get Them

QUALCOMM provides an SDK and a complete set of tools at <http://brew.QUALCOMM.com>, where you can find BREW SDK™ for newer CDMA handsets. BREW is ideal for cdma2000 phones; Samsung and kyocera are suppliers of these early phones.

To write software in BREW, developers use a Windows-based SDK that includes a handset emulator and code development tools. BREW software architecture (Figure 72) supports wireless applications that leverage many interesting elements. In addition to standard applications (e.g., a microbrowser, PIM, and email), the BREW architecture includes a map viewer, a framework for games, sound management, and avatars – a way to generally represent people and services.

Java programmers can also write BREW applications. Although the primary development environment uses C or C++, QUALCOMM offers Java through J2ME licensees such as Redwave, Insignia, and HP. The HP Microchai VM was shown at the BREW developer conference in May 2001. It offers Java APIs for all BREW libraries. The final application is compiled for an ARM target.

Software developers can take advantage of new software functions on a portable device to make many new applications appropriate within 2.5G and 3G networks. Yet, these chips are also useful in LANs and PANs. BREW applications can work offline and when the device is in range of a WAN tower it can reconnect. There is also a good opportunity for middleware libraries to perform data and connection management. After completing development of your application, you must put it through the compatibility testing program. Telco carrier acceptance is necessary for them to pass applications over telcos' networks.

To write a BREW application, you need to obtain a unique class ID from QUALCOMM. You also must get a Verisign class 3 certificate to ensure the kind of security that a telco expects. Next you need the module information file (MIF), which contains the class ID. With Visual C++, create a new project for developing a Win32 dynamic link library (DLL). Names of the directory, project, and DLL must all match. Include the source files AEEAppGen.c and AEEModGen.c. Build the BREW application as a DLL. When it is compiled and linked, launch the BREW emulator and set the application directory to include both the MIF and the application. The VC++ debugger can be used to step through your

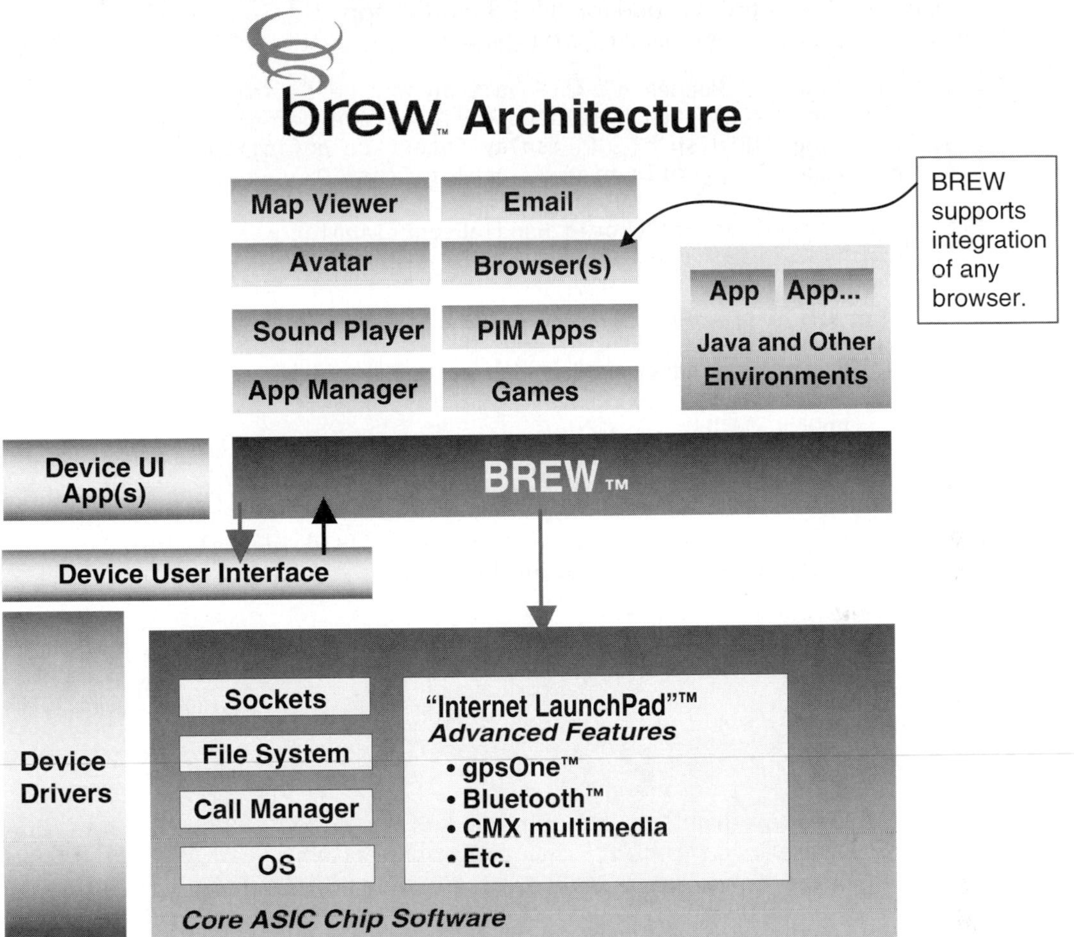

Figure 72 BREW software architecture (*Source:* Copyright © 2001 QUALCOMM, Inc.)

application. The final application is compiled with a code generator for the native ARM processor. Let's look at a basic application in BREW and see how it works.

The BREW Hello-World applet (Example 22) clears the screen, displays the "Hello World" message, and instructs the display interface to update the screen. It uses a simple applet stub source file provided with the BREW SDK. This file is compiled and linked with the applet and provides the necessary interface required to support the IModule and IApplet interfaces. This allows the application developer to focus on handling a few of the BREW events passed to its HandleEvent method.

Example 22 BREW C code for "Hello World" applet
(*Source:* Copyright © 2001 QUALCOMM , Inc.)

```
#include "AEEModGen.h" // Module interface definitions
#include "AEEAppGen.h" // Applet interface definitions
#include "AEEDisp.h" // Display interface definitions
#include "helloworld.bid" // Applet ClassID

static boolean HelloWorld_HandleEvent(IApplet * pi, AEEEvent eCode,
uint16 wParam, uint32 dwParam);

// Applet loading function
int AEEClsCreateInstance(AEECLSID ClsId,IShell * pIShell,
IModule * po,void ** ppObj)
{
   *ppObj = NULL;

   if(ClsId == AEECLSID_HELLOWORLD)
   {
   if(AEEApplet_New(sizeof(AEEApplet), ClsId, pIShell,po,
     (IApplet**)ppObj, (AEEHANDLER)HelloWorld_HandleEvent,
     NULL) == TRUE)
   {
     return (AEE_SUCCESS);
   }
  }
  return (EFAILED);
}

// The event handling function
static boolean HelloWorld_HandleEvent(IApplet * pi, AEEEvent eCode,
uint16 wParam, uint32 dwParam)
{
  AECHAR szBuf[] = {'H','e','l','l','o',' ','W','o','r','l','d','\0'};

  AEEApplet * pMe = (AEEApplet*)pi;

  switch (eCode)
  {
  case EVT_APP_START: // Start Applet event
     IDISPLAY_ClearScreen (pMe->m_pIDisplay); // Erase Screen

     // Display string on the screen
     IDISPLAY_DrawText(pMe->m_pIDisplay, AEE_FONT_BOLD, szBuf,
     -1, 0, 0, 0, IDF_ALIGN_CENTER | IDF_ALIGN_MIDDLE);
     IDISPLAY_Update (pMe->m_pIDisplay); // Flush output to screen

     return(TRUE);
  case EVT_APP_STOP:
     return TRUE;
```

```
48.    default:
49.       break;
50.    }
51.    return FALSE;
52. }
```

This example shows the elementary operations of the BREW application handler. The "Hello World" message is shown when the EVT_APP_START event is received by the applet. This event is received by the application's HandleEvent function when the BREW Application Execution Environment (AEE) starts the applet. BREW isolates all device-specific event processing. Although applets can elect to handle many events, doing so is not a requirement of the AEE. This leaves you to concentrate on the functions required by your application, rather than focusing on any device-specific requirements. The following paragraphs describe by line numbers the "Hello World" application C source code that is shown in Example 22.

Lines 1 through 3 The first four lines include files needed by the Hello-World application.

- The AEEModGen.h and AEEAppGen.h files define the Module and Applet functions.
- The AEEDisp.h file includes the definitions of the IDisplay interface.

Line 4 includes the helloworld.bid file. This file contains the definition of the unique AEECLSID_HELLOWORLD ClassID of the applet. An application developer will have to use a value that is not used by another application. This value is obtained from QUALCOMM BREW Interface Registry and is set by the Module Information File (MIF) Editor.

Lines 6 and 7 Forward declaration of the HandleEvent function prototype.

Lines 10 through 25 These lines define the standard load function that must be provided by all modules.

The Hello World applet is loaded into the BREW Emulator as a DLL. This follows the dynamic loading model that is also used on the target device. In order to support this mechanism, the applet must export a single entry point into the module. From the BREW emulator, this entry point will be exported as a DLL entry point. Under the Device BREW environment, this function must be exported as follows:

- For statically linked modules (.LIB), the entry point must be given a unique name that can be added by the device integrator into the module table.

- For dynamically loaded modules (.MOD), the entry point must be located at the start of the first file linked. The purpose of the AEEClsCreateInstance() function is to create an instance of the AEEApplet data structure for each applet or class supported by the module. The AEEApplet data structure is created by invoking the AEEApplet_New() function with the address of the applet's specific handle event function. The first parameter is the size of the applet's data structure. In this example, there is no data this applet needs to store, so the AEEApplet data structure is used. In the Hello World module, only one applet is supported. At *line 17* the AEEApplet_New() function is invoked to create the AEEApplet data structure of the Hello World module. Upon successful loading of the applet, AEE_SUCCESS is returned.

Lines 28 through 52 The HelloWorld_HandleEvent() function processes all the events the applet receives. The event type, the subevent type, and the event data are passed in the eCode, wParam, and dwParam parameters, respectively.

- The switch statement at *line 35* looks at the main event received by the applet.
- If the event is EVT_APP_START, the applet has received a START event.
- The IDISPLAY_ClearScreen() function erases the whole screen.
- The IDISPLAY_DrawText() function is used to display the text string "Hello World" in the middle of the screen. The flags IDF_ALIGN_CENTER and IDF_ALIGH_MIDDLE are used to place the text string in the center of the screen along the horizontal and vertical display coordinates. Finally, the IDISPLAY_Update() function is used to update the screen.

EVT_APP_START and EVT_APP_STOP are the only two events this application supports. When the user presses the END key on the device, the applet receives the EVT_APP_STOP event. When this event is received by the applet, it needs to do applet-specific cleanup such as saving files and releasing memory allocated by applet. Because the Hello World applet does not allocate resources, there is no cleanup needed when the EVT_APP_STOP event is received.

Unlike the Java phone approach, BREW applications are instantly portable across every device that implements BREW without any code change. For now, this includes all the new handsets using the QUALCOMM CDMA chipsets.

Perhaps the largest advantage BREW developers have over the Java developers is the automatic source of income from BREW's automatic billing mechanism known as the Application Download Server (ADS). The ADS is built into any carrier network running BREW applications, as illustrated later in the BREW distribution model (Figure 89) in chapter 16.

12 Chapter

Developing LAN Interactive Applications

Professional wireless applications are a nearly invisible industry that has been operating in the United States since the late 1980s. These applications are off the radar of popular wireless development, yet these business systems, the machine designs, and the operating system optimizations all provide an incredibly rich source of working wireless examples. Some of their mobile interfaces and utilities are forerunners of many up-and-coming Bluetooth™ and 3G functions.

The industrial handhelds and their networks have even more features to offer a commercial business than an individual consumer. An *industrial handheld* is an integrated handheld software and hardware device that has met IP54 environmental sealing compliance code, which makes it impervious to windblown dust and rain. IP codes (Industrial Protection, the number is the classification) indicate degrees of protection provided by the enclosures for electrical equipment. In the code IP54, for example, IP identifies the standard, the 5 describes the level of protection from solid objects, and the 4 describes the level of protection from liquids. The European Committee for Electrotechnical Standardization (CENELEC) developed these codes. Industrial handhelds like the Symbol Technologies SBT-1700 (Figure 73) can also tolerate a wide range of temperatures and easily withstand a drop to the ground. It is ideal for using the integrated Symbol scanning technology. Industrial handhelds and their manufacturers are listed in Table 45 in chapter 19, the section "Industrial Handhelds."

Figure 73 Symbol SBT-1700 (*Source:* Courtesy of Symbol Technologies.)

Industrial handhelds with modular card slots, first introduced with the communicators by General Magic, Inc., are now popular in handhelds like the Handspring Visor. The Pocket PC or Palm handheld can also be made to perform industrial tasks. Sales Force Automation software is a good example of a Palm OS® application that can synchronize and compete with the heavier-duty wireless LAN handhelds.

Many handhelds can operate in a wireless LAN environment (wireless Ethernet). Not having to pay per minute charges for air access or the costs of wiring a facility can be a cost-effective return on investment for businesses using wireless networks even though they have to buy and configure the wireless access points. Designing wireless LAN applications includes establishing points where mobile workers come into range of the basestations, because most of their work is offline and out of range.

Handheld Industrial Tools and Where to Get Them

Handheld devices require an SDK, which is available directly from the manufacturer. The SDK is designed chiefly to program the client, although there are special sets of libraries to exchange data or synchronize with a server. The Palm OS, PocketPC, Psion, and EPOC operating systems each have at least one SDK.

Symbol <http://www.symbol.com/services/downloads/ppt2700_pocket_pc.html>. Symbol provides handheld applications that use the Microsoft WinCE and the Palm OS development platforms. You must register with Symbol as well as Palm or Microsoft. Symbol provides special drivers for its many communications and scanning devices. Developers largely use the Symbol state-of-the-art, integrated barcode scanning technology.

Palm <http://www.palmos.com/dev/index.html>. Palm developers use the wide range of tools for development of the Palm OS that exists on many mobile platforms.

Microsoft <http://msdn.microsoft.com/cetools/>. Microsoft has many tools that are part of its CD distribution. We will cover its development program shortly.

Linux for handhelds <http://www.handhelds.org/>. Linux developers are also using wireless platforms. To use a Linux OS you have to completely overwrite the OS on the handheld. Handhelds.org is a popular source of a Linux OS for handhelds such as the Compaq iPAQ H3600. Transmeta, the maker of the efficient code-morphing Crusoe chipset, supports Linux and Windows wireless handhelds and tools. The Transmeta developer site is <http://www.transmeta.com/dev/>.

Third-party tools are also made to support development. A well-rounded cross-platform development environment used for many years by wireless Internet developers is CodeWarrior. Other third-party tools, such as Pumatech Satellite Forms®, are listed in the Palm and Pocket PC sections.

Writing Professional Wireless Business Applications

High-bandwidth wireless networks are used widely in business. Although the PocketPC and Palm handhelds are used more and more in business, the established players such as Symbol and Intermec have produced many commercial wireless applications. These companies manufacture rock-solid dependable handhelds that work over reliable networks. Most people have seen Avis, FedEx, and UPS agents use wireless applications to process customers. They use specially built wireless devices that synchronize with corporate dispatch and inventory databases. Handhelds work well in batch-mode (offline) and connect intermittently to synchronize data.

Typical wireless applications use wireless LAN and often take advantage of PAN radio link devices such as the Symbol P300fzy Cordless Scanner (Figure 74) for barcodes, wireless belt printers, and magnetic card readers.

Figure 74 Symbol P300fzy Cordless Scanner (*Source:* Courtesy of Symbol Technologies.)

Real-time data collection, tracking of materials, and access to mission-critical information are primary wireless LAN applications. Businesses enjoy the many advantages of wireless Ethernet. Compared to WAN, the LAN can exchange large amounts of data at a moment's notice, incur no per minute charges, and offer larger screens to facilitate the more comprehensive needs of enterprise information systems. Manufacturers now make IEEE 802.11b cards and server basestations. The standard is so solid that the hardware – whether it comes from 3Com, Lucent, or Apple – is interchangeable. Wireless LAN applications are prominent in U.S. business vertical markets. The best of vertical market applications can be studied as candidates for deployment on smaller Palm and Pocket PC devices.

Wireless handhelds provide operating systems with advanced communication functions. Developers program communication processes that change parts of the application in real time. Their programs branch to other scenes based on user input and the underlying content. Wireless handhelds can connect with many peripheral features to incorporate reading magnetic cards, GPS sensors, and signature capture. In designing business applications, you can program for many potential conditions and operations. For example, in a building inspection application for the handheld, the inspector can select various kinds of systems to inspect. The software can show the relevant building code violations to check for.

Using RAD Tools to Write Wireless Applications

When you approach professional LAN projects, you might consider using a Rapid Application Development (RAD) tool. These tools can dramatically accelerate wireless application construction, which saves development time. Some of the producers of visual RAD tools are Iconverse, Extenta, Speedware, and Aether Systems. A particularly powerful RAD tool that can illustrate how developers produce a wireless handheld project is offered by ICRAS, Inc. ICRAS, the final name of the DataRover spin out of General Magic, created a tool that could model and build a wireless application in minutes while connected to a real database. In 1997a team of engineers, led by Justin Broughton, began building this tool with the colorful name RAK –Remote Access Kit. The RAD application order of development (Table 27) shows the steps involved in professional wireless development. A typical RAD cycle lets you build a prototype in a week.

You begin by pointing the handheld simulation tool at a real database. The tool reads in the tables and schemas and reconstructs an object model in the simulator. It then builds a working forms interface in minutes. The simulator works with live data. At the end of the design, the code is generated and downloaded to the handheld.

A typical project starts, as all wireless projects do, by interviewing current and prospective customers. Notes are taken to construct a persona. Product requirements are formed. Since this is a vertical market application, some understanding of the business is necessary.

In the second stage, handheld scene navigation and data relationships (Figure 75) can be sketched out in one sitting, after the developer has examined current

Table 27 RAD application order of development in six stages

1 **Collect**	2 **Design**	3 **Database**	4 **RAK**	5 **Field**	6 **Distribute**
Web market research Get icon/ graphic Get jargon Get key forms Competitive applications review	Information design Key form layout	Code database Field choices Model for RAK	ODBC config JRUN config ProxyServlet.ini Code RAK laptop Test read/write Format RAK forms	Transfer DB to server JRUN config ODBC config ProxyServlet.ini	Post packages Documentation WEB screen simulation Server HTML
4 hours	4 hours	6 hours	16 hours	4 hours	16 hours

Source: General Magic, Inc.

paper forms and practices. In the early days, developers would post on a white board a diagram of the server, devices, and the wireless network.

The important third stage is not to write code, but to build a working database. During the customer interview process, each paper form was evaluated as to its utility. Some fields are thrown away and others are added. In all cases, simply asking for examples from the field workers provides the base to determine the types and lengths. You have to be thoughtful as to what data really needs to be collected and what is no longer relevant. Every extra piece of field information gathered could mean time lost on the job. Group the data around how the worker actively uses it. This becomes the basis for writing a formal information design document and illustrating screen layouts.

The real work begins with the database. With knowledge of forms and an information design in mind, developers create a model database and load it with preliminary records. You usually get to create a mobile database model based on some snapshots of company data. Even in trial stages, you rarely directly access the company database. As with most wireless new technology, the Information Technology (IT; also known as Management Information System [MIS]) personnel want very little to do with your new-fangled mobile database until the quality of the data is proven, especially if it writes to their database. They prefer to isolate it and have a gateway to control the changes that come and go from the handheld devices. This is good because it gives you much greater latitude as you design the system from scratch; you do not have to negotiate legacy policies, protocols, and data types.

Structured Query Language (SQL) relational databases are largely used in wireless LAN systems, but a small system can be run effectively with MS Access, FoxPro, or other personal computer databases. Typically, Microsoft Access or a similar small database is used because they are easy to run and it is easy to load data into them. This includes building tables with all the right data types and then arranging the tables in the correct schema and relationships to one another. Of course, optimizing tables with indexes is important for larger data sets. Most of them can be scaled up after the beginning. SQL is standardized, although there are vendor differences that ultimately take time to resolve.

The next step is getting real data. Loading data can take time; sometimes it has to be converted from old sources. But getting real data is key for testing input types and data lengths, and to gauge the field time taken to collect it. One important purpose of using real-world data is to determine what can be grouped into pick lists. You have to play with mobile data to see how many choices are enough and what can be optimized.

From the fourth stage on, the process is largely automatic. The server is configured for Java servlets. You can build your application against almost any database by using a JDBC or ODBC server connection to the hosting database. ODBC

(Object Database Connection) or JDBC (Java Database Connection) protocols are universal SQL request-and-response languages that allow any SQL database to be used. This gives your wireless application a generic set of functions to use, and it eases data administration and configuration. Every SQL database today has both ODBC and JDBC connectors.

After a connection is made for the database, some software tools are advanced enough to block out all the work and generate the code. To continue the example of the RAD tool from ICRAS, the RAK is turned on and pointed at the database. It sucks up the data, lays out the forms, builds all the software objects in the simulator, and makes code ready for the device.

The power of professional wireless development tools goes far beyond the phone emulators that most developers work with today. The key lesson is to start with data. *Content builds the application model.* Making a working database first saves enormous amounts of time later in application development.

The RAK example ran on handhelds using the Magic Cap™ operating system. It is fully object oriented and has a complete library of mobile components. It was developed in 1991 by many of the leaders of the Macintosh project at Apple Computer. This mobile object-oriented system could be programmed to do almost any imaginable act. But it was good at writing vertical market applications such as a building inspection application. This is a fine example because it illustrates the wireless development method we have discussed so far.

Handheld Inspection Example

An industrial handheld deserves an industrial application example. The handheld scene navigation and data relationships in Figure 75 show the basic design for a wireless LAN application produced at ICRAS for city building inspectors of major metropolitan areas. Without paper, this application lets an inspector make a report and enforce code, with the ability to issue a general code violation. It had a special provision for elevator inspectors to issue certificates on the spot for immediate posting in the elevator. The wireless application followed the inspector's standard procedures as they went about their work.

This interactive application was developed according to the wireless development method discussed in chapter 6. It began with an examination of the building inspector's process as relayed initially by a city project manager followed by interviews with the lead building inspectors. After looking at paper forms and building some sample data, a developer using a RAD tool generated the project. A storyboard was drawn up using a flowchart that combined application flow, scene navigation, and data associated with each scene. This flowchart (see Figure 75) shows navigation arrows between scenes, and indicates the data relationships of tables accessed by each scene. The double outlined box indicates an indexed list. The

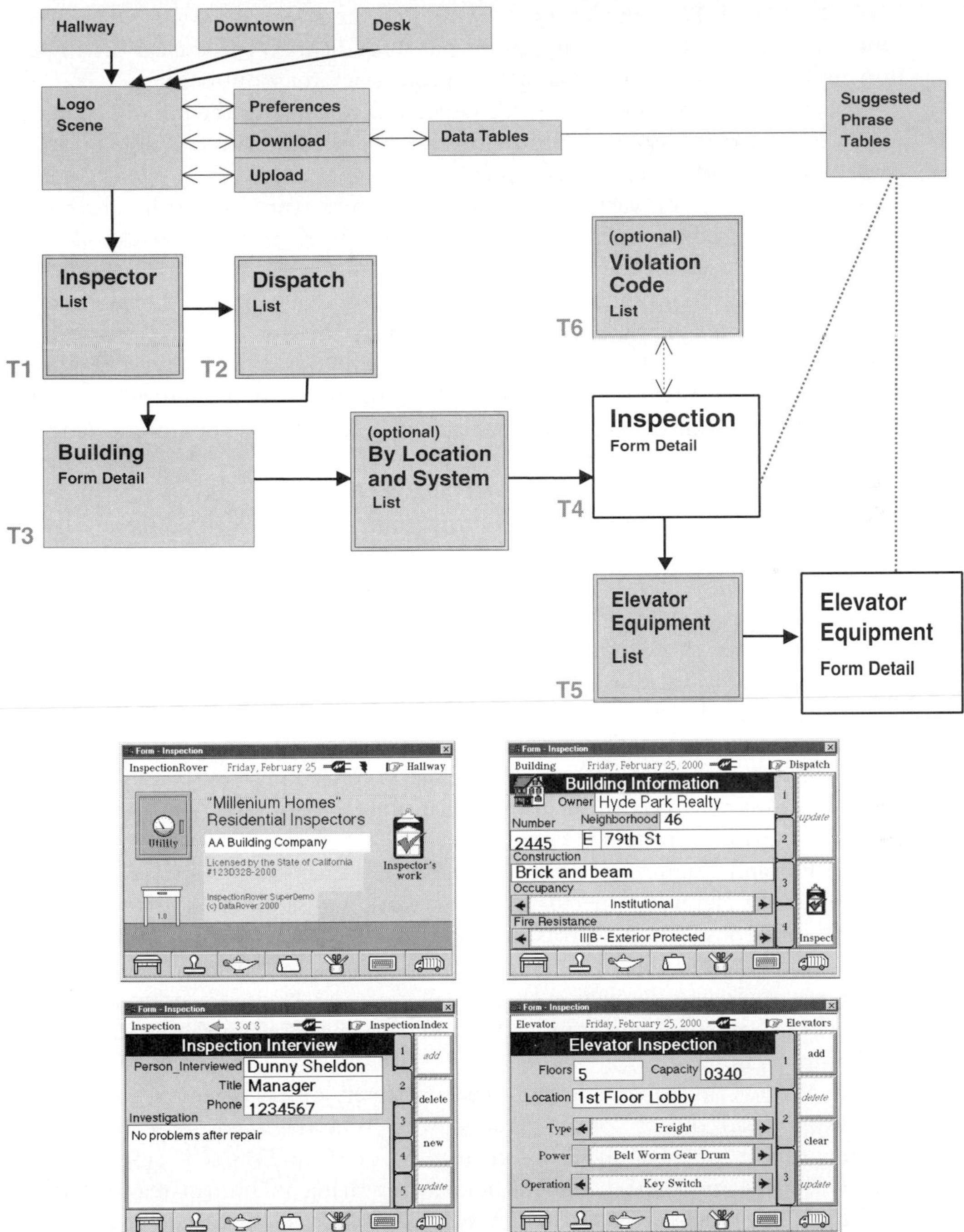

Figure 75 Handheld scene navigation and data relationships (*Source:* Screens courtesy of General Magic, Inc.)

labels T1 through T6 to the left of the boxes indicate tables in the database schema. Only the white boxes allow inspector input. This diagram made clear the inspection application and helped organize the project before layout began.

The first development task for this inspection system was the construction of a database. After that was complete, then real data gathered from a sample inspector database was loaded. The client project manager and lead inspector walked through each field to verify its importance. Some were dropped, a few were added, and any tables with standard choice lists were noted with the standard items for the list. When the database was complete, the RAD tool was pointed to the database. The tool built the wireless application that reflected the data model, laying out and linking each scene as suggested by the flowchart. The application was running within a day, actually exchanging records on the wireless handheld. The largest amount of time was spent refining the interface in the handheld simulator by making fonts bigger, organizing fields, and adding appropriate icons to support the data purpose of the scene.

Four sample scenes of the completed pilot application are shown at the bottom of Figure 75. The flowchart of tables corresponds to implemented scenes. In the Hallway Logo scene in the first screen, an inspector sees the project Logo, taps on the clipboard, and enters a password kept in table T1. This leads to an inspector roster and dispatch list. Choosing a job leads to the Building Form Detail scene; the second screen shows a detailed building information profile kept in table T3. Within the profile, various systems can be inspected. In the Inspection Interview scene in the third screen, the inspector reports on the building and violations using an associated violation code table (T6) that pops up on the screen. The inspector taps in choices and types in observations. Almost every observation is standard and can be tapped in from special word dictionaries. You can also take customer signatures for report verification.

The Elevator Equipment scene in the fourth screen shows a specialized report form based on elevator inspectors' detailed work and equipment codes stored in table T5. Such inspection reports ultimately lead to the elevator repair or direct certification. In one pilot program, inspectors with belt printers were able to report, use a wireless connection to city hall staff, and, having received authorization, print a barcoded certification that could be mounted in the elevator at the time of inspection.

The Magic Cap™ operating system is completely object oriented. You can edit the easy-to-read object format. Example 23 is a fragment of a FormScene resource object for a handheld object from Magic Cap. This is a standard object used within Magic Cap's handheld library. Appearing in human-readable form, the object has bitmasked flag attributes (e.g., viewFlags, screen-centered coordinates, object references, and data values) that are easy to edit.

Example 23 Sample handheld object from Magic Cap™
(*Source:* Courtesy of General Magic, Inc.)

```
instance FormScene form1Scene 'FlightRover';
relativeOrigin: <0.0,-8.0>;
 contentSize: <480.0,256.0>;
 viewFlags: 0x70001200;
 labelStyle: iBook12;
 color: 0xFF333333;
 altColor: 0xFF000000;
 shadow: nilObject;
 sound: nilObject;
 border: nilObject;
(skip)
 stepBackScene: nilObject;
 stepBackSpot: nilObject;
 image: nilObject;
 additions: (SceneAdditions formSceneAdditions);
 screen: nilObject;
 connection: nilObject;
 proxyServerAddress: (Text ref01FD0CAC);
 proxyServerPort: 80;
 proxyServerObject: (Text ref01FD0CB4);
 dbTableName: (Text ref01FD0CBC);
 dbColumnNames: (ObjectList form1ColumnNames);
 dbColumnTypes: (ObjectList form1ColumnTypes);
 dbKeyNames: (ObjectList form1KeyNames);
 recordServerMaxRecords: 4;
 shouldConnectOnAccess: 0;
(skip)
 indexPage: 1;
 persistentID: 0;
 printTemplate: nilObject;
 savedRecord: nilObject;
 subview: (DatabaseButtonBox buttonToolbar);
 subview: (WebProtoCard backgroundCard);
 subview: (TabBox tabBox);
end instance;
```

Developing Palm LAN Applications for Interactive Applications

We have seen how to program a Palm Query Application (PQA) for Web browsing (see chapter 10). Palm handhelds are also useful for standalone interactive applications. The Palm OS® runs wireless devices from Kyocera CDMA smartphones to low-cost Handspring Visors. The classic Palm™ VIIx (see Figure 76 on the next page) handheld uses the Palm.Net® over the Mobitex network. The OmniSky service gives users of the Palm V and Palm III handheld devices a CDPD service that is received by the Novatel Minstrel CDPD modem.

Developers can also write interactive handheld applications with the SDK. The SDK contains Palm software libraries and code in C++. A popular Palm SDK is Code Warrior from Metroworks. This process involves downloading a real-device ROM and running a Palm simulator. The newer Palm m500 handheld series provides an expansion slot for new devices and applications. Content sites must be able to offer content as PQA; however, there are unique applications where advanced development tools are necessary to make interactive Palm applications.

Figure 76 Palm™ VIIx handheld (*Source:* Palm, Inc. Used with permision.)

Advanced programming for the Palm handheld client will require you to use Palm conduits to control data exchange when the end user docks with the desktop and client. Conduits are the means of performing sophisticated record handling, synchronization, and client-server application development.

Palm Handheld Tools and Where to Get Them

The Palm OS Emulator (POSE) works for both Windows and Macintosh. Like all emulators, POSE lets you test your applications before making them available for public use. You need to use a serial cable and sync cradle to develop for a Palm OS handheld. However, to download a debugged ROM for a real device, you need a developer agreement with Palm. The following two Web sites offer useful Palm developer information:

- <http://www.palmos.com/dev/index.html> – Some advice from Palm developer support. Anyone can get a Palm SDK, but you must sign up as soon as you can to complete the formal license agreement, which takes some time for Palm to complete. This agreement lets you legally download the Palm ROM.
- <http://www.codewarrior.com/products/palm/> – Code Warrior is a development environment commonly used by serious Palm developers. It offers many cross-family features.

Some popular third-party tools used to develop Palm applications include:

- Appforge – A Visual Basic programming environment for the Palm OS.
- Satellite Forms – For Palm handheld and competing handheld devices.
- ScoutBuilder – A programming environment similar to the Visual Basic style.

There are many back-end development tools. One of note is the ScoutWare tool from Aether Systems, which lets you look inside the Palm handhelds and operate them remotely. Another set of mail tools is made by ThinAirApps. Many of these server-oriented tools are typically classed as middleware.

Developing with the Microsoft WinCE Devices

Microsoft Corporation offers software engineers many wireless development targets. Its conventional SDK supports Windows XP development for the PC and the up-and-coming TabletPC. Microsoft's Embedded Visual Tools development environment supports the many Pocket PCs (Figure 77), the Handheld PC profiles, and the new Stinger phone. Stinger is very similar to the WinCE SDK, which was used in the 1990s and is still required to support any of the earlier Microsoft mobile systems such as the WinPad and WinCE handhelds.

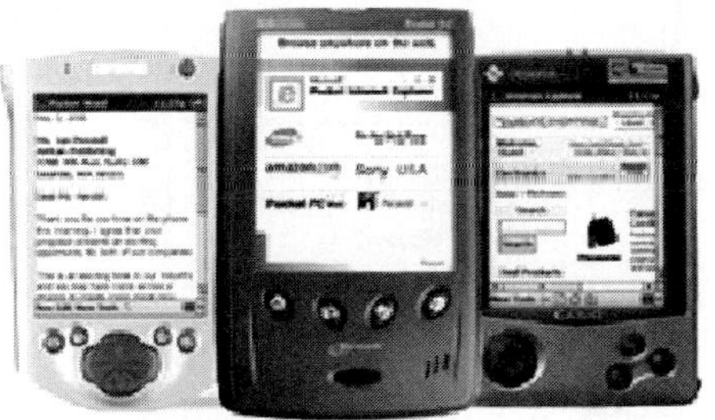

Figure 77 Pocket PCs (*Source:* Copyright © 2001 Hewlett-Packard Company. Reproduced with permission.)

Microsoft Tools and Where to Get Them

Most professional developers sign up to become members of the Microsoft Developers Network (MSDN) in order to get the MSDN Universal subscription. The subscription provides all the Microsoft developer tools, all the office productivity tools, all the server tools, and all the major languages for approximately $2000 per year. It is a good deal, although all this software can be used only for development purposes. Within the distribution are all the necessary Windows CE tools and simulators. Apart from the MSDN Universal distribution, registered developers can get tools from the following two Web sites:

- <http://msdn.microsoft.com/cetools/>
- <http://microsoft.com/mobile/developer>

There are many third-party tools for cross-platform development. CodeWarrior is a low-level development tool. Some of the better high-level tools are PenRight!, MobileBuilder, and Syclo.

Developing WinCE Applications

Within the Visual Studio.NET IDE environment, the main languages are Microsoft C++, CEBasic, and Microsoft's C#, pronounced "c sharp," an alternative

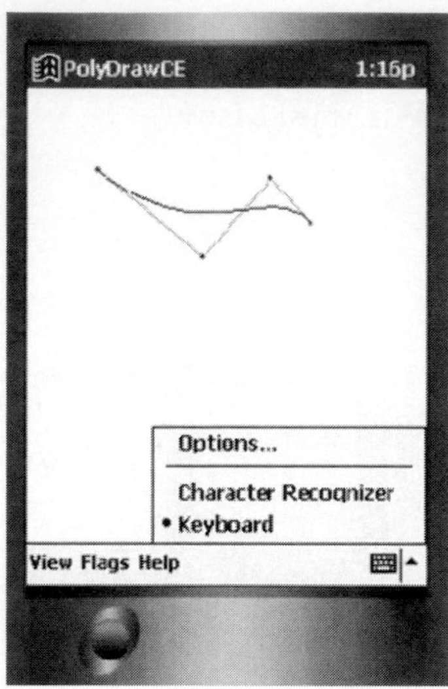

Figure 78 Emulator showing the Casio Cassiopeia E-125 Pocket PC (*Source:* Image courtesy of Casio, Inc.)

to Java. The IDE organizes project files and has a source code debugger, simulators, and interface builder tools for the handheld targets. Microsoft wireless development technology is very low level and not as advanced as the wireless industry. Professional wireless systems excel in low energy-consumption operating systems, wide-ranging communications architecture, and essential mobile components that are easy to use.

Windows CE development relies on the Windows CE Platform SDK, the Microsoft eMbedded Visual C++ 3.0 tools that include a compiler, linker, and desktop build utilities. The Pocket PC Emulator (Figure 78), Windows CE Emulation environments, and remote tools require Windows NT 4.0 or greater. They are not supported on Windows 95/98.

The Pocket PC can be programmed for many kinds of interactive application. Some are modeled on the PC laptop and make use of Microsoft Office documents. Microsoft handhelds and Web phones are well designed to run or communicate with Microsoft Office applications. Advanced services that reach all Microsoft devices as well as others are available from <http://www.wirelessknowledge.com/index.html>.

In the meantime, Microsoft is working on yet another operating system for handhelds and appliances called Talisker. (Talisker is a type of single-malt Scotch whisky.) It offers improved security, a more easily customized user interface and Media Sense, which is a discovery protocol that lets device owners know the types of network connections and devices nearby. Talisker includes connections to Bluetooth™ devices. Talisker will also support connections to its .NET wireless services such as instant messaging and Microsoft Passport authentication.

Using IIS as a Wireless Server

Microsoft servers can support almost any wireless device. In addition to Pocket PCs, Microsoft servers now officially support Palm handhelds. Microsoft is releasing the Mobile Internet Server that was code-named Airstream, and it is targeted for wireless service. Early developer comments during test were that this server is complex and perhaps overengineered for average developers' needs. Using Microsoft's Internet Information Server (IIS), you can program .ASP pages to send database-driven content. (See the example in chapter 7 in the section "Delivering Wireless Content from Databases and Servers.") To have your server support a WAP phone, follow the instructions for setting up the IIS in chapter 10 in the section "Setting up Your WAP Server."

Developing for EPOC Symbian Devices

Symbian, the industry consortium that now comprises Psion, Motorola, Ericsson, Nokia, and Matsushita, began by building upon the Psion EPOC operating system. EPOC is a portable 32-bit operating system that was designed for use in a range of mobile, ROM-based devices including smart phones and communicators. The Ericsson R380 handset (Figure 79) is the first major Web phone based on the Symbian reference model. It runs the EPOC operating system. The Symbian consortium anticipates a mass market for mobile information devices. It provides the development of core software, application frameworks, and development tools to support mobile two principle classes of devices – communicators and smart phones, which are described further in chapter 19, the section "Symbian Limited Wireless Devices."

Figure 79 Ericsson R380 handset (*Source:* Copyright Telefonaktiebolaget LM Ericsson. Photo used with permission.)

Symbian Tools and Where to Get Them

Development toolkits are available from Symbian and its partners such as Ericsson, although access to those kits is limited by agreement with the individual companies. Visit the Web site <http://www.symbiandevnet.com/techlib/techlib.html> for more information.

Programmers can choose C++, Java, or Psion's OPL for applications that run on Symbian platform devices. OPL is a Basic-like language that appeared on the Psion Organizer in 1991. It is used to handle common interface elements. Visual Basic, Visual C++, or Delphi can also be used to develop connectivity applications.

Developers can program for Symbian and Psion mobile devices, although the Psion is no longer made. They can be programmed in Java, PersonalJava, C++, and OPL, although C++ is the most common language. Note that Java is available in Beta form for most Symbian devices.

EPOC comprises an operating system kernel, user libraries, and a user interface framework provided by EIKON. EIKON is a native user interface designed by EPOC for ease of use on handheld machines.

Developing Symbian Applications

Most Symbian developers write customized handheld applications in C++. The Symbian tools are largely derived from the Psion toolset. Components and applications of the Psion and Symbian devices are very similar. Historically, Psion applications have been for professional vertical markets. The recent R380 phone from Ericsson runs EPOC version 5 and is a completely closed system, so you cannot download applications to it.

The EPOC platforms available in Europe are limited to those that were produced by Psion (Psion Revo, Psion 5MX, and Psion Netbook). Both the 5MX and Netbook can run Java code that is compatible with Personal Java 1.1, and with the Revo you can run Java applets.

The Symbian C++ EPOC code to build a window (Example 24) is typical native device code that a developer writes to program handhelds. The EPOC C++ syntax is very similar to that for win32 or Palm handhelds.

Example 24 Symbian C++ EPOC code to build a window (*Source:* Copyright © 1997–2000 Capslock Ltd., Niitykatu 6 C, P.O. Box 114, FIN-02201 Espoo, Finland. All rights reserved.)

```
// Simple.cpp

#include "Simple.h"

// EXPORTed functions

EXPORT_C CApaApplication* NewApplication()
  {
  return new CSimpleApplication;
  }

GLDEF_C TInt E32Dll(TDllReason)
  {
  return KErrNone;
  }

////////////////////////////////////////////////////////////////
// Application class, CSimpleApplication
////////////////////////////////////////////////////////////////

TUid CSimpleApplication::AppDllUid() const
  {
  return KUidSimple;
  }

CApaDocument* CSimpleApplication::CreateDocumentL()
  {
  // Construct the document using its NewL() function, rather
  // than using new(ELeave), because it requires two-phase
  // construction.
  return CSimpleDocument::NewL(*this);
  }

////////////////////////////////////////////////////////////////
// Document class, CSimpleDocument
////////////////////////////////////////////////////////////////
```

```
// C++ constructor
CSimpleDocument::CSimpleDocument(CEikApplication& aApp)
    : CEikDocument(aApp)
  {
}

// The document requires two-phase construction because it
// owns the model (CSimpleEng) and has to allocate memory for it.
CSimpleDocument* CSimpleDocument::NewL(CEikApplication& aApp)
  {
  CSimpleDocument* self = new (ELeave) CSimpleDocument(aApp);
  CleanupStack::PushL(self);
  self->ConstructL();
  self->ResetModelL();
  CleanupStack::Pop();
  return self;
  }

void CSimpleDocument::ConstructL()
  {
  iModel = new (ELeave) CSimpleEng;
  }

// All resources allocated in ConstructL() must be released in
// the destructor.
CSimpleDocument::~CSimpleDocument()
  {
  delete iModel;
  }

void CSimpleDocument::ResetModelL()
  {
  iModel->Reset();
  }

CEikAppUi* CSimpleDocument::CreateAppUiL()
  {
    return new(ELeave) CSimpleAppUi;
  }

/////////////////////////////////////////////////////////////////
// App UI class, CSimpleAppUi
/////////////////////////////////////////////////////////////////
void CSimpleAppUi::ConstructL()
    {
    BaseConstructL();
  iModel = ((CSimpleDocument*)iDocument)->Model();
    iAppView = new(ELeave) CSimpleAppView;
    iAppView->ConstructL(ClientRect(), iModel);
    }
```

```
CSimpleAppUi::~CSimpleAppUi()
  {
    delete iAppView;
  }

void CSimpleAppUi::HandleCommandL(TInt aCommand)
  {
  switch (aCommand)
    {
  case ESimpleCmd1:
    iEikonEnv->InfoMsg(R_SIMPLE_CMD_1);
    break;
  case ESimpleCmd2:
    iEikonEnv->InfoMsg(R_SIMPLE_CMD_2);
    break;
  case ESimpleCmd3:
    iEikonEnv->InfoMsg(R_SIMPLE_CMD_3);
    break;
  case ESimpleCmd4:
    iEikonEnv->InfoMsg(R_SIMPLE_CMD_4);
    break;
  case EEikCmdExit:
    Exit();
    break;
    }
  }

//////////////////////////////////////////////////////////////////
// Application view class, CSimpleAppView
//////////////////////////////////////////////////////////////////

void CSimpleAppView::ConstructL(const TRect& aRect, CSimpleEng* aModel)
    {
  iModel = aModel;
    CreateWindowL();
    SetRect(aRect);
    ActivateL();
    }

void CSimpleAppView::Draw(const TRect& /*aRect*/) const
  {
  CWindowGc& gc = SystemGc();
  // Clear the application view
  gc.Clear();
  // Draw a rectangle round the edge of the application view.
  TRect drawRect=Rect();
  drawRect.Shrink(10,10);
  gc.DrawRect(drawRect);
  // Set the pen size large so the dot is drawn large.
  gc.SetPenSize(TSize(10,10));
  // Draw a dot on the screen at the co-ordinates stored in the model.
```

```
  gc.Plot(iModel->Coords());
  }

// Call this when the user taps the screen in the application view.
void CSimpleAppView::HandlePointerEventL(const TPointerEvent&
                                          aPointerEvent)
  {
  // Update the co-ordinates in the model to the position at
  // which the pointer event occurred.
  iModel->SetCoords(aPointerEvent.iPosition);
  // DrawNow() results in a call to Draw().
  DrawNow();
  }
```

13 Chapter

Developing PAN Device Applications

Most WAN and LAN applications usually connect people, but personal area network (PAN) applications mostly connect devices. In fact, it is the configuration of PAN devices that create some of the most interesting applications. Infrared, the early leader in PAN, established short-range, temporary line-of-sight connections to read barcodes or exchange data. Using the low-power, 10-meter Bluetooth™ PAN, devices exchange very specific kinds of data. Some Bluetooth implementations can exchange voice. Most PAN devices are embedded with radio chips. However, we also include PAN devices that are attached to handhelds provisionally as modular devices. These devices are added on with a slot or sometimes a cable extension. (The IrDA and Bluetooth standards are covered in chapter 4, "PAN Roomwave Applications.")

The personal radio networks provide many rich opportunities for building wireless Internet applications. The emerging wireless Internet will take particular advantage of Bluetooth technology. Three of the interesting wireless application technologies are Bluetooth servers, first demonstrated by Ericsson in December 2000; the much talked-about PAN and WAN applications made possible by the dual-antenna 3G phones; and the synchronization of the many federated Bluetooth devices.

PAN Tools and Where to Get Them

Most Bluetooth, IrDA, and other PAN device driver software is built into the devices such as handhelds and Web phones. Sun Microsystems, Inc., has Jini APIs for the experimental systems, but this particular protocol is not seeing much sign of commercial acceptance. To develop your wireless solution, you may need to use Bluetooth tools. You may also need to acquire some low-level software. Palm Extended Systems offers a number of low-level support packages for Bluetooth development.

- <http://www.bluetooth.com> – The important part is getting a list of the actual Bluetooth device vendors to understand their profiles and protocols.
- <http://www.extendedsystems.com/> – Bluetooth and custom wireless software.
- <http://www.jini.org> – Emerging experimental standard for Sun Microsystems's Jini APIs that can coordinate devices over PANs such as the Bluetooth network.

Developing PAN Applications

The union of the PAN set of devices to provide a unique application is important in itself. Diagramming these configurations, or federations, of devices and understanding their characteristics is the first part of a PAN wireless application. For example, a popular industrial application is reading barcodes with a handheld scanner. Scanner-based applications make use of both PAN and LAN networks. Inventory applications can be done with Bluetooth, IrDA, RFID, or smart-label technology, so you will need to evaluate the tradeoffs of the components. There can be extra details to consider. For example, a handheld inventory application that uses a barcode scanner requires a decision on which barcode format to use. Of course, the kind of barcode you print and the kind of barcode you expect to scan must agree, and these symbols must agree with the standards required by your vendors and customers. You can choose from a great variety of scanning codes for your application to use; Figure 80 shows four sample barcodes used by handheld devices. You will also need matching barcode-printing fonts to test labels, which are not always easy to come by. They are not standard Windows or Macintosh fonts. The device vendors are usually the only source for them.

If you are printing tickets on the spot, you can use Bluetooth or even IrDA networks to send a print file to a printer worn on the belt. Using a Comtec or Cameo printer, you can print on-the-spot receipts. In specialized printing for Bluetooth and IrDA printers, you have to learn the command language, the available fonts, and graphics of the printer. As with all Bluetooth devices, you want to get the vendor's profile document, the device simulator, and testing programs.

When you are writing general applications, a more challenging issue is controlling the dynamic unions of Bluetooth devices so they are useful. How to build Bluetooth interfaces so an average engineer can produce applications for the average

(a) PDF417 (2000 symbolic characters – variable size)

(b) Code 39 – 43 characters

(c) Aztec (up to 3000 characters max)

INTERNAL REVENUE SERVICE
PO BOX 8318
PHILADELPHIA PA 19162-8318

(d) POSTNET US Postal Service propriety 90 characters

Figure 80 Sample barcodes used by handheld devices
(*Source:* Courtesy of the Culver Group.)

person to use is still an open issue. For now, the development community is working on a focused set of Bluetooth profiles, which are discussed in Part I.

Signature Capture

Web phones and pagers try to perform universal handheld functions, but very few of them can provide the right technology to take a customer signature. Signatures are often important for delivery applications.

Handheld software can designate component objects that permit the storage of a pen-written signature. Signatures are stored sometimes as native device formats and at other times as standard bitmaps. You may have to normalize the storage format so that once the signature has been sent to your database server it can be used by other applications. Getting an image that has been stored as a gestural scribble to print in a standard format may require conversion to a GIF format. The handheld digital pen signature of M. Polo (Figure 81) shows the quality of good "software ink."

Figure 81 Handheld digital pen signature

Graphics and signatures were first developed on the GRID tablet and later used on the GO PenPoint notebook computer of the early 1990s. The Microsoft TabletPC demonstrates highly sensitive drawing software with a high digitizing count for signatures. The legality of electronic signatures is still not clear. People can claim they never signed. That is where digital signatures come into play. A digital signature works as an "electronic notary" and acquires the encryption format for the signing components from a trusted source. The final signature is encrypted with the signing component and can be traced to the source with the encrypted value. A real digital signature is actually a separate mechanism from the penned signature; the two signatures can be combined as needed. Check your SDK for signature capture components. Digital signatures and security are discussed later in chapter 15 in the section "Understanding Security."

Smart Card, SIM, SD, and MMC

Figure 82 Smart card for a Web phone

PAN networks do not need a radio to take advantage of nearby devices or data sources. You can physically connect devices or transfer common storage media from one device to another to complete functional personal networks. The international traveler is used to popping out a little SIM chip from one phone and moving it to another. This SIM, or Subscriber Identity Module, is standard in GSM phones. It is also available for iDEN GSM phones. SMS applications make use of this card to store data and execute code. A smart card for a Web phone (Figure 82) can provide secure wireless transactions. The American Express™ Blue card uses software based on the Sun Smart Java Card™ programming environment.

Bluetooth application sets can use smart cards for both voice and data. Bluetooth networks can become a bridge for Internet applications, and a Bluetooth smart card implementation can put a mobile user's personal information in a nearby wireless space for active use. If the customer is in range of a business using a Bluetooth interrogator, then the customer does not need to physically hand over a card. He can conduct authorized transactions wirelessly.

Card Memory Systems

There are many smart card memory devices and formats. There were 100 million SIM cards in existence by the end of 2001 according to industry analysts. CDMA phones refer to these as Removable User Identity Modules (RUIMs). These modules are being produced for the Chinese Unicom phone network. A Unicom subscriber can take a GSM SIM card and pop it into a CDMA phone. A WAP Identity Module (WIM) provides end-to-end security for the WAP networks. Developers can program SIM cards that can use the SIM file system. A leading manufacturer of 3G SIM toolkits is GemPlus. Another company, iButton, makes data chips that can be programmed in Java to perform similar functions.

Compact flash memory that is used in cameras will be around forever. The Sony Memory Stick is standard in many new Sony devices. Some current Sony phones have 64 MB of memory. However, the Memory Stick is a proprietary standard and is not even available for the Sony Playstation 2. The manufacturing industry's answer to the Memory Stick comes in the way of two small card formats introduced in 2001: MultiMediaCard (MMC) and Secure Digital (SD). Each small card needs its own physical package as well as a slot for the receiving device, its own drivers, and special software. It is not clear which standard will prevail for a portable removable flash memory. The most promising seems to be SD, which transfers data at 10 MBps. It provides security for information as well. SD comes in 16 MB, 32 MB, and 64 MB configurations.

The Palm™ m500 handheld with SD expansion card slot (Figure 83) accommodates a postage stamp–sized storage card. This series of handhelds has a new dual-purpose expansion card slot and can hold both SD and MMC cards. The slot can also be used for connecting Bluetooth devices and Ethernet radio modems, cameras, or whatever the industry decides to make. Palm has a large program to support developers and hardware manufacturers who are making the devices that do now and devices that will connect handhelds and smart cards.

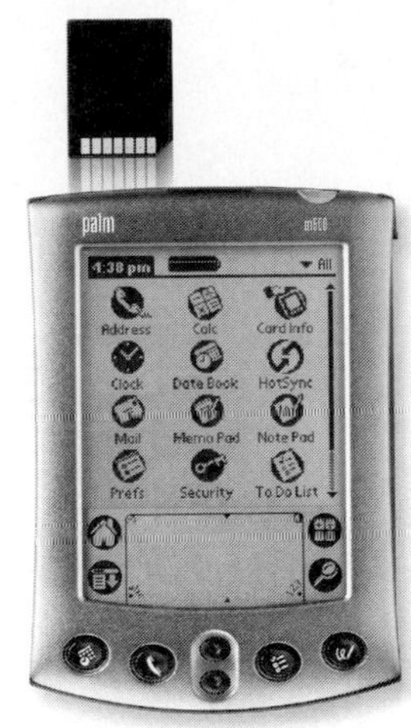

Figure 83 Palm™ m500 with SD card
(Source: Palm, Inc.)

14 Chapter

Developing Voice Portal Applications

Voice portal applications are built with components that range from the highly proprietary to Open Source.[1] The applications depend on a voice gateway that hosts voice markup pages that you write. The voice gateway does the speaking or listening based on your markup direction. These directions are translated to commands that can access your Web site, read messages, and perform limited applications. Wireless Web developers use the open standard VoiceXML™, Voice eXtensible Markup Language. This standard markup language lets you structure a voice dialog. Submitted to the W3C in May 2000, VoiceXML has catapulted the voice industry into the world of the Web programmer.

Voice Portal Tools and Where to Get Them

To end users, a voice portal is a phone number they call to get information. In some cases this phone number connects to a company's voice portal. More often it leads to the voice portal technology provider that hosts the application. Here are some useful Web sites and the key information they offer regarding voice portal technology.

- <http://www-4.ibm.com/software/speech/enterprise/ep_12.html> – IBM site that provides the voice technology for developers to test the alphaworks developer tools project at <http://www.alphaworks.ibm.com/>.

- <http://www.bevocal.com> – BeVocal is a voice portal for developers that is based on Nuance technology.
- <http://www.genmagic.com> – General Magic is a portico service in Sunnyvale, California, that is used in OnStar, the General Motors automotive voice technology.
- <http://java.sun.com/products/java-media/speech/index.html#fordev> – Provides the voice API of Sun Microsystems, Inc.
- <http://www.mya.com> – Motorola voice agent.
- <http://www.nuance.com> – The leading supplier of voice technology, located in Menlo Park, California, Nuance offers V-Builder™, a visual tool to convert a Web site to use Voyager, its voice-recognition technology.
- <http://www.speechworks.com> – A large manufacturer of voice technology, Speechworks is used by FedEx, Etrade, and United Airlines.
- <http://studio.tellme.com> – Tellme is a voice portal company with useful tools and hosting based on the Nuance technology. Its consumer line is 800-555-TELL.
- <http://www.telsurfnetworks.com> – Voice portal. Dial 888-TELSURF for hotline.
- <http://www.voiceXML.org> – The VoiceXML Forum's Web site.
- <http://www.w3.org/Submission/2000/04/> – The W3C definition of VoiceXML.
- <http://www.w3.org/TR/2000/NOTE-voiceXML-20000505/> – The W3C Note about VoiceXML.
- <http://www.wildfire.com> – Wildfire is a voice portal in the United Kingdom, although the service originated in the United States.
- <http://www.voicexmlreview.org/> – An online monthly newsletter from the VoiceXML Forum.

Developing Voice Applications

Writing VoiceXML voice portal applications is a common way to voice-activate content. MobileAria delivers voice-activated and speaking city guides. BeVocal gives business directory information to cellular phone callers. In addition, the wireless Web has many amateur voice applications such as Wine Finder, ATM Locator, Ski Reports, School Closure Reports, Joke of the Minute, Bible Chapter and Verse, and Gossip Corner. Many voice applications use the Nuance speech engine. Nuance speech objects are server-side components that can be programmed in Java and that produce voice applications. Nuance technology is used in the voice portal service of Tellme in Mountain View, California, a company that received a $60 million investment from AT&T in 2000.

Developers write a VoiceXML script to access the general interfaces to create a dialog. The top line of any XML document is a DTD declaration referring to the dialog elements. Unfortunately, many variations of VoiceXML DTDs support different vendor grammars. For example, the IBM emulator supports voicexml1-0.dtd, VOXeo supports nuancevoicexml.dtd, and the TellMe emulator supports vxml-tellme.dtd. Also, there is no standard for the generic verbal commands most people are using to speak to voice portals. Nuance does not have a "menu" command, and you have to define grammars in an external file. The element common to all vendor grammars is that with them you can write dialogs that branch in multiple directions. The "error handling" in voice systems is critical to keeping voice users on the track of your application. During development, make sure you contract with linguists who have an ear for speech and can improve your spoken text by adding such simple things as pauses.

The basic technique of writing voice portal dialogs is to become familiar with the basic flow of speaking. This requires writing prompts, and listening and speaking dialog routines. After you have written your VoiceXML file, you post the form to a voice gateway.

Voice talent is required for advanced voice applications. Simple applications can get by with text converted to synthesized speech; however, it is no substitute for voice talent. A speaking actor works on a soundstage to enunciate words and speak lines of dialog that are recorded as files. Most voice portal companies have these facilities for advanced projects. Recorded voice files replace the positions in the synthesized spoken points in the dialog. Synthesized or spoken, the sound files are referenced in your VoiceXML dialog, as shown in the following examples. Both the VoiceXML dialog file and recorded sound files are all posted to the voice portal.

Many third-party voice portal companies will freely host your application for testing purposes. When the application is ready to run commercially and requires 24x7 support, then the companies begin to charge for that service. Voice portals come in such a wide range of prices that it is wise to compare them before completing your voice portal application. What you get for your money in a good voice portal are improved qualities of voice synthesizers and increased accuracy in speech recognizers. Of course, the ongoing maintenance for an always-up service is required to make sure the servers are not overcome by congestion.

Basic Dialog

We will look at two examples of VoiceXML dialog. The simplest and most common form is one in which each item is executed exactly once, and in sequential order to implement a computer-directed interaction. The more advanced dialogs branch, invoke recorded sound files, and link off to other voice services. Learning to program conversational dialogs that make sense to average people is an art. Linguists are qualified for this. However, the programming principles are simple and best shown in examples.

National Weather Using VoiceXML Dialog

The dialog for getting the weather in VoiceXML (Example 25) shows how a weather information service might be written in VoiceXML. This is a simple example of a VoiceXML application. The basic idea is that a script interpreter continually rescans a form. The interpreter starts at the top checking for true and false conditions of each consecutive block, and taking action on the first false condition. The master form is made of a first block that speaks the main prompt (1) and then sets its form item variable to true.

Example 25 Getting the weather in VoiceXML

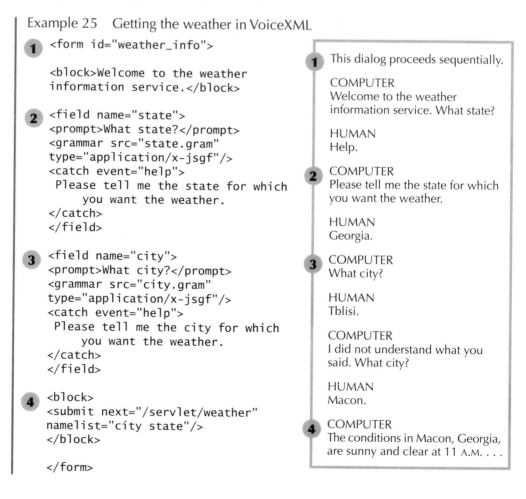

1
```
<form id="weather_info">

<block>Welcome to the weather
information service.</block>
```

2
```
<field name="state">
<prompt>What state?</prompt>
<grammar src="state.gram"
type="application/x-jsgf"/>
<catch event="help">
 Please tell me the state for which
     you want the weather.
</catch>
</field>
```

3
```
<field name="city">
<prompt>What city?</prompt>
<grammar src="city.gram"
type="application/x-jsgf"/>
<catch event="help">
 Please tell me the city for which
     you want the weather.
</catch>
</field>
```

4
```
<block>
<submit next="/servlet/weather"
namelist="city state"/>
</block>

</form>
```

1 This dialog proceeds sequentially.

COMPUTER
Welcome to the weather information service. What state?

HUMAN
Help.

2 COMPUTER
Please tell me the state for which you want the weather.

HUMAN
Georgia.

3 COMPUTER
What city?

HUMAN
Tblisi.

COMPUTER
I did not understand what you said. What city?

HUMAN
Macon.

4 COMPUTER
The conditions in Macon, Georgia, are sunny and clear at 11 A.M. . . .

On the second iteration in Example 25, the interpreter skips the first block because its form item variable is now defined (set to `true`). The `state` field is selected next because the dialog variable `state` is undefined (2). This field prompts the user for the state, and then sets the variable `state` to the answer. The third form iteration prompts and collects the `city` field (3). The fourth iteration executes the final block and transitions to a different URI that submits the gathered `namelist` of the actual city and state. The weather servlet then matches the city-state pair with a current conditions database and will speak a reply (4).

Each field in this example has a prompt that is played in order to elicit a response, a grammar that specifies what to listen for, and an event handler for the Help event. The Help event is thrown whenever the user asks for assistance. The Help event handler catches any event exception and plays a more detailed prompt.

Horoscope Using Tellme VoiceXML Dialog

To get a horoscope in a voice interface, the procedure is similar to the previous example. The VoiceXML horoscope with Tellme dialog (Example 26) has prompts, listening blocks, and speaking responses. With this example, we show what goes on at the server. This application returns a horoscope after the caller states a birthday. A caller gives the month and day. If the person was born between March 21st and April 20th, the computer might respond, "Your birthday is 20 days away. Aries, here is your horoscope today."

Example 26 VoiceXML horoscope with Tellme dialog
(*Source:* Bobby K. Joe, Tellme Studio, Mountain View, California.)

```
<?xml version="1.0"?>

<! -
Tellme Studio Code Example 105
Copyright (C) 2001 Tellme Networks, Inc. All Rights Reserved.

THIS CODE IS MADE AVAILABLE SOLELY ON AN "AS IS" BASIS,
WITHOUT WARRANTY OF ANY KIND, EITHER EXPRESSED OR IMPLIED,
INCLUDING, WITHOUT LIMITATION, WARRANTIES THAT THE CODE IS
FREE OF DEFECTS, MERCHANTABLE, FIT FOR A PARTICULAR PURPOSE
OR NON-INFRINGING.
 - >

<!DOCTYPE vxml PUBLIC "-//Tellme Networks//
    Voice Markup Language 1.0//EN"
"http://resources.tellme.com/toolbox/vxml-tellme.dtd">

<vxml>

<meta name="scoping" content="new"/>
```

```
<var name="ex_105_month"/>
<var name="ex_105_day"/>

<form id="get_month">

<! - This field asks for the caller's month of birth using the intrinsic
     MONTH grammar. The grammar returns the month name in string form
     (e.g., "january", "february"). - >

 <field name="ex_105_month">
 <grammar>MONTH</grammar>
 <prompt>
  <audio>Say the name of the month in which you were born</audio>
 </prompt>

 <default>
  <audio>sorry?</audio>
  <reprompt/>
 </default>

 <filled>
  <audio>i heard you say</audio>
  <pause>200</pause>
  <audio><value expr="ex_105_month"/></audio>
  <assign name="document.ex_105_month" expr="ex_105_month"/>
  <goto next="#get_day"/>
 </filled>
 </field>
</form>

<form id="get_day">

<! - This field asks for the caller's day of birth using the intrinsic
     DAY_OF_MONTH grammar. The grammar returns a number in string form
     (e.g., "1", "2", ... "31"). - >

 <field name="ex_105_day">
 <grammar>DAY_OF_MONTH</grammar>
 <prompt>
  <audio>Say the day of month in which you were born</audio>
 </prompt>

 <default>
  <audio>sorry?</audio>
  <reprompt/>
 </default>

 <filled>
  <audio>i heard you say</audio>
  <pause>200</pause>
```

```
  <audio><value expr="ex_105_day"/></audio>
  <assign name="document.ex_105_day" expr="ex_105_day"/>
  <goto next="#call_cgi"/>
 </filled>
 </field>
</form>

<! - There are two ways to pass parameters to the CGI script: HTTP POST
     and HTTP GET (also known as the URL querystring). This example
     uses the GET method. The general way to use the GET method is to
     construct a querystring and append it to the URL using a "?". URLs
     with querystrings typically look something like this:

http://Webserver/script.pl?input1=value1&input2=value2&input3=value3

Note that this example first constructs the entire querystring and
stores the string into the "ex105_alldata" application variable.
The application variable is in turn passed to the CGI script.
 - >

<form id="call_cgi">
 <block>
 <audio>I am calculating the number of days until your birthday</audio>
 <var name="month" expr="document.ex_105_month"/>
 <var name="day" expr="document.ex_105_day"/>
 <submit next="http://studio.tellme.com/library/code/ex-105/ex-105a.cgi"
              method="POST" namelist="month day"/>

<! - For submitting variables via HTTP GET try:
<submit next="http://studio.tellme.com/library/code/ex-105/ex-105a.cgi"
              method="GET" namelist="month day"/>
 - >
 </block>
</form>

</vxml>
```

On the server, this dialog is processed further. Example 27 shows the server processing a VoiceXML horoscope with Tellme dialog in which a Microsoft IIS server is executing an Active Server Page (ASP written in Visual Basic). The server uses the Request Object to parse out the posted parameters "month" and "day".

Example 27 Server processing of VoiceXML horoscope with Tellme dialog
(*Source:* Bobby K. Joe, Tellme Studio, Mountain View, California.)

```
<%@ LANGUAGE="VBSCRIPT" %>
<%
'declaring variables
dim month_in, day_in, days_to_bDate
```

```
'grabbing values with Request object
month_in = Request("month")
day_in = Request("day")

'array of months
dim months(12)
months(0) = "january"
months(1) = "february"
months(2) = "march"
months(3) = "april"
months(4) = "may"
months(5) = "june"
months(6) = "july"
months(7) = "august"
months(8) = "september"
months(9) = "october"
months(10) = "november"
months(11) = "december"

'Is the month_in value numeric?
If (IsNumeric(month_in)) Then
month_in = months(month_in - 1)
End If

'creating birthdate in date format by concatenating month_in and day_in
bDate = month_in & " " & day_in

'using builtin VBScript function to find out the number of days til
users birthday
'see http://msdn.microsoft.com/scripting/default.htm?/scripting/
vbscript/doc/vsfctDateDiff.htm
days_to_bDate = DateDiff("d", Now, bDate)

'DateDiff returns a negative number if date happened in the past. Add
365 days to calculate days in the future.
If days_to_bDate < 0 Then
days_to_bDate = days_to_bDate + 365
End If

'Response to request in VoiceXML.
%>
<vxml application="http://resources.tellme.com/lib/universals.vxml">
<meta name="scoping" content="new"/>
<form id="result"><block>
<audio>
<%
If days_to_bDate = 0 Then
%>
happy birthday!
<%
Else
```

```
%>
your birthday is <% =days_to_bDate %> days away
<%
End If
%>
</audio>
<goto next="_home"/>
</block></form>
</vxml>
```

The server page takes the caller's birth date, breaks it down, and speaks the number of days back to the caller. It also knows to say "Happy Birthday!" To divine the caller's fortune using a horoscope, the birth date information could be passed on for further processing. The voice portal application could pass the person's birth date to a soothsayer process. You could use Western astrology, which is based on matching the twelve sun signs. You could just as easily use Eastern astrology, which is based on matching the twelve Chinese Zodiac animal spirits.

XML for Voice and Data

You can write wireless applications to send directions to a screen or to a voice server. Using XML you can structure the responses using "drill down" logic so that mobile travelers can get what they need and then request finer levels of detail during the dialog. This is called progressive disclosure; it is the same outlining technique you might use in a text representation to arrange information in a subordinating pattern.

The XML data fragment for routing a driver in Example 28 shows a simple structure for the way to proceed. The driver would see or hear only the level 1 details, but would have access to the next levels of detail on demand. Using a voice portal, you might structure catch responses to listen for something like "more detail." Alternatively, the voice portal interface might sound a tone or show a colored light when there is more detailed information. When the voice portal gets a level 2 request it speaks that line of information in response.

Example 28 XML data fragment for routing a driver

```
<routing>
 <level 1>take US-101 south</level 1>
   <level 2>US-101 south becomes CA-84E</level 2>
 <level 1>exit Broadway</level 1>
</routing>
```

Part III

Wireless Internet Architecture

Wireless architects look ahead to consider the many aspects of the technology and the levels of a project. They are aware of both application and network architecture. These two architectures have elements in common with a building's architecture (see Figure 84): They are long-term structures, represented in the drawing as the column grid of the floor plan. The architects who design wireless applications and networks approach their architecture similarly to the manner of architects who design buildings. They map out the form, in layers, for visual reference. The wireless architect sees at least three levels of issues: long-term, mid-term, and short-term. In the bottom layer of the draft is the only thing that remains the same over time. The long-term issues for a wireless site include the business model and radio technology's capacity. The mid-term tier issues are the capabilities of the Internet server and device's design. The short-term issues concern content values and the points where mobile users make contact with the service.

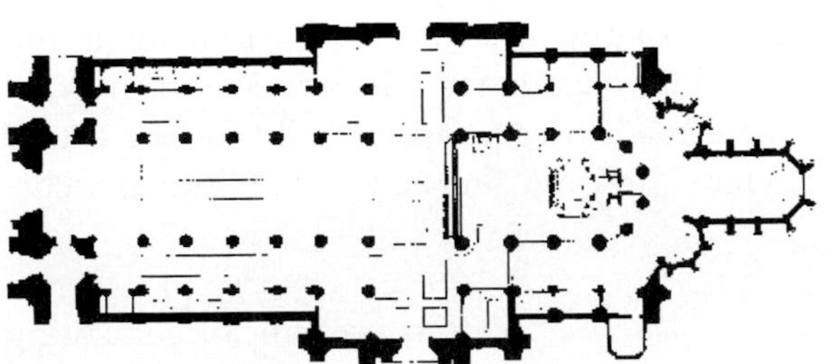

Figure 84 Building Architecture

Up to this point, we have explored the key issues of the wireless Internet. We have seen how wireless applications are made and the parts played by a software team of interaction designers, programmers, engineers, and architects to make these wireless systems. In time, programmers, caught in the zeal of writing wireless code, become the engineers who build powerful development tools. Architects know that special development tools have to be put in place to complete code fast, increase system integrity, and operate the site. Working as a team, architects and engineers must make long-lasting decisions that assist the process of planning, building, and operating a wireless system.

What Is Wireless Internet Architecture?

Wireless Internet architecture is the design of complex systems by arranging elementary materials of wireless Internet technology on a plan that can specify spectrum, networks, servers, applications, devices, content, and individual use. The result is a habitable and useful mobile system determined by aesthetic, practical, and material considerations. A somewhat simpler definition: Wireless Internet architecture is the art, science, and practice of designing and building technical communication structures for mobile life.

The architect, as the first authority, draws up the specifications for the system. Architects of every stripe create structural designs whose grand goal is to impose order, balance, and unity to create a system that has strength, utility, and beauty. The practical work often begins by discerning the kind of application server architecture that is appropriate for the purpose at hand. Although there are many elements to consider, determining and creating good infrastructure is critical to wireless architecture.

The architecture of a wireless system includes the planning for wireless client devices that communicate over wireless air interfaces, the application servers that provide content to them, and protocols to connect everywhere. Consideration of feasible wireless applications and the movement of content throughout the system are part of the planning process. An architect designs the most precise blueprint possible, and suggests materials and the order of development. The architects write the wireless application plan discussed early in Part II that guides programmers, interaction designers, and content engineers.

Grand designs, however, can produce overengineered sites that do not work. Stated goals can be implemented that do not allow for the growth of the inhabitants or the latitude of their own short-term decisions. An architect may inherit an architecture that is flawed, and must make an expert recommendation to the powers-that-be to either rebuild from scratch or rework what exists. Expedient and total costs must be kept in mind. Impending change for a legacy system must be weighed against new capacity. Architects need to responsibly build for the future to ensure adaptability and scalability. Here are some alternative professional architectural strategies and methods.

Construct for use and remember working patterns. Many successful longer lasting systems were built because they were needed at the time – with neither architecture nor a master plan. Berkeley Professor of Architecture Christopher Alexander observed this utility and explained that much construction is passed on from generation to generation as a series of formulas for construction. He illustrated more than 200 patterns that define the goals of structures.[1] To some degree, successful wireless patterns can be encoded in modular software UML diagrams, but we are largely at the beginning of an era that calls into question many of the former computer and telco architectures. It is useful to examine mobile components. It is helpful to use good abstract tools that are effective in wireless deployment and to remember their patterns. Using software tools, architects produce detailed diagrams and specifications. In this part, we look at some UML tools and activity diagrams.

Build for change. Architecture and mobility seem to be at odds. Wireless mobile architects support many devices and networks. They incorporate both voice and data. The size of these networks demands an architectural approach. Deeply entrenched architectural planning, however, can curtail the advantages offered by an emerging, flexible, mobile and in many cases transcending technology. Architecture requires definitive and precise planning to cast a powerful system. If it does not allow for change and revision, it will often be abandoned. To handle many different mobile wireless devices, you need a flexible plan. You need both an architecture and a strategy against architecture. The name of a German musical group expresses the spirit perfectly – *Einstürzende Neubaten,* which means "collapsing reconstruction" (literally, "collapsing new buildings"), which refers to a vigorous reexamination of any architecture. For some, like the sensational Miami architectural firm Arquitechtonica, who made buildings with holes in the middle, rotated buildings on a novel axis, and made visible support elements part of the exterior, deconstructive analysis is inspiring as a revolution that radically challenges assumptions. For others, analysis and reexamination inform the practicality of an ever-changing landscape of devices and services. The important observation is that wireless architectures can "learn" and should be envisioned to allow its owners and operators to grow with their mobile users to allow many short-term changes.

Plan for time. In construction, a building is defined first with a blueprint. A mature plan conceives of a structure that accommodates many interior services and subdivisions of space that change over time. Architects in wireless projects consider the construction and assembly of all elements with a view for the long run; the elements include networks, servers, devices, content and, most important, the space for people to enjoy the technology. Architectural thought evaluates utility first. Form follows function, as the Chicago architect Louis Sullivan made clear. One draws up a full plan for the support structure to carry the load of heavy use over a long time. How architectures "learn" is the key, because a good architect lets a building grow, so that it remains or becomes more comfortable and useful as time passes. Any lasting plan should allow the addition of support as necessary or desired, rather than try to anticipate all possible conditions from the beginning.

Engineer for heavy use. Seasoned contractors or system architects who plan a wireless architecture must put extra engineering thought to produce systems that serve hundreds of thousands of people per day. They look closely at spectrum, bandwidth, air interfaces, how application servers run, the quality of synchronization, the nature of the data, and the detailed capacity of wireless devices. They are concerned about tradeoffs, load-bearing concerns for traffic, all aspects of security, and the ecology of content maintenance and digital publication processes. The defining subjects in wireless architecture include the continued addition of new wireless technology with new features, the effective solution to real-time and synchronized mobile situations, and the many ways to build scalable, distributed, and personalized servers that can handle large amounts of traffic.

Evaluate layered and modular architecture. Reasoning architects who might build a wireless Internet broadcast publication system look at the total system as well as its communicating components. It is healthy to employ deconstructive observation before beginning work. For example, a resulting conclusion might be that the people, not the system, generate the content. This recognition of wireless architecture as Einstürzende Neubaten gives you impetus for a fresh, more differentiated, and general guided wireless architecture that can grow. In spite of a spirit that relishes change, there are many wireless architectural elements to observe and make decisions about. They can be usefully grouped by their capacity to have an effect over time. People who build the "wireless house" must remember that elements have different lifecycles: content changes every day, format changes every few months, new wireless devices appear every few years, new servers appear every five years, new towers can last for a decade, and wireless spectrum is eternal. Different services are available at different intervals.

Consider the long-term effects. Every professional makes responsible decisions that are implemented over various timeframes. As in other aspects of life, decisions that will have long-term impact demand and deserve ample time to conclude. They have to be evaluated from different points of view with sensible, forward-thinking calculations. Anticipating change and growth in the final plan may require some extra construction, but this can lead to an enduring well-loved architecture. You may need to develop special infrastructure. To achieve self-maintaining content, you often need to make tools to manage instantaneous, distributed change including operational systems that include live talent. These can be tall orders. But long-term thinking has a deep-minded sense of purpose.

An architect's decision making can also allow for many fine, short-term decisions that other people will make within your plan. The overall scale of decision making is variable, as the Dean of Architecture and Planning at Massachusetts Institute of Technology (MIT) William Mitchell points out:

> For designers and planners, the task of the twenty-first century will be to build the bitsphere – a worldwide, electronically mediated environment in which networks are everywhere, and most of the artifacts that function within it at every scale, from nano to global, have intelligence and telecommunications capabilities.[2]

15 Chapter

Getting Started with Wireless Internet Architecture

You sometimes build projects from the ground up, and you sometimes get stuck with someone else's mess. As an architect, you will face both situations. You need to be able to recognize when to cut your losses and start over (demolish the building) or when to continue (renovate or expand the building). In all cases, an architect needs to investigate, know, and do certain things to design responsibly for the future.

Not every developer or architect gets to start from scratch to build pure wireless Internet applications. If you have a working Web site and want to add wireless access, then you need to rethink how you build Web software and content. When making architectural decisions, keep in mind that you want to both serve the wireless devices of today and be prepared for the many new ones of tomorrow. (Engineers with an existing Web site who need to get going right away might want to turn to the section "Rebuilding Your Web Site" in chapter 18.)

Making architectural decisions about wireless technology can be challenging because each one involves so many elements. Before making a "wireless blueprint," you have to understand the client's restrictions. For some projects you might have unlimited materials and the client may say, "Build me something great with the new technology. How far can your imagination reach?" Or perhaps, as the market matures, the client may say, "I have some fixed materials. Show me what you can build with them." Your solution needs to be practical, within the limits of technology and the client's objectives. For example, you may have to use only a pager, a certain commercial brand of software, or a specific network. For your client, security is an important issue, but you need to determine the architectural scope and scale of the project and all the elements that may need attention to implement a complete solution.

Understanding Architectural Scope and Scale

The architect looks at networks, devices, servers, coverage patterns, content plans, and end-user interfaces separately and in combination. When planning solutions, an architect looks at elements that have different cycles of input and changes. Some elements have 20-year cycles, others have 2-year cycles, and others have daily cycles. Wireless architecture layers of scope (Table 28) are examined in the following chapters. Each layer has its wireless elements, a range of limits, best uses, and load-bearing architectural values.

Architecture in Layers

Of all the elements in wireless architecture, wireless server specification is perhaps the architect's key task. To understand how server elements are evaluated, it might be useful to compare wireless architecture to the world of building architecture. For buildings, architecture is conceived as layers that are built in stages with different tools and practices. A key point that Stewart Brand makes is that over time a building undergoes various rates of change.[1] From the outside to the inside, a building consists of layers – of site, structure, skin, services, space plan, and stuff. Architectural layering was first formalized by the British architect Frank Duffy. Figure 85 shows the progression, from the bottom up, of the project plan by which most buildings are made. It also indicates for each layer the range of time the elements are expected to last, from the longest lasting (100 to 1,000 years) to the most ephemeral (days, months).

Starting at the bottom of Figure 85, *Site* is the geographical setting that is legally defined with fixed boundaries. The site outlasts the generations of buildings that are erected on the location. It may last 100 years or many thousands of years. The *Structure* is the core plan of an architecture that describes the foundation and all load-bearing elements. Popular construction expects structures to last 30 to 60 years, although many enduring buildings are known to last hundreds of years. The *Skin* is the exterior surface that includes the roof, the façade, and the doors and windows. Skins, which last between 20 and 30 years, proclaim fashion and style, and they give some safety and protection from the environment. The *Services* are the operating parts of a building including wiring for electricity and communications, plumbing, heating, ventilation, and air conditioning (HVAC), as well as elevators and any moving structural parts that provide utility. Services will wear out in 7 to 20 years. The *Space Plan* is the interior design, which shows the layout of the walls, ceilings, floors, stairs, and doors. Commercial building space plans change most often, lasting between 3 and 7 years. *Stuff*, a term Frank Duffy and other architects use to discuss interior design, is the most ephemeral element and includes furniture, phones, paintings, appliances, books, and pencils – all the household goods. Although some stuff lasts decades, most is perishable; it circulates every day, every month, or every season.

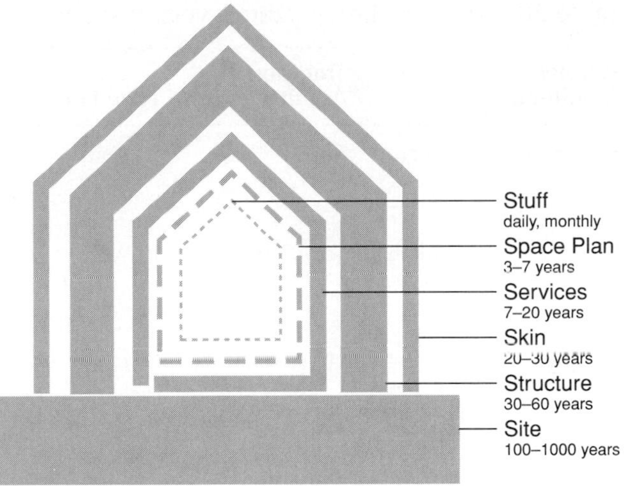

Figure 85 Architectural layering (*Source:* Based on a drawing by Donald Ryan. Reprinted with permission of Stuart Brand.)

Over the life of a building, layers change at different rates and can tear apart a building if the supporting system is not robust. For example, adding a new kind of roof every 20 years, then going in to replace plumbing, HVAC, or wiring every 7 years, or dividing and combining rooms every 5 years can take a toll on a building's structural integrity. Well-chosen sites and structures that permitted growth are more affordable when you look at the cumulative costs incurred over the full life of a building. They also prove more lasting and retain their occupants. Beloved and enduring buildings are designed by architects to allow modification as the many interior layers change throughout the building's lifetime.

On average, a building with a structural life of 50 years will have had replaced two skins, three services, and seven space plans. The replacement costs for changes to the inner part of the building will far outrun the structural costs of the original building. (A graph of the total cost of a building over its lifetime is shown in Figure 100 in chapter 18.) This observation applies well to wireless architecture.

Decisions about each wireless element are based on its engineered capacity to change. These decisions range from long-term decisions about allocation of radio spectrum to short-term decisions about which devices to recommend and how personal content should be used at the moment. Keeping in mind that layers of scope (Table 28) can help wireless architectural engineers understand their tasks with respect to a progressive scale of abstraction and time. To be successful, consider the entire life of the site, examine the elements in each layer, and make appropriate decisions that will allow for growth. Each layer has a different scale of utility in time and space.

This idea of progressive layers of abstraction is somewhat similar to the OSI layered model for network protocols. Progressively each layer abstracts responsibilities from an underlying layer. This concept of layering is depicted in the nine-minute

Table 28 Wireless architecture layers of scope

Wireless Architecture	Traditional Architecture	Time Frame	Developer Issues
Spectrum and power	Site	20 years	Anticipate standards. Evaluate WAN, LAN, and PAN utility. Decide wireless business model.
Tower and network	Structure	10 years	Match application to network data rates.
Server and browser	Service	5 years	Design XML architecture, three-tier services, and application server.
Device	Skin	2 years	Evaluate emulators and SDK. Prepare for devices and chipset capability.
Content	Space	Every season, month, week	Determine publication model, databases, editing workflow, and information design.
People	Stuff	Every day, second	Evaluate user interface, voice, media, and data use.

classic film "Powers of Ten" by Charles and Ray Eames; it is a visual journey that takes the viewer from a hand of a sleeping man at a picnic, out to the edge of space, and then back to a carbon atom within his resting hand – all in a single continuous take. The progressive scope of wireless technology (Figure 86) is similar. In the wireless architectural model, you can follow the content (data) of a cellular phone call out to the planetary sphere of spectrum transmission and back down to the bits being computed and displayed in the device.

Most things, including wireless networks, fall apart with use and time. A rule of thumb in building is, *If repairs and upgrades will cost half the value of a system, then demolish it.* To decide whether to repair or destroy, you need to consider the wear and tear, reliability and failures, and structural usability of all wireless elements.

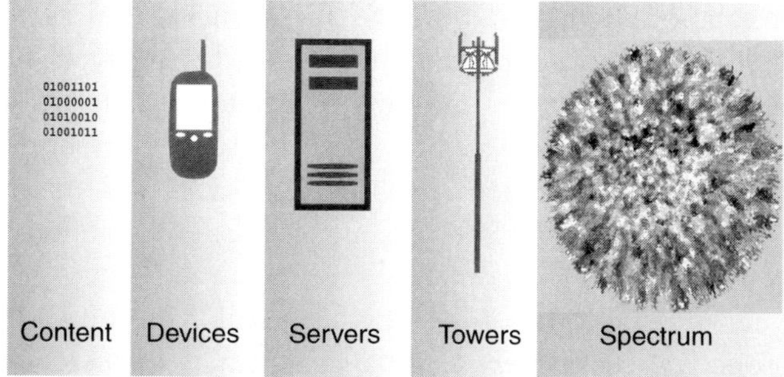

Figure 86 The progressive scope of wireless technology

A wireless application plan is formed from predictions based on experience, but strategy anticipates unforeseeable changes in conditions. A good plan draws up a strategy that leaves the client some maneuvering room. In anticipation of load-bearing data streams or high traffic volume, you may need to engineer technology that does the "heavy lifting." To produce a highly secure system you may need to build or acquire third-party components.

Internet Services and Protocols

Understanding scope and scale is an important part of building the wireless Internet, as many systems perform many services using many protocols. The key network architecture protocols are mostly defined with the seven-layer OSI stack, which we introduced in chapter 4. Table 29 shows the OSI layers with sample protocols and the wireless Internet applications. Each Internet service protocol is designed to operate at one of the seven layers.

In addition to the four primary wireless application families we have covered (i.e., SMS messaging, WML/cHTML/pQA browsing, Java/XML/HTTP interaction, and VoiceXML conversing), there are many Internet applications whose marginal use in wireless applications is still interesting.

People use Internet services to send and receive email, chat online, tour the world from a Web browser, log in to remote computers, download cool applications, shop online, listen to music and share pictures, watch digital videos, and talk with people and computers. Internet application developers see these Internet services as corresponding technical protocols and standards, such as SMTP, POP, and IMAP; newsgroups, IRC, and IM; HTML, HTTP, and TCP/IP; Telnet, FTP, TCL, SSL, and XML; streaming media and SMIL, VoIP, and VoiceXML.

Although not in the wireless mainstream, there are protocols that support other well-known Internet services such as chatting through IRC, logging in to remote computers through Telnet, downloading cool applications through FTP,

Table 29 OSI layers and sample protocols and applications

Layer	Sample Service or Protocol
[7] Application	Netscape, Internet Explorer, newsgroups, Telnet, email
[6] Presentation	HTML, GIF, XML, POP, IMAP, VoiceXML, SMIL, WML, cHMTL
[5] Session	SSL, HTTP, HTTPS, IRC, FTP, LDAP
[4] Transport	TCP, UDP, SMTP, SSL, TCL
[3] Network	IP, UDP, VoIP
[2] Data Link	CSMA/CD for Ethernet, Token-Ring, FDDI, ATM
[1] Physical	Electrical, cable, twisted-pair, fiber-optic, radio frequency, SONET

listening and sharing music and pictures using MP3 and JPG, watching digital videos through AVI, LDAP directory access, and so on. You might even write applications to use these other protocols. For example, from your handheld you might request a fax be sent from your server to a nearby printer.

The traditional OSI application layer crawl – HTML over HTTP over TCP over IP over ATM over SONET – is the way an Internet application works. The source system and the destination system connect, often using gateways, routers, bridges, and relays to shuttle or translate the signal, as illustrated in the section "The Seven Layers of the OSI Model" in chapter 4.

OSI Bottom-Layer Secure Architecture

The OSI layers are checkpoints for wireless security plans as well. The four lower layers of the OSI model handle security in special ways. Wireless networks such as CDPD, i-mode, and WAP implement OSI as follows:

- *Physical layer (1).* An RF carrier signal is digitally modulated to transmit a bit stream. This bit stream incorporates forward error correction, interleaving, and other techniques to mitigate the effects of interference and weak signals that can produce high-bit error rates. The CDMA carrier, using spread spectrum, provides a highly secure radio carrier at the physical layer.
- *Data link layer (2).* This layer is usually a specialized radio access protocol optimized for the radio environment. Most link protocols involve interactions between the wireless modem and a basestation. Mobile units do not communicate directly with each other at this layer.
- *Network layer (3).* Some wireless data WANs, such as Mobitex (RAM Mobile Data in the United Kingdom) and Motient (formerly ARDIS), use network-layer protocols designed specifically for their network, however, the trend is toward using IP. This is the case with CDPD, as well as the packet services being developed for PCS networks including GSM, CDMA, and TDMA.
- *Transport (4) and higher layers (6 and 7).* TCP/IP dates from 1983, and TCP/IP's cousin protocols for security, TLS, SSL, and HTTPS, are very mature in wired use. These layers are often implemented in circuit-switched wireless networks in the upper application layers. Some transports have been designed specifically for wireless networks. Optimization of TCP's timing parameters and algorithms yields better wireless network performance. The WAP Forum specifies the Wireless Transport Communication Protocol (WTCP) to provide a common messaging framework for the Internet to improve transmission control. The Secure Socket Layer (SSL) is the most common wireless low-level protocol that implements security at the transport layer. For more on SSL, visit <http://www.openssl.org/>.

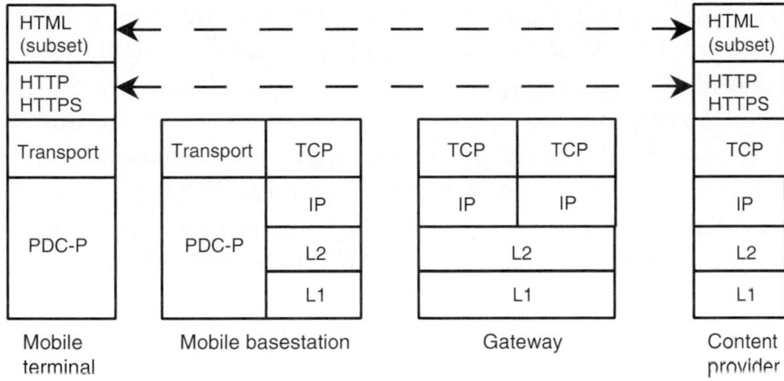

Figure 87 i-mode security HTTPS layer pass-through (*Source:* Copyright © 2001 NTT DoCoMo, Inc. All rights reserved.)

The i-mode and WAP security models can be shown as an OSI stack architecture that handles security in two ways. Figure 87 shows the i-mode security HTTPS layer pass-through, which provides a traditional Internet OSI security model. Layers 1 through 4 for network access are managed by hardware, without software reencoding of the data. To enable one system to talk to another, i-mode uses HTTPS and TLS/SSL. The mobile terminal can receive content directly from the provider without the lower-layer translation and reencryption that WAP requires.

WAP security with reencryption (Figure 88) uses an intermediate gateway and must decrypt the WAP security protocol, WTLS, and then reencrypt it for the Internet security protocol, SSL. During conversion, the data is in the clear for a brief period; this situation has some security risk attached. Analysts also point out that WAP keeps session cookies alive on the server and it is possible for a second application to enter the gateway and read any of the cookie variables.

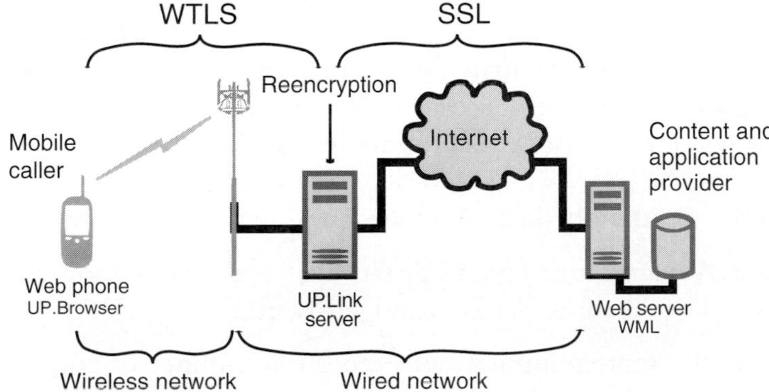

Figure 88 WAP Security with reencryption

WAP has been side-railed with a gateway architecture that unnecessarily put telcos in the security loop. The WAP Forum has had some small challenges convincing the world that its Wireless Transport Layer Security (WTLS) is worth all the trouble. It does not provide an end-to-end security path between the mobile device and the server, which is required by secure applications such as mobile banking. You do have to trust your phone operator to operate a WAP gateway and secure the WTLS and SSL conversion. Nokia and Openwave make secure WAP gateways, which banks use by having their own WAP servers behind a protected LAN. Because telco carriers have to handle all kinds of billing and payment issues, it is doubtful your WAP transmission is in much danger. Openwave has corrected this by providing end-to-end security in WAP 2.0 in 2001 with Dynamic Proxy Navigation. This still requires that you have to buy a WAP server and put it behind your firewall, which is an unnecessary expense in the i-mode architecture.

Understanding Security

Unless you want a no-compromise, secure deployment from end to end and have a fortune at your disposal, you must determine the level of security that is necessary based on the available technology. The memory or processing power of many telephone devices are too limited to implement encryption techniques. Networks are also a problem. Bank of America, which uses 724 Solutions for its wireless channel, has bypassed GSM and SMS networks because of security holes. Small companies license their tools to build end-to-end security systems from scratch. When deploying a wireless end-to-end solution, you have to evaluate the aspects of each device and each of the networks. The scope of security is also important. Determine if you must protect a single application, several applications, or the entire traffic as a virtual private network (VPN).

Wireless Security Concerns

The very aspect that makes wireless devices desirable makes them dangerous. We have them so we can use them anywhere, but that means we can also accidentally leave them anywhere. There are many security aspects to consider – signals being intercepted, a unit being stolen, data being copied, data being destroyed, and so on. The following major wireless security concerns are important.

- *Insider attack.* An insider could obtain a secret key and intercept all messages.
- *Man-in-middle attack.* A transmitter could appear as a "real" basestation and intercept transmissions to obtain secret keys and passwords.
- *Cloning.* A phone can be reprogrammed with the serial number of another phone to impersonate a genuine subscriber and consume paid services.

- *Viruses.* Unchecked programs that execute on the device can do harm and broadcast themselves.
- *Denial-of-service attacks.* A relentless transmission of requests can flood mobile transmissions, crash phones, and lock up basestations. Wireless LAN interference is an innocent version of this.

Wireless Security Model

The elements of a wireless network should interoperate seamlessly, work end to end, and perform efficiently. In an interoperable system, all devices and systems should be accessible. Clients and servers should be able to exchange data without the least intervention of a gateway or processing system to be efficient. There are four good solutions in the wireless security model.

- *Authentication (no forgery).* Verification that both parties in a transaction are who they say they are. This can be assured in multiple ways, including a simple password scheme, certificates, and a Public Key Infrastructure (PKI) scheme. Although useful in the PC Web world, these solutions can add overhead to the time it takes to execute a wireless transaction unless there is hardware support on the device.
- *Integrity (no tampering).* The content transferred on the network has not been altered by anyone. Requiring that content be signed, using keys or certificates, commonly provides integrity.
- *Data privacy (no eavesdropping).* The content transferred on the network cannot be seen by anyone. Privacy is provided by encryption, typically through SSL or WTLS.
- *Nonrepudiation.* All parties to the transaction are noted. A user or a provider cannot deny having performed a transaction. Nonrepudiation is usually ensured by requiring that content be signed with public or private certificates.

Implementing Wireless Security

To alleviate security concerns, there are three levels of wireless security service to implement.

- At level 1, users simply view information, such as bank account information. They cannot exchange information.
- In level 2, closed transactions would be acceptable. For example, information can be exchanged or money can be transferred within the same institution.

- In level 3, the highest level of security, end-to-end encryption allows users to exchange information with other companies or transfer money between financial institutions.

Devices, bandwidth, and wireless security protocols are still evolving. While we expect improvements in all levels of security, making wireless business secure is definitely a greater challenge with the wireless Internet than in the wired world.

Implementing a security protocol in stages is one way to add security over time. With so many ways to add wireless security, deciding how much security to layer on the user can be difficult. You can take the following steps to add security to your system. Each step is more complicated and generally more expensive than the previous step.

- Stage 1 is to secure a connection between the server and the device.
- Stage 2 is to provide certification of the server.
- Stage 3 is to certify the client.

Theft prevention is a constant concern. There are four basic steps to protect your data from being misused.

1. Use a secure air carrier like Code Division Multiple Access (CDMA). Analysts have pointed out that you cannot rely on GSM signal security alone. CDMA is very secure because it uses military spread spectrum. You can put a frequency analyzer on a TDMA or GSM cellular phone call and see the spikes and use a scanner to watch the data stream, in which CDMA appears as pure noise.
2. Deliver content in a microbrowser and store as little as possible on the handheld. Browsers keep all sensitive data resident on the server. This way the mobile user only exposes the browser data for the session on the wireless device. You can design sessions to clear data caches so nothing is stored on the device at all.
3. Use two-way certificates. With two-way certificates, the client must authenticate the server before the password is transmitted over the air. The server then returns an authentication check. This prevents spoofing, in which a user may send a password and upload sensitive data to what he thinks is his network server, but is a phantom server. "There should be mutual authentication before any sensitive information is shared," says Ian Hobbs of 724 Solutions, a security guru who builds wireless infrastructure for major financial institutions.
4. Add an additional layer of encryption for highly secure networks. This must be put on top of the built-in security mechanism. CDMA has strong native security.

Cellular Digital Packet Data (CDPD), Mobitex, and Motient typically need to run an application layer on top of their native security.

Most built-in security is good enough to stop anyone with a scanner from seeing plain text, but computer crackers are always a threat. To thwart them, GSM maintains a database of stolen device serial numbers; however, it takes 48 to 72 hours for notification to take effect in order to lock out known stolen handsets from the network

Security Performance

Security has its price. Security performance is a challenge in wireless systems. Performance and cost versus protection is a classic tradeoff. The more security layers you add, the more transmission and processing degrade. You can expect latency to last anywhere from 15 seconds to as much as 2 minutes per transaction for a fully secure network transmission using strong layers of security. The time to execute security should be reasonable and require as small an amount of code as possible. Implementing client security is a challenge because, unless you have a powerful CPU, sophisticated encryption significantly adds time to a transaction.

Self-destruct Button

Anyone who has ever lost a cell phone, personal digital organizer, or a laptop knows how it feels to mislay a device that contains critical personal or professional information. A famous wireless company's CEO had his laptop snatched at a major trade show in fall 2000, and it triggered a nationwide FBI search. "Self-destruct buttons" are a drastic but useful way to provide security for lost or stolen devices. Japanese inventor Mikio Hasebe of Gyoda, Japan, patented a method of sending an email to a lost or stolen device that will lock the appliance or erase its data. With this method, the owner of a wireless-enabled device chooses a password and a security response. If the laptop is stolen or mislaid, the owner can write the password in the email subject line and send it to the device. The device self-destructs immediately.

Electronic Jamming

The irritation caused by ringing cell phones is common in movie theaters, restaurants, and other public places. Cellular devices can be annoying, used for illegal purposes, and in some instances hazardous. Phones that are positioned to "listen in" to conversations threaten industrial security. Cellular phones can be hazardous by causing interference with equipment including airplanes, hospital equipment, and refueling stations. Some businesses are looking at "antiphone" electronic countermeasures to block cellular devices from operating and to enforce safety. An Israeli company makes a wall-mounted, indoor jamming device for disabling mobile cellular phones in defined areas. It blocks communication between the phones and the cellular basestations. A cell phone silencer, C-Guard, can ward off irritating rings, dangerous interference, and costly eavesdropping for about $600; it is found at <http://www.cguard.com>.

These "cellular firewalls" are currently illegal in the United States. The FCC forbids interfering with stations licensed to transmit radio communications signals. The primary reason this law stands is that a blocking device would scramble *all* calls. Imagine a doctor in a restaurant where such a device prevented incoming emergency calls. In other countries like Japan, it is legal to use cellular jammers in certain special circumstances.

The Bluetooth Stack

Security is only as good as its weakest link. Bluetooth technology is notoriously promiscuous. Wireless devices with Bluetooth transceivers openly discover one another, build communications connections on the fly, and exchange data readily. Each device maker for each Bluetooth profile differs in security implementation. Bluetooth devices can restrict access by other devices, the kind of voice and data connection allowed, and the security protocol requested.

Bluetooth essentially defines the lower four layers in OSI – everything up to the session management layer. The Bluetooth OSI protocol stack includes the RF (radio frequency) baseband (the physical layer), Link Manager, Host Controller Interface (an optional layer in case there is a split between the radio module and the host device), Logical Link Control and Adaptation Protocol (L2CAP) layer, RFComm layer, Telephony Control Protocol (TCS) layer, and Service Discovery Protocol (SDP) layer. The higher layers leading to the application stack are implemented according to the Bluetooth device profile.

16

Chapter

Evaluating Spectrum and Site: Every 20 Years

As a wireless architect, the longest-term decisions you will make are about your business model is the site of all wireless technology. The selection of WAN, LAN, or PAN will condition the reach of your wireless system. The incidental spectrum over which the enterprise operates can be unlicensed, which would expose your solution to interference. The emerging standards can be generally anticipated, especially as the new 3G air interfaces are turned on. As we have pointed out, Japan is in the lead with 3G spectrum and solutions, with Europe following, and the United States as far as two years behind. But the existing cellular 2G PCS bands in the United States are powerful enough for advanced wireless applications. It is helpful to evaluate spectrum characteristics and anticipate 3G networks by studying the five air interfaces and the general standards bodies as you plan a wireless site.

For a traditional architect, a site is a geographical setting, usually an urban location that establishes the grounds for many possible structures. It is a legally defined lot whose boundaries and context outlast generations of buildings.

In Europe, the 3G licenses are granted for 20 years. In the United States, many large FCC licenses are granted for periods of 10, sometimes 20 years. Either these licenses are renewed or the spectrum gets reallocated for other uses. The FCC also mandates that WAN operators offer 10 years of continued service from the date of the last subscriber's purchase of a contract. You can expect a wireless architecture to span 20 years. If you use a good business model, your wireless enterprise may last longer.

The Site: Wireless Business Models

Technology professionals write business plans to clarify purpose, plan operations, and obtain investment. A business plan proposes the product and service concept, achievement objectives, marketing and technical analysis, sales model, the organizational resources required, financial projections, and a legal framework for ownership. A plan that is Internet-based often includes international components. A business plan is more than a project roadmap or a software lifecycle plan.

There is no substitute for a credible business plan. It defines the permanent boundaries of an enterprise. The plan states the goals, and outlines the structure for wireless Internet products and services. The plan relies on a business model, and the business models of companies are worth knowing to become familiar with current marketplace dynamics.

You may be spared from dealing with the mechanics of generating revenue for a wireless project. Even if you are not the project manager dealing with financial or legal aspects of the project, you may need to know how the business works. Renaissance engineers are as curious about details of new business thinking as they are about new technology.

If you are starting from scratch, you begin with the obvious. The wireless Internet is new and depends on many technologies. The technology is changing rapidly, but the market moves slowly because of the expense and time of deploying wireless infrastructure such as wireless network towers and coordinated handsets. Legal regulations on technology license grants, certification, and pricing can add expense and delay. Unlike free markets, communications networks are regulated and the network operators who have purchased spectrum licenses, not the handset makers, define the underlying economic model. On the other hand, it is obvious that the relatively new value of mobile content, personal applications, and the geographical bounds of use can provide unique opportunities.

You may be starting out with a garage-shop idea, forming an independent group in a company, or working in a joint venture in a revenue-sharing opportunity that combines the companies' technology. Plans are created not only for business, but also day-to-day operation and details of core technology.

A wireless technology plan, like wireless architecture, considers many elements. The plan examines hardware: voice and data handsets, radios and antennas, and computer servers. It includes many kinds of software: mobile operating systems, base applications such as messaging and browsing, and custom interactive applications. It devises the use of various voice and data networks in generations of service. It considers many kinds of content: news sources, personal addresses and calendars, corporate data, XML representation, and all kinds of public and commercial content feeds.

The economic return on the combination of these technologies should exceed the cost of the service by at least two times or it is not worth doing. However, the wireless Internet presents a puzzle where free meets expensive. The Internet for consumers is low cost, wired, and an almost free market computer technology. It connects with expensive wireless technology owned largely by the regulated telcos. Free Internet technology companies have largely failed in the stock market. "From now on you've gotta pay" seems to be the lesson. If people want these services, they will have to compensate creators and operators in some manner. Let us look at some credible business models that have shown early signs of success.

What Is a Wireless Business?

A wireless business is one that exchanges Internet content with a network of mobile people via wireless devices. The broad scope of a wireless business includes hardware, software, and suppliers of network products and services, with a special concern for the content as a primary value motivating the end wireless user. Together these elements support wireless industry and commerce. Is there such a thing as a wired business? Of course, wired businesses provide service to everyone who uses the Internet and a telephone. Wireless businesses are companies that use WANs, LANs, and PANs to connect rapidly moving employees and customers via the wireless Internet with many sources of information. Wireless content, rather than the software or hardware, is the primary value in a wireless business.

Initially, a wireless business is viewed as channel for a wired business. In contrast to conventional business models, the uniqueness of wireless consumership lies in a business model where companies must become networks. Unlike in the physical business world, networks allow instantaneous feedback, a quality we will explore later. It is a fact that your business has an operational component to respond to customer email and Web forms, mobile customers, and the movement of fresh Internet content throughout the business. You create a medium that connects a network of subscribers, wherever they happen to be, whatever they happen to be doing. When conceiving a wireless business, consider the customer's new frame of reference. Looking down the road to 3G networks where everyone's antenna is connected, companies are considering different business models as they evolve a wireless identity begun in the current era of wireless channels. Because wireless business markets are not well established, it is difficult to identify superior market dynamics, and supplier relationships, and predict revenue. Money may pass through the content provider or the network provider. You may earn income from transactions, subscriptions, or traffic. While the cauldron of the marketplace finds formulas for a viable wireless business, remember that the technology is in an early stage without full infrastructure in place. The qualities of a viable wireless business will change significantly as the market matures to include the specialist business and the broader yet less forgiving audience.

To broaden the reach of a business or its market share, companies will provide a *wireless channel*. For some companies building a wireless Internet system is simply a cost of doing business to increase commercial access to customers or to other businesses. Some established companies, such as Charles Schwab stock brokerage, offer a wireless channel under the model of extending service to customers. The business goal of "creating a presence" by setting up a Web site has metamorphosed into "extending a relationship" by opening a wireless channel. Currently, companies let customers wirelessly track packages, check on a flight, or make stock trades. For companies offering a wireless channel, wireless technology is simply another form of a business relationship. When you provide a wireless channel to a large company, you must demonstrate how it will increase transactions, add service capacity, or save costs by reducing loads on more expensive parts of the enterprise. A typical cost justification compares the costs of a customer-generated machine transaction with live staff answering telephones or processing the service.

Wireless business is fundamentally about exchanging information of personal value and figuring out how to get machines to handle the routine part of the communication. To share and synchronize content and interests with a wide array of servers is the basis of a wireless business. Both commercial and barter models for personal information are at work. In the long run, the very low-cost, micro-billed subscription for personal content and service is likely to succeed. There are early signs of acceptance for this approach in i-mode.

The Value of Wireless Content

Wireless networks are a medium for popular and enterprise content. Whether it is transmitting voice or data, the wireless Internet is a personal passageway. The idea is to download once and play anywhere. The early trial with Napster was to prove not so much that music can be free (as it is in radio), but that by putting it into an MP3 player, a world library of music can be portable. The cellular jukebox in the hands of listeners is the precursor to many 3G devices and networks.

Traditionally, the publishing industry uses annual subscription, circulation, and advertising revenue as a business model for content. Along with the music industry, it offers original works for one-time sale. Publishers have pretty much been at the mercy of the Internet. As telcos feared, the Internet let the genie out of the bottle. The wish that "everything would be free" was granted and we are living in its aftermath. A global Internet that has no capitalization is unable to sustain service quality. Although the Internet is full of interesting experimental services, much of the actual content is shallow. Sustaining interesting, useful, and ongoing content is an expense, pure and simple.

A prime source of content has always been artists, personalities, and content experts. They sell their art through distribution networks. In the case of music on the Web, Napster has shown that people will access music to make their own music collections. The music industry, rather than work with this new medium, has largely decided to forbid its artists from being part of the new networks. This state of affairs echoes the situation when radio became popular in the 1940s and 1950s. The emerging American Society for Composers, Authors, and Publishers (ASCAP) had formed a system to collect royalties for artists based on repeated use of their work. Until that time, artists sold entire works for a one-time fee. In lobbying for royalties, ASCAP at least provided some income beyond the creative act. During that time, some artists and their attorneys perceived radio as "giving music away for free"; ASCAP sued radio stations and many performers withdrew their work from the airwaves. This is similar to the withdrawal of musicians from the Internet today. Spooked by Napster, some musicians are even suing over downloading ring tones.

One response in the 1950s was that the marginalized music and the garage bands took to the air. Old-time favorites like Gershwin, Al Jolson, and Bing Crosby played only on the radio stations that were willing to pay heavy dues to ASCAP. And they were heard less. Instead, hillbilly music from musicians like Bob Wills, and obscure rock-and-roll artists like Elvis Presley got airplay. They had nothing to lose and the musicians learned to use the new medium as a promotional tool for performances and record sales. In a similar manner, old media is getting in the way of the new, which now confounds the wireless Internet business model for wireless Internet content. The new interactive radio station, personal DJ-ship, the network formed by wireless music fans, and the new access to media are the grounds for new commercial outlets. Combined they provide another cross-media channel for artists. A business model is not yet defined that focuses on providing a means for people to build their own collections from the immense market of digital music. Hopefully, we provide access to new artists once limited by older distribution and outlet models, and to old artists no longer accessible in stores.

For interesting content providers, the opportunity to generate revenue from either a periodic subscription or a pay-as-you-go-when-connected model depends on the wisdom of the network carriers. They collect revenue from subscribers' billing plans that meter cellular phone use. To increase a caller's monthly activity, telcos are considering how to give people wireless Internet connections to any possible content provider. It should be simple. However, if you plan to provide content, then getting the proper agreement with the right network provider is not cut and dried. Except in futuristic wireless cultures like Japan, end users do not pay the publisher directly for wireless content or applications. Wireless carriers continue to make content arrangements on behalf of customers, although they are beginning to consider different plans.

Monthly voice service is the primary revenue generator for carriers. Alternative billing methods for data such as pay-per-bit, pay-per-session, message units, and all-you-can-eat flat rate lie at the root of telco models. NTT DoCoMo offers *value-based pricing* for i-mode subscribers. NTT made the decision with i-mode to cut anyone into the economic model that can keep callers on the air. This is different from the Western approaches whereby only large companies who pay and sign large contracts get to appear as a wireless service. Value-based pricing from network operators lets content companies take a good share of the call revenues. The customer, not the carrier, decides if a service or content is of value. A more comprehensive report of the i-mode business model is in chapter 1, the section "The i-mode Story."

Wireless transactions are another source of revenue. While some information and entertainment services are provided free, many products and services require a transactional service charge. Clearly, the credit card companies and ticketing agencies want to offer wireless services. It is unclear how telcos will work with these companies to factor wireless transaction fees. A Bluetooth pay point application might appear on a credit card or a cell phone bill depending on the business model worked out between the operators and the credit card companies.

Following on the tracks of the DoCoMo value-based pricing model is the QUALCOMM BREW software distribution business model. The i-mode technology lets customers access the Web in a simple manner. With i-appli, DoCoMo offers Java applications. QUALCOMM has described its application BREW distribution model (Figure 89). In the model a BREW developer gets an application

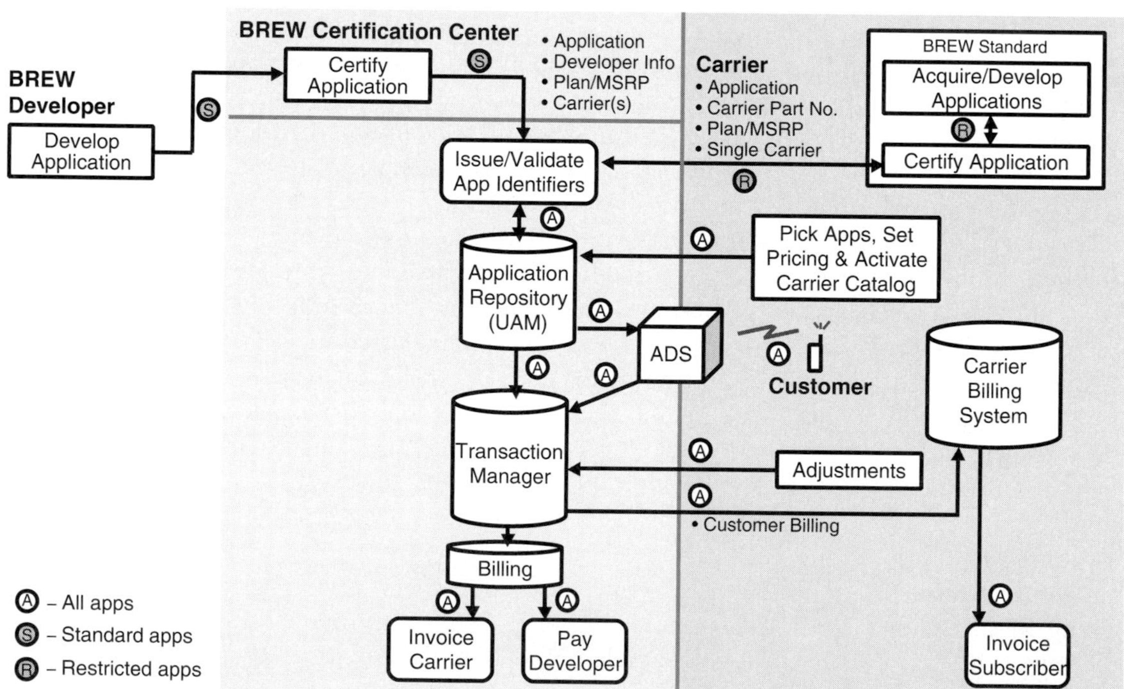

Figure 89 BREW distribution model (*Source:* QUALCOMM. Used with permission.)

certified. It is then placed on a carrier-owned QUALCOMM Application Download Server (ADS). When a customer picks an application, it is loaded over the air and a bill is automatically generated for the carrier, who includes the small service charge in the customer's invoice. The developer is paid automatically through the billing mechanism. The distribution system has a slightly more elaborate path for restricted applications, which require extra certification and security permissions to run.

Now that we understand the use of software as a commodity and the primary value of content to world markets, then it is useful to understand how wireless business works. It is helpful to look at the major wireless business models.

Publication Models

Wireless publishing is clearly a vehicle to deliver content. Content subscriptions are traditional for publishers, but for wireless systems they are not easy to attain without a network operator billing or agreement. Traditional publishers have some of the best sources, although the new smaller, more interactive, networked wireless media formats are bound to favor a mobile publishing industry that "gets it." Magazine publishers accustomed to annual subscription billing may find the i-mode microsubscription model a useful model.

Advertising and sponsorship have proven successful as business models for the broadcasting industry. Advertising-supported Web portals have found limited success over the wireless Internet with mobile portal service. Use of a customer's personal wireless device as a vehicle for advertising is not popular with consumers who pay for every wireless bit they use, coming and going. Targeted mobile personal advertising is in its infancy and there are many wireless avenues. Taxi cabs with electronic billboards that change depending on where they are driving and time of day are indicators of wireless technology to come.

The early stage of invention provides the opportunity to explore a new technology that can have a strong future. Often participating with partners, you jointly prove the basis for a technology and a market. What may start out as a radical Napster-like idea can evolve into a "secure membership-based music distribution system." But most efforts require a pilot; the technology-testing phase is the single-stage theater that anticipates a global play of the market. The pilot lets companies try technology and services, and experiment with business models without making a major financial and marketing commitment. A successful pilot can quickly lead to business relationships and the launch of a larger market.

Vertical Market ROI

Vertical market and select enterprise-wide opportunities are important wireless business opportunities. The best focus is on vertical markets that have a demonstrable return on investment (ROI) that justifies costs. Cerulean (now a division of

Aether Systems) has produced systems for Federal Express and the United States Postal Service. The ROI for these companies came through an increase in productivity and job efficiency. Since the desktop workforce is about as productive as it will ever be, making an effort for mobile users is one of the last major productivity gains for an enterprise. The promise of field technology is that *the one who gets closest to the customer wins* – a cardinal virtue made possible with wireless technology.

Wireless ROI opportunities are the business of many industrial handheld makers producing vertical market applications. A good ROI plan measures an increase in the quantity of work done and improvements in the quality of work. In wireless police-ticketing programs, a work shift can generate more tickets by being able to tap in preloaded information than by taking the time to complete paper forms and then have them rekeyed at the office. Accuracy and quality is improved, since retyping handwritten tickets is error-prone. But the wireless process also shortens the time it takes for ticket submission to reach collection centers. Public safety agencies observe that 40 percent of voice traffic is taken out of dispatch centers using mobile wireless data technology. By pointing to increases in quantity and quality of work done, professionals can do a better job as stewards of their community. An increase in morale is an intangible benefit that results from improved public service. It is clear that identifying mission-critical applications and understanding the entire workflow provide the basis for comparative costs of operation that can justify wireless vertical markets.

One goal of a Chief Information Officer (CIO) is to extend the enterprise and better include the company's field workforce. Making improvements to the desktop now provides minimal return on investment. The mobile workforce is the least productive part of a company. Most large companies have a mobile workforce ranging between 10 and 40 percent of the workers. Mobile workforces offer a key opportunity for companies to provide wireless Internet ROI solutions. After analysis of existing time and resources committed to operations, it is often clear that wireless applications can reduce overall support costs, and increase productivity of mobile activities. Often systems pay back (recoup the investment) within two years. This is particularly true of the wireless LAN projects, like the many wireless vertical markets covered in chapter 5, in the section "Wireless Vertical Market Interactive Applications."

Laptops are the new desktops. Both have required network drops to offices, and retrofitting offices adds substantial expense. All day long the CIO's staff chases, moves, adds, changes, and drops. A small squad goes up into the ceiling, moving tiles and pulling wires on a regular basis. There is an ROI basis for reconsidering the long-term costs of continual rewiring versus going wireless. According to a report by Ford Motor Company, 30 percent of its workforce moves every six months.[1] Think of the project teams, transfers, and turnover of a company. Over three to five years, an ROI calculation of movement costs relative to wireless infrastructure implementation shows dramatic savings. Furthermore, wireless LAN gives capacity to campuses at every possible location, indoor and outdoor.

Finally, vertical markets eventually go horizontal. Companies that have spent years building location-based systems for vehicles have built enough technology that can be made useful for more general transportation.

Telco Network Model

The wireless Internet involves many industries and many business models. Currently, the telcos, not the handset makers, drive the wireless market models. The handset makers produce for operator networks. If you follow the money, subscriber revenue comes from the voice business, with data as an aftermarket. The telcos are comfortable with revenue from monthly subscriber airtime and services packages. The wireless Internet service is a bit of a mystery to them. Data is an upsell since their motive is to keep callers connected, whether it is to other callers or to machines. Other revenue sources include advertising, transaction commission, games, and hosting.

Fundamentally, telcos sell airtime, but they also define the rules of the market. If their price is too high and services too low, however, or if the content is walled in and limited, as is largely the case in the United States, the market stalls. On the other hand, if the telco price is low, the services high, and the content abundant, then the market is lively, as is the case in Japan. Looking ahead to new spectrum and technology, telcos must account for the expense of licensing spectrum, and deploying and upgrading thousands of towers and other plant equipment.

Handset and Handheld Company Hardware Dynamics

Unlike the free market for PC hardware that is driven largely by buyer choice, the telco handset market is closed, regulated, and licensed. This puts network companies who contract for handsets at the head of the wireless economy. Since the radio spectrum is regulated, devices are being made that tune to a specific network. (I am not sure people would buy many radios that tune into only one radio station.) Handset makers must have partnerships with networks to build compatible products. Telcos sometimes give away the handset to get the lucrative monthly service contract. Today it is impossible for consumers to buy any phone and expect it to work with the wireless network of their choice, although there may be some hope with U.S. local number portability (see chapter 22). The U.S. computer industry is experimenting with a more flexible model where a handheld device can add any radio receiver to connect with any network. However, for each radio modem you carry in your pocket, you need a monthly billing plan. Not many people can afford more than one device or have the patience to carry them all. If the FCC approves software-defined radio, then the day may come when you may need only one wireless device anywhere in the world.

Bundling network services and hardware is a common practice in the telco marketplace. Wireless solutions often involve agreements and partnerships. When subscribers buy handsets, they agree to a billing plan and have to prove credit worthiness before getting a phone. When telcos do per-minute billing for voice calls, it is also possible for them to add to the billing plan any wireless purchase that is secured by the account. Credit card companies might integrate with telco networks to fulfill in-store Bluetooth technology–generated retail payments. Many other companies participate in the operation and hosting of network and handset solutions for enterprises.

Software and Tools Revenue Model

The computer industry is used to selling software licenses on a per-user or per-CPU basis. Both software and digital content are distributed through upgrades or new editions. Software has almost become a virtual subscription. As they say in software, version 1.0 is free; version 2.0 is where the money is. Resourceful developers of digital products look beyond the product release to the actual use of the service or content. If they are smart, they study users of their products carefully. Developers can exploit newfound value while increasing a relationship with their users.

Selling "shrink-wrapped" applications is not a clear wireless market option. Instead, we see PIM software bundled, regular subscriber microbilling, and even giveaways for later subscription upsides. Selling subscriptions to content on top of the i-mode phone service has met with great success in Japan and is likely to be a future revenue model for other parts of the world.

The strategy to give away a wireless application that later initiates a billable service worked for Openwave. It provided free microbrowser software to handset makers by agreement with network providers to share revenue when a subscriber makes a connection.

Another good strategy is to focus on singular, repeatable markets. It takes money for software companies to produce custom wireless vertical market applications. Rather than build a wireless system from scratch every time, a company can reuse the technology developed for an earlier successful project such as dispatch or warehousing. This may require more general-purpose development up front so it can be abstracted as a model. Taking a successful shell, you can then build many simple variations. In time, such companies develop reputations as industry domain experts.

The software industry has produced the primary operating systems and tools to develop key software for computers. Producing an operating system for wireless phone and data devices is still in its infancy. Handset or handheld makers have shown they are better than the computer industry in understanding how to manage power, memory, and communications in a robust fail-safe package. But the activity is largely bundled, although companies like Openwave and QUALCOMM have attempted to open the market for radio operating systems.

The software tools model is another successful approach. Wireless tools are needed to rapidly build applications and wireless Web servers, and to shape mobile content. Middleware companies like Aether Systems, fusionOne, and Pumatech have built software tools and many infrastructural tools for administration and synchronization that the market needs. Focusing on any one of these tools for licensing is a viable option.

In the creation of wireless value, it is healthy to continually ask, What can the wireless Internet do that cannot be done on a desktop? When you find value, you should be able to use one of the many business models to continue your plan.

World Spectrum

The need for global radio spectrum has increased. To satisfy this need, spectrum-licensing bodies move up the spectrum to find unused bands. Meanwhile, new technology is applied to increase spectral efficiency, and the cellular systems are subdivided with even smaller cells and lower-power transmitters. The European and Asian countries have agreed on 3G spectrum, which is the basis for the recent auctions and awarding of licenses. The US PCS spectrum already covers a key part of the European 3G spectrum. To add more 3G spectrum and find future areas to harmonize, the ITU held a World Radio Conference, WRC-2000, in Istanbul in the summer of 2000. The members agreed on three common bands to be set aside for future harmonization: 806–960 MHz, 1.710–1.885 MHz, and 2.500–2,690 MHz.

Whatever bands are chosen, the governance and regulation of spectrum through binding agreements guarantee the use of specific frequencies so that any user does not radiate power that interferes with neighbors.

The Power of Your Network

When selecting wireless networks and determining the placement of basestations and access points, it is important to consider the reach of your networks. Broadcasters express a station's *reach* as the population of listeners or viewers within a broadcast area. Technically this is the distance the signal covers. The power of the transmitter determines the number of people you can advertise to. Power is not all there is. Cellular power dynamics are different. In cellular installations you use less power but more towers to cover an area. In highly congested areas, multiple low-power nets increase the number of devices available in a large area.

The output of the wireless networks are ordered by their signal strength WAN > LAN > PAN. Unlike broadcast that could look at a radio tower footprint, the number of cellular towers must be multiplied to predict coverage. The WAN gives great coverage, the LAN only 100 meters, and the PAN 10 meters, expressed in electrical power and signal strength. The radiating signal strength of a cellular tower is measured over the distance of where you happen to be to the tower. The power output of radio stations is measured in decibels (dB). In cell phones it is thousandths of decibels (dBm). Decibels are logarithmic measures of sound or power. A tower signal measure of 10 milliwatts at some distance may be 20 dBm, 100 milliwatts is 40 dBm, 1000 milliwatts is 60 dBm, and so forth. One milliwatt, or .001 W, is the power of most cellular phones.

Although reach is important for a wireless network, sending a clean signal without interference is essential. Only the WAN is regulated. Although 2.4 GHz and 5 GHz are unlicensed, the power output is regulated. Too much power in an unlicensed 2.4 GHz transmitter infringes on the other devices that may be in the area. For any wireless network, congestion must be monitored. Applications must expect intermittent access.

In addition to strictly regulating the use of existing frequencies, guarding against interference, and monitoring the power output of licensed or unlicensed transmitters, the FCC is busy opening spectrum for new use.

Current U.S. Spectrum

Any wireless spectrum eventually gets used up. The U.S. spectrum allocation history (Table 30) shows that since the early days of the Federal Radio Commission (now the FCC), new spectrum has been allocated at increasingly higher frequencies. The FCC and the National Telecommunications and Information Administration (NTIA) jointly plan specific uses of the U.S. spectrum. For example, FM

Table 30 U.S. spectrum allocation history

MHz	Spectrum Use	Time
5.15 to 5.35 5.725 to 5.825	802.11a	2002
2400 to 2483	Bluetooth (802.15)	2001
2400 to 2483	homeRF	2000
2400 to 2483	LAN Ethernet 802.11b	1998
1850 to 1990	PCS cellular phone	1996
806-902	AMPS cellular phone	1980
512-806	UHF TV	1949
54-216	VHF TV	1941
88-108	FM radio	1935
0.535-1.6	AM radio	1921

radio must broadcast under a transmitter license while cellular spectrum can be two-way at very specific frequencies.

The FCC reviews broadcaster content that is in the "public interest," but it cannot review the content of your phone calls (except for justified criminal or security reasons). An FCC license to cellular operators gives them exclusive use of allocated spectrum. Unlicensed use of spectrum for LAN and PAN has the noted problem of interference where they try to coexist. In a busy office environment, interference can be an issue. In the autumn of 2000, the FCC approved homeRF use of the bottom 10 channels of the hopping space formerly used entirely by 802.11 devices. The FCC licenses and gives public trial to new networks on new parts of the spectrum that come online every year. The appendix contains the U.S. frequency allocations, with the complete list of operating and planned U.S. bands.

PCS Bands

The last major U.S. cellular auction was for the 1900 MHz Personal Communications Services (PCS) bands in 1995 through 1996. The U.S. PCS spectrum (Figure 90) relies on paired bands – one band for sending and one band for receiving. They are separated by 80 MHz. All the sending bands, called the uplink, are between 1850 MHz and 1910 MHz. The receiving bands, called the downlink or receiver, are between 1930 MHz and 1990 MHz. PCS spectrum is grouped into major trading blocks for System A and System B providers, each with 15 MHz bandwidth. The other trading blocks are C, and the minor D, E, and F licenses with a 5 MHz bandwidth. In some parts of the country, the C block has been subdivided into many smaller bands. Note the middle section from 1910 to 1930 that is unpaired and unregulated. It is intended for low-power, private PCS use.

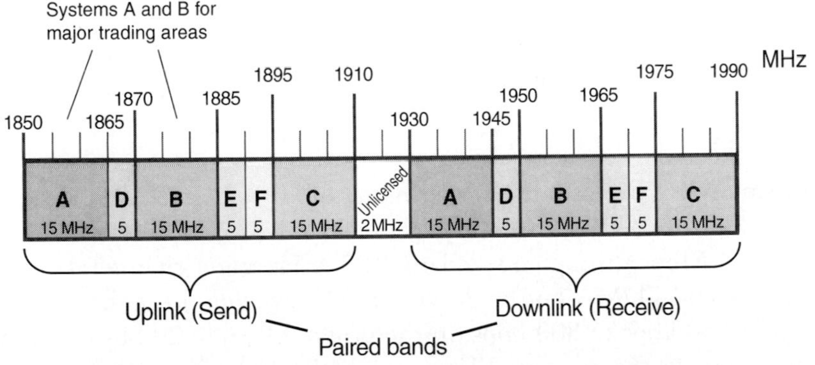

Figure 90 The U.S. PCS spectrum 1996 (*Source:* The Federal Communications Commission)

Filling the Spectrum with CDMA

Once spectrum is licensed, then operators deploy an air interface, build towers, and get handset manufacturers to build devices for their networks. After the PCS auctions of 1995 and 1996 CDMA operators were engaged in all of these efforts. While there were many reasons to maintain the status quo of air interfaces like TDMA and GSM, many operators took advantage of the CDMA technologies that are now the basis for 3G systems.

Major 3G operators are looking to implement air interfaces based on CDMA technology because it has many advantages over other air interfaces, as we mentioned in chapter 4 (see Table 18). Although CDMA evolved from the time of 2G air interfaces, its qualities of security, lower power, and spectral efficiency are now being extended into 3G air interfaces. CDMA can nearly triple TDMA subscriber capacity. Conservation of power is very important. Powerful signals cause interference. When TDMA channel space is recovered and the decision is made to switch a call to an available slot in a channel, then RF qualities are critical. Too much noise (interference) and channels/slots can be temporarily marked as blocked, thus reducing the overall performance and capacity of the system. CDMA spreads the transmission across the spectrum and thereby eliminates self-inflicted performance limitations. For these and other reasons, world telco operators have decided to use CDMA technology in one form or another.

There are a few flavors of CDMA implementations (see Table 31). CDMA is very strong in Korea and Japan. Sprint PCS and Verizon are the largest U.S. CDMA operators. Even Motorola and Nokia have explored a competing version of this technology called 1Xtreme. CDMA in North America has a number of upgrade paths. QUALCOMM has overlapping names for its CDMA releases.

Conventional IS-95A CDMA can send data at 14.4 kbps. Over IS-95B, data is typically transmitted at 64 kbps, although it can reach speeds of 86.4 kbps. Over cdma2000 1x, data can reach 307 kbps. To get serious data throughput that meets the ITU and FCC definition of a 3G data rate, then a data-only, packet-switched channel, 1xEV, is clearly the best technology.

High Data Rate: 1xEV

CDMA 1xEV, or simply EV, replaces the earlier name of High Data Rate (HDR). EV is a high-speed, high-capacity wireless IP data technology that provides Internet access at up to 2.4 Mbps through a standard 1.25 MHz wide channel. It uses CDMA on the uplink and TDMA on the downlink. The average throughput on a loaded sector is from 650 kbps to 800 kbps on the downlink and 220 kbps on the up link. The more people that use an EV channel, the lower is each person's throughput.

EV is a formal ITU standard known as IS-856, "CDMA2000 High Rate Packet Data Air Interface Specification," proposed by the Telecommunications Industry

Table 31 The CDMA Rosetta stone

2G CDMA Technologies

- cdmaOne (IS-95A) – Popular CDMA that can transfer data at 14.4 kbps using a 1.25 MHz bandwidth.

2.5G CDMA Technologies

- cdmaOne (IS-95B) – Advanced CDMA with superior handoff technology. Formerly called 1xRTT, or Radio Transmission Technology, it has a 64 kbps data rate with allowance for 144 kbps packet data using a 1.25 MHz bandwidth.

3G CDMA Technologies

- cdma2000 1x (IS-95C) – Also called CDMA Multi-Carrier (CDMA 1xMC), or simply 1x. This is the entry-level 3G network standard. It doubles capacity and standby times. In use in Korea and expected in the U.S. by the end of 2001, it features 153 kbps and 307 kbps data rates using 1.25 MHz bandwidth.
- cdma2000 EV-DO (IS-856) – (Enhanced Value, Data Only) Data-only channel, also called High Data Rate (HDR), 2.4 Mbps peak, from 650 kbps to 800 kbps shared data rate using a 1.25 MHz bandwidth.
- cdma2000 EV-DV – (Enhanced Value, Data and Voice) Combined voice and data channel featuring HDR using a 1.25 MHz bandwidth.
- cdma2000 3x – U.S. version of W-CDMA for voice and data. 4 Mbps peak, 1 kbps loaded data rate using 3.75 MHz bandwidth. Also called CDMA 3xMC because it combines three 1x 1.25 MHz bands.

Association, which is the communications sector of the Electronic Industries Alliance (TIA/EIA) and developed by the 3GPP2, or Third-Generation Partnership Project 2. Technically EV is a TDMA air interface on the downlink with a dynamically assigned data rate that hops every 1.67 milliseconds.

EV runs as a centralized voice and data service over a CDMA channel where it is called cdma2000 EV-DV (Enhanced Value, Data and Voice). An operator using a centralized approach integrates EV with existing and future IS-95 CDMA cellular systems to provide an optimal voice and data service. It also runs decentralized with other operator air interfaces on its own channel as cdma2000 EV-DO (Enhanced Value, Data Only). Non-CDMA operators can use EV-DO as a separate, high-capacity data channel. EV extends the TIA's cdma2000 standard. EV can be implemented on a separate chipset for handhelds or embedded in Web phone handsets coming from 3G handset makers. The new chipsets from QUALCOMM, such as the MSM5500 (Mobile Station Modem), incorporate EV and should begin appearing in devices in 2002. A closer look at an MSM chip appears in the section "The Revolution in 3G Chips" in chapter 19.

W-CDMA in Europe and Japan

Although QUALCOMM expressly makes a wideband CDMA technology called cdma2000 3x, the name W-CDMA is a third-generation air interface that belongs to the ITU. It now appears there will be a W-CDMA IMT-2000 from Japan, and W-CDMA UMTS from Europe. Although W-CDMA is based on the CDMA technology concept, all of these 3G air interfaces are incompatible.

The 3G Wireless Internet

To lay a foundation in wireless architecture, spectrum needs to be available. Allocation of 3G spectrum is a requirement before towers and receivers can be deployed, and that must happen before services and applications can be made available. The 3G features that are being targeted by international engineers are listed in Table 32.

UMTS and IMT-2000

Internationally, 3G spectrum was decided for Europe and Asia by agreements made through the International Telecommunications Union (ITU). Over the years, the ITU evolved two core 3G standards – UMTS and IMT-2000. Although the two overlap, their objectives differ.

- *IMT-2000.* International Mobile Telecommunication 2000, also called ITU-2000, is international and now refers commonly to Japanese 3G spectrum. It

Table 32 3G target features

3G Feature	3G Detail
High data rates for packet and circuit	144 kbps in vehicles 384 kbps for pedestrians 2 Mbps or higher for indoor use
Always connected	Packet-switched
Voice and data network	Dynamically allocated
Enhanced roaming	Interoperability
Common billing and user profiles	Usage and rate information shared among service providers Standardized recording of call details Standardized user profiles
Determination of geographic position	Via mobile terminal and network
Multimedia services	Bandwidth on demand, variable data rates Multimedia mail store and forward Quality sound

Source: ITU <http://www.itu.int/imt/what_is/imt/> and FCC <http://www.fcc.gov/3G/>.

replaces Future Public Land-Mobile Telephone System (FPLMTS) as the visionary ITU specification of standards for 3G. IMT-2000 is also a family of standards for mixed systems to become interoperable, thereby allowing such things as global roaming. Within the IMT-2000 standards, there are three modes: a direct-sequence mode (DS-WCDMA or UTRA FDD), a multi-carrier mode (cdma2000), and a time division duplex (UTRA TDD) mode. It designates a broad 5 MHz bandwidth to carry voice and high data traffic.

- *UMTS.* Universal Mobile Telecommunications System is used to refer to 3G spectrum in Europe. It is part of the ITU IMT-2000 vision of a global family of 3G mobile communications systems. Developed initially in Europe by the ETSI (like DECT and GSM), the UMTS-Forum and 3GPP developed UMTS to provide a 3G wireless system. UMTS provides a migration path for the GSM industry and uses the UTRA RTT. Building on the success of GSM, UMTS will make the two systems compatible and enable operators to upgrade at relatively low cost.

The two standards are very similar, envisioning a global infrastructure of satellite and terrestrial systems for fixed and mobile devices to deliver voice, data, and multimedia content anywhere in the world. They agree on data transmission rates of 384 kbps for full mobility and up to 2 Mbps for limited movement.

International spectrum allocation (Figure 91) is the result of UMTS auctions in Europe, which took place in 2000 and 2001. The Japanese chose the IMT-2000 designation, although the paired frequency bands for 3G spectrum are identical. For the United States, 3G spectrum is a ways off. The United States has not designated any 3G spectrum yet. The U.S. PCS licenses currently overlay the ITU spectrum area. While the United States finds a location for 3G, it plans to reuse some of the PCS spectrum. While Europe and Japan are developing their own W-CDMAs, the United States is getting ready with CDMA MC also known as CDMA2000,

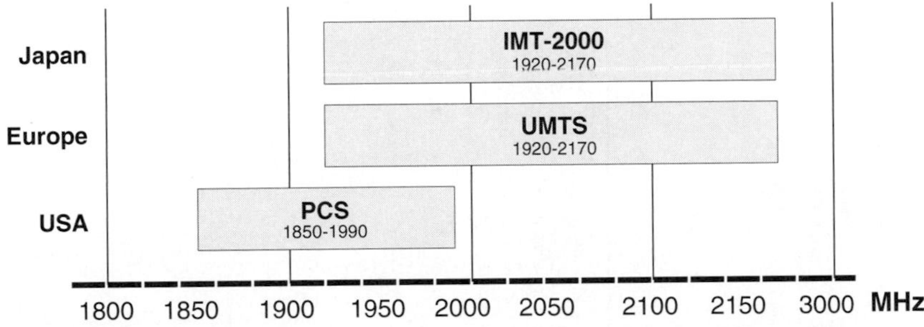

Figure 91 International spectrum allocation. The emphasis is on paired-band ranges.

an upgrade path from cdmaOne. Although alike in theory, all three wideband CDMA interfaces are implemented as divergent interfaces.

3G Spectrum Auctions

At the beginning of 2001, companies had spent more than $110 billion buying 3G spectrum licenses around the world. The United States has yet to specify where 3G will live. Clearly, businesses are convinced of the value of the new services – always on, high data rate, and Internet access.

3G air interfaces (Figure 92) rely on new spectrum that is already available in Japan and Europe, as was discussed in the section "World Spectrum Auctions" in chapter 1. The information about worldwide 3G spectrum auctions in Table 33 was compiled as it came over the newswire. (ITU updates can be found at <http://www.itu.int/osg/spu/ni/3g/resources/licensing_policy>.)

In April 2000, the United Kingdom 3G auction concluded. Vodafone acquired the largest of the four available licenses. On June 12, 2000, the Japanese Ministry of Posts and Telephones awarded licenses to NTT DoCoMo, Japan Telecom, and KDDI for immediate operational testing. KDDI was formed October 2000 as a merger of KDD, Japan's largest international carrier, DDI, a domestic carrier, and IDO, a mobile carrier. NTT DoCoMo offered trial 3G services beginning May 31, 2001, while J-Phone is planning service for June 2002. To continue monitoring the official Japanese position, visit <http://www.mpt.go.jp/eng/>.

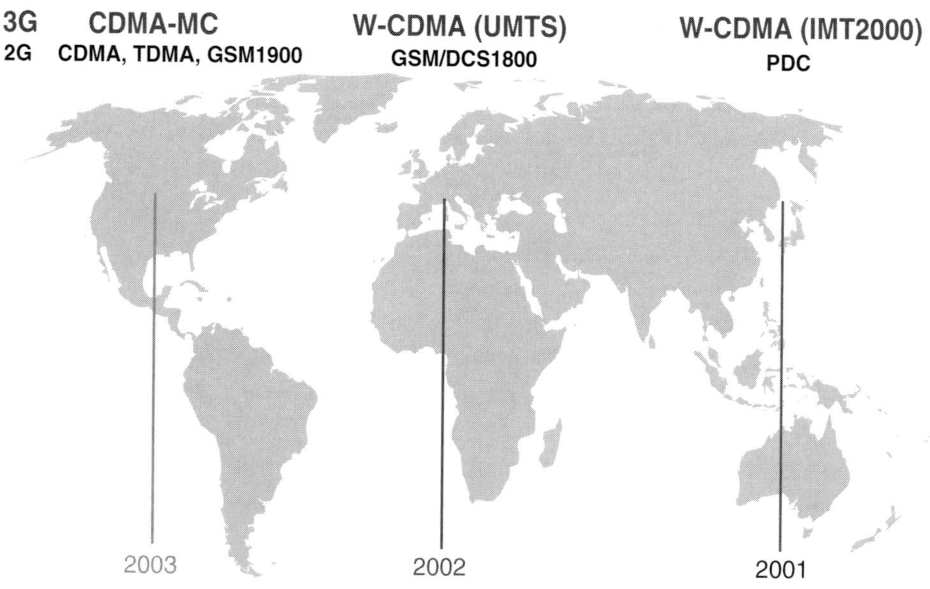

Figure 92 3G air interfaces

Table 33 Worldwide 3G spectrum auctions

Country	Auction Specifics
Finland	Awarded 4 licenses March 2000
Japan	Awarded 3 licenses, June 2000; trial service May 31, 2001
Netherlands	US$2.5 billion, July 2000
Germany	US$46 billion/50.5 Euro for 6 licenses, August 2000
France	Awarded fixed fee US$4 billion/32.5 FF for 4 licenses, September 2000
Italy	US$11 billion contested, October 2000
Austria	US$610 million, November 2000
Sweden	Awarded 4 licenses, November 2000
Spain	Awarded to Telefónica Móviles, November 2000
Switzerland	US$116 million, December 2000
South Korea	US$2.2 billion, December 2000
Canada	US$1.5 billion, January 2001
Australia	US$351.7 million, March 2001
Singapore	US$165.6 million, April 2001
United States	(Auction planned from June to September 2002 may be postponed.)

The U.S. Allocation of 3G Spectrum

The United States has the largest allocation of television spectrum in the world, leaving room for little else. The U.S. government is now busy rethinking the best way to allocate 3G spectrum, especially in the face of the committed allocations of world 3G spectrum. The Clinton administration began worrying about the United States getting left behind in the race to offer 3G services. It began looking at options to "uncover spectrum" from the broadcast industry, members of which strongly protested. The administration issued a directive to the National Telecommunications and Information Agency (NTIA) to study the feasibility of having the Department of Defense (DoD) vacate spectrum. The military spectrum to be examined was the IMT-2000–designated 3G bands of 1755 MHz to 1850 MHz and 2500 MHz to 2690 MHz. The Satellite Industry Association (SIA) had also asked the FCC to allocate the bands from 2500 MHz to 2520 MHz and from 2670 MHz to 2690 MHz for 3G mobile satellite services, all within the IMT-2000 3G band plan. This DoD spectrum is set aside for such things as Air Force communications, intelligence gathering, and the global positioning satellite navigational system. The Pentagon reported that migrating off this spectrum could not be completed until 2010, with space systems remaining until 2017 at a total cost of $4.3 billion.[2]

Another plan calls for reusing television bands. Television broadcasters were given the chunk of airwaves in the band from 747 MHz to 92 MHz for UHF channels 60 through 69. The few television broadcasters using this spectrum have rights to the spectrum through 2006. The FCC plans to move broadcasters to other channels.

The Clinton administration had slated a 3G auction to begin in June and end in September 2002. The Bush administration may delay this. Meanwhile, the FCC is ushering in E911 services to start in 2001 and conclude in 2006, the same year when all broadcast networks are required to transmit HDTV signals. But all of this is subject to revision by the U.S. Congress.

The New Politics of the Wireless Internet

Building the wired Internet is easy in many respects. All you have to do is dig up a street and lay down some fiber. But the wireless Internet requires government support to enter the market and a nod for every increase in its capacity and change of use. With regard to 3G spectrum, the United States lags behind the rest of the world, and there are problems with its process that the free market is pressing home. Spectrum planning thus far has largely been an exercise of the budget committees in the Congress, pressed to generate revenue by selling spectrum licenses. (Historically, cashing in is not policy of the U.S. government; for example, in the 1800s land was given away to pioneering families and railroads to build out the continent.) In addition, device regulation is becoming a problem. The FCC licensing of devices and approval mechanism is under world pressure to match the increased pace of product cycles and ever-increasing changes in spectrum access technology. New device production cycles are down to six to nine months in Asia. Meanwhile, handset makers in the United States find the FCC licensing procedures take almost two years.

To get a sense of the emerging direction of the U.S. with regard to 3G, it is important to study the issues and statements of the industry and FCC leadership. The president and CEO of the CTIA, Tom Wheeler, represents the voices of the cellular telephone and Internet industries. He interviewed Michael Powell, the Chairman of the FCC, who expressed that his organization was, "taking humble stock of what its appropriate role is," and is directing new approaches for the FCC. "Wireless is exciting because it is at the cutting edge of innovation. I think it is at the cutting edge of competitive principles," he said and admitted that, like business, government should rethink its business model.[3] The CTIA member companies are trying to get the FCC to consider their broad positions to help improve the U.S. market:

- Elimination of the wireless tax subsidy for wireline service
- Removal of spectrum caps and easing cross-media ownership

- Vacation or relocation of broadcast and military spectrum for 3G cellular use
- Allowance of spectrum owners to resell their spectrum
- Reduction of FCC approval time for licensing new wireless devices
- Industry privacy code of conduct for FCC approval
- New "revenue-sharing" auction system to allow capital flows later in the process

Powell has begun to respond to some of these issues, stating, "I think the country needs to spend some collective thinking on trying to have a more coherent, nationally harmonized spectrum policy." The FCC can provide a plan, but "Congress has to take a sober role about to what degree it is going to see spectrum policy as a matter of budget policy." In the search for spectrum, the FCC can advocate that the Pentagon free some of it, but as Powell has pointed out, "We can't trivialize the uses of spectrum for our national security and national defense." (An appropriate remark for the son of the four-star General Colin Powell, the U.S. Secretary of State.) As far as relaxing spectrum caps or allowing licensees to resell frequency, the FCC Chairman said, "the Commission recognizes that it has a duty and an obligation to reevaluate and revalidate or get rid of rules that are artificial or put structural constraints on growth." Powell reaffirmed that "Innovation, not regulation, changes the industry. [For example,] Bill McGowen [the founder of MCI] and the use of microwaves circumvented AT&T's long-distance monopoly." Asked whether narrowband rules should apply to new wireless broadband technology, Powell said that legacy systems need support and that the new wireless technology is exploring "our understanding of the kinds of goods and services people will or will not deliver; whether consumers will embrace any of this, despite our techno-ecstasy about all the possibilities."[4]

Chairman Michael Powell continues to help identify additional spectrum for 3G advanced mobile wireless services. He appeared at a Congressional panel on March 29, 2001, reporting that every part of the FCC portfolio is facing some sort of revolution. He observed that the FCC structure that had evolved over the past 70 years was geared toward regulation of established technology, not toward offering services. In the simplest of terms, it is questionable for an agency to stipulate and then regulate the purposes of digital transmission since transmitted bits could be used for television, radio, voice, or digital information. The new wireless broadband technologies challenge the very nature of incumbent voice-centric cellular systems.[5]

In the United States developers work in a complex mix of free market and regulated conditions, while Chairman Powell retools and redirects the FCC to align its operations to services and, with Congress, to form a harmonized national telecommunications plan.

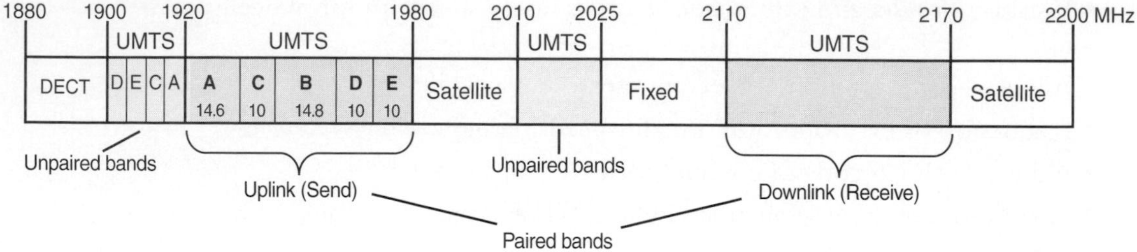

Figure 93 The 3G UMTS spectrum

3G Spectrum Europe

While the clock is ticking as the United States struggles to find its place in a 3G world economy, the ITU International Mobile Telecommunications 2000 (IMT-2000) has already designated 3G UMTS spectrum (Figure 93) based largely on 2G plans. In fact, the IMT-2000 plan generally looks like the U.S. PCS plan that appeared earlier. The UMTS also designates paired bands.

- 1885 MHz through 2010 MHz for uplink
- 2110 MHz through 2200 MHz for downlink

Note that these paired bands include the IMT-2000 satellite component bands 1980 MHz through 2010 MHz and 2170 MHz through 2200 MHz, as well as the Mobile and Fixed Wireless Access (FWA) at 2025 MHz through 2110 MHz.

The Five 3G Air Interfaces

Many companies, including Ericsson, Nortel, and Nokia, are currently conducting trials of UMTS technology, using prototypes of advanced mobile phones and wireless devices. CDMA continues to gain inroads with many advanced digital processing and transmission techniques The technical fate of 3G was decided in May 2000, when the ITU resolved five official air interfaces:

- *W-CDMA, Wideband Code Division Multiple Access.* W-CDMA uses a 5 MHz wide band to handle traffic. Japan IMT-2000 and European UMTS spectrum is assigned to transmit slightly different forms of W-CDMA. W-CDMA is a broadband implementation of the CDMA RTT. The chip rate and framing structure of the initial Japanese and European W-CDMA implementations are different enough that the two CDMA standards are incompatible. European GSM is expected to migrate to W-CDMA. Capable of providing broadband multimedia transmission, the technology will allow a full range of

3G services (e.g., videoconferencing and MPEG4 video). W-CDMA is the basis for next-generation i-mode that began operating in Tokyo in 2001. Its 3G specification incorporates an air interface that is based on Direct Sequence (DS) CDMA technology.

- *CDMA MC, Code Division Multiple Access, Multi Carrier* is the U.S. direction for 3G CDMA with W-CDMA-like properties. It operates on a 3.75 MHz wide band, which can combine three cdma2000 1.25 MHz channels. It is a direct upgrade path from existing CDMA towers. CDMA MC is supported by an entire range of chipsets and products from QUALCOMM, the inventor of the standard. CDMA MC is a 3G standard evolution of IS-95, combining three IS-95 carriers to form one wideband carrier. A useful extension is the 1xEV High Data Rate, which allows data transmissions up to 2 Mbps.
- *TDMA single carrier* is designated by standard UWC-136, Universal Wireless Communications 136. TDMA single carrier is an optional upgrade for European GSM and American TDMA companies. It is a backward-compatible standard to let TDMA equipment run over 3G networks. Although it does not have the qualities of CDMA, it has an installed base and is a force to be reckoned with. It has definite improvements over TDMA. Primary network operators can have a TDMA upgrade path. The UWC group also defines a data carrier called EDGE, or Enhanced Data for GSM Enhancement, that can operate at 384 kbps. D-AMPS and TDMA operators use 200 kHz wide channels, the same width as EDGE. Using a variant called EDGE Compact, D-AMPS operators can use the EDGE data overlay in addition to their voice channel. As much as TDMA operators might consider an upgrade to CDMA, they cannot legally operate a CDMA service that requires a minimal 1.25 MHz bandwidth.
- *CDMA-TD (TDD)* is Time Division Duplex that is ideal for data exchange. Unlike the 3G air interfaces that are Frequency Division Duplex (FDD), meaning the use of paired spectrum bands, TDD simply lets packets come and go through one band using specialized time-sharing protocols. It is the ideal air interface to exchange frames of data used in mobile IP services. I-BURST is a TDD air interface being implemented in the United Kingdom by Marconi.
- *FD-TDMA (DECT)* is Frequency Division Time Division Multiple Access. It is built on an FDD paired-band radio architecture. The purpose of this standard is to have a place for Digital Enhanced Cordless Telephone (DECT). Domestic and small business cordless phones use this air interface over wireless HomeRF and proprietary radio LANs. DECT is one of the transparent roaming standards. Fully transient 3G devices should be able to pass transparent roaming service from FD-TDMA across to a W-CDMA carrier.

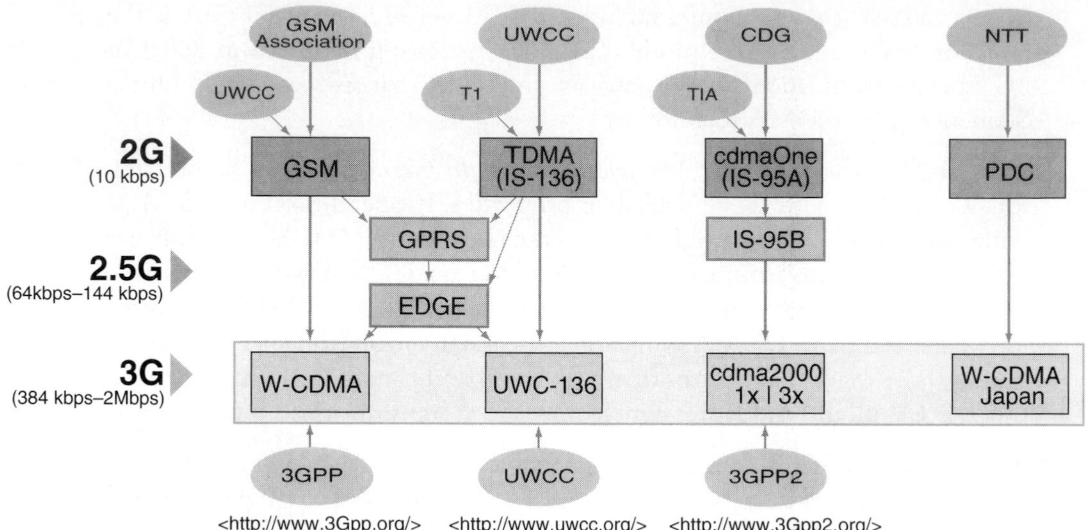

Figure 94 Three ITU standards groups and NTT are defining 3G networks.

Many primary bodies influence each of these 3G standards. Three ITU standards groups and NTT are defining 3G networks (Figure 94). The Third-Generation Partnership Project (3GPP) favors W-CDMA and WAP. The Universal Wireless Communications Consortium (UWCC) favors TDMA. The Third-Generation Partnership Project 2 (3GPP2) favors CDMA MC and Internet protocols. NTT DoCoMo is creating its own W-CDMA standard, which is not compatible with the European version and is derived from PDC, not GSM. There are many migration paths, agendas, and plans for harmonization of these groups.

3G Harmonization

Currently a wide range of standards bodies and companies are defining their plans to create 3G networks. Some have coalesced before the ITU as three working groups: 3GPP, UWCC, and 3GPP2. Three seems to be the lucky number. In addition to the ITU is the Japanese W-CDMA effort.

The ITU recognizes only three standards groups in the development of 3G networks. Each formal 2G specification is being shepherded by multiple standards bodies. In addition, some members of these bodies have multiple affiliations. Another group is working on TDD interfaces. Meanwhile, the following three large consortiums are laying out plans for 3G implementations.

- *Third-Generation Partnership Project (3GPP).* In December 1998, 3GPP was created as a result of an agreement among several international standards-setting bodies: ETSI in Europe, ARIB and TTC in Japan, T1 (ANSI-T1) in the United States, and TTA in Korea. The organizing partners have agreed to cooperate for the production of open, global, technical specifications for a 3G mobile system and services based on the evolved GSM core networks and the Radio Transmission Technologies (RTT) that partners support (i.e., UTRA, both FDD and TDD modes). Since the project started, CWTS in China has joined. In a nutshell, 3GPP provides global specifications for GSM network evolution to 3G and the UTRA RTT.

- *Universal Wireless Communications Consortium (UWCC)*, based in Bellevue, Washington, is an international consortium of more than 100 wireless carriers and vendors that support the TDMA-EDGE technology standards. EDGE has many possible upgrades for TDMA and GSM systems. The UWCC's 3G standard is UWC-136.
- *The Third-Generation Partnership Project 2 (3GPP2)* consists of five telecommunications standards bodies (CWTS in China, ARIB and TTC in Japan, TTA in Korea, and TIA in North America), the Mobile Wireless Internet Forum (MWIF), and the CDMA Development Group (CDG). The 3GPP2 is an effort spearheaded by the ANSI board of directors to counterbalance the GSM-centered 3GPP effort. It evolves U.S.-derived 3G standards such as the cdma2000 by QUALCOMM and the ANSI/TIA/EIA/IS-41 switching infrastructure, and it develops technical specifications for ANSI-based 3G RTTs.

TDD Coalition

One of the ITU 3G air interfaces is Time Division Duplex (TDD). Although not specifically working on ITU specifications, the TDD Coalition was formed to standardize a TDD interface. The TDD Coalition is a group of 12 companies: ArrayComm, IP Wireless, Aperto Networks, Clearwire, Harris, LinkAir, BeamReach Networks, CALY Networks, Malibu Networks, Radiant Networks, Raze Technologies, and Wavion.

These companies are largely using an IP-based, packet-switched protocol. They do not rely on the conventional FDD division of paired spectrum bands found in 2G and planned 3G networks. Instead, a TDD air interface can dynamically adjust transmission in the spectrum band to send and receive data or voice traffic. The spectral efficiency of TDD bandwidth allows it to adapt well to bursty data traffic and the high bandwidth demands made possible with packet data networks. The coalition's initial plan is to get FCC allocation or authorization to use its carrier in any forthcoming U.S. 3G market. The TDD Coalition Web site is <www.tddcoalition.org>.

"4G," New Spectrum, and Emerging Wireless Air Interfaces

It is hard to talk about "4G" when we have not yet resolved how to build 3G. However, each air interface generation appears about ten years apart and initial planning for 4G is taking place. If there is to be a 4G, it will need new spectrum allocation and a technical standard. With a standard, world industries can build towers to cover territory, handset makers can make radio devices for operation, and standards groups can prepare for testing and certification. Like any air interface, it must first increase subscriber capacity. 4G must be useful for voice and digital media. 4G may patch up some of the problems that 3G may not get around to implementing well. For example, 4G may use pure TDD technology, which means it will no longer use a control channel and paired uplink and downlink bands typical of 2G and 3G spectrum plans. It may be entirely IP-based and packet-switched even for voice. The world might insist on one 4G band plan. Other possible 4G requirements might be for optimal connection to IPv6, an extremely ambitious data rate, or for "lambda" interconnects to an all-optical backbone. On the other hand, that could be "5G."

The formal post-3G activities at the ITU are being carried out by exploratory groups such as the ITU WP-8F (Working Party section 8F) chartered to study post–IMT-2000 technology migration. The DoCoMo Yokosuka lab is exploring 4G network possibilities that it hopes to test in 2006. In the name of 4G, many possible air interfaces will come. Although they have no ITU designations, these new commercial spectral air interfaces offer data rates far beyond 3G. The world continues to experiment with bandwidth technology such as UWB, OFDM, HDR, and W-CDMA radio carriers.

Given these many options, operators have to make decisions based on the licensed spectrum in which they may implement air interfaces. They have to decide if they want to continue investing in existing air interface technology to add conventional subscribers or divide some of their owned spectrum and support new air interfaces to attract new customers. It is often easier to hold on and sell what you already know how to sell. But there is always a risk in not offering the new features made possible by new air interfaces. The churn of consumers moving to a transcending technology can be an operator's worst nightmare.

There are other wireless networks, although they are not necessarily mobile. The last mile or the last kilometer, depending on how you count, is the final connection from a fixed network to home and office wireless basestations. Behind the wireless basestation are DSL, cable, fixed broadband wireless, optical fiber, and even satellite. Other wireless Internet networks are fixed broadband wireless carriers that often use high-frequency spectrum such as MMDS, LMDS, and wireless cable. These fixed systems are associated with new wireless spectrum with fixed bands of spectrum. Some are beginning to provide limited mobile wireless access.

While the U.S. government works to establish official 3G spectrum, U.S. technology companies continue to rework the most efficient use of digital spectrum. In the United States, the common parts of the wireless spectrum are found at 800 MHz (AMPS), 1900 MHz (PCS), 2.4 GHz (LAN and PAN), and 5 GHz (LAN). Let us look at the many upper-spectrum wireless technologies in order of increasing data rate.

IPMA @irPointer (20 Mbps) and SDMA I-BURST (40 Mbps)

Making use of smart antennas and IP packet networks in TDD configurations is the work of two companies, SWIFTcomm and Arraycomm.

Mitsubishi Materials created a new division, SWIFTcomm (the first part of the name stands for Smart Wireless Internet for Field Teamwork). SWIFTcomm uses Internet Protocol Multiple Access (IPMA). At the beginning of 2001, Mitsubishi Materials concluded a test of its narrowband 1 Mbps IPMA signal in New York City. The wireless broadband version of this carrier can provide 20 Mbps wireless Internet access and has a handoff speed of 100 mph. Mitsubishi Materials intends to invest $500 million in infrastructure to roll out this network throughout 2002 in the United States.

SWIFTcomm makes the @irPointer, a penlike antenna that accesses IPMA basestations located in cities and along highways. The pointer connects via cable or Bluetooth technology to almost any mobile device. Of course, it is only good as long as there is an IPMA cellular tower nearby. The IPMA tower connects to SWIFTcomm servers and routers, which access the Internet. IPMA competes with CDMA. The company is going after the transportation industry's vertical market. You can read more at <http://www.swiftcomm.net>.

Arraycomm is a specialist in signal processing using Spatial Division Multiple Access (SDMA) to boost signal reception, thereby resulting in a dramatic increase in the number of subscribers per channel. Its IntelliCell® advanced signal-processing software allows a basestation to detect and maintain links with many individual subscribers in a congested and noisy signal environment. ArrayComm I-BURST is an implementation of IntelliCell that can sustain a 1.2 Mbps connection, although it can reach 40 Mbps. (We cover other details of this technology in the section "Spatial Processing and Smart Antennas" in chapter 5.)

W-OFDM (32 Mbps to 155 Mbps)

Another promising technology not yet deployed is Wideband Orthogonal Frequency Division Multiplexing (W-OFDM). W-OFDM is the basis for most implementations of wireless Ethernet 802.11a. This technology uses signal processors to break up the data signal and send it simultaneously down many channels. Wi-LAN, a Canadian company, holds many key patents for this network technology. Wi-LAN has tested W-OFDM reliably at 32 Mbps in a moving vehicle. It is expected to reach a peak rate of 155 Mbps.

LAN Wireless Data Rates (56 Mbps to 100 Mbps)

Many businesses now use wireless Ethernet 802.11b, which runs at 11 Mbps. However, the next-generation standard transmits at breathtaking speeds. Building on the widely used Ethernet protocol, the upgrade for 802.11a in the United States and HiperLAN2 in Europe will transmit initially at 56 Mbps, stepping up to 100 Mbps at the 5 GHz spectrum. (We covered many other details of HiperLAN and 802.11a in the section "Next-Generation Wireless LAN" in chapter 4.)

MMDS Fixed Wireless (5 Mbps to 36 Mbps)

One of the most popular fixed wireless broadband air interfaces is the Multipoint Multichannel Distribution Service (MMDS). MMDS is also known as the Wireless Digital Subscriber Line (WDSL). In the United States, major cities and select rural areas use this wireless air interface for fixed Internet access. MMDS spectrum operates in the range from 2150 MHz to 2162 MHz and from 2500 MHz to 2690 MHz. Because of the collision with ITU 3G spectrum, MMDS may eventually be reallocated.

The original use of MMDS spectrum was to allow for "wireless cable TV," originally authorized only to deliver one-way video programming. Wireless cable TV never took off in the United States. This was apparent in 1998 when the FCC finally redefined the use of the spectrum for two-way Internet service. Sprint and MCI WorldComm own major metropolitan licenses and offer MMDS to households for about $40 per month. Sprint Broadband Direct℠ download speeds begin at 1 Mbps and burst up to 5 Mbps. The uplink is about 256 kbps. Fixed wireless MMDS towers are licensed for power for one-way transmissions to a 30-mile (50-km) radius and can transmit data up to 36 Mbps. Two-way MMDS transmits 6 miles (10 km).

LMDS Fixed Wireless (155 Mbps)

Local Multipoint Distribution Service (LMDS) is a point-to-multipoint broadband technology licensed to operate in the United States at 28 GHz and 31 GHz. In the two bands from 27.5 GHz to 28.35 GHz and from 31.0 GHZ to 31.3 GHz, this microwave service occupies a huge band of spectrum. One 1.3 GHz wide A band can transmit a quarter of a million phone calls. Auctions in 1998 and 1999 offered two licenses per basic trading area. Theoretically, these have a range of 8 kilometers, but because weather interferes with this spectrum, the effective range is often reduced to 2 kilometers on a bad day. LMDS towers are often implemented as sector cells and can reach speeds of 155 Mbps.

Fixed wireless is not standardized. Different countries implement these on different available spectrum. As you might guess, MMDS and LMDS fixed wireless networks are being improved to have mobile characteristics that may put them functionally into the conventional WAN-class carrier service. This situation is similar to that of iDEN, which was originally developed as a dispatch ESMR network into a general WAN subscriber network.

Fixed Wireless (622 Mbps)

The FCC in November 2000 granted a permit to Harmonix to sell devices that use tiny slices of unlicensed 59 GHz to 64 GHz spectrum. These devices connect buildings within a half-mile radius at data rates of between 100 Mbps and OC-12 (622 Mbps). Their modulation of the 60 GHz band of the radio spectrum has some unique characteristics. For example, oxygen molecules in the air absorb most of the energy transmitted, yet it is powerful enough to cover transmitters within half a mile. The FCC sponsored line-of-sight energy tests of the 60 GHz Harmonix radios and the company showed that the units radiate about 1/100th to 1/400th as much energy as a typical cell phone. Small consumer receivers can sit in windows aimed at a transmitting device on a nearby telephone pole to bring in nearly optical-speed connections or "slow" connections that are several times faster than cable modems or digital subscriber lines. The receivers use the Harmonix GigaLink beam that operates as a short-range beam of microwave with a range of 400 to 1400 meters. Customers do not have to purchase an FCC license like other high-speed data transmission technology. The Harmonix Web site is <http://www.hxi.com/>.

Ultra Wideband (1 Gbps)

Ultra Wideband (UWB) uses the entire spectrum in a random, low-power manner and can offer a dramatic increase in wireless capacity. UWB does not use frequency band to modulate a carrier. It works by firing pulses of low energy over a wide spectral band. UWB is sometimes called pulse radio.

Military and intelligence establishments have been using ultra wideband frequency radio for many years. Original UWB applications were developed for radar imaging of objects buried under the ground or behind walls; they are now evolved to provide short-range, high-speed data transmissions suitable for broadband access to the Internet. Since a UWB energy band can travel through floors, it is ideal for use in buildings.

Time Domain's PulsON chipset-based wireless Ethernet uses UWB technology. It generates extremely low-power pulses at 50 millionths of a watt, scattered over 1 GHz to 4 GHz. Transmitters send out 40 million pulses per second at precise intervals, each one able to carry 10 megabits per second. In the lab, this has been tested to transfer data at 1 gigabit per second. The downside is that these transmissions can cause interference raising a noise floor with many devices depending on clean UWB frequencies. Some devices see pulse radio as noise and filter it out, but others can be overloaded and fail to operate. This promising scatter-spectrum approach is many years away from general use. The UWB market has had little commercial development because of regulatory barriers. In May 2000, the FCC granted permission for wide-range testing of UWB technology on an unlicensed basis. The Ultra Wideband Working Group (UWBWG) Web site is <http://www.uwb.org/>.

Other High-Frequency Wireless Technologies (155 Mbps to 10 Gbps)

Conventional microwave dishes have been in use for decades. They require a license to operate, and can transmit data at 155 Mbps within a typical range of 45 km. They operate at many bands between 2 GHz and 50 GHz. Like many higher-frequency media, weather can shorten the effective distance. Compared to a cellular antenna, a dish is generally smaller and easier to deploy.

In 2000, the FCC auctioned the 39 GHz licenses that provide fixed communications for point-to-point and point-to-multipoint communications. The 38.6 GHz to 40.0 GHz band was divided into 14 symmetrically paired bands with 50 MHz uplink and 50 MHz downlink. Some of the winners are Advanced Radio Telecom, AT&T Wireless, Hyperion Communications, Milkyway Multipoint, and TRW; they will use the spectrum to extend wireless broadband connections from their fiber networks.

Other companies besides Harmonix use unlicensed areas of the spectrum. One good place is the low end of the visible spectrum between 200 THz and 400 THz (terahertz) – the place where lasers roam. Terabeam calls this fiberless optic technology and commercially operates systems between 5 Mbps and 100 Mbps with line-of-sight connections between lasers and telescopic photodetection "antennas." Fiberless optic systems have a range of 4 km, but are restricted by bad weather, especially fog. Lab tests for short-range systems have reached up to 10 Gbps.

17
Chapter

Planning Towers and Network as a Structure: Every 10 Years

Ten years is an interesting interval in the wireless Internet. The intervals between the introduction of 1G and 2G, and between 2G and 3G air interfaces are roughly 10 years. No communications satellite lasts for more than 10 years. All telco network operators in the United States are legally obligated by their FCC licenses to continue support of their service for up to 10 years after they have signed up their last subscriber.

Structure in the wireless Internet is formed by elements such as towers, wires, effective coverage patterns, and the bandwidth of the working spectrum. These elements are like the load-bearing structures one would see as the first pieces on a construction site for a building. These structural elements are expensive to change and set the fundamental quality of the building.

The transceivers mounted on the towers are changed out to support generations of wireless air interface. The cellular radius of the network is extended by the addition of nearby towers. Ten years is a practical duration for a wireless air interface. It is doubtful that carriers who must change transceivers, IT (Information Technology) departments who must afford new equipment, much less society in general, could digest a much faster period of innovation for wireless transmission technology.

The Internet is, inherently, an open platform. Yet, the structure of modern telecommunications network architecture is fundamentally closed. The carrier currently owns the network, the pipe "|" that determines the devices that connect, a measure of the content, and to a large extent, the customer. It is useful for developers to know telco subscriber statistics to anticipate congestion, coverage patterns to plan for availability, technical air interfaces to plan device support, and data network bandwidths to determine throughput. All these points are essential to evaluating choices. An understanding of network qualities such as enhanced roaming, LBS, and packet-based architecture for voice and data is essential to planning next-generation wireless application architecture.

Network air interfaces do not matter to most software developers. But they do matter to an architect, especially when, as an alternative to telcos, we build our own towers. It took nearly six years for 2 Mbps 802.11 to become 11 Mbps 802.11b in 1998. Now we look forward to 54 Mbps 802.11a.

Putting up Towers

Wireless architecture begins with the physical location of towers. The number of cellular towers in an area is a key measure of capacity. To add subscribers, you must increase tower capacity, which is different from the old days of broadcast when to increase reach, you simply boosted power to your signal. Two-way, low-power cellular transmitters use multiple towers. To increase capacity in congested areas, a tower has to grow new antennas with special properties or the tower has to be replaced by a set of smaller towers in a technique called cell splitting. Cellular WAN operators traditionally have split cells. Splitting cells means adding antennas and often erecting new towers. One approach is to replace a strong macrocell antenna with many lower-power picocell antennas. Another way to increase traffic capacity is to add antennas and tune them, which would require reducing the sector size of the antenna to focus energy in narrow cones. At other times, new antennas are added as an upgrade to carry a new frequency. New operators using smart antennas can simply add more of them and the signal-processing software figures out how to spatially process the traffic.

The FCC does not regulate or approve tower locations for cellular companies. State and local zoning boards handle tower location. The Telecommunications Act instructs the FCC to ensure that the state and local zoning boards do not unreasonably delay the construction of towers or the approval of sites.

It takes time to upgrade tower basestations. One of the risks of providing a new WAN air interface is destroying the loyalties of the existing subscribers. Preserving backward compatibility can be costly when creating a new customer base, even when companies offering new handsets try to move subscribers to the new wireless network. On the other hand, upgrading can also be costly because it involves writing off years of capital investment in earlier technology. There is always a tradeoff between adding capacity to a familiar technology and upgrading to a new one. In a move from 1G to 2G, TDMA towers were upgraded from IS-56 to IS-136. CDMA towers are moving from IS-95A to IS-95C and remain backward compatible. Upgrades to transmitters and handsets are often required. The new transceivers usually sit on the pole with the old transceivers. The new handsets are dual-mode; they retain older circuitry when new service towers are not yet available.

Deploying Fixed Wireless Access Towers

Combinations of fixed wireless basestations and access points (Figure 95) can be deployed in buildings as a fixed wireless access system. The Fixed Wireless Access (FWA) transmitter is mounted on the building's roof. It communicates outside to a centrally located antenna that serves as the gateway into the Internet or the PSTN. This setup replaces the "last mile" of copper wire that traditionally provides customers with telecommunications services. This final segment is also referred to as the Wireless Local Loop (WLL) competing with traditional wire line service providers.

The WLL tower transmits microwaves (like MMDS) to the building's FWA basestation, which is connected to a wireless LAN or Bluetooth access point in the building. The roaming Web phone can transmit voice and data either to the building's access point or over a conventional WAN air interface to a cellular tower.

Inside the building, a wireless access point transmits via either LAN wireless Ethernet or PAN Bluetooth network to reach all wireless devices in range. To continue wireless service from the building to outside requires a handoff to a cellular tower – the transparent roaming goal of 3G networks. Although operators provide FWA equipment, consumers and small businesses can buy their own.

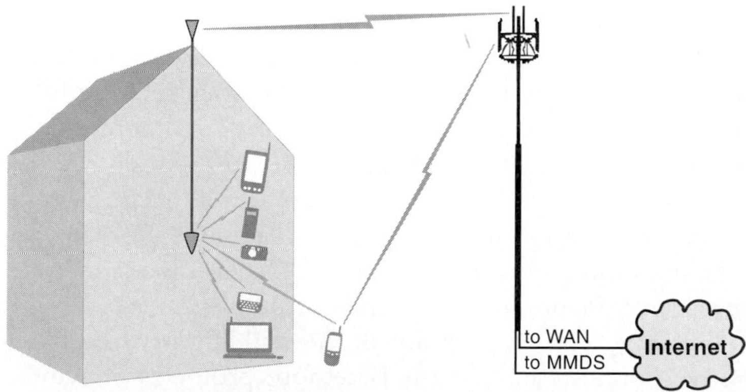

Figure 95 Fixed wireless basestation and access point

Deploying LAN and PAN Towers

You might want to put up your own LAN or PAN access points in order to provide access to local wireless devices. The access point can be connected to a rooftop FWA basestation, cabled directly to the Internet, or connected with a fixed wireless access point that reaches the Internet from inside the building. Companies such as SOMA Networks are beginning to offer low-cost and highly portable MMDS fixed wireless transceivers for small businesses that can provide between 5 Mbps and 12 Mbps connections for local devices.

Trying to locate basestations, one soon learns a healthy respect for physics and the law. Maybe law should come first. Telcos pay a license to let you use spectrum without interference. The cost of a nationally auctioned license is often far beyond the physical costs of a network. To put up a WAN from the start in the United States costs up to $14 billion in physical plant equipment. An upgrade to the network is about $600 million. The FCC assures there will be no interference. The carrier only has to handle congestion. On the other hand, when you use your own LAN and PAN access points, which operate without a spectrum license, any maker of access points and wireless devices can use and perhaps interfere with others in that spectrum.

Other legal aspects of locating a basestation include determining right of way and abiding by local ordinances. Historically, railroads and large utilities were given rights of way of physical property to run their services. Companies today purchase rights of way to run wires, cables, and erect towers. In addition to the land required, putting up dishes and towers often requires licenses to use building tops. Most businesses can usually do what they want with gear, but in the possibly interfering worlds to come, businesses must make sure you have permission to use a location and check ordinances for telecommunications transmitters.

Physics is easier than politics. Many of the WAN tower lessons apply to placing your own LAN basestations. Always take the high ground. Altitude is critical for tower transmission. You have to plan lines of sight and consider physical sources of interference. Outdoors, signals find that trees turn into walls when they are full of wet leaves. Street lamps radiate all kinds of nasty electromagnetic interference. Indoors, depending on your spectrum and modulation technology, walls can be a problem. For example, in deploying 802.11b, UWB works easily through walls, but conventional 2.4 GHz transmission technology has limitations. Typically, you space office LAN basestations from the corners of rooms and at 100-meter intervals.

Wireless LAN access points (Figure 96) and even Bluetooth PAN access points are easily deployed in buildings. The access point in the building is wired to the Internet. The roaming Web phone can transmit Bluetooth protocols or wireless Ethernet (data or VoIP) to the building's basestation. Outside it can transmit over a conventional WAN air interface to a cellular tower.

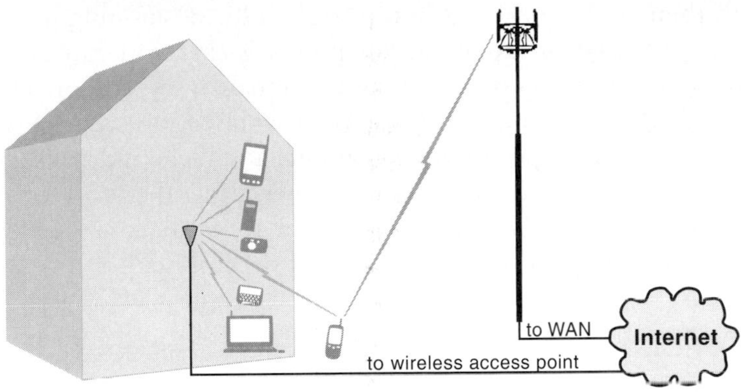

Figure 96 Wireless LAN access point

Cisco Systems began providing mobile VoIP phones in 2001 to go with its IP phone network. These mobile phones can transmit voice and data. Cisco's IP phones use WML display technology. The Cisco routers are designed to hand off the call within the network. Depending on the handset, it can use outside WAN cellular towers, although continuing the call requires transient service agreements with the carriers. AT&T and WorldCom also provide mobile IP phones.

The topology for access points must include the sources for power. If outdoors, power can be solar assisted. Although these access points provide wireless access for nearby devices, the access point must reach the Internet. Some are wired to the Internet with an ordinary RJ-45 Ethernet wire sometimes through DSL or a cable TV modem. Other access points have a separate antenna to reach nearby microwave towers, which can use microwave relays that beam from pole to pole until they reach a switching center that connects to the Internet. Yet another solution is to have the access point connect directly to a satellite with a dish.

We do not always need towers, basestations, access points, or relays for wireless solutions. Small mobile networks, such as PAN and personal radio, operate device to device. For some architectural plans, it is feasible to have a device "shuttle" periodically in and out of range of a wireless Internet basestation to synchronize data on demand.

Moveable Access Points

Fixed basestations can be moved manually or put inside vehicles. These access points can be moved and reattached to the Internet in new temporary locations or simply connected to a server that acts as a content hub to coordinate all wireless devices. The server is later connected to the Internet. Wireless mobile teams communicate with these access points. As they move from site to site, people carry their access points with them and connect to laptops or handhelds running interactive applications. The advantage of mobile access points is that you can place them in buildings where reception to outside wireless signals is very poor. The other advantage secure is high-speed connections without connection costs.

Truck-mounted access points are also used by mobile installers and package delivery people. These access points can run wireless Ethernet to the workforce. The truck often uses a secondary high-power transmitter to connect as needed with the central office via a data network such as Motient or Mobitex.

Understanding Cellular Networks

Cellular wireless air interfaces (Table 34) have evolved over three generations since 1979. First-generation analog voice is the most used interface for voice calls. Worldwide, European GSM is the leading second-generation network standard. 3G air interfaces are undergoing trials.

Reaching Subscribers

Ideally, wireless application can be received by a subscriber in a city, in the countryside, out at sea, in the air, and across continents. Some automobiles now have wireless connections. Your wireless Internet applications need to play to all manner of roaming customers. Your content can give roamers access to competing or foreign cellular public WAN towers as well as to private LAN and PAN systems. As a mobile subscriber moves from a WAN to a LAN, transparent roaming networks can use multimode modems. However, to use transparent roaming points, the architect might have to build in special-session transitions. Also, you may need to arrange billing agreements with WAN telcos.

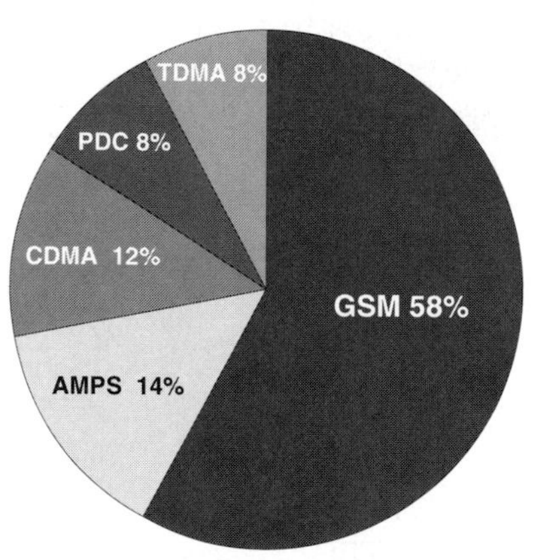

Figure 97 Worldwide mobile cellular subscribers (*Source:* Based on data in the EMC World Cellular Database, <http://www.e-searchwireless.com/>.)

According to statistics gathered by ITU in 2000, GSM is the majority air interface among worldwide mobile cellular subscribers (Figure 97). Although telcos are generally not forthcoming with such information, information is more freely available because companies are now being run as Internet companies; for example, DoCoMo posts its weekly subscriber count.

In the United States, the FCC provides detailed annual reports of the telco industry. One of the most useful for wireless planners is the report that studies commercial mobile radio services. In July 2001, the FCC issued the *Sixth Report*, which explains wireless technology and standards and gives maps and statistics

Table 34 Cellular wireless air interfaces

Generation	Interface	Name	Frequency	Region
1G Analog Cellular 1979	**AMPS**	Advanced Mobile Phone Service	824 MHz–894 MHz	**US*** **EU*** **JP***
	Analog cellular voice service using Frequency Division Multiple Access (FDMA) was introduced in the first national network in Japan in 1979. These phones in Europe, Asia, and the United States were all incompatible, voice-only, national networks. Today Digital AMPS (D-AMPS) is the upgrade for this voice-only network.			
2G Digital Circuit-Switched Cellular 1990	**TDMA**	Time Division Multiple Access IS-54/IS-136	824 MHz–894 MHz 1850 MHz–1990 MHz (PCS)	**US**
	Introduced in 1984, TDMA shares callers in one channel with a division of time slots. TDMA networks can support circuit-switched data at 9.6 kbps, although most carriers have opted for CDPD, a separate data overlay.			
	GSM	Global System for Mobile Communications	880 MHz–960 MHz 1710 MHz–1880 MHz (DCS)	**EU** **US**
	The European Union agreed on GSM in 1990. Based on TDMA technology, GSM supports circuit-switched data services from 9.6 kbps to 14.4 kbps and Short Message Service (SMS), a bidirectional service for short text messages. An extension to GSM is DCS1800, Digital Communication System. A data upgrade for GSM is General Packet Radio Service (GPRS), which allows 20 kbps to 100 kbps. U.S. offers PCS GSM1900.			
	CDMA	Code Division Multiple Access IS-95, IS-136	824 MHz–894 MHz 1850 MHz–1990 MHz (PCS)	**US**
	In 1993 QUALCOMM introduced spread-spectrum, lower-power cell technology, first in Korea and then in the United States. CDMAOne offers circuit-switched data at 14.4 kbps with an upgrade of faster packet-data rates of 104 kbps, using IS-95B. Even faster IS-95C reaches 307 kbps.			
	PDC	Personal Digital Cellular	810 MHz–956 MHz 1429 MHz–1501 MHz	**JP**
	Japan-only TDMA technology. Personal HandyPhone Service (PHS) for data.			
3G Digital Packet-Switched Cellular 2001	**CDMA-MC**	Multi-Carrier (formerly cdma2000)	Reuse of PCS	**US**
	With early deployment in 2002, this network combines superior voice, location-based, always-on, broadband service with enhanced roaming. The 2.4 Mbps data rate is implemented in 1xEV (IS-856).			
	WCDMA	Wideband Code Division Multiple Access	1885 MHz–2200 MHz	**JP** **EU**
	UWC-136, CDMA TDD, TDMA FDD are other 3G standards. With early deployment in 2003, the 384 kbps data network component intends to step up to an always-on, superior voice, 2 Mbps, always-on, enhanced roaming system.			

* **US** = United States; **EU** = European Union; **JP** = Japan.

Table 34 Estimated U.S. digital mobile telephone subscribers

Technology	1997 Subs*	1998 Subs	97/98 Percent Change	1999 Subs	97/98 Percent Change	Pecent of Total Digital Subs
GSM	1,200,000	2,700,000	125%	5,400,000	100%	12%
TDMA	3,800,000	8,700,000	129%	18,300,000	110%	41%
CDMA	1,400,000	6,400,000	357%	15,800,000	147%	36%
iDEN	1,300,000	2,900,000	123%	4,800,000	65%	11%
Total Digital	7,700,000	20,700,000	169%	44,300,000	114%	
Percent of Total	14%	30%	115%	52%	73%	
Analog Cellular	47,600,000	48,500,000	2%	41,700,000	–14%	
Percent of Total	86%	70%	–19%	48%	–31%	
Total Mobile Phone Subscribers	55,300,000	69,200,000	25%	86,000,000	24%	

Source: FCC, *Sixth Report* 2001.
* Subs = subscribers.

of coverage and subscriber growth. The FCC has been counting U.S. digital mobile telephone subscribers since 1997 (Table 35). The FCC noted that iDEN, formerly a dispatch network, is now a large-growth public WAN. The report shows for the first time that CDMA is dominant and is the fastest growing subscriber base. Sprint and Verizon are the primary CDMA carriers in the United States.[1]

Mobile Virtual Network Operator

Another emerging carrier concept and business model is the Mobile Virtual Network Operator (MVNO), which provides integrated value-added services and resells carrier access to a select audience, not the general public. The MVNO can brand its own handsets and operate over multiple networks. An MVNO might contract for billions of minutes of spectrum for many years from a regular WAN operator. MVNOs actually want to sublicense their own spectrum, although this is prohibited by the FCC and most international agencies. The MVNO can offer its own network interface and APIs to developers for the special wireless services it offers to its devices. This lets people access their network (not just the carrier) over which they deliver unique services. For example, Orange in the United Kingdom is providing experimental MVNO services to fully integrated home appliances and information systems. Virgin, also in the United Kingdom, is branding teen phone and prepaid billing plans as MVNOs and is planning on service with Sprint in 2002. Since the Internet is global, an MVNO can include foreign networks and expand member coverage beyond the territorial and regulatory limits of carriers. While the regular WAN operator has to offer general public service, the MVNO can deliver personalized and exclusive services to a unique population.

Telco Wireless Internet Subscribers

In the U.S. market, at the beginning of 2001 there were about 3 million wireless Internet subscribers, excluding the data-only carriers like Motient and Mobitex. Sprint PCS had already accumulated 1,000,000 wireless Internet WAN subscribers by the end of 2000.

Coverage Maps

The wireless Internet is limited by its availability. Telco coverage maps are like highway roadmaps of the wireless Internet. They show the extent of wireless network coverage not only by city, but also within a city. These maps are so hard to come by that some companies hire special agencies to measure coverage within a city. Most carriers conceal the details of their national coverage, which they view as "strategic information." This approach may be useful in blinding the competition, but it is a problem for subscribers. When they sell a plan, telcos try to assure subscribers of coverage by zip code. Later when subscribers travel they are often uncertain of coverage. Determining coverage by zip code is often not detailed enough. On the other hand, some carriers are more forthcoming about details of their deployment. The CDPD organization readily provides national service maps based on the locations of participating first-generation AMPS towers. Since these 1G networks are phasing out, planners should not expect much growth in CDPD coverage. The Motient network shows current detailed coverage maps at <http://www.motient.com/find/>. Then there is the FCC, who shares all it knows.

CDMA, TDMA, GSM, and iDEN in the United States

The maps of U.S. WAN coverage (Figure 98) show each network's national distribution of subscribers. National maps for WAN interfaces show the extent of county coverage, which gives some sense of carrier presence in states and cities. As you can see on the maps of CDMA, TDMA, iDEN, and GSM, there is quite a lot of white space in the United States. Detailed coverage patterns within cities generally require independent reporting because telcos protect this information.

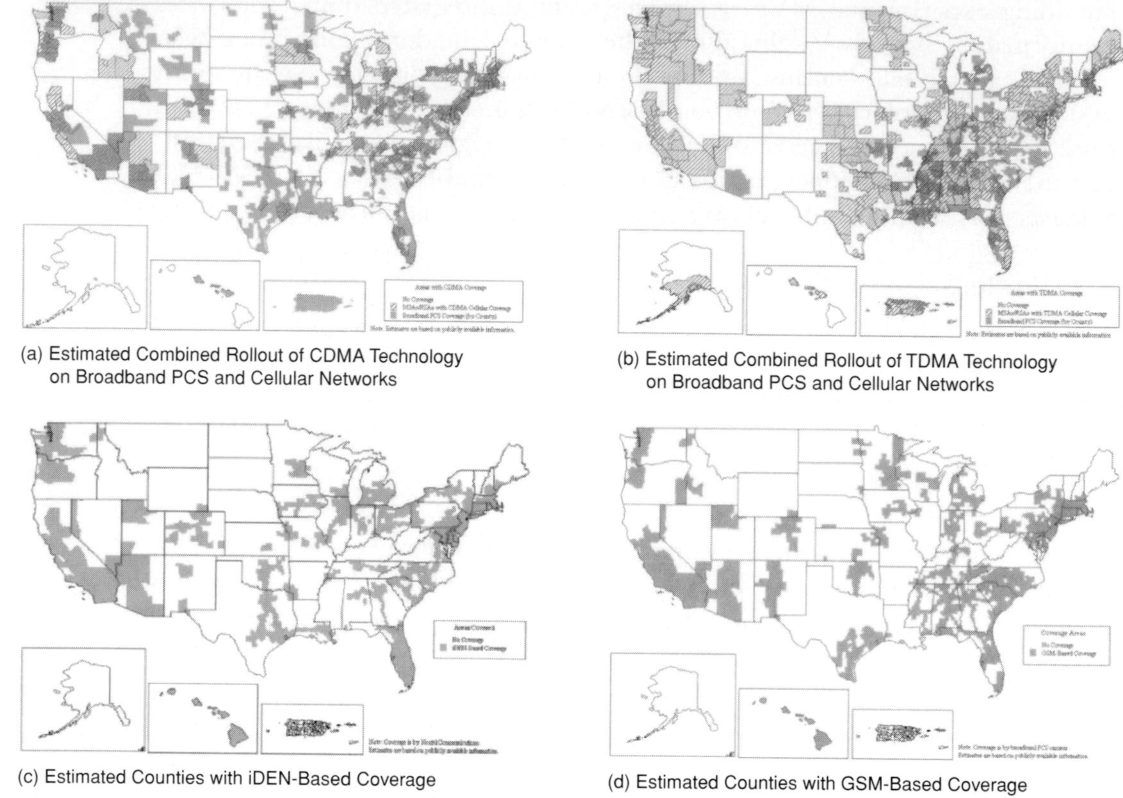

Figure 98 WAN coverage in the United States (*Source:* FCC, *Sixth Report,* 2001.)

Planning Data Network Architecture

Architects planning for the wireless Internet need to know coverage and network data rates. Although many programmers work independently of the underlying network, knowledge of data capacities may be required to know the kinds of application content that can be delivered. Older networks generally have more coverage but lower data rates. If you are building your own towers or a very large system, you sometimes plan wired connections and use trunk hierarchy tables in the section "Evaluating Wired Bandwidth" later in this chapter. To plan the capacity for the network, you fit trunk rates with network router and switch data rates, which is useful when you are building towers.

Worldwide Wireless Data Migration

The Japanese 2G networks use Personal Digital Cellular (PDC) and Personal HandyPhone Service (PHS). They went live with 3G W-CDMA tests in May

2001. The initial data rate for trial testing is expected to run at 64 kbps uplink and a maximum of 384 kbps downlink.

The Europeans have announced many 2.5G wireless data network upgrades in the GSM network. It is unclear which network will prevail, although GPRS is favored for 2002. It is important to realize that there are many competing standards and it takes two to three years before networks, line cards, and towers can be upgraded. The full range of current standards and future upgrades for emerging wireless data protocols is shown in Table 36, along with a best-guess time frame for general public availability. Keep in mind that early pilots stage the technology one to three years ahead of general deployment. In Europe, WAP may be able to use HSCSD, GPRS, EDGE, and eventually 3G UMTS, but the choice of protocol is up to the carrier. Data use competes with voice; for most operators, voice gets the priority. Because voice transmission cannot have latency, data calls are shuffled around on networks. Data latency often builds in congested areas. The United States continues to use a multitude of competing wireless data protocols.

Table 36 Wireless data protocols

Service	Date	Data Rate	Notes
Circuit-switched	Today	9.6 kbps data and fax	Data overlay service available from most GSM operators today.
Circuit-switched Compressed	Today	14.4 kbps circuit-switched data and fax	Works identically to 9.6 kbps service, but at higher speed; V.42 BIS compression can double throughput.
IP Access	Today	19.2 kbps circuit or packet-switched connecting directly to Internet	Reduces call set-up time and provides a stepping-stone to packet data; can also work with high-speed circuit-switched data services.
HSCSD High-Speed Circuit-Switched Data	2001	56 kbps circuit data	A software-only upgrade for carriers; operators need to decide whether to offer this service or GPRS or both.
GPRS General Packet Radio Service	2001	100 kbps packet data; average 20 kbps to 40 kbps	High-speed packet data; solid yet flexible mobile communications; requires new chipset.
1xEV (HDR) High Data Rate	2001	2 Mbps high-speed packet data; average 660 kbps	Integrated with CDMA carriers or as separate data channel; in U.S. and Asian markets; it should appear 1 year later in European markets.

continued

Table 36 Wireless data protocols *(continued)*

Service	Date	Data Rate	Notes
i-BURST	2002	40 Mbps high-speed packet data; average 1 Mbps	3G TDD airlink; Spatial Division Multiple Access (SDMA) is an optional upgrade for GSM and CDMA; available in Europe and Japan in 2003.
IPMA	2002	IP packed data; 1 Mbps to 20 Mbps	Experimental network enhancement; IPMA has a 100 mph handoff speed.
802.11a HiperLAN2	2002	6 Mbps to 100 Mbps	Experimental network enhancement; approved by FCC to operate at 5 GHz; uses OFDM.
UWB	2003	10 Mbps to 1 Gbps	Experimental network enhancement; approved by FCC for device testing; 802.11b versions exist today.
EDGE Enhanced Data for GSM Enhancement	2003	384 kbps high-speed packet data; average 120 kbps	Final high-speed data technology for existing GSM networks and traditional IS-136 TDMA networks.
3G W-CDMA Third-generation cellular (UMTS)	2004	2 Mbps high-speed packet data; average 100 kbps to 1 Mbps	Completely new airlink; multiple standards; theoretically the 5 GHz band can reach 5 Mbps.

North American 2G Data Networks: CDPD, Mobitex, and Motient

The three major North American data networks – CDPD, Mobitex, and Motient – are used by data-dedicated devices. Each wireless data network is overseen and directed by industry operator associations.

Cellular Digital Packet Data (CDPD) is an IP packet protocol that has been designed as a packet data overlay system that operates on the aging, analog, cellular voice system 800 MHz AMPS. Its bandwidth is advertised at 19.2 kbps, but you may get only 12 k user bits. More than 10 cellular carriers in North America offer CDPD network services. OmniSky service on the PalmV and PalmIII handhelds is a CDPD service that is received by the Novatel Minstrel CDPD modem. Another popular CDPD carrier is AT&T Digital PocketNet. Motorola is a supplier of CDPD 1.1 network equipment.

Mobitex was developed by Ericsson originally for the Swedish phone company Telia. It is operated in the United States by Cingular Interactive (formerly Bell South Wireless Division). In the United Kingdom, it is operated by Transcom (formerly RAM Mobile Data). Mobitex offers packet data communication rates of 8 kbps. Mobitex does indeed push packets to client devices that are "on," that is, registered as active with the network. This makes paging applications possible.

Mobitex packet data network services are offered in 28 networks operating in 22 countries. The popular RIM BlackBerry™ 950 and 957 two-way pagers in the United States use Mobitex. There are three families of frequencies: 80 MHz, 400 MHz, and 900 MHz. Generally speaking, the European, Australian, and Asian networks operate at 400 MHz and the American networks at 900 MHz. Ericsson licenses and supplies all network infrastructure. The PalmVII Palm.Net uses the Mobitex network. Broadbeam and RIM are among the members of the Mobitex Operators Association, whose Web site is <http://www.mobitex.org>.

Motient actually uses the Motorola DataTAC network. The popular business RF network service, begun in 1990 and originally called Ardis, was the joint effort of IBM and Motorola to serve mobile business needs. In 1998 Ardis was sold to American Mobile Satellite, who rebranded the service as Motient. Motient towers typically have a 10-mile radius. The network services are based on the Motorola Radio Data Link Access Protocol (RD-LAP), an open protocol specification used by wireless data network operators around the world. The DataTAC network supports over-the-air data communication rates ranging from 4.8 kbps to 19.2 kbps, depending on the region. The bandwidth advertised at 19.2 kbps serves about half as many user bits. Each data network carrier advertises raw air interface rates. But when you include error correction, billing, and other network overhead, the actual *user bits* are significantly lower, often half as much as advertised. Motorola provides wireless data subscriber hardware for DataTAC network operators.

Which data standard is best? CDPD is IP based and the easiest to program. But the CDPD IP network has a lot of overhead, which means that the amount of actual user bits delivered is low. CDPD shares AMPS voice channels, and its service latency is the highest of all. CDPD does not have paging or signaling protocols, so it is used largely as a data channel. Mobitex and Motient can push packets to you over their paging/data channels at a generally constant rate. One-way pagers use paging protocols over networks like ReFLEX.

The Motient DataTAC network offers the most efficient use of the data bandwidth. There is significant programming overhead in Mobitex and Motient, which makes record handling with error recovery an extra chore. Many developers use toolkits from Broadbeam or RIM for these networks. Prices for the service differ depending on the carrier and promotional bundling.

Many North American Web phones get data service as an overlay. American carriers such as Sprint and Verizon have adopted CDMA to provide data overlay services for their Web phones. AT&T uses the TDMA air interface. Because TDMA does not support data transmission, AT&T uses the CDPD overlay format to provide Internet access through its cell phone network. VoiceStream Wireless and Pacific Bell, a unit of SBC Communications, use the European-style GSM air interface. GSM networks are expected to have European-style 2.5G data air interfaces such as GPRS.

Examining Qualities of Cellular Networks

When cellular WANs are upgraded, they increase the number of subscribers and improve service. The best services hand off a signal cleanly and are efficient in reuse of frequency. A good service should not drop calls, but this sometimes depends on how fast you are traveling. Metricom (128 kbps service) advertised 70-mph handoffs, and SWIFTcomm IPMA operates 100-mph handoffs. The older Japanese PDC Personal HandyPhone can hand off a signal at the speed of a pedestrian bicycle. In addition to good coverage, you want predictable connections with no dead spaces. The ability to handle available bandwidth dynamically is necessary for circuits that allow voice and data. Providing location to the calling device is an important feature of the wireless Internet. Interference is not an issue on regulated WANs, but it can be an issue on the unregulated ISM bands.

Rate plans can vary widely. In 2001, U.S. subscription plans typically charge $50 per month for 500 minutes, with possible extra charges for roaming or long distance. You can generally get low-cost service for calling during off-peak hours. Some networks allow free calling to anyone within the same network; however, sometimes it is free for only the first minute. CallerID, the PCS feature that shows the calling phone number as the phone rings, is often an extra charge. Wireless Internet access is often an extra charge, which can limit the wider use of wireless applications.

To eliminate per-minute charges of a WAN, some applications use 802.11b wireless Ethernet LAN. For a business, 802.11b can be the last-mile wireless Internet solution. These private networks work quite well to form a useful enclave. An *enclave* is a provincial network that provides harmonized devices and network features. Enclaves are important because they often provide maximum exploitation of new services overlooked by the general market. iDEN uses free, always-connected, push-to-talk calling to members of its network. SMS in Europe lets everyone exchange messages affordably. Cybiko Web phones for kids talk freely to other Cybiko phones. Nokia mail is free for any other Nokia subscriber. The Japanese government has taken advantage of an enclave of cultural insularity – i-mode blankets a complete geographical area, roughly the size of California. From a subscriber's point of view, the benefit is hardware perfectly matched with software and content. Enclaves unify standards and devices for one audience.

Network Storage for the Wireless Internet

Another dimension to wireless technology is the use of more powerful storage technology. Sometimes architects have to plan for the volume of data, its security, and redundancy. As disk capacity increases, and fiber network architecture spreads the distance between the bus and the server, new storage architectures must be planned. Fiber data rates measured in megabits per second meet the storage capacity measured in gigabytes of memory and terabytes of disk. Storage companies now offer storage on demand.

Network Attached Storage (NAS) is a feature of most major disk-storage companies. The drives are measured in terabytes. NAS operates as a high-speed fileserver responsible only for sending and receiving data via IP protocols. Another more affordable option to consider is a storage area network.

A storage area network (SAN) is a specialized configuration of drives connected over optical fiber to form high-speed backbone transmission at the lowest cost. It can be complicated to configure and administer; it is worthwhile to consult hosting companies such as Exodus and new wireless companies like M7 to get the maximum utility and security.

Evaluating Wired Bandwidth

The wireless Internet eventually leads back to wiring systems. By most estimates, 80 percent of the large businesses in the United States are connected to the Internet with nothing more than a T1 (1.5 Mbps wire). Wired trunk hierarchies (Table 37) are standard data rates used in planning and diagramming large networks. The United States uses the T (trunk) designation and sometimes the DS (Digital Service) designation that is used in Japan. Europeans use the E series designation for their lines.

Table 37 Wired trunk hierarchies

Digital Service (DS) Hierarchy		U.S. Trunks (T) Hierarchy		European Trunks (E) Hierarchy		Optical Carrier (OC) Hierarchy		Ethernet Hierarchy	
Service	Rate	Service	Rate	Service	Rate	Service	Rate	Service	Rate
DS0	64 kbps	T1	1.54 Mbps	E1	2 Mbps	OC1	51.8 Mbps	10BASE-T	10 Mbps
DS1	1.54 Mbps	T3	45 Mbps	E2	8.4 Mbps	OC3	155.5 Mbps	100BASE-T	100 Mbps
DS2	6.3 Mbps	T4	274 Mbps	E3	34 Mbps	OC12	622 Mbps	1000BASE-T	1 Gbps
DS3	45 Mbps			E4	140 Mbps	OC48	2.5 Gbps	10 Gigabit Ethernet	10 Gbps
DS4	274 Mbps					OC192	9.95 Gbps		
						OC256	13.3 Gbps		
						OC768	40 Gbps		

Finally, we should note that Ethernet has its own set of data rates. It comes in 10BASE-T, 10 Mbps, 100BASE-T, 100 Mbps, and 1000BASE-T, 1 Gbps also called Gigabit Ethernet, IEEE 802.3z. In mid-2002, 10 Gigabit Ethernet, known as 10 Gbps IEEE 802.3ae, should be adopted. The Web site is <http://www.10gea.org>.

Using Satellites

It is helpful to know about satellites, although their connection rates, high costs, and special deployment equipment puts them beyond the scope of most wireless applications in this book. Satellites are useful wherever air interfaces and wires do not reach. Service is available worldwide and does not depend on national telco policies of limited regional range. Satellite spectrum is enormous for broadcast, but the narrowband uplink is a weak signal from portable wireless devices. End user satellite transmitters are most often found fixed to a dish or in vehicle-mounted systems. Another limitation is that satellite reception is almost nonexistent inside buildings. Voice has latency problems, and the delay takes some getting used to. Satellite connections are useful for data, for email, and certainly for outdoor GPS applications. They have proved ideal for international paging.

In 2000 there were no more than 450,000 Internet satellite subscribers, who used them for both data and voice. Satellite wireless applications can provide access to far-ranging travelers and businesses. The Globalstar phone service is used for voice calls anywhere on the planet. Internet radio broadcast also comes from satellites. In 2001, XM Internet radio and Sirius Satellite radio became available in North America. These radio nets feature about 100 channels, require a special receiver, and are directed to car owners at a cost of about $10 a month. The great advantage of satellites is that you can connect to them from anywhere, and as long as you are outdoors and away from buildings, you can get a clean signal.

The big investment picture is that the overall national cost for a terrestrial cellular system is about $14 billion. The FCC estimates the cumulative wireless terrestrial cellular for all generations of technology to be $70 billion. A $1 billion satellite network is a comparative bargain, especially considering it can reach the maximum number of possible subscribers.[2]

Satellites are graded by their altitude of orbit from sea level – GEO, MEO, and LEO. As any rocket scientist knows, spacecrafts must avoid the orbits from 1,000 km to 5000 km and from 15,000 km to 20,000 km where the deadly Van Allen radiation belts occur. The radiation is so strong that it can annihilate a satellite. The Van Allen belts form the major divisions for the satellites, which all fly over the lowly space shuttle's 400 km orbit. Sometimes satellites are built to transmit to one another. Many are designed with a simple transponder that is said to offer a "bent pipe" to relay data from one point on Earth to another.

GEO (35,785 km)

The Geosynchronous Earth Orbiting (GEO) satellite has an orbital speed that matches the earth's rotation. This forms a geosynchronous parking orbit at 22,282 miles from Earth, also called Clarke's orbit.[3] A GEO is expensive to launch and position, but it takes only three GEOs to cover the globe. They have been in use since the 1960s to transmit data, video, voice, and fax. The average GEO satellite lasts 12 years and travels 6875 miles per hour to keep a perfect orbit. Today about 75,000 subscribers use two-way wireless data access to high-orbit GEO satellites. They typically get between 300 kbps and 900 kbps downlink and 50 kbps to 150 kbps uplink data rates.

One of the most successful GEO operators is QUALCOMM, which offers the OmniTRACS Fleet management service. This application provides automatic vehicle location, two-way voice and data, and vehicle telemetry – a full range of tracking, dispatch, and messaging services. To give you an idea of the service, for about $50 per month a subscriber gets a vehicle location report every hour and 180 messages. The trucking company that owns or operates a fleet must also purchase a satellite transceiver at $3000 to $4500 per truck. It has coverage in the United States, Europe, and East Asia. Motient, formerly American Mobile Satellite, has been operating since 1992 and offers a GEO data service at 4800 bps. The GEO is not ideal for voice because of a physical delay. To traverse at the speed of light – 186,282 miles per second – it takes half a second to complete a geosynchronous call. Voice conversations are very choppy with half-second delays. This is one reason to use a lower orbit and cheaper satellite.

MEO (10,000 km)

The Medium Earth Orbiting (MEO) satellite is not as popular as GEO and LEO, but offer some compromise benefits. A MEO operates in the range from 5,000 km to 15,000 km, between the Van Allen belts. It takes 10 MEO satellites to cover the planet, but the lower altitude LEO takes 48. The circuit delay is 0.1 second; a LEO's delay is 0.05 second.

LEO (1,000 km)

Low Earth Orbiting (LEOs) satellites have the advantage of minimal latency because they operate between 400 miles and 1,000 miles above the earth. A LEO is not as expensive as a GEO to launch, because it is smaller, easier to launch, and does not have to be built to endure. A LEO stays up for about 7 years. Globalstar has a system of 48 LEOs. ORBCOMM operates 35 satellites that function as "orbiting packet routers," sending traffic from earth station to earth station. Loral/QUALCOMM, VITASAT, and FAISAT also operate LEO systems. Typical LEO service is $30 per month for the transmission of 3500 characters. The equipment costs less than $1000 per terminal. LEO data rates are typically 4800 bps. The Motorola Iridium LEO sends 2400 bps TDMA data traffic. LEO satellites experience atmospheric drag and need onboard rockets to maintain altitude. They quickly fall to Earth when their fuel tanks are emptied.

By 2005, every cellular phone will probably use a satellite, but none of the satellites mentioned so far. Phones will be listening to the GPS Navstar constellation, and it will change the wireless Internet forever.

Anticipating Location-Based Network Features

The FCC requires that by 2006 every handset made and every operating network provide precise caller location information for emergency use as part of the FCC E911 mandate. The Navstar satellite (Figure 99) is part of the U.S. Global Positioning System (GPS) satellite constellation, which provides high-precision location signals first tested in 1973. Although it is not a requirement to use GPS satellites to deliver location-based services, the market will likely favor them for their precision. GPS processors are being built into common handsets to process the signal. And the signal is freely available.

Figure 99 Navstar GPS satellite (*Source:* <http://www.fas.org/spp/military/program/nav/gps.htm>)

By 2005, a developer's servers will need location-based components, and telecommunication and software engineers with geocoding skills will be very busy. It will not be long before there is a rush to provide the precision location technology that differentiates your services. There is nothing lousier than being directed to somewhere and getting lost. Some background on the E911 mandate, the network servers, and location providers is in order.

The E911 Mandate

Although the market is likely to accelerate the value for the precision of location, the stimulus for location is not being driven by location-based fantasies. It is being driven by fear – the necessity for life-saving and emergency capability. The FCC E911, or Emergency 911, mandate exists to save lives. It has been implemented in two phases. Phase 1 is fully implemented and lets any cell phone have immediate access to a Public Safety Answering Point (PSAP) for emergency calls.

In 1996 the FCC defined the Phase 2 caller location requirement. It requires "the location of all 911 calls by longitude and latitude," or as developers say, a geocode, that is to be transmitted to a PSAP. Either the cellular network operator or the handset manufacturer must provide Automatic Location Identification (ALI). When a 911 call is placed using a wireless handset, the dispatcher at the 911 PSAP gets location information. The PSAP transmits the call and location to emergency response teams. The E911 mandate specifies that caller location be disclosed so that emergency police, fire, and medical teams can assist a person in distress.

A series of E911 Reconsideration Orders now replace the original 1996 FCC E911 Phase 2 caller location requirement. Originally, the location of a caller was to be determined within a radius of 125 meters in 67 percent of cases. The FCC E911 Phase 2 calling precision schedule (Table 38) shows networks and handset targets for caller location beginning October 1, 2001. At that point, the industry was to begin selling and activating ALI-capable handsets and network operators and activate some degree of caller location service. The schedule of requirements is likely to be refined as government and industry determine the optimal course of implementation. For more on the changing status of E911 requirements, check <http://www.fcc.gov/e911>.

Some companies may stall implementation while privacy issues are settled. However, smart companies will find a way to provide this life-saving and valuable location-based technology. Developers should expect networks and handsets to provide your wireless application with geocodes. Whether you use a high-end geospatial system or roll your own location technology, it is useful to know a few things about GPS technology.

Table 38 FCC E911 Phase 2 calling precision schedule

Date	Action	Precision
October 1, 2001	Network activation	67% of callers within 100 meters 95% of callers within 300 meters
	Handset activation	67% of callers within 50 meters 95% of callers within 150 meters
	Begin selling and activating ALI-capable handsets.	
December 31, 2001	25% of new handsets activated are to be ALI-capable.	
June 30, 2002	50% of new handsets activated are to be ALI-capable.	
December 31, 2002	100% of new digital handsets are to be ALI-capable.	
October 1, 2006	95% of handsets must be ALI compliant.	100% of callers within 40 feet for longitude and latitude; vertical location to be 90% accurate.

Source: FCC, <http://www.fcc.gov/e911/>. Accessed November 2000.

GPS Satellites

A GPS provides precise location information. From a constellation of 24 satellites, mobile devices worldwide can receive latitude, longitude, altitude, and the atomic time for their current location. Because they are sampling the signal, mobile devices can calculate exactly the speed you are traveling.

On May 1, 2000, the U.S. government ordered the military to turn off SA (Selective Availability) dithering to produce the finest-precision signal to arrive at any commercial-grade GPS receiver. SA was used to scramble the signal for security purposes and the military retains the authority to restore SA to any part of the globe. (Users might get lost when times are bad.) ALI-capable handsets with GPS chips and U.S. automobile in-vehicle navigation systems with GPS antennas can deliver high-precision location to the mobile user. They can identify a location within 10 meters to 20 meters, as opposed to 100 meters when SA was turned on. When the towers and basestations are fixed and receiving differential GPS information, the location within 1 meter can be calculated.

Although the number of satellites in range of a person varies, the orbital design ensures that three satellites are always visible. The combined impetus of E911 and GPS gives wireless developers in the United States an enormous opportunity to exploit new location-based services (LBS). GPS technology depends on network operators' Mobile Positioning Systems (MPS), also called Position Determination Equipment (PDE), or a GPS receiver to pick up and decode the locations of wireless devices. New cellular phones are being made with the GPS receiver built into the standard communication chip.

GPS satellites transmit on two L band frequencies, L1 (1575.42 MHz) and L2 (1227.6 MHz). L1 carries a coarse acquisition code along with a precise (P) code. L2 carries only a P code. An ephemeris almanac is downloaded from the satellites with location information. When three sets of L1 and L2 signals are combined and time differential calculations are made, then a precision location can be determined. Once all the satellite signals are acquired, new telemetry is received and the handset owner's location and velocity can be determined quite accurately.

Geocodes

A geocode is a pair of geographic coordinates, latitude first and longitude second (latlon), that fix exact locations on the surface of Earth. Databases store decimal geocodes as latitude followed by longitude given in fractional degrees (for example, `36.973200–122.02458` marks a building in Santa Cruz, California). Geocoded data uses latitude and longitude for points in a database, rather than a street address or phone number. You can purchase geocoded data, have your data geocoded by a service, or buy a geocoder for ongoing conversions. Geocoders convert street addresses and sometimes phone numbers to latlon points. (For a full primer on geocodes, GIS, and location-based applications read the section "All about Geocodes" in chapter 7.)

On the back end, a Geographic Information System (GIS) can quickly process complex, multilayered location-based content. The GIS can retrieve, convert, and overlay many geographic data sets. Geospatial information based on data sets is often presented as thematic layers such as street geometries and icons for buildings or people. (GIS and location-aware applications are covered in more detail "GIS and Location Servers" in chapter 8.)

GPS, LBS, and MPS, ANI Technology

Location-based services (LBS) depend on a number of technologies. GPS satellites deliver raw location telemetry to the traveler and the network. The network operators use MPS to also locate the source of the signal. Later calls are combined with Automatic Number and Identification (ANI) servers that bill users based on their location. The actual caller location is determined by two general technologies. Some handsets are equipped with GPS antennas and signal processors and can transmit the satellite telemetry. Handsets that do not have GPS technology can have the network towers triangulate location through a number of techniques.

- *Cell of origin (COO), or CellID.* A cellular phone network already knows which tower a subscriber handset is near. This is required to get billing information, as well as to route the call correctly. COO can get as close as 200 meters. Although easy to implement, the precision is the lowest.
- *Time of arrival (TOA).* Related to time difference of arrival (TDOA). The network measures the time of receipt of a transmission from the mobile device. This time is measured at three or more basestations. The network can convert these times into distances and triangulate the caller's location. This method works with existing GSM mobiles since the network can force the necessary transmission from the mobile by "faking" a hand-over between basestations. TOA works only when a call is active.
- *Angle of arrival (AOA).* The angle of arrival is computed by two towers that use trigonometry to calculate distance based on the exact angle at which the signal arrives. AOA is ideal in rural areas where there are fewer towers with more distance between them than in urban areas. It usually requires extra antennas and processing time, which makes it a more costly process.
- *Enhanced observed time (EOT).* The cellular device measures signal strength from three basestations. The mobile device reports observed time differences from the network location of the MPS calculated by the network center's computer. The mobile device looks at the clock time as transmitted by three or more basestations. The difference between clock times gives the difference in distance from the basestations. A slight refinement is the enhanced

observed time difference (EOTD). Both techniques look at TDMA and the time advance within the signal. Typically, the advance is 550 meters, but time advance resolutions with EOTD can be 16 times higher. This method requires changes to both network infrastructure and mobile devices.

- *Assisted GPS (AGPS).* AGPS uses a handset and towers to calculate position. The MPS stores known orbits of the satellites and accurate clocks, as mentioned earlier. Assisted GPS enhances the accuracy of the mobile device's GPS computation by transmitting satellite ephemera and differential telemetry from the MPS.

Automatic location identification technologies (Table 39) offer cost-effective solutions for networks to offer LBS, but more precise location is made available through handset makers.

The 3G handsets now include GPS processors. Recent QUALCOMM CDMA chipsets now include its gpsOne processor. A handset with this chip can speed GPS location by using an AGPS method, by which the assisting network operator transmits telemetry that can eliminate satellite acquisition times, speeding GPS response times.

Despite the enormous potential for location services, some wireless network operators have not determined where to start because there are so many variables. There is some question as to which technology should be deployed first. The precision of location is certainly important, but it requires that Internet information be geocoded at the right level of detail. The Location Interoperability Forum defines categories of service for increasing accuracy:

- Category 1 supports a legacy handset and uses COO.
- Category 2, enhanced, is for new handsets and uses EOTD and TOA.
- Category 3, extended, offers the best precision with AGPS.[4]

Table 39 Automatic location identification technologies

Network Accuracy	Technique	Cost
200 m – 2500 m	COO	Lowest
30 m – 550 m	TOA	Very low
50 m – 125 m	AOA	High
Handset Accuracy		
50 m	EOT	Low
5 m – 20 m	AGPS	Medium

Location Service Providers

Location service providers (Table 40) employ location technology to give a caller's location to a network. There are many location server platforms and techniques, most of which are connected to mobile positioning equipment supplied to a WAN carrier. Location service providers generally supply an XML interface to access information from their spatial servers. Engineers can customize their content servers to deliver location-relevant information with geocodes that will operate with the location service provider's XML schema and remote-invocation APIs.

Fortunately, the architecture being adopted today by many network operators and used by many infrastructure vendors can adapt to varying grades of location precision. A component called the Mobile Location Center (MLC) separates the location technology from the application. Since many applications can function quite well with cellular sector granularity, network operators can deploy variable location technology gradually, rather than wait for 100 percent coverage to offer new services.

In addition to the government mandate, and media examples of how lives are saved, five elements will fuel the evolution of location services: location accuracy, wireless device integration, intelligent network development, geocoded content, and standards. With incremental improvements in the supporting technology, location services will continue to proliferate. The services offered by wireless network operators begin with safety, billing, and information services. But the market will grow with tracking, navigation, and integrated data products. If the FCC schedule holds up, then by 2006 location will be a standard element of the wireless Internet.

Table 40 Location service providers

- SignalSoft
- Cell-Loc
- XYPoint
- SnapTrack
- Vicinity
- Airflash
- OmniPoint
- Cambridge Positioning Systems
- Grayson Wireless
- SigmaOne
- Televigation
- True Position
- U.S. Wireless
- Integrated Data Communications
- KSI
- Aerial Communications
- FocuSystems

Europeans are developing location technology as well. In October 1998, Nokia made a $3 million strategic investment in SiRF (*Si* refers to silicon and *RF* refers to radio frequency.) Ericsson licensed the SiRF GPS technology for a wide range of wireless handheld devices. Meanwhile, the prices of GPS handset chips of one of SiRF's competitors, Snaptrack, have fallen to as low as $5 for large-volume orders.

Geographic and Location Standards

To alleviate the proprietary nature of competing location-based systems, Motorola, Nokia, and Ericsson founded the Location Interoperability Forum (LIF) in

2000. There are many open and commercial geographic and location-based standards in use.

- *Spatial Location Protocol (SLoP)* is a strong standard that specifies two-way authentication between client and server. It is specified at <http://www.ietf.org/ietf/1id-abstracts.txt>.
- *Open GIS Consortium (OGC)* of Wayland, Massachusetts, provides an abstract model and useful documents, which can be read at <http://www.opengis.org>.
- *Location Interoperability Forum (LIF)* is a forum for handset makers. Its standards are published at <http://www.locationforum.org/>.
- *Geography Markup Language (GML)* uses WGS-84 geodetic datum as a reference system for latlon.
- *LandXML,* an XML schema for exchange of geographic information is specified at <http://www.landxml.org/>.
- *arcXML* is a markup language from ESRI to exchange mapping and geographic data.
- *Point of Interest Exchange (POIX)* is a descriptive language for locations; it was specified June 1999 by the W3C.
- *Mobile Positioning Protocol (MPP)* is an Ericsson HTTP protocol for Java servlets. The MPP format of positioning response includes latlon and a sector arc for inner radius, outer radius, start, and stop angle.

Finally, privacy is an issue because the network always has your location. The principle for using location information should be simple. Callers control the visibility of their location. This is how callerID is managed. When handset users run LBS, they are warned that their location will be given to a vendor. After the warning, the user has the option to cancel the service.

Location with LAN and PAN

WAN GPS systems can provide wide area coverage, but it is possible to get useful location information from well-placed LAN or even Bluetooth PAN basestations. Consider a traveling woman lost in an airport, on a large corporate campus, or in a convention center. Chances are she cannot get a decent WAN GPS location signal. Since Bluetooth and wireless Ethernet networks are short range, then the network basestation is a marker for the caller's location. Using the right software, your application can help the traveler by showing nearby services. The application can use landmarks to guide her to the destination.

Messaging Networks and Protocols

There have been paging protocols to transmit text since the 1980s. ReFLEX is the most common paging standard today. Data networks such as Motient, Mobitex, and CDPD are being pushed into paging service. Sprint QNC (Quick Net Connect) provides two-way messaging via its CDMA phones. QNC provides rapid packet-like connections and runs at 14.4 kbps. It can send variable-length messaging that uses IP addresses.

Sending text on Web phones began in the late 1990s with short messages with SMS, the messaging part of the GSM cellular network. All GSM handsets can receive SMS and many can send them. Although SMS was specified in the PCS service in the United States, no carriers implemented it initially. SMS networks have different limits on message size:

- GSM – 160 characters
- CDMA – 256 characters
- iDEN– 140 characters
- TETRA – 260 characters
- PDC – 160 characters

European SMS sends characters at 300 bps using an 8-bit GSM header and footer frame within the control channel. When a phone is in low-power mode, it has to listen for the time sync so that when a caller decides to make a call it is ready in an instant. The phone is also listening to the GSM (TDMA) signal and waiting for its phone number to be called. When it is signaled, it usually rings, but for SMS the processor looks for SMS text frames and will store them when they come in. At 8 bits per frame, messages accumulate until it gets a final checksum and beeps you for a complete message.

Push server architecture is in its infancy. Push servers send sophisticated messages through circuit-switched systems. Push can be networked with mailbox or SMS exchanges. Push servers can also be added to text decision information systems. In response option or decision support systems, text can be sent along with the appropriate checkoffs for the "next people in the loop" who depend on the decision the person makes about a message.

The Future of SMS

Oddly enough, the ever-popular SMS was omitted from the European ITU 3G specifications. However, there is a new bearer, Unstructured Supplementary Services Data (USSD), and new services EMS and MMS.

A standard defined by 3GPP, USSD and the services that run on it are expected to replace SMS as the new messaging bearer. USSD is very similar to SMS, but it has new connection protocols to expedite transmission of the data on the control channel. USSD is a bearer that allows very short messages to be sent over the signaling channel. If you enter *#100#<send> into your handset on an Ericsson network, it will return your own number.

Enhanced Messaging Service (EMS) is a set of services that can run on top of USSD. EMS has a rich set of combined text, imagery, and sound achieved by bundling SMS packets on current networks. Multimedia Messaging Service (MMS) can also use USSD. MMS sends animated images, pictures, audio, and text and potentially streaming media. Nokia is developing MMS platforms. A key MMS site is <http://www.mobileussd.com/>.

Europeans are the masters of wireless messaging, judging by the enormous traffic. Person-to-person messaging will continue as an important part of 3G. The new messaging services are expected to build on the successes, which include a billing model, low prices, free messages for the receiver, operator roaming agreements, ease of use with no action required by the receiver, and standard inclusion in all makes of handset. The new models will guarantee that messages are received with a delivery report message. Consumers who use telephone, email, fax, and messaging services can benefit from integrated services, which is the objective of unified messaging (see chapter 22).

18 Chapter

Building Servers and Matching Client Applications: Every 5 Years

In wireless systems, the most critical piece of technology for architects is the server. It spans both network and application architecture. The server and client device must agree on session management, Internet protocols, proper security handshaking, the exchange of XML content, and formatting. Implementing servers and gateways requires programmers and database engineers to have a common knowledge of networks, hardware, software, and content. Computer languages, operating systems, communication, and database technology are brought together at the server to deliver wireless content.

In planning the construction of a building, after the architect determines its structure, the services within are specified. Services are the working guts of a building. They involve wiring, plumbing, air conditioning, heating, and mechanical equipment. The service elements need maintenance until the point at which they are beyond repair or become obsolete.

Servers also age. As new wireless devices come along with new capabilities, services are put in jeopardy. This is largely what is happening to the older, established application server architectures such as ATG or BEA. Although fine for large-scale eCommerce servers, many established server assumptions are facing the challenges of the volume of new devices, the underlying protocols for wireless messaging, shared XML content, the distributed operation of field-generated content, multipass SQL queries, how granular personalization works over myriad devices, and how intermittent wireless connections and caching work. The remaining sections essentially explain how a developer can answer the server's changing purpose created by the wireless Internet:

- Rebuild sites and servers.
- Specify server and gateway architecture.
- Serve multiple devices.
- Implement application servers
- Use XML content.
- Decide on interactive models.

Servers are a family and include Web servers, gateways, application servers, content servers (databases), proxy servers, and dedicated servers (i.e., dedicated to commerce, personalization, ad management, and other special functions). Application servers are probably the most important to understand. They are often set up as content generators, and function as distributed "switches," which are able to connect to banks of servers in a scalable architecture to manage presentation, business logic, and databases. They must be set up to handle wireless session management, to add and drop new breeds of devices with widely varying capabilities, and to get out of the way when low-level voice and streaming media are exchanged.

Server hardware and operating system software generally last for 5 to 7 years. More exactly, the rate of change in hardware server design is significant enough within 5 years that replacing them provides significant advantages. If the hardware changed any faster, information technology departments could not keep up with the system support required.

We have moved from mainframe architecture of the 1960s, to client/server of the 1990s, into the emerging wireless distributed and peer-to-peer computing architectures of today. Engineers coordinate client and server by managing the connection, session, and application interfaces through the well-conceived Microsoft ISAPI or the Java NAPI software libraries. Sometimes wireless software must be built that directly accesses an OSI protocol.

Connection and session management for mobile users are unique because the connection to the server may come and go. Whereas a PC server will keep alive a connection and sufficient local resources to manage a servlet long enough for a standard application to complete, it has to be prepared to put aside everything as devices intermittently come and go. The special intermittent dance of client and server challenges cache optimization.

Sites are made of servers, and although any software-built Web site is easily modifiable, you should aim to construct a stable navigation interface supported by key services. Like a building, stable, well-known passageways between areas of the structure are necessary for the crowd to repeatedly use the facility. Like Yahoo's directory hierarchy or Amazon's service categories, once decided, these services should remain for at least 5 years of business. Changes on the server for wireless navigation can be extremely disorienting. As visitors become familiar with the layout, they are able to travel about more quickly. Early mobile users are very good at remembering key sequences.

The wireless Internet, with ever more powerful hardware, changing content, and variable user requirements, puts great stress on conventional server architecture. The adds and drops of system elements can be dramatic enough to break up a system that does not have a solid structure capable of operational changes and staging versions of the system. A well-planned system like the one at CNet is designed for new advertising campaigns or editorial sections to be introduced to their Internet servers. Each service manages personalization and content databases differently. The overall editorial and content changes are introduced on a staging server where they are tested and authorized. Once running, the new additions are made to the public operational server.

Rebuilding Your Web Site

As you begin to add wireless services to your Web site, it may be easier to get started with simple changes such as reworking images, simplifying pages, and offering text. But a long-term change that reconstructs your server architecture may take you further. Even before wireless times, some Web server architects offered their sites with text-only views as well as the rich HTML views. What appears as providing either basic information or beautiful content for the mobile traveler amounts to fast or slow service. You are now delivering streamlined content to small screens to people who no longer have plenty of time to study a PC screen. This kind of thinking is the basic idea of offering a wireless channel. Whether you go short- or long-term, here are some changes to consider when rebuilding a Web site for wireless access.

Rework images. If you plan to reuse images, think through their purpose and attraction for the mobile audience. On a small device, images are no longer ornamental; they usually take over the entire screen. Because the screens are small, often black and white, or gray scale, many applications use only text. Text is certainly kinder to transmit over the air to the paying receiver. The reality is that images are rarely as effective as text when users are on the go. If you do reuse images, you will need to resize them and reduce their color maps.

They should be converted to four-level gray-scale or black-and-white images. A useful batch-editing tool for processing images is Debabelizer from Equilibrium or even Adobe Photoshop. Consider the editorial step of choosing new images that are appropriate for the mobile audience.

Write a mobile use flowchart. Adding a mobile channel to a Web site will cause you at a minimum to think through the new steps mobile users will take and to imagine what screens will match their actions. The simplest thing to do is to diagram the processes with a flowchart. Put verbs to it. A WAP storyboard has standard navigation choices: Accept, Cancel, Select, Scroll, and Menu. The storyboard, derived from scenarios and persona, goes hand in hand with activity diagrams and useful notation.

Look again at text. Also new to most Web developers is the special consideration to be given to text. For users on the go, text is the essential means through which they get what they need. With text transmissions, essential and important information appears first. Details and narrative follow. Other techniques are covered in the section "Text: The Medium of Wireless" in chapter 7.

Simplify pages and remove fancy elements. Web sites often compete by showing the newest most elaborate features of HTML. These elements add overhead for mobile Web content and spell disaster. What may be a sizzling PC attractor simply takes too long to download and may not even be interpreted on a mobile device. You need to eliminate tables, frames, cascading style sheets, and other dynamic elements. Simplifying page composition is essential. Professional Web phone sites remove comments, HTML META tags, and DTDs. Nested tables are eliminated and often are reduced to lists or are converted to pure text with spaces.

Uplevel your HTML to XHTML. As you rework HTML pages, go ahead and convert HTML to be XHTML compliant. Every tag must be terminated and some elements are deprecated. For example, Java code, once tagged as Applet must now be called Object. The transformed pages should appear the same as the original pages and will be valid for new XML-based browsers. The important point about valid XML-formed pages is that they can transmit optimal amounts of XML data. Run it through an XHTML verifier to be sure. Some browsers throw away invalid pages.

Other reconstruction tasks common to converting an existing site include checking and fixing broken hyperlinks. If a database is to be converted, care has to be taken not only with the database, but also with the way it is called and mixed within Web pages. The subject is detailed further in the section "Converting Databases" in chapter 20.

Architectural Reconstruction

Studying the cost of retrofitting buildings can teach a good lesson to Web architects. In almost every case, the original cost of a building (Figure 100) is less expensive than the combined cost of incremental changes to structure, services, room reorganization, and interior redesign over the life of the entire system. Overarching the traditional "capital costs" at the beginning of development are the actual cumulative costs incurred during the building's lifetime. Clearly, it is important to allow for changes in the service (server) and space plan (content) without too much pain. It is the mark of a great architect not to overengineer a structure, to avoid specifying too many subsystems, and to allow for its growth over time. If the service design of a building is embedded too deeply in the structure, it is more cost-efficient to demolish the building and start anew than to redesign.

Similarly in server architecture, if the protocols and designs are embedded too deeply, the hardware must be replaced. The design of the WAP gateway that transmits special binary encoding, maintains proprietary security mechanisms, and restricts session management requires of its owners a tough server upgrade, probably total replacement.

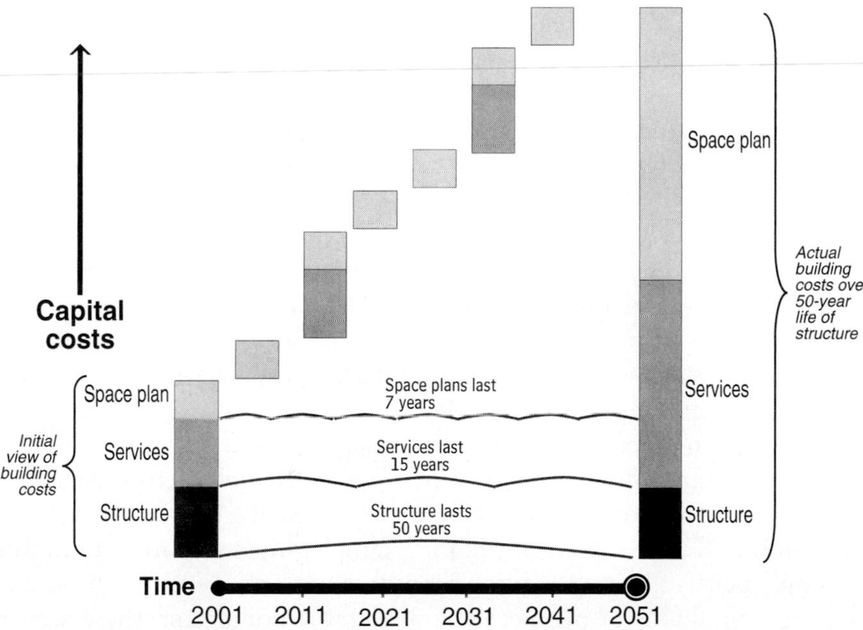

Figure 100 Total cost of a building (*Source:* Adapted from a drawing in *How Buildings Learn* by permission of Stuart Brand, which originally appeared in *The Changing City* by Frank Duffy.)

The utility of legacy systems and knowledge of previous models for running wired networks keep us tending to old technology. Wireless networks intensify the stresses of older capacities and purposes; however, the inevitable breakdown of older systems can mean opportunities.

On the other hand, without enough integrity in the original architectural plan, too many necessary future modifications will be made, causing inevitable reconstruction to take place. As we saw in the drawing of architectural layering (in chapter 15, Figure 85), the changes to site, structure, skin, services, space plan, and stuff practically destroy a building whose elements are not planned to accommodate those changes.

Understanding Server Architecture

You can understand server systems by considering three levels of increasing complexity. The architectural approach and development tools required for each system are different. Designing higher-volume systems requires making tradeoff decisions for all components and tools.

In the beginning, you may design a simple wireless Web site. The early ones are little more than a system that fetches pages from a file system. The URL is a path to every page on the file system. This is a *one-tier system* built with a simple page editor to produce a set of pages for one kind of device.

Next, you might move to a Web server that makes use of a database-driven architecture where the content is generated on request. The pages are templates that are filled in with data as the request comes in. This is a *two-tier* system – one tier for presentation and one tier for data. You might design the site to reach a few wireless devices. The URL is a path, often with an appended query string to direct the special processing of a page on the file system.

Next, you may advance to an application server. These servers can reach many kinds of devices simultaneously and effectively. These *three-tier* systems have one tier for presentation, one tier for programming logic, and one tier for data. The URL no longer accesses a file system, but is an entry point to a program that generates pages. If you are successful, you arrive at a heavy-duty, data-flow transaction server that delivers to millions of users per day.

Heavy traffic is often a goal, but it must be anticipated. The number of people who visit a site determines the endpoint of many wireless architecture decisions. The solutions have degrees of assured reliability and security. Large-scale systems based on Inktomi or Kabira architectures, for example, must sustain a minimum of 250,000 people per day. Each person performs many transactions. Such systems are built to support millions of people. To ensure traffic conditions, these servers use software development tools covered in the section "Heavy-Duty Application Servers" later in this chapter.

Supporting Multiple Devices and Networks

Multiple wireless devices of differing quality will appear at the door of your Web server. And many new ones will be invented in the years to come. Part II explains how to program wireless applications for each of kind of device and network. Now you need to be able support multiple devices, old and new, from one server.

Whether creating or rebuilding a Web site, think long-term and keep in mind the total cost of building the system and how it will be operated as devices are added. Keeping that in mind, an architect can choose from a number of approaches to get a server to handle wireless devices.

- *Select one wireless server.* An approach for beginners is to pick one wireless device and support it side by side with a running wired Web site. Amazon chose this approach and has supported only HDML Web phones for many years. It is a good way to begin if you have to understand important distinctions about wireless service relative to your Web server. Although you limit your potential audience of wireless clients, this approach is the least expensive to implement.
- *Build multiple wireless servers.* Another method is to develop and support as many servers as you have devices by a modular server approach. It does not mean you have to buy a server box for each device; your Web server can run multiple processes. The difficulty with this approach is that multiple servers are hard to maintain. An application change needs to be replicated and in many cases translated across the server for each device. As your wireless service moves forward, changes have to be made to each server module. Pioneers such as Yahoo have encountered this problem.
- *Put a translator on the server.* Yet another way to support multiple devices is to use a translator to convert content from the normal PC Web server to work as a mobile Web server. Most developers report that this is a stopgap measure, not a substitute for mobile design. Using the server translation method, which some companies refer to as transcoding, you can run into a number of problems. The "one-solution-fits-all-devices" approach means that you try to use on the mobile version of sites many of the styles, layouts, and content sizes conceived for the PC Web. However, mobile use is fundamentally different from Web browsing. You have to partition data differently on mobile devices and on wired networks. Another serious issue is copyright problems. You cannot automatically translate copyrighted source streams. The reduction of material often violates the terms of copyright assertion. An exception is with graphics that can legally be resampled without violating the original value of the mark. If you use iAS Wireless Edition XML Oracle 9, the server

will translate your content into every device format that hits it. OracleMobile uses this engine coupled with its universal XML stream for all wireless devices. It is a great idea. The results, however, are not always predictable. OracleMobile suggests that if mobile customers write in the Oracle dialect of XML, they can embed branching and presentation as needed.

- *Use an application server.* This approach provides a complete three-tier application server to handle all your wireless devices at once. By *three-tier,* we mean having separate modules in the application server for handling presentation, logic, and data. The advantage of using an application server is that it is the most efficient way to handle wired and the entire milieu of wireless device and network traffic. Not all application servers permit wireless tiers to operate efficiently. It takes more engineering to implement. We will look at how application servers process wireless traffic in the next few pages.

Each of the four server strategy approaches requires an escalating commitment in engineering skill. But only the application server provides a truly scalable wireless publishing model that can accommodate new devices readily while providing the best mobile experience. Regardless of the approach you take, your Web server plan should generate both wired Web pages and wireless pages, even though the wireless mobile branch will need to be designed to handle unique needs. To make sure that the content going to either branch will be appropriate, you must make a number of changes to the way the content is generated.

Separate Content and Style

Once you have made the essential server strategy decision, then it is time to look at how the content is generated. If you look carefully at a typical Web page, the HTML style tags and the literal content appear together. They must be broken apart to reach different devices. Theoretically, you could use of one wireless server and one PC Web server. However, if you do not make the separation of content and style, any significant changes in your application flow will have to be faithfully implemented in parallel. You want your total site to deliver the same basic content to all devices. You can make the server software format the style for each device. This can be accomplished initially by having production tools generate different styles of Web pages, by having server-side includes for content, or more commonly by having a database-driven approach. With this two-tier model, content comes from databases and the server uses it with presentation templates to generate Web pages.

Always keep in mind that the needs of mobile and PC Web users are different. It may be simpler to have two completely different server designs initially. Once you engineer the method for separating style and content, you can effectively provide a wired channel and a wireless channel. With some thoughtful engineering, you can add other wireless channels for new devices by simply adding a presentation layer to the server. We will look into effective engineering server techniques to add multiple wireless devices shortly.

Here is an example of separating style and content. You might serve HTML pages from your server by having Active Server Pages (or Perl or JavaServer Pages) merge the appropriate HTML style tags with your content. You can serve wireless Internet WML presentation for a Nokia device using the same server-side architecture that merges the WML style tags with the same content calls to the same database. You could extend this for an HDML presentation for a Motorola device, and an XML DTD presentation for a Java phone. Whether you use an XML data architecture or not, you will still be doing the primary job of separating style and content. We will look at an especially efficient technique for separating style and content called XMLC in the upcoming section "Application Server Manipulation of a Wireless DOM."

Specifying Server and Gateway Architecture

There are many possible wireless architectures including servers, gateways, and their connections to clients. A *gateway* connects two networks. A WAP gateway translates requests and responses between the wired Internet and the wireless protocols of WAP phones. Unlike traditional gateways, a WAP gateway also maintains WSP session states and is truly a *proxy server* that performs services between the client and server. A proxy server typically caches and filters content. It also helps optimize server connections. An *origin server,* also called a content server, is a full Web server and generates content on demand, often formatting presentation based on the profile of the requester. In the *peer-to-peer* model, wireless devices can exchange voice or data directly, skipping any gateway or server with perhaps the aid of a relay. This is in contrast to a client/server model exemplified by the Web server that holds all data for devices to access.

Application servers are designed to deliver optimal Web traffic response. For heavier traffic, the application server can *scale* the solution by adding server boxes as needed with little change to the software. When multiple boxes are connected, if one dies, then fail-over logic will route the connection to the other application servers. Advanced server architectures require scaling of a solution to allow adding multiple servers or clustering secondary servers. Installations can also add on special servers to take care of personalization, content management, geographic information, and ad management. Servers can connect with WAP and voice gateways to obtain support for their branches of wireless device service. With varying levels of support for the wireless Internet device families, some popular servers are IBM Websphere, BEA Weblogic/Clicklock, ATG, HP Bluestone, Lutris Enhydra, Microsoft Mobile Internet Server, and Nokia Activ server.

You may need to consider building your own tools that will administer and perform record synchronization. Over many wireless networks, you can rely on HTTP as the standard low-level API for record exchange. However, low-level tools for record handling and synchronization need to be built or bought from middleware companies. Back-end administration tools are commonly required to administer the front-end wireless client. Sometimes you can set up PC Web pages for the end user to administer or graze information for later mobile use.

Supporting multiple wireless devices and networks can be a challenge. Web servers send files to one specific device. Database-driven sites pass data directly from the database, usually with SQL expressions. Supporting one wireless device from a server is a beginning. To support many devices simultaneously, many developers start with crafty gateway server programming and eventually progress to a somewhat more complex, but ultimately more maintainable, approach. You can program an application server to manage variable device presentations, which can be scaled to serve thousands of visitors simultaneously.

Wireless Publishing Framework

To reach many kinds of wireless devices from your server, you must be able to handle each device efficiently as a presentation device. There are a few useful approaches, such as using a server for each device, a page translator, or an XML application server. An XML application server publishing framework (Figure 101) provides the maximum coverage and is the easiest setup to maintain in the long

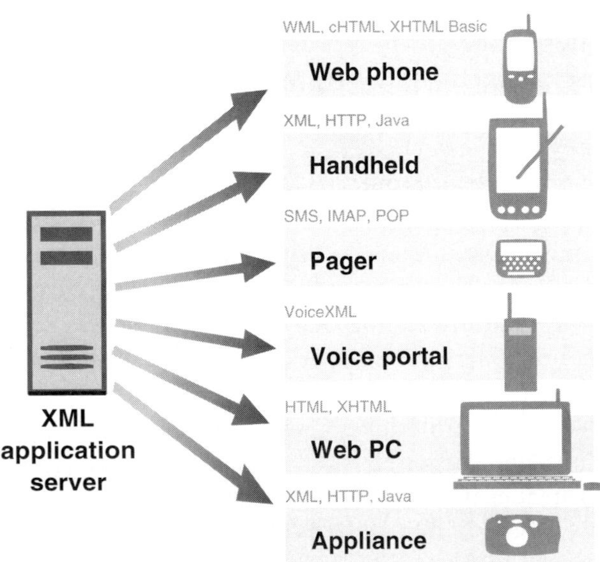

Figure 101 XML application server publishing framework

run. Some companies use a page translator. It is simple to do, but the end product has not been received well by mobile users. People need an application built for them with content edited to suit their mobile devices.

We use XML because it has great flexibility and can deliver portable content from application servers. Server programming gives the most control. Servers will take care of all the device detection and make XML requests of your content server. The database sends up XML content that the presentation tier can reformat for each device. This XML stream is generally useful and requires special development at the presentation tier so that the display and input to the mobile traveler will be optimal. Content must be measured out optimally for each form factor.

All Web servers have a programmable gateway. Programmers have many choices – CGI, Perl, ASP, JSP, and even Java. When the site is hit by a large variety of wireless devices, then programming is essential. Each request must be treated as a special case depending on the type of device.

The key to many of these advanced systems is session management. Within the server, the user session is monitored and contexts are set as the user navigates to various parts of the site and requests different services.

Device Detection and Content Service

Solaris, NT, or Linux Web servers can detect the device browser. From this they generate dynamic responses. Detection and response is handled in code through a few popular techniques, such as a Perl script running on a CGI gateway, an ASP or JSP server-side page processor, and directly with Java code in an application server.

It is important to know how your Web server senses the device before you return Web pages. Of course, there can be impersonators or multimode devices where users demand a preferred device mode. When any browser or device makes a connection to a server, before the application is started, the browser starts a low-level HTTP protocol where the device registers itself as a USER_AGENT with the server. Examining the details of this protocol is the most common way to determine the device. As devices evolve, so do the HTTP protocols.

How does the server find out about the capabilities of the wireless device that is making requests on it? From the device's view, how can it inform the server of its capabilities? The server must know about the capabilities of individual devices to serve them best. For example, the server must know that a mobile phone with a very small display, rather than a large-screen laptop computer, is requesting a Web page. If your server can transmit a complex page as pictures, sound, or text, then you need to figure out when to transmit which media to the right devices. Server software detects devices as part of information embedded in the HTTP header; having done so, the server can be programmed to route service to respond exactly to the incoming wireless device's signature.

There are a couple of techniques to match the client request and server content. You could give to mobile users a URL that delivers content specifically for their kind of device. This way the user is in control and can access the /wml part of your server to get WML content from your file system. Web sites were first built with this approach in mind. Another technique is to use server-side programming with a database-driven approach. This can be done by having the server construct and then send differently formatted device pages with data computed on the fly. This technique gives developers control over all requests through one piece of code.

Three standard Web protocols are designed for device detection. The protocol used by most Web servers reads the User Agent header. An emerging W3C standard called Composite Capabilities and Personality Profile (CC/PP) fully qualifies the mobile device, microbrowser, network, and user. A subset of this is User Agent Profiles (UAProf), which WAP Web phones implement. CC/PP appears to be the future. All three protocols use HTTP as the transport mechanism for Internet-related information with mechanisms for header management and session caching.

User Agent Detection

Devices can be identified as WAP capable or HTML capable without CC/PP. The most common way for a Web server to identify the inquiring browser and the protocols the viewer accepts is to read the User Agent and Accept headers. You make calls to the server to read the lower HTTP session block for details to help you determine what streams or browser pages to return. The example of reading a User Agent header (Example 29) shows how a Microsoft IIS server processes an ASP page. When the server comes to the Request.ServerVariables line, it requests the header variable HTTP_USER_AGENT, and a string is returned of the current values.

Example 29 Reading a User Agent header

```
<% ' Server side access of the browser
browsing = Request.ServerVariables("HTTP_USER_AGENT")
%>
This HTTP_USER_AGENT is:
<%= browsing %>
```

In the example, Microsoft Explorer version 5.0 is attempting to browse the server. IIS provides an HTTP_ACCEPT header call that can be used in the IIS server to determine what content streams the requester can receive, such as WML, HTML, and XML. A sample return is:

```
HTTP_ACCEPT =image/gif, image/x-xbitmap, image/jpeg,
application/pdf, application/x-comet, */*
```

Composite Capabilities and Personality Profile

Composite Capabilities and Personality Profile (CC/PP) is an emerging W3C standard that defines a framework for content negotiation involving a mobile client, a server, and a user. The goal of the CC/PP framework is to completely specify the capabilities and preferences of different client devices. The way CC/PP works (Figure 102) is that a device sends a user agent profile as a URI to a content server (the origin server). The content server decodes the user agent profile, perhaps having to fetch further information from the URI to understand how to produce content appropriate to the client device. Complete data about the profile of each device and the preferences of its user is stored in a relational database located on a Web server.

A closer look at how CC/PP works shows that a wireless device requests a document unique to its form factor.

1. A device makes a request for a Web page. It requests the Web URI page in the usual way, but also sends a second URI to indicate where its mobile device profile can be found. The URI location of the device profile is sent with a request for a Web page.

   If the server does not have the URI stored, it transmits the URI device profile, a CC/PP repository that returns the profile. The server stores the detailed list of fields about the device.

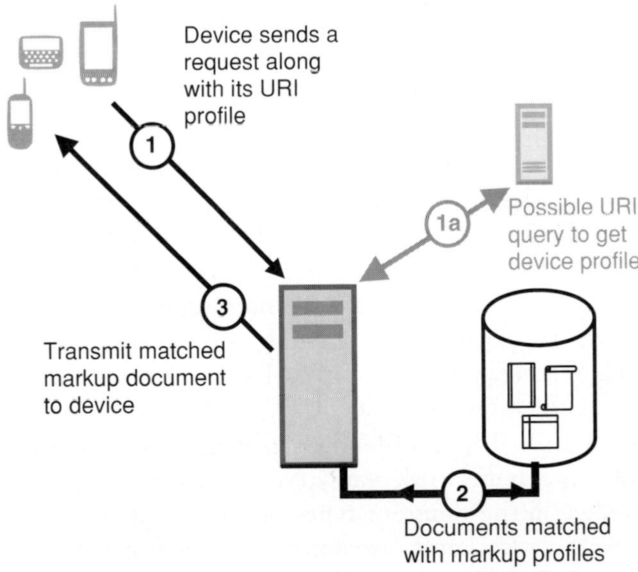

Figure 102 How CC/PP works

2. On the basis of the device profile, a Web server can choose the right content. Most wireless requests will be for an XHTML document. The server matches the right version of Web information in terms of assembling the right markup and style, and XML data. From a document point of view, CC/PP works by accessing modules within the XML language. XHTML is designed as a series of modules associated with different functionality: text, tables, forms, images, and so on. Cascading Style Sheets (CSS) and Synchronized Multimedia Integration Language (SMIL) specifications have similar modular constructions. If a content provider wants information to be available for different devices, then different versions of that content can be generated. For example, the modules for text only or the modules for full graphics with scripting might be chosen. In its document profile, the expected capabilities of the browser are specified in terms of XHTML modules, style sheet support, and so on. When the device profile is unknown, the server can reject service, send back a default page, or interpolate the characteristics of the device.

3. The document and device profiles are compared to determine the best fit between the two. The exact document or a variation of it would be generated. The server then transmits the proper style of document in response to the original device request.

Composite Capabilities and Personality Profile is written in the Resource Description Framework (RDF), W3C's XML application language for modeling metadata. RDF is a language that provides a standard way of using XML to represent metadata properties and relationships of items on the Web.

The W3C issued requirements for CC/PP in February 2000. The RDF framework describes a standardized set of CC/PP attributes that express a user agent profile in terms of device capabilities. It defines a generic user agent profile for each device. The client device may be a workstation, personal computer, mobile terminal, or set-top box. CC/PP can also describe the users' particular preferences. The CC/PP collection of device information describes capabilities, hardware, system software, and applications. It includes a preferred language, sound on/off, images on/off, class of device (e.g., phone, PC, printer, screen size, available bandwidth, version of HTML supported), and more. A good content server can send a high-density page that features a large, complex layout and graphics, as well as the low-resolution mode with simple text.

Composite Capabilities and Personality Profile does not limit the possible wireless functions of handhelds. The framework was designed to be extensible because it is not possible to predict all the different types of wireless devices that may come. New descriptions can be added and distributed. It does not rely on a central registry, which might make it inflexible. On the other hand, CC/PP appears to be somewhat overengineered, like many of the recent W3C mobile wireless technical specifications. Many of the distinctions may not be meaningful, and other critical mobile distinctions are not covered. The wireless traveler may want to determine the presentation, rather than leave it to the automated CC/PP system. Even with a fancy device, the mobile user might like to see the text-only, low-bandwidth version of a page. Often the Internet is clogged or the server is too busy and a person prefers a text-only page. A mobile traveler may choose voice rather than text on a multimode device. The current definitions of CC/PP are covered at <http://www.w3.org/Mobile/CCPP/>.

WAP UAProf

The Wireless Application Protocol implements a subset of CC/PP called UAProf. An early version of UAProf is sometimes referred to as Capability and Preference Information (CPI). UAProf is implemented as a lengthy extension of a classic HTTP User Agent. A WAP gateway can forward the HTTP request and generate the CC/PP HTTP Profile and Profile-Diff headers. The WAP Forum and the W3C are working jointly to write the database model and likely fields that CC/PP will contain. The plan for WAP UAProf consists of description blocks for the following key components:

- *HardwarePlatform.* A collection of properties that adequately describe the hardware characteristics of the terminal device. Descriptions include the type of device, ModelNumber, Vendor, ScreenSize, CPU, Keyboard, SoundOutputCapable, and other input and output methods.
- *SoftwarePlatform.* A collection of attributes that describe the operating environment of the device. Attributes provide information on the operating system's software, video and audio encoders supported by the device, and user's language preferences. Examples include JVMVersion, OSName, and OSVersion.
- *NetworkCharacteristics.* These characteristics include information about the network-related infrastructure and environment such as bearer. These attributes often influence the resulting content, as a result of the variation in the network's infrastructural qualities such as bandwidth and device accessibility. Examples are CurrentBearerService and SecuritySupport.
- *BrowserUA.* This block describes a set of browser application attributes such as BrowserName, BrowserVersion, TablesCapable, and XHTMLModules.
- *WAPCharacteristics.* This block is a set of attributes that describe WAP device capabilities, including qualities of the WML Browser, WAPVersion, WMLDeckSize, WMLVersion, WAPPushMsgPriority, and so forth.

The UAProf header signals to the client that the CPI is being cached by the WAP gateway and will be effective for the lifetime of the session. The client device may update the CPI at any time during the session. Details of WAP CC/PP appear at <http://www.w3.org/Mobile/posdep/ericsson-position-paper.htm>.

Stopping the WAP Cache

A common problem in WAP server development is stopping device caching. WAP phones are designed to keep data around to conserve trips over the air. It turns out that both the Web phone gateway and the phone do caching: They put WML content into the phone memory cache and use it again rather than call your server. If your site generates dynamic content, you may need to disable caching on the phone. To disable microbrowser document caching, send these HTTP headers:

```
Expires: Tue, 01 Jan 1980 1:00 GMT
Cache-Control: max-age=0
Cache-Control: must-revalidate
```

The WML cache cancellation code in Example 30 shows how to get a gateway to stop caching data.

Example 30 WML cache cancellation code

```
<head>
 <meta forua="true" http-equiv="Cache-Control" content="must-revalidate"/>
 <meta forua="true" http-equiv="Expires" content="Tue, 01 Jan 1980
          1:00:00 GMT"/>
 <meta forua="true" http-equiv="Cache-Control" content="max-age=0"/>
</head>
```

The meta tags specify three attributes:

- *forua,* "for user-agent," specifies that the content of the meta tag should be passed on to the microbrowser. If forua is true, the meta tag is passed on to the wireless device; otherwise, the WAP gateway is to follow any directives of the meta tag, and then remove it from the document.
- *http-equiv,* "http equivalent," specifies an HTTP header value. We set the value of the standard HTTP variable "Cache-Control" content to 0 seconds, so that any data in the cache will time out and expire. The microbrowser is supposed to request new versions of expired content. To make extra sure, we submit the "Expires" directive with a bogus early date.
- *content.* "max-age=0" for the http-equiv "Cache-Control" is one of the acceptable paired values that goes with the header response.

If you have entered these lines, the gateway should not process the headers. However, some combinations of gateway and device insist on caching pages in spite of your directives. The only way to flush a page cache is to append a bogus random string to every URL on your WML site. Usually a timer is random enough so that every requested page appears new. This is enough to force both the phone and WAP gateway to think they are getting a unique page every time. Sadly, this is the kind of black magic (I mean design feature) that is necessary to get your pages to work on the various makes of WAP gateways and WAP devices.

Implementing Wireless Application Servers

Most wireless portals let mobile users personalize the mobile experience from a PC. You set up start pages for them so they can set personal preferences. You can also let them mark up content and store their choices to make their future mobile visits easier. Europe has many dedicated wireless mobile portals. U.S. companies like OracleMobile, Yahoo, and Amazon are examples of Web sites that have a mobile portal page for the end user. Big-screen PC Web access is part of the application design. It gives mobile users a home port. The point of designing mobile settings and editable preferences is to minimize input and reduce complexity when the user is mobile. It is useful to have "common phrase list" files that can be exchanged to help users make rapid notation. For example, an inspector might have an "elevator defect list" or a diner might have a "superlative rating qualities list." Although a network of users can maintain and administer such lists centrally, it is also possible to distribute the information with an XML DTD to allow client-to-client synchronization and exchange of data.

Using XSL or DOM for Presentation

An application server is the workhorse of Internet servers. It uses many technologies to deliver content rapidly to a volume of requesting devices. When a traveler requests a mobile Web page, a URL is sent to a server. The application server, rather than go to a file system, computes an in-memory version of a page, which is delivered rapidly in response.

Application servers use two techniques to generate pages for the plethora of wireless devices. One technique is the use of XSL, a procedural language approach; the other is to use DOM, a programming approach. Both of these approaches transform XML content into pages that wireless and wired devices can read. If you use XML Style Language Translation (XSLT), an application server matches style codes with underlying XML content. There is one XSLT template for each device. The server uses a parser such as SAX to marry XML content and XSLT style.

The Document Object Model (DOM) uses a powerful abstraction model to reproduce a hierarchy of XML documents. A DOM represents any kind of Web page in memory. An application server takes the DOM, a coded representation of a page, and plugs in XML data on the fly. Application servers manipulate all types of wireless DOM, mixing the data with the presentation format requested, and can produce any marked-up page such as XHTML, cHTML, and WML.

Because XSLT is a little easier to show, we will look at an example of it. When XML content is generated, the data must be associated with a presentation to be viewed. A corresponding style sheet is one way to do this. Style sheets can be compiled into DOM systems, or they can exist as separate files. XSLT is a style sheet that can present XML to result in pages for HTML, WML, or cHTML. HTML programmers who are familiar with CSS to style Web pages understand this idea. The limitation of CSS is that it must match the order in which the XML appears on the page.

Let us look at an example of creating a WML page. The XSLT process uses a parser that takes the content of an XML Account Record (Example 31) and merges it with an XSLT style sheet for WML page generation (Example 32). The process is directed by the parser and uses XSLT styling codes to form a complete markup page. There can be multiple input and output documents. The resulting WML card and deck can display on a WAP phone. XSLT pages are designed for only one presentation device and are often called templates.

Example 31 XML account record

```
<?XML version="1.0" ?>
<accountrecord>
 <balancerecord>
 <owner>Dave Doer</owner>
 <acctnum>0000 to 1234</acctnum>
 <balance>100.20</balance>
 </balancerecord>
</accountrecord>
```

Example 32 XSLT style sheet for WML page generation

```
<xsl:stylesheet XMLns:xsl="http://www.w3.org/1999/XSL/Transform"
                          version="1.0">
 <xsl:output method="XML" omit-XML-declaration="no" />
 <xsl:output doctype-system="http://www.wapforum.org/DTD/wml_1.1.XML"
      doctype-public="-//WAPFORUM// DTD WML 1.1//EN" />
 <xsl:template match="/">
 <wml>
 <xsl:apply-templates />
 </wml>
 </xsl:template>
 <xsl:template match="accountrecord/balancerecord">
```

```
<card>
<p>
<xsl:apply-templates />
</p>
</card>
</xsl:template>
<xsl:template match="balancerecord/owner">
<em>
Name:
<xsl:value-of select="." />
</em>
<br />
</xsl:template>
<xsl:template match="balancerecord/acctnum">
<em>
Acct#
<xsl:value-of select="." />
</em>
<br />
</xsl:template>
<xsl:template match="balancerecord/balance">
<em>
Bal: $$
<xsl:value-of select="." />
</em>
<br />
</xsl:template>
</xsl:stylesheet>
```

To execute this example, your server does require an XSLT parser to be running. Popular XSLT parsers are Saxon, Xalan, and MSXML3 from Microsoft – all freely available at the following Web sites: <http://users.iclway.co.uk/mhkay/saxon/>, <http://xml.apache.org/xalan/overview.html>, and <http://msdn.microsoft.com/downloads/technology/xml/mxsml.asp>.

Application Server Manipulation of a Wireless DOM

Although XSLT is easy to read, it is not easy to write. It is very hard for interaction designers to lay out the navigation without the help of experienced XSLT programmers. An alternative to using XSLT is to use XMLC to create DOM classes.

A special Open Source tool from Enhydra.org called XMLC, or XML Compiler, can construct DOMs automatically from any Web page. For beginners, XMLC compiles any markup page language, such as HTML or WML, to generate Java class representations of the page. The server manipulates these classes as DOM representations of the document. If tags are embedded in the original page, the compiled DOM will create Java classes with getter and setter methods automatically named for the tagged elements.

When the markup page line with XMLC span tag (Example 33) is written, a name is chosen to represent the entire paragraph. It is delimited by a spanning ID meta tag. The name `ownerTitle` is the symbolic name where content will appear in the place of "Dave Doer is my name."

Example 33 Markup page line with XMLC span tag

```
<P ID="ownerTitle">Dave Doer is my name</P>
```

When the file of this markup page runs through XMLC, the compiler removes the actual text and automatically creates a setText and getText method for every tag. This tag generates a method, setTextOwnerTitle(), that you can use to set its value. This lets you program multitudes of different styled pages. Each page makes a call for content when the application server executes it. This is ideal in the middle tier where business logic or an Enterprise Java Bean (EJB) container exists. For more information about XMLC, which is in the Open Source public domain, visit the Enhydra site at <http://www.enhydra.org>.

The power of the DOM approach is it provides clean separation of layers (presentation layer, business layer, and the database layer) for the people responsible for contributing those elements. This is a goal of three-tier application server architecture. Programmers find that DOM models give them far more control than they have with a parser approach. It also lets designers use whatever tools they like. The downside of DOM manipulation is that it takes more memory, although this can be an advantage since the server can now return pages faster. On the other hand, because XSLT is declarative, programmers have to keep their code in the same order as the XML DTD, and that can create all kinds of problems when the publication changes. Another important advantage to DOM/XMLC is that the people who have to operate a Web site find it easier to revise and maintain than writing XSLT with a SAX parser would be.

In addition to XMLC, Lutris Technologies provides useful tools such as an application server debugger and administration console tools that let you debug request and responses in detail and check session and state of the server. Lutris has also integrated Borland JBuilder, a good Java IDE that permits debugging a live application server that is running servlets. You can drill down and step through source code while watching connection traces on the server debugger.

Wireless Server Configuration for MIME Types

To set up your Web server for wireless traffic, the MIME types being requested by the devices have to be registered on the server. This registration has to be done only once. Although we showed how to set up your WAP server for Apache and IIS (chapter 10), Table 41 shows a complete range of wireless server extensions, which are used with various wireless devices.

Table 40 Wireless server extensions

File Type	Extension	MIME Type
WML	`.wml`	`text/vnd.wap.wml`
Compiled WML	`.wmlc`	`application/vnd.wap.wmlc`
WMLScript	`.wmls`	`text/vnd.wap.wmlscript`
Compiled WMLScript	`.wmlsc`	`application/vnd.wap.wmlscriptc`
Wireless bitmap	`.wbmp`	`image/vnd.wap.wbmp`
Compact HTML	`.chtml,`	`text/chtml`
XHTML	`xhtml`	`text/xhtml`
XML	`.XML`	`text/XML`
MIDP application	`.jad`	`text/vnd.sun.j2me.app-descriptor`
DTD	`.dtd`	`text/plain`

Wireless Server Performance

When writing code and delivering content, keep in mind new wireless server characteristics. Unlike conventional Web servers, wireless Internet servers must use their application, session, and connection mechanisms differently to work well for mobile users. Here are some things to watch for in your wireless server that can be solved with low-level server engineering, database tuning, or eliminating caches and states that are managed on your server.

- Wireless traffic will request a large variation in potential result sets from your database. This invalidates the standard 90 to 10 caching architecture. There is a high probability of cache misses for wireless mobile content requests because queries are so fine-grained and "personal."
- In general, the cache control model should be customized and is application dependent.
- A clean separation between presentation and data is necessary to reduce cache sizes.
- There are more multipass queries when processing wireless content.
- Wireless interactive applications work best by transmitting multidimensional models that mix code and data. Users get the result set and play with the model. The server must deliver code and data sets.
- The design of a persistent session manager model is different for mobile wireless use. Over the wireless Internet, the server should allow long-term

sessions. It should be built to anticipate out-of-service periods. The connection can switch off at any time and resume hours later when the user expects a full context restored.

- Location-based content and user profiles are key indexes to data and often require special management.
- To serve large amounts of traffic, use memory rather than disk – especially for a cache-database design. Consider putting an object database in memory to manage the operation of the server.
- Separate objects that might cache time-based media such as voice or streaming SMIL components.

Wireless Middleware for Large Systems

Wireless middleware companies offer tools for synchronizing, provisioning, and handling data. They also provide complete software to design applications as well as to manage and track devices for large organizations. You may need this kind of "heavy lifting." It is good to become familiar with the companies and their products, because each company bundles exclusive and different technologies.

The leading wireless middleware company is Broadbeam, which was Nettech until June 2000. Broadbeam makes ExpressQ. Aether, the number two wireless middleware company, is known for expert provisioning gear. Other companies and their specialties are IBM Websphere, which uses the Secureway Wireless Gateway, formerly Artour, Tivoli, MQ Series, and an application server; AlterEgo hosts and replicates servers on NOCs; AvantGo has a wireless channel; and GoAmerica is known for a Web browser on the RIM Pager. These are just the highlights. Each system has many components.

Wireless Internet traffic is expensive and data usage is inefficient. Most wireless devices do not have powerful applications for messaging, browsing, and interaction. The wireless middleware companies provide comprehensive packages to connect wireless devices to servers over networks and complete missing pieces of a wireless solution. They operate in many different ways and are invisible to most mobile end users.

Wireless middleware companies offer the following features:

- Data compression. To eliminate redundant header information, they reform packets and use compression to send more bits down the wire.
- Security. Through various forms of encryption and authentication, they provide end-to-end security between mobile devices and servers.
- Microbrowser and proxy server software. Each middleware company makes a microbrowser that handles HTML or WML requests. If your request is for a

common URL, then middleware companies often have a proxy server that reformats, compresses, truncates the page, and compresses it as data returned to the middleware browser.

- Cross-platform development tools are designed to produce multiple-platform targets from one application.
- Web hosting and server replication at network access points are provided.
- Messaging readers. Store-and-forward message queuing, Push message delivery, and security services are provided. The middleware will take care of validation and certification of messages.
- Roaming across data networks keep service transparent to your application.
- Administrative tools like network management, provisioning, and remote administration for large numbers of devices.

Middleware security modules provide end-to-end encryption for secure use of the Virtual Private Network (VPN) that the middleware can create for a company.

The AvantGo wireless channel is very popular with mobile subscribers. A wireless channel is a distribution vehicle that provides a broad spread of popular content that mobile users like such as sports, weather, news, and other wireless portal items. As a developer, you give a larger audience access to a site by making it part of the AvantGo channel. When checking traffic logs, wireless developers are often surprised to see the uptake from such middleware channels. Middleware companies know how to send a lot more data down the pipe, thereby attracting mobile users.

Serving International Languages Locally

The Internet is a global medium – the server can be in Chicago and the inquiring device could be calling from a restaurant in Lausanne, Switzerland, or a taxi in Osaka, Japan. This reality means that your server must format data for international devices. To transmit foreign languages, a mobile user must receive a "localized" version of your site. If your content is to be seen in multiple languages, your server may need a foreign-language, string-management system. Such application localization involves many issues. In addition to language translation and terminology, you have to consider converting currency, date formats, measurement, use of icons, and sometimes even color. Some devices permit downloading of language translation tools for the mobile traveler, but most require that the server perform these feats.

Although Unicode is an ideal text format for the world's languages, the transmission requirements usually force mapping the 16-bit Unicode character to some familiar 8-bit format on the wireless device. Third-party companies can provide a translation engine, a native content server, or language translation to convert content. It is very important to use native translators to give credibility to your content. Companies such as AT&T have multilingual staff to help mobile travelers translate conversations in real time while the foreign person they are visiting listens on a cellular phone. Many translation companies are available over the Internet.

Heavy-Duty Application Servers

It is useful to understand the development and operation of high-traffic wireless application servers. In many ways, the heavy-duty automatic tools, the server data flow, and memory architectures are the future for wireless systems to come.

Sometimes people love a service so much that it quits working. This is a polite way of saying that your servers are jammed and you are oversubscribed. This happens to everyone including AOL, NTT DoCoMo, and stock-trading brokerages. To respond, companies use a scalable system that lets them add servers as traffic increases. Popular wireless sites require the ultimate in wireless architecture – heavy-duty servers built for telco carrier-grade service. This often requires a redesign of wireless server architecture. These servers must be highly reliable because they must be able to support at least 1 million visitors per day.

Programming at this level can be very complicated or very simple, depending on the tools you use. Dealing with complex details by having to code very large systems, programmers are kept from their main focus of writing business logic. Who can write software for middleware, database maintenance, operating systems, presentation interfaces, infrastructure, billing, account database, and a customer relationship management system?

With complex projects, teams of software programmers try, but automatic tools succeed. A Uniform Modeling Language (UML) program is often used at this level. Rational Rose is a UML tool that lets architects build high-level diagrams of software models. Think of it as a design for what, not how. UML models typically generate C++ code. Once the code is generated, programmers do not touch it. Each module contains code that handles such items as TCP/IP session drop and recovery, race conditions, circuit drops, and security checks. There are no hand-coded modules; it all flows from the diagrams. This automatic code generation enforces many important ideas for high-level robust server development. One key to efficient software architecture is a system that does not create multiple copies of data. Data is never trapped inside the application. There are no pointers, no local variables; therefore, it is all stack and no heap. All system variables are indirect. Whenever possible, modules should be reentrant so the system is not wasting memory. There can be no deadlocks. Threads are programmed with the proper scooping-rule logic.

Designers specify objects, and diagram behaviors that generate code. Good UML tools never let the code get out of phase with the models. A key to good mobile design at this level is to use UML schemes with useful action semantics. There are many that have been developed by the Object Management Group (OMG). (See the section "Wireless Activity Diagrams in Development" in chapter 21, which illustrates the most valuable of these diagrammatic languages.) Like code on any system, you design it, model it, run it, and change the model as needed.

Etrade hit the wall with its large number of transactions. They needed to handle heavy traffic, do stream handling, provide ultra-high performance, and use fast business logic. The old Etrade was 150,000 lines of code and could handle 300 transactions per second. The new Etrade was rebuilt from the ground up using UML tools. The running system ended up with 1500 UML models. The resulting system had higher reliability, handling 7,000 transactions per second. All the work was done in a matter of months with the Kabira Design Center UML tools. These CASE-style tools are emerging more and more in wireless solutions, as we saw in the section "Using RAD Tools to Write Wireless Applications" in chapter 12.

To get maximum speed, everything must be kept in memory. Disk access speed is 10,000 times slower than memory. A data flow architecture makes use of a hyperchannel, which is a telco carrier-class system and uses large cache memory. All transactions happen in memory. You might see this implemented in an Oracle 9i database using Inktomi caches. Stock quotes are multicast; they are published once. Viewers "subscribe" to their location. You do not want 30,000 copies on the network. On financial messaging systems, you need to know the message was received for security purposes. To be truly secure, the system must make sure there is one copy only.

High-capacity servers pump all the content out to all possible receiving server processors or gateways. The gateway responder throws away data it does not need. When an origin server of this magnitude sends wireless content to a WAP gateway, the gateway must reduce an enormous amount of data.

The Swedish White Pages needed such a fast hyperchannel architecture. It hosts all 3 million pages in Kabira "object switches," which are generated network objects from UML models. All of these objects are in memory. There is no disk. The UML system generated 25 million lines of self-testing code. This system uses a real-time cache architecture that is nothing like traditional page caches.

Server and Gateway Locations

Physical server and gateway locations can be important, especially when you are reaching broader audiences with high performance. WAP architecture is designed to use multiple telco proxy-serving gateways. Alternatively, WAP will let you make a long-distance direct call to a private WAP gateway.

To get maximum response, and to reduce the number of hops that routers take, you can put gateways near the basestations and move your server to Network Operation Centers (NOCs) or Network Access Points (NAPs) – the major on ramp to the backbone of the Internet. This is where high-volume servers are located to use maximum bandwidth before routers hop to other routers and the traffic becomes congested. Large hosting companies such as Exodus run global NOCs to host servers in highly secure centers that are guaranteed never to lose power. Hosting companies have peering arrangements to connect by fiber, via redundantly collocated servers throughout the network.

Personalization Engines

On complex systems, information is delivered as the result of multiple systems. Site personalization is a very important component subsystem for wireless servers. Third-party personalization systems take care of most of the complex details. Implemented correctly, these systems can significantly increase commercial use of a server. Commercial *personalization servers,* which are often supplied as component servers, range widely in functions such as the following:

- An *ad management* system rotates banner ads from outside sources, tracks customer activity, and provides commercial reporting and campaign management. It sends advertisement to the people most likely to react to the ad. Companies that produce ad management systems are 24/7 Media, DoubleClick, Engage, Mediaplex, and Real Media. Known more for campaign management are Epiphany, MatchLogic, Unica, and WellConnected.
- A *collaborative filtering system* is personalization technology that generates and recommends choices. Some key companies here are Net Perceptions, Alkindi, and Macromedia (Andromedia).
- A *content management system* controls the production and staging of large bodies of changing content. It is good at matching information to customers. Vignette (StoryServer), Interwoven, ATG (Dynamo), Autonomy, Edify, and YellowBrix make content management systems.
- An *eCommerce system* handles purchases and shipping. Key eCommerce vendors are Ariba, ATG, Blue Martini, Broadvision, Intershop, Totality, Verity, and YOUpowered.
- A *rules engine* is personalization technology that administers business logic based on the activities of the person and the characterization of the content. Some companies are Be Free, Blaze Software, Manna (FrontMind), Personify, PrimeCloud, ResponseLogic, and Applied Predictive Systems.

- An *analytics engine* looks at the entire system and its logs and generates traffic and usage reports. Some of these companies are NetGenesis, HotData, Magnify, EmotionEngine, Quadstone, SPSS, and WhiteCross Systems.

Personalization engines often cost more than $100,000 per component. Administering the rules and coding the content incur further costs. But these engines can often save large companies more than $1 million dollars per year. A little history helps explain the key difference between two approaches to personalization – collaborative filtering engines and rules engines.

Collaborative filtering began in 1987 when a small company called Neonics patented a kiosk-operated recommendation system. Neonics became Live Minds, which merged with Andromedia, which Macromedia acquired. Also in the early 1990s, students at the University of Minnesota started the GroupLens Project, which used technology to recommend news and information sources. At the same time, people at MIT were working on a technology known as Firefly that could recommend books and music. Microsoft acquired Firefly some years later. What all these companies have in common is the development of a personalization technique called collaborative filtering. This application makes personal recommendations based on previous transactions and compares a user's choices to people with similar profiles who seem to be interested in the same content. The end user has no control over this implied profile, and the hosting company does not really know who the people are and what is being recommended.

Rules engines take a different approach. These systems let administrators and users edit profiles and put into play rules of logic. Usability studies show that people rarely edit their profiles, so these rules have to be administered. A rules-based system knows customer segments and content. It adds intelligence to decisions about what should be marketed to the visitor, and specializes in real-time personalization. Dynamically, it can "reference sell" products. The reference sale appears as a rapidly constructed wireless page that is based on the apparent interest by looking at the history of selected links or prior purchasing patterns.

The ability for end users to personalize a mobile experience is often worth returning for. A premium-personalized site may run upwards of $5 million. For more information on personalization, visit <http://www.personalization.org>.

The pioneers of personalization are now producing an XML DTD Mobile Profile to get devices in the street to synchronize with diverse systems in back offices. The leading personalization companies formed the Customer Profile Exchange (CPEX) as an open standard for personalization in June 2000. Developers can use this standard method to create, store, and exchange data about Web users. One of CPEX's goals was to produce an XML standard for online and offline data repository. This enables a single view of the customer within multiple enterprise applications. The CPEX standard originated from Vignette, although the group now involves Siebel Systems, net.Genesis, Andromedia, and Oracle. The standard is defined at <http://www.cpexchange.org/>.

Planning XML Architecture for Content

We have seen that XML architecture is important to wireless presentation. It is also important for data exchange between businesses. XML forces the separation of content from style and gives wireless devices flexibility for interpretation. In large projects, a database architect develops schemas for tables. For XML, you must write DTDs and XML code in order for a Web server to efficiently present, synchronize, or exchange data between wireless devices or Web servers.

Servers send mobile content through XML protocols. XML can be exchanged among databases on multiple systems with presentation on wireless devices. An XML schema might need to be defined, or an established DTD might need to be transformed to access a relational database on the server. XML content analysis is required to improve mobility, partition wireless data, and form the correct data types for location, time, and personalization.

An interesting property of XML is that you can synchronize data between wireless client and server quite efficiently. This is a good technique to reach wildly different ranges of devices, while you are generating only one XML stream. Once the server and client agree on the DTD, they can exchange data with very little overhead, as we discussed in the section "Wireless XML Browsers" in chapter 11.

For portable and distributed data, FusionOne, PumaTech, and AvantGo are leading providers of synchronizing software. SyncML is a standard to synchronize Web content. An efficient synchronization server will simply transmit any changes relative to data on your device storage. Wireless devices can sync over the air or, for periodically refreshing large amounts of data or code, they can use a cable.

XML Data Portability and Exchange

Separation of content, style, and logic is key to advanced server architecture. If you are generating content from the server dynamically with ASP or JSP, then you are probably using processing logic in most of your pages. In the generation of Web pages, content, style, and logic are distinct classes in application servers that operate on data objects, presentation objects, and the business objects that control it all.

Servers need to operate on and, in some cases, generate XML data streams. These streams may appear in JSP or ASP pages, or be generated from objects. Higher-level protocols that use XML are now the basis for business. eCommerce standards are largely XML based. U.S. companies already exchange data via Electronic Data Interchange (EDI) protocols, and some are converting to higher-level XML protocols. A whole series of new XML-based protocols is emerging under the general name of Web services. The two Web services implemented most often are SOAP and UDDI.

Simple Object Access Protocol (SOAP) serves as a standard for enterprise server interfaces. SOAP is a lightweight protocol that defines a uniform way of passing XML-encoded data. It is ideal for the exchange of information in a decentralized, distributed environment. SOAP is an XML-based protocol that consists of three parts: an envelope that defines a framework for describing what is in a message and how to process it, a set of encoding rules for expressing instances of application-defined data types, and a convention for representing remote procedure calls and responses. SOAP may be absorbed by the XML Protocols Working Group. The SOAP site is <http://www.w3.org/TR/SOAP/>.

Universal Description Discovery Integration (UDDI) is another important electronic marketplace standard. UDDI provides a mechanism for clients to dynamically find other Web services. It is a kind of DNS of application services and is effective in connecting to services provided by external business partners. UDDI is layered over SOAP. If you send a SOAP message that requests "find_business Microsoft," your request will get a long XML-encoded UDDI response that details all the Microsoft services that can be used later for SOAP exchange. UDDI was defined by Ariba, IBM, and Microsoft. *e-speak* is another Open Source XML-based eCommerce standard, defined by Hewlett Packard.

Electronic Commerce Modeling Language (ECML) is a key mCommerce standard. It lets the user store billing, payment, and shipping information on a mobile phone. This information can be automatically filled into Web forms that conform to the ECML specification, with no need to enter the information manually. More information about E-wallets and ECML is at <http://www.ecml.org>.

Rethinking the Wireless Client/Server Relationship

We have looked at server techniques to connect mobile devices to obtain a broad set of wireless Internet services (i.e., messaging, browsing, interactivity, and voice). Engineers are thinking through new relationships between the wireless client and server. For example, city guides are using new handheld interactive models with different caching, storage, and data-exchange protocols.

Radio operating computers have brought many challenges to conventional thinking. Developers and architects are asking, How should sessions be managed by devices? How should microbrowsers work? Where should data reside? How should messaging be integrated? How should XML be transmitted? How should OSI layers operate between devices and servers? The premises behind distributed systems, or peer-to-peer protocols, are that every device can have server functionality and that a large part of wireless architecture is to switch and coordinate.

Conventional Web phone microbrowsers work only when they are connected. Mobile environments where connections come and go and where data and services are aggregated between sets of devices defy the conventional assumptions of how to maintain an OSI Web session. With wireless handhelds, the entire application can work offline. Going online, often a smart transaction needs to be resumed with the server.

Java phone architecture (see Figure 69 in chapter 11) already recognizes that servers can run a Java applet and need send only XML data. The same is true for BREW device architecture. The style of the data presentation can be entirely handled by the mobile device. For XML synchronization to be efficient, the presentation should not be computed on the server, as it is now in WAP, in i-mode, and on most wireless microbrowsers. The XML data should be transmitted to an onboard XML-defined style sheet or object processor.

Architects at work on wireless session management between the OSI stack of the client and server must manage the connection and caching better than the conventional wired PC system. *Rather than form complex objects and cache pages on the server, cache objects in the client.* The Palm PQA shows that keeping the front end of a Web site can cut down over-the-air traffic. PQA pages are the kind of pages a browser would normally cache. Microbrowser memory caching often creates more problems than it solves. It is more efficient to cache not browser pages, but the subelements, the objects. Web caching on the phone is a big problem; developers must determine architectures that leave enough code and data on the device to be useful in environments where connections come and go. Expecting the mobile user to "purge unused Web pages" is not reasonable. New browsers and matching servers are experimenting with smart object caching in the microbrowser to minimize over-the-air transmission time. This caching can reuse images and objects within the Web page. XHTML can properly encode and manage Web server document objects.

When servers transmit content to a wide range of wireless devices, some have high page densities; others have low page densities. Conventionally, the server computes the receiving device's Web display. The latency of a normal Computer Gateway Interface (CGI) when using Perl, ASP, or JSP can be dramatically improved with an application server, but systems still build pages and use caching schemes that are reaching a practical upper limit on the number of accessing devices coming from the wireless Internet. Looking at current systems as *Einstürzende Neubaten* (a structure that collapses to become a new one), we may begin to realize what mobile applications do: They are the repositories of personal content by the millions, they use complex distributed objects that must avoid roundtrips in the air, and they consume XML devoid of style. Assembled on a device, these objects form an application. The application is a small simulation, a model of the nearby real world. Complex XML data streams connect all wireless models, each with serverlike qualities. Data exchanges consist mainly of differences and intelligent commands. A good example of this emerging class of software is a digital city guide.

City Guides as Models

It is not quite SimCity™, but having a personal city guide is like having a simulated city in your hands. Simulating a city based on personal data points is an example of model-based software. If you plan the application architecture for a travel guide, it can be done through a messaging system, a browser, an interactive application, or even a voice portal. The simplest approach for developers is to send content to an ordinary microbrowser. The mobile traveler can point his or her microbrowser at your site. This is how pda.guide.com, hdml.guide.com, and wap.guide.com work on Web phones. City guides that depend on browser, messaging, or conversations do not work unless there is a connection. To be able to show content without a connection, you must produce an interactive guide.

To make a guide work interactively, a developer writes some custom client code for the operating system of a wireless device, usually a handheld device. Interactive mapping software can be built from the device operating system graphic libraries. The content engineer localizes data, as the traveling end user requires. This is how CitySync, Jungleport, Vindigo, and WCITIES work. They provide interactive wireless applications that work effectively offline. These rudimentary models and their content are compiled for specific target devices.

Note the pitfalls of creating guides with conventional browsing models. Multiple pages have to be loaded, often with redundant and irrelevant data. Objects are cached that are not needed, and objects that you really need are not cached. In short, the microbrowser does not have a meaningful "refresh" technology. Interesting objects created as applets can be shown interactively. But an interactive applet like a Map requires an underlying store of data to be interesting. Solutions for server and client that use models are numerous.

A mobile traveler ideally wants to make a connection, load local guide pages, and then work offline. This means you electronically distribute the application model for the devices that can synchronize with content. It also means that if you supply the content – a good idea because it is an ongoing revenue stream – then you should do an information design and work on data-partitioning plans. Partitioning of the data is essential because you cannot load the entire current database of content. The application model and the content should also be available from a PC so the traveler has a way to "mobilize" the Web site, perhaps marking up information for later mobile use. Participating travelers can modify a guide with notes or other elements. When the connection is synchronized, the changed information is passed back to the network. Of course, the mobile device must have storage and processing power.

New companies like Pixo are rethinking the way browsers cache their objects, use over-the-air transmission, and make use of brand-new capability on board the new devices. Microsoft's Stinger browser does not do any special tricks. It simply delivers useful connections to HTML sites over the WinCE operating system. But it has sufficient power to write interesting applications, as does the Symbian platform, the J2ME, and the QUALCOMM BREW platform.

Bluetooth Servers

In some networks, such as those that use Bluetooth devices, there may be no radio towers and any wireless device can interact directly with any other with the PAN. A set of Bluetooth radio devices can connect with Bluetooth access points that are almost never connected to the Internet, but are always connected to one another. As a group, these devices can be moved as a unit and set up by work teams to continue local work. A Bluetooth application server can operate as an application hub.

The Bluetooth end-to-end solution over the Internet is particularly interesting. It can make use of telco voice and Internet data, perhaps using VoIP to bypass the telco, but capable of making voice-assisted data and data-enabled voice applications possible. Ericsson showed an early WAP Bluetooth server in December 2000; it connected Bluetooth phones with WAP browsers using a Bluetooth protocol to the Internet to read WML content.

19

Chapter

Working with Devices as Skins: Every 2 Years

Little squares of light shine your content at mobile users. The windows on your wireless server are now in motion. The exterior surfaces of your wireless server are carried around by mobile users, framed by all manner of consumer hardware that changes about every two years. Like the exteriors of buildings, these devices, the exterior of your site, are always under assault by the elements. Button numbers rub away, lids break off, and antennas get mashed. Old pagers and cell phones are often discarded, replaced by new mobile devices that with every new generation look a little deeper at content, take on new wireless functions, and often operate with other new small devices.

We will consider general, commercial, and industrial device families. To anticipate 3G technologies, we will use the technique of looking at the chips that implement the technology. We provide a six-family programming model to reign in the madness of the confusing landscape of wireless devices.

Building architects are commissioned to change a building's skins perhaps two or three times over the life of a building. Façades, roofs, doors, and windows are the skins of buildings that let in light, air, and people, and protect against natural elements. They are often statements more of fashion than engineering necessity.

On the wireless Web, a *skin* is the wireless developers' term for a device emulator; the same word is used for the variable visual interfaces of Internet music players such as Winamp. Developers bring up an ever-increasing variety of wireless device skins in their emulators. For devices with new page densities, windows and entrances are moved. For color devices, new façades are made.

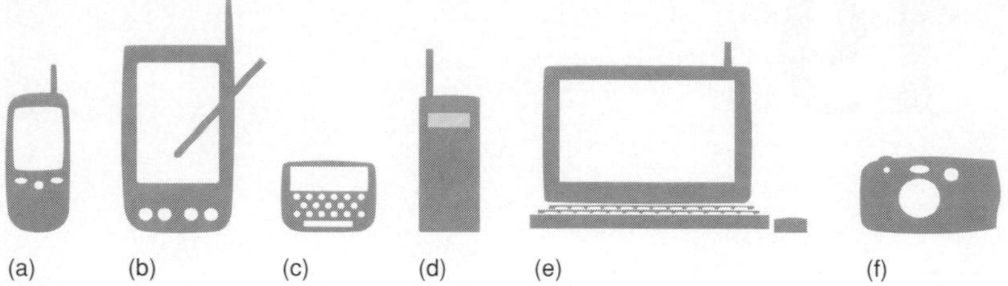

Figure 103 Six wireless device families: (*a*) Web phone, (*b*) handheld, (*c*) pager, (*d*) voice portal, (*e*) Web PC, and (*f*) communicating appliance.

Six-Family Programming Model

The total landscape of wireless devices is staggering. Device vendors focus on promoting their product lines, but developers must obtain a realistic view of the entire market for wireless devices. It must make sense to the Web developer whose server generates a wide range of content. The six wireless device families in Figure 103 cover the general device and form factors available on the wireless Internet. The new devices, even though they cross functions, still use one of these six models. For example, the older HDML phone has increased its display sizes to become a WAP phone, such as the Nokia 7110. Both belong to the Web phone family. The new Ericsson Symbian phone that lets you write on the screen, the new Java phone, and the two-way Java pager are all devices that belong to the handheld family, which are most useful in an interactive, application programming model.

There is an important matched relationship between the utility of devices and servers. Developers create the navigational entrance and access methods to a server. But the device is the entry mechanism and its navigational entrance should be planned and set with care. The wireless Internet has a lot of skin. Developers match the various skins to their servers. Good server architecture can last for many generations of wireless devices. Only when devices of considerable difference, such as a Bluetooth device or a GPS handset, become available do you need to reevaluate the purpose of your applications and the entry point to the server. Using a CC/PP agent, developers can manage the many new windows into their site.

The Changing Device Landscape

Popular wireless networks arrive about every 10 years, providing key services for devices. Suitable devices are succeeded by better devices about every 2 years. For example, the first models of the Palm handheld replaced the Newton. The configurable Handspring Visor may well overrun the nonconfigurable Palm handhelds. It is said that Japanese production and consumer cycles are falling to within 1 year. New mobile user interfaces must be developed as new devices evolve. To take advantage of new network features like GPRS, HDR, GPS, and Bluetooth technology, the device and sometimes the server need upgrades.

There are many possible devices to consider and it is important to keep track of the new arrivals on the scene. You might read about new devices in a magazine advertised months ahead of production or browse the Internet to survey the ever-changing wireless device landscape. An up-to-date survey is published at CNET. Wireless developer portals periodically update comparisons. Developer and vendor portals often provide advance wireless device emulators for early testing.

The nature of wireless devices is changing. Sometimes it is a phone, a data terminal, a computer, a pager, a remote controller, a spell checker, a "location radar," a pay point, an electronic room key, or a personal information system. Versatility is one of the qualities of software machines. Through reprogramming, they change purpose; but physical design is a challenge. Sometimes the new look is like the change of a building façade – just a fashion statement. As with a car, some people find style the reason to buy. Handsets and handhelds are combining voice and data. Often these combination devices are disappointing to use; users complain they cannot see the screen as they talk or they expect software to behave more naturally. While the ideal form is elusive, new features are rampant and you need to exploit the best of them. Devices are evolving to provide remote controls, location services, and the ability to use other devices. Some devices specialize in music, do messaging, let you play interactive games, feature multiple styles of Web browsing, or have voice interfaces. Industrial devices are built to take drops and not wear down.

Do not become seduced by a device's capabilities. Consider starting with what a person wants to get done first and explore how these devices can be used to perform the application within the available wireless network. Reflect on the primary content and the user's interest in it. Should it be voice, data, or both? Consider the software and network to accomplish the tasks, and finally match the device that best delivers the application. In the Total Cost of Ownership (TCO) consider device costs, long-life batteries, rechargers, and replacements.

GPRS Handsets

Some devices can use network data protocols such as GPRS, HDR, and EDGE. It takes years to deploy data networks, which appear first in pilot cities. Even though the devices are ready, it takes years before developers can expect any market to provide revenue. General Packet Radio System (GPRS) is a 2.5G data upgrade for GSM and TDMA networks. GPRS handsets are an important opportunity in Europe. GPRS devices differ by the number of 14.4-kbps uplink and downlink slots the device supports. These slots are additive and are allocated dynamically depending on the current number of users in a cell. Theoretically, a GPRS handset using a maximum of eight slots can transfer data at 115 kbps.

Within the data packets of a 20-kbps link, the actual user bits turn out to be 10 kbps, so multiple slots are needed to obtain decent speeds. Unfortunately, if the device travels too far from a basestation and uses many slots, it needs a lot of power. In early testing, it appears that using more than three slots can exceed legal power transmission limits and will certainly drain the battery.

There are 29 classes of GPRS handsets to consider. They differ largely by slot configuration and compatibility with High Speed Circuit-Switched Data (HSCSD). Most handsets are asymmetric; that is, they have a greater downlink or down slot than uplink or up slot data rate. The Motorola Timeport, Ericsson R520, Mitsubishi Trium, and the Mitsubishi Mondo support 1 up slot and 2 down slots. The Sagem/Microsoft WA3050 supports 1 up and 3 down. The Samsung SGH Q100 is a 1-up, 4-down GPRS handset. The 4-slot subscribers may get service only if they are near a tower when the slots are available. After a year in trial, many operators testing GPRS are experimenting more with HSCSD fallback because GPRS is not implemented everywhere. The downside is that HSCSD requires 20 to 30 seconds for a dial-up connection.

GPRS is the first available 2.5G packet-switched standard. To a developer, emulators are helpful, but reality is defined by deployment and operation. The next best thing for developers is using a GPRS testing center and a local trial. There is one testing center on every continent. Check the schedules of the GPRS Applications Alliance (GAA) at its site <http://www.gprsworld.com/>.

Bluetooth and ALI Devices

A Web browser interface is no longer sufficient because there are new functions for which no interface exists. In a roomful of Bluetooth wireless devices able to connect with one another, the Bluetooth profiles that are compatible provide special services. Mobile users discover what devices are available to use and what devices are requesting service from the owner. Proximity of nearby information is also a feature of Automatic Location Identification (ALI) handsets. As we move about with ALI devices, it may be very useful to show location and nearby items of interest perhaps through an iconic display. Closing in, then the mobile user could acquire nearby products or services, perhaps switching to the Bluetooth network. New kinds of interfaces are important when the traveler starts "surveying" with any wireless device. Examples of thematic and starfield displays are promising.

Commercial and Industrial Devices

While the W3C continues to define basic functionality of wireless devices and mobile applications, the world of devices and uses from consumer to business is wide ranging and not easily summarized. An ongoing list is available at <http://www.w3.org/Mobile/Activity>.

The six-family programming model covers the breadth of wireless Internet devices. Also, commercial and industrial classifications are important. Sun, Microsoft, and Symbian have platform families of wireless devices for their markets, and even Motorola and other telco companies are offering more than cellular phones and pagers. Wireless developers still have to mitigate the large holes in vendors' product lines and network offerings.

Sun Microsystems Wireless Devices

The wireless devices and the terminology used at Sun Microsystems (Table 42) speak to the hard-core Java developer working on Sun products. Sun specifies two general wireless mobile platforms – a medium-bandwidth Connected Device Configuration (CDC) platform and a low-bandwidth Connected Limited Device Configuration (CLDC) platform. In order to call devices CDC or CLDC, manufacturers of such devices must be licensed and certified by Sun.

The categorization of Sun platforms is based on a device's memory size and estimated wireless bandwidth constraints. Each device specified by Sun has a configuration for the device family and a set of profiles for each device group within

Table 42 Sun Microsystems wireless devices

Devices	Terminology
	**CDC – JVM – greater than 1 MB memory** CDC devices are information devices such as handhelds, high-end communicators, fixed set-top boxes, Internet TVs, and Internet screen phones. Applications run on the Java Virtual Machine (JVM).
	**CLDC – kVM – less than 512 kb memory** The bottom-end CLDC devices for personal use are good for highly mobile information. Examples are cell phones, pagers, and personal organizers. The CLDC devices run the Java Kilobyte Virtual Machine (kVM) and have low memory and network bandwidth. Sun targets these as having no more than 512 kilobytes of memory including both RAM and ROM. They are low-bandwidth, with intermittent low-bandwidth network connections of 9600 bps or less.
	**SmartCard – CardVM – 32 kb memory** Smart cards are used for security and transactions. Sun classifies the SmartCard as running a Java CardVM. A Java Card API and SIM Toolkit have been developed by GemPlus.

the family. This hardware-oriented viewpoint is good for the experimental developer, although it does not offer a natural model that conforms to the reality of products and networks that face the wireless development community.

Java2 Micro Edition (J2ME) is the premier wireless developer's environment. With it, you can write a Mobile Internet Device (MIDlet) application, which is suitable for the low-end CLDC highly mobile information devices such as cell phones, pagers, and personal organizers. These run the Java kVM and have low memory and limited network bandwidth. The high-end CDC devices are shared, sometimes fixed information devices including high-end communicators, handhelds, set-top boxes, Internet TVs, and Internet screen phones. But each wireless solution is unique.

Wireless Internet programmers develop content with Sun platform servers. Although Sun offers iPlanet, the company has no *unified* server architecture for the six devices of the wireless programming model. To navigate the Sun technology lineup better and see how to program Java phones, read chapter 11, "Developing WAN Interactive Applications in Java."

Microsoft Corporation's Wireless Devices

Microsoft Corporation offers a number of generations of wireless devices (Table 43). These initiatives go back many years. Today, developers build primarily for the PocketPC OS that covers a Handheld PC as well. There are also have three prototyping operating systems – the Stinger OS for select Web phones, the experimental TabletPC, and the recent Talisker system for new embedded devices. An original equipment manufacturer (OEM) licenses one of these Microsoft operating systems so developers can create applications for wireless devices.

Wireless Internet developers delivering content from their servers are used to developing solutions on top of Microsoft platforms. They have no strong architecture for pager and voice portals. Developers write their own Web PC interfaces. Because Microsoft has not yet produced a grand model to unify all its wireless devices, each device must be programmed with separate tools of different quality. The architecture of the .NET Mobile Internet Server, formerly known as Airstream, is intended to address back-end connection services, but some developers prefer the Wireless Knowledge product codeveloped by Microsoft that more generally covers the general "non-Microsoft" technologies and market opportunities that face wireless developers.

Symbian Limited Wireless Devices

The Symbian consortium, based in the United Kingdom, specifies two devices – a communicator and a smartphone. The smartphone is a cellular voice-centric handset and the communicator is a data-centric handheld. Symbian wireless devices

Table 43 Microsoft Corporation wireless devices

Devices	Terminology
	HPC, PPC – WinCE OS Microsoft has a long history of making Windows-based operating systems for handheld platforms. The current WinCE development environment builds final applications for a PocketPC, a Palm PC, and a handheld PC. The Compaq iPAQ with a wireless Ethernet sled is a popular PocketPC.
	"Stinger" Devices – WinCE OS "Stinger" is an internal code name for cell phones that use experimental extensions to WinCE. There are many "Stinger" makers including Ericsson, which makes a phone in Asia. The Stinger phone runs the Mobile Internet Explorer Web browser.
	WebPC, TabletPC – Windows XP Professional Microsoft developers are used to the Windows SDK, now called Windows XP Professional. The evolution of the Microsoft laptop is the TabletPC to appear in 2002. The TabletPC has all the power and capability of a fully programmable PC. The TabletPC includes special handwriting processing software and is a refocusing of Microsoft's early 1990s Winpad, which was its answer to the many tablet PCs such as the GO PenPoint tablet.
	Appliances – "Talisker" OS Microsoft's operating system for Internet appliances is called Talisker. It offers a new user interface, security, and Media Sense, a discovery protocol that lets device owners know what types of network connections and devices are nearby. Talisker includes connections to Bluetooth network devices.

(Table 44) provide three reference devices using the EPOC operating system. Symbian is based on the original Psion handheld architecture.

Communicators are information-centric products with voice capability. Mobile by nature, communicators include richer functionality than smartphones. The communicator includes keyboard input facilities and the ability to link seamlessly with a PC, with printers, and with the Internet to send and receive files, to synchronize seamlessly, and to be practical to carry around. In effect, the communicator is a full-featured palmtop and digital phone in one unit. Symbian has implemented two reference designs based on the communicator concept. Application suites

Table 44 Symbian Limited wireless devices

Devices	Terminology
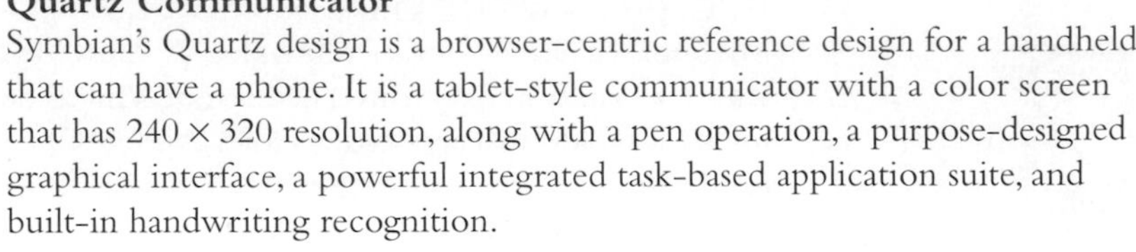	**Quartz Communicator** Symbian's Quartz design is a browser-centric reference design for a handheld that can have a phone. It is a tablet-style communicator with a color screen that has 240 × 320 resolution, along with a pen operation, a purpose-designed graphical interface, a powerful integrated task-based application suite, and built-in handwriting recognition.
	**Crystal Communicator (WID)** Symbian's Crystal is an information-centric reference design for a keyboard-based handheld with a 640 × 200 screen, with soft keys. Symbian calls it a Wireless Information Device (WID). It has an integrated application suite meant for advanced mobile professionals who need more conventional lap-top-like computer power.
	**Pearl Smartphone** Symbian's Pearl smartphone reference design is voice-centric with advanced information capabilities. Its smartphones are advanced Web phones that use wireless GSM networks. They are consumer focused and can let owners browse the Internet, play games, receive and send faxes, SMS, and email. They also have built-in scheduling and contact management software. Because of the wide range of requirements required for smartphones by licensees, Symbian provides a suite of applications and generic technology.

shared by Quartz and Crystal include contacts, schedule, to-do list, sketch, word processor, messaging, WAP and Web browsing, and voice recorder, as well as viewers for external data formats including Microsoft Word email attachments.

Wireless Internet developers delivering content from their servers will find the Symbian product model has no answers for pagers. The first Symbian smartphone was the Ericsson R380 handset pictured in Figure 79 in chapter 12.

Industrial Handhelds

As popular as they are, the Palm handhelds and Pocket PC are relatively recent additions to the wireless market. In the late 1980s corporations began using devices with longer battery life, more rugged characteristics, and specially designed software. The industrial handheld manufacturers and devices (Table 45) include the leader Symbol, Telxon (now owned by Symbol), Psion, Intermec, and Norand (now owned by Intermec).

In evaluating professional handhelds, you have to look closely at their special features. The most important feature is that the device must stay powered

Table 45 Industrial handheld manufacturers and devices

Company	Handheld
Amrel	Rocky II
Casio	IT 2000
Cruise Technologies	CruisePad, CruisePad NXT
Cycomm	PCMobile
Dolphin	UPS
Dauphin	Orasis
DES	MiniWriter, ScriptWriter XL
Epson	EHT-40
Fujitsu Personal Systems	Point 510, Stylistic 1200, Point 1600, Stylistic 2300
Fujitsu-ICL	TeamPad 7100, 7600
Granite	VideoPad VP7
Icras/General Magic	DataRover
Intermec	Trakker Adara, 6110
Itronix/Dynatech	X-C 6000/6250, T-5200
Melard	SCOUT2
MetroBook	SLT
MicroSlate	MSL3000, Datellite 500V
Mitsubishi	AMiTY VP
Motorola	Forte CommPad
Norand	Pen*Key 6100, 6110, 6210, 6360, 6620, 6632
Palmax	PD-1000
Panasonic	CF-01, Toughbook xx
PGI Data	Nightingale, P7, Road Runner
Ramline	Frisbee/Integra
Symbol	SPT-1500, PPT 4xxx
TelePad	3
Telxon (Symbol)	PTC-1124, PTC-1124 Java, PTC-2124, PTC-2134, PTC-960M
TouchStar	Eagle
WalkAbout	Hammerhead P-233
WPI Husky	FC-486P, fex21, FC-PX5
Xplore	Genesys

throughout a worker's shift without a battery change. It also must be rugged. Having multiple batteries is not only expensive, but people just do not like to tote them around. Here is a good checklist to compare industrial handhelds:

- *Battery life* – three days or better in average use.
- *Rugged* – IP54 or better. IP is Industrial Protection environmental sealing code, which makes a device impervious to windblown dust and rain. They also can be dropped without harm.
- *Communication architecture* – ease of access and changing among WAN, LAN, and PAN. It should support simultaneous voice and data traffic.
- *Display* – bright and large enough to read text comfortably.
- *Handwriting* – ability to take signatures, draw, and actually write text. You need to be able to correct mistakes easily.
- *Keyboard* – facilities to suit rapid typing and for large fingers.
- *Location aware* – sometimes requires cooperation of the wireless network.
- *Modular slots* – ability to add devices without having to buy a new unit.
- *Peripherals* – ability to efficiently use barcode scanners, cameras, belt printers, WAN, LAN, Bluetooth, GPS; no dangling wires; and proper drivers.
- *Radio modem* – Whether the modems are built in or can be attached via a modular slot, the handheld manufacturer must provide a device driver.
- *Touch screen* – software programmable displays allow more interface choices.
- *Upgradeable operating system* – avoid masked ROM devices that cannot be upgraded.
- *Voice* – supported directly and integrated with applications.

Look for a solid communication architecture that lets you connect to multiple networks and intelligently handles storage and synchronizes content. Voice and data should be integrated, although data may be the only purpose for the device. Symbol's Spectrum 24 network integrates voice and data over a LAN and can make end-to-end connections. To accommodate voice, some devices use iDEN and TETRA networks. Bluetooth technology can also provide voice and integrate a much wider group of devices. (For more information on industrial handhelds, read the section in chapter 12, "Developing LAN Interactive Applications.")

Handset and Handheld Design Excellence

There have been many beautiful wireless devices with interesting features. We can expect many more to come. But the invisible element, dearly loved, is battery and long life. It is an endearing quality of the pager and the Palm family of handhelds. Device screens are definitely improving in size and quality. Mass-produced Web phones are ultimately built for their local population and have native keys and language sets burnt into their ROMs. An i-mode handset is designed for Japanese language use. Some new phones are losing their keyboards to work like handhelds with projected keypad displays. But color, large screen, and multiple antenna features are coming at the dearest price of all – shorter operational time for the mobile user.

Devices have a personality that matches the owner. The hobbyist looks for function and pocket power, rather than fashion and flair. The fashion-conscious owner looks for a cool skin. Your wireless applications and content can match personal profiles with clever server programming. But it is best to program flexible user choices, rather than assume that one CC/PP profile will work for everyone.

Some devices worth studying are the Palm V™, the DoCoMo i-mode color phone, the Apple Newton, the RIM 957, Ericsson R380, and the Kyocera smartphone. Aside from the "essential device" that combines the features of the handset and handheld, there are special features to look for in mobile wireless design.

Java in silicon. The Java phones of 2001 are entirely implemented in software. By putting the Java processing on a chip, the performance can be increased at least 50 times. The hardware can also implement multiple threading, which is not implemented in software because of the overhead. Java hardware accelerators include Zucotto Xpresso™, inSilicon JVXtreme™ Accelerator, ARM® Jazelle, and Nazomi JSTAR™.

Handwriting. The mobile user interface is undergoing many changes. Even "electronic ink" is breaking its latency barrier. Most people are sensitive to the fact that entering text with an electronic stylus does not keep up to their writing speed. When you are taking notes in front of someone you are aware how slow electronic ink can be. Any latency longer than 30 milliseconds is noticeable in average hand-eye coordination. It is similar to the problem where laptop keyboards cannot keep up with high-speed typists. It appears that a device like the Microsoft Tablet PC will eventually have the horsepower to deliver fluid writing. Until then, make sure your mobile users can use the handheld typing software, which is faster than handwriting software. Anoto and other radio pen makers provide an alternative handwriting technology.

Pingers. Not only quality, but also quantity of devices manufactured is creating opportunity for wireless Internet applications. Soon they will put a heavy load on your server. The architecture for cellular devices is undergoing tremendous revision. On the one hand, there is a convergence of voice and data leading to a quality consumer device with complex media interface requirements. Then there are devices with no interface at all such as smart cards, small beacons, pingers, and active badges. Experts expect there to be at least three times as many of these devices as Web phones, pagers, and handhelds by the year 2010. These devices will provide telemetry coming and going. In your wireless applications, these "lesser" devices can complete the architecture for content and sensor telemetry.

Reprogrammable Devices

The biggest secret of all is software, the ability to reprogram a machine to do yet something else. Wireless architectures can take advantage of reprogrammability in software-defined radio, as well as in general-purpose radio operating systems. It is interesting to note that when a space probe is built, it has a huge software component. Software programs operate the craft differently from the way designers might first have imagined. While in space, programmers transmit final programs to cause all the subcomponents to work effectively when the probe reaches its destination. This flexible design strategy allows some room for error; you do not have to get everything right the first time. For the wireless Internet, this strategy is an assurance that "the future is built in."

Compared to the planned obsolescence of specialized handsets and handhelds, this software flexibility is ecologically beneficial. But it takes underlying hardware to succeed. If you look under the hood at the chipsets of the newest handsets, you will see Bluetooth, GPS, and other useful 3G functions.

The Revolution in 3G Chips

In order for the 3G wireless Internet to work, devices have to be "defined in silicon." In 2000, QUALCOMM, Inc., began producing the Mobile Station Modem chipsets and system software. The first full-featured 3G chip was the MSM5500™, a single-chip, baseband processor modem that integrates both digital and analog functions including processing multiband CDMA, PCS, and AMPS cellular signals. It also delivers 1x cdma2000 and has a High Data Rate (HDR) circuit. It also includes other exotic 3G technologies.

You do not have to be an electrical engineer to appreciate the features of the chip, as illustrated in the MSM5500 functional block diagram (Figure 104). You can see many 3G wireless Internet features. Note the three antennas (the upside down triangles): the WAN antenna transmits AMPS and CDMA, another receives GPS signals, and the third antenna is for a Bluetooth PAN. The multiple antennas can permit the 3G quality of transparent roaming, which allows a subscriber to

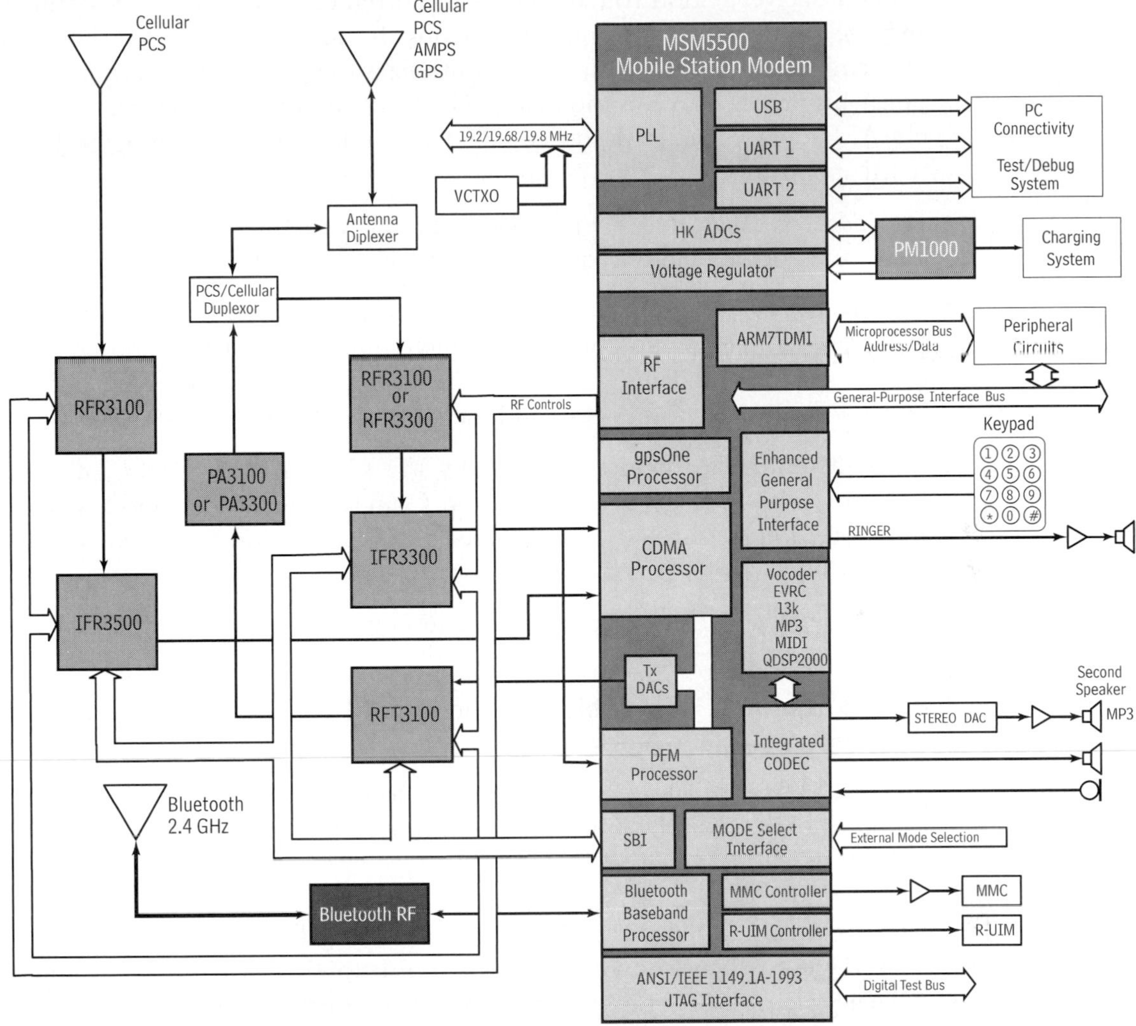

Figure 104 MSM5500 functional block diagram. Note the triangular antennas for Bluetooth network, GPS, and CDMA as well as other multimedia services. (*Source:* QUALCOMM, Incorporated.)

keep conversations going as the person moves between a WAN tower and a Bluetooth PAN access point.

The new MSM5500 chips feature:

- *gpsOne position location processor.* The gpsOne processor merges GPS satellite and network information to provide a high-precision data coordinate. The base transceiver station (BTS) collects measurements from the GPS satellites and the cellular PCS network, then sends the information to the Position Determination Entity (PDE), which optimizes the position location calculation. This processor meets the FCC E911 mandate for manufacturers to supply ALI-capable handsets and is a key technology for precision location-based applications.

- *Embedded Bluetooth baseband processor* complies with Bluetooth 1.0 standard. This can negotiate radio frequency. It has led to a Bluetooth antenna.
- *IS-95B compliant* to support High-Speed Packet Data (HSPD) transfer and processing. The chip also contains complete digital modulation and demodulation systems (modems) for both CDMA and AMPS cellular standards, as specified in IS-95A and IS-95B and the new cdma2000 1x (IS-95C).
- *Audio.* Multimedia support provided by the Qtunes MP3 player software, multimedia-processing software based on Compact Media Extension (CMX) and a MIDI processor. Also included are Voice Recognition (VR) and vocoder processors.
- *MMC controller* – Integrated mass-storage controller for a MultiMediaCard (MMC).
- *R-UIM controller* – Removable User Interface Module compatible with SIM cards.
- *QDSP2000 digital signal processor core* in the low-power chip, which assists on advanced chip processors like GPS position location and Bluetooth network activation.

The device contains an MSM5500 modem, an analog baseband-to-RF upconverter, an IF-to-baseband downconverter, an RF-to-IF downconverter, and a power management ASIC. The MSM5500 device performs baseband digital signal processing and executes the subscriber unit's system software. System software is executed by an embedded ARM7 microprocessor, which is the central interface device in the subscriber's unit, connecting RF and baseband circuits as well as memory and user interface ports. The user interface of a subscriber's unit includes the standard keypad, LCD display, ringer, microphone, and earpiece.

This chip delivers voice, high-speed data, music, and video over wireless networks to make entertainment and information applications possible. The MSM5500, supports cdma2000 1x, as well as HDR technology. It doubles the overall capacity of callers using IS-95A and IS-95B, and it adds a 2.4 Mbps HDR processor, thereby fully realizing the convergence of cellular and Internet technologies and services. The chip has been produced in quantity since August 2001.

Communication Software in Wireless Devices

Chips with new features lead to new devices that can make possible many interesting applications. Developers need to get hold of these underlying processors and subsystems to exploit the technology. To provide access to chip features, QUALCOMM created a software development environment called BREW™ (Binary Runtime Environment for Wireless). The BREW software development library exposes the software interfaces to all of the chip components. To read more about BREW development, turn to the section "Developing WAN Interactive BREW™ Applications in C++ and Java" at the end of chapter 11.

A wireless device needs solid communication architecture. This means software has to support the silicon design to execute both radio signal and network protocol processing. Professional and military devices have implemented designs to handle different protocols and signal sources interchangeably. Unfortunately, many devices on the market today are still stuck in phone-think or computer-think. Handhelds are still designed with communication as an afterthought. An early exception, still worth study, was the proprietary General Magic communication architecture. Software application programmers enjoyed the multithreaded, low-level communication architecture that abstracted every communication interface and provided libraries for all public and private networks. With effective communication software and well-considered development tools, it is easier for developers to build applications that transmit content over the wireless Internet.

20 Chapter

Making Content, Defining Space: Every Season, Every Month, Every Week

All wireless content originates from the Internet. Wireless devices are now sources and receivers forming a greater wireless Internet of content. Wireless content is a unique architectural element. As an architect, you are responsible for embodying systems that define it, allow for it, contain it, and manage it. The run-of-the-mill Internet site never had to deal with the richness or precision of wireless Internet content, which has to be synchronized, distributed, and made available to multitudes of mobile visual displays and voice portals. There is more of it, there are more sources for it, and it changes more frequently.

As we discussed in chapter 5, personal content drives the wireless Internet. Content is the dominant value over software and hardware in the wireless 3G economy. When it comes to wireless content, it is helpful for architects to understand the nature of wireless Internet production and the frequency with which digital content will be produced. You can capitalize on the new media and their data types, and make decisions about the tools, content management engines, and system designs that expedite production.

Time frames for content generation are important. Consider traditional architecture for a moment – in a building, space planning for the interior determines where the walls, doors, and rugs go. Architects write space plans that define the general utility of rooms. Space plans change every 3 to 7 years, although sedate homes may stay the same for up to 30 years. A plan for wireless Internet content is analogous to a traditional architectural plan for a building's space. While a database server lasts 5 or more years, the content the database operates on cycles at a rapid pace. The server and many wireless mobile clients share the life of the content.

The turnover of wireless content is an operational activity that the architect also takes into consideration. An effective Internet staff can keep content under control on a seasonal, monthly, or weekly schedule, although individuals work with the stuff on a daily basis. You can frame these cycles in a content plan, as you will soon see.

The Value of Wireless Content

The general value of a wireless system is ultimately derived from its content. Because good content makes a wireless system personable, content needs to be selected and managed well. When wireless technology evolves, it is a medium, and the content, not the device, takes the foreground of people's interest. In a similar way, we speak of television shows without giving much thought to broadcast technology. What goes on in the television station and the wireless Internet server is of interest only to engineers. Content, not control-room techo-ecstasy, ultimately drives the audience.

In the middle 1990s, developers of wireless systems at Sony Software used content from industrial feeds such as the stock market, television guides, and airline information systems. But they found that content could get dangerously out of hand in mobile use. Content such as personal news feeds flooded the memory of handhelds. If you are transmitting data from a large database, it is essential to set boundaries and, if possible, disclose information progressively, as needed, to the mobile traveler. Systems like Marimba and AvantGo give the mobile device an information sandbox where a channel of data such as a magazine source can be refreshed periodically.

Content is the lure that draws people. Valid content matters. Businesses that do not keep their Web sites up to date quickly lose credibility. Dead links pointing to content that is no longer available can be a problem as sources come and go over the Internet. The content of good sites changes often; content of wireless sites more often. Content also has a shelf life. Clearly, recent travel guides are more useful than older ones. To revalidate content, developers use operational feedback in the wireless Internet, as we shall soon see. Using the technology of the wireless Internet, mobile users and editorial staff can keep the collection of information fresh, up to date, original, and precise. Editors need to be provided semiautomated tools so they can easily check the operational system.

Leveraging Feedback and Creating Mobile User Identity

One key to any successful wireless content system is allowing space for the assertion of a personal identity. The traveling persona is fed mobile content, but when mobile, he or she can also feed content to the rest of the wireless network. If your architecture permits the development of personal content, then it can also allow for the housing and sharing of content by the network of users. Bringing together the traveler and the sources of content forms an effective feedback loop. In traditional media, feedback allows readers to ask questions and a publication to follow up with responses. Live musicians instinctively gauge audience feedback so they can adjust the emotional tone of their performance. Social feedback creates natural dialogs that a good Internet architect will extend so that the entire community is in the loop.

Social media contain many feedback systems. Voting is a powerful feedback technique. Rating systems also provide helpful feedback. The letter to the editor and the call-in portion of a radio show are familiar responses to media content. Digital networks are an opportunity for rapid feedback when the content producer and consumer are brought closer together. In electronic networks, the cause and the effect happen so close to each other that it redefines commercial and personal relationships. It changes the nature of applications and human activity. As the communications teacher Marshall McLuhan observed in a 1965 broadcast:

> We have laid out our own electric networks on a global scale by cables, by telegrams, by radio, by all sorts of electric means. These circuits are loaded with data that move instantly and which have become indispensable to all decision making in the Western world; in business, in education, and in politics. These circuits have a peculiar character not just of *connecting* us with one another but also of *involving* us with one another. It is because of the speed. With circuitry the feedback from anything occurs at the same moment that the event occurs.[1]

The way to take advantage of the speedy increase in mobile network feedback depends on an appropriate wireless publishing model. Over the wireless Internet, media production and audience response are almost immediately connected. Feedback loops must be tighter and more responsive in wireless networks than in wired ones. Content that took weeks to collect for publishing now can be gathered in minutes. With alerts and anytime messaging the tempo of feedback with wireless networks creates a greater demand on the content system and the people who operate it. Immediate feedback creates a more direct digital relationship between a business and its customer. In Japan, most i-mode businesses have a special i-mode person on staff now who answers when an i-mode customer presses the standard Phone-to response button. The mobile person's query will connect precisely and rapidly; your operation is a success if you have precision content and a mobile service staff to match. The antenna gives a business service-gain if you have put into place the architecture to prepare it to process the signals of its mobile customers. The culture of the wireless Internet is one of action and immediate response.

Gauging the Frequency of Wireless Publishing

Producers of wireless Internet content want to know how often their audience expects to be "refreshed." The wireless architect can help determine the primary production cycle for content that will best serve the expectations of the mobile audience and set the schedule for the production staff. The selection depends on the nature of the wireless content being gathered and generated, the production effort required, and the time it takes for the audience to provide feedback. It is helpful to examine conventional media as a model; for example, there is some science to the frequency of periodicals.

Consider the range of broadcast media – movies, newspapers, books, TV shows, catalogs, magazines, and radio programs. Some media are produced more frequently than others. Some take more capital and time to produce. Some are consumed more rapidly by the public. Some have global and others have local appeal. Publishing media can be graded according to the time it takes for them to produce content, which generally corresponds to the time it takes for the public to digest the content. The frequency of publishing major media and the typical intervals an audience has to digest the content before receiving "next editions" appear in Figure 105.

One way to evaluate wireless publishing is to examine the amount of time it takes to produce it. Quality media with exceptional talent can take months to create and produce. Each media has its own deadlines (e.g., monthly magazines, daily newspapers, and hourly radio programs), which are the necessary result of the kinds of talent, tools of production, and means of distribution. A wireless publisher needs to know where to draw the line for staff and how to form the circle for the audience.

People expect media to appear at regular intervals. Subscribers get used to this timing. They expect newspapers daily, magazines monthly, television series seasonally, radio news reports hourly, and movies from a studio at least every couple of years. All media can be graded by a sense of immediacy, interactivity, and frequency. At one point the publication is made, at another the audience buys. The tempo of the production process increases in digital wireless systems.

Comparing media by subscribership is useful. On the Web, we measure traffic. In print media, the measurement is circulation. In movies, it is box office receipts. Ratings can provide feedback. Each communication medium has agencies that

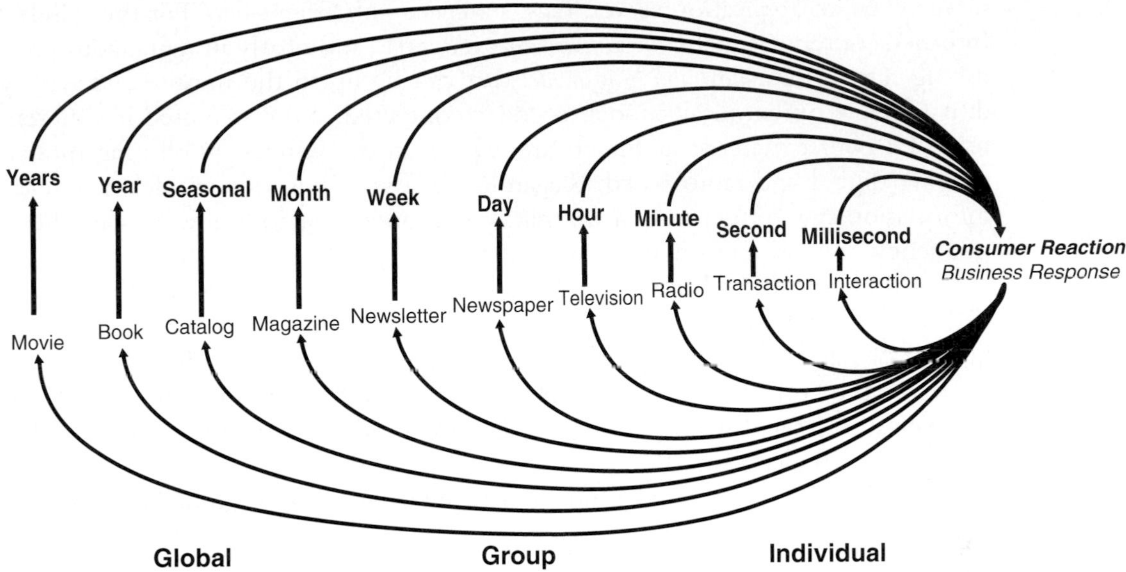

Figure 105 Frequency of media publishing and response

measure its reception in the marketplace and often produce awards to stimulate interest. Other effective audience feedback mechanisms include letters to the editor and critical reviews, some amateur and others professional.

We established that it is best to think of early wireless media as read-only, which is one dimension of the medium. Mobile users cannot be expected to write in, although it is easy for them to gather telemetry. Most people respond immediately, but the assimilation of responses and the distribution of media take time. Movies have a few months to run before the public film format is converted for televised and then private sale. Magazines and books take a while to distribute and for readers to digest. Media have variable frequency formats of operation. For example, a TV show may have a one-hour viewing format, but the "line-up" is seasonal with reruns to follow. TV interjects breaking news and commercials that last only a few minutes, but in general, the audience expects to be entertained on the hour. Readers and viewers of broadcast media have expectations about how often they will receive new material, and your wireless Internet site needs to establish its own frequency of publication.

Radio Publishing Model

Computer servers produce content largely through file systems. This *electronic publishing model* replaces a print publication model. Content of any high frequency, monthly or more often, is best produced from a dynamic database-driven Web server, even an application server. This is a *digital publishing model*. For the wireless Internet, content frequency is a week or even a day, and nearly instantaneous publishing requires a *radio publishing model* that can be up to the minute and widely distributed. Content in all models is collected, edited, and distributed in different ways. Of course, wireless architects are experts in the wireless publishing models that are digital and radio-based. Regardless of the publication model, a wireless information system uses a database that issues content periodically. It establishes a frequency of consumption and production.

For the radio publishing of content, it is important to understand the various cycles of production. The feedback loop is part of the operation, as is the frequency of publishing. Like all radio publishing in 2001, the broadcast territory is fixed and the content within those boundaries is of primary value to consumers. To really understand where radio publishing is headed, we need an example. Let us consider a travel guide.

Consider what it takes to produce a comprehensive city guide that provides personal views. There are many sources of information about travel destinations and travelers who benefit from this knowledge, often orienting their purpose toward guides who share their views. On a seasonal basis, production of such a guide is manageable; on a weekly basis, it starts to become challenging. Wireless architecture for this site needs a solution for a Web server and wireless devices that is responsive to the demands of production as well as to the site's audience. Let us consider what looks like an impossible task. What would it take to produce an international travel guide that covers every hotel, restaurant, shop, and sight and that is updated hourly? The means that, on the hour, the information about every establishment and destination is up to date, all over the world, and available with wireless Internet technology. Realize that the information exists right now; it just is not in your pocket. At this moment all over the world travelers are finding this information; businesses present this information in many media formats. Think small; think personal. A wireless architect would tell you that this information is cellular or, in computer language, distributed. The operational plan for providing information through the system is of special importance. A database engineer would size the data and traffic. An interaction designer would construct one persona for a traveler and one for the owner of a destination. This radio-published guide must work within cells, perhaps with the content remaining available at the sources in a digital format. The operation should probably start with a lower frequency commitment, perhaps seasonally. To demonstrate how a system works, it is helpful to understand a working example. Two organizations that produce the breadth of national content today are the Michelin Guide in France and the American Automobile Association (AAA) guide in the United States.

An architect designs according to a territory and a frequency of publishing the content. Michelin and the AAA can afford a member-supported, national, annual travel guide. They pay professionals to canvas hotels and restaurants, sweeping parts of the country randomly. Combined with maps and a database of business listings, the content appears to stay fairly well up to date. The annual AAA guides are massive, multivolume publications. To move from annual to weekly or daily publication would strain the staff, destroy the presses, and probably risk the credibility of the membership. Ahh, but what about the Internet? Engineers can use some of the production techniques of the annually produced guides to produce a site that offers national travel information, but with more frequent publication.

Let us look at one feature of the travel guide business – restaurants. The production process of a precision global restaurant guide published hourly over the wireless Internet needs to consider resources for reviewers, editors, their travel, production time, cross-indexing, and comparative rating. It appears impossible to do on a global scale. It would cost a fortune to publish with high frequency and keep it up to date. Even a national guide takes a year to assemble for print. On the other hand, this volume of wireless Internet content is virtually free. In the architect's mind is a model of the globe based in reality. At any given second, 3 million people are eating in a restaurant somewhere in the world. Almost every one of them will have a wireless Internet device by 2010. As the world turns, how is it possible to guide these diners?

To answer this, we will examine content tools and methods, and at the end of the chapter continue the example to address how we can be of service to global travelers.

Operating the Cycles of Content

Wireless architects establish the complete identity of a wireless system. The plans, diagrams, and early prototypes help the developers of the system and the operating staff to understand responsibilities. But the wireless architect must go on, because content matters to the business. In constructing the content system, the architect establishes the mechanisms and responsibilities for operations, which include all requirements to obtain, develop, and dispatch content during the periodic cycle. In the example of the world radio guide, the frequency of publication must be set, whether it is seasonal or up to the minute. The frequency of publication implies the frequency of effort to produce the information. Increased frequency of publication adds to the cost of production and the value of the service. It may require more effort to check the facts on a hotel every day than to do so every month, but the traveler will turn to the more current source. Increased frequency of publication generates value. It is important to look at wireless architecture to defray the expense.

Determining the staff and tools it takes to ensure frequent mobile content requires estimates of the development expenses and operational effort. This number can get pretty big using traditional publishing models. But this picture will change when we start to consider wireless participation of the sources of content.

The architect must direct the builders to put in place the right tools for a business to keep content up to date, determine the navigation of the site with the kind of face that delivers the desired content, and set the right timing expectations for the interactive mobile audience. The face of mobile information will not be as large as a television display, but the multitude of wireless digital devices in the hands of mobile users is expected to be one of the most frequently published sources of content ever.

The originator of wireless Internet content transcends the conventional broadcasting model. Rather than transmit media broadly for general reception, a system to generate personal content factors in specific values and often involves the audience in content generation. The exact location of the mobile user, the precise time of day, and the accurate interests of traveling mobile users are not on the radar of broadcasting companies. But these qualities are unique to radio-published, mobile Internet content servers. Consider traditional radio traffic broadcasting in cities. Announcers describe large areas; perhaps every 30 minutes they cover a vast body of commuter information that is relevant only to travelers in specific areas. You have to listen to "everybody's problem" before they get to you. Also wasting time is the "information channel" for most cable TV guides that slowly scrolls over 100 channels every three or four minutes before the endless loop starts again. A wireless Internet channel with good information design can quickly direct users to their desired services.

Wireless Internet Content as Media

Publishing is going through a bit of an identity crisis as it faces the wireless Internet channels. All new communication media start out by doing the work of the old. Motion pictures capture theater performance; television shows movies; print replaces handwriting; and the written word expresses speech. New media technology repurposes and initially adopts the patterns of their parents. An Internet newspaper comes out once a day. It does not have to. And the wireless Internet will do the work of the wired. But it does not have to. Selecting the frequency of content generation is an important decision for a wireless architect, but the setting is totally fluid. Once set, though, your audience will form a network loop based on the timing. To be safe, start slowly and increase the tempo *molto allegro*.[2]

If your chosen content stream mixes text, audio, pictures, and video, it is important to understand the technology and effect of the media. For a creative crash course in comparative media, grab a copy of *Understanding Media* by Marshall McLuhan.[3]

Although the frequency of wireless Internet publication has not been determined, it is clear that mobile travelers will require wireless Internet content to be more frequently generated than prior media forms. To assume that wireless Internet content should do the work of the wired Internet is predictable. But leave that to the PC Internet; wireless content provides new opportunities.

Qualities of Wireless Internet Content

Television and radio broadcasters "program" their seasonal schedules. The term *programming* has different meanings to television professionals and software professionals. But, as we move more to a world of content, software developers can borrow concepts from TV and radio broadcasters. For broadcasters, programming is the art of timing, placement, selecting the talent, and choosing the sources that will satisfy the network of viewers. Interactive digital "programming" (in the broadcast sense) is another dimension content design.

Wireless networks favor spontaneous, frequent, and precise content. The content, which can also be very personal, develops with interactive networks of mobile users. This pattern has emerged from early wireless experience with handheld city guides. It takes perception and time to understand any new media. As all the wireless technology for wireless content comes into play (e.g., voice, audio, images, and text), the ultimate wireless content servers will convert and generate any wireless media form that the mobile user needs at the time. The quality of media convertbility is heightened by mobility, and it will make wireless Internet content distinguish itself from its predecessors. We will look at the ultimate wireless content signal in "Transcoding the Scalable Signal" in chapter 22.

Architects of media are aware that any medium can be offered in a real-time synchronous or delayed asynchronous form. For example, email and voice mail are asynchronous, and instant messaging and a live phone call are synchronous. Escalating media to a real-time audience initially increases the involvement of the owners of the site. However, when the audience is streaming voice and media to one another, the server must get out of the way and simply become a switch.

Mere information becomes important when it is applied. Giving it context and relevance is the frame of location, time, and personality made possible with wireless technology. The fundamental volatility of wireless information can be an advantage over other publications. One problem with traditional media is that once the medium is distributed, it cannot be recalled. Broadcast media do not have the advantage of revising ephemera. Once Internet content is published, if there are mistakes, you can fix the content online eventually – *legato*. With wireless Internet, changes can be made from the field immediately – *molto vivace.*

There is space for history in the lifecycle of wireless content. You probably do not want to show travelers a mobile guide with restaurants that no longer exist. However, it would be tragic for a respectable travel reference to purge forever the restaurant details so carefully gathered – the great recipes, vibrant culture, and memorable stories of fable and legend. Good culture can live on. Most mobile travelers appreciate good culture in all areas of their lives. Travelers often review their trips, the events of their past. One miracle of digital content is that each book is unbound and the bookshelf has infinite length. Databases can show relevant content by any time criterion – now or years ago. Mobile use and later reflection are important profiles in the life of wireless content. History is the piling up of what was once news. An enduring content architectute builds a treasury of historic content from the currency of news.

News is driven by events. Often the headlines of a local newspaper are more important than the global headlines. To the reader, any difference that makes a difference constitutes important information. But each person has a different sense of what matters. As a content developer, you want to be able to provide both nearby and simple changes taking place as well as globally significant ones. Targeting the news to a mobile person can be automatic when information is matched with geocodes and time frames. Personal filters and past interests are often helpful. The newness of news freshens content. Generally, news is best delivered live from the event, as close to the source as possible. Bringing the viewer closer to the source is one of the interesting capabilities of wireless applications.

Designing a Content System

Developers employ a number of tools for use in wireless content architectures. Databases must be planned for servers and devices using XML as a standard bridge. Large databases and servers can benefit from third-party tools such as a content engine. Wireless content is different enough from the wired variety that you should consider creating your own content model.

If you are an information architect or interaction designer, you have used the information design principles described in Part II. These principles help your content make sense to end users, and they can be applied in designing the flow content through the site.

Wireless content can include code, data, and real-time media sources. Bringing this range of content to mobile travelers requires more than database skills. It is sometimes a software design issue. It most often requires editorial talent to keep content alive. But unlike professionally broadcast content, personal content serves personal needs, so the editorial skills and the space in which it is produced are unique. People value direct access to good personal content.

Selecting Content Tools

The wireless development method shown in Part II depends on building a database before writing a wireless application. If you are building interactive applications, then you may be lucky and have a speedy RAD tool to simplify the process of wireless application development. Even these tools depend on your having built a database first. A simple database serves the initial purpose of feeding data to your application so the application can be built and the logic tested. In the first attempts, the database can be changed quickly as you see what mobile content is actually used. It is often a mistake to overspecify databases. Much is learned in the field. Remember the mobile user needs only little bits.

Database experts are the best people to select the final database. As far as physical location of the machine within the server complex, many security aspects will mandate the placement. Database servers are more often placed in Storage Area Networks (SANs) that attach servers and databases with fiber switches that can be hundreds of miles apart. The computer bus that is inches long is now becoming an optical bus of fiber that reaches for miles. Software engineers now learn the database tools for creating tables, defining fields, and generating mobile forms. You may have a mobile content expert take care of defining XML markup and writing DTDs.

Content can be transmitted purely without formatting information. Using an XML browser, the mobile device does its own formatting by simply reading transmitted XML from your content server. This beats the old style of having the server translate XML pages and compute the entire image on the server for each device. Of the many issues that architects consider in designing distribution of content, keeping copies down and using references as much as possible are essential. Database servers are good places to pull together device content; however, there can be many small databases in use. In PAN systems, every device can be a point source for content, all made more convenient with XML Browsers.

Using Databases

The chief content tool is the database. The purpose of any database is not to store data, but to retrieve content easily. Good database architects agonize over the optimal ways to form tables, indexes, and joins to match optimal retrieval patterns. As we saw in chapter 8, the data types for wireless use have to be formed carefully for ready retrieval in interactive maps.

Distributed content ultimately lives in many SQL relational or object databases. Data is often clustered on servers to be able to handle the high traffic loads of primary servers. Content is often encoded in XML, and each presentation device requires an agreed-upon style sheet that can be coordinated by the DTD.

Converting Databases

Converting databases for wireless use requires attention to many elements. If you are converting server-side pages, you may need to extract hard data and dynamic data sources that are embedded in old ASP or JSP pages. You might need to redirect data in the old pages that is fed from an external XML stream and have it "called" within your new page compositions. In redesigning wireless Internet databases, architects or database administrators know the familiar tasks of sizing the data, estimating its volatility, and determining the best data typing; based on how much volume the database must serve, they recommend the best scalable arrangement of devices.

Some time must go into planning how the content is to be cleaned and scrubbed. There are everyday issues of how null values will be handled and how data types are converted to a new wireless data format. A reexamination of sources of the content is important to determine if data conversion or "repurposing" is the best plan. Some editorial and technical content can be repurposed. Often it must be created, which is usually the case with any new media. Wireless content can be acquired by new means.

Obviously, once built, the site must be operated. This is often overlooked in many wireless development plans that emphasize the novelty of end use rather than the realities of ongoing operation. Someone new "owns" the data and must maintain it. On wireless servers, the data changes more frequently than on wired servers. The increased frequency of change may be an added organizational responsibility. A chief engineer or architect must make decisions about whether special tools need to be built to keep content flowing. Good administration server tools may take time to develop initially, but over the total cost of the operation, they usually save significant time. Just like UML tools for code, modeling tools for data like Erwin are invaluable. Some modeling tools will even generate SQL code and tables. As the conversion progresses, the system must be load tested and made ready for 24 × 7 use. The database is tuned, collocation plans are evaluated, and a maintenance program for data is put in place.

Although databases can be repurposed, mobile Internet content is different enough that it needs to be built from scratch. We might get by, by repurposing existing content, but it is better to create new digital content. Experience shows that new technology needs new content. The older formats are not so precise as the new formats, nor are they tuned for retrieval by the new technology. New wireless data types will be undefined in your legacy database. We already pointed out that collections of time-tagged events provide interesting challenges. Also new wireless content depends on new wireless sources.

Studying Newspaper Systems

Content systems require operations. Architects need to separate the working areas required for various professionals who contribute to the steps involved in making content. Writers and editors need useful tools to work within the server. They need to work with content in various stages of development before its release. To get content to reach any device, the data has to be reformatted in XML. Depending on our presentation strategy, the server must retrieve the correct amount of content and present it in the appropriate style. The edition must be staged and the work scheduled. Looking at the way established content systems operate is helpful.

Information flow is important to the architecture of large systems. Because wireless servers largely deliver text, they can make use of content management systems. Electronic newspaper systems pioneered many of the systems and operations now found in content management systems. The newspaper industry has evolved complete systems that are similar to those of many wireless content businesses. The industry reports news stories and creates content with very short deadlines. The stories are edited in stages, authorized, laid out for printing, and then finally distributed. Editions are staged in various draft forms. Stories are held back for a better time, to fill specials or empty areas, to allow space for more important stories, and to fit in all the ads. Editors accept advertising as part of the layout process. The ATG story server is a highly regarded content management system used by some of the most visited Web sites. It is ideal for editorial work.

Content Management Engines

The content management system is useful for large-scale development of many sources of content. The goal of a content management system is to be able to regularly produce a standard publication. As a developer, you may need to work with such a system. Even if you do not use a commercial content management system, they are useful models to study. Although they serve content to the Internet well, they are built for people involved in the process of building, publishing, and maintaining content.

Content engines are useful for large efforts that require quality management and staging of information for digital publication. These systems can manage print and digital versions of a publication. Content architectures must take into account staging sources, editions, and presentations. A newsletter and a newspaper are ink on paper or phosphors behind glass. The production of big media has to deal with significant issues of scale. Personal and mass media all have something to say, but when there are more voices talking – reporters, content experts, news feeds, advertisers, and an audience – a system is required.

A key purpose of content management systems is to coordinate people in the production of content. Reporters create stories, editors compose them, and designers lay out pages. Together they build an edition that is staged for various kinds of approval. To manage the process of coordinating people, system software applies schedules to professional roles and keeps a flow of various content streams organized. The system often stages the publication in various states of readiness as decisions about copy, story length, placement of pictures, writing headlines, and integrating advertising are made. The makers of content management systems include ATG, Vignette, and Interwoven, among others, as mentioned in the section "Personalization Engines" in chapter 18.

These content management systems work by a kind of paint-by-numbers approach to content production. First, a Web developer creates templates to contain content, then lays them out, and finally styles them. Then a database designer defines data control records that point to content sources in a database. Regardless of the way the data stream is stored, it is transmitted as XML. When templates and data control records are merged, they generate publication by streaming files from the database server into the template holes sometimes called portlets. The advantage of this approach is that templates can keep an ongoing style, while data sources can change. This separation of style and content is a cardinal rule of server architecture, but content management may be a more elaborate architecture than most wireless servers need. You can often get by with an XML application server model.

Creating Self-Maintaining Content Systems

Wireless architects are needed to design self-maintaining wireless content systems. If you are lucky enough to originate a content system, there are new tools and practices in wireless content design to use. You want to look at not only the new data elements, but also the topology for distributed data, synchronization points, and application models, as well as your underlying content plan made manifest in an XML DTD.

Digital wireless networks can be hungry beasts to feed. Content happens faster and in greater volume than can be edited and approved. Rather than staff an entire organization to produce content, some Internet businesses involve the consumers of the content in its production. The goal of a content-laden Web information service is to make the content self-regulated so it will not become the casualty of overpowered production methods.

Tools for instantaneously distributed change are fundamentally needed in a vibrant wireless content system. The technical tools are for travelers and administrators. For example, if you were to make a business directory, you would want a way for people to submit their business listings and have an external means to maintain the listings. Otherwise, you would have to hire people to beat the streets and edit everything. The accuracy, quality, and validation of content qualify as important assets. But the production values must be cultivated. Maintaining content requires editorial checks, of course, and editors may use analytical techniques to make information coherent.

Making data collection easy for anyone is essential. Games probably channel more data collection power than any digital technology imaginable, and you have to wonder why their data collection techniques are so fun to use. Using wireless wizardry, the process of collecting information may become far simpler. Perhaps enjoyable. Perhaps invisible. Especially if wireless technology is automatically adding location, times, and machine identifiers in the telemetry.

To help distribute content instantaneously, you can design and make available your XML DTD, thereby establishing your own private, yet common, language for any device. If you post your XML vocabulary, divergent devices and systems will know how to synchronize their content with any devices or servers using that DTD. These posting protocols are part of the .NET server strategy that implements SOAP and UDDI.

Five Rules of Wireless Content Systems

Designing original wireless content systems can benefit from five rules. They give purpose to content and define the relationship between the user and the content, as well as the need for time and allowance for growth.

1. *Understand the use of the content.* Wireless content is meant for use. Contemplating the utility of content is not as obvious as it seems. Content has inherent value and interesting qualities derived from its source. To a content builder, what matters is not what the content is, but how it will be used. Perhaps working with an interaction designer, you will realize what the mobile user will find valuable about it. Then you make decisions about how it is best stored for retrieval and what data type or index will make it relevant or expedite its use.
2. *Direct users to their content.* Mobile users often know what they want. Giving them what they want at any given moment is a key challenge. "Finding" interfaces can get in the way. For every user to be able to connect with her content, classic information design is required. Classic techniques produce useful navigation or indexing systems. Engineers can then cluster content and provide topical classifications to guide users to familiar territory.
3. *Direct content to its users.* It is important that content find its intended audience. Books are written for people, but getting one book in millions to the right audience is a challenge. If content is grouped in clusters, a user will be able to find relevant choices. If you are looking for a great Chinese restaurant, you may already know one. If you ask a good search engine about the one you know, it should return listings of other similar good or nearby Chinese restaurants. This is the difference between a listing and a useful guide. A guide knows how to direct relevant content. If there are places for the audience to organize and make its common values known, then the content can be directed and made available.
4. *Save the user's time.* Search engines and indexes can be effective, but if information is not well organized, it takes multiple requests to find things using traditional search engines, indexing, and browsing techniques. Saving time for your clients is a classic goal of engineering. As we pointed out earlier, the mobile user often knows what she wants, but your study of the user's persona will

reveal more. Engineers simply figure out the shortest path to get desired content to the users.

5. *Allow for the growth of content.* Content is a growing organism. Every content system devised has a chink in its armor. The matter will change. All categories and classifications can be called into question. Effective sources of content of any system need user involvement in maintenance and creation. This leads to the observation that self-regulating content creates effective information systems.

These rules are based loosely on the work of library scientist S. R. Ranganathan who wrote the *Five Laws of Library Science* in 1931.[4] His Indic parables and insights into knowledge classification are highly recommended for students of information architecture. His major achievement, colon classification (i.e., the ":"colon notation used to facet and relate subjects), was complex to implement for librarians. Although rarely used, it is a powerful content-clustering technique, appropriate to personal digital wireless storage systems that need to retrieve information along multiple lines of inquiry.

Involving Users with Content

Content is tied to personal use. To create self-maintaining wireless content, the architectural plan must make room for personal involvement. To most people, geocodes, time formats, and profile keys mean nothing. But the services they yield are the rewards for the involved audience. Content can often be made more relevant with content conversion or lookup functions. Good geocoders magically convert a phone number into an address, and an address into a map.

If the mobile audience grows and wants ever more precisely located and up-to-date content, perhaps the only economical way to increase the content database is to involve users in its creation and development.

Feedback is important to the mobile user, as it is to the developer. Unlike the broadcast model, the wireless network has a rapid return channel, so the system design should include feedback. Monitor feedback and change the loop as needed. But let users see themselves reflected in their personal content and on the stage of the public network. In other words, try to create architecture for participation.

Voting is a playful and powerful feedback mechanism. Showing feedback to a voter during the voting process works wonders. Displaying a vote immediately after it is cast, stacked against all other choices, is not only informative and instructive; it also gives a sense of relationship with others.

Making content a social experience is often engaging to the participants. To sort user-supplied content, the data needs to be identified, tagged, and filtered. The architect may decide on the best techniques for the user to sort and match personal filters to the content. Content has social value when it provides relevant and desired information for others in the network.

Let us return to our example of the hourly published, international radio travel guide. The sense that a site is in touch with the world, with actual people and real places, is special. Travelers can identify with that. Now that travel guides are global, it is not possible even for a set of editors to eat at every restaurant or sleep in every hotel to provide some kind of rating. Somehow, it will take a global exchange of people to establish useful ratings. Personal values are useful and interesting as well. For example, on late-night Napster prowls, you might have thought you were finding an obscure tune by typing in an artist or a title. Yet as you looked further at the collector's music library, you discovered the new tastes of the world. And the content was distributed, living in no particular central database.

Participation in sharing content is gratifying to network members. And it is a wireless architect's job to make sure a system is in place to build and extend content easily. For massive systems, you want users to be part owners of the information. For example, a user can make a note on a handheld of a particularly good dish at a restaurant, and then transmit this to your servers during the next sync. This is the model of Vindigo with Palm PQA and WAP travel information. But the business owners and artists who are sources of this information need involvement as well. Almost everyone is on board the Internet. Being available through the wireless Internet and being on the right search engines, directories, and rating services are necessary for promotion. But larger participatory services almost defy description as they become distinguishable publishing models that are more of an exchange of information between the consumer and the producer.

Quality is always an issue in popular forums, however. You can raise standards, have member certification, and open editorial codes for those who are qualified to produce it. To produce a global guide, it is necessary to train a cadre of people who share common standards. One of the things that make any local guide work is knowledge of the reviewers. You look forward to information from known reviewers because as they work at ferreting out the good and the bad, you know their values.

Criticism of large wireless content sources, like personal Web sites, is as pointless as criticizing a phone conversation. These are presences, for better or for worse. A phone conversation is not content. It is stuff. The difference for engineers is that content is cached and stored, and stuff is not.

21 Chapter

Allowing Personal Stuff: Every Day, Every Moment

The architecture that makes social computing possible is fundamental to the wireless Internet. To plan radio networks via which people will converse, exchange data, map interactively, and control devices remotely requires architects to think in terms of daily activity. They must appreciate how mobile users live the wireless Internet; every day puts new demands on production methods. Tools such as activity diagrams help construct the interactive application for a persona. Personas form mobile networks of people. These mobile networks have important properties for architects. In this chapter, we look at the mobile network's effect on individuals. Their active experiences determine mobile interfaces. They relate to content and personalize their world. Giving mobile travelers a launch pad of a PC start page to customize mobile experiences is a useful addition for developers of wireless sites.

For the architects of buildings, *stuff* refers to the interior design of the changing environment. It includes furniture, throw rugs, desks, phones, pictures, appliances, lamps, and all the things that change position daily or monthly. It is all the stuff on tables (e.g., pens, papers, drinks, notes, magazines) and the books on shelves – all the personal effects that make a working space come alive. As all buildings grow, the burden of stuff taxes the space plan. The warmth and habitability of a structure is determined at this level. In a similar way, the wireless Internet can fill up with stuff (Figure 106).

♦ Just locating my friends ♦ Making an appointment ♦ Talking to people ♦ Checking email ♦ Creating spontaneous networks on the fly ♦ Chatting online ♦ Forming new Bluetooth connections ♦ Listening to DJs ♦ Watching videos ♦ Hearing a newscast ♦ Buying a soft drink ♦ Playing mobile games ♦ Reading cartoons ♦ Making little notes ♦ Checking the sports scoreboard ♦ Turning on a light ♦ Just staying in touch ♦ Listening to music ♦ Show you what I am seeing now ♦ Cutting and pasting messages ♦ Forward hot content like wildfire ♦ Syncing my calendar to stay up to date ♦ Getting direct access to a guide ♦ Keeping people on the air ♦ Beaming a business card ♦ Uploading my shift of parking tickets ♦ Acknowledging you have passed security and printing your portable boarding pass

Figure 106 Wall of wireless stuff

To do what they like whenever they want, to get content on the fly, to make decisions anywhere and anytime, mobile users create their own worlds. In a techno-ecstasy, they send their "stuff" flying through the networks. Personal stuff includes communications such as chat, appointments, cut-and-pastes, beamings – all the ephemera that people live with minute by minute, connected to their friends, family, and professional lives. It almost sounds like I am saying that users are babblers who just want to hear themselves talk. If you believe Marshall McLuhan, who proclaimed that "the medium is the message,"[1] content makes no difference. After all, it is just bits that fill the air. There is a difference, however, in the content of messages. Having something to say attracts like a magnet. In other words, messages differ in their power to build audiences, form feedback loops, and generate traffic. Your voice and your content are heard by listeners who expect that the message will contain something of value to them, that is, a reason to stay tuned. For example, we will listen to a scratchy AM radio station for a special announcement or use a staticky cell phone to get emergency information. In speech, the music of emotion has a universal appeal, more than elocution or logic. Nevertheless, it is important that architects of wireless network technology make transmission of all this "stuff" civil and simple. Getting people to the final interesting bits – the payload of communication – and simplifying personal life is a chief outcome of successful wireless architecture.

Building a Mobile Architecture

The best "buildings" in wireless architecture are adaptable and enduring. Planning must anticipate the shifts and changes in the lives of mobile people and the burden of content they must have at their fingertips. In addition, server architectures must learn when and how to ignore content. For example, you certainly do not want to cache a voice conversation. Content is being created as it is happening so that the person I am connected to sees what I am seeing and hears what I am hearing *now*. Wireless applications are the means to transmit experiences, but these ephemera are rarely stored. There are further shifts in architecture caused by the great mobility of the wireless Internet.

Mobile servers. One new architectural emphasis brought on by mobile use is that connection and session management needs an entirely new approach. Mobile users connect, disconnect, and reconnect in unpredictable ways. Telco architecture once ensured a voice circuit with a distinct beginning and a distinct end; the circuit was either opened or closed. Now a user might run off in the middle of a data call without indicating that he is finished. Computer architecture once delimited a session over a physically established wire between two machines. Now the user might run off in the middle of the session and return 30 minutes later expecting to pick up where he left off. In the meantime, the user may have changed to another device or a different connection topology. New memory caching, client software, event volumes, media calls, and dependent messaging require new and robust server software.

More robust server. We have discussed how wireless networks increase the tempo of digital content and that there is much more of it to store. People expect rapid service networks to be up all the time and, if they ever go down, to be repaired immediately. The system has to be ready at all times and must keep working. To provide 24-hour service, the network and server architecture must be robust.

Feeding the Internet. One other new activity created by new wireless technology is that devices now feed the Internet. Consumers can take on the roll of producers. Wireless cameras and other mobile Internet devices will continue to provide increased content. The vertical markets already deploy wireless handhelds as data-gathering tools to feed a wireless Internet server. A person making a phone call is engaging in a kind of "voice publishing." At the same time, these devices provide common points on the Internet to coordinate people.

Wireless content lifecycle. Probably the greatest architectural challenges of our times are to determine the user content worth preserving and to design a lasting medium for storage. Digital standards and computer systems are notoriously obsolescent. What original software or important contract written on a 5¼" disk from the 1980s can be read today without going to a museum of computing devices? Stewart Brand's *The Clock of the Long Now* reflects deeply on the subject as he describes the project to construct the world's slowest computer – a clock that keeps time for 10,000 years.[2]

Whole persons. Another shift important to wireless architects, identified in 1991 by the General Magic team led by Marc Porat, is the idea of "whole person thinking." This shift involved moving from a specialist and segmented "work here" and "personal activity there" approach to system design resulting in integrated approaches to managing information, news, communication, and one's time. The team's mission was to create a communicator to integrate all parts of one's life. Today, wireless applications include personal and business software and content. Devices let mobile travelers stay in touch using voice and messaging to both personal and corporate networks. Having all your information comfortably on you is important. Data architectures and applications that share content are essential. For a long time, systems like Lotus Notes have provided group calendars and contact management software. It is important to evaluate realistically how well your architecture accommodates the daily life of the whole person – your end user. Mobile living integrates everything.

Keeping Content Alive

To keep content interesting and relevant, your architecture should include operators, their operating tools, and talent. Consider staffing for a "wireless DJ," who, like disk jockeys (DJs) in radio stations, would program the content and play the "music" people want to hear. The wireless architect must be aware that, although much thought is put into engineering the delivery of wireless Internet technology, further thinking should go into workflow and "control room" tools for the operating staff to deliver live and interesting content on a momentary basis. To excel, a network may need real-time components, shared data spaces, location-shared and time-shared data streams, and media streams.

New Sources of Content

As we learned in Part II, it is best to develop content early in a wireless project. The real world is made of massive volumes of information. It is fun to build these kinds of systems. But the project needs to start with only a representative sample.

The new digital content is demanding. Consider guides. Mobile wireless Internet information is far more precise, as well as efficient with time and space, than data in earlier types of publication. New digital content systems are being updated constantly with times, locations, and deep content that would be prohibitively expensive in an older editing and distribution model. New systems are up to the minute, while older ones are often out of date. Conventional travel guide information is simply not tracked closely enough, nor maintained often enough, for a mobile digital audience.

The public may provide content, if your architecture permits. The mobile network of people can help a system achieve the goal of broad, useful content based on direct experience. People with live wireless devices might have peculiar identifiers that CC/PP agents transfer. Your data structures must encode new device attributes and owners' qualities; your workflow needs to handle the many paths of data. The emerging effect of the wireless Internet is that *you are the next mobile application*. Developers might build a restaurant guide listing every restaurant in the world, but without a formation of diners, the network will have limits. The content and the system suffer unless people contribute content on some level. The network becomes the source for the latest word. Your database may store the table talk, the ratings, the reviews of hundreds of diners per restaurant, but you will need the tools of information design covered in Part II to bring forward the content in a meaningful way.

When we take wireless architecture out to the edge of the network – away from servers and gateways – to the place where people actually use it on a moment-by-moment basis, wireless applications become interesting. This is where you beam your business card to a friend, where you make a call, or where you change a calendar appointment. The product requirement for this kind of infrastructure is not as clear as that of an inspection system that processes wireless records or of a Bluetooth printer that generates a traffic ticket. But such personal tools make a wireless system dear to the hearts of the network of mobile users.

Building Networks for Mobile People

As people walk and talk, on the go, they are busy with things every hour of the day. Part of the social pattern to consider when making mobile applications is the amount of time people have on their hands. While commuting on public transportation, people may want to pass time with games and messages. If they commute by driving, they may be receptive only to stories and conversation. Many others periods during the day also offer opportunities for assistance.

People Relate to Content

Architects can structure the application flow so that mobile users (1) find the information, (2) understand the information, and (3) trust the source of the information. Ultimately, a content network is valued because the content is informative or entertaining. In networks, a good "DJ personality" cultivates relations and interests that can increase subscribers.

When relying on the content of others in the network, it is important to create a way to qualify your sources. When you read a review, one of the first things to ask is, "Who says so?" Some ranking of credibility or identity affiliation of viewers is helpful. Knowing the cultural value of a good reviewer in your network can save you a lot of time because networks have their own social and cultural order. They are often served well by many points of view; however, too many opinions and views can become confusing, and leave the network uniformed or ill informed.

Technology can spark popular interest. If it is too complex, however, it can stall. The iDEN phone system is popular because it lets people speak without dialing. The simple technology of shared voice circuits simplifies the conventional point-to-point WAN circuit call. It appears WAP is too complex to succeed. i-mode is too simple to fail.

Personal interests often spark communication technology. Inventors sometimes fool around in the lab and are inspired by the raw technology. For example, Samuel Morse, the inventor of telegraphy, was an artist enthralled with the idea of electricity. Although he misunderstood electricity, his intuitive sense of its value for communication was right. At other times inventors look to build the services and interactions that people want. For example, Alexander Graham Bell invented the telephone while attempting to create a device that could communicate with his deaf mother. Likewise, the Internet web was designed just to be able to exchange documents in a research lab. These three inventions have proved useful beyond their origins and evolved beyond expectations as a result of human needs and desires. Look at a few people you know and consider their networks of people. Their basic needs are constant and simple. Awareness of human necessity is the mother of many inventions.

One goal of wireless architecture is to make sure that wireless devices and servers allow a person to do daily things easily. Of course, a person often coordinates with other lives and other systems. Wireless distributed architecture is designed initially to serve mobile individuals. Its circle of influence is small. When the circle spreads, then group qualities become important. And there are multiple groups that need to be served. A week of business calendar appointments come and go fluidly through a group server like Domino. To use them effectively, a person needs to coordinate with clients, family, and friends. Important events require coordination. The whole person needs attention.

Wireless architecture exists to make the wireless life better, one aspect of which is security. Think through the network's structure of security. Is it necessary or is it too onerous to get anything done? Unlike business NT systems that assume hostile intent, artists openly connect and use Apple computers and security is added later. Security measures that are difficult to use are sometimes discarded by their owners, which leaves systems open to attack.

Demographics, Profiles, Personas, Identities

When designing the primary persona for a project, it is useful to look generally at people as a group and allow for specific values of personal identity. A broad sense of demographics and profiles is helpful. *Demographics* is the study of statistical grouping of a population's characteristics. The technology adoption curve (Figure 9 in chapter 2) shapes itself to a progression of mobile users, each with a demographic profile. A technology runs its course from youthful hobbyist, to businessperson, to general consumer, to skeptical conservatives. The progression is said to be hobbyist experimenters looking for breakthroughs, early adopting visionaries, early majority practical shoppers, late majority conservatives, and the traditional skeptics. The overall trend shows an increasing lack of interest in becoming competent in technology. It is essential when building technology to match the available technology and application interfaces to the appropriate profile of user.

Motorola, Inc., works with four mobile user profiles: technophile, businessperson, fashion-conscious, and family-oriented. The technophile is enthusiastic about advanced function and utility. The businessperson looks for technology that will pay for itself, and she is attracted to time and information-management features. The fashion-conscious person makes social impressions and wants to connect with status and style. The family-oriented member wants unification, security, and communication that benefit the whole family.

There are as many good reasons to make your product have broad appeal as there are reasons to target it to a profile of users. Early technology products that are targeted are more successful because they do not have to answer a longer requirements list, which can have conflicting needs in a broad population. Products for men or products for women are often more effective than a gender-neutral approach. For example, targeting advertisements of pickup trucks to men has a very strong effect. Another characteristic worth considering is age, which can meaningfully target a product by its appeal to infant, youth, teenage, starting adults, working adults, or retired consumers. Further, ethnicity can be a defining consideration. For example, people go to an Italian restaurant or listen to soul music because of the cultures. Belief systems also indicate strong populations according to religious, moral and ethical inclination; married or single orientation; professional and economic status; and other points of interest. Profiles set general boundaries for use, but are often too general to specify the needs of a wireless application. Ultimately, a project needs to construct a persona and to envision specific behavior and employ development tools to plan its system accordingly.

A key realization is that although developers build for a mobile persona as a separate entity, the mobile persona is often a manifestation of our desktop self. *We are different personas at different times*. When we look for a cheap meal, it is not necessarily because we are poor. We are multidimensional. We are not stereotypes. We are identities. We change aspects of our persona often. It is as if we have special masks, change hats, or put on new clothing to wear our information in a different way. weaving the mobile persona's fabric is the wireless architect's key to success.

The Active Experience in the User Interface

We have observed that the mobile user is unique, so we develop personas to identify the characteristics to build applications. Engineers can build the persona application with advanced tools that map out the persona's activity, describe actions, and measure interfaces. Wireless development has its own language, its own notation. Like any revolution, thinking precedes action; language precedes formed thought; notation precedes social communication; and play is the root of all scribbling. Wireless projects evolve from playful imagining on a whiteboard to the discovery of revolutionary concepts through the help of useful notation and modeling tools.

Wireless Notation and Tools

Many professionals start planning projects by drawing on whiteboards with erasable markers. As other people look on and contribute, it is easy to add and subtract the interoperating elements of a sketched conceptual model. When we build models, we structure our thoughts.

Location is now a part of application architecture, so let us look at the whiteboard for a wireless location application (Figure 107), which illustrates the key elements of a location-based mobile transaction system. This figure has the key elements you want to see in a sketch: people, devices, networks, and servers. A collection of whiteboard drawings would show entirely different gestures, figures, and cartooning because professionals develop their own standardized notation to help them clarify the various elements they are working to form into one system. Regardless of the notation you use, whatever you do, always put a person in the picture.

Here are some helpful notes on working with whiteboards:

- Blue ink erasable markers are generally the most visible and easiest to erase. You can mount 4 × 8–foot sheets of construction-grade, white bath panel for projects.
- Draw with your arm, not with your wrist, so that people at the back of the room will see your image. Practice.
- To develop your own iconography, study notation and cartooning. *Understanding Comics* by Scott McCloud and *Notes on Graphic Design and Visual Communication* by Gregg Berryman are helpful.

Figure 107 Whiteboard for a wireless location application

- If your drawing is shaky, have a deck of cards printed with the common iconic elements (e.g., CDMA tower, GPRS handset, and telco switch). Label each illustration.

The depiction of wireless Internet applications matures during the process: first, get it going; next develop the basic solution; and finally provide the operating service. To get things going, it is helpful to illustrate the server and client and where input, processing, and output take place. For reference in developing the solution and implementing the service, the sketch can be redrawn as a UML (Unified Modeling Language) diagram. UML systems provide excellent professional notation for wireless Internet projects. UML defines classes and objects, and can show sequence and collaboration. A number of diagram techniques show different views of the system at hand and let an architect define the components and their relationships, examine the logic, and show concurrency, change of state, and deployment. Other development tools that have useful diagrammatic qualities include editors, emulators, SDKs, IDEs, and RAD tools. For complex systems, the UML code modeling tools such as Rational Rose, Together J, and Visio are ideal. Most of these tools have code generators. But the important part for architects is that they provide multiple notation systems that let them model the individual persona's activity. The activity diagram is the most used notation system in wireless architecture.

Wireless Activity Diagrams in Development

A number of UML interaction diagrams are useful for wireless development. The most useful wireless application diagrams include activity, sequence, and collaboration diagrams. The activity diagram is particularly useful because the notation articulates a flow of activities involved in a single process. The activity diagram shows how activities depend on one another, as well as all the components and transactions in order. It describes the action-based interfaces of wireless applications.

Lets look at the activity diagram (Figure 108) that corresponds to our whiteboard notation for a wireless location application (Figure 107). On the whiteboard, the wireless location application shows that a traveler accesses and navigates a location-based content server that returns maps and merchant coupons for transactions on a merchant's Bluetooth register. The activity diagram for a wireless application shows how these things happen. The top of the diagram shows the four involved classes of activity: Traveler, Web phone, Network, and Guide server. The lines trace the activities of a traveler as they are guided to a destination merchant using location-based network and device technology.

The process begins at the black Start circle at the top and ends at the concentric white/black Stop circles at the bottom. Activity diagrams can be divided into

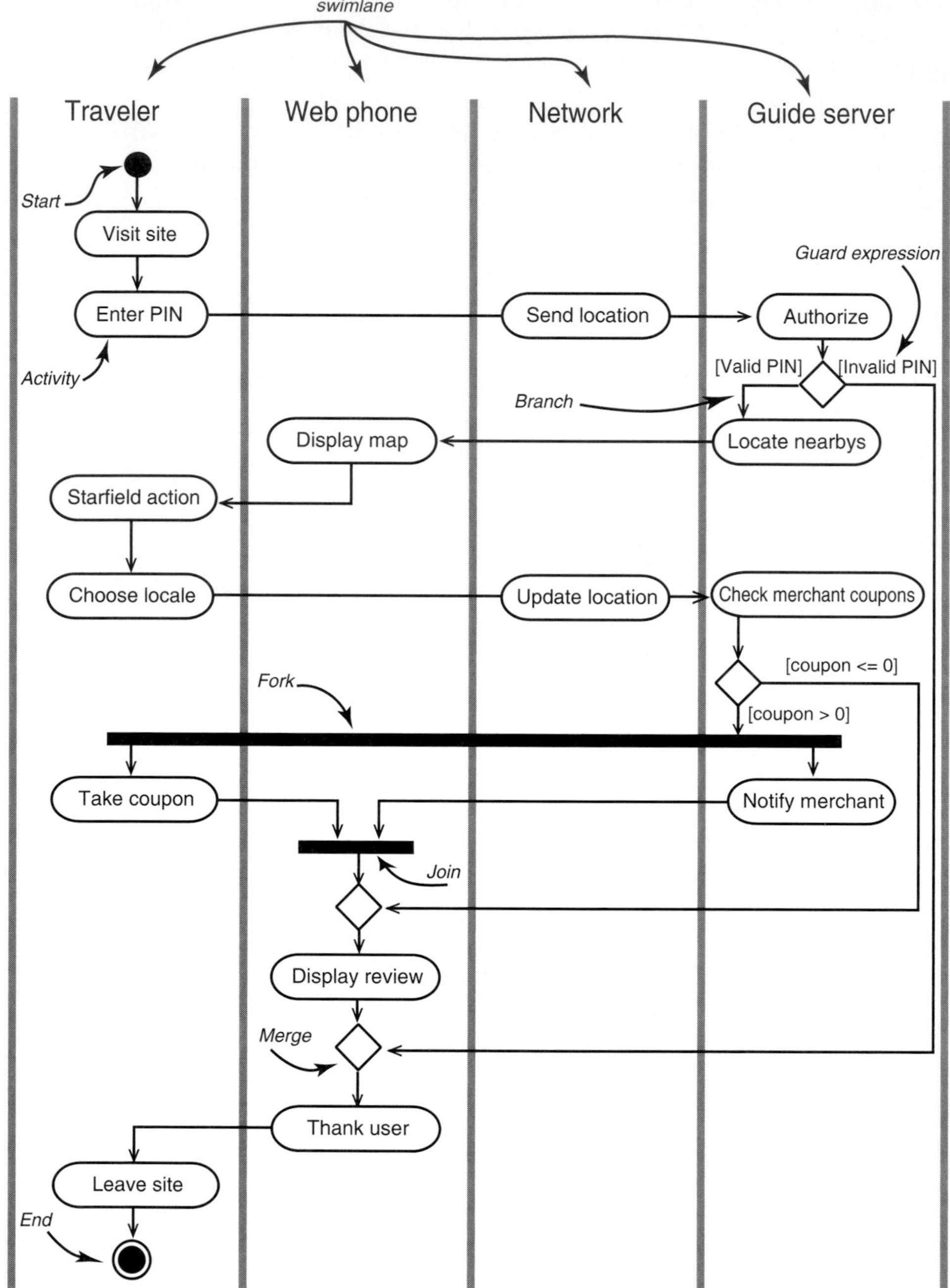

Figure 108 Activity diagram for a wireless location application

class "swim lanes" that determine which object is responsible for which activity. The activities are represented by rounded rectangles. A single transition comes out of each activity, connecting it to the next activity. The single transition may branch, shown in the diagram as a diamond, into facets of mutually exclusive transitions. The branched transitions are labeled by guard expressions inside brackets [ ] with the label for each branch. A subsequent merge marks the end of a branch, also shown as a diamond. A transition may fork into two or more parallel activities, shown in the figure as a solid bar. The bar may fork transitions or be matched by a bar that joins the threads of the first fork.

For more information on modeling languages and automatic tools, visit <www.omg.net> and <http://www.rational.com>. Activity and other UML diagrams are discussed at <http://www.togethersoft.com/services/UMLShortCourse/index.html>.

Studying Users in Motion

The overall purpose of your application is not to get people to talk or type, but get them to act. Your application and content exist to facilitate user action. Users rely on a user interface. A computer interface traditionally is made of a user conceptual model, a display interface, and a command interface. Users build a model of the environment in their minds. An environment must be consistent and predictable so that it easy to use. For example, dynamic displays on wireless devices can provide meaningful output. Great interaction design and information architecture can be the groundwork for engineering a successful interface. Interfaces can be as natural as talking on a cellular phone; at other times a skill like typing or handwriting can be learned. The simple Palm OS® and the visual Magic Cap™ operating system are fine examples of useful and appealing mobile user interfaces. The best wireless interfaces and architecture are invisible. You do not "boot" a phone; the interface design would not permit it and telco engineers spent a long time figuring out how to make communication devices as automatic and bulletproof as possible. Measuring command user-interface methods against goals and objects can improve the efficiency of interfaces.

Measuring Interfaces

Planning for user interaction and "putting a face" to the persona is an effective method to define and focus a project. Sometimes you have to conduct usability studies to analytically compare and qualify alternative interfaces. Some commonsense rules of interface are based in engineering study. A classic rule is *Fitt's law,* based on research done at Xerox Corporation's PARC (Palo Alto Research Center) for the first mouse-based Alto and Star desktop computers. A study was made of people using the mouse and graphical display. The law quantified that people are more successful when the targets are bigger and they move shorter distances. Restated, make frequently accessed areas bigger and closer.

Jeff Raskin, who made key usability decisions for the Apple Macintosh project, describes classic rules and techniques to improve interface. Having observed the continued success for simple and intuitive solutions, he explains, "The first law of interface design should be: A computer shall not harm your work or, through inaction, allow your work to come to harm."[3] Raskin reminds us of a technique to measure interfaces that can be applied to alternative wireless interfaces. Applied to large systems, it can help us make better decisions for the mobile user. In 1983 Card, Moran, and Newell documented a method to measure key interface components: GOMS – goals, objects, methods, and selection rules (Table 46). When a person uses software, you measure the time for all activities – every key press, use of a graphic input device (GID) such as a mouse or pen, and even time for mental preparation. Standard wireless network activities can be extrapolated to the model (Table 47), although latency is a highly variable factor.

In practice, the numbers in Tables 46 and 47 vary widely depending on the actual device, the content, and the user's experience. For example, K can be 0.1 sec for a skilled typist who types 120 words per minute (wpm), 0.2 sec for a more typical typist with a rate of 55 wpm, or 1.2 sec for a beginning typist. Also, network latency for packets can take 5 sec or 10 sec depending on numbers of subscribers. Circuit connect latency can actually reach 30 to 60 seconds for the first call. By using these numbers, it is easy to see why a shift from circuit-switched networks to packet-switched networks is popular. In the time it takes to operate

Table 46 Goal, Object, Method, Selection

Code	Time (sec)	Activity	Explanation
K	0.2	Keying	The time it takes to tap a key on the keyboard
P	1.1	Pointing	The time it takes a user to point to a position on a display
H	0.4	Homing	The time it takes a user's hand to move from the keyboard to the GID or from the GID to the keyboard
M	1.35	Mentally preparing	The time it takes a user to prepare mentally for the next step

Source: Raskin, J. *The Humane Interface.* Copyright © 2000 AMC Press. Reprinted by permission of Pearson Education, Inc., pages 73–74.

Table 47 GOMS applied to wireless networks

Code	Time (sec)	Activity	Explanation
W	1	Web phone keying	The time it takes to multitap an average key on a Web phone
D	2	Digital packet latency	The time a user must wait for a digital packet reply or connection
A	10	Analog latency	The time a user must wait for a circuit network to reply to input
C	20	Circuit connect	The time a user must wait for a circuit network to open a connection

one circuit-switched application, you could complete at least two packet-switched applications.

These calculations may look like bean counting, but it is sometimes important to account for *all* the time it takes to use a wireless application. With this tool, you can summarize competing interfaces. For example, it takes 363 keystrokes to buy a book on Amazon.com on a WAP phone, which adds up to nearly 5 minutes. For wireless applications, note the improved latency and connection times of a 3G packet network over a 2G circuit network. Save users' time. To achieve that end, work with them to see if entire screens can be eliminated and how they might act more directly with the content.

Putting the Internet in Motion with Live Sources

Television does not get any more exciting than reading black-and-white text on a color screen. In 1968 four words – "Live from the Moon"– appeared on the bottom of the telecast during the historic visit. Place and time can have a special magic. As the science fiction writer Arthur C. Clarke wrote, "Any sufficiently advanced technology is indistinguishable from magic."[4] And magic is exactly what GPS is. It is invisible and available, informing interfaces and challenging content makers to be more precise.

Using mobile location-based and time-based content, you can create live mobile experiences with emerging location-based applications. As your wireless applications mix PAN configurations of sensors, scanners, magnetic card readers, interrogators, and other exotic antennaed devices, they feed content live to the wireless Internet.

Coordinating and sharing content in real time requires server software and client software. The Ricoh i700m wireless Internet camera can take a digital picture, email a picture, surf the Web, send pictures with FTP, and edit an HTML picture book. Infotrends of Boston forecasts that 80 million people worldwide will transmit mobile wireless photos by 2004.[5] Having gone to the trouble of capturing a memory, people do not want to lose it. Sharing voice circuits and media streams are other good choices. Deploying this kind of technology needs a lasting architecture for content management and classification.

Anticipating the Personal Value of Networks

The value of networks increases as more people connect and technology improves. The increasing power of network, bandwidth, computers, and storage is having a dramatic effect on the evolution of the wireless Internet. The following "laws" of digital technology are used by analysts to make general plans.

- Law of computer value: *Computer processing power doubles every eighteen months.* This law was stated by Gordon Moore of Intel Corporation, based on historical analysis of the number of components per chip. It is also called Moore's law, or the law of the microcosm.
- Law of network value: *The value of the network rises as the square of the number of participants.* This law was first stated by Bob Metcalfe, one of the inventors of Ethernet. One fax machine is useless, two are useful, and the more there are, the better. The value of a network increases with the number of users. Metcalfe originally formulated this concept in 1973 at Xerox PARC.[6] He observed that in the beginning when the cost of technology is fixed, and the number of people is additive, there is a crossover point when the multiplied value exceeds the fixed value. At this point, the market explodes, as more people want to take advantage of this newly created value. Also called Metcalfe's law, or the law of telecosm.
- Law of disk storage: *Disk storage density doubles every year.* A statement by industry analysts in 1996 based on historical trends in density of manufactured disks. In 1998 worldwide digital storage capacity exceeded the amount of information in the world. EMC estimates that today there are about 10 exobytes of information spread over the Internet. This is up from 200 terabytes in 1995.[7]
- Law of bandwidth: *Bandwidth grows at least three times faster than computer power.* George Gilder stated this law in 2000 in his book *Telecosm*.[8] As the power of terminals, bandwidth and storage capacity rise simultaneously, so does the value of accessing them. His analysis is that the Internet increases in value one thousand times every 5 years. Also called Gilder's law.

- Law of wireless network capacity: *Wireless network capacity doubles every 30 months.* As stated by Martin Cooper in 2001.[9] This is based on the analysis of the number of voice and data transceivers since 1900, as illustrated in the diagram in the next chapter, "Increasing usage of wireless spectrum" (Figure 110). The Law of wireless network capacity is also called Cooper's law.

If only batteries and power had a matching exponential rule. As mobile wireless devices introduce more powerful processors, brighter and more colorful screens, higher-bandwidth modems, increased memory and disk storage, and are in service longer to connect to more people and services with more than one antenna on a device, then their battery life goes down, down, down. This reminds me of a famous wireless Internet joke told in Silicon Valley.

> A wireless device inventor walks into the lobby of a hotel and puts down his suitcase to play with his new contraption. The thing is remarkable. It is thin as a card, has a bright color screen, and fits the hand. The inventor taps on his email inbox, and reads messages by clicking on a link that displays some Internet pages in full color. A crowd of businesspeople gathers. Someone asks the inventor for an Internet map of the city. The inventor holds up the device and speaks to it, "Turn down the lights and show me the neighborhood." The device emits a remote control signal that dims the lobby lights and a colorful map appears, lit up with dots in the area. He commands, "Print it." As the fax machine at the front desk whirs off the map, he tunes the device to a color television station, and then to an XM satellite radio to get some music. People start handing over their business cards. He passes them over the screen, which reads them in. The venture capitalist takes him aside and says, "Gee, that is the most amazing personal device I have ever seen. How much do you want for it?" The inventor says, "Well, this is the only one ever made. I guess I could sell it for $5000." The investor writes out a check and darts off with his prize. The inventor shouts, "Hey, you forgot the suitcase," pointing down to the large, 50-pound suitcase he had brought in. "It has the battery and the antenna."

An amazing amount of personal technology is coming our way. The explosive growth of network technology we are building has an effect on both society at large and people as individuals. We have already seen how digital media, governed by frequency of publication, creates a tempo of feedback that increases the responsibilities of enterprises and the participation of individuals. The networks, ethereal and remote, now speed the voice and content of electric personae to people. On a personal level, phone conversations can lack substance. To encounter a "phony" derives its meaning from the impersonal and sometimes dishonest impersonations of telephone callers. The cool personalizing quality of the wireless Internet technology can restore identity that has been made impersonal ever since the invention of electric networks. Marshall McLuhan metaphrased Walter Cronkite, the popular CBS news anchor of the time.

> Look, when Mr. Cronkite says, "That is the way it is," he is charismatically telling you what sort of a fantasy world you are living in. Because at the speed of light there is no reality – it is all fantasy. There is no real world at the speed of light. It is ALL fantasy. Science fiction is the only reality left to us because we live at the speed of light. At the speed of light, we do not have physical bodies. We also do not have identity. And when you do not have an identity, you become very upset. And you become very violent in your quest for identity. But we live in a very violent age, which is eager to find out who are we – what are we made of.[10]

Asserting an identity through a persona is the revolutionary promise of the wireless Internet. As feedback loops tighten, the content that used to take weeks to collect now takes only minutes. The alert message and the mobile query connect precisely and rapidly, if you have precision content to meet the match. The culture of the wireless Internet is one of immediate response. Bureaucratic and corporate accountability can no longer be systematically delayed.

Our wireless technology can drive people to distraction and put them in strange states of consciousness. You can walk into a room where you see a man seemingly talking to himself. He is a perfectly dressed business professional in a white shirt and tie who is flailing his arms, gesturing to strange places in the room, and speaking random phrases out loud, and then turning to gaze toward the horizon like some lost actor on a stage. He is oblivious to your presence. You might as well be a ghost or an angel passing through his life. Up close, you see little ear-bud headsets and an R380 cellular microphone dangling by his mouth. You do not need supernatural powers to read people's thoughts (like the angels in the movie *Wings of Desire*). Today's cellular conversation is all laid out for the world to hear and judge. Walking into the next room, you might see a woman talking aloud with her finger in her ear. She is using the "bone phones" that transmit conversation through her hand. NTT has shown these for a few years now. At other times professionals who are talking with you normally, might grip and squint at an electronic clipboard; they are keeping the electronic handwriting software up to speed as they listen and write what you are saying. A car comes into view with an animated driver talking into a cell phone. As the car speeds by, a kid in the back seat happily waves at you. To break from the somnambulistic technology trance and realize the world around – that may be the un–killer application.

Increasing Awareness to Facilitate Participation

As you develop wireless applications, you can add social qualities to increase participation. Often the programming is easy, but you need to stop and consider the social effects of your work. Social experiences make people aware of one another; for example, audiences laugh, sports fans cheer. The need to share social awareness is true of wireless networks. As you build messaging, browsing, interactive, and voice portal applications, remember to provide a collective view for the participants. People like to see themselves. Give them "mirrors." Give them visibility. Networked chorus effects achieved with instant messaging enhance the value people derive from using your network. Here are some examples. Network games are far more popular when they have a messaging window for players to talk with one another as they play. When people answer a survey, immediately show how they voted with respect to everyone else. Web Crawler was one of the first Internet search engines that showed the latest query. It was fun just to watch what other people were asking and it was trivial to program. Amazon shows you what the best sellers are in your city. Visibility of the activity of social networks is perhaps a deep-rooted tribal value, especially if we are living now in a global village.

Personalizing the World

Your architecture must provide the means to support personalization. Mobile users thrive on it. Palm OS handheld owners depend on having personal information with them at all times. An architect makes sure that the PC start page, the mobile components, and the general service delivers personal value. Mobile users personalize their site for mobile use. Wireless portals like OracleMobile, Yahoo, and Verizon use the PC as a primary interface for customers to use their wireless devices. You can give the mobile user a view of the Web on the go.

Let users speak with your portal or type input, browse it, or run a model of it. It is their time. They perfer to use their language when they can or your language if they have to. They may use a personal gisting vocabulary, their own notations, and their own commands to get things done. Their mobile culture includes messages, maps, and discovered information. Their personal wireless devices connect with other wireless devices.

The inevitable trend toward personalization and the sheer multiplicity of options were made clear in 1970 when Alvin Toffler's best-seller *Future Shock* was published. In the chapter "The Origins of Overchoice," Toffler refers to McLuhan's observation made in 1967 that "it will be just about as cheap to turn out a million differing objects as a million exact duplicates. The only limits on production and consumption will be the human imagination."[11] The frontier of personalization continues to be pushed on the Internet. This trend from standardized production to personal creation is the story of photography. Many people now take their own pictures rather than hire professionals or use stock photographs. The movement from mass manufacture to extreme personalization continues. For example, today you can create customized clothing over the Internet. The Customatix shoe site lets the PC viewer simulate billions of combinations of athletic shoe designs. Viewers can make many choices and create personal designs. The plan is transmitted via XML to China where the templates are printed in Chinese. Your personalized shoes are shipped to your address.

When building wireless Internet technology, consider the culture of the mobile network, a plan for personalization, and the many issues of personal and device identity. The Internet lets people shop remotely. The wireless Internet lets people participate directly.

Personalization Engines and Agents

The masses of unique mobile individuals use wireless personalization technology. If the number of mobile users is small, you can implement a solution by defining profiles. Both mobile users and services can be defined in tables that live in SQL databases. Use personalization engines to handle heavy traffic. These engines provide optimal service that matches choices against products, ads, editorial content, and the selections of other users. For a more comprehensive technical discussion of personalization, read the section "Personalization Engines" in chapter 18.

Where does personalization lead us on the wireless Internet? The architectural mastery of personalization and customization underscores digital presence. A presence is qualified by time, location, and identity for people, machines, and services. The services of intimate tailoring are major components of mobile commerce systems. Convenient commerce depends on the selective revelation of intimate details of your life. The frontiers of personalization are rooted in personal identity. The development of a personal agent can relieve the tedious reentry of personal information. Perhaps a rebirth of personal culture stems from this extreme personalization.

In the ultimate electronic marketplace, XML is the blanket we are weaving over which merchandise, buyers, and sellers meet. As we define digital personas and define the processes of their activation, the evolution is toward an agent process. The process represents buyers and sellers through dialogs and protocols of discovery, negotiation, and transaction. In a full extension, agents manifest your presence and can be given parameters to make choices, which is what the General Magic Telescript system did in the early 1990s. The Telescript agent could be told to shop for something in a certain price range, visit any Telescript server, and execute a best price transaction. It never reached the public because this ultimate eCommerce system was extremely difficult to program, even for expert software engineers. Meanwhile at CERN, Tim Berners-Lee had just finished making his first Web page an invention so simple that millions can use it.

Personal agents may manifest presences as standardized avatars. An avatar is a full representation of a person or object in cyberspace. In the "Metaverse"

Bali Ha'i
May call you,
Any night, any day.
In your heart
You'll hear it call you
"Come away, come away."

Bali Ha'i
Will whisper
On the wind of the sea,
"Here am I,
Your special island
Come to me, come to me!"

Your own special hopes,
Your own special dreams
Bloom on the hillside
And shine in the streams.

If you try,
You'll find me
Where the sky meets the sea,
"Here am I,
Your special island!
Come to me, come to me!"

Figure 109 Bali Ha'i (*Source:* Lyric excerpt from "Bali Ha' i" by Richard Rodgers and Oscar Hammerstein II. Copyright ©1949 Richard Rodgers and Oscar Hammerstein II. Copyright renewed by Williamson Music, owner of publication and allied rights throughout the world. International copyrights reserved. Reprinted by permission. All rights reserved.)

depicted by Neal Stephenson, people regularly use microcoded avatar identities in cyberspace to accomplish the commercial and social tasks of the real world.[12]

As for personalized culture, individuals collect and then make their private art. For a brief period, the history of all the music in the world was available at Napster. The massive overdose of officially acceptable broadcast media can stimulate a personal cultural response. In the end, a musical band can only sing their songs. An individual's songs are unfound and unsung. The active traveling persona searches the wireless world with a magic wand, an Internet dipstick for an alternative culture. The wireless Internet is the newest vehicle in the call to new worlds.

Mythology is full of beckoning voices for travelers; the muses tested Odysseus, and Bali Ha'i called sailors and artists (Figure 109). The banker Paul Gauguin soaked in "official culture," abandoned it, and escaped to become a painter in pursuit of the exotic; he replaced one culture with another.

With or without digital devices, when people travel, they learn about culture. Others are stimulated to return with new ideas, even misunderstood ideas, that lead to their own inventions. To create the place that is traveled to, with every imaginable personal detail – that is the destiny of wireless architecture.

If wireless architecture does not get in the way, personality in content will grow. People may create their own special islands. The wireless Internet can be filled with individual presence as choices and tailoring create cultures. The outcomes may include the world of individual clarity suggested by Ayn Rand in the *Objectivist Epistemology,*[13] and the reinvestigation of global values postulated by Theodore Roszak in *Person/Planet.*[14]

The essential part about "wireless stuff" is that architects, software engineers, and interaction designers must envision mobile details, and allow for content personalization and operational tools to let active people create.

22 Chapter

The Future of Wireless Technology

Of course, the future of wireless technology is not written, and where things will go depends on one's knowledge of technology and one's imagination. Earlier we introduced a complete list of emerging wireless transmission technologies such as UWB, OFDM, HDR, and MMDS. These and other technologies are already influencing corporate timetables through the next 5 years. Companies are looking to Open Source software that spreads technology worldwide. They are aware of new communicating networks of devices and the next-generation Internet backbone IPv6. A universal transcodable digital signal is ultimately important to the future of content development and distribution, as well as universal spectrum access, and the all-optical networking systems.

A technology time line (Table 48) shows that the mobile wireless Internet has a heritage in transportation, communication, and information technology. Along these lines the future is being drawn.

Back in 1948 Arthur C. Clarke calculated the geosynchronous orbit of satellites (22,282 miles). Finally in 1967 a Syncom communications satellite parked itself in Clarke's orbit as the world's first geosynchronous orbiting craft. Also in that year Clarke completed a book based on the screenplay he wrote with Stanley Kubrick; both the movie and book were titled *2001: A Space Odyssey.*[1] In the poetic silence of space, this science fiction movie visualized many still developing technologies. But Clarke's earlier 1963 book, *Profiles of the Future,* more boldly predicted the magical technology beyond 2001.[2] The mindbender included a timetable that leads to the year 2100. It is remarkable to reread his deductions and

Table 48 Technology time line

Year	Transportation	Communication	Information
		Camera	
		Telegraph	
1850			
		Telephone	
	Automobile	Phonograph	Typewriter
1900	Airplane		Adding machine
		Vacuum tube	
1910			
		Radio	
1920			
1930			
		TV	
1940	Jet	Radar	
		Tape recorder	
1950	Satellite		Computer
		Laser	
1960	Spacecraft	Communication satellite	Minicomputer
1970	Lunar Landing		Electronic mail
		Cellular phone	
1980			Personal computer
1990			Internet Web
2000			
	International Space Station		3G wireless Internet
2010			

timings of the personal radio, the immortality of genetics, the "world brain" that is the Internet, and the embedding of memory in silicon that is now the unconscious rehearsal for building robots. The world brain is now a fan of wireless antenna, digesting the perceptions of our "programming." But we have a more humble time line to follow – the one that is creating a 3G world architecture.

In the name of 3G, telecommunications and computer history overlap in many significant ways. The time line for markets of key wireless cellular air interfaces (Table 49) shows that everything wireless is no more than 20 years old. The dates are somewhat problematic because the first commercial service is listed first. We

Table 49 Time line for markets of key wireless cellular air interfaces

	Year	North America	Europe	Japan	Data Rate
1G	1979			J-TACS	None
	1981		NMT, TACS, CNet, MATS-E		None
	1983	AMPS			None
	1984–1985	Cellular licenses 800 MHz–900 MHz			None
	1986	Mobitex	Mobitex		8 kbps
2G	1990		GSM		300 bps–4.4 kbps
	1991	TDMA ARDIS/Motient (data)			 8 kbps–19.2 kbps
	1992	CDPD (data)			8 kbps–19.2 kbps
	1993	CDMA Korea, IS-95		PDC	9.2 kbps–14.4 kbps
	1995–1996	PCS auctions 1900 MHz.			
	1997	UP.HDML (data)			9.2 kbps–14.4 kbps
	1998		WAP (data)		9.2 kbps–14.4 kbps
	1999			i-mode (data)	9.2 kbps
	2001		GPRS (data)		20 kbps–115 kbps
3G				(J)W-CDMA	40 kbps–384 kbps
	2001	CDMA2000 1x			64 kbps–144 kbps
	2002	i-BURST(data)			1 Mbps–40 Mbps
		CDMA2000 1x EV			650 kbps–2.4 Mbps
		HDR (data)			
	2003		EDGE (data)		64 kbps–384 kbps
	2004	3G CDMA2000 3x			1 Mbps?– 7 Mbps?
	2005		3G W-CDMA		384 kbps?–4 Mbps?

Note: Information beyond 2001 results from educated guesses of technology and capability. Contact vendors for their claims.

often mix proof of concept dates with market establishment dates. This table shows first markets. For example, GPRS was introduced in 1999, but the market for the devices and networks starts in 2001. The telco market continues to grow, taking between 2 and 3 years from the time a standard is agreed upon until the technology is generally deployed. Overall, we note an increased user capacity, greater mobility, and higher data rates.

The Future of World Spectrum

The future of global spectrum, like its history, is based on freeing spectrum and implementing new radio technology on top of the old. This is a common pattern in wireless technology. Today, segments of the radio frequency spectrum go unused or underused in the face of radically new radio technology.

One way to examine the increasing usage of wireless spectrum (Figure 110) is to imagine the following. How many people can get on the air at the same time? More technically, what is the theoretical number of simultaneous two-way conversations, voice and data, that can be held within the entire useful radio frequency spectrum over the entire world at any given moment? The figure illustrates the number of conversations historically to show the increase in spectrum usage.

Outdated utilization rules for telecommunication spectrum created over 50 years ago, based on then-current analog technology for systems like television, now limit modern technology. Even television broadcast technology was a radical division of spectrum when the world had only one channel. The energy from the original Marconi transmitter used in the first transatlantic transmission in 1901 blanketed an area of millions of square miles. It was capable of sending only a few bits per second and occupied the entire usable radio spectrum. In fact, only a single such transmission could be accommodated on the surface of the earth using that technology.

Increasing usage of wireless spectrum was achieved over the next 80 years by rigidly allocating spectrum bands for each broadcast transmission technology. Recent efficiency was achieved with two important shifts realized as inventions in the 1980s – the development of miniaturized digital computing technology and the treatment of spectrum as a cellular phenomenon. Digital devices could be reprogrammed to do many different things. It is the basis for software-defined radio. Digital formats have extraordinary efficiencies far beyond analog capabilities including IP-based, packet-switched protocols.

The other important shift was cellular thinking. This gives the illusion of using the same frequency for different purposes. In one city, for example, ten people in neighboring cells typically reuse exactly the same frequency. This idea of distributing the spectrum through cellular technology was implemented by Martin Cooper

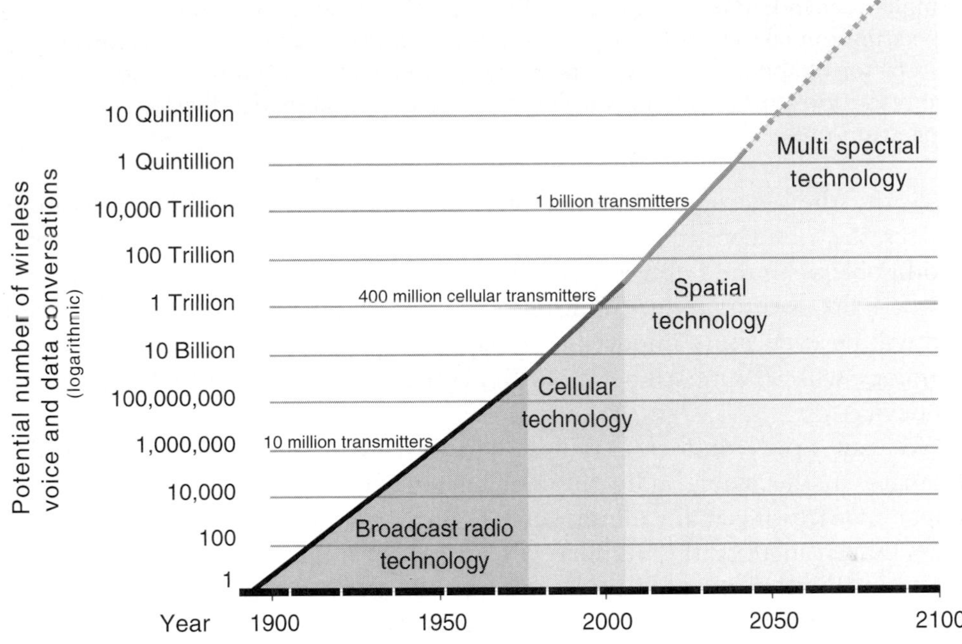

Figure 110 Increasing usage of wireless spectrum (*Source:* Martin Cooper. Based on a drawing "Cooper's Law." Used with permission of ArrayComm, Inc.)

for Motorola in 1973. As a key inventor of cellular era technology, his company is now developing next-generation, spatial processing technology that will dramatically increase spectral efficiency. Spatial processing of the spectrum can increase the density of devices able to share spectrum. We currently use digital rather than electromechanical devices and digital rather than analog transmission. Modern digital radio technology could free up two-thirds or more of dead spectrum that is currently assigned for use.

How many conversations can there be at once? On average, the number of channels has doubled every 30 months since 1895. This is Cooper's law. There have been about 40 doublings in the number of channels in the last century. In the twentieth century the effectiveness of spectrum utilization in personal communications has improved by a factor of a trillion. Cooper writes,

> Focusing on the most recent period, it improved a million times since 1950. Of that million-times improvement, roughly 15× was the result of being able to use more spectrum. In 1950, devices transmitted over 150 MHz of bandwidth. Today they transmit over 3 GHz. Another improvement of 5× was from using

> frequency division, that is, the ability to divide the radio spectrum into narrower slices (25 kHz channels vs. 120 kHz channels). Modulation techniques like FM, single sideband, time-division multiplexing, and various approaches to spread spectrum can take credit for another 5×. But the lion's share of the improvement – a factor of about 2700 – was the result of effectively confining individual conversations to smaller and smaller areas–what we call spatial division, or spectrum reuse.[3]

Clearly, the addition of Bluetooth technology and WLAN basestations increases the number of wireless Internet conversations. It is possible to pass smoothly between the bubbles of WAN/LAN/PAN spectrum with dynamic signal processors, smart antennas, and software-defined radio. In the future, spectrum reuse will be even more important, perhaps to a point where multiple-spectrum technology will permit each person with many devices to have a subfrequency for each device.

"We can now conduct a million voice conversations, or equivalent data exchanges, in the usable radio spectrum in one location," according to Martin Cooper.[4] Decreasing radio transmission power and using the spatial location of frequency can increase the number of conversations. Rather than think of a cell tower, you think of moving users surrounded by their variable bubbles of energy continuously processing and being processed spatially.

The wireless Internet increases in size with the addition of new lower-power networks. Many devices are added to the spectrum through low-power wireless Ethernet LAN cells. Even more devices are available through lower-power Bluetooth PAN cells.

An attractive air interface that can unify cellular spectrum and simplify protocols is Time Division Duplex (TDD). To perform cellular service, 2G systems need three parts of the spectrum. An operator has to run an uplink channel, a downlink channel, and a control channel. TDD simply uses one piece of spectrum for all traffic coming and going. It is how wireless Ethernet and newer networks operate. For more on the subject, see the section "TDD Coalition" in chapter 16.

Ringing the last bit out of a hertz of spectrum has just about reached its limit. A 25 kHz AMPS channel could deliver about 10 kbps. The upper limit of data throughput of Shannon's law (1 Hz = 1 bit) has been surpassed by new modulation techniques. By splitting and reshaping waves, sending multiple fragments of different parts of the spectrum simultaneously, and performing sideband calculus, a transmitter can get between a 4-fold and 16-fold improvement per Hz. But with spatial signal processing, the reuse of radio spectrum is unbounded. With advances in hardware digital signal processors and software spatial processing techniques, we can dramatically increase capacity. A combination of spatial processing technology can span WAN, LAN, and PAN power ranges and spectral use to create reliable, broadband wireless connections between any pairs of points. Those points can be miles away or a few feet apart. Theoretically, the effectiveness of spectrum use can be increased by 10 million times over today's capabilities. The technology of adaptive array processing is appearing in commercial cellular and high-speed Internet access systems using spatial processing technology to ascend the spectrum.

The Internet of the Future

The Internet of today has pretty much reached its architectural limits. The heavy traffic, poor handling of voice and media, and highly variable quality of service have sent the inventors, the Internet Engineering Task Force (IETF), back to the drawing board. The original fear of running out of IP addresses was put to rest with routers and domains. Essentially the world sees all the employees of a company as one IP address. Behind the firewall, the actual devices are given internal addresses. For example, email sent to `you@company.com` is received by the mail gateway that redistributes the message to an actual machine address. As people move out from behind the firewall with wireless devices, then the technical limits of IP addressing become an issue again.

Internet IPv6

Internet Protocol Version 6 (IPv6) is the "next-generation" protocol designed by the IETF to replace the current version Internet Protocol, IPv4. (There was an IPv5 protocol; it was used to define a header for an experimental and now rarely used non-IP streaming format called ST.) IPv6 answers most of the shortcomings of the current Internet backbone and is compatible with all the important parts of its predecessor's specifications. The Internet defines a voice service called Voice-over IP (VoIP). However, the Quality of Service (QoS) is very poor on wireless packet services that use conventional IPv4. The problem is that return voice timing is unpredictable using IPv4 routing and addressing. Until a 3G packet-based network is implemented on IPv6, we are not likely to see much improvement in VoIP systems. Cisco is already shipping IPv6 switching technology and many companies offer new qualities of VoIP service, including IP cellular service.

Some of the features of IPv6 are enlarged name space, improved security, real-time use, and compatibility with IPv4. IPv6 uses a 128-bit address space. This is four times longer than IPv4, allowing access to a nearly infinite number of devices (to be exact, 2^{128}, or 300 million google, a number that is explained in appendix A in the section "Bits, Hertz, and Prefixes of Magnitude"). The IPv6 core specification includes secure packet encryption featuring both Encapsulated Security Payload and source authentication through an Authentication Header. To support real-time traffic such as video conferencing or voice-grade quality of service, IPv6 implements a flow label, so a router can know which end-to-end flow a packet belongs to, and then find out the packet that belongs to real-time traffic streams.

IPv6 includes autoconfiguration of addresses, which should help the users connect their machines to a network.

The university-led Internet2 and the U.S. government–led next-generation Internet (NGI) are parallel and complementary initiatives based in the United States. Both groups are testing IPv6. Through participation in the National Science Foundation's (NSF's) NGI program, more than 150 universities competed and were awarded grants to support connections to advanced backbone networks such as Abilene and the very high performance Backbone Network Service. Internet2 universities are forming partnerships with related networking initiatives around the world. For more information about Internet2, visit <http://www.internet2.edu/html/faqs.html>. The NGI site is <http://www.ngi.gov/>.

Universal Messages

In building wireless messaging applications, you have to keep track of the phone number, the IP address, the machine identity of a wireless device, and user details. A unique identifier for a device, a network account, a user name, or a user handle is important for system design. Many businesses work best with absolute numbers that identify devices. They can also have numbers that can be forwarded from device to device, from service to service. Businesses use email addresses, phone numbers, fax numbers, IP addresses, social security numbers, and actual names. But we are entering an era where a user has multiple devices – some general and some personal, some public, and some private.

Local Number Portability

The Telecommunications Act of 1996 established a wide range of actions to continue the deregulation of the telecommunications industry. It established a national framework to structure competition and reduce regulation. The U.S. Congress realized that bringing competition to the local telephone marketplace reduces prices and motivates telephone companies to provide high-quality service, to deploy advanced services, and to provide more choices for customers. This was "regulated competition."

One of the technical barriers to competition was the inability of customers to switch from one telephone company to another and keep the same telephone number. Congress directed local telephone companies to offer "telephone number portability" to be administered according to the requirements determined by the FCC.

Local number portability (LNP) is a service that provides residential and business telephone customers with the ability to retain, at the same location, their existing local telephone numbers when switching from one local telephone service provider to another. In order to provide the telephone number portability envisioned by Congress, telephone companies have had to invest in upgrades to their networks. In 1998 the FCC determined what types of costs local telephone companies will be allowed to recover through separate charges that establish and provide telephone number portability service. They specified which LNP costs must be treated as part of the overall cost of doing business. The FCC determined that incumbent local telephone companies were allowed to recover the costs of implementing and providing LNP through two kinds of charges: (1) charges paid by other telephone companies that use a telephone company's number portability facilities to process own calls, and (2) a small, fixed monthly charge assessed on subscribers. Local telephone companies may continue to assess an LNP charge on customer telephone bills for a period of 5 years from the date the local telephone company first begins collecting the charge. At the end of that period, the local telephone company must stop assessing the charge.

Unified Messaging

We are still in the infancy of integration of communications. Personal communications and corporate communication systems rarely overlap. The standards, needs for security, and styles of use for all the media and services are difficult to unify in one desirable product. Commercial history has shown cross-vendor compatibility unlikely to be a success story. If the Internet has taught us anything, it is protocols like HTTP that work to integrate different systems. Integration of systems is more difficult as new communication machines are invented. A strong messaging and signaling protocol and architecture is sorely needed. Until that time, legacy vendor systems must be integrated.

Messages can be spoken or appear printed on a display. Giving a "Follow me" command, the content will track mobile users, for example, calling the right phone at the right time. This service attempts to integrate phones, faxes, and emails. The routing options to your destination device are changed on demand or preprogrammed by the time of day and day of the week. Training all your client devices to follow you by giving them your schedule can be tedious and time consuming as your schedule changes. The system requires unique identities and a portable architecture. The interfaces are not easily learned and can produce unintended results, sometimes sending calls to places you have decided not to go. Until technology and the economy settle, let the sender decide. Give the sender choices such as the option to leave a message or route calls to other voice mailboxes, to cell phones, to a 24-hour operator, to pagers, and so on.

Openwave Systems is engaged in developing such wireless Internet services. Integrating the many commercial protocols and technical standards is the daunting task of *unified messaging*. As engineers, we know these are all bits underneath, but the protocols for signaling, storing, and accounting are all unique and owned by vastly different companies. Many companies have tried to offer combined services, but it is difficult to cross carrier boundaries. Openwave has decided to create unified messaging accounts that will be managed by telcos. Another company, Etrieve, provides an integrated voice portal and text messaging system that manages large amounts of secure content for businesses.

ENUM

Although people can use their computers to call out using VoIP, no one can call them. One effort, called ENUM, integrates phone numbers and IP addresses. With ENUM, anyone can place a phone call to a computer. Internet devices do not have telephone numbers. To join Internet IP addresses and the telco phone numbers, the IETF ENUM effort got under way with the sponsorship of VeriSign and Telcordia. The ENUM system converts phone numbers into IP addresses by keeping the domain name registry in sync with the associated phone number. The directory is <http://www.enumworld.com>.

The Wireless Internet and Open Source

Many Internet companies consider Open Source an important asset. Open Source puts software source code in the public domain. Developers can use source code under a license that essentially says that if you make changes, you are to contribute them to the originating Open Source group. It is important to reflect on Open Source because it is so fundamentally part of the mechanics of the Internet. Anyone can view the source of a Web page. Select "View Source" from your Web browser and voilà – HTML source code. This ease of openly sharing HTML source code catapulted Web site development and was key to accelerating the Internet industry. Any developer could learn from the best tips and tricks from any site in the world. The two key parts of the Internet, the client and the server, exist in many Open Source forms, the chief ones being the Mozilla (Netscape) browser and the Apache Web server. Other examples include the Linux operating system, the MySQL database, the Mosaic browser, SendMail, TCP/IP, HTTP transmission, CVS source code control, the Perl language, StarOffice applications, the Apache Tomcat application server, and the Enhydra application server. Open Source is very popular. The Apache Web server operates more than half of the Internet Web servers. Linux is found in 20 percent of corporate computer systems, according to industry estimates in 2000.

The Open Source Internet

The popular Internet originally came into being as a do-it-yourself means to allow different networks to connect. It was all self-assembling.

Many open processes are used to put technology into the public domain and grow the computer industry. One process is to take a commercial standard and open the specification, or "Open Source" the implementation. For example, IBM

Corporation had worked on a relational database called SEQUEL, then realized the industry needed standardization and declared SQL an open standard for relational databases. The world database market now almost exclusively uses SQL. You can now get Open Source MySQL or InstantDB and compile the code for your own working SQL database engine.

Sun Microsystems uses a guarded process for controlling its Open Source releases. It owns the Java Community Process (JCP) used to establish, evolve, and endorse new wireless technology that guides a complex set of overlapping wireless standards – J2ME, MIDP, kVM, CLDC, CDC, and JINI.

It often takes the vision of one or two inventors to define a base technology. After TCP/IP was defined as an information protocol, companies wrote their own compliant TCP/IP stacks. Ethernet was defined as a standard that wired computers into local networks. These technologies caught on in the 1980s. As open standards, no single company owned them and many firms improved on the implementations. Wireless Ethernet as an open IEEE 802.11b specification now runs interchangeably on all kinds of hardware.

Finally, the most guarded software source, the operating system, was made open with the Linux operating system. Its inventor, Linux Torvalds, made the source code for this derivative of the UNIX™ OS freely available since 1991. Linux now runs on PCs, Macintoshes, and UNIX boxes. Wireless handhelds such as the iPAQ and Pocket PC can run Linux.

Qualities of Open Source

The pace for wireless development is increasing with Open Source. Already Open Source operating systems are appearing on wireless devices. Open Source application servers are driving wireless architectures. The Internet industry has found many important qualities of Open Source:

- *Speed.* Ahead of the market, the independent Open Source Internet development community continues to innovate and introduce new solutions. Features are driven by discussion, contribution, and consensus, not by lengthy product planning cycles compromised by restricted resources. Corporate confidentiality has slowed many past projects. Open Source is the opposite. Having source code means that you do not have to wait for the revision and release cycle of a particular vendor's product.
- *Asset.* The entire source code can be secured as an asset. In large contracts, code is locked in a vault as escrow in case the supplying company fails. Open Source code is a legal entity that lives beyond the fortunes of any company.
- *Ownership.* Open Source code is your own code to use, although you are obligated to return to the community any intellectual property you may

develop. The source code can be extended to match the technology needed by a company. A company using Open Source is not beholden to a supplying vendor whose releases often contain unpleasant surprises that cannot legally be changed.

- *Community.* The ongoing collaboration and peer review enlarges the quality of the source and the solutions that get applied to it. Open Source has proved to be a quick method to address bugs and deficiencies worldwide. Consider that you can find a developer any hour of the day somewhere in the world to solve your problem. There are many sources for support and services. Changes are often made by working with the Open Source community. However, a company in a pinch can modify the code directly. While one company may develop a successful system, it may not get all the parts of it right. Companies and individuals apply the Internet itself – code repositories, mail lists, newsgroup support – to fill in the missing parts. Together they validate the strengths and trim the weaknesses of implementations.

- *Cost.* Obviously Open Source is free. Open Source also lowers compound redistribution costs. From a financial viewpoint of development expenses, Open Source spreads the cost of ongoing development among the world community.

- *Quality.* Many developers examine the Open Source code. As we have seen in XP team programming or buddied CVS check-in systems, checked software development consistently produces code with the fewest defects. Open Source means that all phases of work – specification, implementation, and testing – are developed by many minds not just the best in a single company. Open Source implementations are often superior to closed sources. There is now greater recognition that a viable internationally acceptable industry standard will come from Open Source.

- *Talent.* Companies are finding they are able to hire from a wide pool of Open Source talent. Open Source programmers are often drawn from universities. This is partly because educational institutions do not have the budgets to keep up with the many new commercially licensed products. However, Open Source is a leading-edge experimental test bed of wireless Internet technology. It is a good match for the youthful and passionate breed of technologist. Open Source is nonthreatening and engineers find great freedom in using it. It is a good way to train and retain staff. Open Source systems have large followings and are becoming a vehicle to leverage the software development community.

Implementing Standards with Open Source

Open Source and standards often go hand in hand. The difference between standards and Open Source is that a standard does not specify an implementation. Open Source not only supplies source code, it is often a software development methodology. An Open Source community can truly establish a robust, feature-rich, and adaptable working system. Using the Internet, they can advocate it and easily correct or distribute any part. Open Source makes use of other open standards such as XML, HTML HTTP, and TCP/IP.

The standards process also has its complexities. Designs by committee can be haphazard. Without a real-world purpose, the members can usurp the stated goals of a standard with their self-serving submissions that do nothing more than match existing company products and objectives. Rather than create a new market, they extend an old one. This has also been a problem with some W3C wireless Internet mobile standards in recent years. It appears W3C mobile standards are being drafted as complicated specifications with commercial interest more than vision guiding the process. They are a long way from a clear and simple mobile wireless reference model that solves real developers' problems and creates clear technical opportunities. Open Source can be an alternative to standards bodies. The Open Source community is driven by pragmatic needs and pioneering ideas. It implements solutions, and generally does not get too far ahead of anticipated technology.

Making money with Open Source is a challenge for the inventors. Although core software is free, Open Source companies often charge for hardware, services, training, support, documentation, licensed content, and masterful implementation of an integrated solution. For example, a company can consult or integrate system parts in a wireless Internet architecture built by bundling many Open Source systems. From an Open Source master, special software components or extensions can be built that optimize or perform unique functions. This often leads to a branded and certified version of the Open Source main product. Companies sometimes turn to the original Open Source companies to bring products to market quickly, because it takes time and talent to figure out the optimal uses of the source code. Some companies produce an Open Source entry-level product but charge for the more robust and scalable versions. The general observation is that, because price is no longer a barrier, Open Source accelerates the market and increases the tempo of technology acceptance.

Wireless Open Source Technology

Many analysts believe that one of the reasons i-mode is more successful than WAP is that cHTML was registered openly with the W3C and it highly leveraged knowledge of how Internet content is delivered. The service openly compensated any Internet provider who could produce interesting content that kept a customer on the air. The open standard made it easy for developers to produce content and motivated them to do so. In contrast, the WAP Forum of telcos guards closed implementation and licenses complex specifications produced only after consortium consensus, which usually takes a considerable length of time to reach. The Open Source community is endeavoring to change this dynamic.

Wireless Open Source projects include WAP gateways, application servers, phone microbrowsers including XML parsers, and other tools. Open Source WAP servers are available from Wapit.com who sponsors kannel.org and from 5NINE hosts at <http://www.waplinux.org/>. Open Source technology also includes the Amaya markup editor, the Jigsaw Web server, and Eclipse development tools.

Open Source is popular. Perhaps people like to see companies using Open Source because it means all the cards are on the table, there are no secrets, and it uses the technology and talent of the worldwide Internet to build a common market in which everyone can participate.

Open Content

The full encoding of the U.S. street system as TIGER GIS files is in the public domain. Business listings are generally in the private domain. With some public organization, Open Content for the Internet might become a rich counterpart to Open Source for software. A global distribution of one application that runs on every Bluetooth network or small radio device might perform the task of appending every location to a global listing.

Content may have some free qualities, as suggested by the Napster episode, but clearly compensation to creators is an issue. It may be that a very low-cost subscription model for content will provide the proper vehicle not only for artists, but also for wireless Internet software developers, content producers, and even average mobile users.

Transcoding the Scalable Signal

Transcoding is the conversion of one media format to another. The meaning has been temporarily abused by wireless software companies who attempt to do nothing more than translate old Web page markup languages to wireless versions. Transcoding has a far richer future.

The original use of the word was in telecommunications. Signals were either transcoded in switches so they could be combined in digital trunks or transcoded in gateways where they were converted from one media encoding to another. For example, a circuit-switched, time division, multiplexed video signal could be transcoded to a packet-switched, Ethernet LAN video signal.

Nicholas Negroponte at the MIT Media Laboratory in the 1980s directed projects that asserted the possibility that any media type could be transcoded to another. Computers ordinarily perform simple media transcoding such as text to speech. The Media Lab's transcoding experiments were far more interesting, going so far as to attempt to generate movies from text.[5] To achieve this end, some researchers approached movie encoding by looking at the Music Instrument Digital Interface (MIDI), the encoding format for music; others explored time-variable viewers; and others toyed with advanced user interfaces. But they never hit the nail on the head. Perhaps it is not an advanced interface, but a commonsense interface that is needed. In everyday life, media transcoding is what happens when you try to explain pictures to someone over the phone. It also happens while reading a book, when you form a movie in your mind. The theoretical challenge of transcoding paperbacks to movies remains.

Future transcodable signals fundamentally need a base multimedia encoding. Such an encoding has a natural basis both experientially and in physics. Physiologically people experience all senses simultaneously. We are born as multimedia creatures. It is over time that we are taught to break apart sensorial and motor connections of experience, as Dr. Richard Cytowik points out. The neurologist observed cases of synesthesia where the perceptual aspects of one sense were experienced as another. In the lead study, a person experienced intense flavors as sharp points. Cytowik explains that the design of the brain seems to have large elements that synthesize sensations and that the largest portion is not so much for rationality as it is for emotion – another synesthetic function.[6] Technically, it may be natural to encode media in a simultaneous time-stream format. If you look again at the electromagnetic spectrum chart in chapter 3 (Figure 15), you might appreciate that video cameras are machines that simultaneously record two narrow intervals of the electromagnetic spectrum: 20 Hz to 20 kHz for hearing and the interval around 1 petahertz for seeing. (Why stop with ear and eye? A media recorder could record other parts of the spectrum where the effects of electromagnetic-related sensations occur – heat and possibly a spatially controlled electromagnetic interface to the sensors for taste and smell.) The arts show us that anything important to experience, memory, and dreams is worth encoding. At the same moment add to the record an automatic location identification and precision time stream and you have a thoroughly multimedia encoding. These perceptual telegrams, with proper encoding, might transform the wireless Internet into a full-sensation Internet. But what do you do with it?

Wireless Internet servers are showing multichannel solutions that answer the question. People sometimes like to read news in a newspaper, hear the news through radio, or watch the news reports on television. (Sometimes people use various devices that record various sources.) Clearly, there are times when people want information legible, audible, or visible. Digital transcodable content can be adapted by command of the individual. Today you can build an Internet server to deliver directions as a list of turns. This list can be either spoken as a live guide would or displayed as a graphical map. The media encoding for the underlying directions uses XML, possibly SMIL, or Flash. The industry is coming to a point in wireless device technology where the user can summon any media encoded in a portable format. It is facilitated with standards like CC/PP that help mediate device, user, and content characteristics.

Storing the "creator" is far more efficient than storing the performance. A MIDI recording gives listeners a new way to hear music. It records the gestures of the creators, not the resulting waveforms. MIDI can store the same amount of data to a sound file in 5 KB that it takes a waveform 50 Mb to store. Likewise, typed text requires far less time to store than spoken form does. In the 4 KHz wireless bandwidth devoted to a human speaking for 1 second, 8,000 characters can be sent. Consider encoding the source of the media, or more exactly, the emanator rather than the resulting emanation – it is often more efficient.

Savings in digitizing are not all they seem. Something gets lost in the translation. When we read text, we no longer see the flourish of the hand. Words are a poor substitute for the music of a speaker's voice; with digital data, clues to emotion and the identity of the source are lost. Voice carries the musical overtones and pacing of text, which are often critical pieces of communication. With some research, technologists experiment in restoring personal qualities and emotional characteristics to digital media. Using *voice fonts* is an experimental technique that presents a person's text in an individualized font that is weighted, italicized, and styled to express emotion.

Encoding a speaker's tonality and identity can be done on the cheap. In simple text messages, people add emoticons to indicate feeling and occasional humor; however, with a limited selection or language, much gets lost in translation. We know that translating the spoken language of one culture to another can change meanings. Continuing translation to yet other cultures can produce strange results. Sentences can become unrecognizable and sometimes laughable. There is nothing like a good misunderstanding. However, when translating languages, always strive to retain the meaning, with as much of the cultural nuances, overtones, and undertones as possible.

Media translation presents many technical challenges. Computers already convert some media types. For example, text to speech and speech to text happens in voice portals. Optical Character Recognition (OCR) scanners convert printed to computerized text. Handwriting Recognizers (HWR) scanners convert gesture to text. Keyboard music can be converted to MIDI very efficiently. A number of key cross-media transforms exist in the world's transcoding library, but many conversions are unknown. See Table 50.

Each medium has its own vocabulary, its architectural limits. When translated, the qualities are often mapped incorrectly. This is clear by watching popular computer music programs like WINAMP that offer visualization plug-ins that transcode

Table 50 Cross-media transforms

The Known	The Unknown
Text to speech	Text to movie
Speech to text	Video to music
Handwriting to text	Movie to speech
Type to text	Voice to handwriting
Sound waves to animated images	Animation to text
	Photo to text

music as creative animations. They are fun to watch. Ironically, in the WINAMP program, the music composer's notationn reads *allegro molto vivace,* which means "very lively," but even with this direction to the program, Tchaikovsky looks just like Miles Davis. The major human values of emotion, feeling, mood, and tempo are overlooked. It is not clear that rhythm maps best to shapes and melody shows best in color. The whole study of synesthetic perception and cross-media encoding suggests that the notation for the emanator for all-media encoding and the new composer's authoring tool have a very long way to go.

Theoretically, all types of digital media can be converted from one to another. The permutations of media include text, photos, drawn images, sound, music, voice, animation, television, movie, gesture, dance, and even digital smell. It is possible that we will have a media artifact-encoding format inclusive of media types. The playout will be up to the viewer. The transmission of a compound digital media signal that carries all the media formats to play on any scale of end-receiving device may work like television signals. Broadcast television transmissions in color can play even on dinky black-and-white devices. The end device "throws away" the color information. It is clear that a highly encoded digital carrier – perhaps XML-, SMIL-, or QuickTime-based – can carry an enormously powerful multimedia stream that can easily be stripped away by gateways as the display is computed on the receiver.

Simultaneous media interfaces present choices and interfaces for interacting at the same time. Combining media in the interfaces without careful study is not recommended. A lesson from usability is that people interact best with only one media channel for an entire transaction. Testing of interactive systems shows that with multimodal interfaces people do not know when to speak, when to listen, when to handwrite, or when to type, unless you provide a moderator who prompts the interaction. However, combining interfaces can be learned over time.

Some interfaces have higher bandwidths than others. For the mobile user, speaking and listening to someone is faster than typing messages and reading responses. Transmitting interactive streams of digital text with time-based media is in its infancy. When you get phone service off a Cisco IP phone, you get a combination of voice service and visual service that appears on a faceplate as you take a live call or process a recorded message. These coordinated transactions of text accompanying voice streams offer promising, time-saving services.

Given a fully transcodable media signal, the interface question is, If you want to read, listen, watch, view, or interact, which medium is best? But for the content-minded developer, the real question is, Which source is best?

True Source

In his life-long study and exposition of primitive Indian culture and arts, Ananda Coomaraswamy asked some important questions about all art. The Sri Lankan Hindu might ask something like, "When you listen to a live performance, what are you listening to? The musical instrument, the performer's interpretation, the composer who wrote it, or the source that inspired the composer?"[7] When we are making digital content, it is important to make careful decisions about the sources. When the source is transcoded for transmission, what will get lost in translation and which medium will deliver the intent and character of the source best? A personal note written in ink is quite different from typed text. The color of the spoken word is a far cry from a printed one.

Some people are visual, some oral, and some textual. When people receive messages, they "get it" differently. People learn that they can see quicker than they can hear. Of course, interacting and being able to navigate through media as well as through a face-to-face dialog is the goal.

Over the wireless Internet, try to use the true sources. The original sources are generally more efficient and trusted. We respect the source. Consider the difference between the impressions you receive from seeing original paintings and reprints. Once you have seen the wild, sculpted, colorful paint in Vincent Van Gogh's work, then printed reproductions pale in comparison. Why endure the Roman retelling of the story of Ulysses when the original Greek story of Odysseus is set in the right culture with the proper motives? In the end, our culture is what we choose to repeat.

An interesting clue to how sources of content can be transcoded technically is found in the observation that "the 'content' of any medium is always another medium."[8] The content of writing is speech. The content of print is the written word, and so on. Essentially, any communication technology contains antecedent communication technology. This implies that transcoders can take advantage of original media sources. Ken Burns, in his televised series *Civil War,* uses narrative and photographs, as do many documentary filmmakers. But he chose also to use handwritten letters and have them spoken by a person representing the personality (so far as he could determine) of the one who wrote the letter. Content contains; what is revealed is the stuff that makes it interesting – personality.

The wireless Internet will grow as content is chosen and sources are made available in compelling formats. Handwritten gestures can be very expressive; they reveal emotion and energy. A handwriting analyst sees entire personalities in ink. We all read books, but it is amazing to look at the original handwriting of great works. If you are ever in Austin, Texas, hop up to the top of the main library of the University of Texas and enter the James Michener Museum. Look at the handwritten manuscripts of Michener, Ernest Hemingway, or Mark Twain. You might be able to feel the extraordinary turmoil, reflection, nuance, and variety of experiences in the original manuscripts that are sadly lost when reduced to type. Maybe that is for the best, but the human dimension expressed in handwriting on paper still lives.

Sometimes you have to make choices about when to use voice, when to use text, and when to use images, but mobile digital medium can be open-ended. Ultimately, the mobile user should be in control of wireless media. This is different from the broadcast technology that requires (by FCC regulation) that media be transmitted in a fixed format. Mobile users want to select the format they need now.

In the 1980s, newspapers experimented with sending Teletext to homes. Dwellers could view color-television transmission of newspaper content. The text was legible, but Teletext was not popular. Interviews revealed some obvious lessons. Although it could be said that people do not like to read on the television, trial customers said they would rather have the news spoken to them. Today, Internet newspapers are effectively digitized and voice portals can read any text on demand. But automatic voices do not compare well to radio voice talent, which uses emphasis and emotion to portray personality. It may not be merely a matter of technical interpretation, but also one of trust in personality.

Your site content in some eventual format should be able to present all media forms, preserving media nuance in a hefty digital signal transmission over the Internet. Viewers will extract the parts they want and throw away the rest. Some XML descendent may encode content that can be printed as text, formed as pictures, or effectively spoken. However, XML will travel another direction, making most of this fancy multimedia interface irrelevant. In the future, we may not be looking or listening to any devices.

They may be representing us in a machine-to-machine, agent-mediated interface. Today in the electronic marketplace we are seeing that XML is defining the content, the exchange protocol, and the buyer and seller profiles that are mediated in various agent processes. The entire agent process, discussed in the section "Personalization Engines and Agents" in chapter 21, can represent mobile users in a silent manner. We will still use our devices to communicate. Not so much for person to person, but machine to machine. Only they will be communicating in their own language.

Communicating Devices

A businessperson has a phone to take a call, a fax machine to send and receive important documents, email to get the latest word, a Web site for content, and voice mail to get messages. The emerging field of unified messaging promises to consolidate these many forms of communication.

Bluetooth technology suggests the direction of next-generation devices where everything communicates. It is a wireless mobile Internet that grounds an individual in personal physical experiences. It is not like the "immersive" electronic media – the telephone, television, or PC network – where the user is engulfed. Immersion, taken to its science fiction extreme, requires data gloves and goggles where the user experiences virtual reality, a synthetic world that surrounds the senses. In the 1980s, the "father of ubiquitous computing," Mark Weiser, research scientist at Xerox PARC, began experimenting with small, communicating wireless devices. In his experiments, users worked in the real world moving about rooms where dozens of communicating devices combined whiteboard displays, tablets, audio, various kinds of input, and location information to give teams of mobile users dynamic mobile information.[9] Configurations of devices were used for collaboration. He spoke of this world as virtual reality turned inside out. In his language, the goal is to create "embodied virtuality," not virtual reality. Rather than turn people into disembodied discarnate beings wrapped in goggles and gloves, the real-world wireless artifices of communication let people relate directly to the daily world. The mobile audience relies on only brief use of mobile technology as it acts and transacts. Unlike prior electric networks, the wireless Internet enhances physical presence. It underscores active personal identity.

Theoretically, a premier communicating device can replace every wall switch or sign around you. The issues in interface and interaction design for master communicating devices remain. The current exchange of media content and formats is piecemeal. Consider performing bank transactions. You can punch them up on an ATM display, converse through an IVR voice portal, graphically view and click with a Web PC, and tap keys from a Web phone. From the server point of view, this is all manageable with techniques already discussed. Reaching the end user in a consolidated manner is new territory, especially the interfaces for coordinating devices. A personal device communicates with other machines and it functions in some cases as a mini radar screen showing services around you, and at other times as a remote control in a peering and commanding manner with supplied interfaces from neighboring devices. Service transactions may be the path that unifies interfaces and protocols as mCommerce solutions set the bar for uniform interfaces.

Universal Spectrum, Ultrafast Data, and All-Optical Networks

It takes too long to lay wires, even longer to lay them again when new, higher-capacity wire technology comes along. Many wireless technologies are coming that will run faster than the wired connections we get today. Given that Ultra Wideband (UWB) wireless can transmit at 1 gigabit per second, the world will desperately need a high-speed network backbone to handle this cellular capacity. Conventional networks today stream voice synchronously and transmit data in asynchronous packets. With software-defined radio, we will be able to travel worldwide and tune into any 3G network. 3G is a network of packets and CDMA technologies are in the lead as the air interface. After this long trek to get packeted service, all-optical network research is now suggesting a return to circuit-switched topology.

Optical fiber is the highest bandwidth transmission technology. A conventional SONET network optical router using OC-12c reaches 622 Mbps and up to 2.5 Gbps using OC-48c. The SONET standard reaches theoretical speeds of 10 Gbps (OC192) and 40 Gbps (OC768). Terabit speeds are here with the announcement of the Nortel's 80 Gbps × 80 lambda single fiber, which uses an entirely different technology from SONET. This means 6.4 terabits per second on a single strand. A Lucent AccuRibbon 864-strand optical cable is able to carry 28.6 petabits per second. This is done by transmitting 10 Gbps per lambda over the total cable capacity of 2.86 million lambdas. One Lucent AccuRibbon cable can transmit in 1 second the entire monthly traffic of the Internet worldwide in 1995. And it appears that these speeds will triple by the end of 2002.

In current tests, an optical 10 Gbps signal travels 3000 km without a repeater using wave-guide fabrication of the optical fiber. But SONET routers require header decoding and rerouting network traffic. New technology from companies like Avanex provides pure optical switching without logical header recoding software or electronics.

The basic idea for optical end-to-end connection is to dial a color. The color combines with other colors passing through an immensely large optical network of nearly infinite bandwidth. This future of an all-optical network with no routers is being made possible with exolasers, tunable color lasers. Each device might have its own color coordinated to its own frequency or subfrequency. Everyone has a personal optical circuit. There is limited "switching" because connections are everywhere and bandwidth is wasted. However, incumbent technology, vested interests, and recovery of investment in deployed technology must inevitably delay acceptance.

Within 10 years, an all-optical network and protocol set may replace conventional telecommunications architecture. Perhaps the industry will move back to an optical, circuit-switched architecture. Using tunable lasers and tunable radio, every possible wireless device connects through the optical core as each person dials his or her color. George Gilder reports monthly on these changes to the Telecosm in his newsletter, *The Gilder Technology Report.*[10]

We are on the verge of a communications Renaissance stirred by the prospect of the new wireless Internet. The latent potential has been building; technology is being distributed all over the world; Internet content is building once again. The conditions are similar to conditions at the time when Tim Berners-Lee provided a simple technology that released the pent-up content on the world's file systems. So we ask ourselves, What content is useful? What is the source? Which mobile medium communicates best? New devices feed sources of new content, filling the Internet and stimulating a new look at old information and the purpose of that information.

Common GPS technology, location-based services, and mapping databases suggest a market for personal spots and personal maps. The new map of the world is in everyone's handheld as the active mobile user digitally draws the interior continent of living. The value of the new maps is comparable to that of the original ship-going maps of the 1400s that were desperately sought after, traded like securities. The original ancient nautical maps were more like diaries of adventures and experiences than painstakingly drawn geographies. The visuals were secondary. Experience was primary. With the wireless Internet, we will help people map their own spaces and create their own special worlds. The historian Arnold Toynbee observes that societies are given historical challenges. The response may be noble or decadent; this is what defines civilization.[11] It also defines personal character. The challenges for developers become the shared challenges of society and the individual: the control of digital presences; where a mobile user goes; and what he or she does. The response of civilization to the world that will be formed is unknown. But success surely depends on the imagination and technical will power of the wireless engineers and architects who understand and create the wireless Internet

Appendices

Wireless Internet Resources

A

Appendix

Codes and Conventions

ASCII Text for WAP and i-mode

Developers constantly refer to encoding in wireless technology. The American Standard Code for Information Interchange (ASCII) is the 8-bit code used as the transmission standard for text in most wireless phones. This chart is handy to decode Wireless Application Protocol (WAP) byte streams, Japanese emoji icon values, and memory references.

Char	Hex	Oct	Dec	Bin	Char	Hex	Oct	Dec	Bin	Char	Hex	Oct	Dec	Bin	Char	Hex	Oct	Dec	Bin
NUL	0	0	0	00000000	Space	20	40	32	00100000	@	40	100	64	01000000	`	60	140	96	01100000
SOH	1	1	1	00000001	!	21	41	33	00100001	A	41	101	65	01000001	a	61	141	97	01100001
STX	2	2	2	00000010	"	22	42	34	00100010	B	42	102	66	01000010	b	62	142	98	01100010
ETX	3	3	3	00000011	#	23	43	35	00100011	C	43	103	67	01000011	c	63	143	99	01100011
EOT	4	4	4	00000100	$	24	44	36	00100100	D	44	104	68	01000100	d	64	144	100	01100100
ENQ	5	5	5	00000101	%	25	45	37	00100101	E	45	105	69	01000101	e	65	145	101	01100101
ACK	6	6	6	00000110	&	26	46	38	00100110	F	46	106	70	01000110	f	66	146	102	01100110
BEL	7	7	7	00000111	'	27	47	39	00100111	G	47	107	71	01000111	g	67	147	103	01100111
BS	8	10	8	00001000	(	28	50	40	00101000	H	48	110	72	01001000	h	68	150	104	01101000
HT	9	11	9	00001001	)	29	51	41	00101001	I	49	111	73	01001001	i	69	151	105	01101001
LF	0a	12	10	00001010	*	2a	52	42	00101010	J	4a	112	74	01001010	j	6a	152	106	01101010
VT	0b	13	11	00001011	+	2b	53	43	00101011	K	4b	113	75	01001011	k	6b	153	107	01101011
FF	0c	14	12	00001100	,	2c	54	44	00101100	L	4c	114	76	01001100	l	6c	154	108	01101100
CR	0d	15	13	00001101	-	2d	55	45	00101101	M	4d	115	77	01001101	m	6d	155	109	01101101
SO	0e	16	14	00001110	.	2e	56	46	00101110	N	4e	116	78	01001110	n	6e	156	110	01101110
SI	0f	17	15	00001111	/	2f	57	47	00101111	O	4f	117	79	01001111	o	6f	157	111	01101111
DLE	10	20	16	00010000	0	30	60	48	00110000	P	50	120	80	01010000	p	70	160	112	01110000
DCI	11	21	17	00010001	1	31	61	49	00110001	Q	51	121	81	01010001	q	71	161	113	01110001
DC2	12	22	18	00010010	2	32	62	50	00110010	R	52	122	82	01010010	r	72	162	114	01110010
DC3	13	23	19	00010011	3	33	63	51	00110011	S	53	123	83	01010011	s	73	163	115	01110011
DC4	14	24	20	00010100	4	34	64	52	00110100	T	54	124	84	01010100	t	74	164	116	01110100
NAK	15	25	21	00010101	5	35	65	53	00110101	U	55	125	85	01010101	u	75	165	117	01110101
SYN	16	26	22	00010110	6	36	66	54	00110110	V	56	126	86	01010110	v	76	166	118	01110110
ETB	17	27	23	00010111	7	37	67	55	00110111	W	57	127	87	01010111	w	77	167	119	01110111
CAN	18	30	24	00011000	8	38	70	56	00111000	X	58	130	88	01011000	x	78	170	120	01111000
EM	19	31	25	00011001	9	39	71	57	00111001	Y	59	131	89	01011001	y	79	171	121	01111001
SUB	1a	32	26	00011010	:	3a	72	58	00111010	Z	5a	132	90	01011010	z	7a	172	122	01111010
ESC	1b	33	27	00011011	;	3b	73	59	00111011	[	5b	133	91	01011011	{	7b	173	123	01111011
FS	1c	34	28	00011100	<	3c	74	60	00111100	\	5c	134	92	01011100	|	7c	174	124	01111100
GS	1d	35	29	00011101	=	3d	75	61	00111101	]	5d	135	93	01011101	}	7d	175	125	01111101
RS	1e	36	30	00011110	>	3e	76	62	00111110	^	5e	136	94	01011110	~	7e	176	126	01111110
US	**1f**	**37**	**31**	**00011111**	**?**	**3f**	**77**	**63**	00111111	_	**5f**	**137**	**95**	01011111	**Del**	**7f**	**177**	**127**	01111111

Soundex for Gisting

Rather than insist that everyone spell a name the same way, such as Mark or Marc, you need a technique so that words that sound like other words can be found. Soundex is a means to phonetically encode words. The National Archives devised the Soundex phonetic system in 1880 to index the U.S. census. It was devised to provide a means to retrieve complex spellings of surnames with similar sounds but various spellings. Soundex codes begin with the first letter of the name followed by a three-digit code that represents the next three consonants.

Soundex Coding Guide

1 = B, P, F, V

2 = C, S, G, J, K, Q, X, Z

3 = D, T

4 = L

5 = M, N

6 = R

The letters A, E, I, O, U, Y, H, and W are not coded. For example, coded in Soundex the names Smith and Smythe are both S530. SMS messengers who create gisting libraries for SMS messages use the Soundex system. On SMS GSM phones, a gister reduces this to SMTH.

The entry `SOUNDEX` is a standard call in the SQL application library that takes a word and returns the standard Soundex codes.

Emoticons

Sometimes called "smileys," emoticons convey emotion with a sense of humor. These common signatures are icons composed by combining various keyboard characters; they are added to messages to convey the sender's feelings about the content. For wireless messaging, short letter emoticons are commonly used. It is interesting to observe how a simple form can insert or restore some level of emotion to digital text.

Feeling is often as important to communicate as the basic message itself. The restoration of emotional identity to digital communication is one of the qualities of media covered in such technology as "voice fonts" and transcoding (see chapter 22). :)

Happy	Sad
:)	%-(
(^^	:(
%)	:[
:-D	:-(
:]	:-/
:-)	:_(
:->	>:-(
:-\	
:]~	
:o)	

Tempo

In email and messages, people also convey feeling and emotion with terms used on musical scores to indicate tempo. For example, the term *molto vivace* says the feeling is extremely lively.

Term	Emotion
adagio	slow, slowly
allegro	lively, fast
allegro con brio	fast, energetic
brio	with "spirit" or "fire"
con fuoco	with "fire"
fuoco	"fire," fiery
giocoso	light, humorous
grave	slowly, solemnly
grazioso	graceful
largo	slow, broad
legato	smoothly
lento	slowly
moderato	moderately, at a moderate pace
molto	much, very
molto lento	very slowly
moto	motion
non tanto	not very
pesante	heavy, ponderous
piacevole	pleasant, agreeable
presto	very fast
risoluto	resolute, in a determined manner
sotto voce	extremely quiet, softly
stepitoso	loud, noisy, boisterous
tanto, troppo	so much, too much (e.g., allegro non tanto means fast but not very fast)
veloce	rapid
vivace	lively, very fast

International Morse Code

Some wireless messages have snips of Morse code in their messages. It has the flourish of an emoticon. Of course, seeing this code horrifies telegraphers who know this to be an audible, not a visual, system. To the right is the world's first electronic software code.

Letter	Morse
A	.-
B	-...
C	-.-.
D	-..
E	.
F	..-.
G	--.
H	....
I	..
J	.---
K	-.-
L	.-..
M	--
N	-.
O	---
P	.--.
Q	--.-
R	.-.
S	...
T	-
U	..-
V	...-
W	.--
X	-..-
Y	-.--
Z	--..

Digit	Morse
0	-----
1	.----
2	..---
3	...--
4	....-
5	.....
6	-....
7	--...
8	---..
9	----.

Punctuation	Morse
Full-stop (period)	.-.-.-
Comma	--..--
Colon	---...
Question mark	..--..
Apostrophe	.----.
Hyphen	-....-
Fraction bar	-..-.
Parenthesis	-.--.-
Quotation mark	.-..-.

Accent	Morse
Ä umlaut	.-.-
Á accent	-- -
Å angstorm	.--.-
É accent	..-..
Ñ tilde	--.--
Ö umlaut	---.
Ü umlaut	..--

Since Morse code is not a visual, but an aural, language, the pattern and pace of the clicks are meant to be heard. To telegraph Morse code, the duration of a dot is taken to be one unit and the dash is three units. The space between the components of one character is one unit, between characters is three units, and between words is seven units. To indicate that a mistake has been made and for the receiver to delete the last word, send · · · · · · · · (eight dots).

Any good telegrapher will tell you not to look at a written table of the Morse code before starting to learn it. Never attempt to memorize it from a written table; learn Morse code by sound. Do not use software that shows you Morse characters on the screen. Do not use training systems that ask you to listen to successions of dots and dashes, or parts of characters, or to "count the dots and dashes" in characters. Listen only to complete, correctly sent words. Try using Morse at 12 words per minute or faster, if possible.

At the origin of the Morse code is the telegraph. The code was the first piece of electronic software. Without it, the telegraph was useless. It is interesting that the inventor, Samuel Finley Breese Morse, spent most of his time creating an encoder for words, not characters. He finally yielded to simplicity. Mr. Morse was born on April 27, 1791, in Charlestown, Massachusetts. Morse was a painter who, in 1832, was returning by sea from a period of art study in Europe. While at sea, discouraged with his art career, he heard about the newly discovered electromagnet and conceived of an idea for an electric telegraph. He mistakenly thought that the idea of such a telegraph was new, thus helping to give him the impetus to push the idea forward. Inspired, he experimented with different kinds of apparatus. He brought in two partners to help develop his telegraph and applied for a patent for his new telegraph in 1837, which he described as including a dot and dash code to represent numbers, a dictionary to turn numbers into words, and a method for sending sawtooth electrical signals. By 1838, at an exhibition of his telegraph in New York, Morse transmitted 10 words per minute. Morse assumed he could generate coded words with a dictionary because it had worked well for the previous generations of communication technology. For example, the French Chappe brothers gave us the visual semaphore, which is a system of signaling by positioning flags. With the complex apparatus of the semaphore, two signals in a row could represent more than 8000 words. It gave Napoleon a successful battle edge for some time. Morse soon dropped the notion of encoding words and ended up with a far simpler dot-dash code to represent letters. For many years, he faced considerable skepticism that any message could really be sent from city to city over wire. In fact, his two partners lost interest and left him.

With little help, Morse finally secured funds from Congress in 1843 to construct the first telegraph line in the United States from Baltimore to Washington, D.C. In May 1884, after Morse directed the wires to be set on poles, the first intercity electromagnetic telegraph line in the world was ready. From the Capitol building in Washington, Morse sent a Biblical quotation, "What Hath God Wrought!" as the first formal message on the telegraph line to Baltimore, a message that revealed his own sense of wonder at this new use of electricity. He later returned to his favorite role as an artist, painting miniature portraits. Further information on Morse can be found at <http://www.morsehistoricsite.org>. (A short history of telecommunication appears in chapter 1.)

Bits, Hertz, and Prefixes of Magnitude

Bits measure data rates. Hertz measure wavelengths of spectrum. Every few years the language adds a larger multiple. The prefixes are taken from the International System of Units (SI, Système International), the metric system, which has been adopted by most nations. The following table shows common prefixes that indicate decimal multiples and submultiples of SI units. One thousand bits per second could be represented as 1 kbps, or expressed as kilobits per second. The same prefix is used for counting hertz. A PCS band that runs at 1900 MHz is 1.9 billion hertz. Note "M" is capitalized and "k" is not.

Telecommunication systems measure data rates in bits per second, never in bytes. Computer storage simply measures bytes. Binary notation such as 2^{xxxx} is exponential notation for the string of 1s or 0s that follow. In byte speak, 1MB is 1,048,576 bytes, or about 2^{20}.

2^{32} – 4400000000 is the IPv4 address size. The maximum number of devices that can be addressed is about 4.4 billion.

2^{128} – 300000000000000000000000000000000000000 is the IPv6 address size, which is four times the length of IPv4. The maximum number of devices that can be addressed is about 3 by 38 zeroes or 300,000,000 google.

Symbol	Prefix	U.S. Name	~Bits	Tens	Decimal
y	yocto			10^{-24}	0.000 000 000 000 000 000 000 001
a	zepto			10^{-21}	0.000 000 000 000 000 000 001
a	atto			10^{-18}	0.000 000 000 000 000 001
f	femto			10^{-15}	0.000 000 000 000 001
p	pico			10^{-12}	0.000 000 000 001
Å	angstrom	ångström		10^{-10}	0.000 000 001
n	nano			10^{-9}	0.000 000 001
μ	micro	micron, micromillimeter		10^{-6}	0.000 001
m	milli	thousandth, millimeter		10^{-3}	0.001
c	centi	hundredth		10^{-2}	0.01
d	deci	tenth		10^{-1}	0.1
	one		2^{0}	10^{0}	1
da	deka, deca	ten	2^{4}	10^{1}	10
h	hecto	hundred	2^{7}	10^{2}	100
k	kilo	thousand	2^{10}	10^{3}	1,000
M	mega	million	2^{20}	10^{6}	1,000,000
G	giga	billion	2^{30}	10^{9}	1,000,000,000
T	tera	trillion	2^{40}	10^{12}	1,000,000,000,000
P	peta	quadrillion	2^{50}	10^{15}	1,000,000,000,000,000
E	exa	quintillion	2^{60}	10^{18}	1,000,000,000,000,000,000
Z	zetta	sextillion	2^{70}	10^{21}	1,000,000,000,000,000,000,000
Y	yotta	septillion	2^{80}	10^{24}	1,000,000,000,000,000,000,000,000
G	googl	nonillion	2^{100}	10^{30}	1,000,000,000,000,000,000,000,000,000,000

Working Frequency Standards

Wide area networks (WANs) and local area networks (LANs) that are in use have specific transmission characteristics. All WANs transmit and receive in paired bands as Full Division Duplex (FDD). Most LANs share traffic in Time Division Duplex (TDD). The transmission bandwidth is divided into channels with one user per channel in 1G technology, and multiple users per channel in later technology. The radio frequency modulation technique varies from simple Frequency Modulation (FM), to Frequency Shift Keying (FSK), to elaborate Gaussian Minimum Shift Keying (GMSK), and to Differential Quadrature Phase Shift Keying (DQPSK). The channel bit rate is the maximum use of the channel using that modulation technique. User capacity is the product of the number of channels and the number of users per channel. (See the table that follows.)

Standard	Transmit	Receive	Channels	Users per Channel	Spacing	Modulation	Channel Bit Rate	User Capacity
1G Analog Cellular WAN								
AMPS	824–849	869–894	832	1	30 kHz	FM	na	832
N-AMPS	824–849	869–894	2496	1	10 kHz	FM	na	2496
2G Digital Cellular WAN								
TDMA	824–849	869–894	832	3	30 kHz	DQPSK	48.6 kbps	2496
CDMA	824–849	869–894	20	798	1.25 MHz	QPSK	1.2288 Mbps	15960
GSM	880–915	925–960	124	8	200 kHz	GMSK	270.833 kbps	992
PDC	940–956 1477–1501	810–826 1429–1453	1600	3	25 kHz	DQPSK	42 kbps	4800
DCS 1800	1710–1785	1805–1880	374	8	200 kHz	GMSK	270.833 kbps	2992
PCS*	1850–1910	1930–1990						
Data 2G WAN								
CDPD	824–849	869–894	832		30 kHz	GMSK	19.2 kbps	832
RAM - Mobitex	896–902	935–941	480		12.5 kHz	GMSK	8 kbps	480
Ardis - Motient	806–824	851–869	720		25 kHz	FSK	19.2 kbps	720
Data 2G LAN								
IEEE 802.11 FHSS	2400–2483**		79		1 MHz	GFSK	1 to 2 Mbps	79
IEEE 802.11 DSSS	2400–2483**		11		11 MHz	DQPSK	1 to 2 Mbps	255
Cordless Phones								
DECT	1880–1900**		10	12	1.728 MHz	GFSK	1.152 Mbps	120
PHS	1895–1918**		300	4	300 kHz	GMSK	384 kbps	1200

* PCS includes PCS TDMA, PCS CDMA, PCS GSM1900, wideband CDMA, PACS (PHS), DCT-U (DECT), composite CDMA/TDMA (HDR).

** TDD

FCC Spectrum Allocation

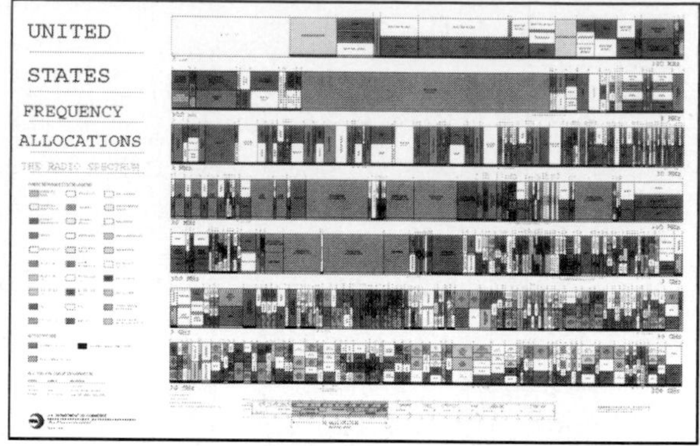

If somehow you could see every wireless signal in the air at once, you would see something like the U.S. Frequency Allocation chart. This chart is helpful in tracking various spectrum allocation technologies. We have reprinted the 1996 spectrum wall chart first, and then present one enlarged band per page. The original is available for purchase (stock # 003-000 to 00652-2; $6.00, non-U.S. $7.50) from the U.S. Government Printing Office, Post Office Box 371954, Pittsburgh, Pennsylvania, 15250-7954. The Web site is <http://www.ntia.doc.gov/osmhome/allochrt.html>.

Note that the bands are color coded, although the colors are represented in gray scale here.

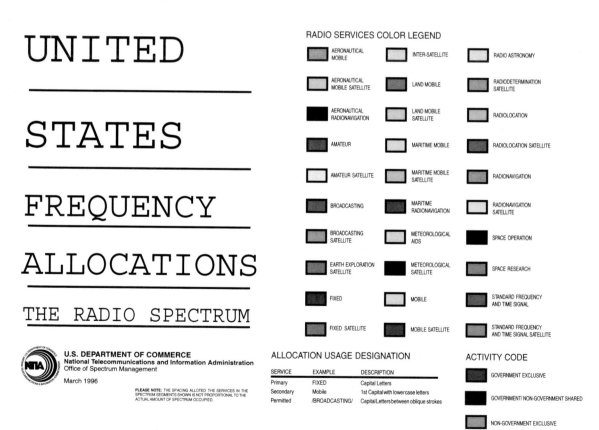

UNITED

STATES

FREQUENCY

ALLOCATIONS

THE RADIO SPECTRUM

U.S. DEPARTMENT OF COMMERCE
National Telecommunications and Information Administration
Office of Spectrum Management

March 1996

PLEASE NOTE: THE SPACING ALLOTED THE SERVICES IN THE SPECTRUM SEGMENTS SHOWN IS NOT PROPORTIONAL TO THE ACTUAL AMOUNT OF SPECTRUM OCCUPIED.

RADIO SERVICES COLOR LEGEND

- AERONAUTICAL MOBILE
- AERONAUTICAL MOBILE SATELLITE
- AERONAUTICAL RADIONAVIGATION
- AMATEUR
- AMATEUR SATELLITE
- BROADCASTING
- BROADCASTING SATELLITE
- EARTH EXPLORATION SATELLITE
- FIXED
- FIXED SATELLITE
- INTER-SATELLITE
- LAND MOBILE
- LAND MOBILE SATELLITE
- MARITIME MOBILE
- MARITIME MOBILE SATELLITE
- MARITIME RADIONAVIGATION
- METEOROLOGICAL AIDS
- METEOROLOGICAL SATELLITE
- MOBILE
- MOBILE SATELLITE
- RADIO ASTRONOMY
- RADIODETERMINATION SATELLITE
- RADIOLOCATION
- RADIOLOCATION SATELLITE
- RADIONAVIGATION
- RADIONAVIGATION SATELLITE
- SPACE OPERATION
- SPACE RESEARCH
- STANDARD FREQUENCY AND TIME SIGNAL
- STANDARD FREQUENCY AND TIME SIGNAL SATELLITE

ALLOCATION USAGE DESIGNATION

SERVICE	EXAMPLE	DESCRIPTION
Primary	FIXED	Capital Letters
Secondary	Mobile	1st Capital with lowercase letters
Permitted	/BROADCASTING/	Capital Letters between oblique strokes

ACTIVITY CODE

- GOVERNMENT EXCLUSIVE
- GOVERNMENT/ NON-GOVERNMENT SHARED
- NON-GOVERNMENT EXCLUSIVE

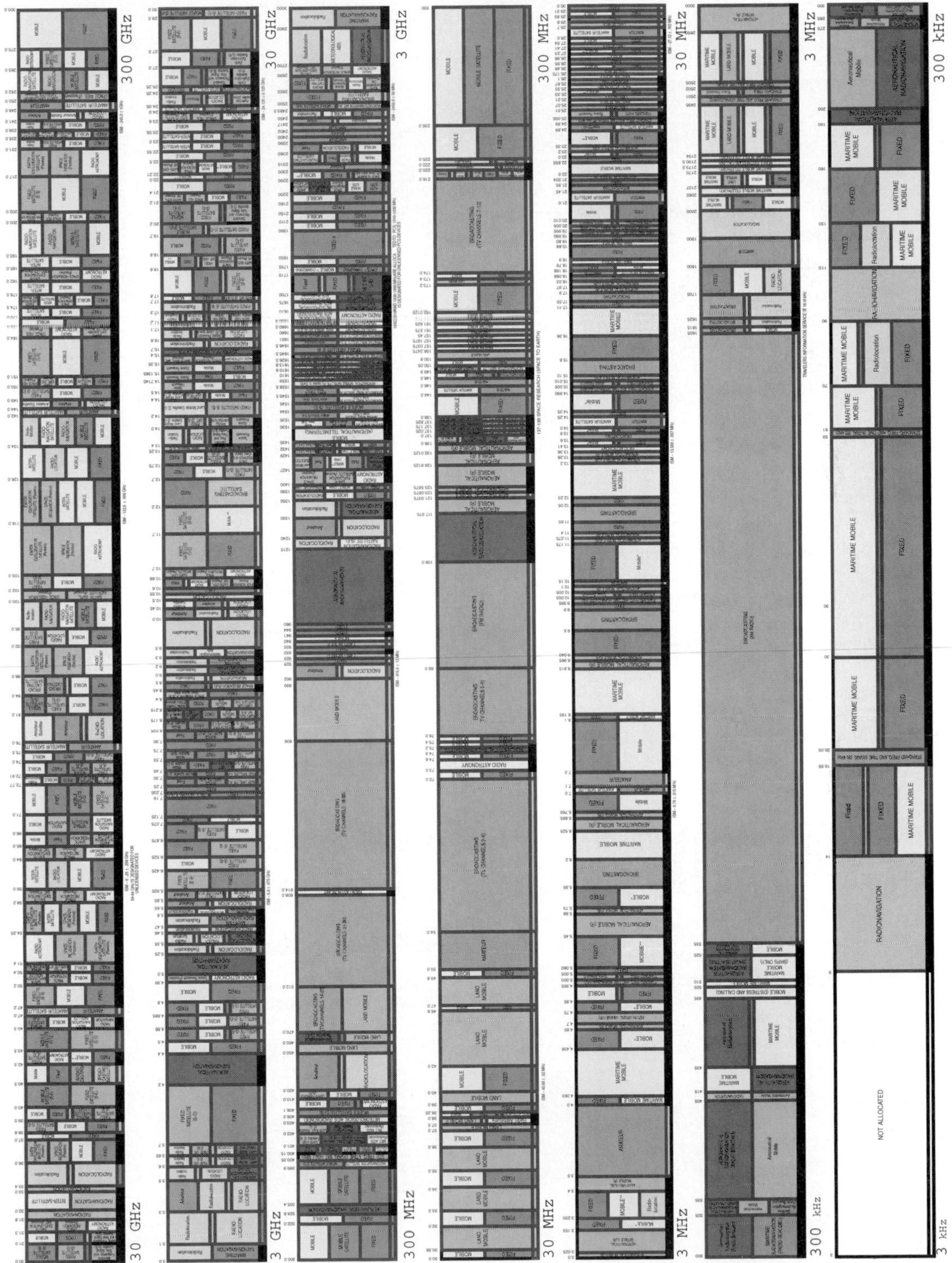

Band 1 – (3 KHz–300 KHz) Submarine and Maritime

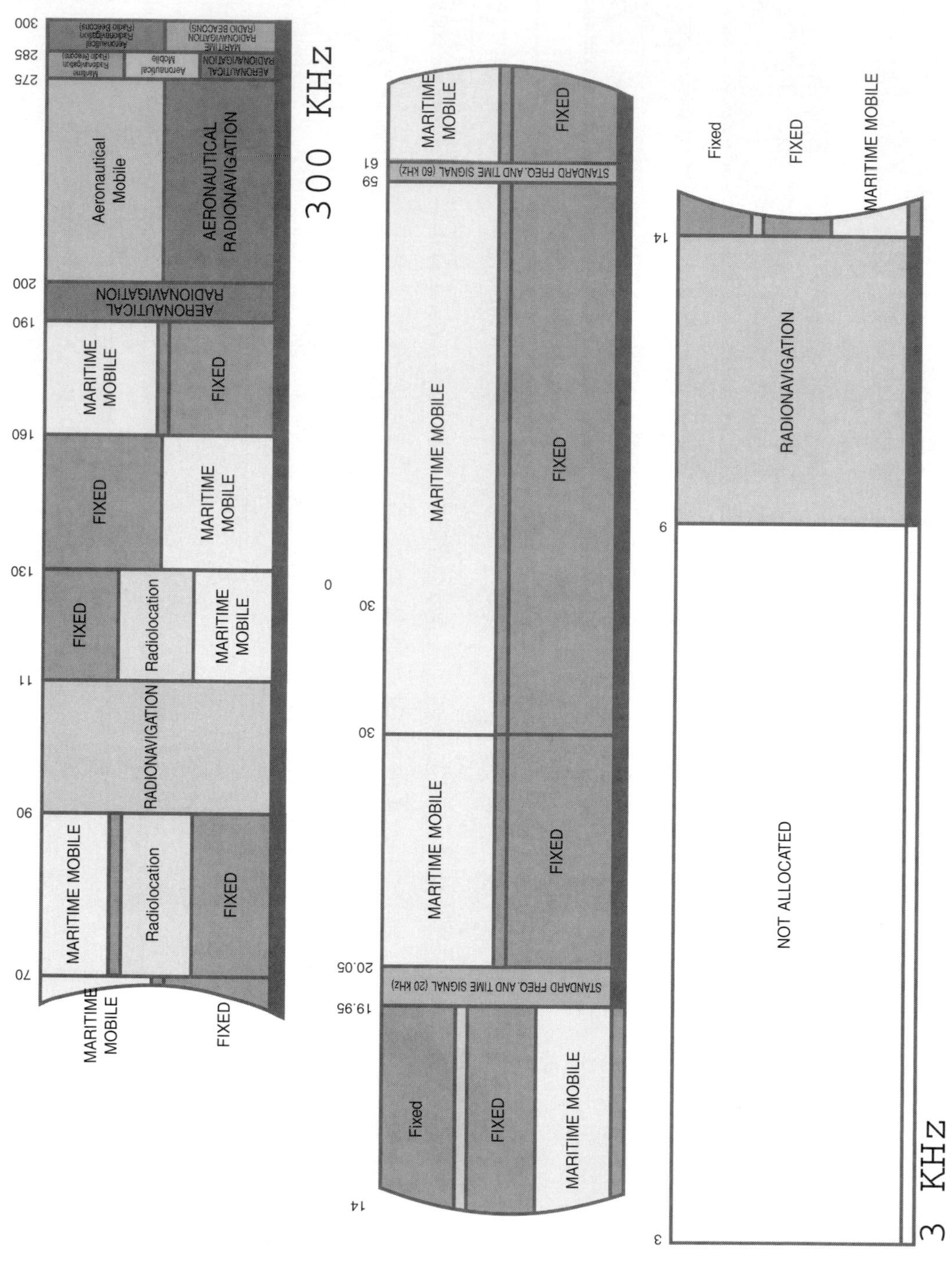

Band 2 – (300 KHz–3 MHz) AM Radio

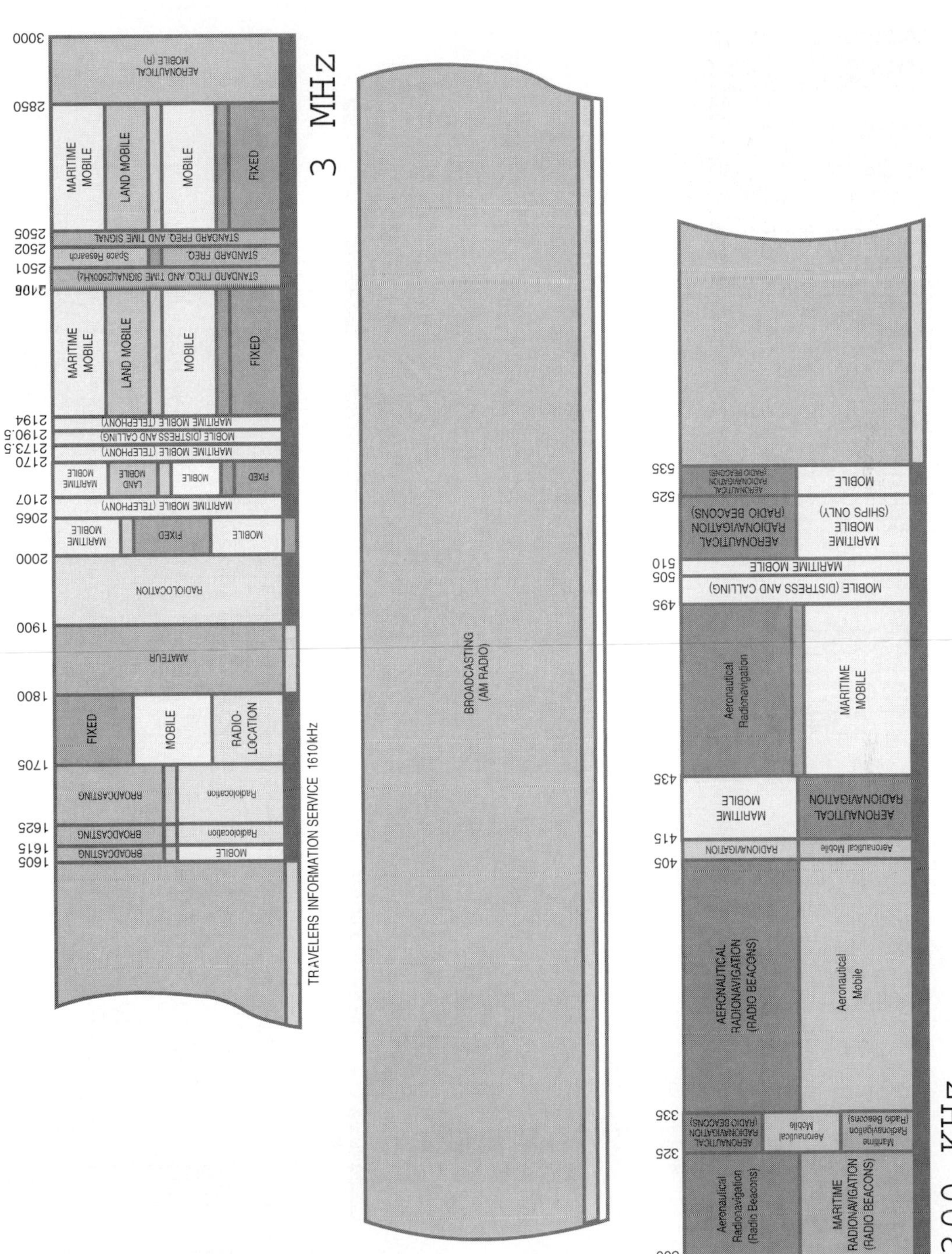

Band 3 – (3 MHz–30 MHz) Maritime and Air

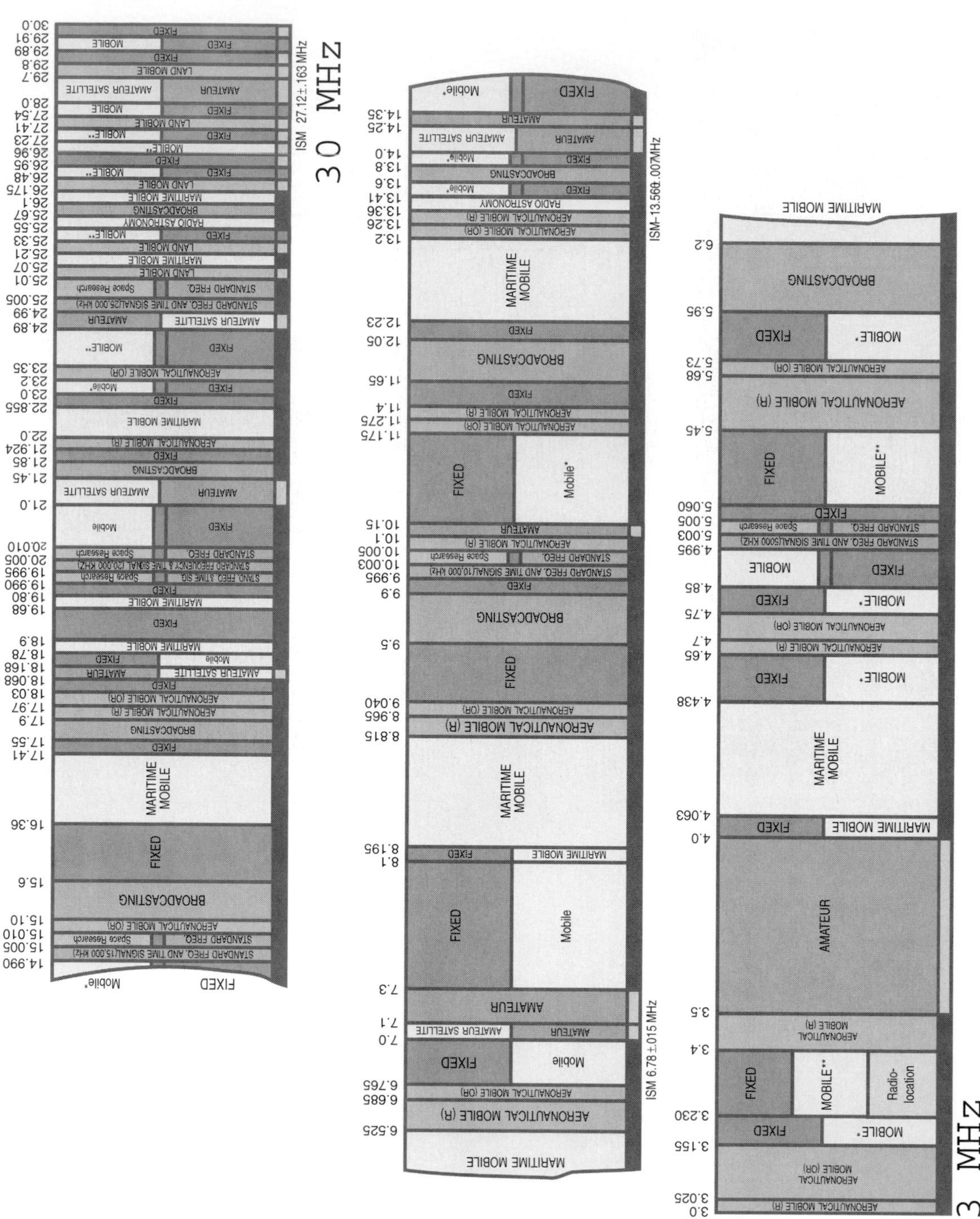

Band 4 – (30 MHz–300 MHz) SMR, Paging, FM Radio, VHF TV

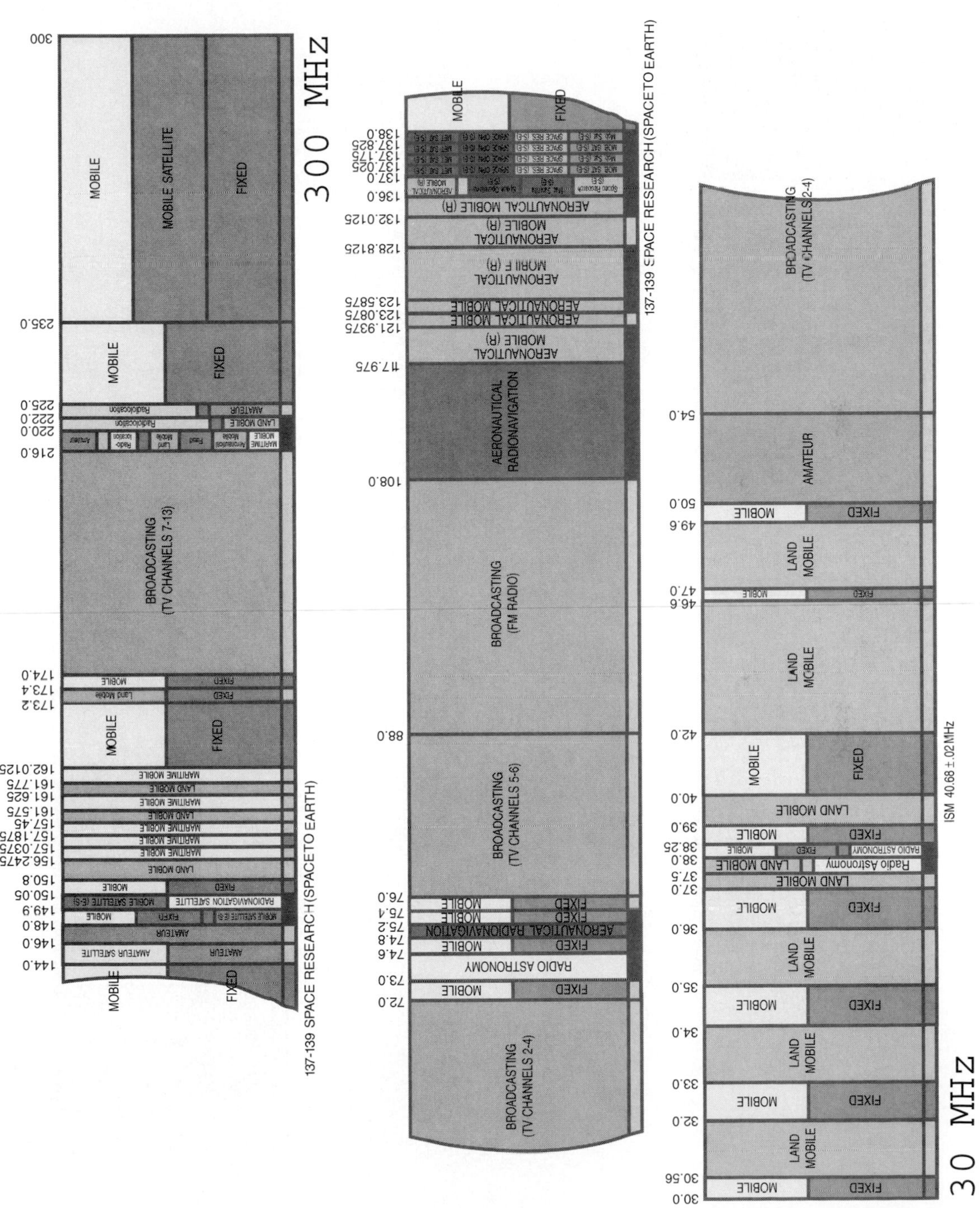

Band 5 – (300 MHz–3 GHz) IG Cellular, 2G PCS, 3G, ISM, GPS, 002.11, MMDS, and Bluetooth

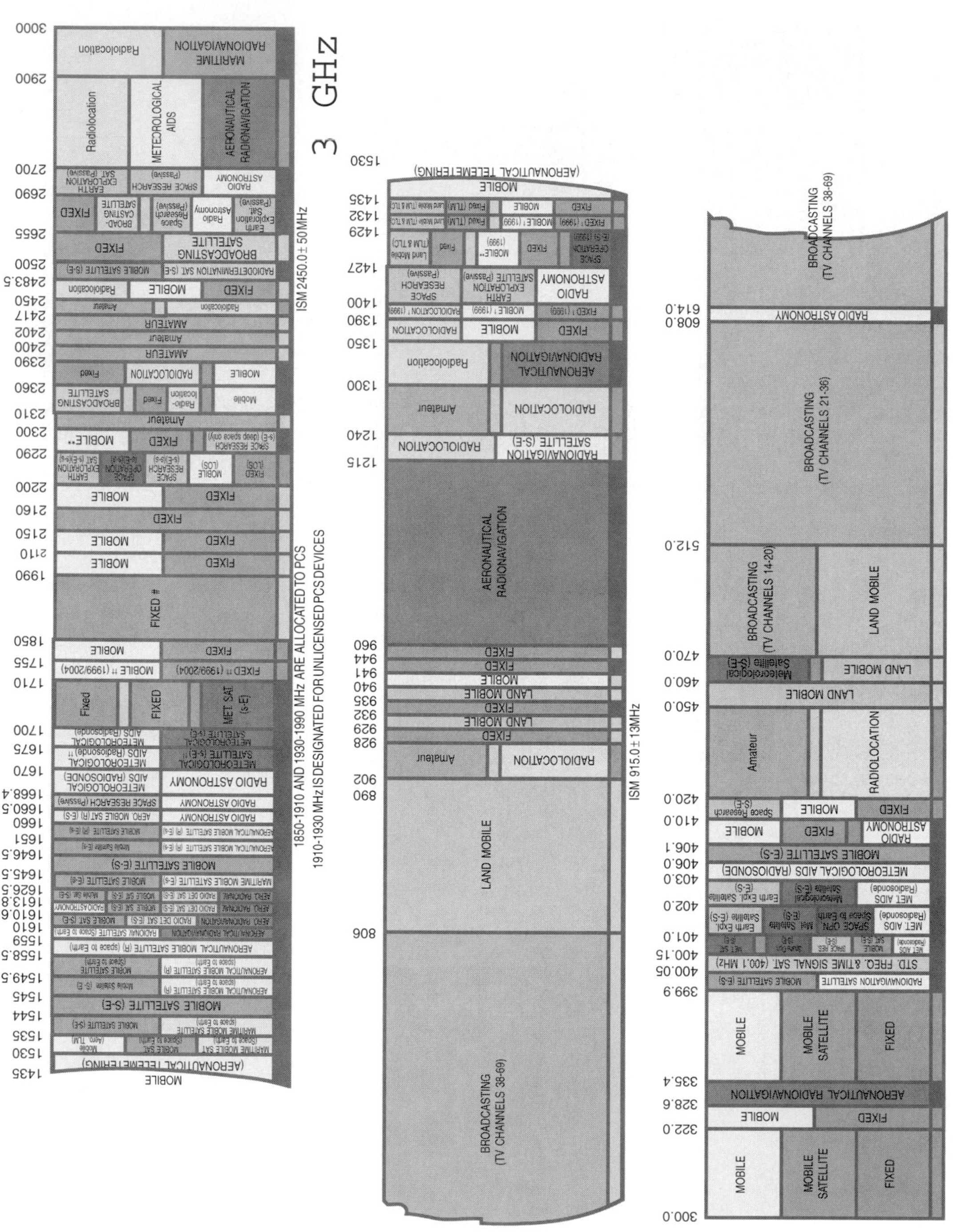

Band 6 – (3 GHz–30 GHz) 802.11a, HyperLAN2, LMDS

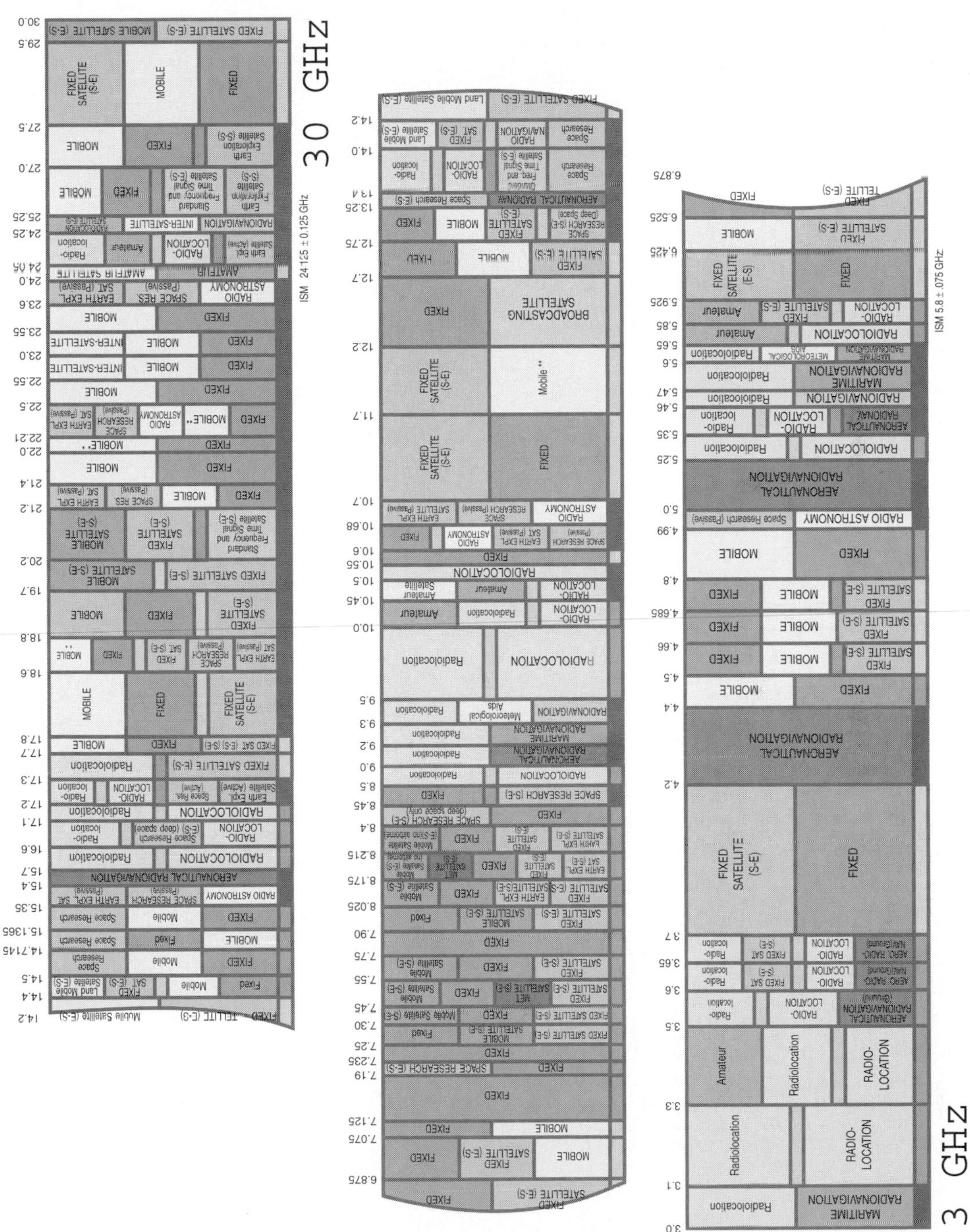

Appendix B

Research and Standards

Research about the wireless Internet can be challenging. Much of the application research is not scientific, not measured, and lies in the field of use.

Wireless Research

Some research companies have reasonable insight into wireless technology and markets. They occasionally compile surveys and first-order reports. Notable research companies, some of which post industry reports at their Web sites, include:

ARC Group	<http://www.the-arc-group.com>
Cahner's In-Stat	<http://www.instat.com>
Dataquest	<http://www3.gartner.com>
Durlacher	< http://www.durlacher.com>
Forrester	<http://www.forrester.com>
Gartner	<http://www3.gartner.com>
George Gilder Technology Report	<http://www.gildertech.com>
IDC	<http://www.idc.com>
Meta Group	<http://www.metagroup.com/>
Strategis Group	<http://www.strategisgroup.com>
Yankee Group	< http://www.yankeegroup.com/>
Datamonitor	<http://www.datamonitor.com>

Mobilestreams <http://www.mobilestreams.com>
Ovum <http://www.ovum.com>
Strategy Analytics <http://www.strategyanalytics.com>

Consulting firms, such as Price-Waterhouse and Frost & Sullivan, and banking and brokerage firms, such as ING Barrings and Hambrecht, post illuminating reports from time to time.

Standards Bodies

The following national and international groups are setting the standards for the wireless Internet. They are listed alphabetically by their familiar acronyms, followed by their Web addresses, their full names, and the location of their headquarters.

3GPP: <http://www.3gpp.org/> Third-Generation Partnership Project. A partnership, not a legal entity.

ANSI: <http://Web.ansi.org/> American National Standards Institute, New York City

ATIS: <http://www.atis.org/> Alliance for Telecommunications Industry Solutions, Washington, D.C.

ARIB: < http://www.santa-cri.com/cc/arib/> Association of Radio Industries and Businesses, Chiyoda-ku, Tokyo. Japanese commercial standards group.

Bluetooth: <http://www.bluetooth.com/> Bluetooth Consortium, Stockholm, Sweden

CDG: <http://www.cdg.org/> CDMA Development Group, Anaheim, California. A consortium of more than 100 companies who use CDMA technology.

CTIA: <http://www.ctia.net> Cellular Telecommunications and Internet Association, Washington, D.C.

ETSI: <http://www.etsi.org/> European Telecommunications Standards Institute, Sophia Antipolis, France. European technical and commercial standards group.

FCC: <http://www.fcc.gov/> Federal Communications Commission, Washington, D.C. The FCC works closely with the NTIA in assigning spectrum.

GSM: <http://www.gsmworld.com/> GSM Association, Dublin, Ireland, and London, England. GSM is the European source of standards and statistics.

IEEE: <http://www.ieee.org> Institute of Electrical and Electronics Engineers, Washington, D.C. The IEEE (spoken as "I triple E") is a premiere U.S. standards body.

IETF: <http://www.ietf.cnri.reston.va.us/home.html> Internet Engineering Task Force, Reston, Virginia.

ISO: <http://www.iso.ch/> International Organization for Standardization (UN) Geneva, Switzerland. ISO is part of the United Nations.

ISOC: <http://www.isoc.org/> Internet Society, Geneva, Switzerland

ITU: <http://www.itu.int> International Telecommunication Union, Geneva, Switzerland. This worldwide standards body sanctions all international communications standards such as IS-95(CDMA), IS-154(TDMA), GSM. IS stands for Interim Standard. Founded in 1865 to moderate telegraphy standards, ITU now standardizes technology and negotiates spectrum for global use.

NTIA: <http://www.ntia.doc.gov/> National Telecommunications and Information Administration, Washington, D.C. A chapter of the U.S. Department of Commerce that registers spectrum use.

PCIA: <http://www.pcia.com> Personal Communications Industry Association, Alexandria, Virginia.

T1: <http://www.t1.org> Telecommunications 1. Committee T1 was established in February 1984. T1 develops technical standards and reports regarding interconnection and interoperability of telecommunications networks at interfaces with end-user systems. T1 is sponsored by ATIS and is accredited by ANSI. T1 is an organizational partner of the 3GPP.

TIA: <http://www.tiaonline.org/> Telecommunications Industry Association, Arlington, Virginia.

TTA: <http://www.tta.or.kr/index.html Telecommunications Technology Association, Seoul, Korea. Commercial and technical organization promoting Korean standards.

TTC: <http://www.ttc.or.jp/> Telecommunications Technology Committee, Tokyo, Japan. Commercial and technical organization that promotes Japanese standards.

UNICODE: <http://www.unicode.org/> The Unicode Consortium, Sunnyvale, California

UWC: <http://www.uwcc.org/> Universal Wireless Communications Consortium, Bellevue, Washington. This international consortium comprises more than 100 wireless carriers and vendors that support the TDMA-EDGE and WIN technology standards.

W3C: <http://www.w3.org/> World Wide Web Consortium, New York City. This is the Internet community standards body that specifies HTML, XML, and Compact HTML among many other standards. W3C is active in defining mobile standards.

WAP Forum: <http://www.wapforum.org> Wireless Access Protocol Forum, Sunnyvale, California. The WAP Forum is the owner of the telco-centric WAP standards.

WTO: <http://www.wto.org> World Trade Organization, Geneva, Switzerland. The WTO makes recommendations about global eCommerce, language, and international personalization.

C
Appendix

Wireless Companies

The wireless Internet is served by many wireless companies. There are three useful groups: client, server, and middleware. We have listed them in these categories, with some basic information and their Web addresses.

Wireless Client Companies

Wireless client companies produce browsers. They often produce an optimal server or gateway that supports their browser.

Access

Access Systems America, Inc., is a wholly owned subsidiary of Access Co., Ltd., of Tokyo, Japan. Access develops and licenses software technology for manufacturers of consumer information appliances including NetFront, the popular i-mode browser. Access created open standards and specifications such as Compact HTML and XHTML Basic. <http://www.access-us-inc.com/>

Openwave Systems

Openwave is the result of the merger of Phone.com and Software.com. Alain Rossman, a French-born entrepreneur and former executive at Apple Computer, Inc., founded the company in late 1994. It was initially known as Libris, Inc., and based in Redwood City, California. The name changed to Unwired Planet, then changed again to Phone.com, Inc. Phone.com established the leading North American Web phone browser and was contracted to produce the basic technology for WAP Forum. It also provides gateways. Software.com was known for providing email systems to telcos for their subscribers. It is now working on a Unified Messaging System for telcos. <http://www.openwave.com>

Pixo

Pixo develops wireless software platform and services for wireless phone manufacturers, carriers, and content providers. The Pixo OS platform integrates Pixo phone software with Internet services. Its platform is ideal for pioneering developers to produce new wireless Internet applications for Web-enabled phones. <http://www.pixo.com>

Wireless Server Companies

Wireless server companies make servers that enable content companies to reach wireless networks and devices. Although BEA Weblogic and IBM WebSphere are the most popular application servers, the following systems are useful wireless application servers.

ATG

Advanced Technology Group is known for its eCommerce system, Dynamo. Because of its advanced personalization components, it is ideal to manage mobile application accounts. <http://www.atg.com/>

Everypath

Everypath can mobilize a Web site for the wireless Internet in only a couple of weeks without changing the underlying site. <http://www.everypath.com/>

Lutris

Lutris Technologies is an Open Source enterprise software and services company that makes an Open Source Java™/XML application server called Lutris Enhydra. The application server delivers wired and wireless Web applications through a unique page compiler called XMLC. <http://www.lutris.com>

Wireless Middleware Companies

Wireless middleware companies provide intermediate channel services that are shaping the wireless Internet.

724 Solutions

Begun in Toronto in July 1997, 724 quickly established wireless Internet infrastructure software for financial institutions with companies such as Bank of America.

Its Financial Services Platform provides secure access to Web phones, handhelds, two-way pagers, and personal computers. <http://www.724.com>

Aether Systems

Aether Systems provides wireless development software tools and implementations for large-scale wireless solutions. It provides Web hosting services and software for wireless development and deployment. Aether Intelligent Messaging (AIM) is an integrated, wireless software development environment and a suite of software development toolkits to build client-server applications that seamlessly operate over a variety of wireless networks. ScoutWare is a development tool for mobile synchronization, management, and development software. Vertical market offerings include solutions for the financial, health care, logistics, and mobile government markets. <http://www.aethersystems.com>

Air2Web

Air2Web provides a Mobile Internet platform for large companies and wireless application hosting services. Its middleware is useful to reach major brands of Web phone, handheld, and pager using a special Air2Web markup language (A2WML). It delivers wireless vertical market applications such as Enterprise Application Integration (EAI), Sales Force Automation (SFA), Customer Relationship Management (CRM), Enterprise Resource Planning (ERP), and Supply Chain Management (SCM). <http://www.air2Web.com>

AvantGo

AvantGo offers mobile infrastructure software, services, and solutions for all wireless architectures. It provides to subscribers a wireless AvantGo browser and channel that feature mobile content and services. The AvantGo Enterprise software is for business information and applications from mobile devices to accelerate information flow between companies and their mobile employees, customers, suppliers, and business partners. AvantGo Mobile Internet service (AMI) provides consumers with interactive and personalized Internet content and Web-based applications on mobile devices from more than 600 content sources or channels. <http://avantgo.com>

Brience

Brience™ provides Mobile Processing Server, a universal delivery platform for wireless and broadband solutions, allowing customers to use new Web-enabled business opportunities. As a server, it provides parsing modules for the key commercial application server components. Integrated Experience Studio is a visual development tool to build wireless applications. Brience was founded in March 2000. <http://www.brience.com/>

Broadbeam

Broadbeam is the largest provider of worldwide wireless infrastructure. Developers can write to its platform SystemsGO to build large, enterprise applications. Tools offer end-to-end security between mobile devices and enterprise server applications. ExpressQ™ is the mobile messaging. In June 2000 Broadbeam changed its name from Nettech. <http://www.broadbeam.com>

FusionOne

FusionOne offers synchronization software for wireless devices and servers. FusionOne was founded in 1998 and is a pioneer in the development of Internet Sync, which is software that makes information access seamless across multiple communications and computing devices using its centralized storage services. This company is a leading sponsor of SyncML. <http://www.fusionone.com>

Go America

Go America is a national wireless Internet service provider founded in 1996. Its Go.Web℠ browser and email system run on pagers and handhelds. Its middleware can access intranet or enterprise systems from mobile locations through the use of the efficient and secure wireless Virtual Private Network (VPN). <http://www.goamerica.com/>

Neomar

Neomar delivers an end-to-end WAP solution that runs on RIM wireless handhelds and a WAP gateway to connect the Web with any wireless network. It specializes in security. <http://www.neomar.com/>

PumaTech

PumaTech provides software infrastructure for wireless personal communication platforms. It provides low-level, end-to-end mobile device management systems for synchronization, custom applications, centralized backup, security, information flow control, notification, eCommerce, and browsing. PumaTech is known for its Intellisync synchronization software used by Palm in its devices, Windows CE, and other mobile platforms. Satellite Forms is a leading RAD tool to build applications for a variety of mobile devices. <http://www.PumaTech.com/>

Wireless Knowledge

Wireless Knowledge was founded in 1998 as a joint effort of Microsoft and QUALCOMM. Its Workstyle™ family of server products is used for mobile business wireless solutions that access Microsoft Exchange as well as Lotus Domino and other back-end systems. <http://www.wirelessknowledge.com>

D Appendix

Further Reading

The wireless Internet encompasses many disciplines, and information about it comes in many forms. We have listed useful resources in four categories: books and periodicals, white papers and reports, articles on the Web, and Web sites especially useful for developers.

Books and Periodicals

Alexander, C. *A Pattern Language.* Oxford UK: Oxford University Press, 1977.

Arehart, C., et al. *Professional WAP.* Birmingham, UK: Wrox Press, 2000. 814 pages.

Bates, Regis, and Gregory, Donald. *Voice and Data Communications Handbook,* 3rd ed. New York: McGraw Hill, 2000. 999 pages.

Beck, Kent, and Gamma, Emma. *Extreme Programming Explained: Embrace Change.* Reading, Mass.: Addison-Wesley, 1999. 224 pages.

Brand, Stewart. *Media Lab: Inventing the Future at MIT.* New York: Viking-Penguin, 1987. 285 pages.

___. *How Buildings Learn: What Happens after They're Built.* New York: Viking-Penguin (in UK: Orion Books), 1994. 243 pages.

___. *The Clock of the Long Now: Time and Responsibility: The Ideas Behind the World's Slowest Computer.* Cambridge, Mass.: Perseus Books, 1999. 198 pages.

Clarke, A. C. *Profiles of the Future.* New York: Harper & Row, 1963. 235 pages.

Coomaraswamy, Ananda K. *The Transformation of Nature in Art.* New York: Dover, 1934. 245 pages.

Cooper, A. *The Inmates Are Running the Asylum: Why High Tech Products Drive Us Crazy and How to Restore the Sanity.* Indianapolis, Ind.: Sams, 1999. 261 pages.

Cytowik, Richard. *The Man Who Tasted Shapes.* Los Angeles: Tacher/Putnam, 1993. 252 pages.

___. *The Neurological Side of Neuropsychology.* Cambridge, Mass.: Bradford Book/ MIT Press, 1996. 529 pages.

Dodd, Annabel. *The Essential Guide to Telecommunications,* 2nd ed. Upper Saddle River, N.J.: Prentice-Hall, 2000. 365 pages.

Duffy, Francis, and Henney, Alex. *The Changing City.* London: Bullstrode, 1989.

Dunlop, Beth. *Arquitectonica.* Washington, D.C.: The American Institute of Architects Press, 1991. 214 pages. (The Architecture of Bernardo Fort-Brescia and Laurinda Spear).

Eames, Charles, and Eames, Ray. *Powers of Ten: A Film Dealing with the Relative Size of Things in the Universe and the Effect of Adding Another Zero. 9.5 minutes.* Pyramid Films, Santa Monica, California, 1978. (Film)

Finch, Christopher. *Highways to Heaven: The AUTO Biography of America.* New York: HarperCollins, 1992. 416 pages.

Gershenfeld, Neil. *When Things Start to Think.* New York: Henry Holt, 1999. 225 pages.

Gilder, George. *Telecosm: How Infinite Bandwidth Will Revolutionize Our World.* New York: Free Press, 2000. 353 pages.

Jacobson, Robert E. (ed.). *Information Design.* Cambridge, Mass.: MIT Press, 1999. 373 pages.

McCloud, Scott. *Understanding Comic.* Northampton, Mass.: Kitchen Sink Press, 1993. 216 pages.

McLaughlin, Brett. *Java and XML.* Sebastopol, Calif.: O'Reilly, June 2000. 479 pages.

McLuhan, Marshall. *Understanding Media: The Extensions of Man.* New York: McGraw-Hill, 1964. 318 pages.

___. *War and Peace in the Global Village.* New York: McGraw-Hill, 1968. 192 pages.

Mitchell, William J. *City of Bits: Space, Place, and the Infobahn*. Cambridge, Mass.: MIT Press, November 1996.

Moore, Geoffrey A. *Crossing the Chasm: Marketing and Selling High-Tech Products to Mainstream Customers*. New York: HarperBusiness, 1999. 227 pages.

Morrison, Phillip, Eames, Charles, and Eames, Ray. *Powers of Ten: About the Relative Size of Things in the Universe.* New York: Scientific American Press, 1982.

Negroponte, Nicholas. *Being Digital.* New York: Knopf, 1995. 243 pages.

Newton, Harry. *Newton's Telecom Dictionary,* 16th ed. Gilroy, Calif.: Telecom Books, 2000. 992 pages.

Rand, Ayn. *Introduction to Objectivist Epistemology.* New York: Meridian, 1990. 314 pages.

Ranganathan, S. R. *Five Laws of Library Science.* Bangalore: Sarada Ranganathan Endowment for Library Science, 1999 (originally published in 1931). 449 pages.

Raskin, Jeff. *The Humane Interface.* Boston, Mass.: Addison-Wesley, 2000. 233 pages.

Rodgers, R, and Hammerstein, O. *South Pacific.* New York: Random House, 1959.

Rowsome, Frank, Jr. *Think Small. The Story of Those Volkswagen Ads.* New York: Ballantine Books, 1971. 128 pages.

Singhal, Sandeep, et al. *The Wireless Application Protocol.* Boston: Addison-Wesley, 2000. 678 pages.

Stephenson, Neal. *Snow Crash.* New York: Bantam, 1992. 471 pages.

Toffler, Alvin. *Future Shock.* New York: Bantam, 1970. 562 pages.

Tufte, Edward. *The Visual Display of Quantitative Information.* Cheshire, Conn.: Graphics Press, 1983. 199 Pages.

___. *Envisioning Information.* Cheshire, Conn.: Graphics Press, 1990.

White Papers and Reports

Wireless Data Networks: A Guide to Mobile Computing. Revision 6. Kalamazoo, Mich.: The Bishop Company, September 1999.

Young, W. R. "Advanced Mobile Phone Service: Introduction, Background, and Objectives." *The Bell System Technical Journal,* Vol 58, No 1, January 1979.

Articles on the Web

Barcode information: <http://www.theculvergroup.com/barcodes.html>

DoD Spectrum Report: "Department of Defense Investigation of the Feasibility of Accommodating the International Mobile Telecommunications (IMT) 2000 within the 1755-1850 MHz Band." <http://www.ntia.doc.gov/ntiahome/threeg/33001/dodassessment.pdf>

Hedy Lamarr, actress and wireless heroine: <http://www.hedylamarr.at/>

Location-based information: <http://tcs-prod.Weblabs.com/issues/199910/tcs/location.html>

Radio in the early days <http://home.luna.nl/~arjan-muil/radio/history.html>

Scientific American's wireless articles: <www.sciam.com/2000/1000issue/1000alpert.html>

SIM supplier: <http://www.gemplus.com>

Sixth Report: FCC 00-289 July 2001: <http://www.fcc.gov>, <http://hraunfoss.fcc.gov/edocs_public/attachmatch/FCC-01-192A1.pdf>

Spectrum auction information: <http://www.fcc.gov/wtb/auctions/>, <http://www.zaborski.com/cdma/forecasting.html>, and <http://www.ntia.gov/>

WAP phone illustration of restaurant application: <http://www.smartmoney.com/techmarket/index.cfm?story=20001011>

WAP report: "W* Effect Considered Harmful" appears at <http://www.4k-associates.com/IEEE-L7-WAP-BIG.html>

Developer Resources

The following sites are useful developer resources and development portals. The CTIA listserver is an invaluable resource for news compiled daily. The ayg.com site is particularly helpful to early wireless developers.

Allnetdevices: <http://www.allnetdevices.com>, wireless developer portal with information.

Anywhereyougo: <http://www.anywhereyougo.com> and <http://www.ayg.com>, useful wireless developer portal with tools and information.

Cellmania: <http://www.cellmania.com>, wireless developer portal with information.

CNET: <http://download.cnet.com/>, good source of wireless tools and device information.

CTIA: <http://www.wow-com.com/news/now/>, excellent daily wireless news feed from CTIA.

FreeNetworks: <http://www.freenetworks.org/>, Wireless LAN.

Gelon: <http://www.gelon.net>, WAP search engine with emulators to test site.

Geo Community: <http://www.geocomm.com>, developers in location based technology.

Global Sources: <http://www.globalsources.com>, wireless developer portal with information. <http://wireless.cnet.com>.

Global Mobile Suppliers Association (GSA): <http://www.gsacom.com>, GSM/3G industry.

GPRS Applications Alliance (GAA): <http://www.gprsworld.com/>.

GSM Association Web: <http://www.gsmworld.com/technology/gprs.html>.

Mobileinfo: <http://www.mobileinfo.com>, wireless developer portal with information.

Mobile Media Japan: <http://www.mobilemediajapan.com/resources>, good source of information and tools.

Mobitex: <ttp://www.mobitex.webmaster.se/mobitex_ny/Kampanj/gateway_mobitex.asp>, good crash course.

Motorola iDEN: <http://www.idendev.com>, iDEN Java developer tools.

Nokia: <http://www.nokia.com>, WAP developer tools and servers.

NTT DoCoMo: <http://www.nttdocomo.com/>, information and cHTML notes.

Olabs: <http://www.olabs.com>, wireless developer testing information.

Openwave: <http://www.openwave.com>, HDML and WAP developer tools, gateways, servers, and information.

Philips: <http://www.semiconductors.philips.com/>, device and chip information.

Signalsoft: <http://www.signalsoftcorp.com/>, location-based tools for this vendor.

SmartRay: <http://www.smartRay.com>, wireless developer portal with information.

WAP Forum: <http://www.wapforum.org>, general WAP developer tools and information.

WAP Forum: <http://www.wapforum.org/what/whitepapers.htm>, WAP white papers with developer information.

WAP gateway: <http://www.wapit.com>, wireless WAP developer portal with information.

Wapholesun: <http://www.wapholesun.com>, wireless developer portal with information.

Wapit: <http://www.kannel.org/>, Open Source.

Wapland: <http://www.wapland.com>, WAP developer portal with information.

Waplinks: <http://www.waplinks.com>, WAP search engine and portal.

Wirelessdeveloper: <http://www.wirelessdeveloper.com>, simple wireless information portal.

Wirelessdevnet: <http://www.wirelessdevnet.com>, wireless developer portal with information.

Endnotes

Part 1

[1] "IBM Teams with Top Interactive Firms to Deliver M-Business Solutions." IBM press release June 2, 2000. Available: <http://www.ibm.com/Press/prnews.nsf/jan/FC958519E9E4F8C4852568F20041F7A9>.

Chapter 1

[1] Webb, Janiece. Keynote presentation at the PCIA Global Xchange, Chicago, Illinois. September 2000.

[2] Homer. *The Odyssey.* Robert Fagles (translator). New York: Viking Press, 1996, p. 277.

[3] Council of Economic Advisors. *The Economic Impact of Third-Generation Wireless Technology.* Washington, D.C.: U.S. Government Printing Office, October 2000.

[4] Bill Gates. Question and answer session at the "Forum 2000." Redmond, Washington, June 22, 2000.

[5] Levenson, Lisa. "Advanced Wireless Networks May Cost $751 Billion, Study Says." [Online]. Available: <http://quote.bloomberg.com/fgcgi.cgi?ptitle=Technology%20News&s1=blk&tp=ad_topright_tech&T=markets_fgcgi_content99.ht&s2=blk&bt=ad_bottom_tech&bt2=ad_position1_technology&middle=ad_frame2_technology&s=AOlxuRRTwQWR2YW5j>. Accessed: January 10, 2001.

[6] Eurotechnology-Japan Corp. "i-mode – mobile computing & ecommerce, mcommerce, UMTS, i-mode in Japan." [Online]. Available: < http://www.eurotechnology.com/imode/>. Accessed: January 2001.

[7] Japanese Ministry of Posts and Telecommunications. Home page statistics. Available: <http://www.mpt.go.jp/eng/>. Accessed: December 2000.

[8] Guth, Robert. "Japanese Cell-Phone Companies Are Pushing Wireless Internet." [Online]. Dow Jones & Company. [Online]. Available: < http://www.tkai.com/press/000327_wsj.htm>. Accessed: March 2000.

[9] Uda, Yoshinori. Keynote presentation at PCIA Global Xchange. Chicago, Illinois, September 28, 2000.

[10] Durlacher. *Mobile Commerce Report 1999.* [Online]. Available: <http://www.durlacher.com/fr-research-reps.htm>. Accessed: November 2000.

[11] Riivari, J. "Nokia WAP Security." Presented at Wireless Live! e-Security for a Wireless World Events 2000, sponsored by RSA, Santa Clara, California. October 5, 2000.

[12] FCC 00-289. *Sixth Report.* July 2001. [Online]. Available: <http://www.fcc.gov>, <http://hraunfoss.fcc.gov:8888/edocs_public/attachmatch/FCC-00 to 289A1.pdf>.

[13] Ploskina, Brian. "Wireless LANs to Roam Free." *Interactive Week.* May 7, 2001, quoting IDC statistics.

[14] SignalSoft home page. [Online]. Available: <http://www.signalsoftcorp.com/>. Accessed: November 2000.

[15] Japanese Ministry of Posts and Telecommunications. Home page statistics. Available: <http://www.mpt.go.jp/eng/>. Accessed: December 2000.

[16] Ibid.

[17] Robert Badavas, former CEO of Cerulean Technology (now owned by Aether Systems) discussed this information with the author during a telephone conversation on February 24, 2001.

[18] Ploskina, Brian. Op. cit.

[19] HiperLAN2. Home page statistics. [Online]. Available: <http://www.hiperlan2.com/>. Accessed: February 2001.

[20] The derivation of this saying is William Gibson's comment to Paul Saffo, "The future has already arrived; it is just not evenly distributed yet."

Chapter 2

[1] Moore, G. A. *Crossing the Chasm: Marketing and Selling High-Tech Products to Mainstream Consumers.* New York: HarperBusiness, 1999.

[2] Christensen, C. *The Innovator's Dilemma.* Boston: Harvard Business School Publishing, 1997.

Chapter 3

[1] Cellular Telephone and Internet Association, 2001.

[2] "Wireless Portable Devices World Market for 2G, 2.5G and 3G Devices and Connectivity to the Wireless Internet." *Allied Business Intelligence.* 1Q. Oyster Bay, New York. 2001.

[3] "VoiceXML in the Enterprise: Facts and Fiction." [Online]. Tellme Networks, Inc., 2000. Available: <http://www.tellme.com>. Accessed: January 2001.

Chapter 4

[1] Federal Communications Commission. *Sixth Report* (FCC 00-289). July 2001. Available: <http://www.fcc.gov>, <http://hraunfoss.fcc.gov:8888/edocs_public/attachmatch/FCC-00 to 289A1.pdf>.

[2] The Bluetooth trademarks are owned by Bluetooth SIG, Inc., U.S.A.

[3] Gartner, Inc. "Bluetooth Industry Conference." Open house conferences, San Jose, California. November-December 2000.

[4] Infrared Data Association. [Online]. Available: <http://www.irda.org/about/background.asp>. Accessed: November 2000.

[5] Symbol Technologies, Inc. Home page. [Online]. Available: <http://www.symbol.com>. Accessed: January 2001.

Chapter 5

[1] Shimbun, Yomiuri. *Daily Yomiuri.* April 29, 2000. [Online]. Available: < http://www.yomiuri.co.jp/>. Accessed: April 2000.

[2] Patrick, Dennis. President, AOL Wireless, America Online, Inc. Keynote presentation at PCIA Global Xchange, Chicago, Illinois. September 28, 2000.

[3] Wheeler, Thomas. President, CTIA. Keynote presentation at CTIA Global Wireless 2001, Las Vegas, Nevada. March 20, 2001.

[4] GSM Association. [Online]. Available: <http://www.gsmworld.com/technology/sms.html>. Accessed: July 2001.

[5] Patrick, Dennis. Op. cit.

[6] Cahners In-Stat Group. "Wireless Data Users to Reach 1.3 Billion by 2004." September 12, 2000. [Online]. Available: <http://www.instat.com/pr/2000/md0003md_pr.htm>. Accessed: July 2001.

[7] Bell, David. CEO, Chasma, Inc. "Winning the Gen Y Appeal." BREW 2001 Developer & 3G Technology Conference, San Diego, California. May 9, 2001.

[8] NTT Docomo. "Increase of Subscriber Number of i-mode." [Online]. Available: <http://www.nttdocomo.com/i/i_m_scr.html> Accessed: November, 2000.

[9] Gilder, George. *Telecosm: How Infinite Bandwidth Will Revolutionize Our World.* New York: Free Press, 2000. Prologue, p. 1.

[10] Used with permission from "Digital Cities Restaurant Guide: Spring 1994," published by Digital Lantern, a company that is no longer in business.

[11] Ibid.

[12] Cooper, Martin. "Telecommunications in the Next 1000 Years." Attachment to a private letter, April 4, 2001.

Chapter 6

[1] Beck, Kent, and Erich Gamma. *Extreme Programming Explained: Embrace Change.* Reading, Mass.: Addison-Wesley, 1999.

[2] Raskin, Jeff. *The Humane Interface.* Boston: Addison-Wesley, 2000, p. 6.

[3] Cooper, Alan. *The Inmates Are Running the Asylum: Why High-Tech Products Drive Us Crazy and How to Restore the Sanity.* Indianapolis, IN: Sams, 1999.

Chapter 7

[1] Tufte, Edward. *The Visual Display of Quantitative Information* (1983) and *Envisioning Information* (1990), both published by Graphics Press in Cheshire, Connecticut.

Chapter 8

[1] Kreth, Will. "Digital Guide Done Right" (Illustrated), *Wired Magazine*, July 1991; and Kreth, Will. "Digital Guide Done Right" (Illustrated), *Wired Magazine*, July 1993.

[2] The LBS algorithm depends on polar coordinate math functions. Some computers do not have a complete math library. The following example shows you how to compute the inverse cosine, which is necessary for polar coordinate calculations.

Example 34 Algorithm for arccosine

```
Function Arccos (ByVal X As Double)
' Compute the Arccosine of X - returns inverse cossine
If X = 1 Then
 Arccos = 0
Else
 Arccos = Atn(-X / Sqr( X * X + 1)) + 1.5708
End If
End Function
```

Chapter 14

[1] "Open Source" refers to source code that has been placed in the public domain for common development; it is usually bound by a license to oblige contributions." For more information about Open Source, see chapter 22.

Part III

[1] Alexander, Christopher. *A Pattern Language*. Oxford, UK: Oxford University Press, 1977.

[2] Mitchell, William J. *City of Bits: Space, Place, and the Infobahn*. Cambridge, Mass.: MIT Press, 1968, p. 167.

Chapter 15

[1] Brand, Stewart. *How Buildings Learn: What Happens after They're Built*. New York: Viking-Penguin (in United Kingdom, Orion Books), 1994.

Chapter 16

[1] Robert Badavas, former CEO of Cerulean Technology (now owned by Aether Systems) discussed this information with the author during a telephone conversation on February 24, 2001.

[2] Department of Defense papers and ongoing status of U.S. 3G spectrum planning can be monitored at <http://www.ntia.doc.gov/ntiahome/threeg/index.html>.

[3] Michael Powell, Chairman of the FCC, was interviewed by Thomas Wheeler, president and CEO of the CTIA, at the annual Cellular Telephone and Internet Association conference, Las Vegas. March 20, 2001.

[4] Ibid.

[5] Powell, Michael. Compiled quotes from FCC testimony, statements, and press releases from March through August 2001. All available at: <http://www.fcc.gov/commissioners/powell/mkp_statements_2001.html>.

Chapter 17

[1] Federal Communications Commission. *Sixth Report* (FCC 01-192). July 27, 2001. [Online]. Available: <http://www.fcc.gov>; Available: <http://hraunfoss.fcc.gov/edocs_public/attachmatch/FCC-01-192A1.pdf>.

[2] Ibid.

[3] Clarke's orbit is named after the scientist and writer who predicted its properties in the article "Extra-Terrestrial Relays," published in October 1945 in *Wireless World*, a British magazine.

[4] Location Interoperability Forum, February 2001. Available: <http://www.locationforum.org/>.

Chapter 20

[1] McLuhan, Marshall. *Take Thirty*, April 1, 1965. Interview televised by CBS.

[2] For musical terms, see the section "Tempo" in this book's appendix A.

[3] McLuhan, Marshall. *Understanding Media: The Extensions of Man*. New York: McGraw-Hill, 1964.

[4] Ranganathan, S. R. *Five Laws of Library Science* (originally published in 1931). Columbia, Mo.: South Asia Books, 1996.

Chapter 21

[1] McLuhan, Marshall. *Understanding Media: The Extensions of Man*. New York: McGraw-Hill, 1964. "The Medium Is the Message" is the oft-quoted title of a chapter in this book, which is similar to the title of his popular book *The Medium Is the Massage* (New York: Bantam Books, 1967).

[2] Brand, Stewart. *The Clock of the Long Now: Time and Responsibility: The Ideas Behind the World's Slowest Computer*. Cambridge, Mass.: Perseus Books, 1999.

[3] Raskin, Jeff. *The Humane Interface*. Boston: Addison-Wesley, 2000, p. 6.

[4] Clarke, Arthur C. *Profiles of the Future: An Inquiry into the Limits of the Possible*. New York: Harper & Row, 1963, p. 19.

[5] Infotrends. Boston. Home page. Accessed: February 2001. [Online]. Available: <http://www.infotrends-rgi.com/press/index.html>.

[6] Metcalfe, Robert. "The Systematic Value of Compatibly Communicating Devices Grows as the Square of Their Numbers." Paper published at Xerox PARC, 1973.

[7] *Gilder Technology Report,* Vol. 6, No. 6. Great Barrington, Mass.: Gilder Publishing, June 2001.

[8] Gilder, George. *Telecosm: How Infinite Bandwidth Will Revolutionize Our World.* New York: Free Press, 2000.

[9] Cooper, Martin. Keynote address at Internet World, New York City, February 21, 2001.

[10] McLuhan, Marshall. *McLuhan: The Medium Is the Message.* CD Time Again Productions, 1994. Based on a CBS Television interview in the late 1970s.

[11] Toffler, Alvin. *Future Shock.* New York: Bantam, 1970, p. 269.

[12] Stephenson, Neal. *Snow Crash.* New York: Bantam Books, 1992.

[13] Rand, Ayn. *Introduction to Objectivist Epistemology.* New York: Meridian, 1990. This book grew from a series of essays in *The Objectivist* newsletter, 1966–1967.

[14] Roszak, Theodore. *Person/Planet: The Creative Disintegration of Industrial Society.* New York: Anchor Press/Doubleday Books, 1979.

Chapter 22

[1] Clarke, A. C. *2001: A Space Odyssey, Based on a Screenplay by Stanley Kubrick and Arthur C. Clarke.* New York: New American Library, 1968.

[2] ___. *Profiles of the Future: An Inquiry into the Limits of the Possible.* New York: Harper & Row, 1963.

[3] Cooper, Martin. "The Myth, the Law, and the Spectrum." Attachment to a private letter, February 26, 2001.

[4] Ibid.

[5] Brand, Stewart. *Media Lab: Inventing the Future at MIT.* New York: Viking-Penguin, 1987.

[6] Cytowic, Richard. *The Man Who Tasted Shapes.* Los Angeles: Tacher/Putnam, 1993.

[7] For more information on these ideas, see Coomaraswamy, A. K. *The Transformation of Nature in Art*. New York: Dover, 1934.

[8] McLuhan, Marshall. *Understanding Media,* p. 23.

[9] Weiser, Mark. "The Computer of the 21st Century." *Scientific American*. September 1991. This is essential reading for people entering the field of mobile computing.

[10] *Gilder Technology Report*. Great Barrington, Mass.: Gilder Publishing. Monthly. Available online at <http://www.gildertech.com>.

[11] Toynbee, Arnold J. *Change and Habit: The Challenge of Our Time*. London: Oxford University Press, 1966. Toynbee established the concept of cultural challenge and response.

Index and Glossary

Note: G: and sans serif typeface denotes the defination of a term; **bold** numbers denote detailed information about the entry.

A

G: On a client, the executable code and interface used by a mobile persona to complete tasks. It generally connects with a server that defines a business layer composed of object models and database schemas.

G: Scalable programmable Internet computer running software capable of serving information to heavy traffic loads. Whereas Web servers were originally Internet file servers, the application server is programmable and keeps frequently used content in memory. Application servers are typically three tier – one for presentation, one for programming logic, and one for data.

B

C

cdma2000 3x air interface; 373
G: U.S. version of W-CDMA for voice and data; 4 Mbps peak, 1 kbps average data rate using 3.75 MHz bandwidth. Also called CDMA 3xMC because it combines three 1x 1.25 MHz bands.
cdma2000 air interface; 373
G: CDMA 1x (IS-95C) – One of five 3G network standards. It doubles prior CDMA capacity and standby times and it features 153 kbps and 307 kbps peak data rates using 1.25 MHz bandwidth. Also called 1x.
as 3G air interface; 110
properties of (table); 395
technical overview; **381**
cdma2000 EV-DO air interface; 373
G: CDMA Enhanced Value, Data Only (IS-856) – WAN packet data-only channel featuring 2.4 Mbps peak, 650 kbps–800 kbps shared data rate, using a 1.25 MHz bandwidth. Also called HDR.
cdma2000 EV-DV air interface
G: CDMA Enhanced Value, Data and Voice. WAN that combines CDMA 1x voice and HDR packet data within a 1.25 MHz bandwidth.
as CDMA family member (table); 373
cdmaOne air interface, 373
G: Original CDMA air interface (IS-95A and IS95-B) – The original IS-95A can transfer data at 14.4 kbps using a 1.25 MHz bandwidth.
KDDI use; 33
CDPD (Cellular Digital Packet Data)
G: A system overlay for transmitting and receiving data over older AMPS cellular networks.
as 2G data network; 112
coverage information provided by; 397
effective data rate; 249
paging service; 413
properties of; 395, **400**
pros and cons of using; 401
as pure digital system; 92
specification (table); 533
CEBasic language
G: Microsoft Basic for mobile devices.
CeBIT trade show, Bluetooth problems; 124
cell splitting; 390
Cell-Loc company, as location service provider; 230, 411
CellID; 409
Cellmania company; 554
cellular
air interfaces; 8
market time line (table); 503
wireless, properties of (table); 395
Band 5 spectrum allocation; 540
data rate, text transfer and (table); 82
handoff (figure); 103
Internet, social impact contrasted with broadcast networks; 100
networks; **394, 402**
phones; **6**
handheld features starting to appear on; 67
pager indoor reception compared with; 68
principles of operation; **102**
as radios; **101**
Web phones as modified versions of; 62
x; **119**
radio, broadcast differences; 91
towers; 88, 100, **101**
WANs; 91, **100**
Cellular One System A; 8
Cellular Telecommunications and Internet Association. *See* CTIA
CENELEC (European Committee for Electrotechnical Standardization)
G: Hardware certification group necessary for devices to be sold in Europe.
as IP54 code developer; 307
CEPT (Conférence des Administrations Européenes des Postes et Télécommunications), paging standard activities; 16
Cerulean Technology [Aether Systems division]
government services provided by; 43
vertical market ROI of; 365
change, building for, in wireless Internet architecture design; **343**
channel; 85
control (term description); 91
data capacity relative to bandwidth; 111
transmission (term description); 91
wireless; 437
children, tracking applications; 234
Christensen, Clayton; 559
disruptive technology studies; 51
cHTML (compact HTML); 149, 150
G: Compact HTML is a markup language subset from HTML that delivers simple text and graphics for use by mobile wireless devices.
development; 279, 280
HTML differences; 280
i-mode access key use (example); 282
i-mode applications, writing; **278**
i-mode pages, creating; **280**

D

F

H

HiperAccess; 120
HiperLAN2; 120
G: European standard for a high-speed wireless LAN similar to 802.11a.
Band 6 spectrum allocation; 541
data rate and properties (table); 400
as European 155 Mbps LAN standard; 120
properties of; 120
HiperLAN2 Global Forum (H2GF); 120
wireless LAN projection; 44
HiperLink; 120
Hiragana
Japanese use; 217
as phonetic form of Kanji; 65
history, wireless Internet (chapter); **3**
hits
G: Web traffic at a site that generally corresponds to number of pages viewed.
Homer; 557
Sirens as exemplars of voice appeal; 13
HomeRF
G: Wireless radio standard for audio and data that runs at 2.4 GHz.
interference with Bluetooth and IEEE 802.11b; 118
properties and backers (table); 119
voice specification in; 119
HomeRF Forum; 118
HomeRF™ Working Group, Inc.; 117, 119
hop; 118
horizontal markets; 51
enabling conditions for; 52
position in wireless marketing strategy; 51
horoscope example
server processing of Tellme VoiceXML dialog; 337
Tellme VoiceXML dialog; **335**
host ID, as IP address component; 95
HotData company, as analytics engine supplier; 441
HotSync® [Palm], handheld data synchronization; 153
HP company. *See* Hewlett Packard
HPC (Handheld PC) [Microsoft]; 64
WinCE operating system use with (table); 453
HSCSD (High Speed Circuit-Switched Data)
G: 56 Kbps standard for GSM in Europe.
data rate and properties (table); 399
GPRS handset compatibility; 450
properties of; 113
HSPD (High Speed Packet Data), MSM5500 support; 460
HTML (Hypertext Markup Language); 147
G: A markup standard for pages so that they can be published on the Web. Any browser can read these pages which include text style, graphics, and hyperlinks that navigate to other HTML pages.
applications, converting Web sites to PQA (example); **286**
cHTML differences; 280
microbrowser application use; **268**
OSI layer used by (table); 99
WWW publishing role; 20
HTTP (Hypertext Transfer Protocol). *See also* URL
G: An Internet protocol used between a Web server and client application to exchange data.
OSI layer used by (table); 99
HTTP_USER_AGENT. *See* User Agent protocol
HTTPS (Hypertext Transfer Protocol Secure)
i-mode use; 280
as Internet security protocol; 243
layer, i-mode security (figure); 353
OSI layer used by (table); 99
hubs
OSI level 1 use; 98
properties of; 98
Hurley, Bob, as prototypical vertical market handheld persona; 196
Husky company. *See* Itronix
HWR (handwriting recognition) software
handheld use; 65, 258
media translation use; 516
HyperCard hypertext language [Apple]
Digital Restaurant Guide use; 236
presentation design use; 206
hyperchannel architecture
G: Signal Computing System Architecture that bundles timeslots to increase data rates.
data flow architecture use; 439
Hyperion Communications company, wireless broadband connections to fiber development; 388
Hz (Hertz). *See* Hertz

I

i-appli Java service
G: Java application service complementing i-mode browser service from DoCoMo; launched in January 2001.
Sun Java MIDP vs.; **294**

interoperability
as 3G goal; 169
international telephone networks, ITU maintenance of; 92
wireless application importance; 25
interpreter
G: An application that processes code and data for a computer as it comes in realtime; interpreted applications execute slower than compiled ones.
interrogators; 126
G: Wireless sensing device that probes nearby wireless tags and devices.
identification application use; 233
Intershop company, as eCommerce system supplier; 440
interviews, personal development use; 196
Interwoven company, as content management system supplier; 440
intranet; 92
G: Private business Internet network used behind a firewall.
Intuit company, checkbook metaphor use; 56
inventory, as mobile data application; 131
IP codes
G: Industrial Protection codes that certify the ruggedness of devices; the codes were established by CENELEC.
IP54 code, industrial handheld conformance to; 307
IP (Intellectual Property)
G: Often called IPR, Intellectual Property Rights.
IP (Internet Protocol)
G: Transport protocol for networks.
access service, data rate and properties (table); 399
addresses
IANA role; 45
phone numbers and; **94**
properties of; 95
cellular phones; **119**
data packets, packet-switched network use; 93
EV high data rate IP access; **372**
mobile phone, private computer network use; 62
OSI layer used by (table); 99
phone network, Cisco Systems VoIP phones; 393
IP (Internet Protocol) address
G: A 32-bit number that identifies each sender or receiver of information across the Internet. An IP address has two parts: the identifier of a particular network on the Internet and an identifier for a device within that network.
IP54 code
G: IPC for rugged handhelds.
industrial handheld, conformance to; 307
iPAQ handheld [Compaq]
as extensible handheld; 66
Linux OS; 258
MP3 player; 143
PIM applications; 67
WinCE operating system use (table); 453
iPlanet [Sun] server, wireless device use; 452
IPMA (Internet Protocol Multiple Access) [SWIFTcomm]; 39, **167**
data rate and properties (table); 400
handoff speed; 402
@irPointer antenna for; **385**
IPR (Intellectual Property Rights)
G: Original or creative technology or content that can be legally protected.
IPv4 (Internet Protocol version 4)
G: Standard Internet based on 32-bit IP addresses.
IPv6 (Internet Protocol version 6); 507
G: Next-generation Internet based on 128-bit addresses.
as emerging technology; 169
Internet2 and NGI initiatives testing of; 508
QoS issues; 507
IRC (Internet Relay Chat)
G: Internet protocol that provides instant messaging allowing many users to connect to the same network node and chat in real time.
IrDA (Infrared Data Association); 125. *See also* PAN
handhelds use for wireless device links; 65
Jini compatibility with; 125
standard published by; 125
Iridium
G: LEO satellite network designed by Motorola.
IS (Interim Standards)
G: Registered by the ITU; IS-95 is the CDMA standard.
ITU wireless air carrier standards; 45
IS-136 standard
G: TDMA, U.S. cellular standard; also known as D-AMPS.
GPRS as upgrade for; 114
IS-41 (SS7) standard, U.S. use; 104
IS-54 standard
G: TDMA – the original specification.
as TDMA standard (table); 395
IS-856 standard. *See* CDMA, 1xEV
G: High Rate Packet Data Air Interface; also known as HDR or 1xEV-DA.
IS-95 standard, CDMA ITU standard; 45
IS-95A standard
G: CDMA version A – the original PCS implementation.

J

K

L

location-based applications; 231
G: Spatially sensitive applications that take advantage of GPS wireless devices. Chapter 8 covers the key location-based applications: identifying, directing, emergency assisting, asset tracking, presence detecting, area service requesting, friend finding, list serving, area informing, triggering nearby services, mapping, surveying.
as concept that drives wireless business; **178**
Location Interoperability Forum. *See* LIF
LON. *See* longitude
long-term use, as wireless Internet architecture design consideration; **344**
longitude
G: Global degrees measured east and west of Greenwich – +180 to the east, and –180 to the west.
geocode definition use; 219
geocoding use; 159, 218
latlon proximity algorithm use; 239
location definition use; 231
location-based network use; 406, 408
Loral Space & Communications, LEO use; 405
LoS (line-of-sight) antennas, mobile terminal use; 85
Lotus 1-2-3™, IBM PC sales impact; 156
loyal users; 242
Lucent company, as IEEE 802.11b backer; 119
Lutris Technologies; 548
application server tools; 434
email application storyboard; 200
Enhydra, as wireless server architecture; 423, 433

M

M. *See* magnitude prefixes
G: Mega million (1,000,000).
m500 [Palm], with SD card (figure); 329
M7, as SAN hosting company; 403
macrocells; 88
G: Long-range cellular tower used in a WAN.
Macromedia company
ActiveScript; 214
as collaborative filtering system supplier; 440
Flash™, multimedia use; 214
FLASH, streaming animation use; 152
Magic Cap operating system [General Magic]
handheld device use; 312
in inspection application for handheld devices; 314
Maginot line, as metaphor of how not to approach wireless design; 53
MAGNET (Motorola Applications Global Network); 298
Magnify company, as analytics engine supplier; 441
magnitude prefixes; 530
man-in-middle attack, as wireless security concern; **354**
Manna, FrontMind, as rules engine; 440
manufacturing, as wireless LAN application; 116
MAP (Mobile Application Part), GSM use; 104
MapQuest, commercial geocoding source; 220
Marconi; 6
maritime band, Bands 1 and 3 spectrum allocation; 536, 538
market
forecast, wireless Internet; **42**
growth, hardware, software, and content relationships(figure); 156
world, projections for wireless mobile users; 3
markup languages; 145
cHTML; **149**
HTML; **147**
microbrowser, for devices; **146**
migration (figure); 151
selecting for mobile applications; **151**
VoiceXML; 152
of wireless publishing; **145**
XHTML; **150**
XML; **147**
mast, as UK term for tower; 88
MatchLogic company, as campaign management system supplier; 440
MATS
G: Early 1G European analog cellular protocol.
MATS-E, as 1G protocol; 105
Matsushita Communication Industrial. *See* Panasonic
Max Headroom TV series, voice portal personality example; 72
Mb
G: Megabyte.
MBCK (M-ary Bicoded Keying)
advanced LAN use; 120
as modulation technique; 90
Mbps
G: Megabits per second (not megabytes).
mBusiness (mobile business). *See* mCommerce
McCloud, Scott; 488, 552
MCDN (Ricochet Microcellular Data Network) [Metricom, Inc.]. *See* Ricochet, network
MCI, *See* WorldCom/UUNet

N

O

P

PAP (Push Access Protocol), push model defined in; 135
PAQ. *See* PQA
PARC. *See* Xerox PARC (Palo Alto Research Center)
participation, increasing; 496
partitioning
algorithms, content structuring use; 267
content, as microbrowser application guideline; 269
data; 224
mobile vs. desktop Web use; 421
wireless data; **223**
patterns, wireless Internet architecture use; **342**
PBX (Private Branch Exchange). *See also* PABX
current limitations compared to digital services; 169
PC (Personal Computer), differences in use from wireless devices; 53
PCIA (Personal Communications Internet Association); 545
G: Telco member association.
Bluetooth conference, issues highlighted; 124
PCM (pulse code modulation), bit encoding use; 89
PCMCIA (Personal Computer Memory Card International Association) card
1G data network use; 112
handheld use of; 66
PCS (Personal Communications Services) bands
G: North American 2G mobile telephone services that feature digital voice, messaging and data service. PCS primarily operates in the 1900 MHz frequency band and is largely CDMA based.
1900 MHz; 79, 106
1994 auctions; 9
Band 5 spectrum allocation; 540
iDEN relationship to; 108
phones, dual mode; 9
specification (table); 533
United States; **371**
PDA (Personal Digital Assistant); 10, 12
G: A handheld device that has a pen user interface.
as name for handhelds; 64
Profile, as handheld profile; 293
PDC (Personal Digital Cellular) air interface
G: A Japanese-only 2G air interface. Sometimes called Japanese Digital Cellular (JDC).
as 2G air interface; 106
as 2G Japanese network; 398
bandwidth channel capacity for data (table); 111
DoCoMo use; 33
properties of; 107, 395
SMS message limits; 413
specification (table); 533
PDC-P Japanese transport layer
G: Japanese i-mode protocol that corresponds to TCP/IP.
OSI layer used by (table); 99
PDE (Position Determination Equipment)
G: Location determination equipment used by carriers and often coupled with GPS systems.
PDF417 barcode; 126
G: Military 2D barcode standard.
peak rate
G: The highest data rate a network is capable of reaching; rarely possible with ordinary traffic.
Pearl OS operating system [Symbian], as mobile operating system (table); 251
Pearl smartphone reference model [Symbian]; 454
peer
G: A terminal that communicates with other terminals without intermediate protocol conversion.
peer-to-peer
connections, as part of Bluetooth promise; 141
information transfer, in PAN operations; 121
model; 423
properties of; 95
OSI communication, properties of; 99
PenPoint™ handheld tablet [GO]
adoption curve, impact on; 51
Microsoft impact on; 40
Microsoft Winpad as competitor for (table); 453
signature capture use; 327
performance, wireless security strategy impact on; **357**
Perl
G: An Open Source programming script that is run as a Web server process. Started by Larry Wall in 1987, it is derived from the C programming language, Lisp, sed, awk, and various UNIX shell languages.
CGI use, application server advantages over; 444
content development in; 210
as Open Source example; 510
server application use; 423
server programmable gateway use; 425
persistence, URN guarantee of; 95
persona(s); 55, 188, **193**
G: Characterization of the most important mobile user for a wireless application prior to development.
background studies for development of; **195**
design, demographics in; **486**
development; **197**, 202
field test use, in wireless application development; 190

Q

R

S

U

V

W

security; **354**, **355**
"shadows," as big city wireless network limitation; 76
spectrum; **78**, **370**
technology, future (chapter); **501**
users, complaints (figure); 57
vertical markets (table); 139
XML, as potent data exchange format; **153**

wireless application

G: Software that runs on a wireless device that exchanges content over a wireless network; there are four application types: messaging, browsing, interacting, and conversing.

wireless business models

G: The operational plan for a wireless Internet architecture. Examples are value-based model, publication model, vertical market ROI model, telco subscriber model, telco OEM model, software revenue model.

Wireless Communications Services. *See* WCS

wireless development method

G: The software development process for building a mobile application. It begins with the user, information design, storyboard, content, server design, and device refinement.

wireless devices

G: There are six main types of wireless devices: Web phones, handhelds, pagers, voice portals, Web PCs, and embedded Internet appliances.

Wireless Digital Subscriber Line (WDSL), *See* MMDS

wireless Internet

G: The global network of radio-connected devices and servers exchanging voice, data, and providing mobile Internet services.

Wireless Knowledge company; 318, 550

wireless programming model

G: The selection of programming methods to develop a wireless application to run on one of the six classes of wireless mobile devices: Web phone, handheld, pager, voice portal, embedded device, and laptop.
device families; **61**, 62, **448**

wireless publishing model

G: The cycle of media production and network feedback that determines the frequency of content accountability in a wireless Internet system.

wireless vertical markets

G: Distinct mobile wireless markets that are generally divided into mechanical, field force, and industrial; examples include fleet management, salesforce automation. or package delivery.

Wirelessdeveloper.com; 556

Wirelessdevnet.com; 556

WLAN (Wireless Local Area Network)
Bluetooth relationship; 506
impact on channel density; 506
LAN specification relationship to; 115

WLL (Wireless Local Loop)

G: A fixed service that competes with or replaces last-mile local wired phone service.
as last-mile wireless alternative; 391

WML (Wireless Markup Language)

G: An XML-defined markup language defined by the WAP Forum; rather than a Web page it uses a deck of cards as its publishing model.
browser applications, guidelines for writing; **269**
cache cancellation code (example); 430
European WAP use; 146
HDML applications vs.; **270**
HDML relationship to; **148**
migration from HDML to; 266, 270
OSI presentation layer use; 98, 99
permission forms; 149
variables, programming use of (example); **273**
WAP development in; 36
WAP MIME extension; 275
Web phone programming issues; 256, 257
as XML derivative; 148
XSLT page generation (example); 432

wmlc WAP MIME extension; 275

wmls WAP MIME extension; 275

wmlsc WAP MIME extension; 275

WMLScript scripting language, WML use; 275

word processor, as adoption curve market progression example; 51

Wordwise (Eatoni), as predictive input system; 254

Workstyle™ [Wireless Knowledge], wireless servers; 550

world
market, projections for wireless mobile users; 3
spectrum, overview; **369**
wireless Internet status (chapter); **3**

World Trade Organization. *See* WTO

World Wide Web Consortium. *See* W3C

World Wide Web. *See* Web

WorldCom (UUNet) company, mobile IP cellular phones; 14, 393

WRC (World Radio Conference), ITU spectrum activities at; 369

WRC (World Radio Congress)

G: International body that convenes every few years to designate international spectrum bands and their usage.

writing
i-mode cHTML applications; **278**
i-mode cHTML pages, creating; **280**

writing *continued*
Java phone applications; **295**
journalistic style; **215**
messages; **215**
Pixo cHTML applications; **284**
PQA wireless browsing applications; **285**
wireless applications, with RAD tools; **310**
wireless business applications, guidelines; **309**
WSP (Wireless Session Protocol). *See also* WAP
OSI layer used by (table); 99
WTAI (Wireless Telephony Application Interface), WAP phone call use; 273
WTCP (Wireless Transport Control Protocol), WAP Forum specification of; 352
WTLS (Wireless Transport Layer Security)
OSI layer used by (table); 99
security issues; 37
WAP security use; 243
WTO (World Trade Organization); 546
WTP (Wireless Transfer Protocol). *See also* WAP
OSI layer used by (table); 99
Wurman, Richard Saul, SMART Yellow Pages® designer; 212
WWW (World Wide Web). *See* Web

X

Xalan, as XSLT parser; 433
Xerox PARC (Palo Alto Research Center)
Fitt's Law; 491
as major research lab; 46
Mark Weiser's work on ubiquitous computing; 520
Metcalfe's law; 494
whiteboard use; 488
XHTML Basic, WAP phone use; 269
XHTML (eXtensible HTML); 150
G: Reformulation of HTML as an application of XML.
converting Web sites to, advantages and issues; **418**
as HTML successor that uses XML; 147
XHTML (eXtensible HTML) Basic; 150
XM Internet radio, digital distributor; 170
XML (eXtensible Markup Language); 147, 148
G: XML is a portable data language. It can also define all other markup languages.
application server, publishing framework (figure); 424
architecture, content planning; **442**
data; **339**, **442**
as data exchange language; 210
describing data with; **226**
metadata modeling, RDF use for; 428
parsers, for Java phone application development; 301
properties of; 145
as root markup language for wireless publishing; 145
servers, software independence; **152**
as SMIL foundation; 151
vocabulary, including domain jargon in; 216
voice; **339**
wireless, as potent data exchange format; **153**
wireless browsers; **300**
WWW publishing role; 20
XML Schema
G: Similar to a DTD, this specifies how XML will be interpreted or styled.
XMLC [enhydra.org] XML compiler; 433
XP (Extreme Programming), as wireless application development model; 184
Xpresso™ [Zucotto], as Java-in-silicon handset; 457
XSL (XML Style Language)
application server use; **431**
properties of; 148
XSLT (eXtensible Stylesheet Language Transformation)
G: A processor that combines XML with XSL, producing a general markup language. Apache Xalan is an XSLT tool.
XSLT (XSL Transformations)
WML page creation; 432
WML page generation (example); 432
XYPoint company, as location service provider; 411

Y

Yahoo company, as early wireless full portal; 131
Yankee Group; 543
yellow pages, as wireless application; 24
YellowBrix company, as content management system supplier; 440
Yokosuka Telecom Research Park, site for W-CDMA experiments; 33
YOUpowered company, as eCommerce system supplier; 440

Z

zoning laws, basestation location issues; 392
Zucotto company, Xpresso™, as Java-in-silicon handset; 457